PICTISH SOURCEBOOK

PICTISH SOURCEBOOK

Documents of Medieval Legend
and Dark Age History

J.M.P. Calise

Documentary Reference Collections

GREENWOOD PRESS
Westport, Connecticut • London

Library of Congress Cataloging-in-Publication Data

Pictish sourcebook : documents of medieval legend and Dark Age history / [compiled, edited, and translated by] J.M.P. Calise.
      p.   cm.—(Documentary reference collections)
   Includes bibliographical references (p.   ) and index.
   ISBN 0–313–32295–3 (alk. paper)
   1. Picts—Sources.   2. Ethnology—Scotland—Sources.   3. Scotland—History—To 1057—Sources.   4. Manuscripts, Medieval—Scotland.   I. Calise, J. M. P., 1969–
II. Series.
DA774.P528   2002
941.101—dc21   2002072643

British Library Cataloguing in Publication Data is available.

Library of Congress Catalog Card Number: 2002072643
ISBN: 0–313–32295–3

First published in 2002

Greenwood Press, 88 Post Road West, Westport, CT 06881
An imprint of Greenwood Publishing Group, Inc.
www.greenwood.com

Printed in the United States of America

The paper used in this book complies with the
Permanent Paper Standard issued by the National
Information Standards Organization (Z39.48–1984).

10 9 8 7 6 5 4 3 2 1

Do mo mháthair

CONTENTS

PREFACE

The Picts (whom the Medieval Irish called "Cruithni," a name which has caused some confusion because it was also used for an unrelated Irish population) were native inhabitants of Dark Age Scotland, whose existence as an independent population can be dated c.300-c.850. Prior to this period, the ancestors of the Picts have been called "Proto-Picts." After this period, the Picts ceased to be an independent kingdom when they were united with the Scots, who had migrated from Ireland. Unfortunately, no written documents definitely attributable to the Picts are now extant, aside from a list of Pictish kings which may derive from a Pictish source. The Picts did, however, leave behind a wealth of stone monuments which have been the subject of much study. With these facts in mind, one can safely say that the history of the Picts has been written by non-Picts, particularly by the other inhabitants of Medieval Britain and Ireland. Therefore, much that Medieval authors recorded about the Picts was a blend of the mythological, legendary, and historical.

Many scholars have written narrative histories of the Picts and studies of their monumental sculptures. This book is neither of these. Instead, it is a reference work designed to address the various forms of Medieval documentary sources concerning Pictish matters and an attempt to distinguish the historical from the mythological and legendary. To this end, in Chapters 2 and 3, I have collected, edited, and translated Medieval Irish texts relating to the Picts in single manuscript editions rather than in composite editions compiled from several manuscripts. Many of these texts had previously been edited by scholars, most notably by William F. Skene in his monumental 1867 tome *Chronicles of the Picts, Chronicles of the Scots*. Skene's work was ambitious and groundbreaking, but his editorial technique was inconsistent and not always at a level in keeping with modern standards. These texts have also been discussed by modern scholars, most notably by Gearóid S. Mac Eoin in his

1964 article "On the Irish Legend of the Origin of the Picts" and in the works of T.F. O'Rahilly, H.M. Chadwick, Marjorie O. Anderson, and Molly Miller. However, many of the texts have never been edited. For the first time, this book edits them in single manuscript versions in a consistent manner and presents them in one volume, enabling scholars to compare and contrast their content. In Chapters 5 and 6, I have provided a cross-referenced dictionary of about 500 personal, population, and place names associated with the Picts and the Medieval texts in which they appear. Specific details of these texts and the methodology of the edited texts and dictionary can be found in the Introduction provided in Chapter 1.

I would like to thank the following for their contributions to the realization of this work: Professor Philip Lockhart of Dickinson College for giving me a background in Old Irish. Professor William Gillies of Edinburgh University for his constructive criticism concerning the finer points of translation. Mr. Ronald Black for introducing me to the world of palaeography. Dr. Thomas Owen Clancy for introducing me to a wide variety of Medieval Celtic Literature. Gearóid S. Mac Eoin, whose pioneering "On the Irish Legend of the Origin of the Picts" provided me with the initial impetus for this work. Rachel Bromwich, whose *Trioedd Ynys Prydein* was the inspiration for the format of this work. The examiners of earlier versions of my work, Dr. Séamus Mac Mathúna and Dr. Alex Woolf, for their advice and comments. Mr. Warren Priest and the staff of the Royal Irish Academy for diligently tracking down obscure texts and manuscripts and providing me with photocopies and microfilm printouts. Mr. Stuart Ó Seanóir, Ms. Jane Maxwell, Ms. Felicity O'Mahony, and the rest of the staff of Trinity College Dublin Library for providing textual references and microfilm printouts of manuscripts. Ms. Patricia Buckingham and the staff of the Bodleian Library at Oxford for supplying microfilm printouts. Ms. Elizabeth Kirwan, Mr. Thomas Desmond, and the rest of the staff of the National Library of Ireland for providing microfilm of manuscripts. Prof. Fergus Kelly of the Dublin Institute for Advanced Studies for supplying manuscript references. Mr. Gene Devlin, Mr. Andrew Fal, and the rest of the staff at the Berlin Peck Memorial Library in Kensington, Connecticut for their interlibrary loan services. Professor Benjamin T. Hudson of Penn State University for reading my typescript and providing me with invaluable comments. Mr. Chris Foran for his technical assistance with the preparation of the camera-ready copy of the book. All my friends and relatives for their moral support. Ms. Cynthia Harris and Ms. Jane Lerner and the rest of Greenwood Publishing Group for helping this work to see the light of day. Most of all, my parents whose constant fostering of my intellectual faculties made this endeavor possible.

1

INTRODUCTION

But most the modern Pict's ignoble boast,
To rive what Goth, and Turk, and Time hath spared:
Cold as the crags upon his native coast,
His mind as barren and his heart as hard,
Is he whose head conceived, whose hand prepared,
Aught to displace Athena's poor remains:
Her sons, too weak the sacred shrine to guard,
Yet felt some portion of their mother's pains,
And never knew, till then, the weight of Despot's chains.

Lord Byron,
Childe Harold's Pilgrimage
Canto II, xii.[1]

Byron's sentiments provide an ideal starting point for discussing the Celtic view of the people of Dark Age Scotland who have come to be known as "Picts." The "modern Pict" in question here is, of course, Lord Elgin who acquired several friezes from the Parthenon not long before Byron wrote this. In choosing the term "Pict" to describe Lord Elgin, Byron is not merely using an ethnically based derisive term in the manner of "Philistine." He is obviously aware of Elgin itself as having been in an area of Scotland which was a home to the Picts, a fact that is corroborated by the presence of Pictish symbol stones.[2] By grouping this "Pict" along with "Goth, and Turk, and Time," Byron has revealed the connotation that the term "Pict" holds for him. Because "Goth, and Turk, and Time" can be viewed as three things which have helped to "ravage" Classical civilization, he obviously sees the "Pict" as the barbaric enemy of the Classical world. In fact the "Pict" is even worse because he had succeeded in doing something that the others had failed to do. Lord Elgin's patrimony and actions make Byron's representation of the Picts as barbarians both geographically and poetically apt. In this, Byron is similar to the Medieval Irish learned class called the *filid*, who attempted to preserve the traditions of the Irish past.[3] Despite the many differences between them, Byron's view of the acquisition of the "Elgin Marbles" and the Medieval *filid*'s view of the Picts have one thing in common: a marked ignorance of the historical Picts. Byron uses a Classical-centered stereotype of the Picts as barbarians to create his "modern Pict," and the *filid* use their Ireland-centered bias to create mythical and legendary "Picts."

During the present, writing about the Picts has flourished as part of the current interest in "esoteric" subjects. Yet, knowledge has not progressed in every area. Although there have been advances in archaeology, epigraphy, and art history, the Picts continue to incite much controversy and speculation. Even though F.T. Wainwright's collaborative volume *The Problem of the Picts* was published over four decades ago,[4] the word "problem" is still used in discussions of the Picts. In particular, there has been no systematic analysis of the various Medieval Celtic literary sources discussing the Picts and their culture. This work is designed to fill that gap by presenting in full and analyzing these literary materials.

The presentation of the materials is in three main parts. The first part (Chapter 2 and Chapter 3) contains texts which concern the Picts. These texts are widely represented in the manuscripts, and many have not been recently (if at all) edited and translated. The aim here is to make as many of them as possible available in one place with a consistent system of designation and one level of explication. The texts in Chapter 2 consist of Origin Legends, which describe in different ways how the Picts came to be in Scotland. The Irish versions of these tales have been briefly discussed by Gearóid Mac Eoin.[5] The texts in Chapter 3 consist of Pictish and Scottish Regnal Lists which have not been previously (or recently) edited separately. The texts and versions of the Pictish Origin Legends in Irish are labelled in a manner designed to show both the chronological sequence of the several versions recognized and to clarify by content and textual status. Therefore, the Irish texts with essentially the same narrative content and format (i.e., poetry or prose) receive the same letter designation plus further identification to show their source manuscripts. Legends with the same content but with different formats receive entirely separate letter designations. The edited texts are followed by a brief analysis of their content, specifially considering the relationship of the Origin legends with Pictish regnal succession. The second part (Chapter 4) consists of appendices of supplemental material which present information concerning Pictish matters. The third part (Chapter 5 and Chapter 6) is an attempt to place the Pictish Origin Legends into the wider context of Medieval insular texts (mostly Celtic) which refer to the Picts in a broad sense through the personal, population and place names which they contain. To this end, several major categories of Medieval texts have been selected for examination. This should give at least a representative sample of the range and variety of texts within the great body of Medieval insular literature. "Origin Legends," "Genealogies," "Annals," "Regnal Lists," "Hagiographies," and "History and Literature" are the six categories chosen for this study.

Origin Legends are those tales which claim to explain where the Picts originated. Some of these accounts occur in the Medieval Irish text known as the *Lebor Gabála*.[6] According to the analysis by R. Mark Scowcroft, which is followed here, this text exists in four Medieval recensions in about 22 manuscripts.[7] Other variations occur in the Middle Irish translation of the Latin *Historia Brittonum* called the *Lebor Bretnach*, which exists in about 16 manuscripts.[8]

Genealogies are texts which purport to give the ancestry of particular families and individuals. These texts provide pedigrees for many individuals who feature in early Medieval Scottish history. This study will examine the early ninth century Welsh genealogies from *Harleian MS. 3859* (c.1100), the twelfth century Irish *Rawlinson B. 502*,[9] the twelfth century Irish *Book of Leinster*,[10] the thirteenth century Welsh genealogies from *Jesus College MS. 20*, the fifteenth century Irish *Book of Lecan* and *Laud 610*,[11] and various transcripts of the genealogies of Mac Firbis,[12] which were composed in the seventeenth century and are currently in the process of being edited.[13]

Annals are documents which record historical events in chronological order. Their compilation and use in the Middle Ages derived from ancient times, when annalists were distinct from historians and annals with their presentation of bare facts were separate from histories.[14] This study discusses seven different annalistic compilations. The *Annales Cambriae*, the earliest of these, is a tenth century text.[15] It originated in Wales, and its history has been extensively analysed by Kathleen Hughes, who states that its primarily secular content distinguishes it from the Irish Annals.[16] The remaining Annals were written in Ireland. These are the *Annals of Inisfallen*, written in Latin with some Irish material c.1091; the *Annals of Tigernach*, written in Latin with some Irish material c.1100/1120; the *Annals of Clonmacnoise*, probably written in Irish c.1408 but existing only in a seventeenth century English translation; the *Annals of Ulster*, written in Irish before 1498; the *Annals of the Four Masters*, written in Irish 1632-1636; and the *Chronicum Scotorum*, written in Irish 1660-1666.[17] The relationships of these various Annals have also been extensively analyzed by Kathleen Hughes.[18]

Regnal Lists are sequential rosters of the rulers of certain peoples and areas. The Pictish Regnal Lists are found in two distinct varieties, each of which records kings whose reigns add up to over a thousand years. M.O. Anderson has called these lists P and Q and indicates that they share a common source until about 724.[19] In this study, the P lists are included in what Molly Miller designates the "Series Longior" (SL) and labelled accordingly with some altered designations owing to the inclusion of a number of lists not discussed by

Miller. Chapter 3 includes the texts of those versions of these lists which have not been recently (or at all) separately edited.[20] The Q lists are labelled using M.O. Anderson's designations.[21] Regnal List N is a list of Scottish Kings which contains some information relevant to the Picts.[22]

Hagiographies are literary works giving the details of saints' lives. In this study, the Hagiographies are addressed in the chronological order of the time in which the saints are reputed to have flourished. Kathleen Hughes indicates that hagiographical tales were written for a variety of purposes, of which history was not the primary one. Hence, they are filled with paranormal activities.[23] However, the lives of those saints who had contact with the Picts provide another source of information about the Picts. The earliest of these saints is Bishop Ninian (5th or 6th century) of Whithorn,[24] who features in the late eighth century Latin poem *Miracula Ninie Episcopi*, which exists in the eleventh century manuscript *Codex Bambergensis*.[25] Ninian is also the subject of the twelfth century *Vita Niniani*, which is included in the twelfth century manuscript *Laud Misc. 668*.[26] Another saint who had contact with the Picts was the sixth century Welsh abbot Cadoc.[27] The *Vita Cadoci* exists in the c.1200 manuscript *Cotton Vespasian A.XIV*.[28] There is also Abbot Columba of Iona (521-97), who travelled into Pictland.[29] *Vita Columbae* written by Adomnán dates from before 704 and survives in several manuscripts, the earliest of which is not later than 713.[30] *Betha Coluim Cille Incipit*, written in Irish independently of Adomnán's *Vita*, seems to have existed before 1200, although its current form dates from the sixteenth century.[31] Two hagiographical works written about Bishop Cuthbert of Lindisfarne (d.687) refer to the Picts: *Vita Sancti Cuthberti Auctore Anonymo* (c.699-705) and Bede's *Vita Sancti Cudberti* (c.721).[32] Eddius Stephanus wrote his *Life of Wilfrid* in 720. This historical biography, the first written by an Anglo-Saxon, of Bishop Wilfrid of Northumbria and Hexham (634-709) often discusses the Picts.[33] The thirteenth century *Life of Servanus* states that the bishop Servanus, who lived sometime between 450 and 700, journeyed into Pictland.[34]

History and Literature consist of those texts which give historical information in narrative accounts and which do not fit into the other categories. They are given a single category because they were written during a period in which distinctions between history and literature were often blurred. Beryl Smalley asserts that to the Medieval writer, "a history differed from annals in being a literary composition."[35] Particular texts were chosen for either their importance to Medieval literature or for their importance to the study of the Picts. While the majority of the texts can be considered of Celtic origin, those which are not have been included because they contain enough relevant information to be worth consideration. Gildas's *De Excidio Britonum* (*Concerning the Ruin of Britain/the Britons*) was written c.540 and gives some accounts of the Picts, whom Gildas considered barbaric.[36] The seventh century Welsh poem *Y Gododdin* recounts an ill-fated battle fought c.600 by Britons whose center of power was Din Edyn (Edinburgh). It exists in the thirteenth century *Book of Aneirin*.[37] Bede's important *Ecclesiastical History of the English People* finished in 735 includes much significant information about Pictish matters.[38] The *Táin Bó Fraích* dates from the eighth century and occurs in the twelfth century *Book of Leinster*, the fourteenth century *Yellow Book of Lecan*, the sixteenth century *Egerton 1782*, and the sixteenth century National Library of Scotland, *Gael. MS. XL*.[39] *Historia Brittonum* was first written in the early ninth century, and the eariest text is *Harleian MS 3859* of 828/829.[40] *Senchus Fer nAlban* tells of the early Irish settlers in Scotland and their descendants. Its current form dates from the tenth century but may have been compiled in the mid-seventh. It exists in several manuscripts, which have been discussed by John Bannerman.[41] *Duan Albanach* is a poem about various rulers of Scotland. The earliest extant text dates from the seventeenth century but seems to have been composed in the eleventh.[42] *Longes Chonaill Chuirc* relates the story of how Conall Corc (c.400), future King of Munster, was exiled to Scotland. It was probably composed during the eleventh century.[43] Another tale with a Scottish dimension is *Scéla Cano Meic Gartnáin*, which only occurs in the *Yellow Book of Lecan*. The present form text dates from the eleventh century but may have existed in an earlier form in the ninth.[44] Around 1136 Geoffrey of Monmouth completed his pseudo-historical *History of the Kings of Britain*, a work that makes frequent references to Scotland.[45] The text used for this study is the late twelfth century *Bern, Bürgerbibliothek, MS. 568*, an early text of Geoffrey's work.[46] *Trioedd Ynys Prydein* (*Triads of the Island of Britain* or *Welsh Triads*) are collections of significant items arranged in groups of three written in Welsh and which were used by bards. They come from *Peniarth MS. 16*, the *Black Book of Carmarthen*, *Llyfr Gwyn Rhydderch*, *Peniarth MS. 47*, and the *Red Book of Hergest* and appear to have been composed by the beginning of twelfth century.[47]

It has been deemed useful to undertake an analysis of these texts in the form of Notes in Chapters 5 and 6, which relate them to one another through the personal, population and place names which these texts connect to the Picts in various degrees. These Notes attempt to identify those personal, population, and place names and to give an account of their roles within the texts. The Notes are designed to include every textual reference which has some relation to the Picts. Some references are omitted when they are not specifically concerned with the Picts. Within these criteria of inclusion, the names are as complete as possible.

Standardized forms of names are given according to *Corpus Genealogiarum Hiberniae*,[48] *Persons: Ecclesiastics and Laypeople*, Vol. 3 in *Arthurian Period Sources*,[49] or *Onomasticon Goedelicum*,[50] when the name occurs in one of these sources. Pictish names are given according to *Kings and Kingship in Early Scotland*[51] or Kenneth Jackson.[52] Variations are given in parentheses after the name in the Notes. The Notes are arranged by category of text, and the texts in each category are arranged in chronological order by composition as far as this can be ascertained. The notes consist of three parts: the identification of the given name, the textual references, and relevant commentary (if any).

TEXTS

Origin Legends - see Chapter 2. Pictish Origin Legends

Genealogies

Harl. 3859: Egerton Phillimore, "The *Annales Cambriae* and Old Welsh Genealogies," in John Morris, *Genealogies and Texts*.[53]

Rawl. B. 502: "Genealogies from Rawlinson B. 502" in M.A. O'Brien, *Corpus Genealogiarum Hiberniae*.[54]

Book of Leinster: Anne O'Sullivan, *The Book of Leinster*. Vol. VI.[55] and M.A. O'Brien, *Corpus Genealogiarum Hiberniae*.[56]

Jes. 20: Egerton Phillimore, "Pedigrees from Jesus College MS. 20," in John Morris, *Genealogies and Texts*.[57]

Book of Lecan: Mulchrone, *Book of Lecan*.[58]

Laud 610: Kuno Meyer, "The Laud Genealogies and Tribal Histories" in *Zeitschrift für Celtische Philologie*.Vol. VIII.[59]

MacFirbis Genealogies: Elizabeth FitzPatrick, "Mac Firbis's Book of Genealogies" in *Catalogue of Irish Manuscripts*.Fasciculi XI-XV.[60]

MacFirbis Abstract: Elizabeth FitzPatrick, "Mac Firbis's Genealogical Abstract" in *Catalogue of Irish Manuscripts*.Fasciculi XI-XV.[61]

Annals

Annales Cambriae (ACam.): Egerton Phillimore, "*Annales Cambriae*" in *Genealogies and Texts*.[62] John Morris, "Annales Cambriae" in *Nennius*.[63]

Annals of Inisfallen (AI): Seán Mac Airt. (ed. and trans), *The Annals of Inisfallen (MS. Rawlinson B. 503)*.[64]

Annals of Tigernach (AT): Whitley Stokes, "The Annals of Tigernach" in *Revue Celtique*. Vol. XVII.[65] Donnchad Ó Corráin, *The Annals of Tigernach: CELT Edition*.[66] Kathryn Grabowski and David Dumville, *Chronicles and Annals of Medieval Ireland and Wales*.[67]

Annals of Clonmacnoise (AC): Denis Murphy. (ed.), *The Annals of Clonmacnoise*.[68]

Annals of Ulster (AU): Seán Mac Airt and Gearóid Mac Niocaill (eds.), *The Annals of Ulster*.[69]

Annals of the Four Masters (AFM): Donnchadh Ó Corráin, *The Annals of the Four Masters: CELT Edition*.[70]

Chronicum Scotorum (CS): William M. Hennesy, *Chronicum Scotorum*.[71]

Regnal Lists[72]

Regnal List SL1: Facsimile and edition in W.F. Skene, *Chronicles of the Picts, Chronicles of the Scots.*[73] Edition in M.O. Anderson, "Scottish Pieces from the Poppleton MS" in *Kings and Kingship in Early Scotland.*[74]

Regnal List SL2 M: R.A.S. MacAlister, *Book of Uí Maine* and Van Hamel (ed.), *Lebor Bretnach.*[75]

Regnal List SL2 O: M.O. Anderson, "List B" in *Kings and Kingship in Early Scotland.*[76]

Regnal List SL2 H: T.C.D., *MS. #1336*. W.F. Skene, *Chronicles of the Picts, Chronicles of the Scots*[77] and A.G. Van Hamel (ed.), *Lebor Bretnach.*[78]

Regnal List SL3(Lec.1): K. Mulchrone, *Book of Lecan.* (M. Miller's SL3 L)[79]

Regnal List SL3(Lec.2): K. Mulchrone, *Book of Lecan.* (M. Miller's SL3 La)[80]

Regnal List SL3(Lec.3): K. Mulchrone, *Book of Lecan.* (M. Miller's SL3 Lb)[81]

Regnal List SL3(Lec.4): K. Mulchrone, *Book of Lecan.* (M. Miller's SL3 M)[82]

Regnal List SL3(Bal.1): R. Atkinson, *Book of Ballymote.* (Miller's SL3 Bii)[83]

Regnal List SL3(Bal.2): R. Atkinson, *Book of Ballymote.* (Miller's SL3 Bi)[84]

Regnal List SL3(D.iv.1): R.I.A., *MS. Stowe D.iv.1.* (Miller's SL3 V)[85]

Regnal List SL3(24.P.13): R.I.A., *MS. Stowe 24.P.13.*[86]

Regnal List SL3(23.G.4): R.I.A., *MS. Stowe 23.G.4.*[87]

Regnal List SL3(1295.1): T.C.D., *MS. #1295.*[88]

Regnal List SL3(1295.2): T.C.D., *MS. #1295.*[89]

Regnal List SL3(1289): T.C.D., *MS. #1289.*[90]

Regnal List SL3(D.iii.2): R.I.A., *MS. Stowe D.iii.2.*[91]

Regnal List SL3(G47): N.L.I., *Gaelic MS. G 47.*[92]

Regnal List D: M.O. Anderson, "List D" in *Kings and Kingship in Early Scotland.*[93]

Regnal List F1: M.O. Anderson, "List F: *F(Innes,* 1729)" in *Kings and Kingship in Early Scotland.*[94]

Regnal List F2: M.O. Anderson, "List F: *Variant readings* in *Harleian* 4628" in *Kings and Kingship in Early Scotland.*[95]

Regnal List I: M.O. Anderson, "List I" in *Kings and Kingship in Early Scotland.*[96]

Regnal List K: M.O. Anderson, "List K" in *Kings and Kingship in Early Scotland.*[97]

Regnal List N: M.O. Anderson, "List N" in *Kings and Kingship in Early Scotland.*[98]

Fordun's List: Molly Miller, "The Disputed Historical Horizon of the Pictish King-lists" in *The Scottish Historical Review.* Vol. 58. and M.O. Anderson, "Fordun" in *Kings and Kingship in Early Scotland.*[99]

Hagiographies

Miracula Ninie: John and Winifred MacQueen, "The Miracles of Bishop Nynia (*Miracula Ninie Episcopi*)" in *St.Nynia*.[100]

Vita Niniani: Alexander P. Forbes, "Vita Niniani," in *St. Ninian and St. Kentigern*. John and Winifred MacQueen, "The Life of Ninian (*Vita Niniani by Ailred of Rievaulx*)" in *St. Nynia*.[101]

Vita Cadoci: A.W. Wade-Evans, "Vita Sancti Cadoci/The Life of Saint Cadog" in *Vitae Sanctorum Britanniae et Genealogiae*.[102]

Vita Columbae: William Reeves, *Life of Saint Columba*[103] and A.O. and M.O. Anderson, *Adomnán's Life of Columba* (1961); *Adomnán's Life of Columba* (1991).[104] Adomnán of Iona. Richard Sharpe (trans.), *Life of St Columba*.[105]

Betha Coluim Cille: Máire Herbert, "Betha Coluim Cille Incipit" in *Iona, Kells, and Derry*.[106]

Anonymous Cuthbert: Bertram Colgrave, "Vita Sancti CuthbertiAuctore Anonymo/The Life of St. Cuthbert by an Anonymous Author" in *Two Lives of Saint Cuthbert*.[107]

Bede's Cuthbert: Bertram Colgrave, "Vita Sancti Cuthberti Auctore Beda/Bede's Life of St. Cuthbert by Bede" in *Two Lives of Saint Cuthbert*.[108]

Life of Wilfrid: J.F. Webb and D.H. Farmer, "Eddius Stephanus: Life of Wilfrid" in *Age of Bede*.[109]

Life of Servanus: W.F. Skene, "Life of Saint Servanus" in *Chronicles of the Picts, Chronicles of the Scots*.[110]

Félire Óengusso: Whitley Stokes, *Félire Óengusso Céli Dé: The Martyrology of Oengus the Culdee*.[111]

Martyrology of Tallaght (Lein.): Anne O'Sullivan, "[Martyrology of Tallaght]," in Anne O'Sullivan, *Book of Leinster*, Vol. VI.[112]

History and Literature

Epistola: A.B.E. Hood, "*Epistola*" and "Letter," in A.B.E. Hood, *St. Patrick*[113]

Gildas: Michael Winterbottom. (ed.), *Gildas: The Ruin of Britain and Other Works*.[114]

Y Gododdin: Ifor Williams, Canu Aneirin. A.O.H. Jarman, *Aneirin: Y Gododdin*.[115]

Bede: Bede, *Historia Ecclesiastica Gentis Anglorum* (*HEGA*), in Bede, *Historical Works*, 2 Vols. ed. and trans J.E. King. Bede, *Ecclesiastical History of the English People* (*EHEP*), ed. and trans. Leo Sherley-Price and D.H. Farmer.[116]

TBF: Wolfgang Meid. (ed.), *Táin Bó Fraích* and R.I. Best and M.A. O'Brien, "Táin Bó Fraich," *Book of Leinster*, Vol. V.[117]

Historia Brittonum: John Morris, "Historia Brittonum" in *Nennius*.[118]

Senchus Fer nAlban: John Bannerman, "Senchus Fer nAlban" in *Studies in the History of Dalriada*.[119]
Duan Albanach: Kenneth Jackson, "The Duan Albanach" in *The Scottish Historical Review*. Vol. 36. and Kenneth Jackson, "The Poem *A Eolcha Alban Uile*" in *Celtica*. Vol. III.[120]
Longes Chonaill: Best and O'Brien, "Longes Chonaill Chuirc," *Book of Leinster*, Vol. V. Vernam Hull, "Exile of Conall Corc" in *Publications of the Modern Language Association of America*. Vol. 56.[121]
Scéla Cano: D.A. Binchy, *Scéla Cano Meic Gartnáin*.[122]
Culhwch and Olwen: Rachel Bromwich and D. Simon Evans, *Culhwch and Olwen*. Patrick K. Ford, "Culhwch and Olwen," in Patrick K. Ford, *The Mabinogi*.[123]
Geoffrey of Monmouth: Neil Wright (ed.), *The Historia Regum Britannie of Geoffrey of Monmouth* and Geoffrey of Monmouth. Lewis Thorpe (trans.), *The History of the Kings of Britain*.[124]
Welsh Triads: Rachel Bromwich (ed. and trans.), *Trioedd Ynys Prydein: The Welsh Triads*.[125]

ABBREVIATIONS AND METHODS

ALOC: A.O. and M.O. Anderson, *Adomnán's Life of Columba*.
CGH: M.A. O'Brien, *Corpus Genealogiarum Hiberniae*.
CPS: W.F. Skene, *Chronicles of the Picts, Chronicles of the Scots*.
d.: died
EIHM: T.F. O'Rahilly, *Early Irish History and Mythology*.
ESSH: A.O. Anderson, *Early Sources of Scottish History*.
f.: filius (son of)
fl.: flourished
fr.: frater (brother of)
HCPNS: W.J. Watson, *History of the Celtic Place-Names of Scotland*.
KKES: M.O. Anderson, *Kings and Kingship in Early Scotland*.
n.: nepos (nephew of/grandson of)
P: Pictish Origin Legend
q.v.: used after personal, population, and place names in order to cross-reference them to the Notes contained in Chapters 5 and 6.
SIHD: John Bannerman, *Studies in the History of Dalriada*.
TR.: Text which has been transcribed from single manuscript by someone other than this author. This is followed by initials of the transcriber.
VSBG: A.W. Wade-Evans, *Vitae Sanctorum Britanniae et Genealogiae*
?: In texts and translations, there is some question about the content or the meaning of a word or phrase. Otherwise, there is a question of the presence of an item in a text or its identification.

': After a letter in an edited text, this represents a dot over the letter in the text. It is often difficult to determine if a mark is a dot, a superscripted "h," a stray ink blot, or a stain.

{ }: When placed around a letter in an edited text, this represents a dot under a letter in the text. This is usually an indication that the letter is meant to be deleted.

- : When placed after a letter in an edited text, this represents a line over the letter in the text.

[ ]: Represents a corrupt passage in a text or an emendation in a translation.

//: Represents a caesura in a line of poetry.

Underlining indicates the expansion of contractions, suprascripts, and subscripts. Proper names have been capitalized. The rest of the capitalization is according to the text as it appears in the manuscript. Every effort has been made to accurately interpret and transcribe the contents of the original texts; however, this author will be the first to admit that mistakes may have occurred either because of the quality of the original or through palaeographical misinterpretaion.

Note on the translations: Every effort has been made in the translations to balance accuracy, intelligibility, and logic although this is difficult and not always possible due to the nature of the original texts. In order to minimize confusion, the names in the translations have been standardized as in the Notes regardless of the form in the text.

Note: In order to limit the quantity of endnotes and limit repetition of references, the texts of the Origin Legends and the Annals are only referenced at their initial appearance.

MANUSCRIPTS

Bal.: *Book of Ballymote* (facsimile)
B 506: Bodleian *MS. Rawlinson B 506* (microfilm printout)
B 512: Bodleian *MS. Rawlinson B 512* (microfilm printout)
B.iii.1: R.I.A. *MS. Stowe B.iii.1* (microfilm printout)
C.vi.2: R.I.A. *MS. Stowe C.vi.2* (microfilm printout)
D.i.3: R.I.A. *MS. Stowe D.i.3* (microfilm printout)
D.ii.2: R.I.A. *MS. Stowe D.ii.2* (microfilm printout)
D.iii.1: R.I.A. *MS. Stowe D.iii.1* (microfilm printout)
D.iii.2: R.I.A. *MS. Stowe D.iii.2* (microfilm printout)
D.iv.1: R.I.A. *MS. Stowe D.iv.1* (microfilm printout)
G47: N.L.I. *Gaelic MS. 47* (microfilm)
G131: N.L.I. *Gaelic MS. 131* (microfilm)
Lec.: *Book of Lecan* (facsimile)
Lein.: *Book of Leinster* (facsimile)
Ren.: *Rennes Ms.*
1336: T.C.D. *MS. #1336* (microfilm printout)
1322: T.C.D. *MS. #1322* (microfilm)
1289: T.C.D. *MS. #1289* (microfilm printout)
1295: T.C.D. *MS. #1295* (microfilm printout)
24.P.13: R.I.A. *MS. 24.P.13* (microfilm printout)
23.G.4: R.I.A. *MS. 23.G.4* (microfilm printout)
Uí Ma.: *Book of Uí Maine* (facsimile)

2

PICTISH ORIGIN LEGENDS

DATES AND KNOWN MANUSCRIPTS

(Texts marked with '*' are not printed in this work)

P#A(B 506): Early 9th century. (Mac Eoin's Version 2(a), archetype Vx, c.600). Bodleian Library, *MS Rawlinson B 506*, 3vbb31-4rb9 (pre-1373, scribe: Seán Ó Cianáin).[1]

P#A(Uí Ma.): Early 9th century. (Mac Eoin's Version 2(a), archetype Vx, c.600). *Book of Uí Maine*, 15[67]ra8-61 (1392-1397(?), scribe: Faelán Mac a' Ghabhann (d.1423)).[2]

P#A(Lec.): Early 9th century. (Mac Eoin's Version 2(a), archetype Vx, c.600). *Book of Lecan*, 131vb[2]50-132ra49 (1418, scribe: Gilla Isu Mac Fir Bhisigh).[3]

P#A(C.vi.2): Early 9th century. (Mac Eoin's Version 2(a), archetype Vx, c.600). Royal Irish Academy *MS. C.vi.2*, 298b16-299b4 (1715-1716, scribe: Semus Mhaguidhir. This is a transcript of Mac Firbis's Book of Genealogies).[4]

P#B(Lec.): Early 9th century. (Mac Eoin's Version 2(b), archetype Vx, c.600). *Book of Lecan*, 270rb2-12 (1417-1418, scribe: Gilla Isu Mac Fir Bhisigh). Part of Recension c of the *Lebor Gabála*.[5]

P#B(Bal.): Early 9th century. (Mac Eoin's Version 2(b), archetype Vx, c.600). *Book of Ballymote*, 19a39-47 (1384-1406, scribe: Magnus Ó Duibgennáin). Part of Recension c of *Lebor Gabála*.[6]

P#B(1295): Early 9th century. (Mac Eoin's Version 2(b), archetype Vx, c.600). T.C.D. *MS. #1295* (formerly H.2.4), 40 ll.19-23 (1728, scribe: Richard Tipper. Copy of *Book of Ballymote*). Recension c of *Lebor Gabála*.[7]

P#B(1289): Early 9th century. (Mac Eoin's Version 2(b), archetype Vx, c.600). T.C.D. *MS. 1289* (formerly H.1.15), 41 ll.19-24 (c.1745, scribe: Tadhg Ó Neachtain. This is a copy of *Book of Ballymote*). Part of Recension c of *Lebor Gabála*.[8]

P#B(D.iii.2): Early 9th century. (Mac Eoin's Version 2(b), archetype Vx, c.600). R.I.A *MS. Stowe D.iii.2* (#619), 20 ll.20-27 (1746, scribe: Aodh Ó Dálaigh. This is a copy of *Book of Ballymote*). Part of Recension c of *Lebor Gabála*.[9]

P#C(Lein.): Pre-887. (Mac Eoin's Version 1, archetype O. pre-600). *Book of Leinster*, 134a48-b21 (Late 12th century, scribe: Aed mac Crimthainn).[10]

P#C(Uí Ma.): Pre-887. (Mac Eoin's Version 1, archetype O. pre-600). *Book of Uí Maine*, 150[208]ra20-43 (14th century).[11]

P#C(Lec.): Pre-887. (Mac Eoin's Version 1, archetype O, pre-600). *Book of Lecan*, 144vb46-145a20 (1416-1418, scribe: Gilla Isu Mac Fir Bhisigh).[12]

P#C(G131): Pre-887. (Mac Eoin's Version 1, archetype O, pre-600). National Library of Ireland, *Gaelic Manuscript G 131*, 28v[52] l.6-29r[53] l.4 (c.1650-59, main scribe: Cú Chóiríche Ó Cléirigh).[13]

P#D(D.iv.1): Mid-11th century. (Mac Eoin's Version 4(d), archetype Vy, pre-700). R.I.A. *MS. Stowe D.iv.1*, 3rb46-3va6 (1391-1399, part of original Yellow Book of Lecan (?)). Recension b of *Lebor Gabála*.[14]

P#D(Lec.1): Mid-11th century. (Mac Eoin's Version 4(d), archetype Vy, pre-700). *Book of Lecan*, 5ra17-28 (1418, scribe: Adamh Ó Cuirnín). Part of Recension b of *Lebor Gabála*.[15]

P#D(Lec.2): Mid-11th century. (Mac Eoin's Version 4(d), archetype Vy, pre-700). *Book of Lecan*, 287rb11-23 (1417-1418, scribe: Gilla Isu Mac Fir Bhisigh). Part of Recension c of *Lebor Gabála*.[16]

P#D(Bal.): Mid-11th century. (Mac Eoin's Version 4(d), archetype Vy, pre-700). *Book of Ballymote*, 43a56-43b12 (1384-1406, scribe: Magnus Ó Duibgennáin). Part of Recension c of *Lebor Gabála*.[17]

P#D(24.P.13): Mid-11th century. (Mac Eoin's Version 4(d), archetype Vy, pre-700). R.I.A. *MS. 24.P.13* (#1068), 27 ll.8-19 (1621, scribe: Luán (mhac) Taidg). Part of Recension c of *Lebor Gabála*.[18]

P#D(1295): Mid-11th century. (Mac Eoin's Version 4(d), archetype Vy, pre-700). T.C.D. *MS. #1295* (formerly H.2.4), 84 ll.15-24 (1728, scribe: Richard Tipper). Part of Recension c of *Lebor Gabála*.[19]

P#D(1289): Mid-11th century. (Mac Eoin's Version 4(d), archetype Vy, pre-700). T.C.D. *MS. #1289* (formerly H.1.15), 93 l.38-94 l.8 (1745, scribe: Tadhg Ó Neachtain). Part of Recension c of *Lebor Gabála*.[20]

P#D(D.iii.2): Mid-11th century. (Mac Eoin's Version 4(d), archetype Vy, pre-700). R.I.A. *MS. Stowe D.iii.2 (#619)*, 97 ll.12-21 (1746, scribe: Aodh Ó Dálaigh). Part of Recension c of *Lebor Gabála*.[21]

P#E(Lec.): Mid-11th century. (Mac Eoin's Version 4(f), archetype Vy, pre-700). *Book of Lecan*, 144ra14-144va6 (1416-1418, scribe: Gilla Isu Mac Fir Bhisigh). Part of *Lebor Bretnach*.[22]

P#E(Bal.): Mid-11th century. (Mac Eoin's Version 4(f), archetype Vy, pre-700). *Book of Ballymote*, 204a34-205a24 (1384-1406, scribe: Robeartus mac Sithigh). Part of *Lebor Bretnach*.[23]

P#E(B 512): Mid-11th century. (Mac Eoin's Version 4(f), archetype Vy, pre-700). Bodleian *MS. Rawlinson B 512*, 95rb29-32 (15th-early 16th century). Part of Recension m of *Lebor Gabála*.[24]

P#E(1295): Mid-11th century. (Mac Eoin's Version 4(f), archetype Vy, pre-700). T.C.D. *MS. #1295*, 380 l.1-381 l.9 (1728, scribe: Richard Tipper). Part of *Lebor Bretnach*.[25]

P#F(D.iv.1): Late-11th century. (Mac Eoin's Version 4(a), archetype Vy, pre-700). R.I.A. *MS. Stowe D.iv.1*, 3rb22-45, 3va7-28 (1391-1399, possibly part of original Yellow Book of Lecan). Part of Recension b of *Lebor Gabála*.[26]

P#F(Lec.1): Late-11th century. (Mac Eoin's Version 4(a), archetype Vy, pre-700). *Book of Lecan*, 4vb50-5ra16, 5ra29-49 (1418, scribe: Adam Ó Cuirnín). Part of Recension b of *Lebor Gabála*.[27]

P#F(Lec.2): Late-11th century. (Mac Eoin's Version 4(a), archetype Vy, pre-700). *Book of Lecan*, 287ra33-rb10, 287rb24-287va4 (1417-1418, scribe: Gilla Isu Mac Fir Bhisigh). Part of Recension c of *Lebor Gabála*.[28]

P#F(Bal.): Late-11th century. (Mac Eoin's Version 4(a), archetype Vy, pre-700). *Book of Ballymote*, 43a33-55, 43b13-32 (1384-1406, scribe: Magnus Ó Duibgennáin). Part of Recension c of *Lebor Gabála*.[29]

P#F(24.P.13): Late-11th century. (Mac Eoin's Version 4(a), archetype Vy, pre-700). R.I.A. *MS. 24.P.13*, 26 1.21-27 1.8, 27 1.20-28 1.4 (1621, scribe: Luán (mhac) Taidg). Part of Recension c of *Lebor Gabála*.[30]

P#F(1295): Late-11th century. (Mac Eoin's Version 4(a), archetype Vy, pre-700). T.C.D. *MS. #1295*, 83 1.41-84 1.14, 84 11.25-39 (1728, scribe: Richard Tipper). Part of Recension c of *Lebor Gabála*.[31]

P#F(1289): Late-11th century. (Mac Eoin's Version 4(a), archetype Vy, pre-700). T.C.D. *MS. #1289*, 93 11.22-37, 94 11.9-20 (c.1745, scribe: Tadhg Ó Neachtain). Part of Recension c of *Lebor Gabála*.[32]

P#F(D.iii.2): Late-11th century. (Mac Eoin's Version 4(a), archetype Vy, pre-700). R.I.A. *MS. Stowe D.iii.2*, 96 1.21-97 1.11, 97 11.22-37 (1746, scribe: Aodh Ó Dálaigh). Part of Recension c of *Lebor Gabála*.[33]

P#G(Lec.): Late-11th century. (Mac Eoin's Version 4(b), archetype Vy, pre-700). *Book of Lecan*, 143vb11-144ra3 (1418, scribe: Gilla Isu Mac Fir Bhisigh). Part of *Lebor Bretnach*.[34]

P#G(Bal.): Late-11th century. (Mac Eoin's Version 4(b), archetype Vy, pre-700). *Book of Ballymote*, 203c37-204a33 (1384-1406, scribe: Robeartus mac Sithigh). Part of *Lebor Bretnach*.[35]

P#G(B 512): Late-11th century. (Mac Eoin's Version 4(b), archetype Vy, pre-700). Bodleian *MS. Rawlinson B 512*, 95ra18-b29 (15th-early 16th century). Part of Recension m of *Lebor Gabála*.[36]

P#G(1295): Late-11th century. (Mac Eoin's Version 4(b), archetype Vy, pre-700). T.C.D. *MS. #1295*, 379 11.13-40 (1728, scribe: Richard Tipper). Part of *Lebor Bretnach*.[37]

P#H(Lein.): Late-11th century. (Mac Eoin's Version 4(c) (includes 3(a)), archetype Vy, pre-700). *Book of Leinster*, 15a22-37 (Late 12th century, scribe: Aed mac Crimthainn). Recension a of *Lebor Gabála*.[38]

P#H(D.iii.1): Late-11th century. (Mac Eoin's Version 4(c)), archetype Vy, pre-700). R.I.A. *MS. Stowe D.iii.1*, 1vb38-2ra18 (pre-1374, scribe: Adam Ó Cianáin (d.AFM 1374)). Recension a of *Lebor Gabála*.[39]

P#H(D.i.3): Late-11th century. (Mac Eoin's Version 4(c), archetype Vy, pre-700). R.I.A. *MS. Stowe D.i.3*, 3rb13-23 (1391-1399, possibly part of original Yellow Book of Lecan). Recension m of *Lebor Gabála*.[40]

P#H(Lec.): Late-11th century. (Mac Eoin's Version 4(c), archetype Vy, pre-700). *Book of Lecan*, 20va6-16 (1418, scribe: Adam Ó Cuirnín). Part of Recension m of *Lebor Gabála*.[41]

P#H(B 512): Late-11th century,. (Mac Eoin's Version 4(c), archetype Vy, pre-700). Bodl. *MS. B 512*, 95ra1-18 (15th-early 16th century). Part of Recension m of *Lebor Gabála*.[42]

P#I(Lein.): Mid-11th century. (Mac Eoin's Version 4(e), archetype Vy, pre-700). *Book of Leinster*, 196a11-31 (Late 12th century, scribe: Aed mac Crimthainn).[43]

P#I(Uí Ma.): Mid-11th century. (Mac Eoin's Version 4(e), archetype Vy, pre-700). *Book of Uí Maine*, 93[152]vb6-21 (Late-14th century).[44]

P#I(Lec.): Mid-11th century. (Mac Eoin's Version 4(e), archetype Vy, pre-700). *Book of Lecan*, 234va12-35 (1418, scribe: Gilla Isu Mac Fir Bhisigh).[45]

P#I(Bal.): Mid-11th century. (Mac Eoin's Version 4(e), archetype Vy, pre-700). *Book of Ballymote*, 370b1-25 (1384-1406, scribe: Magnus Ó Duibgennáin).[46]

*P#I(Ren.): Mid-11th century. (Mac Eoin's Version 4(e), archetype Vy, pre-700). Rennes Bibliotheque MS. (14-15th century).[47] I have not examined this text. This Variation of P#I may follow its Variation of P#J (see below) as is the case with other Variations of this text.

P#I(D.ii.2): Mid-11th century. (Mac Eoin's Version 4(e), archetype Vy, pre-700). R.I.A. *MS. Stowe D.ii.2*, 26vb23-27ra22 (16th century (?), scribe: Muiris Ó Clérigh).[48]

P#I(1322): Mid-11th century. (Mac Eoin's Version 4(e), archetype Vy, pre-700). T.C.D. *MS. #1322* (formerly H.3.3), 24b3-20 (c.1548).[49]

P#I(B.iii.1): Mid-11th century. (Mac Eoin's Version 4(e), archetype Vy, pre-700). R.I.A. *MS. Stowe B.iii.1*, 30v l.26-31r l.14 (17th century, scribes: two Donegal O'Clerys(?)).[50]

P#J(Uí Ma.): Late-11th century. (Mac Eoin's Version 4(e), archeptype Vy, pre-700). *Book of Uí Maine*, 93[152]va51-b5 (Late-14th century).[51]

P#J(Lec.): Late-11th century. (Mac Eoin's Version 4(e), archeptype Vy, pre-700). *Book of Lecan*, 234rb43-234va11 (1418, scribe: Gilla Isu Mac Fir Bhisigh).[52]

P#J(Bal.): Late-11th century. (Mac Eoin's Version 4(e), archeptype Vy, pre-700). *Book of Ballymote*, 370a38-51 (1384-1406, scribe: Magnus Ó Duibgennáin).[53]

P#J(Ren.)(TR.WS): Late-11th cent. (Mac Eoin's Version 4(e), archeptype Vy, pre-700). Rennes Bibliotheque MS. (14-15th cent.). The W. Stokes edition is re-printed in this work.[54] I have not examined the original. This P#J may precede its P#I (see above) as in other manuscripts.

P#J(D.ii.2): Late-11th century. (Mac Eoin's Version 4(e), archeptype Vy, pre-700). R.I.A. *MS. Stowe D.ii.2*, 26va26-b22 (16th century(?), scribe: Muiris Ó Clérigh).[55]

P#J(1322): Late-11th century. (Mac Eoin's Version 4(e), archeptype Vy, pre-700). T.C.D. *MS. #1322*, 24a36-b2 (c.1548).[56]

P#J(B.iii.1): Late-11th century. (Mac Eoin's Version 4(e), archeptype Vy, pre-700). R.I.A. *MS. Stowe B.iii.1*, 30v ll.17-25. (17th century, scribe: two Donegal O'Clerys(?)).[56a]

P#K(D.iv.1): c.1100. (Mac Eoin's Version 3(b), archetype Vy/Vz, pre-700/post-900). R.I.A. *MS. Stowe D.iv.1*, 3va35-46 (1391-1399, original Yellow Book of Lecan(?)). Recension b of *Lebor Gabála*.[57]

P#K(Lec.1): c.1100. (Mac Eoin's Version 3(b), archetype Vy/Vz, pre-700/post-900). *Book of Lecan*, 5rb2-12 (1418, scribe: Adam Ó Cuirnín). Part of Recension b of *Lebor Gabála*.[58]

P#K(Lec.2): c.1100. (Mac Eoin's Version 3(b), archetype Vy/Vz, pre-700/post-900). *Book of Lecan*, 144ra4-14 (1416-1418, scribe: Gilla Isu Mac Fir Bhisigh). Part of *Lebor Bretnach*.[59]

P#K(Bal.): c.1100. (Mac Eoin's Version 3(b), archetype Vy/Vz, pre-700/post-900). *Book of Ballymote*, 43b49-44a3 (1384-1406, scribe: Magnus Ó Duibgennáin). Recension c of *Lebor Gabála*.[60]

P#K(24.P.13): c.1100. (Mac Eoin's Version 3(b), archetype Vy/Vz, pre-700/post-900). R.I.A. *MS. 24.P.13*, 28 ll.16-25 (1621, scribe: Luán (mhac) Taidg). Part of Recension c of *Lebor Gabála*.[61]

P#K(1295): c.1100. (Mac Eoin's Version 3(b), archetype Vy/Vz, pre-700/post-900). T.C.D. *MS. #1295*, 85 ll.10-17 (1728, scribe: Richard Tipper). Part of Recension c of *Lebor Gabála*.[62]

P#K(1289): c.1100. (Mac Eoin's Version 3(b), archetype Vy/Vz, pre-700/post-900). T.C.D. *MS. #1289*, 94 l.34-95 l.2 (1745, scribe: Tadhg Ó Neachtain). Part of Recension c of *Lebor Gabála*.[63]

P#K(D.iii.2): c.1100. (Mac Eoin's Version 3(b), archetype Vy/Vz, pre-700/post-900). R.I.A. *MS. Stowe D.iii.2*, 98 ll.20-31 (1746, scribe: Aodh Ó Dálaigh). Part of Recension c of *Lebor Gabála*.[64]

P#L(Uí Ma.): Post-1100?. (Mac Eoin's Version 5, post-900?). *Book of Uí Maine*, 36[92]ra44-65 (Late-14th century). Part of *Lebor Bretnach*.[65]

P#L(Lec.): Post-1100?. (Mac Eoin's Version 5, post-900?). *Book of Lecan*, 141ra15-43 (1416-1418, scribe: Gilla Isu Mac Fir Bhisigh). Part of *Lebor Bretnach*.[66]

P#L(Bal.): Post-1100?. (Mac Eoin's Version 5, post-900?). *Book of Ballymote*, 206a25-48 (1384-1406, scribe: Robeartus mac Sithigh). Part of *Lebor Bretnach*.[67]

P#L(1336): Post-1100?. (Mac Eoin's Version 5, post-900?). T.C.D. *MS. #1336* (H.3.17), cols. 809 l.36-810 l.21 (c.1500). Part of *Lebor Bretnach*.[68]

P#L(1295): Post-1100?. (Mac Eoin's Version 5, post-900?). T.C.D. *MS. #1295*, 382 ll.27-40 (1728, scribe: Richard Tipper). Part of *Lebor Bretnach*.[69]

P#L(G47): Post-1100?. (Mac Eoin's Version 5, post-900?). N.L.I. *Gaelic MS. 47*, 10 l.13-11 l.6 (1807). Part of *Lebor Bretnach*.[70]

EDITIONS OF PICTISH ORIGIN LEGENDS IN IRISH

P#A: Skene, *Chronicles of the Picts and Scots*, prints a composite text with translation from *Rawl. B. 506* and *Book of Lecan*.

    M.E. Dobbs, "The History of the Descendants of Ir," prints a composite text with translation from *Rawl. B 506, Book of Uí Maine* (*Stowe D.ii.1*), *Book of Lecan, Book of Ballymote, Mac Firbis' Genealogies.*[71]

P#B: Skene, *Chronicles of the Picts and Scots*, prints this text with translation from *Book of Ballymote*.

    MacAlister, *Lebor Gabála, Part II*, prints a composite text with translation from *Book of Lecan* and *Book of Ballymote.*[72]

P#C: Todd, *Irish Version of the Historia Brittonum*, prints a text with translation from the *Book of Leinster* and the Book of Lecan.

    Skene, *Chronicles of the Picts and Scots*, prints a composite text with translation from *Book of Leinster* and *Book of Lecan*.

    Best, *Book of Leinster*, prints diplomatic edition.[73]

P#D: Todd, *Irish Version of the Historia Brittonum*, prints a text with translation from the *Book of Ballymote* with readings from *Book of Lecan*.

    Skene, *Chronicles of the Picts and Scots*, prints a composite text with translation from the two versions in the *Book of Lecan*.

    MacAlister, *Lebor Gabála, Part V*, prints a composite text with translation from several manuscripts.[74]

P#E: Todd, *Irish Version of the Historia Brittonum*, prints a text with translation from the *Book of Ballymote* with readings from *Book of Lecan*.

    Skene, *Chronicles of the Picts and Scots*, prints a composite text with translation from *Book of Lecan* and *Book of Ballymote*.

    Van Hamel, *Lebor Bretnach*, prints separate texts from *Book of Lecan* and *Book of Ballymote* without translations.[75]

P#F: Todd, *Irish Version of the Historia Brittonum*, prints a text with translation from the *Book of Ballymote* with readings from *Book of Lecan*.

    Skene, *Chronicles of the Picts and Scots*, print composite texts with translation from several manuscripts.

    MacAlister, *Lebor Gabála, Part V*, prints a composite text with translation from *Stowe D.iv.3., Book of Lecan, Book of Ballymote, Stowe D.iv.1., Stowe D.iii.2.*[76]

P#G: Todd, *Irish Version of the Historia Brittonum*, prints a text with translation from the *Book of Ballymote* with readings from *Book of Lecan*.

Skene, *Chronicles of the Picts and Scots*, prints a composite text with translation from *Book of Lecan* and *Book of Ballymote*.

Van Hamel, *Lebor Bretnach*, prints text from *Book ofLecan* with readings from *Book of Ballymote* without translation.[77]

P#H: Skene, *Chronicles of the Picts and Scots*, prints text with translation from *Book of Leinster*.

MacAlister, *Lebor Gabála, Part V*, prints a composite text with translation from *Book of Leinster, D.iii.1, Rawl. B 512, Stowe D.i.3, Book of Lecan*.

Best, *Book of Leinster*, prints diplomatic edition.[78]

P#I: E.G. Gwynn, *Metrical Dindshenchas, Part III*, prints a composite text with translation from *Book of Leinster, Rennes MS., Book of Ballymote, Book of Lecan, T.C.D. #1322*(H.3.3), *Book of Uí Maine, Stowe D.ii.2, Stowe B.iii.1*.

Best, *Book of Leinster*, prints diplomatic edition.[79]

P#J: Stokes, "The Prose Dindshenchas in the Rennes MS.," prints text with translation from *Rennes MS.*[80]

P#K: Todd, *Irish Version of the Historia Brittonum*, prints a text with translation from the *Book of Lecan*.

Skene, *Chronicles of the Picts and Scots*, prints a composite text with translation from the two versions in *Book of Lecan*.

MacAlister, *Lebor Gabála, Part V*, prints composite texts with translations from several manuscripts.[81]

P#L: Skene, *Chronicles*, prints composite text with translation from *Book of Lecan* and *Book of Ballymote*.

Van Hamel, *Lebor Bretnach*, prints text without translation from *T.C.D. #1336*(H.3.17) with readings from *Book of Uí Maine, Book of Lecan, Book of Ballymote*.[82]

TEXTS AND TRANSLATIONS

<u>VARIATION P#A(B 506)</u>

De ge<u>nel</u>ach Dal Araid<u>h</u>e ·i· Fiacha <u>A</u>raid<u>h</u>e Cland Conaill C<u>e</u>rnaich ·i· Dal nAraide <u>o</u> carraic i<u>n</u>dber u<u>ac</u>ht. co li<u>n</u>d huachalla Ai<u>n</u>m naile doib Cr<u>ui</u>thníg ·i· ni<u>ath</u> cruthaige <u>no</u> nia Crodai· u<u>t</u> poeta d<u>ixit</u>

A Maildui<u>n</u> anasrubairt <u>frith</u> rui<u>n</u> i<u>m</u>rubairt
do gae cruaith rodamar do lobor buaith <u>no</u> trenfir

Cr<u>o</u>dai <u>for</u> Irial Glu<u>n</u>mar m<u>ac</u> <u>Co</u>naill C<u>e</u>rnaich <u>for</u>ceta <u>ar</u> ba cr<u>u</u>th Cruithniu ·i· nia Cruithne ·i· m<u>ac</u> seath<u>ar</u> Cruit<u>h</u>ne Lonchetnae. i<u>n</u>gean Echd<u>h</u>i Echbeoil dia Albae a math<u>air</u>· IThe abbae donacht Cu C<u>ul</u>aind ⁊ Cu Roi m<u>ac</u> Daire a Albae i nEri<u>n</u>d Colgu m<u>ac</u> Mongai<u>n</u> d<u>ixit</u>·

MAsa co<u>m</u>ram <u>con</u>daigi cuideas. eacna ru<u>n</u>mar
coica catha derruaid rofich Irial Glu<u>n</u>mar

Da nocht dec milead de thuaib Tr<u>ai</u>ciae Da lotar ar cea<u>n</u>d loingse m<u>ei</u>c Miledh Easpai<u>n</u>e do Gearma<u>n</u> dob<u>er</u>tadar leo co mbat<u>ar</u> him militeacht· leo ni taultatar mna leo statim <u>con</u>id do s<u>il</u> m<u>ei</u>c Mil<u>ed</u> arro fr<u>oe</u>tar mna iarsi<u>n</u> to brith i<u>n</u>geiní oigtigear<u>n</u> daaib o flaithnio hEri<u>n</u>d ⁊ ar nglanad a claideabtir doib alle IT<u>er</u> Bretnaib .i. Mag F<u>or</u>trei<u>n</u> pri<u>m</u>o ⁊ Mag Cirgi<u>n</u> ·i· fo <u>con</u>id iar mathru gabait flaith ⁊ cach comarb<u>us</u> olc<u>h</u>eana ar naisa <u>for</u>ru o f<u>er</u>aib Eri<u>n</u>d ·i· t<u>ri</u> caicat i<u>n</u>ge<u>n</u>a ro huicset a hEre<u>nn</u> do maithrib m<u>ac</u> i<u>n</u>de aldi<u>n</u>d na hi<u>n</u>gi i cr<u>i</u>ch Dail Araid<u>h</u>e

T<u>ri</u>ca rig do Cruithnib <u>for</u> Eri<u>n</u>d ⁊ Albai<u>n</u> ·i· do Cruithnib Alba<u>n</u> ⁊ Ere<u>nn</u> ·i· di Dail Airad<u>h</u>e Ota Ollaman diata Mur nOllam<u>h</u>an hi Te<u>am</u>air Coirrici Fiachni m<u>ac</u> Baetai<u>n</u> ronenaisc sid<u>h</u>e giallu Ere<u>nn</u> ⁊ Alba<u>n</u> seact riga da<u>no</u> do Cruithnneac<u>h</u>aib Alba<u>n</u> rofollamnaigeastair Ere<u>nn</u> a Tem<u>air</u> Ollam<u>h</u> aí<u>n</u>m ·i· c· rig rogab ⁊ a Cruachnaib ·xxx· and is de ata Mur nOllama<u>n</u> hi Tem<u>air</u> his leis ceta nd<u>er</u>nad feis Temrach

Heilím ollfinsnechta taeis<u>i</u> nOllaman ri <u>for</u> Eiri<u>n</u>d uili a Te<u>am</u>air ·xxx· an<u>n</u>is· na laithsid<u>h</u>e f<u>ear</u>ais. ín snecta fína co tímteth f<u>er</u> isan gai<u>m</u>riath

Of the Genealogy of Dál n-Araide: that is, Fiachu nAraide. The children of Conall Cernach: that is, the Dál n-Araide from cold(?) Carrac Inbhir to Lind Uachaill. Another name for them, Cruithni: that is, shapely warrior or nephew of Crodai. As the poet said:

Oh Mael Duin, // what you have said was obtained in secret(?),
you have wielded your hard spear, // you have given victory to a sick man.

Cródai ("hardy warrior"). Upon Irél Glúnmár, son of Conall Cernach; it was enjoined (or "prophesied"), for he was the charioteer (?) of the Cruithni: that is, the nephew of Cruithne. That is: Lonceta, daughter of Echde Eachbheoil of Alba, his mother. It was her (his?) cows which Cú Chulainn and Cu Rai mac Dáire drove from Alba to Ireland. Colcu mac Mongáin said:

If it is a contest you seek // (the one) that proves knowledge of secrets,
fifty battles to Es Ruaid(?) (Assaroe) // Irél Glúnmár fought.

Two companies of eighteen soldiers from the tribes of Thrace came to meet the fleet of the Sons of Mil of Spain to Germany. They brought [them] with them so that they were [kept] for the sake of soldiers. Women did not come with them initially so that it was from the descendants of the Sons of Míl that they accepted women. Afterwards the daughters of young lords from the nobility of Ireland (?) were brought to them and after the purification of their sword-land for them yonder among the Britons: that is, the Plain of Fortriu first and the Plain of Circhend. It was so that it was according to [men's] mothers [that they] held the sovereignty and every succession besides for the sake of that being pledged ("enjoined") upon them by the men of Ireland. That is, the one hundred and fifty maidens whom they brought from Ireland to be mothers of sons (Whence Alt na n-ingen ("Cliff of the Maidens") in the territory of Dál n-Araide).

Thirty kings of the Cruithni over Ireland and Alba: that is, of the Cruithni of Alba and of Ireland (that is, of Dál n-Araide). From Ollam (from him is Mur n-Ollaman ("Wall of Ollam") at Temair) to Fiachna mac Báetáin. The last mentioned bound the hostages from Ireland and Alba. Thence seven kings of the Cruithni of Alba ruled Ireland in Temair. Ollam the name of the first king who ruled for thirty years at Temair and at Cruachu. From him is Mur n-Ollaman in Temair. It is by him the Feast of Temair was first accomplished/held.

Eilim ollfhinachta was after Ollam king of all Ireland at Temair for thirty years. In his reign the wine-snow fell so that the grass decayed in winter-time.

Findoll cisirne tareissi nEilim ·xxx· annis· hi Teamair ocus i ceann nach nad rogenair ina flaithusidhe robo ceanand is de ata Ceanandas· ina lochtae

Geithe ollgothach ina diaisidhe i Teamair 7 for Fainlaibi hi tirib Mogornai rofallnastar ·xxx· annis· ína flaithsidhe ba bindníthir· la cach guth araili bidh crot ar med in cainchomraich ina flaitha sidhe

Slanoll tareissi nGeith is na flaíthus ni raib gallra for dainib in Ere roallnastair hi Teamair 7 slan for Ere ·xxx· annis.

Bagag ollfiacha taeisi Slanuill rofallnastair for Erind i Teamair ·xxx· is na flaith sidhe tinscanta coicce in Ere

Bearngal tareisi ·in· b· rofallnastair for Ere a Teamair ·xxx· annis· is na flaithnus sidhe a rocuir ith a in Ere acht miach co leith ar med in coicthe in Erind 7 ar a lin

it e sin na ·uíí· riga rogabsat Erenn di Cruthnib Alban di Cruithnib Erind din di Dal nAraidhe· na ·uíí· Laichre Laig[ean]· 7 na ·uíí· Sodhain Erind 7 cach Conailli fil in Erind. De genelach Dail nAraidhe

Findoll cisirne after Eilim for thirty years at Temair, and in the end every cow born in his reign was white-headed. It is from that that Ceanannus is ("a place of ..."?).

Géde Ollgothach then ruled after him in Temair and over Fain-laibe of the lands of Mugdorn for thirty years. In his reign everyone regarded every voice as being as melodious as a lute on account of the fine conversation during his reign.

Slanoll after Géde. It was in his reign that no one was ill in Ireland. He ruled at Temair and wholeness [was] over Ireland for thirty years.

Bagag ollfiacha after Slanoll. He ruled over Ireland at Temair thirty years. It is in his reign [that] wars were instituted in Ireland.

Berngal after that Bagag. He ruled over Ireland at Temair thiry years. It is in his reign [that] corn in Ireland was destroyed except a sack (or "bushel") and a half through the scale and frequency/abundance of warring in Ireland.

Those, then, are the seven kings from the Cruithni of Alba who ruled Ireland. From the Cruithni of Ireland, therefore, from the Dál n-Araide: that is, the seven Laigsi (s. Laigis) of Laigin and the seven Sodain of Ireland and all Conailli who are in Ireland. Of the genealogy of Dál n-Araide.

VARIATION P#A(Uí Ma.)

Da cland Conaill C'earnaig Dal Araig'i o Carraig nisoe co lind
hUac'aill Ainm eile dal Dhal Araighi ·i· Cruithnigh ·i· cruthaichthe no i Nad'
Crodui ut· poeta· dixit·

A Mailduin anasrubart frith iruin amrubairt
da gai cruaich crodamar do lobar brait no treinfir

Crodai for Irial nGlunmar meic Conaill Cearnaig for ceda ar ba rad
Cruithni ·i· nia Cruithni ·i· mac seathar Cruithni Loincheada ingean Eachach
Eachbeoil dia Alba a mathair at e abae i danocht Cu Culaind ₇ Cu Rai mac
Dairi di Alba a nErind Colca mac Mongan ·dixit·

Masa chomrair conaighi cruites ecna runmar
caeca catha co heas ruaigh rosfigh uaig Irial Glumar

Da nocht deg milidh da thuathaib Traigia da lodar ar ceand loingse
meic Milead Esbaine da Gherman dosbeartadar leo co mbadair a milteacht ₇ ni
taultadar mna leo statim conad da sil meic Mileadh nair rof[']eadar mna Iarsin
da breatha ingena oigtigearn doibh o f'laith Erind ₇ ar nglanadh a cloigeamhtir
doib' allae eudir breatnaib ·i· Mag Fortrenn primo ₇ Magh Cirgin ·i· po conad
iar mathra gabsad flaithear ₇ gach comarbus olceana ar nascad forro o fearaib'
Erind ·i· Tri caegad· ingean rugsad a hEiri da maithrib' a mac a hAlt na
nIngean a c'rich Dal Araighi
        ·XXX· rig do Cruithnibh for Erind ₇ Albain ·i· do Cruithnibh Alban ₇
Erind ·i· Dal Araigi Ota Ollom Fodla connici Fiacna mac mBuaedain Ronaisc
sige mgiallu Erend ₇ Alban· Uii· rig do- do Chruithnib Alban da follnastair
Erind a Teamair Ollom ainm an ced rig rogob Erind a Teamair ₇ Cruachnaibh
·xxx· ann is de ata Mur nOllaman a Teamhair is leis cedna ndearnadh feis
Teamhrach artus
        Ollam' ollfinsneachta areis Ollomon a rrigi for Erind uili a Teamair
·xxx· and· IS na flaitus sigein fearais in sneachta finna conad romeath in fer
isan geim'readh
        Findoll cisirni tareis nOlloman ·xxx· annos a Teamair ₇ gach ad'
rogenair ina flaitus sigein robo ceananda is de ata Ceanandas a na loctgi

The children of Conall Cernach of Dál n-Araide from Carrac Inbhir to Lind Uachaill. Another name [for] the sept of Dál n-Araide: that is, Cruithni. That is, shapely warrior or in(?) Nat Crodu, as the poet said:

Oh Mael Duin, // what you have said was obtained in secret(?),
you have wielded your hard spear, // you have given victory to a sick man.

Cródai ("hardy warrior"). Upon Irél Glúnmár, son of Conall Cernach; it was enjoined (or "prophesied"), for he was the charioteer (?) of the Cruithni: that is, the nephew of Cruithne; that is, son of the sister of Cruithne. Lonceta, daughter of Echde eachbheoil of Alba, his mother. It was her (his?) cows which Cú Chulainn and Cu Roi mac Dáire drove from Alba to Ireland. Colcu mac Mongáin said:

If it is the casket you seek // (the one) that creates knowledge of secrets,
fifty battles to Eas Ruaid // Irél Glúnmár fought.

Two companies of eighteen soldiers from the tribes of Thrace came to meet the fleet of the Sons of Míl of Spain to Germany. They brought them with them so that they were their soldiers. Women did not come with them initially so that it was from the descendants of noble Míl that they accepted women. Afterwards the daughters of young lords from the nobility of Ireland (?) were brought to them and after the purification of their sword-land for them yonder among the Britons: that is, the Plain of Fortriu first and the Plain of Circhend. That is, it was so that it was according to [men's] mothers [that they] held the sovereignty and every succession besides by reason of that being pledged ("enjoined") upon them by the men of Ireland. That is, the one hundred and fifty maidens whom they brought from Ireland to be mothers of sons (Whence Alt na n-ingen ("Cliff of the Maidens") in the territory of Dál n-Araide).

Thirty kings of the Cruithni over Ireland and Alba: that is, of the Cruithni of Alba and Ireland (that is, of Dál n-Araide). Thence Ollam Fotla to Fiachna mac Báetáin. The last mentioned bound the hostages from Ireland and Alba. Thence seven kings of the Cruithni of Alba ruled Ireland in Temair. Ollam the name of the first king who ruled in Ireland for thirty years at Temair and Cruachu. It is from him is [named] Mur n-Ollaman in Temair. It is by him the Feast of Temair was first done.

Eilim ollfhinachta after Ollam in the sovereignty of all Ireland at Temair for thirty years. It is in his reign [that] the wine-snow fell so that the grass decayed in winter-time (for them?).

Findoll cisirne after Eilim for thirty years at Temair. Every cow born in his reign was white-headed. It is from that that Ceanannus is ("a place of ..."?).

Geid'e ollgothach ina d'iaid' sigein a Teamhair ₇ for Fainlaib'e a tirib Mudhorna rofallnastair ·xxx· and. is na flaithsighe ba beindicear la guth alaili amail meandcrot ar med an caenchom'raic bai na flaitus sighein

Slanoll tareis G'eidhi is na flaitus sin nach raibi galar for duini a nEiri ₇ Robo slan fir Erind re lind ·xxx· annos

IN Badach ollfiacha tareis t'Slanuill rofallnastair for Eiri i Teamair ·xxx· annos. is na flaithisighein tindscomtea coicthe artus a nEirend

Bearng'al tareis in Bagaig' rof'allnastar for Eiri a Teamair ·xxx· annis· is na flaitus sein adrocair ith a hErend acht miach co leith ar med in coicht'e ₇ ar liu

aithi Agsin tra na ·uii· rig dag gabsad Erind da Cruithnibh Alban ₇ Da Cruitnibh nErind da Dal Araigi na ·uii· Laic'se Laigean ₇ ·uii· Sogain Erind ₇ gach a Conailli fil a nErind

Géde Ollgothach then ruled after him at Temair and over Fain-Laibe of the lands of Mugdorn for thirty years. In his reign it was made melodious with every other voice as a lute on account of the fine conversation during his own reign.

Slanoll after Géde. It was in his reign that no one was ill in Ireland, and wholeness was over Ireland for thirty years.

The Bagag ollfiacha after Slanoll. He ruled over Ireland at Temair thirty years. It is in his reign [that] wars were first instituted in Ireland.

Berngal after that Bagag. He ruled over Ireland at Temair thiry years. In his reign corn in Ireland was destroyed except a sack (or "bushel") and a half through the scale and frequency/abundance of warring.

Those, then, are the seven kings from the Cruithni of Alba who ruled Ireland. From the Cruithni of Alba and from the Cruithni of Ireland from the Dál n-Araide: that is, the seven Laigsi of Laigin and the seven Sodain of Ireland and all Conailli who are in Ireland.

VARIATION P#A(Lec.)

genelach Dal Araidi· Fiachaid
Cland Chonaill Chearnaig ·i· Dal nAraidi o charraic indbeir uisqi co lind
Uachaill ainm naili doib Cruithnig nó Nat Crodu ut poeta dixit·

A Mailduin anas rubairt· frith iruin imrubairt
do gae cruaith rodamair do lobar buaith Nó trenfear

Crodai for Irial nGlunmar mac Conaill Cernaig for ceta ar ba rath
Cruithni ·i· nia Cruithni ·i· Lonceta inghean Eachach Eachbeoil di Albain a
mathair in Ireoil IT e abbae do nacht Cuchulaind 7 Curai mac Dairi di Albain
in nErind Colca mac Monga[i]n dixit·

Masa comrair conaigi cruitheas eagna runmar·
caeca catha co hEas Ruaid rofich Irel glunmar

Da n'ocht dec milead do thuathaib Traicia do lotar ar ceand loingse
mac Milead Espaine do Germain dosbertadar leo co mbadar a militacht ni
taltadar mna leo statim conad do shil mac Milead arro faetar mna iarsin do
breith ingena oigthighernna doaib o flaithnia Erind 7 ar nglanad a claideamtir
doib allae iter Breatnaib ·i· Mag Fortrenn primo 7 Mag Cirgin ·i· po conad iar
mathra gabait flaith 7 cach comarbus olcheana iarna nascad forru o fearaib
Erind ·i· tri chaeca inghean roucsad a hEre do maithrib mac inde Alt na nIngen
a crich Dal nAraidi isead lotar leo
Tricha rig do Cruithnib for Erind 7 Albain .i. do Cruithnib Alban 7
do Cruithnib Erind ·i· di Dail Araidi Ota di-· Ollumain dia ta Mur nOllaman i
Temair conige   Fiachna mac Baedain ronaisc side giallu Erend 7 Alban Secht
rig didiu do Chruithnib Alban ro fallnastair Erind i Temair Ollam ainm in
chetna rig rogob Erind a Temair 7 a Cruachnaib tricha bliadain and is de ata
Mur nOllaman i Temair is leis cetna dernad feis Temrach
Ailill ollfindachta tareis nOllaman a rigi for Eirind uili a Temair
tricha and isin flaithside fearais in sneachta fina con demeth a fer isin
gaimriuth

Genealogy of Dál n-Araide· Fiacha

The children of Conall Cernach: that is, the Dál n-Araide from Carrac Inbhir all the way to Lind Uachaill. Another name for them: Cruithni. Or Nat Crodu, as the poet said:

Oh Mael Duin, // what you have said was obtained in secret(?),
you have wielded your hard spear, // you have given victory to a sick man.

Cródai ("hardy warrior"). Upon Irél Glúnmár, son of Conall Cernach; it was enjoined (or "prophesied"), for he was the charioteer (?) of the Cruithni: that is, the nephew of Cruithne. That is: Lonceta, daughter of Echde eachbheoil of Alba, mother of that Irél. It was her (his?) cows which Cú Chulainn and Cú Roi mac Dáire drove from Alba to Ireland. Colcu mac Mongáin said:

If it is the casket you seek // (the one) that creates knowledge of secrets,
fifty battles to Eas Ruaid // Irél Glúnmár fought.

Two companies of eighteen soldiers from the tribes of Thrace came to meet the fleet of the Sons of Míl of Spain to Germany. They brought them with them so that they were their soldiers. Women did not come with them initially so that it was from the descendants of the Sons of Míl that they accepted women. Afterwards the daughters of young lords from the nobility of Ireland (?) were brought to them and after the purification of their sword-land for them yonder among the Britons: that is, the Plain of Fortriu first and the Plain of Circhend. That is, it was so that it was according to [men's] mothers [that they] held the sovereignty and every succession besides by reason of that being pledged ("enjoined") upon them by the men of Ireland. That is, the one hundred and fifty maidens whom they brought from Ireland to be mothers of sons (Whence Alt na n-ingen ("Cliff of the Maidens") in the territory of Dál n-Araide) were the ones who went with them.

Thirty kings of Cruithni over Ireland and Alba: that is, of the Cruithni of Alba and of Cruithni of Ireland (that is, of Dál n-Araide). Thence from Ollam (from him is the Wall of Ollam at Temair) to Fiachna mac Báetáin. The last mentioned bound the hostages from Ireland and Alba. Thence seven kings of the Cruithni of Alba ruled Ireland in Temair. Ollam the name of the first king who ruled in Ireland for thirty years at Temair and at Cruachu. From him is [named] Mur n-Ollaman in Temair. It is by him the Feast of Temair was first accomplished/held.

Eilim ollfhinachta was [established] after Ollam in the sovereignty of all Ireland at Temair for thirty years. In his reign the wine-snow fell so that the grass decayed in winter-time (for them?).

Findoll cisirne tareisi nAililla tricha annos(?) a Temair ⁊ i cend nach nag rogenair ina flaithside robo cheaninda is de ita cenannus ina lochte

Geide ollgothach ina diaidsid'e i Temair ⁊ for Fainlaibe a tirib Mugdorna ro follnastair tricha and IS [sic] ina flaithside ba bindithir la cach alaile amail bid chrot ar met in chaincomhraic bai ina flaith

Slanoll tareisi nGeithi is ina flaithside ni raibe galar for duine i nEire rofollnastair a Temair ⁊ slan for Eire tricha ann

Bagag ollfiacha tareis Slanuill ro follnastair for Eri a Temair tricha annis ina flaithside tindscanta coicthi i nEire

Bearngal tareis in Bagaig ro follnastair for Eiri a Temair tricha andis ina flaithside arro chuir ith a hEri acht miach ar med in choicthe in Ere ⁊ ara lin

IT e sin tra na ·uii· rig rogabsat Erind do Chruithnib Alban Do Chruithnib Erind didiu di Dal' Araidi ·i· na ·uii· Laigsi Laigen ⁊ ·uii· Sogain Erind ⁊ cach Conailli fil a nErind

Findoll cisirne [came] after Eilim for thirty years at Temair, and in the end (or "and at Cruachu"?) every cow born in his reign was white-headed. It is from that that Ceanannus is ("a place of ..."?).

Géde Ollgothach then ruled after him in Temair and over Fain-Laibe of the lands of Mugdorn for thirty years. In his reign everyone regarded everyone else as being as melodious as a lute on account of the fine conversation during his reign.

Slanoll after Géde. It was in his reign that no one was ill in Ireland. He ruled at Temair and wholeness [was] over Ireland for thirty years.

Bagag ollfiacha after Slanoll. He ruled over Ireland at Temair thirty years. In his reign wars were instituted in Ireland.

Berngal after that Bagag. He ruled over Ireland at Temair thiry years. In his reign corn in Ireland was destroyed except a sack (or "bushel") through the scale and frequency/abundance of warring in Ireland.

Those, then, are the seven kings from the Cruithni of Alba who ruled Ireland. From the Cruithni of Ireland, therefore, from the Dál n-Araide: that is, the seven Laigsi of Laigin and the seven Sodain of Ireland and all Conailli who are in Ireland.

VARIATION P#A(C.vi.2)

Do c'lannaib' Conaill C'ernaig' Dál Araid'e o c'arruig Indber uisge go linn
Uac'aill, Ainm eile do D'al Araid'e ·i· Cruit'nig'e ·i· dat' crut'aict'e, no niad'
Crodíu· ut poeta dixit

A Mailduin anasrubairt da g'ai, cruaic' crod'amar
do lobar buait'· [text apparently meant for deletion]
A Mailduin anasrubairt frit a ruín· [deleted text] ambrubairt
da g'ai cruaic' crod'amar do lobar buait'· no trenf'ir

      Crod'a for IRial Glúnm'ar (mac Conaill C'ernaig') forceda ar ba rad
Cruit'ne ·i· nia Cruithne) ·i· mac sethar Cruit'ne Loinc'eada ·ingeane Eac'ac'
Eac'beoil do Alba a mat'air mel até abaoi no adnacht danocht Cu c'ulaind ┐ Cu
raoi mac Daire di Albae a nErind· Colga mac Mongain· dixit·

Masa com'rair conaig'e cruit'eas eacna ru[mn]ar·
Caeca cat'a co hEas Ruaid', rosfig IRial Glunmar

      Da noc't deg milead' da tuat'uaib' Traigia, do lottar (ar cenn loingsi=
meic= Míled' Easpaine) go Gearmain dosbertadar leo, go mbadar a miltecht ┐
leo ni taultadar mna leó, statim, Conad' do s'iol meic Milead', uair roeadadar
mná iarsin do bret'a [in]g'ena oigthig'ernaig' dóib' o f'lait' nEírind· Et iar
nglanad' a claid'im't'ire d'oip' allae edir B'ret'naib' ·i· Mag' Foirtreann primo ┐
Magh Cirgin primo· gonad' iar mat'rib' gabsad flait'eas ┐ gach com'orbus
olc'ena, ar nasgad' forra o f'eraib ·Erind· ·i· tri c'aogad ing'en ragsat a hEir[ind]
da mait'rib' a mac, a hAlt na ning'en a c'rich Dal Araid'he·
      TRioc'a ríg' do C'ruit'nib' for Erind ┐ Albain ·i· do C'ruit'nib' Alban ┐
Eirind ·i· Dal Araid'e (otta Ollam Fodla gonuige Fiac'na mac Baodáin)
ronnaisg sid'eíhe gialla Eirend ┐ Alban, seacht ríg' do Chruit'nib' Alban
dfollam'naig'estar Eirind a Tem'air· Oillam ainm an c'eid rig' dogab' Eirind a
Tem'air ┐ Cruathnaib' ·30· bliad'uin, as de ata Múr nOllam'an a Tem'rac', as
leis cenna dernad' feis Tem'rac' artús·
      Ollamh ollfinns'neachta tareís Ollam'an a ríg'e for Eirind
uili a Tem'air ·30· bliad'uin· as na flaithios sid'ein ferais an sneachta fiona,
conad' rom'et' an fér isin ngeim'read'·

Of the descendants of Conall Cernach: that is, the Dál n-Araide from Carrac Inbhir all the way(?) (water?) to Lind Uachaill. Another name of Dál n-Araide: that is, Cruithni. That is, or nephew of Crodai, as the poet said:

Oh Mael Duin, // what you have said
you have wielded your hard spear, // you have given victory
Oh Mael Duin, // what you have said was obtained in secret(?),you have wielded your hard spear, // you have given victory

Cródai ("hardy warrior"). Upon Irél Glúnmár, son of Conall Cernach; it was enjoined (or "prophesied"), for he was the charioteer (?) of the Cruithni: that is, the nephew of Cruithne. That is, son of the sister of Cruithne. Lonceta, daughter of Echde eachbheoil from Alba, his mother. It was her (his?) cows, or burial, which Cú Cuchulainn and Cú Roi mac Dáire drove from Alba to Ireland. Colcu mac Mongáin said:

If it is the casket you seek // (the one) that createsknowledge of secrets,
fifty battles to Eas Ruaid // Irél Glúnmár fought.

Two companies of eighteen soldiers from the tribes of Thrace came to meet the fleet of the Sons of Míl of Spain to Germany. They brought them with them so that they were their soldiers. And with them (*sic*) women did not come with them initially so that it was from the descendants of the Sons of Míl that they accepted women. Afterwards the daughters of young lords from the nobility of Ireland (?) were brought to them and after the purification of their sword-land for them yonder among the Britons: that is, the Plain of Fortriu first and the Plain of Circhend first. So that it was according to [men's] mothers [that they] held the sovereignty and every succession besides by reason of that being pledged ("enjoined") upon them by the men of Ireland. That is, the one hundred and fifty maidens whom they brought from Ireland to be mothers of sons. Alt na n-ingen in the territory of Dál n-Araide.

Thirty kings of the Cruithni over Ireland and Alba: that is, of the Cruithni of Alba and Ireland (that is, Dál n-Araide). Thence Ollam to Fiachna mac Báetáin. The last mentioned bound from Ireland and Alba. Seven kings of the Cruithni of Alba ruled Ireland in Temair. Ollam the name of the first king who ruled in Ireland for thirty years at Temair and at Cruachu(?). From him is [named] Mur n-Ollaman as Temair. It is by him the Feast of Temair was first accomplished/held.

Eilim ollfhinachta after Ollam in the sovereignty of all Ireland at Temair for thirty years. In his own reign the wine-snow fell so that the grass decayed in winter-time (for them?).

Fionnoll Cisirne tareis nOllam'an ·30· bliad'uin· a Tem'air ⁊ gac' nág' rogenair na f'lait'esid'eín, roba cenanna as de atá Cenannas ana loic'tge·

Geid'e ollg'aothac' na d'iaig'sid'ein a Tem'air ⁊ for Fainlaib'e a tírib' Mudhorn rofalnastar 30· bliad'uin· as na f'lait'sid'ein ba binnig't'ar la cách gut' aláile amail mennc'rot ar m'ed an c'om'craic baoi na f'lait'ios sid'eín·

Slanoll tareis G'eid'e, as na f'laít'ios sin nac' raib' galar ar d'uine a nEire, ⁊ roba slan fir Eirenn re a linn ·30· bliad'uin·

IN Bád'ac' ollfiac'a táreis Slanoill rof'ollnastair for Eir[enn] ·30· bliad'uin is na f'lait'iossid'eín tionsganta coict'e artús i nEir[e]·

Bearng'al tareis an b'ág'aid' rof'ollnastar for Éir[e] a Tem'air ·30· bliad'uin· as na f'lait'iossid'e adroc'air iot' a hEirinn, acht míac' go leit' ar med' an coict'e ⁊ ar a liona

it'e· ag sin tra na secht riog'a dog'ab'sad Éire do C'ruithnib' Alban ⁊ do C'ruithnib' Éirind· do D'al Araid'e na seacht Laic'hri Laig'en ⁊ seacht Sog'ain Eirind ⁊ gac' Conaille fil i nEirinn·

Findoll cisirne after Eilim for thirty years at Temair, and every cow born in his reign was white-headed. It is from that that Ceanannus is ("a place of ..."?).

Géde Ollgothach then ruled after him in Temair and over Fain-laibe of the lands of Mugdorn for thirty years. In his reign everyone regarded everyone else's voice as being as melodious as a lute on account of the fine conversation during his own reign.

Slanoll after Géde. It was in his reign that no one was ill in Ireland, And there was wholeness over Ireland from his ale(?) thirty years.

Bagag ollfiacha after Slanoll. He ruled over Ireland thirty years. It is in his reign [that] wars were instituted in Ireland.

Berngal after that Bagag. He ruled over Ireland at Temair thiry years. In his reign corn in Ireland was destroyed except a sack (or "bushel") and a half through the scale and frequency/abundance of warring.

Those, then, are the seven kings from the Cruithni of Alba who ruled Ireland. From the Cruithni of Ireland from the Dál n-Araide: the seven Laigsi of Laigin and the seven Sodain of Ireland and all Conailli who are in Ireland.

VARIATION P#B(Lec.)

IN tan don· tanic loinges Meic Milead cor
gabsad in Germain isin nairther Do lotar da nocht milead do mileadaib na
Traigia for loinges co Macaib Milead ·i· fo clu ⁊ airrdercus na loingsi sin
combadar a naentaich Mac Milead ⁊ do rairngirsead faidi doib seam saigid thiri
leo dia ngabdair fesin tir IS de sin tra ro selgadar Gaeidil ar eigin in tir a
fuilead the Cruithnig a niu IN milig sin tra do lodar do lodar a Tragia i
Cruitheantuaith

VARIATION P#B(Bal.)

IN tan don t'ainig loingis Meic Milidh gur gabsad i nGearmain ina
hoirrtur Do lodar da nocht deg milid' do mileadaib' Traicia for loingeas gu
Macu Milidh .i. fo clu uirdracus na loingsi combadar in naentaidh Meic Milidh
⁊ do rarngairseadar said'e doib'sium soig'e t'ire leo dia ng'ab'dais tir feisin de
sin tra rot'sealgadar Gaid'il ar eigin in tir a f'ilead Cruit'neachu IN mileid' sin
tra do lodar a Traicia i Cruit'eantuait'

VARIATION P#B(1295)

IN tan don t'ainig loingios Meic Miliod'· gur g'ab'sad ín G'earmáin ina
hoirrteri· do lodar dá noc't deg m'ilid' do m'ilead'aib' Traicía for loingeas go
Macaib' Miliod' ·i· fo clú urrdearcus na loingsi [c]ombadar i naentaid' Mic
Miliod'· ⁊ do rugairseadair said'e d'oib'sium soig'e t'ire léo dia ngab'daois tír
feisin de sin trá rót's'ealgadar Gaid'il ar eigín ín tír a a f'ilead' Crúit'neac'ú· IN
mileid' sin trá do lodair a Trac'ia i Cruit'enc'túait'

VARIATION P#B(1289)

IN tan do ráinic loingis Mhac Milead' gur g'ab'sat i nG'ermáin ionna
hoirt'er do lodar da nocht dég milib' do m'ilib' - Tracia for loingis go Macaib'
Milead' ·i· fo c'lu oirdeirces na loingsig' gomb'adar i naon[t]ad' M'ic Milead', ⁊
go rarngairsedar said'e doib'sium soig'e thire leo dia ng'ab'daois tir feisin, de
sin trat' ros'algadar Gaoid'il ar eigin in tir a b'f'ilead Cruitnec'ad' In milead' sin
trat' lodar i Tracia i Cruithnec'tuath

VARIATION P#B(D.iii.2)

IN tan do rainic loingis Mac Miled' gur g'ab'sat
in g'ermain ionna hoirt'eri do lodar da nocht deg m'ilib' do m'ilib' Tracia f'or
l'oigin go Macaib' Miled' ·i· fo clú oirdeirces na loingsig' gombadair i naóntad'
M'ic Milead', ⁊ go rairngairseda[u]r said'e d'oib'sium soig'e t'ire leo ndia
nga[?]b'dís tír feisin dé sin trát' ros'algadair Gaoid'il air eigin in tir a ab' filead'
Cruit'nec'ad'· in milead' sin trat' lodair a Tracia ig Cuitnec'atuáit'

<Now when the fleet of the Sons of Míl came and attacked Germany in its east, two times eighteen soldiers from the soldiers of Thrace came on a naval expedition to the Sons of Míl: that is, through the reputation of the splendor of the fleet until they were united with the Sons of Míl. And the latter promised them a sufficiency of lands with them if they themselves should conquer land hence. It is as a consequence of that, then, Gaels cleared(?) by compulsion the land in which are the Cruithni. Those soldiers then came from Thrace into Pictland.>

<Now when the fleet of the Sons of Míl came and attacked Germany in its east, two times eighteen soldiers from the soldiers of Thrace came on a naval expedition to the Sons of Míl: that is, through the reputation of the splendor of the fleet until they were united with the Sons of Míl. And the latter promised them a sufficiency of lands with them if they themselves should conquer land hence. As a consequence of that, then, Gaels cleared(?) by compulsion the land in which are the Cruithni. Those soldiers then came from Thrace into Pictland.>

<Now when the fleet of the Sons of Míl came and attacked Germany in its east, Two times eighteen soldiers from the soldiers of Thrace came on a naval expedition to the Sons of Míl: that is, through the reputation of the splendor of the fleet until they were united with the Sons of Míl. And the latter promised them a sufficiency of lands with them if they themselves should conquer land hence. As a consequence of that, then, Gaels cleared(?) by compulsion the land in which are the Cruithni. Those soldiers then came from Thrace into Pictland.>

<Now when the fleet of the Sons of Míl came and attacked Germany in its east, Two times eighteen soldiers from the soldiers of Thrace came on a naval expedition to the Sons of Míl: that is, through the reputation of the splendor of the fleet until they were united with the Sons of Míl. And the latter promised them a sufficiency of lands with them if they themselves should conquer land hence. As a consequence of that, then, Gaels cleared(?) by compulsion the land in which are the Cruithni. Those soldiers then came from Thrace into Pictland.>

<Now when the fleet of the Sons of Míl came and attacked Germany in its east, two times eighteen soldiers from the soldiers of Thrace came on a naval expedition to the Sons of Míl: that is, through the reputation of the splendor of the fleet until they were united with the Sons of Míl. And the latter promised them a sufficiency of lands with them if they themselves should conquer land hence. As a consequence of that, then, Gaels cleared(?) by compulsion the land in which are the Cruithni. Those soldiers then came from Thrace into Pictland.>

VARIATION P#C(Lein.)

Ruc Cruithne mac Cin'ge a mná úadib róssair n'dírech .'
in'ge Tea ben hErimóin meic Miled.

Mór saethair césait uili for cach m'buadre
la mná Bresse la mna B'asse la mná Buaigne.

Banba a Sléib Miss cona s'luagaib siriuch tuislech
Fót{h}la i nEblinne asnach hEriu i nUisniuch.

A docorsat Tuatha Dea tria chert clithach
o tír tidach dar noí tonnaib don lir lethan.

Ro gab hErimón co lleith in ts'luaig iar nurd tolgdai
timchell atúaid ba gen mergle dInber Cholpthai.

Ro gab Dond cosin leith aile iar nurd innaiss.
ba marb ic ascnam cen chomais descert hIrraiss.

Co tuarcbad carn la lia a cheneoil as lir lethach
sentreb tontech conid Tech Duinn de dongarar.

Ba hésin a hedacht adbul dia chlaind chetaich
cucum dom tic tissaid uili iarbar n-écaib.

IC Inbiur Scene ro scuirset scél cen dúnad
sruth dían dermar inros fothraic Fíal ben Lugdach.

Ros dailset fo hErind oraig mar atberid.
gníset córa fri Firu Bolg fri claind Nemid

Nís bátar mná soirbe soíre cea no glea .'
ar n'gait a mban gabsat clemnas Tuath Dea.

Dobreth dóib leth cech arba co muir medbas.
iarsin charddine chóir chomdes iarsin chlemnas.

Cruithne mac Cinge has carried their wives from them, it is directly   stated(?),
except Tea, wife of Éremón son of Míl;

Great difficulty they all suffer in respect of every disturbance
with the wives of Bres, Basse, and Buaigne;

Banba by Sliab Mis with its hosts wandering about, stumbling,
Fotla at ribbed Eiblinn, Eire at Uisnech;

The Tuatha De have placed them(?) on account of the protective law
from the firm(?) land across nine waves into the wide sea;

Éremón has proceeded with half of the host according to a powerful order
round from the north, it was a bright, spirited laugh, to Inber Colptha;

Donn has taken with the other half according to a settled order;
he died while contending, without ability, for the southern part of Erris;

Till a cairn was set up with a stone of his race [arising] out of the divided
        sea(?);
an ancient, wave-tossed house which is hence called Tech Duinn;

That was his great bequest to his hundredfold children:
"towards me, to my house, you may all come after your deaths;"

At Inber Scene they disembarked, a story without closing;
a huge, swift river in which Fial, wife of Lugaid, bathed herself;

They spread themselves through Ireland of the coastline as you(pl.) say;
they made amities with the Fir Bolg, with the children of Nemed;

There were not charming, noble women for them, whoever may clarify [the
        question];
after the theft of their women, they took a marriage alliance with the Tuatha
        De;

There was given to them half of all land to the burgeoning sea
after the proper, equitable amity, after the alliance;

VARIATION P#C(Uí Ma.)

Rug Cruitne mac Cing mna uaidhib' in drong dire[a]ch
  Tea a taeib geal bean Eiremoin móir meic Mileadh

Mor saethar ceasaidís uílí tre gach mbuaid're
  la mnai Breisi la mnai Buaisí la mnai Buaíg'ne

Banb'a i Sleib Mís gona sluaig'aib' seirgh tuiseal
  is Fodla i nEblind na ngaisgead' Eren a nUisneach

A gairsead['] iad Tuatha Dea a tre cheart creacach
  a cur o tir tar nai tonna tar lear leathan

Luig' Ereamon gu leith in ts'luaig' iar tuind
  timhceall Er[end/ind] ba gan mearcla dInnber Colpta

Gabais Donn gusin leith ele iar ndord ninnais
  ba marb' e ag asgnam gan cungaís deíscert irraís

Da togb'ad' carn do le cenel uas lear laim'theach
  santreib' toimthig' gunad e Teach nDuind gnath gaírthear

IS ísin a oigead ad'bal dia cloind cedaigh
  lim ata fisaigel sgailteach iar na negaib'

An Innber Seme rosguirsead sgel gan dubnath
  sruth dían dei[m]nech ar fotraic Fial deig' bean Lugdach

Luig' Eremon du Inber Boínne ba thoirm ndeini
  gabais Éimear o sar Duind an Innber Feile

Fo gailsead fo i Eírind uili go dearb deimin
  gnisid cora fri Ferab' Bolg fri cloind Neimidh

Nis badar mna saibri saera giarba gleaa
  iar ngaid a ban rogabsad cleamnas Tuath nDeaa

Darad' ad' doib leath gach orba go muir mead'rais
  iarsin gairdine cain combras siarsar cleamnas

Cruithne mac Cinge has carried their wives from them, the straight band,
Tea, from fair of form, wife of great Éremón son of Míl;

Great difficulty they all suffer in respect of every disturbance
with the wives of Bres, Basse, and Buaigne;

Banba by Sliab Mis with its hosts wandering about, stumbling,
It is Fotla at Eiblinn of the weapons(?), Eire at Uisnech;

The Tuatha De sent them forth through marauding right
in putting from the land across nine waves across the wide sea;

Éremón went with half of the host across the wave
round Ireland, it was a bright, spirited laugh, to Inber Colptha;

Donn took with the other half according to a settled order(?);
he died himself while contending, without companionship(?), for the southern
    part of Erris;

A cairn was set up from a stone(?) of [his] race over of the daring sea;
Of the special, billowy(?) house so that it came about that it is called Tech
    Duinn;

That is his great hospitality(?) to his hundredfold children:
"with me, it is tidings of them, to the shadow house(?) after their deaths;"

At Inber Scene they disembarked, a story without black verse(?);
a certain, swift river before which Fial, wife of Lugaid, bathed;

Éremón went to Inber Bóinne ("mouth of the Boyne") through sudden tumult,
Éber took from excellent Donn to Inber Feile;

They spread through all Ireland, that is downwright certain;
they made amities with the Fir Bolg, with the children of Nemed;

There were not charming, noble women for them, whoever it was who(?)
    may clarify [the question];
after the theft of their women, they took a marriage alliance with the Tuatha
    De;

There has been given to them half of all land to the mirthful sea
after the fair, vigorous amity, after the alliance;

VARIATION P#C(Lec.)

Ruc Cruithne mac In'ge a mna uaidib serech ndirec'
inge Tha ben ba hEremon meic Milead

Mor saethair chesaisit uile tre cach mbuaidre
la mna Bresi la mn'a Baise la mna Buaise

Banba i Sleb[e] Mis co sluaigaib serech tuslead·
Fotla i nEblinde asnach hEri in Uisneach

Ata coirsead Tuatha Dea tre chert['] crecach·
o thir thaithlech tar noi tonda tar ler lethach

Luid hEremon co leath in tluaig iar tuind tolcda·
timcheall an tuaith ba in can merga dInber Cholptha

Gabais Dond cosin leith aile iar ndurd indais·
ba marb hic tascnam cen tungais deiscert hIrrais

Ar tocbad carn do lia cheineoil uas lear laimtheach·
sentreib sontach conad Tech nDuind dogairther

Combai tetacht adbul dia claind chedaich·
chucum chom thaich tisad uile iarbar negaib·

A nIndber Scene ruscoirsed scel can dubnad·
sruth dian dermair hi fothraic Fial fa bean Lugdach

Luid Eremon do Inber Boinde fa toirm ndene
gabais Emer o sar duind do inber file

Fo dailsed fo hErind oraid or adberid·
gnisead coro fri Firu Bolc fri cloind Nemid

Nis mbadar mna saidbri saera cia ro nglea·
tard gairt a mban ros gabsad clemnas Tuath Dea

Dorat a doib le'ath cach forba co muir meblas·
iarsin chairt michaim chombrus iarsin cleamnos

Cruithne mac Cinge has carried their wives from them, a direct
  deprivation(?),
except Tea, wife of Éremón son of Míl;

Great difficulty they all suffer through every disturbance
with the wives of Bres, Basse, and Buaigne;

Banba by Sliab Mis with its hosts wandering about, stumbling,
Fotla at ribbed Eiblinn, Eire at Uisnech;

The Tuatha De have placed them(?) through marauding might
from the shining land across nine waves into the wide sea;

Éremón went with half of the host according to a powerful order
round from the north, it was a bright, spirited laugh, to Inber Colptha;

Donn took with the other half according to a settled wave;
he died while contending, without companionship(?), for the southern part of
  Erris;

Since [then] a cairn [was] set up from a stone of his race out of the daring
  sea;
an ancient, vigorous house which is hence called Tech Duinn;

So that was his great bequest to his hundredfold children:
"towards me, to my house, you may all come after your deaths;"

At Inber Scene they disembarked, a story without black verse(?);
a huge, swift river in which Fial, wife of Lugaid, bathed;

Éremón went to Inber Bóinne through sudden tumult,
Éber took from excellent Donn to Inber Feile;

They spread themselves through Ireland of the coastline since you(pl.) say;
they made amities with the Fir Bolg, with the children of Nemed;

There were not charming, noble women for them, whoever may clarify [the
  question];
concerning the theft (?) of their women, they took a marriage alliance with
  the Tuatha De;

It has given to them half of all land to the treacherous(?) sea
after the affable(?), vigorous pact, after the alliance.

VARIATION P#C(G131)

Ruc Cruitne mac Cinca a mna hoaidaib rosi tirech
 inge Tea ben ba Erimoin meic Miledh

Mor saetor ro cesaset uili tre gach mbuaidre .
 la mna Breisi la mna Buaisi la mna Buaigne

Banbae i Sleib Mis co sluagaib serech tuslead·
 Fodla i nEblinne asnach, Eriu ind isneach ·

Ata coirset Tuatha De tria chert crechach
 o tir tithac tar noi tonna tar ler let[an]

Luid Erimon co let a ntluaigh ier tuinn tolgda·
 timcheall Er[end/ind] ba cen mergdai dInber Colbtha

Gapais Donn cusinn leth aile ier nurd indais·
 ba marb ag ascnam cen comais descert Iorrais

Ar ocbad carn do lia c[eneoil] os ler laimtech
 sentreabh sontach conid Teach nDuinn dogairter

Comba siaedacht adbal dia cloinn cetaib
 cugom dom toigh tiesat uile iernar neccaibh

I ndIndber Scene roscorsiut scel cen dubhnad
 srut' dian dermar· hi fotraic Fial ben Lugdach

Luid Erimon do Inber Boinne ba torm ndene
 gabas Eber o sarn dune i ndin[nber] fele

Fos ndailset fo Eirinn noraig ar atbermait
 gniset coru fri Tuatha De fri cloinn Cermait

Nis batar mna saidbri soera cia ru gleo
 ierd ngait a mban gabsat clemnas fri Tuath Deo

Dorat doib leth cech orba co muir medras
 iersin cairdne cor comdhas. iarsin cleamnas

Cruithne mac Cinge has carried their wives from them, a direct
   deprivation(?),
except Tea, wife of Éremón son of Míl;

Great difficulty they all suffer through every disturbance
with the wives of Bres, Basse, and Buaigne;

Banba by Sliab Mis with its hosts wandering about, stumbling,
Fotla at ribbed Eiblinn, Eire at Uisnech;

The Tuatha De have placed them(?) through marauding might
from the shining land across nine waves into the wide sea;

Éremón went with half of the host according to a powerful order
round Ireland, it was a bright, spirited laugh, to Inber Colptha;

Donn took with the other half according to a settled wave;
he died while contending, without companionship(?), for the southern part of
   Erris;

Since [then] a cairn [was] set up from a stone of his race out of the daring
   sea;
an ancient, vigorous house which is hence called Tech Duinn;

So that was his great bequest to his hundredfold children:
"towards me, to my house, you may all come after your deaths;"

At Inber Scene they disembarked, a story without black verse(?);
a huge, swift river in which Fial, wife of Lugaid, bathed;

Éremón went to Inber Bóinne through sudden tumult,
Éber took from excellent Donn to Inber Feile;

They spread themselves through Ireland of the coastline since you(pl.) say;
they made amities with the Tuatha De, with the children of Cermait(?);

There were not charming, noble women for them, whoever may clarify [the
   question];
concerning the theft (?) of their women, they took a marriage alliance with
   the Tuatha De;

It has given to them half of all land to the treacherous(?) sea
after the affable(?), vigorous pact, after the alliance;

VARIATION P#D(D.iv.1)

(P#F(D.iv.1))...
ARD Lemnachta as tirsi tess finnat gach aen bus eces
   cret dar len in tainm is sloinn rosgab o aimsir Crimthainn

Crimthand Sciathbel é rogab da saeradh ar chath cruadh
   da ndin ar neimib na narm na nathach nuathmar nagarb

Seiser Cruithnech rocinn dia· tancatar a tir Tra[cia]
   Solen Ulpa Nechtan nar Aengus Ledene is Drostan

Ro thinnlaic dia doib tre thus· dia ndin dia ndil dia nutrus
   d[i]a ndin ar n[em]ib a narm naithach nuathmar nagarb

IS e eolus do [uair] doib [drai] na Cruithnech nir begoir
   tri ·l· bo mael don m[ui]g· do blegan do a naen chuithig

Ro cuiredh in cat co cacht mon cuithigh imbi in lemnacht
   ro moigh in cath co calma for aithechaib ard Banba ·ard·
                        (continuation of P#F(D.iv.1))...

Ard Lemnacht in this land in the South, let every luminary, every poet know,
why did the name and designation stick with it, which it took it from the age
      of Crimthann?

Crimthann Shield-mouth, who uttered it, he [who] delivered in hard battle,
to their defense against the poisons of their weapons, [of] the dreadful, fierce
      giants.

Six Cruithni whom God appointed came from the land of Thrace:
Solen, Ulfa/Ulpa, noble Nechtan, Óengus, Letenn and Drostan.

God gave to them through precedence for their defense for their requital for
      their sickness(?)
for their protection against poisons of their weapons, dreadful, fierce giants.

This is the charm which he got for them, druid of the Cruithni, he was
      no enemy(?),
one hundred and fifty hornless cows from the plain for milking for him into
      one pit (or "receptacle"?).

The battle was fought with great intensity about the pit in which the milk
      was.
The battle bravely turned against the spectres/giants of noble Banba.

VARIATION P#D(Lec.1)

(P#F(Lec.1))...

Ard Lemnachta as tirsi thess finnat gach aen b[us eces]
  cret dar len in tainm sin sloinn · ro gab o aimsir Crimthainn

Crimthann Sciathbel· e ro gabh dar saerad ar [chath] cruadh
  da ndin air neimib na narm na nathach nuathm[har] nargarbh

Seisser Cruithnech ro cinn dia tancatar a tir Traicia
  Solen Ulpa Nechtan nar Aengus Ledenn is Drostan

Ro thinnlaic di[a] doib tre t[lus] dia ndin dia ndil dia nutrus
  dia ndin air nemib a narm na naithach nuath[mhar] na garb·

IS e eolus do uair doib drai na Cruithnech nir b[']esgoir
  tri ·l· bo mael don muigh do blegon do a naen chuithidh

Ro cuire[a]dh an cath co cacht mon cuithigh imbi lemnacht·
  ro moigh in cath co calma for aithe[a]chaib ard Banba· ard·
                 (continuation of P#F(Lec.1))...

Ard Lemnacht in this land in the South, let every luminary, every poet know,
why did the name and designation stick, which it took it from the age of
          Crimthann?

Crimthann Shield-mouth, who uttered it, he [who] delivered in hard battle,
to their defense against the poisons of their weapons, [of] the dreadful, fierce
          giants.

Six Cruithni whom God appointed came from the land of Thrace:
Solen, Ulfa/Ulpa, noble Nechtan, Óengus, Letenn and Drostan.

God gave to them in his kindness for their protection for their requital for
          their sickness(?)
for their protection against poisons of their weapons, those dreadful, fierce
          giants.

This is the charm which he got for them, druid of the Cruithni, he was no
          enemy,
one hundred and fifty hornless cows from the plain for milking for him into
          one pit (or "receptacle"?).

The battle was fought with great intensity about the pit in which the milk
          was.
The battle bravely turned against the spectres/giants of noble Banba.

VARIATION P#D(Lec.2)
(P#F(Lec.2))...
Ard Leamnachta is tir sea theas findad cach an cach eiges·
craed dar lean in tainm i sloind rosgab o aimsir Crimthoind

Crimthand Sciathbel he rogab da tharaid ar chath curad·
cen din ar neimib a narm na fuathach nuathmar nagarb

Seiser Cruithneach rochind dia tancadar i tir Tragia·
Solen Ulpa Nechtain nar Aengus Leithcend is Trostan

Ro thidlaic dia doib tre tlus d,ia ndil is dia nduthurus
dia ndin ar nemib a narm na naithach neitig nagarb

Is e eolus do uair doib drai na Cruithneach fo cetoir·
tri ·l· bo mael don muig do blaegan do an aen chuithig

Ro curead in cuco cacht mor chuitig a mbai in lemnacht
ro maid in cath co calma for athachaib ard Banba ·A·
(continuation of P#F(Lec.2))...

Ard Lemnacht in this land in the South, let every luminary, every poet know,
why did the name and designation stick with it, which it took it from the age
        of Crimthann?

Crimthann Shield-mouth, [it was] who uttered it, he [who] intervened in
        battle of warriors,
without defense against the poisons of their weapons, [of] the dreadful, fierce
        spectres/giants.

Six Cruithni whom God appointed came from the land of Thrace:
Solen, Ulpa, noble Nechtan, Óengus, Letenn and Drostan.

God gave to them in his kindness for their requital and for their reward(?)
for their protection against poisons of their weapons, those repulsive, fierce
        spectres/giants.

This is the charm which he got for them, druid of the Cruithni, straight
        away,
one hundred and fifty hornless cows from the plain for milking for him into
        one pit (or "receptacle"?).

The battle was fought with great intensity about the pit in which the milk
        was.
The battle bravely turned against the spectres/giants of noble Banba.

VARIATION P#D(Bal.)
(P#F(Bal.))...
Ard Leamhnachta is tirsea theas findadh gach an sgach eigeas.
cred dar lean in tainm o sloind rosgab o aimsir Creamhthoind

Creamhtand Sciathb'el he roghabh. da saeradh ar cath curadh
da ndhin ar neimib a narm na nathach nuathmar nagarbh

Seisear Cruithneach ro chind dia. tangadhar a sin Traigia
Solen Ulpa Nechtan nár. Aengus Leidean is Trosdan

Ro thindhnaich dia doibh tre thlus. dia ndhin dia ndhil dia nuthrus
dia ndhin ar neimib' a narm na nathach nuathmar nagarbh

IS e eolas do fuair doib'. drai na Cruithneach nír bégoir.
tri caegad bo mael don maigh. do bleadhan do i naen chuithigh

Ro cuiridh in cath go cacht. mon guighithigh i mbí in leamhnacht.
ro moidh in cath co calma for aithechaibh ard Banba Ard Leamhnachta
(continuation of P#F(Bal.))...

Ard Lemnacht in this land in the South, let every luminary, every poet know,
why did the name and designation stick with it, which it took it from the age
        of Crimthann?

Crimthann Shield-mouth, who uttered it, he delivered in battle of warriors,
to their defense against poisons of their weapons, [of] the dreadful, fierce
        giants.

Six Cruithni whom God appointed came from the land of Thrace:
Solen, Ulfa/Ulpa, noble Nechtan, Óengus, Letenn and Drostan.

God gave to them in his kindness for their protection for their requital for
        their sickness(?)
for their protection against poisons of their weapons, those dreadful, fierce
        giants.

This is the charm which he prepared for them, druid of the Cruithni, he was
        no enemy,
one hundred and fifty hornless cows from the plain for milking for him into
        one pit (or "receptacle"?).

The battle was fought with great intensity about the pit in which the milk
        was.
The battle bravely turned against the spectres/giants of noble Banba.

VARIATION P#D(24.P.13)
(P#F(24.P.13))...
Ard Lemhnacht in tirsi t'es. finnaicch gach aon gach eicces.
cia dar len in tainm is sloind. rogab' o aimas Criomhtainn.

Criomhtann Sciathbel é dogab'. do tarraidh ar cath curadh
cin din ar neim'ib' a narm· na nathach nuadhmar naccgarb'·

Seisior cruithneach do cinn dia· tangadar a tir Traiccia
Solen Elpo Nechtain nar Aongus Leitteann is Orcan.

Do tidhmaic dia doib' tre gus· día ndiol, ₇ dia nuthrus·
dia ndhin ar neimhib' a narm. na natheac nuathmar naccgarb'

IS é eolas do fhuair doib'. draoi na Cruithneach fo ·cetoir.
tri fichit bo maol don muig[h]. do bledccan a naon cuithidh·

Do cuirid' in cath co cecht. mor cuithe ambidh in lemhnecht·
do cuirid' in cath co calmo· For aithechaib' ard Banba. A-R-
(continuation of P#F(24.P.13))...

Ard Lemnacht in this land in the South, let every luminary, every poet know,
why did the name and designation stick, which it took it from the age of
              Crimthann?

Crimthann Shield-mouth, who uttered it, he delivered in battle of warriors,
to their defense against the poisons of their weapons, [of] the dreadful, fierce
              giants.

Six Cruithni whom God appointed came from the land of Thrace:
Solen, Ulfa/Ulpa, noble Nechtan, Óengus, Letenn and Drostan.

God gave to them in his kindness for their protection for their requital for
              their sickness(?)
for their protection against poisons of their weapons, those dreadful, fierce
              giants.

This is the charm which he prepared for them, the druid of the Cruithni, he
              was no enemy,
one hundred and fifty hornless cows from the plain for milking for him into
              one pit (or "receptacle"?).

The battle was fought with great intensity about the pit in which the milk
              was.
The battle was fought bravely against the spectres/giants of noble Banba.

VARIATION P#D(1295)
(P#F(1295))...

Ard Leam'nachta is tirsea t'es: findad' gac' áen sgac' eigeas
crét dar lean in tainim o sloind: rosgab' ó aimsir C'reaom't'oinnd

Crem't'onn Sciat'b'el he rog'ab: dá saerad' ar [c]at' curad'
da ndín ar neim'ib' a narm: na nat'ac' nuat'm'ar nag'arb

Seisear Cruit'neac' ro c'ind día: t'angadar a sin Tragía
Solen Ulpa Neac'tain nár· Aeng'us Leidean· 7 Trosdan

Ro t'id'naic' día doib' tre t'lus: día nd'in día día nd'il nut'rus
día ndín ar neim'ib' a narm· na nat'ac' nuat'm'ar natg'airb'

IS e eolas do fuair doib'· draoid' nar na C'rúit'neac' b'egóir
trí caogad bó mael don m'aig'· do b'lead'on an [ ]aen c'uit'ig'

Ro cuirid' in cat' go cac't mon guit'ig' imbí in leam'nacht
ro móid in cath go calma for ait'ec'aib' ard Banba. Ard Leamnachta·
(continuation of P#F(1295))...

Ard Lemnacht in this land in the South, let every luminary, every poet know,
why did the name and designation stick with it, which it took it from the age
        of Crimthann?

Crimthann Shield-mouth, who uttered it, he delivered in battle of warriors,
to their defense against the poisons of their weapons, [of] the dreadful, fierce
        giants.

Six Cruithni whom God appointed came from the land of Thrace:
Solen, Ulfa/Ulpa, noble Nechtan, Óengus, Letenn and Drostan.

God gave to them in his kindness for their protection for their requital for
        their sickness(?)
for their protection against poisons of their weapons, those dreadful, fierce
        giants.

This is the charm which he prepared for them, druid of the Cruithni, [he]
        was [no] enemy,
one hundred and fifty hornless cows from the plain for milking for him into
        one pit (or "receptacle"?).

The battle was fought with great intensity about the pit in which the milk
        was.
The battle bravely turned against the spectres/giants of noble Banba.

VARIATION P#D(1289)
(P#F(1289))...
Ard Lem'nachtad' is tírsed' t'es· fionnad' gac' aon, is gac' eiges
cred dar lean in tainim ó sloinn. rosgab' ó aimsir Criom'tuinn·
[Criom':]

Criomht'ann sgit'b'eal he róghab'. dá saorad' ar c'ath curad'
da ndíon ar neim' a narm· na nfat'ac' nuat'm'ar nat'gharb'

Seiser Cruineac'aib' ro c'inn dia· t'angadar a sin Traicia
Solen, Ulpa, Neachtain nár· Aongus, Liden, ₇ Trostán

Ro diod'nac' día daoib' trea t'lus. dia ndíon, dia ndil, dia nut'rus
dia ndíon ar neim'ib' a narm· na nat'ac' nuathm'ar nathgharb'

Is é eolus do fuair dóib'. draoid' nag Cruineac' chedóir
trí c'aogad' bó m'aol don mhaig'. do b'lead'an an aon c'uit'aig'
(continuation of P#F(1289))...

Ard Lemnacht in this land in the South, let every luminary, [and] every poet
        know,
why did the name and designation stick with it, which it took it from the age
        of Crimthann?

Crimthann Shield-mouth, [it was] who uttered it, he [who] delivered in the
        battle of warriors,
to their defense against the poisons of their weapons, [of] the dreadful, fierce
        spectres/giants.

Six Cruithni whom God appointed came from the land of Thrace:
Solen, Ulfa/Ulpa, noble Nechtan, Óengus, Letenn and Drostan.

God gave to them in his kindness for their protection for their requital for
        their sickness(?)
for their protection against poisons of their weapons, those dreadful, fierce
        giants.

This is the charm which he prepared for them, the druid of the Cruithni,
        straight away,
one hundred and fifty hornless cows from the plain for milking for him into
        one pit (or "receptacle"?).

VARIATION P#D(D.iii.2)

(P#F(D.iii.2))...
Ard Leam'nachtad' is tirsed' t'es· fionnad' gac' aon is gac' eiges
cred dar lean in tainim o sloinn. rosg'ab' o aimsir
    Creiom't'uin. c

Criot'm't'uin s'git'b'eal he róg'abh. dá saorad' air c'at' curad'
da ndíon air neim' a nairm· na nfat'ac' nuat'm'ar nat'g'arbh·

Seiser Cruineac'aib' ro c'inn dia· Tangadar a sin Traicía
 Solen, Ulpa, Nechtain nár· Aongus· Liden, ₇ Trostán

Ro diod'nac' dia daoib' trea t'lus, dia ndil, dia nut'rus
 dia ndíon air neim'ib' a nairm· na nat'ac' nuat'm'air nat'g'airb'

IS é eolus do fuair doibh· draoid' nag Cruineac' c'edoír·
 tri c'aogad' bo m'aol don maig'· do b'leadan an aon c'uit'aig'
          (continuation of P#F(D.iii.2)...

Ard Lemnacht in this land in the South,   let every luminary, [and] every
       poet know,
why did the name and designation stick with it, which it took it from the age
       of Crimthann?

Crimthann Shield-mouth, [it was] who uttered it, he [who] delivered in the
       battle of warriors,
without defense against the poisons of their weapons, [of] the dreadful, fierce
       spectres/giants.

Six Cruithni whom God appointed came from the land of Thrace:
Solen, Ulfa/Ulpa, noble Nechtan, Óengus, Letenn and Drostan.

God gave to them in his kindness for their requital for their sickness(?)
for their protection against poisons of their weapons, those dreadful, fierce
       giants.

This is the charm which he prepared for them, the druid of the Cruithni,
       straight away,
one hundred and fifty hornless cows from the plain for milking for him into
       one pit (or "receptacle"?).

VARIATION P#E(Lec.)

(P#K(Lec.2))...

Cruithnich cid dusforglaim a niath Alban amra·
cona mbrig bil belga cia tir asa targa

Cia fochaind rusfogluais o crichaib in chocaid·
fri snim tond tar sreathar cia lin long dolodar

Cia sloindead re tiachtain do riachtain na rigi·
asa narm bo dene is cia hainm a tiri

Traicia ainm a tiri co siri roseolta·
iarna tairchill techta a noirthear na hEorpa

Agthairius a nanmand amrand Ercail itbi·
o chearbthar dia chucli adbearrthar cid Picli

Picti ind aicme aitrib rosodaidne thechtmuir·
ced-gnim nercaill notchaid sil nEolchoin meic Ercail

Huaithir seser brathar ria lathar cen liud·
do sercblaid co soad in sechtmad a siur

Soilen Ulfa Nechtain Drostan deachain dreadell·
a nanmand a naebus Aengus ₇ Leitend

Lan ri Traicia trebtha do cheathra a siur sochla·
robo damna debtha can tarba can tochra

Tancadar lea in deigfir o thirib o thredaib·
lucht tri long co lor mud nonbur ar tri cetaib

Cingsed seach tund crichi Frangcu fichu falgais·
gnid cathraid airm aiblis diarbo ainm Pictabis

Pictabis a pictus adberdis a cathraid·
fa slondud slan sochraid iarum tarsin rathmuir

The Cruithni, what has assembled them in the country of marvelous Alba
With auspicious Belgic(?) might; what land will it come from?

What cause has set them in motion from the lands of war,
To meet trouble over the saddle(?) of the waves? In what number of ships
       did they come?

What were they called before their coming to reach the sovereignty?
Whose weapons were strongest; and what is the name of their land?

Thrace the name of their land, ceaselessly their voyaging continued
After their circuit of travelling in the east of Europe.

Agathyrsi their names, in the part of Ercal-Itbi (Amrand, Ercal and Itbi??);
Because of the cutting of their beautiful form(?) they are called Picts.

Picts, the colonizing race; the possession-rich sea sparkled for them (?);
The first deed of the unlucky(?) Ercal, descendant of Eolchu son of Ercal.

They are united, a company of six brothers, with vigor, without accusation,
From love of undying fame; the seventh their sister.

Solen, Ulfa/Ulpa, Nechtan, Drostan, Deachan's(?) favorite(?)
Their names, their delightfulness(?); Óengus and Letenn.

The full king of populous Thrace sullied(?) their honorable sister --
This was a reason for strife -- without benefit, without bride-price.

They escaped with her, the noble men, from lands, from flocks;
Cargo of nine ships with sufficient (ample?) honor, three hundred and nine
       people.

They marched past the sea [... ?], they were covering the territories of the
       Franks;
They construct a city -- a place of bright enclosure-- the name of which was
       Pictabis.

Pictabis, from "pictus," they called their city;
It was a noble, seemly act of naming; afterwards over the auspicious ocean.

Ri rochar a shiair tria gliaid co ng'gairgi·
dia fochaid a fergi a dothfonn for fairrgi

For tracht mara mebaid long lelig lucht lathair·
anais ara feser acin seser brathair

Batar a Bictaue co ngraine dia nglenair·
a nainm ro bo df_ada airm i raba elair

Elaid asa chele co ndeni fo diud·
cinta la co lochta adbath a co a siur

Seoch Bretnaib na reimim co hErind na hani·
rothagsad a tindrum gabsad Innbear Slaine

Slaigsed sluaig Fea foglach dia fognam i [nemni?/ndemnacht?]
tria glundu garga i cath Arda Lemnacht

Laich an'gbaidi f'aidbe co ngairbe re pudar·
co nainib co ndecraib do Breatnaib a mbunad

Ba marb nech notheigdis acht teilgdis a fuile·
combo tru de sene cid cu no cid duine

Drui Cruithnech ni chardais fuair ingcheas amlaid·
lemnech isan alad fri tamad· for talmain

Tuctha tainti trebh cland la Creamthand coir cetbalc·
co tomlacht a rachnem ic Ard Lemnacht

Slaigsed sluaig fa faebrach can trebad can torad·
ro chobrad dian dith gliaid Cremthand Sciathbel scoraich

Cuirid and tri maigi na Cruithnich co n'gairi·
cumthar eagla f'aebair na Gaeigil co nglaine

Gar iarsin co n'gabad ceathrar brathar bladach·
Solen Nechtan Drostan Oengus fostan fathach

The king who had desired their(?) sister through combat with a fierceness,
From the calamity(?) of his wrath their pursuit over the ocean.

Upon the seashore broke up the ship; vigorous crew survived;
They stayed, that you may know, with the six brothers.

They were in Pictaue without emnity(?), whence originated
Their name, it was appropriate in the place where Elair was(?).

They escaped asunder with swiftness eventually;
At the end(?) of two days of resistance(?) their sister died with them.

Past the Britons in their course to Ireland in its splendor
They chose their voyage; they took possession of Inber Slaine.

The hosts struck down predatory Fea, despite her service in nothing (magic?)
Through their bold deeds in the Battle of Ard Lemnacht.

Fierce warriors of vengeance(spoils?) with toughness plus mischief,
With privations, with struggles; of the Britons their origin.

Anyone was dead whom they may attack, if they as so much as draw his
        blood,
So that he was doomed therefrom, whether dog or human.

A druid of the Cruithni --they didn't love [him for it]-- found a cure for the
        illness thus:
New milk(?) in the wound against death on the earth (any form of death?).

Herds of cattle of households were brought by just, foremost, battle-strong
        Crimthann,
So that [...?] were milked at Ard Lemnacht.

Hosts who were sharp-edged wrought destruction without cultivating, without
        harvest;
Was saved from the destructive battle Crimthann Shield-mouth, abounding
        in horses (?).

They sowed three plains there, the Cruithni with filial affection
So that they were fearful with respect to their blades, the Gaels with
        purity/brightness.

A short time after there were taken four renowned brothers,
Solen, Nechtan, Drostan, Óengus, steady, possessed of knowledge.

Rof̲ai andes Ulfa iar nurchra a charad·
in Rachrand a mBregaib an̲n ru̲s̲mebaid mal̲art

Marbt̲h̲air aco Catluan nirbo a truag i̲n̲d aire·
da rig foraib uile re ndul a tir naile

A dubrad riu erim si̲n̲ neri̲n̲d si̲n̲ nec̲h̲tair·
a[rna] dernsad debaid imon Tem̲air̲ tec̲h̲taich

Tri chet ban do breatha doib ru̲s̲tetha tlathaig·
gid ead robo tuachail cach ben co̲n̲a brathair

Badar rat̲h̲a f̲or̲o fri demnu fri diriu·
co̲n̲ad saera a mbad̲ar̲ ru̲s̲gnathgab in rigu

Rerdaig isan eri̲n̲d ina remi̲m̲ rathgli̲n̲d·
can mu̲ir̲er can mar cluag in Catluan m̲a̲c̲ Cait[{i}n]i̲n̲d

Cadnolod̲or̲ clecht is Catainlacach cnapruaid·
bad̲ar̲ gilli glana glorda da m̲a̲c̲ croda Chatluain

A choraid cruaid chom̲n̲ert fa trom̲balc a t̲air̲m seom·
cind co cerd dia cerd seom· [Im·?/uii·?] [m̲a̲c̲?/me̲ic̲?] Pirt a nai̲n̲m seom̲

Huaisnem ai̲n̲m an f̲ilead ro siread in set gen·
robo ru̲s̲ dia milib Crus m̲a̲c̲ Cirig cheitlem

Cruithnig m̲a̲c̲ coir Gi̲n̲ga doib ro thi̲n̲cha tochmorc·
co ruc ban̲ntrac̲h̲t blat̲h̲glan dar Athmag dar Athgort

Anaid dib a nealga co lin cerd is cu̲r̲ach·
nad cesead for Breagm[ ]ach seser demnach druaad

Dr̲'aidecht ₇ idlac̲h̲t maith inailc mi̲n̲glan̲·
murgla̲n̲ barc dibergi duai̲n̲gil is uaib rib romu̲n̲a[dh̲]

Ulfa/Ulpa went(?) from the south after the death of his kinsmen;
In Rachru in Brega there destruction arose to him.

Cathluan was killed among them; he was not wretched, that noble;
Two kings upon them all before going into another country.

It was told to them to move on whether in Ireland, or overseas(?),
In order that they might not contend for Temair of property.

Three hundred women were given to them --it placated them(?)--
Yet, it was cunning, each woman with her brother.

There were pledges(?) upon them against assurance, against honor-price
With the noble status attached to them (?) that the sovereignty became
        customary to them.

He sailed out of Ireland in his securely pledged course
Without a retinue without horsemen that Cathluan, son of Caitnind.

Experienced Cadnolodor, Catainlacach (Catain, death-dealing?),
        hard-knobbed(?)
They were bright, resplendent lads, two valiant sons of Cathluan.

His warriors of hardy strength, their tumult was heavy and strong;
Cing, with a craft to match their craft, [Im?/seven?] son(s) of Pern/Pert,
        [were] their names.

Uaisnem the name of the seer; he would search for the way of favor;
He was a sage to their warriors, Crus, son of Cirig the Weak(?) (Crus the
        Weak, son of Cirig?).

Cruithne, proper son of Cing; for them he took care of courtship
In that he brought a company of bright and loving women across Athmagh,
        across Athgort.

There remained of them in Ealga, with a full complement of artisans and
        boats,
Those that would not step beyond Bregmach: six demonic druids.

Druidic lore and idolatry, augury, fine-clean, pure-protective;
Pirate ships (?) that give rise to bright songs; it is from them that [each of
        these] was taught.

Morad sred is mana raga si<u>n</u> amsona·
got<u>h</u>a en da f<u>a</u>iri· cairi cach ceol cona

Cnuic is coirc<u>h</u>i ar cora can troga tuath toilli
tuar gaibsed dia ti<u>n</u>dru<u>m</u> sund a ni<u>ndber</u> Bon<u>n</u>i

Ba headar <u>lodar</u> uai<u>n</u>di co ngluairi na <u>g</u>ribi·
ima taig co trene a tir maisech ile

IS as gabsad Albai<u>n</u> ard glai<u>n</u> is leis gabt<u>h</u>a·
cen dith luc<u>ht</u> la trebthu o c<u>r</u>ich Chat co Forcu

[Ro]bris Catluan cathu can tacha cen tec<u>h</u>tu·
nirbo hind ard tucthu no cor indarb Bretnu

Ba de gabsad Cruithnig Albai<u>n</u> tu<u>r</u>thig tlac<u>h</u>tmi<u>n</u>·
a nerclod amlael co Ci<u>n</u>aed m<u>ac</u> Ailpi<u>n</u>

Ar cechnad nard naichnich for aichib cen uchnem·
ni celt<u>ar</u> na cochlaid as de adb<u>erthar</u> Cruichnich· C ·RU⁻·

Exalting of sneezes and portents, choosing of elements (portents?), fortunate
       times,
Watching for voices of birds, the melody/melodies of every sort of music
       moreover(?).

Mounds and standing stones (?) in proper manner without misery, people of
       reckoning (battlements?);
They raised them up for their serving here at the Boyne's mouth

It was that they who went from us with swiftness of falcon
Concerning their dwelling with strength in the fine land of Ile.

It is from there they captured Alba, noble and pure, it is by him they were
       seized
Without loss, contents along with residences, from the territory of Cat (Cats?)
to Fortriu(?).

Cathluan won battles without scarcity without possessions;
It was not an end, -- noble stratagem -- until he expelled Britons.

It was from that that the Cruithni took fertile Alba, gentle and smooth,
Their noble vanquishing, their numerous broods(?) until Cináed mac Alpín.

Upon [.?.] of famous heights face to face and without sorrow(?),
The [.?.] (hooded ones?) are not concealed; that is why they are called
       Cruithni.

VARIATION P#E(Bal.)

(P#G(Bal.))...

Cruit'níg' dosfarclam i niat' Alban nam'ra
gona mbrig' bil beld'a cia tir as nac' tarlla·

Cia foconn fosrogluaís o crichaib' ín cogaid'.
cia lín long as teagar. fri snim tond dolodar

Cia slondud fria tiac'tain. do riactain na ríge.
asa nairm fad'e is cía nainm a tíre

Traícía ainm a tíre go sire a seolta.
iarna tairc'íul techta a nairt'íur na hEorpa

Agantirsi a nanmann amrand erc'tb'hí.
o cearptar dia cuctlí adbertar cid Picti

Picti in aicme atraib' rostaitne techtmuír
gan gnim nd'eireoil ndodc'aid' sil nGeleoin meic Ercoil.

Huadib' seisear brathar. fri lat'ar gan líuu.
do sercblad' go sood'. in sechtmad' a siur

Solen Ulp'a Nechtain Drostan. dec'tain dret'ell
a nanmand. a n-aebdus Aengus 7 Leít'end

Lan ri Traigía treab't'a· do dec'ra a siair soc'la
robo damna deab't'a gan tarba gan toc'ra

Tangadar lea in deig'f'ir o t'irib' o treab'aib'.
luc't nae long go llor-mud'. nonb'ur ar tri cedáib'

Cíngset seac' ann chríc'u Frangcu fiachu failgís
gunt cat'raig' aírm aiblís. diarbo ainm Píctabís

Pictabis a pictís atbertís a cat'raig'.
ba slonnud' slan soc'hraid'. iarum darsin rat'muír

Cruithni, [what] brought them into the territory of marvelous Alba
With their fortunate Belgic/Belgian(?) power; what land from which have
        they not launched?

What underlying cause has set them in motion from the territories of war?
[In] what number and gathering of ships towards contending of waves have
        they come?

What is their lineage before their coming to reach the kingdom
From their own place and what is the name of their land?

Thrace the name of their land, so that you may seek their voyagings
After their circuit of travelling in the east of Europe.

Agathyrsi their name; in the part of Erchtbhi(?) (Ercal?);
Since they are disfigured of their beautiful form they are called Picts.

Picts, the colonizing race -- the richly endowed sea appeared attractive to
        them--
Without insignificant, unfortunate works, the descendants of Gelon, son of
        Ercal.

Six brothers from them with(?) vigor without accusation,
To beloved fame they turn; the seventh their sister.

Solen, Ulfa/Ulpa, Nechtan, Drostan, Dechtan's(?) favorite;
Their names, their heroic appearance(?), Óengus and Letenn.

The full king of cultivated Thrace, set his heart on their honorable sister --
It was a matter of strife -- without benefit, without bride-price.

The noble men came with her from lands, from houses;
Complement of nine ships with sufficient honor, three hundred and nine
        people.

They proceeded past [...?] territories, they got engaged in overthrowing (?)
        the villages of the Franks;
A place of bright enclosure, the name of which was Pictabis.

Pictabis from "pictis"(?) they called their city;
It was an attractive(?) name afterwards across the auspicious ocean.

Ri roc'ar a siair tre gliaíd' go nairge.
di foconn a ferge a tofund for fairge.

For trac't mara mead'b'aid'. long lelaig' luc't lat'air
anaís ara feísíur accu in seisead' brat'air

Badar in Pictaue gen grane. dia nglenail.
a nainm robo aed'a. airm í rraba Elair

Elaid assa c'ele co nd'ene fo díud.
cínd dala gac' lactu. atbat' accu a síur

Seac' B'reatnaib' na reímim. co hErinn na haine.
rotog'sat a tindremh. gob'sat Inber Slaine

Slígsit sluag foglac' dia fognad' a ndemnac't
dria nanglungnu garga i cath Arda Leamnac't

Laic' angbaíd'e amble. fea faidb'e fudar
gona danaib' go nd'ec'raib' do B'reatnaib' a bunad'

Ba marb' nec' nosectis acht teilgteis a f'uile.
gobom tru do enne cid' cu no cid' dune

Druí Cruit'nec' ín cardais fuair ic aíntis amlaíd'
lemlac't isin nalad ri a mit'amad' fortamail

Tugt'a tainte treab' clann. la Crem'tand coir cennb'alc.
co tom'lac't a naicmid'. for faic't'i Ard Lemnac't

Sligfeat sluag' Fea febac'. gan treib' is gan tobac'
roc'ob'rad' don tuat' gliaid'. Cremt'and Sciat'bel sc'orac'

Sguirsit ann ín Cruíthníg'. for tuirtib' tri maig'e.
comd'ar ecla. oibil na Gaeidil go ngloine

Gar iarsin go napad' cet'ur blat'ach brat'ar.
Solen Ulpha Drostan. Aengus fosdan fat'ac'

The king who had fallen in love with their sister in hostility, without
      mildness,
In consequence of his wrath their being pursued upon the ocean.

Upon the shore of the sea was broken a ship, its vigorous crew survived;
He stayed, that you may know, with them, the sixth brother.

They were in Pictaue without emnity, whence became fixed
Their name, it was enduring in the place where Elair was.

They evaded easily asunder with swiftness ultimately;
At the end of two days (heading for a tryst?), each company/crew(?), their
      sister died with them.

Beyond the Britons in their course to Ireland of splendor
They chose their voyage; they captured Inber Slaine.

They struck down a predatory host, whose magic used to serve them (despite
      the service of their magic?),
Through their great exploits of fierceness in the Battle of Ard Lemnacht.

Fierce, dumb (other-worldly?) warriors of Fea, mischief of spoils,
With their skills, with wonders; from the Britons their source.

He was a dead person, anyone they reached, if they but spilled his blood
So that he was a doomed man from [it?], whether dog or man.

A druid of the Cruithni -- they loved him [not](?)-- provided a cure whenever
      they were attacked thus:
New milk in the wound to prevent death for a while (?).

Herds of the clan household were brought by Crimthann, just and
      strong-headed,
So that his clan milked [them] upon the green of Ard Lemnacht.

They smote the excellent host of Fea without settlement (husbandry?), without
      tribute;
Was saved from the ill-omened/ominous combat Crimthann Shield-mouth
      rich in horses.

The Cruithni encamped there upon the harvestings of three plains
Until they were aflame with fear, the glorious Gaels.

A short time after that died foursome(?) of the renowned brothers,
Solen, Ulfa/Ulpa, Drostan, Óengus, steady and skillful/wise.

Rofait' and'eas Ulfa iar nurc'ra a c'arad
ina c'arnn i mBreagaib' and romeadair malart

Mort'ar occaib Cat'luain nirbo a truag aire.
do rig oraib' uile ria ndul a tír naile

Ar asbert friu erim asín erim sechtar.
arna dearndaís deabaíd' immon Teamair tectaid'h

Tri cet ban dobreat'a doib'. roscet'ea tlat'aig'
cid' ead' robo triuac'ail g'ac' bean gona brat'air.

Badar rat'a erru fri drennu fri díre.
conid' soire a mat'ar rognat'aig í rríg'e

Rerdair asin nErinn. ina reimím rat'glind.
gen mureír gan marcluag'. ím Cat'luan m'ac Caítínd

Cat'molod'or cnapcruaid'. is Cat'mac'an crapgluair.
b'adar gillí glord'a. da mac croda Cat'luain

A coraid' cruaid' com'nart. ba dornnbalc a t'oirm seom'.
Cíng co cernn dia cerrn seomh Im mac Perrnn a hainm seom'

Huaísem ainm a filed nosired ín sedgin
robo rus dia milíd' Crus mac Círíg' cetlím

Cruithne mac coir Cínca rotínca at' c'oc' mór
co tuc banntroc't mblathglan dar Athgort

Anait dib' melga go lín cerda is cruan.
na roceised Breagmac' seisear demnac' druad'

D'ruíd'echt is idlact mat' marc. minbalc murglan
gles diberga duangil is uaidib' romunad'

Ulfa departed from the south after the death of his kinsmen
In his cairn in Brega, there destruction was pondered (?).

Cathluan was exalted amongst them; he was not a wretched noble
He ruled upon them all before going into another country.

For he told to them a course from Ireland(?) beyond,
So that they might not make conflict concerning Temair of property.

Three hundred women were given to them; gentle ones were ejected(?)
Yet, it was cunning, each woman with her brother.

There were pledges for them against quarrels against honor-price
So that it is the nobility of their mothers that has become customary in
        kingship.

They(?) sailed from Ireland in their(?) firmly pledged movement
Without a retinue without horsemen around Cathluan, son of Caitnind.

Cadnolodor knobbly hard(?) and Catainlacach of crumpling reputation(?);
They were resplendent lads, two brave sons of Cathluan.

Their(?) warriors of hardy strength, their tumult was strong-fisted;
Cing, carrying victory to match their victory, Im, son of Pern/Pert, their(?)
        names.

Uaisnem [was] the name of their seer -- he would search the way(?) of favor(?)
He was a sage to their warrior, Crus, son of Cirig the Weak(?) (Crus the
        Weak, son of Cirig?).

Cruithne, proper son of Cing, he took care of [...?],
Until he brought a female retinue of bright, flourishing appearance [...?]
        across Athgort.

There stayed from them in Ireland with a full complement of artisans and
        enamellers(?)
Who would not settle Bregmach, six demonic druids.

Druidic lore and idolatry, augury, fine-strong, pure-protective;
The practice of plunder, which gave rise to bright songs were taught by
        them.

Morad' sleag' is mana rog'a sén ní sona
gotha en do aire chaire gan cel cona

Cnuíc as c'oirt'e ar chora cen troga tuath taille.
ro rotogsat a tíndremh. gabsat ínber mB'oinde

Ba head' lodar huaine go ngluaire na grib'e.
imma iat' co drene i tir iat' seac' Íle

IS as gabsat Albain ardglain ailes thoirt'íu
cen díth tlac't la treb'tu o chric' Ath co Foirc'íu

Robris Cathluan cat'u gen tac'u cen treb't'u
nírbo ín garg tuícíu co romarb Breatnu

Ba de gabsat Albain ardglaín talcain tlac'min
co nimad amlaeb' in Chinaet' mac nAilp'in

Ar creac'ad' nard naic'nid' for aítc'ib' cen uchneím
ni celldar in coclaig' as de adberar Cruit'nig'.

Coeca rig' ceím crec'ac' maraen do sil Ec'dac'
o Feargus rofirad. co mac mbrigac' mB'retach

Se riga ar se deic'ib' dib' fri feit'ím. fuilcrech
carsat sithe suic'lech gabsat rige Cruit'neac'

Cruithnig' dosfarclam.

Mustering of spears and omens, choice of signs and anything lucky,
Observation of the voices of birds; fault without concealment, besides.

Mounds(?) and standing-stones aright without misery, people of
      battlements/reckoning(?);
They selected their [mode of] service/servitude; they seized the mouth of the
      Boyne.

It was that they went from us with the swiftness of falcon
Which encloses/circles with strength, in the land (into Tiree?) past Ile.

It is from there they took Alba, noble and pure, which nourishes crops
Without lack of mildness, with residences from the boundary of Ath to
      Fortriu(?).

Cathluan won battles without scarcity without dwellings;
There were no fierce onsets(?), until he slew the Britons.

It was from that they seized Alba, noble and pure, pleasant, vigorous   peace(?)
With much success, not fraudulent(?), that Cináed mac Alpín.

Upon plundering famous heights face to face and without sorrow(?),
The hooded ones(?) are not concealed that is why they are called Cruithni.

Fifty kings, a marauding sequence, altogether the descendants of
      Eochaid/Eochu;
From Fergus it was shown to be true to the mighty son of Bretach.

Sixty-six kings of them set to observe bloody raids;
They loved the peace treaties of liberal men (?); they accepted the kingship of
      the Cruithni.
Cruithni [...?] assembled themselves.

VARIATION P#E(B 512)

(P#G(B 512))...
Flann cecenit ·i· Mainistrech·
Cruithnig cid dusfarclam· i niath nAlban namra·
cona mbrig bil beldu· Cia tir as nas tarla· Et Reliqua

<Flann sang; that is, Manistrech:
The Cruithni, what has assembled them in the country of marvelous Alba
With auspicious Belgic(?) (fortunate?) might; what land from which have
      they not launched themselves? And the rest>

VARIATION P#E(1295)

(P#G(1295))...

Cruit'nig' dosfarcla[m]· í niat' Alban nam'ra:
gona mbrig' bil belda cía tir as nac' tarlla

Cia foconn fosrógluais ó cric'aib' ín cogaid':
cía lín long as teagar fri sním tonn dolodar.

Cia slonnud' fria tíac'tain do riac'tain na rig'e:
asa nairm fad'e is nainm a t'íre

Traic'ía ainm a t'ire go síre a seolta:
iarna tairc'íul t'echta. a nairt'íur na hEorpa.

Agat'irsi a nanman amran Erc'tb'i.
ó cearptair dia cuc'tlí adbertar cíd Picti

Pictí, ín aicme atraib' rostaitne techtmuir.
gan gnim' nd'eireoil ndodc'aid' sil nGeleoin meic Ercoil·

Huadib' seisear brat'air. fri lat'air gan línu.
do s'ercb'lad' go sood'. ín sechtmad' a síur

Solen. Ulpa. Nechtain. Drostan dret'all, dec'tain
a nanmand: a n-aeb'dus Aengus. ⁊ Leit'end

Lan rí Traigía treab't'a; do dec'ra a siair soc'la·
robo dam'na deabt'a gan tarb'a gan toc'ra;

Tangadair lea ín deig'f'ir· o t'írib' ó t'reab'aib'.
luc't nae long go ll.or-mud'. nonb.ur ar tri c'edaib'

Cíngset seac' ann cric'u Frangcú fiac'ú failgís.
gunt cat'raig' aírm aiblís. diarbó ainm Pictab'is

Pictab'is a pictis atbertís a cat'raig'.
ba sloinnud' slán soc'hraig'. íarum darsin rat'm'uir

Cruithni, [what] brought them into the territory of marvelous Alba
With their fortunate Belgic/Belgian(?) power; what land from which have
        they not launched?

What underlying cause has set them in motion from the territories of war?
[In] what number and gathering of ships towards contending of waves have
        they come?

What is their lineage before their coming to reach the kingdom
From their own place and the name of their land?

Thrace the name of their land, so that you may seek their voyagings
After their circuit of travelling in the east of Europe.

Agathyrsi their name; in the part of Erchtbhi (?);
Since they are disfigured of their beautiful form they are called Picts.

Picts, the colonizing race -- the richly endowed sea appeared attractive to
        them--
Without insignificant, unfortunate works, the descendants of Gelon, son of
        Ercal.

Six brothers from them with(?) vigor without accusation,
To beloved fame they turn; the seventh their sister.

Solen, Ulfa/Ulpa, Nechtan, favorite Drostan, of Dechtan(?);
Their names, their heroic appearance(?), Óengus and Lethenn.

The full king of cultivated Thrace, set his heart on their honorable sister --
It was a matter of strife -- without benefit, without bride-price.

The noble men came with her from lands, from houses;
Complement of nine ships with sufficient honor, three hundred and nine
        people.

They proceeded past [...?] territories, they got engaged in overthrowing (?)
        the villages of the Franks;
A place of bright enclosure, the name of which was Pictabis.

Pictabis from "picti"(?) they called their city;
It was an attractive(?) name afterwards across the auspicious ocean.

Rí roc'air a siair tre glíad' go nairge.
dí foc'on a ferge a tófund for fairge

For trac't mara meab'aid'· long lelaig' luc't lat'air
anais ara feisíur accu ín seisead' brat'air

B'adair in Pictaue gen grane. día nglenail:
a nainm robo aed'a airm í rraba Eláir

Elaid assa cele co nd'ene fo d'iud:
cínd dala gac lac'tu atbat' accú a síur

Seac't, B'ret'naib' na reimim. co hErinn na haine:
rót'og'sat a tindrem'. g'ab'sat Inb'ir Sláine

Slígsit sluaig' fog'lac'. día fog'nad' a ndemnac't:
dria nanglungnú gairga í cat' Arda Leam'nac't

Laic' angbaid'e amble. fea faidb'e fudar.
gona danaib go nd'ec'raib dó B'ret'naib' a bunad'

Ba marb' nec' nosectis. as teilgteis a fuile.
gobom tru do enne cid' cú no cid' dune·

Drúi Cruit'nec' ín cardais: fuair íc aíntís am'laid':
lem'lac't isin nalad' ri a [mi]t'amad' fortam'ail.

Tugt'a táinte treab' c'lann. la Crem't'and cóir cennb'alc:
co tom'lac't a naicmid'. for faic't'i nArd Lemnac't

Sligfét sluag' Fea febac' gan treib' is gan tobac':
róc'ob'rad' don tuat' gliaid'. Crem't'and Sciat'b'el sc'orac'

Sguirsit ann ín Cruit'nig': for tuirt'ib' tri maig'e
com'd'ar ecla. oibil na Gaeidi go ngloine:

Iarsin go na cet'ur. blat'ach brat'air:
Solen Ulpha Drostan: Aeng'us fosdan fat'ac'

The king who had fallen in love with their sister in hostility, without
      mildness,
In consequence of his wrath their being pursued upon the ocean.

Upon the shore of the sea was broken a ship, its vigorous crew survived;
He stayed, that you may know, with them, the sixth brother.

They were in Pictaue without emnity, whence became fixed
Their name, it was enduring in the place where Elair was.

They evaded easily asunder with swiftness ultimately;
At the end of two days (heading for a tryst?), each company/crew(?), their
      sister died with them.

Beyond the Britons in their course to Ireland of splendor
They chose their voyage; they captured Inber Slaine.

They struck down a predatory host, whose magic used to serve them (despite
      the service of their magic?),
Through their great exploits of fierceness in the Battle of Ard Lemnacht.

Fierce, dumb (other-worldly?) warriors of Fea, mischief of spoils,
With their skills, with wonders; from the Britons their source.

He was a dead person, anyone they reached, if they [but] spilled his blood
So that he was a doomed man from [it?], whether dog or man.

A druid of the Cruithni -- they loved him [not](?)-- provided a cure whenever
      they were attacked thus:
New milk in the wound to prevent death for a while (?).

Herds of the clan household were brought by Crimthann, just and
      strong-headed,
So that his clan milked [them] upon the green of Ard Lemnacht.

They smote the excellent host of Fea without settlement (husbandry?), without
      tribute;
Was saved from the ill-omened/ominous combat Crimthann Shield-mouth,
      rich in horses.

The Cruithni encamped there upon the harvestings of three plains
Until they were aflame with fear, the glorious Gaels.

A short time after that died a foursome(?) of the renowned brothers,
Solen, Ulfa/Ulpa, Drostan, Óengus, steady and skillful/wise.

Rófait' andeas Ulfa: iar nurc'ra a c'arad:
ina c'arnn i mBreag'aib' and romeadair malairt·

Mort'or occaib' Cat'luain· nírbo a truag' aire:
do rig' oraib' uile ría ndul a tír naile·

Ar asbert fríu erim: asin erim sechtar:
arna dearndais deabaid' immon Tem'air tec'aid'

Trí cet ban dob'reat'a doib': roscetea tlat'aig':
cid' ed' róbó tuac'áil· g'ac' ben gona brat'air.

B'adar rat'a errú frí drenna fri díre.
conid' sdire a mat'air: róg'nat'aig' í rrig'e.

Rerdair asin nErinn. ina réimim rat'g'lind:
gen mureir gan marcluag'. im Cat'luan m'ac Caítínd·

Cat'molod'or cnapcruaid': is Cat'mac'an crapg'luair:
badar gillí glord'a: da mac crod'a Cat'luain

A coraid' cruaid' com'nart: ba dornnb'alc a toirm seom':
Cing co cernn dia cerrn seom' Im mac Perrim a haim seom'·

Huaisem ainm a filed'. nosired ín sedgín:
robo rus dia m'ilid': Crus mac Cirig cet'lím

Cruit'ne mac cor Cínca. rotínc'a at' c'oc' mor:
co tuc banntroc't mblat'glan dar At'gort·

Anaít dib' melga go lín cerda is crúan:
na róteised Bregmac' seiseor dem'nac' druad'·

Druid'acht is idlac't mat' marc mínbalc múrg'lan:
gles diberga duangil: is uaid'ib' rómunad'.

Ulfa departed from the south after the death of his kinsmen
in his cairn in Brega, there destruction was pondered (?).

Cathluan was exalted amongst them; he was not a wretched noble
He ruled upon them all before going into another country.

For he told to them a course from Ireland(?) beyond,
So that they might not make conflict concerning Temair of property.

Three hundred women were given to them; gentle ones were ejected(?)
Yet, it was cunning, each woman with her brother.

There were pledges for them against quarrels against honor-price
So that it is the nobility of their mothers that has become customary in
      kingship.

They(?) sailed from Ireland in their(?) firmly pledged movement
Without retinue without horsemen around Cathluan, son of Caitnind;

Cadnolodor knobbly hard(?) and Catainlacach of crumpling reputation(?);
They were resplendent lads, two brave sons of Cathluan.

Their(?) warriors of hardy strength, their tumult was strong-fisted;
Cing, carrying victory to match their victory, Im, son of Pern/Pert, their(?)
      names.

Uaisnem [was] the name of their seer -- he would search the way(?) of
      favor(?)
He was a sage to their warrior, Crus, son of Cirig the Weak(?)
      (Crus the Weak, son of Cirig?).

Cruithne, proper son of Cing, he took care of [...?],
Until he brought a female retinue of bright, flourishing
      appearance [...?] across Athgort.

There stayed from them in Ireland with a full complement of artisans and
      enamellers(?)
Who would not settle Bregmach, six demonic druids.

Druidic lore and idolatry, augury, fine-strong, pure-protective;
The practice of plunder, which gave rise to bright songs were taught by
      them.

Morad' sleg' is mana: rog'a séin ní sona:
got'a en do aire: c'aire gan cel cona.

Cnuíc as c'oirt'e ar cora: cen trog'a tuat' taille:
ro rotogsat a tindrem'. gabsat ínb'ir mBoinde:

Ba hed' lodar huaine go ngluaire na grib'e:
imma iat' co drene i tír iat' seac' Íle·

IS as g'ab'sat Albáinn. ardgláin ailes t'oirt'íu:
cen dit' tlac't la treb't'u. ó c'ric' at' co Foirc'íu

Robris Cat'luan cat'u: gen tac'u cen treab't'u:
nírbó ín garg tuícíu co róm'arb' Bret'nu:

Ba de g'ab'sat Albáin ardgláin talcáin tlac'min:
co nimad amlaeb' in Chinaet' mac nAilp'ín

Ar creac'ad' nard naic.nid'. for aitc'ib' cen uc'neim':
ní celldar in coc'laig' as de adbertar Cruit'níg'·

Coeca rig' ceim creac'ac'. maráen do sil Ec'dac':
ó Fergus rofirad'. co mac mbrigac' mB'ret'ac'

Se riog'a ar se deic'ib'. dib' fri feit'im fuilc'rec':
carsad sit'e suic'leac': g'ab'sat rig'e Cruit'neac':

Cruithnig' dosfarclá[m];

Mustering of spears and omens, choice of sign and anything lucky,
Observation of the voices of birds; fault without concealment, besides.

Mounds(?) and standing-stones aright without misery, people of
      battlements/reckoning(?);
They selected their [mode of] service/servitude; they seized the mouth of the
      Boyne.

It was that they went from us with the swiftness of falcon
Which encloses/circles with strength, in the land (Tiree?) past Ile.

It is from there they took Alba, noble and pure, which nourishes crops
Without lack of mildness, with residences from the boundary of Ath to
      Fortriu(?).

Cathluan won battles without scarcity without dwellings;
There were no fierce onsets(?), until he slew the Britons.

It was from that they seized Alba, noble and pure, pleasant, vigorous peace(?)
With much success, not fraudulent(?), that Cináed mac Alpín.

Upon plundering famous heights face to face and without sorrow(?),
The hooded ones(?) are not concealed that is why they are called Cruithni.

Fifty kings, a marauding sequence, altogether Eochaid's descendants;
From Fergus it was shown to be true to the mighty son of Bretach.

Sixty-six kings of them set to observe bloody raids;
They loved the peace treaties of liberal men (?); they accepted the kingship
      of the Cruithni.

Cruithni [...?] assembled themselves.

VARIATION P#F(D.iv.1)

Seis'er toisech tancatar co hErinn ·i· ui· braithre Solen· Ulpa· Nechtan· Trostan· Oengus· Letenn· fáth a tiachtana ·i· Pilicornus rig Tracía do rat grad día siair c'or triall a breith cen tochra· lotar iarsin t[ar] Romanc'u co Fran'gco ⁊ cumtaigsit cathair [o and] ·i· Pictairius a pictus ·i· o na randaib ⁊ do r[ad] righi Frangc grad' dia siair· lotar for muir ar [nec] in tseisid' brathar ·i· Letend i cind da la iar ndul ar muir atbath a siur· Gabsat Cruithnigh a nInber Slaine a nIb Cennsilaigh· Atbert friu C[r]emthand Sciathbel rig Laigen do berad failte doib ar dícor Tuaithe Figdha doib· Atbert Drostan drai Cruithnech riu co foirfedh iat ar logh dfagbail ⁊ isse in leiges ·i· blegan ·uíí·xx· bo find mael do dortadh i faili ferfaigthe in cath doib unde cath Arda Lem'nachta a nIb Cendsilaigh re Tuaithaib Figda ·i· tuath do Bretnaib robúi i F'othardaib ⁊ neim ara narmaib marb cach aenar a ndergtais ⁊ ni gebdis acht iarnaidhi neim impu cach aenar a ndergtais do Laig[nib] isin cath ni dentais acht loighi isin lemnocht ⁊ ni cuimg'etiss neim ni doibh· Ro marbtha iarsin Tuath Fidba· Marb cetrar iarsin do Cruithen tuaith ·i· Drostan· Solen· Nechtan· Ulpa ⁊ isin [duain] asbert

(P#D(D.iv.1))...

ET issin aims'ir sin Erimoin gabais Gub ⁊ a mac ·i· Cathluan mac Guib ·i· ri Cruithnech nert m'or for Erind no co rusindarb Erimon a hErind ⁊ co ndernsat sid iarsin ⁊ co tard Erimon doib mna na fer ro baiged maille Donn ·i· mna Bres ⁊ mna Buais ⁊ Buaigne ratha ngrene ⁊ esca ⁊ conabudh lughu do gebthai do rigi ⁊ du domun o mnaib inais o feraib a Cruithentuaith co brath ⁊ anais seisir dib os Bregmuig' ⁊ is uaithaib gach geis ⁊ gach sen ⁊ gach sregh gotha én ⁊ gach mana ⁊ gach upaidh· Cat'luan ba hairdrig' forro uile ⁊ isse ·c· rig rogab Albain dib ·lxx· rig dib for Albain o Cat'luan co Constantin ⁊ isse Cruithneach deiginach rogab dib Da mac Cathluain ·i· Catanolodar ⁊ Catanalachan· A da curaidh im- mac Pirrn ⁊ Cing atair Cruithne· A da sruith ·i· Cruis ⁊ Ciric· A da milidh· Uasnem a fili· Cruithne a cerd· Domnall mac Ailpin ise a taisech ⁊ ised atberait araile comad' he Cruithne mac Lochit mac Cinge tisad do cun[dg]id ban for Erimon ⁊ comad do do berad Erimon mna na fear do baitea maill fri Donn

A company of six leaders came to Ireland, that is, six brothers: Solen, Ulfa/Ulpa, Nechtan, Drostan, Óengus, Letenn. The reason of their arrival in Ireland: Policornus, king of Thrace, gave love to their(?) sister, so that he attempted to carry her off without a bride-price. They then went past the Romans to the Franks, and they built a city there: that is, Pictabis was its name, from "pictus," i.e "from the points"(?). And the king of the Franks gave love to their sister. They went upon the sea after the death of the sixth brother: that is, Letenn. At the end of two days after proceeding on the sea, their sister died. The Cruithni took Inber Slaine in Uí Cennselaig. Crimthann Shield-mouth, king of the Laigin, told them that he would welcome them in return for their banishing the Tuath Fidga. Drostan, druid of the Cruithni, said to them that he would help in return for receiving a payment; and this is the cure: that is, the milking of one hundred forty white, hornless cows to be poured in the place in which the battle would be fought by them. Whence the Battle of Ard Lemnacht in Uí Cennselaig against the Tuath Fidga: that is, a tribe of the Britons who were in Fotharta, who used to put poison upon their weapons. Dead was anyone whom they would wound, and they would not attire themselves with any but poisoned weapons. Any one of the Laigin who was wounded in the battle, they would do nothing but lie in the milk, and the poison would not be able [to do] anything to them. The Tuath Fidga were killed after that. After that four from Pictland died too: that is, Drostan, Solen, Nechtan, Ulfa/Ulpa and in that poem it said:

....

And in that age of Éremón, Gub and his son (that is, Cathluan son of Gub: that is, king of the Cruithni) attacked Ireland [with a] great force/army, until Éremón expelled them from Ireland, and until they made peace afterwards. And so that Éremón gave to them the wives of the men who drowned with Donn: that is, the wife of Bres and the wife of Basse and Buaigne. Sureties [were given] of the sun and moon so that women should not partake of rule and sovereignty any less than men in Pictland forever (lit. "so that it should not be less that would be got of kingship or of world by women than by men in Pictland till Judgment."). And six from them stayed over Bregmach, and it is from them every spell and every charm/amulet and every prophetic sneeze, and augury of birds, and every omen, every charm [that is made]. Cathluan was high-king upon them all, and he was the first king from them who ruled over Alba. Seventy kings from them over Alba from Cathluan to Constantine(?), and he was the last Cruithnian who ruled from them. Two sons of Cathluan: that is, Cadnolodor and Catainlacach, Their two heroes: moreover (Im?), son of Pern/Pert and Cing father of Cruithne. Their two elders: that is, Crus and Cirig. Their two soldiers: Uaisnem, their seer, and Cruithne, their artisan. Domnall mac Alpín was their leader, and it is this that others say, that it was Cruithne son of Loichet son of Cing who should have come to request wives from Éremón, and that it was to him that Éremón should have given the wives of the men who had been drowned together with Donn.

VARIATION P#F(Lec.1)

Seissir toisech tancatar co hErind ·i· u[i] braithre Solen Ulpa Nechtan
Dro[stan] Oengus ⁊ Letenn· fath a tiachtana ·i· P[olicor]nus righ Tracia do rat
gradh dia siair cor t[riall] a breith cen tochra· lotar iarsin [tar] R[om]anchu co
Francco ⁊ cumdaigsit [caitir] and ·i· Pictairus a pictus ·i· o na rannaib ⁊ do rat
righ Frangc grad dia siair· lotar for muir iar nec in tseisidh brathar ·i· Lethenn i
cind da la iar ndul ar muir atbath a siur Gabsat Cruithnigh a nInber Slaine a
nIb Cennsilaigh Atbert friu Cremthann Sgiathbel rig Laigen· do berad failte
doib ar dicur Tuaithe Figdha doib' Atbert Drostan drai Cruithnech riu co
foirfedh iat ar log dfagbail ⁊ ise med ·i· bleghan an uij· xx^it· bo find mael do
dortadh i faili f[er]faige in cath doib unde· cath Arda Lemnachta an Ib
Cennsilaigh re Tuaithaib Figda ·i· tuath do Bretnaib robui hi F'othardaib ⁊
[neim] ar armaib marb cach oenar a ndergtais do Laigen isin cath ni dentais
acht loighi isin lemnacht ⁊ ni cuimgitis neim doib Ro marbtha iarsin Tuatha
Figda marb cetrar iarsin do Cruthentuaith ·i· Drostan Solen Nechtan Ulpa
isbert [isin duain]

(P#D(Lec.1))...

ET issin aimsir hErimoin gabais Gub ⁊ a mac ·i· Cathluan mac Guib
·i· ri Cruithnech nert mor for Erind no cor rusinnarb hErimon a hErind ⁊ con
dernsat sidh iarsin ⁊ co tard hErimon doib mna na fer ro baighedh maill Donn
·i· mna Bress ⁊ mna Buais ⁊ Buaigne ratha ngrene ⁊ esca conabugh lugu do
gebthai do rigi ⁊ du domun o mnaib' inas o feraib a Cruith'entuaith co brath ⁊
anais seissir dib os Bregmuigh ⁊ is uaithib gach geiss ⁊ cach sen ⁊ gach sregh
gotha en ⁊ gach mana ⁊ gach upaidh Cathluan im⁻ ba hairdri forro uile ⁊ ise ·c·
righ rogab Albain dib lxx· rig dib for Albain o Chathluan co Constantin ⁊ ise
Cruithnech deigenach rogab dib Da mac Cathluain ·i· Cat[ai]nolodar ⁊
Catanalachan A da curaidh im⁻· mac Pirrn ⁊ Cing athair Cruithni· [a da] sruith
·i· Crus ⁊ Ciric A da milidh· Uasnem [a fili] Cruithne a cerd Domnall mac
Ailpin [ise] a taisech ⁊ isadh asberait araile comadh he Cruithne mac Loichit
mac Cinge tisadh do chuindgid ban for Erimon ⁊ comad[h] do do berad
[E]rimon mna na fer do baitea maill fri Donn

A company of six leaders came to Ireland, that is, six brothers: Solen, Ulfa/Ulpa, Nechtan, Drostan, Óengus, Letenn. The reason of their arrival in Ireland: Policornus, king of Thrace, gave love to their(?) sister, so that he attempted to carry her off without a bride-price. They then went past the Romans to the Franks, and they built a city there: that is, Pictabis was its name, from "pictus," i.e "from the points"(?). And the king of the Franks gave love to their sister. They went upon the sea after the death of the sixth brother: that is, Letenn. At the end of two days after proceeding on the sea, their sister died. The Cruithni took Inber Slaine in Uí Cennselaig. Crimthann Shield-mouth, king of the Laigin, told them that he would welcome them in return for their banishing the Tuath Fidga. Drostan, druid of the Cruithni, said to them that he would help in return for receiving a payment; and this is the means: that is, the milking of one hundred forty white, hornless cows to be poured in the place in which the battle would be fought by them. Whence the Battle of Ard Lemnacht in Uí Cennselaig against the Tuath Fidga: that is, a tribe of the Britons who were in Fotharta, who used to put poison upon their weapons. Dead was anyone whom they would wound. [Any one] of the Laigin who was wounded in the battle, they would do nothing but lie in the milk, and the poison would not be able [to do] anything to them. The Tuath Fidga were killed after that. After that four from Pictland died too: that is, Drostan, Solen, Nechtan, Ulfa/Ulpa. and it said in that poem:

....

And in that age of Éremón, Gub and his son (that is, Cathluan son of Gub: that is, king of the Cruithni) attacked Ireland [with a] great force/army, until Éremón expelled them from Ireland, and until they made peace afterwards. And so that Éremón gave to them the wives of the men who drowned with Donn: that is, the wife of Bres and the wife of Basse and Buaigne. Sureties [were given] of the sun and moon so that women should not partake of rule and sovereignty any less than men in Pictland forever. And six from them stayed over Bregmach, and it is from them every spell and every charm/amulet and every prophetic sneeze, and augury of birds, and every omen, every charm that is made. Cathluan, however, was high-king upon them all, and he was the first king from them who ruled over Alba. Seventy kings from them over Alba from Cathluan to Constantine(?), and he was the last Cruithnian who ruled from them. Two sons of Cathluan: that is, Cadnolodor and Catainlacach, Their two heroes: moreover, Pern/Pert and Cing father of Cruithne. Their two elders: Crus and Cirig. Their two soldiers: Uaisnem, their seer, and Cruithne, their artisan. Domnall mac Alpín was their leader, and it is this that others say, that it was Cruithne son of Loichet son of Cing who should have come to request wives from Éremón, and that it was to him that Éremón should have given the wives of the men who had been drowned together with Donn.

VARIATION P#F(Lec.2)

Seisear taiseach tancadar co hErind ·i· sesear dear braithri ·i· Soilen·
Ulpa· Nechtain· Trostan· Aengus· Leitend Fath a tiachta a nErind· im¯·
Polornus ri Traicia do rad grad dia shiair co ro triall a breith can tochra Lotar
iarsin co ro triallsad tar Romanchu co Frangcu ꝟ ro cumdaigsead cathair and ·i·
Pictairis a pictus a hainm ·i· o na reandaib ꝟ do rad rig Frangc grad dia siair
Lotar for muir iar neg in chuiced brathar ·i· Laitenn I cind da la iar ndul ar
muir adbath a siur Gabsad Cruithnig a nIndber tlaine a nIb Cendsealaig
Atbeart friu Cremthand Sciathbel rig Laigen do berad failti doib ar dichur
Tuaithi Fidga doib Adbeart tra Trostan drai Cruithneach riu co foirfead iad ar
log df_agbail ꝟ ise leiges ·i· bleogan ·uii· fichit bo mael finn do dortadi fail a
fearfaidea in cath doib ·i· cath Ard Leamnachta an Ib Cendsealaich re
Tuathaibh Figda ·i· tuath do Breatnaib ro bai i Fothartaib ꝟ nem ar a narmaib
marb cach aen fer ar a ndeargdais ꝟ ni gebdis acht iarnaidi nemi umpu cach
aen dogobtha do Laignib isin chath ni dendais acht laigi sin leamnacht ꝟ ni
cumgid nem ni doib Ro marbtha iarsin Tuath F'idga Marb ceathrar iarsin do
Cruithneachaib ·i· Trostan· Solen· Nechtain· Ulptha iar ndichar in chatha
conad doib sin rochan in senchaid so
(P#D(Lec.2))...

ISin aimsir hEreamon ro gobustair Guba ꝟ a mac ·i· Cathluan mac
Guba ·i· ri Cruithneach neart mor for Eirind No corusindarb Eremon a hErind
ꝟ co ndernsad sid iarsin No is o macaib Miled fen dochuaid Cruithneachan
mac In'gi la Breatnu Foirtreand do chathugud· re S{c}axanchu ꝟ ro sellad a
clann ꝟ a claideamthir doib ·i· Cruitheantuath ised ni robadar accu ar adbath
bandtrocht Alban do gall roib Doluid dono ar a cul dochum mac Miled ꝟ
rogabad nem ꝟ talam· grian ꝟ esca· muir ꝟ tir beith do maith riu flaith forro co
brath ꝟ adbert di mnai dec for craid do badar la tascur mac Milead in Erind
uair ro baitea a fir isa nairrgi tshiar maraen re Donn

Translation

A company of six leaders came to Ireland, that is, six brothers: that is, Solen, Ulpa, Nechtan, Drostan, Óengus, Letenn. The reason of their arrival in Ireland: Policornus, king of Thrace, gave love to their(?) sister, so that he attempted to carry her off without a bride-price. They then journeyed past the Romans to the Franks, and they built a city there: that is, Pictabis was its name, from "pictus," i.e "from the points"(?). And the king of the Franks gave love to their sister. They went upon the sea after the death of the fifth brother: that is, Letenn. At the end of two days after proceeding on the sea, their sister died. The Cruithni took Inber Slaine in Uí Cennselaig. Crimthann Shield-mouth, King of the Laigin, told them that he would welcome them in return for their banishing the Tuath Fidga. Drostan, druid of the Cruithni, said to them that he would help in return for receiving a payment; and this is the cure: that is, the milking of one hundred forty white, hornless cows to be poured in the place in which the battle would be fought by them. That is, the Battle of Ard Lemnacht in Uí Cennselaig against the Tuath Fidga: that is, a tribe of the Britons who were in Fotharta, who used to put poison upon their weapons. Dead was anyone whom they would wound, and they would not attire themselves with any but poisoned weapons. Any one of the Laigin who was wounded (struck down?) in the battle, they would do nothing but lie in the milk, and the poison would not be able [to do] anything to them. The Tuath Fidga were killed after that. After that four of the Cruithni died too: that is, Drostan, Solen, Nechtan, Ulfa/Ulpa after the expulsion of the [hostile] army, and it is for them that the shennachie ("reciter of lore") sang:

....

In that age of Éremón, Gub and his son (that is, Cathluan son of Gub: that is, king of the Cruithni) attacked Ireland [with a] great force/army, until Erimon expelled them from Ireland, and until they made peace afterwards. Or it is from the Sons of Míl themselves that Cruithne[chan], son of Cing himself, went with the Britons of Fortriu to give battle against the Saxons; and he and his children carved out sword-land for them: that is, Pictland. They had no [wives] with them because the womenfolk of Alba had died from diseases. He came back again to the Sons of Míl, and the sky and earth, sun and moon, sea and land were invoked [that] the sovereignty would be *to their advantage forever.* And he said (or "they take," reading "do-berat") twelve women who were in excess with/along with the company of the Sons of Míl in Ireland when their husbands had been drowned in the western ocean together with Donn.

*‾*Reading "co maith friu" for "do maith riu" with confused syntax. Alternately, "do maithrib" ("from mothers")

conad o feraib Erenn flaith for Cruithentuaith do gres iar foirind Mna Bresi·
im⁻· ꞓ Buaidne ꞓ Buaisi ꞓ na taisech ro baitea uile Ocus anais seser dib os
Bregmaig ꞓ is uathib cach ges ꞓ cach sen ꞓ cach sred ꞓ gotha en ꞓ cach mana
ꞓ cach obair do gnithear Catluan ise ba rig orrtho uile ꞓ ise cet rig rogob Albain
dib ·lxx· rig for Albain dib o Chatluan co Consantin ise Cruithnech deiginach
rosgob dib Da mac Catluain ·i· Cotanolotar ꞓ Catalacach a da curaid ·im⁻· Pirn
ꞓ Cing athair Cruithnich a da sruith ·i· Crus ꞓ Ciric a da Milidh ·i· Uasnem a
filig ꞓ cruithne a cerd Domnall mac Ailpin ise a taisech ꞓ ised adberaid aroile
comad he Cruithne mac Loichit mac In'ge fen tisad do chuindgid ban for
Eremon ꞓ comad do do beread Eremon mna na fer do baitea maille re Donn

So that the sovereignty of Pictland derives from the men of Ireland from then on. Members of the group [were] the wives of Bres, moreover, and Buaigne and Basse, and all the princes who were drowned. And six from them stayed over Bregmach, and it is from them every spell and every charm/amulet and every prophetic sneeze, and augury of birds, and every omen, every work(?) that is made. Cathluan, however, was high-king upon them all, and he was the first king from them who ruled over Alba. Seventy kings from them over Alba from Cathluan to Constantine(?), he himself was the last Cruithnian who ruled from them. Two sons of Cathluan: that is Cadnolodor and Catainlacach, Their two heroes: moreover, Pern/Pert and Cing father of Cruithne. Their two elders: Crus and Cirig. Their two soldiers: Uaisnem, their seer, and Cruithne, their artisan. Domnall mac Alpín was their leader, and it is this that others say, that it was Cruithne son of Loichet son of Cing who should have come to request wives from Éremón, and that it was to him that Éremón should have given the wives of the men who had been drowned together with Donn.

VARIATION P#F(Bal.)

Seissiur toisseach tangadar go hErind .i. uí. braíthre Solen Ulpa. Nechtain Trosdan. Aengus Leídeand Fath a tiachtana .i. Poliornus rí Traigia dorad graidh da siair gor triall a breíth gan tochra Lodar iarsin tar Romanachu gu Frangchu ᚐ cumdaighsead cáthair and .i. Pictairius a pictís i. o na randaib' ᚐ dorad righ Frangc gradh dia siaír Lodar for muír iar neg in seisead brathar ·i· Leideand i cind dá lá iar ndhul ar muir adbath a siur Gabsat Cruithneigh i nInber Slaine i nUibh Ceindselaigh Atbert fríu Creamthond Sciathbel righ Laigen do berad failti doibh ar díchur Tuaithi Fidhbha doibh Atbert Trostan drui Cruithneach riu co foirfeadh íad ar log do fhaghbail ᚐ ise in leighís .i. bleaghon .uíí.xx. bo mael find do dhortadh i fhail i fearthea ín cath doib .i. Cath Arda Leamnachta in Uibh Ceíndsealaigh re Tuaith Fidhbha .i. tuath do Breatnaibh robaí i Fothartaibh ᚐ neim ara narmaibh marbh gach aen ar a ndergdaís ᚐ ni geibdís acht iarnaighi umpu gach aen dogonta do Laignib' isin chath, ni dendais· acht loígí isin leamhnacht ᚐ ni cuimgidís neímh ní doibh Ro marbhtha iar sin Tuath Fidhbha[h] Marbh ceatrar iarsin do Chrutheantaith .i· Trosdan Solen Neachtain Ulpa Et ísin doibh sin ro chan in sencaid' ín duan sa sis

(P#D(Bal.))...

Et isin naimsir sin Erímon gabhas Gub ᚐ a mac .i· Cathluan mac Guíb .i. rí Cruithneach mór neart for Erinn. no gorosíndarb Erimon ᚐ co nd'earnsat sidh. iarsin ᚐ go tard Erimon doib mná na fear ro baitea maille re Dond i. mnai Breis ᚐ mnai B'uaís ᚐ mnai Buaighne ᚐ ratha grene ᚐ esca conabad' mo do ríg'e ᚐ do d'oman do gebhta o feraibh nas o mnaibh i Cruthtuaithaib' go brath ᚐ anais seisear dibh os Breagmaigh ᚐ is uadhaibh gach géis ᚐ gach sén ᚐ gach sredh ᚐ gotha en ᚐ gac' upaid'ᚐ gach mana Cathluan ba hairdrig forro uile ᚐ is e c. rígh rogab Albain díbh .lxx. ríg' dib for Albain o Chathluan gu Consta[n]tin ise Cruithneach rosgab' dib' Da mac C'athluain .i· Catanolodar ᚐ Catanalachan. a dhá curaid' im⁻. mac Pírn ᚐ Cíng at'air Cruit'ni a dha sruíth Crus ᚐ Ciríg a dha milid' hUaisneamh a file Cruithni a ceard. Domnall mac Ailpin is e a toiseach ᚐ ised adberaidh aroile gomadh he Cruithne mac Loichít mac Cínge fein tisad' do chuindgidh ban for Erímon ᚐ comad' do do berad Erimon mna na fear ro baitea maille re Donn.

A company of six leaders came to Ireland, that is, six brothers: Solen, Ulfa/Ulpa, Nechtan, Drostan, Óengus, Letenn. The reason of their arrival in Ireland: Policornus, king of Thrace, gave love to their(?) sister, so that he attempted to carry her off without a bride-price. They then journeyed past the Romans to the Franks, and they built a city there: that is, Pictabis was its name, from "pictis," i.e. "from the points"(?). And the king of the Franks gave love to their sister. They went upon the sea after the death of the sixth brother: that is, Letenn. At the end of two days after proceeding on the sea, their sister died. The Cruithni took Inber Slaine in Uí Cennselaig. Crimthann Shield-mouth, king of the Laigin, told them that he would welcome them in return for their banishing the Tuath Fidga for them. Drostan, druid of the Cruithni, said to them that he would help in return for receiving a payment; and this is the cure: that is, the milking of one hundred forty white, hornless cows to be poured in the place in which the battle would be fought by them. That is, the Battle of Ard Lemnacht in Uí Cennselaig against the Tuath Fidga: that is, a tribe of the Britons who were in Fotharta, who used to put poison upon their weapons. Dead was anyone whom they would wound, and they would not attire themselves with any but [poisoned?] weapons. Any one of the Laigin who was wounded in the battle, they would do nothing but lie in the milk, and the poison would not be able [to do] anything to them. The Tuath Fidga were killed after that. After that four of the Cruithni died too: that is, Drostan, Solen, Nechtan, Ulfa/Ulpa and is to them that the shennachie sang the following poem:

....

And in that age of Éremón, Gub and his son (that is, Cathluan son of Gub: that is, king of the Cruithni) attacked Ireland [with a] great force/army, until Éremón expelled them, and until they made peace afterwards. And so that Éremón gave to them the wives of the men who drowned with Donn: that is, the wife of Bress and the wife of Basse and the wife of Buaigne. Sureties [were given] of the sun and the moon so that men should not partake of rule and sovereignty any more than women in Pictland forever (lit. "so that it should not be greater that would be got of kingship or of world by men than by women till Judgment"). And six from them stayed over Bregmach, and it is from them every spell and every charm/amulet and every prophetic sneeze, and augury of birds, and every charm, every omen [that is made]. Cathluan, however, was high-king upon them all, and he was the first king from them who ruled over Alba. Seventy kings from them over Alba from Cathluan to Constantine(?), he himself was the Cruithnian who ruled from them. Two sons of Cathluan: that is Cadnolodor and Catainlacach. Their two heroes: moreover, Pern/Pert and Cing father of Cruithne. Their two elders: Crus and Cirig. Their two soldiers: Uaisnem, their seer, Cruithne, their artisan. Domnall mac Alpín was their leader, and it is this that others say, that it was Cruithne son of Loichet son of Cing who should have come himself to request wives from Éremón, and that it was to him that Éremón should have given the wives of the men who had been drowned together with Donn.

VARIATION P#F(24.P.13)

.ui. tais<u>i</u>cch tancad<u>ar</u> go her<u>ind</u> .i. ui. b<u>ra</u>tri. Sole<u>n</u> Ulpa Ne<u>ch</u>tain Trostan Aengus lei<u>th</u>cend.   Fath a te<u>ch</u>tana .i. Poliorn<u>us</u> ri T<u>rai</u>g<u>h</u>ia dorad gradh dia s<u>i</u>air g<u>or</u> t<u>ri</u>all a breíth ca<u>n</u> toc<u>ra</u>. Lodar iars<u>in</u> tar Rom<u>h</u>anchu go F<u>ra</u>ncu .₇ cum<u>h</u>daichs<u>it</u> caithir an<u>n</u> .i. Pictairi<u>us</u> a pictus .i. o na ran<u>n</u>aib' dorad rig F<u>ra</u>nc gradh dia s<u>i</u>air. Lodor for muir iar necc in ts<u>h</u>eisedh brathair itcean<u>n</u> a cin<u>d</u> da lá iar ndul ar muir atba<u>th</u> a s<u>i</u>ur gab'sud Crui<u>th</u>nicch a nInb<u>er</u> Slaing<u>h</u>e a nIub' Cendsela<u>ig</u>'. átb<u>er</u>t fríu Criom<u>h</u>tann Scia<u>th</u>b<u>é</u>l ri Laicc<u>en</u> do bera<u>dh</u> failti doib' ar di<u>ch</u>ur Tuaithe Ficch[<u>da</u>] Atbert tru T<u>ro</u>stan draoi Cruithneach friu co foirfeadh iad ar locch dfucc[<u>bail</u>] .₇ ise leithis do rinde doib' .i. bled<u>gh</u>an .uii.xx<u>it</u> bo mael find do dort<u>ad</u>' a fail a ferfaid<u>h</u>e in cath .i. cath Arda Leam<u>h</u>a<u>ch</u>ta a nIb' Cei<u>n</u>dsela<u>ig</u>' re Tuaith Ficcd<u>h</u>á .₇ tuaith do Breatn<u>aib</u>' dobi Fot<u>h</u>ortaib' .₇ nei[m]h ar a narm<u>a</u>ib' .₇ ba marb'h ga<u>ch</u> aon ar a nd'erccdis .₇ ni geib'dís a<u>ch</u>t iarnaid'e neim<u>h</u>e umpo gach aon dagontai n<u>ó</u> da ngab'ta is<u>i</u>n cath s<u>i</u>n do Laiccnib' ni dendais a<u>ch</u>t loicche is<u>i</u>n lemn<u>ach</u>t .₇ ni cuimgidis neim<u>h</u>e ní doib' marb't<u>ar</u> iars<u>i</u>n Tuatha Ficc[da] Marb'tar cetror do Chruithintuaith .i. Trostán Solen Ne<u>ch</u>tain .₇ Ulpa is ís doib' sin ro can in sencha<u>id</u>'i in Duan So.

(P#D(24.P.13))...

ET is naim<u>a</u>s s<u>i</u>n Eirim<u>h</u>oin gab'as Gub' .₇ a m<u>a</u>c .i· Cathluan m<u>a</u>c Guib' .i. ri Cruithneach nert mor for Eirin<u>n</u> n<u>o</u> g<u>o</u>roin<u>n</u>arb Erim<u>h</u>on a hErínd iad et co nd<u>e</u>ratt s<u>it</u>' iars<u>i</u>n et go t<u>a</u>rd Erim<u>h</u>on doib<u>h</u> mná na f<u>er</u> do baith ₇ maill[e re] Don<u>n</u> .i. mnai Breisi .₇ B'<u>ua</u>is<u>i</u> et Buaid'ne ₇ rat<u>h</u>a Greine agas esca g'u na ba lug'a do geb't'a do i na dom<u>h</u>an o a mnaib<u>h</u> na ca f<u>er</u>aib<u>h</u> ac Cru<u>i</u>t<u>h</u>in{thin}tuataib<u>h</u> co brat<u>h</u> agas an'a<u>is</u> se[<u>iser</u>] doib<u>h</u> os Breccmuig' et is uathoib' ga<u>ch</u> geis et sr<u>e</u>odh .₇ gothae eun. Cathluan ba ri orra uile et is e ·c· ri dogab' Alb<u>ain</u> diob' .lxx. ri for Albain diob' o Cathluan cu <u>C</u>onsantin ise Cruithnech deg<u>h</u>in dogab' dib' <u>Consantin Da</u> m<u>a</u>c Cathluain .i. Cathanoloda<u>r</u> .₇ Cathala<u>ch</u>an. a da cur<u>aid</u>' .u<u>o</u>. .i. mac Pirn' .₇ Cing athair Cruith<u>n</u>e a d<u>h</u>a sruíth .i. C<u>ru</u>s.₇ Cirig A d<u>h</u>a mil<u>id</u>' Uasnema a f<u>h</u>il<u>ed</u>' Cruithne a c<u>er</u>d. Dom'nall mac Ailpín is e a tais<u>i</u>cc .₇ is<u>ed</u>' atberuit aroile gomad<u>h</u> é Cruithnech m<u>a</u>c Loichit m<u>a</u>c Cinge fén do cuing<u>id</u>' ban ar Eirim<u>h</u>ón .₇ comad' do do bera<u>dh</u> Eirim<u>h</u>ón mna na fer do baite maill[<u>e re</u>] Don<u>n</u>.

A company of six leaders came to Ireland, that is, six brothers: Solen, Ulfa/Ulpa, Nechtan, Drostan, Óengus, Letenn. The reason of their arrival in Ireland: Policornus, king of Thrace, gave love to their(?) sister, so that he attempted to carry her off without a bride-price. They then journeyed past the Romans to the Franks, and they built a city there: that is, Pictabis was its name, from "pictus," i.e "from the points"(?). The king of the Franks gave love to their sister. They went upon the sea after the death of the sixth brother: Letenn. At the end of two days after proceeding on the sea, their sister died. The Cruithni took Inber Slaine in Uí Cennselaig. Crimthann Shield-mouth, king of the Laigin, told them that he would welcome them in return for their banishing the Tuath Fidga. Drostan, druid of the Cruithni, said to them that he would help in return for receiving a payment; and this is the cure(?): that is, the milking of one hundred forty white, hornless cows to be poured in the place in which the battle would be fought. That is, the Battle of Ard Lemnacht in Uí Cennselaig against the Tuath Fidga: that is, a tribe of the Britons who were in Fotharta, who used to put poison upon their weapons. And dead was anyone whom they would wound, and they would not attire themselves with any but poisoned weapons. Any one of the Laigin who was wounded or struck down(?) in the battle, they would do nothing but lie in the milk, and the poison would not be able [to do] anything to them. The Tuath Fidga were killed after that. After that four of the Cruithni died too: that is, Drostan, Solen, Nechtan, and Ulfa/Ulpa and is to them that the shennachie sang this poem:

....

And in that age of Éremón, Gub and his son (that is, Cathluan son of Gub: that is, king of the Cruithni) attacked Ireland [with a] great force/army, until Éremón expelled [them] from Ireland, and until they made peace afterwards. And so that Éremón gave to them the wives of the men who drowned and with Donn: that is, the wife of Bress and the wife of Basse and Buaigne. Sureties [were given] of the sun and the moon so that women should not partake of rule and sovereignty any less than men in Pictland forever (lit. "so that it should not be less that would be got of kingship or of world by woman than by men till Judgment"). And six from them stayed over Bregmach, and it is from them every spell and every prophetic sneeze, and augury of birds [that is made]. Cathluan, however, was high-king upon them all, and he was the first king from them who ruled over Alba. Seventy kings from them over Alba from Cathluan to Constantine(?), he himself was the last Cruithnian who ruled from them. Constantine(?). Two sons of Cathluan: that is Cadnolodor and Catainlacach. Their two heroes: moreover, that is, son of Pern/Pert and Cing father of Cruithne. Their two elders: Crus and Cirig. Their two soldiers: Uaisnem, their seer, and Cruithne, their artisan. Domnall mac Alpín was their leader, and it is this that others say, that it was Cruithne son of Loichet son of Cing who should have come himself to request wives from Éremón, and that it was to him that Éremón should have given the wives of the men who had been drowned together with Donn.

VARIATION P#F(1295)

Seisiur toíseac' tangadair go hEirin ·i· uí. braít're· Solen Ulpa·
Neachtaín· Trosdan· Aengus Leideand· Fat'{a} a tia[s]ana ·i· Poliornus rí
Tragía dorad graid' da siar gor triall a breít' gan toc'ra Lodar iarsin tar
Rom'anac'u gu Frangcú· ⁊ cum'daig'sead cat'air ann ·i· Pictairius a pictis ·i· o
na randaib' ·⁊ dorad rig' Frangc grad' dia siair Lodair for muir iar nég ín
seisead' brat'air ·i· Leideand i cind da la iar ndul ar muir adbat' a s'iur g'ab'sad
Cruit'neig' i nInb'ir Sláine i nUib' C'einnselaig' atbert friu Creamt'ond Sciat'b'el
rig' Laig'en do beraid' failtí d'oib' ar dic'ur Tuait'i Fid'b'a d'oib' atbert Trosdan
drui Cruit'neac' ríu co foirfead' iad ar log do f'ag'b'ail ·⁊ isein leig'is ·i· bleag'on
secht ·xx bo m'ael f'ionn do d'ortad' i f'ail i feart'ea in cat' d'oib' ·i· Cat' Arda
Leam'nachta in Uib' C'eansealaig' ré Tuait' Fid'b'a ·i· tuat' do B'reatnuib'h ró
b'ái í Fot'artaib' .⁊ neim' ar a narmaib' marb' gac' aenar a ndergdis ·⁊ ní
g'eaib'dís acht iarnaig'i umpu gac'h áen do{n}gonta do Laig'nib' isin c'at' ní
g'endís acht loig'í isin leam'nacht ·⁊ ní cuimgididís neim' ní doib'· Ro marb't'a
iar sin Tuat' Fid'b'a· Marb' ceatrar iarsin do Cruit'entuat' ·i· Trosdan Solen
Neac'táin Ulpa ·⁊ is doib' sin ro c'an in senc'aid' in duan si:

(P#D(1295))...

·⁊ isin aimsir sin Eirim'on gab'us Gub ·⁊ a mac ·i· Cat'lua'n mac Gub
·i· rí Cruithneac' móir nert for Eirinn no gorosinarb' Eirim'oin a hEirinn ·⁊ co
nd'earnsat sid' iarsin ·⁊ go tard Erim'on doib' mna na fear ro bait'ea maille re
Dond i. mnái Breas· ⁊ mnái Buais ·⁊ mnái Buaig'ne ·⁊ reta greine ·⁊ esca
conadbad' mo do rig'i ·⁊ do d'om'an do g'eab't'a ó f'earaib' nas o m'naib' i
Cruit'entuait'aib' go brat' ·⁊ anais seisear doib' os Breag'm'aig' ·⁊ is uad'aib' gac'
geis ·⁊ gac' sén ·⁊ gac' sred' ⁊ got'a én ⁊ gac' nupaid ·⁊ gach mana· Cat'luan ba
hairdrig' forro uile ⁊ is e ·c· ríg' rog'ab' Albáin dib'·lxx. rig' diob' for Albáin go
Constantin ise Cruit'neac' rosgab' dib'· Da mac Cat'luain ·i· Catanalodair ·⁊
Catanalacán. a d'a ad' a cuiraid' im⁻. mac Pírn ·⁊ Cíng at'air a d'a⁻ sruít'· Crus
·⁊ Cirig a dá m'ilid' hUaisneam' a file· Cruit'ni a ceard· Dom'nall mac Ailp is e
a toiseac' ·⁊ ise adberaid' aroile gomad' hé Cruitne mac Loic'it mac Cinge fein
tisad do cuingid' ban for Eirim'oin ·⁊comad' do do berad Erim'oin mna na fear
ro bait'ea maille re Donn.

A company of six leaders came to Ireland, that is, six brothers: Solen, Ulfa/Ulpa, Nechtan, Drostan, Óengus, Letenn. The reason of their arrival in Ireland: Policornus, king of Thrace, gave love to their(?) sister, so that he attempted to carry her off without a bride-price. They then journeyed past the Romans to the Franks, and they built a city there: that is, Pictabis was its name, from "pictis," i.e "from the points"(?). And the king of the Franks gave love to their sister. They went upon the sea after the death of the fifth brother: that is, Letenn. At the end of two days after proceeding on the sea, their sister died. The Cruithni took Inber Slaine in Uí Cennselaig. Crimthann Shield-mouth, king of the Laigin, told them that he would welcome them in return for their banishing the Tuath Fidga. Drostan, druid of the Cruithni, said to them that he would help in return for receiving a payment; and this is the cure: that is, the milking of one hundred forty white, hornless cows to be poured in the place in which the battle would be fought by them. That is, the Battle of Ard Lemnacht in Uí Cennselaig against the Tuath Fidga: that is, a tribe of the Britons who were in Fotharta, who used to put poison upon their weapons. Dead was anyone whom they would wound, and they would not attire themselves with any but poisoned weapons. Any one of the Laigin who was wounded (struck down?) in the battle, they would do nothing but lie in the milk, and the poison would not be able [to do] anything to them. The Tuath Fidga were killed after that. After that four of the Cruithni died too: that is, Drostan, Solen, Nechtan, Ulfa/Ulpa and is to them that the shennachie sang the following poem:

....

And in that age of Éremón, Gub and his son (that is, Cathluan son of Gub: that is, king of the Cruithni) attacked Ireland [with a] great force/army, until Éremón expelled them from Ireland, and until they made peace afterwards. And so that Éremón gave to them the wives of the men who drowned with Donn: that is, the wife of Bress and the wife of Basse and the wife of Buaigne. Sureties [were given] of the sun and the moon so that men should not partake of rule and sovereignty any less than women in Pictland forever (lit. "so that it should not be less that would be got of kingship or of world by men than by women till Judgment"). And six from them stayed over Bregmach, and it is from them every spell and every charm/amulet and every prophetic sneeze, and augury of birds, and every omen, every charm that is made. Cathluan, however, was high-king upon them all, and he was the first king from them who ruled over Alba. Seventy kings from them over Alba from Cathluan to Constantine(?), he himself was the last Cruithnian who ruled from them. Two sons of Cathluan: that is Cadnolodor and Catainlacach, Their two heroes: [moreover?/Im?], son of Pern/Pert and Cing father. Their two elders: Crus and Cirig. Their two soldiers: Uaisnem, their seer, and Cruithne, their artisan. Domnall mac Alpín was their leader, and it is this that others say, that it was Cruithne son of Loichet son of Cing who should have come to request wives from Éremón, and that it was to him that Éremón should have given the wives of the men who had been drowned together with Donn.

VARIATION P#F(1289)

Seiser taoisec' tangadar go hEirinn ·i· se<u>ch</u>t brait'<u>r</u>e· Solen, Ulpa, Nea<u>ch</u>tu<u>i</u>n, Trostan, Aongus Leiden<u>n</u> Fat'<u>a</u> A tia[<u>ch</u>t]ana ·i· Poliornu<u>s</u> rig' T<u>r</u>aigía dorad grád' da s'<u>i</u>ár gor t'<u>r</u>iall a breit'<u>_</u> gan toc'ra, Lodar iars<u>i</u>n ta<u>r</u> Rom'anc'aib' go Frangcaib'· et ro com'daig'sed cat'<u>air</u> an<u>n</u> ·i· Picta<u>i</u>rius, o na pictib' ·i· o na ran<u>n</u>aib', ₇ dorad' rig' Frangc grád' da s<u>i</u>ár, lodar tar mu<u>i</u>r ia<u>r</u> nég in seis<u>i</u>ug'ad' brat'<u>air</u> ·i· Leiden<u>n</u> ag cion<u>n</u> da lá iar ndul ta<u>r</u> mu<u>i</u>r adbat'<u>_</u> a s<u>i</u>ár, g'ab'sat iars<u>i</u>n portan In<u>n</u>b'er Slá<u>i</u>ne a nUib' Cein<u>n</u>s<u>i</u>ollac'. Atbert friu Criom<u>ht'u</u>in<u>n</u> Sgit'b'e<u>a</u>l rig' Laig'en failte,da ndioc'<u>ar</u> dis Tuait<u>h</u>a Fiod'b'ad', adbert Trostan draoid' Cru<u>i</u>tn<u>neac</u>' fris go b'<u>f</u>oirfed' ·i· tuat'<u>_</u> do B'<u>r</u>et'<u>n</u>aib' iád ro b'asa b'F'<u>o</u>t'<u>ar</u>taib', neim' for a narmaib' gur m<u>ar</u>b' gac' aon <u>ar</u> a ndergadaois, ní g'<u>e</u>ab'ad' leig'es aon do gon'iaoid' da Laig'nib' isin gcat'<u>_</u>, tre <u>ar</u>bert Trostan se<u>ach</u>t b'<u>f</u>id'c'it bó maoil f<u>i</u>on do c'rú an aon log a b'<u>f</u>ertaid' cat'<u>_</u> etiorrad', ₇ gac' gon[t]ad' e féin din<u>n</u>ioll isin log, goma slán <u>ar</u> nim' na n<u>ar</u>[m']aib' iád. cu<u>i</u>rer cat'<u>_</u> Arda Lem'na<u>ch</u>t i nUib' Cin<u>n</u>siollac' ettorrad' ion<u>n</u>ar m<u>ar</u>b'ad' Tuat'<u>_</u> Fiod'b'ad', m<u>ar</u>b' s<u>i</u>n cet'<u>r</u>ar do C'<u>r</u>u<u>i</u>t'<u>i</u>ntuat'<u>_</u> .i. Trostan Solen, Ne<u>ch</u>tu<u>i</u>n, Ulpa, ₇ is diob' s<u>i</u> ro c'an an senc'aid' an duan so.

(P#D(1289))...

As isin ams<u>i</u>rir Eirem'oin ro g'ab' Gub', ₇ a m<u>h</u>ac Cat<u>h</u>luain ·i· ríg' C<u>h</u>ru<u>i</u>t<u>h</u>neac' moir nert for Eirin<u>n</u>, gondernsat sit<u>h</u> re HEiremon, ₇ gus ail mnaib' f<u>ai</u>r, ₇ go ta<u>r</u>d Eiremhón doib', mnaib' na b'fer ro bait'<u>e</u>d', ag ro<u>ch</u>tain Eiren<u>n</u> do m'acu Miliod', ₇ retad' grían, ₇ easg s<u>i</u>t<u>h</u> ré <u>ar</u>oile go brát<u>h</u>, ₇ anas seiser diob' os Breag'm'oig', ₇ is uat'<u>a</u>d' gac' geis, gac' sén, gac' sred, ₇ got<u>h</u>ad' éin, ₇ ga<u>ch</u> Upaide<u>ch</u>t, ₇ gac' mana

Cat<u>h</u>luain ba h<u>ai</u>rdrigh for C<u>h</u>ru<u>i</u>t<u>h</u>nib' é, ₇ ced ríg<u>h</u> díob' rog<u>h</u>ab' Albu<u>i</u>n, se<u>ch</u>tmhod<u>h</u> rig'ib' díob' for Albu<u>i</u>n, go Constantain· dá m<u>h</u>acu Cat<u>h</u>luain ·i· Cat<u>h</u>analodar, ₇ Catanala<u>ch</u>an. [a d'a] a d'a c'u<u>i</u>rid' ·i· Maic Pirn, ₇ Cing Ad<u>air</u> [.?.] ad<u>h</u>á S'<u>r</u>u<u>i</u>t<u>h</u> Crus, ₇ Cirig', a d<u>h</u>a m<u>h</u>iliod', Uaisne<u>a</u>m' a' f<u>h</u>ile. Cru<u>i</u>tin a cerd· Dom'nall m<u>h</u>ac Ailp is é a t'<u>a</u>oisec, ₇ ise ab'ertaid' <u>ar</u>oile. gomad' he Cru<u>i</u>t'<u>n</u>e m'ac Loicit m<u>h</u>ic Cing féin,

A company of six leaders came to Ireland, that is, six brothers: Solen, Ulfa/Ulpa, Nechtan, Drostan, Óengus, Letenn. The reason of their arrival in Ireland: Policornus, king of Thrace, gave love to their(?) sister, so that he attempted to carry her off without a bride-price. They then journeyed past the Romans to the Franks, and they built a city there: that is, Pictabis was its name, from "pictib'," i.e "from the points"(?). And the king of the Franks gave love to their sister. They went upon the sea after the death of the fifth brother: that is, Letenn. At the end of two days after proceeding on the sea, their sister died. They took the place Inber Slaine in Uí Cennselaig. Crimthann Shield-mouth, king of the Laigin, told them that he would welcome them in return for their banishing the Tuath Fidga. Drostan, druid of the Cruithni, said to them that he would help. That is, a tribe of the Britons who were in Fotharta, who used to put poison upon their weapons. Dead was anyone whom they would wound, and no cure would work(?) for any of the Laigin who was wounded in the battle. Drostan proposed one hundred forty white, hornless cows for violent death which is the one cure(?).   The battle was fought amidst honor and every [one] wounded immersed(?) himself in that cure, so that he was sound after the poison of their weapons. The Battle of Ard Lemnacht in Uí Cennselaig was waged amidst honor. The Tuath Fidga were killed after that. After that four of the Cruithni died too: that is, Drostan, Solen, Nechtan, Ulfa/Ulpa, and it is for them that the shennachie sang the following poem:

....

And in that age of Éremón, Gub and his son (that is, Cathluan son of Gub: that is, king of the Cruithni) attacked Ireland [with a] great force/army, until Éremón expelled them, and until they made peace afterwards. And so that Éremón gave to them the wives of the men who drowned, the case of reaching Ireland by the Sons of Míl. Sureties/guarantees [were given] of the sun and moon themselves against others forever. And six from them stayed over Bregmach, and it is from them every spell and every charm/amulet and every prophetic sneeze, and augury of birds, and every omen, every work(?) that is made. Cathluan, however, was high-king upon the Cruithni, and he was the first king from them who ruled over Alba. Seventy kings from them over Alba to Constantine(?).   Two sons of Cathluan: that is Cadnolodor and Catainlacach,   Their two heroes: that is, son of Pern/Pert and Cing father [of.?.]. Their two elders: Crus and Cirig. Their two soldiers: Uaisnem, their seer, and Cruithne, their artisan. Domnall mac Alpín was their leader, and it is this that others say, that it was Cruithne son of Loichet son of Cing who should have come himself.

VARIATION P#F(D.iii.2)

Seiser taoisec' tangadair go hEirinn ·i· seser brait're. Solen, Ulpa, Neachtuin Trostan, Aongus Leidenn Fat'a A tiasana ·i· Poliornus righ Traigia dorad gradh da s'íar gor triall a breit' gan toc'ra, Lodar iarsin tair Rom'anac'aib' go Frangcaib' et ro comhdaig'sed cat'air ann ·i· Pictairius o na pictib' ·i· o na rannaib', ⁊ dorád rig' Frangc grad' dá siár Lodar tair Muir iar neg in seisiug'ad' brat'air ·i· Leidenn ag cionn da lá iar ndu'l tair muir adbat' a siar, g'ab'sat iairsin port a nInnb'er Slaine a nUib'· Ceindsiollac'· Adbert['] fríu - Criom't'uinn Sgit'b'eal rig' Laig'en failte, da failte, da ndiochair a dis Tuat'a Fiod'b'ad', adbert Trostan draoid' Cruinneac' fris go b'foirfet' ·i· tuat' do B'retnac'aib' íad ró b'ar ab' fog't'aib', ⁊ neim' for a narmaib' gus mairbh gac' aonn air a ndergadais, ní geab'ad' leig'es aonn do gon[i]od' dá Laignib' isin gcat' tré air bert Trostán seacht b'fit'c'it bo máol fonn do C'ru⁻ an áon lag ab'fertaidh cat' eattorrad' Et gac' gontad' é féin dinnioll isin log['], ⁊ goma slán aur nim' na nairmaibh iad Cuirer Cat' Arda Leam'nacht in Uibh Cinnsiollac' eattorradh ionnair mairbhad' Tuat' Fiod'b'ad', marb'ad' iairsin cet'rair do C'ruit'nec' t'uait' ·i· Trostan, Solen, Nechtuin, ⁊ Ulpa, ⁊ is diobh sin ro Chan an senc'aidh an duan sa·

(P#D(D.iii.2))...

As isin aimsirsi EIREm'oin rogab', ⁊ a mac ·i· Cat'luan ·i· rig' Cruit'neac' moir nert for Erinn gonersat sit' re Heirem'on, ⁊ gus ail mnaib' fair, ⁊ go taird Eirem'onn doib' mnaib' na b'fer ro bait'ed', ag rochtain Eirenn do m'ac= Milead', ⁊ sectad' grián, ⁊ easg sit' re air oile go brát' agus anas Seiserr dhiobh os Breag'm'aig', ⁊ is uat'ad' gac' géis, gac' sén, gac' sred, ⁊ got'ad' ein, ⁊ gac' Upaid'echt ocus gac' mana Cat'lúain ba hardrig' for Cruit'nib' é, ⁊ ced rígh dhiobh rog'ab' Albuin, sechtm'od' rig'ib' diobh for Albuin go Constantain· Da mhacu Cat'luain ·i· Cat'analodair, ⁊ Catanalac'an a d'a c'uirid' ·i· Maic Pirn, ocus Cing Adair d'á shruit' Crus, ⁊ Cirig' a d'a m'ileadh Uisneam' a file Cruitini a c'erd· Dom'nall mac Ailp is e a taoisec', ⁊ ise ab'ertaid airoile gomad' he Cruit'ne m'ac Loicit mic Cing fein·

A company of six leaders came to Ireland, that is, six brothers: Solen, Ulfa/Ulpa, Nechtan, Drostan, Óengus, Letenn. The reason of their arrival in Ireland: Policornus, king of Thrace, gave love to their(?) sister, so that he attempted to carry her off without a bride-price. They then journeyed past the Romans to the Franks, and they built a city there: that is, Pictabis was its name, from "pictib'," i.e "from the points"(?). And the king of the Franks gave love to their sister. They went upon the sea after the death of the fifth brother: that is, Letenn. At the end of two days after proceeding on the sea, their sister died. They took the place Inber Slaine in Uí Cennselaig. Crimthann Shield-mouth, king of the Laigin, told them that he would welcome them in return for their banishing the Tuath Fidga. Drostan, druid of the Cruithni, said to them that he would help. That is, a tribe of the Britons who were in Fotharta, who used to put poison upon their weapons. Dead was anyone whom they would wound, and no cure would work(?) for any of the Laigin who was wounded in the battle. Drostan proposed one hundred forty white, hornless cows for violent death which is the one cure(?). The battle was fought amidst honor and every [one] wounded immersed(?) himself in that cure, so that he was sound after the poison of their weapons. The Battle of Ard Lemnacht in Uí Cennselaig was waged amidst honor. The Tuath Fidga were killed after that. After that four of the Cruithni died too: that is, Drostan, Solen, Nechtan, Ulfa/Ulpa, and it is for them that the shennachie sang the following poem:

....

And in that age of Éremón, Gub and his son (that is, Cathluan son of Gub: that is, king of the Cruithni) attacked Ireland [with a] great force/army, until Éremón expelled them, and until they made peace afterwards. And so that Éremón gave to them the wives of the men who drowned, the case of reaching Ireland by the Sons of Míl. Sureties/guarantees [were given] of the sun and moon themselves against others forever. And six from them stayed over Bregmach, and it is from them every spell and every charm/amulet and every prophetic sneeze, and augury of birds, and every omen, every work(?) that is made. Cathluan, however, was high-king upon the Cruithni, and he was the first king from them who ruled over Alba. Seventy kings from them over Alba to Constantine(?). Two sons of Cathluan: that is, Cadnolodor and Catainlacach, Their two heroes: that is, son of Pern/Pert and Cing father [of.?.]. Their two elders: Crus and Cirig. Their two soldiers: Uaisnem, their seer, and Cruithne, their artisan. Domnall mac Alpín was their leader, and it is this that others say, that it was Cruithne son of Loichet son of Cing who should have come himself.

VARIATION P#G(Lec.)

Do Chruithnechaib andseo do reir na neolac' A tir Traicia tra thancadar Cruichnich ·i· clanda Gueleoin meic Ercail iat Agathirsi a nanmanda seser taisech tancadar ·i· Solen Ulfa Nechtan Drostan Aengus Leithenn Fath a tiachtana Poilicornius ri Traicia dorad grad dia siair co ro thriall a bith cen shochraidi Lodar iarsin tar Romanchu co Frangcu ⁊ cumdaigsed cathair ann .i. Pietauis a pegtis ·i· o narmthaib ⁊ dorad rig Frangc grad dia siair Lotar for muir iar neg in ts'innsir brathar ·i· Leitind i cind da laa iar ndul tar muir adbath a siur Gabsad Cruithnich inn Inber Slane i nUib Cendselaich Adbathadar friu Cremthand Sciathbel rig Laigen do berad failti doib ar ndichur Thuaithi Figda. Atbert Drostan drai Cruithnech bleganh ·uii· fichit mbo find do dortad baile i fearfaidi in cath Do rondad sin ⁊ doradad in cath doib .i. cath Arda leamnachta i nUib Cendselaig Cach aen no gondais no laiged isin lemnacht ni cumgaid i nem ni do neoch dia eis Ro marbtha iar tain Tuatha Figba Marb ceathror iarsin do Chruithnechaib ·i· Drostan, Rolen Nechtain Ulfa Gabais Gib ⁊ a mac ·i· Catluan nert mor i nErinn corusindarbsad hEremon ⁊ co tard mna doib na fer ro baitea imailli fri Donn ·i· mna Bresi ⁊ mna Buaise et reliqua Doan seser dib ·h· Breagmaig ⁊ is uathib cach nges ⁊ cach sen ⁊ cach sred ⁊ gotha hen ⁊ cach mana archena Catluan is e fa hairdrig forro huili ⁊ is e rig rogob dib i nAlbain ·lxx· rig dib for Albain o Chatluan co Constantin is e Cruithnech deidenach rusgob Da mac Catluain rogobsad Cruith[nechu?] ·i· Catinoladar or ⁊ Catinalachan Na da churaid ·im⁻· Im mac Pirn ⁊ [Chind] athar Chruithne Crus mac Cirich a milig Uisnem a file Cruithne a cert Domnall mac Ailpil is e taisech rogob co ro marb Brittus mnai Isacon Clanda Nemid [ro] gobsad iar mBrittus ·i· Iargalu (iar Galu?) Cruithnich rogob[sa]d iar techtain doib a hErind Gaedil im⁻. rogabsa[d] iar sin ·i· meic Erc meic Echach (P#K(Lec.2))...

Of the Cruithni here then according to the learning. Out of the land of Thrace, then, came the Cruithni; that is, the children of Gelon son of Ercal [were] they. Agathyrsi their name. Six leaders came: that is, Solen, Ulfa/Ulpa, Nechtan, Drostan, Aengus, Leithenn. The cause of their coming: Policornus, king of Thrace, had given love to their sister so that he attempted her carrying(?) away without a bride-price (treaty?). Then they went past the Romans to the Franks. And they constructed a city there: that is, Pictabis from "pegtis"; that is, from their battle-equipment. And the king of the Franks fell in love with their sister. They went across the sea after the death of the eldest brother: that is, Letenn. At the end of two days after going across the sea, their sister perished. The Cruithni settled Inber Slaine in Ui Cennselaig. Crimthann Shield-mouth, king of Laigin, told them(?) that he would give welcome to them in return for the extirpation of the Tuath Figda. Drostan, druid of the Cruithni, said that the milking of seven score of white cows should be poured in the place in which the battle would be fought. That was done and the battle was given to them: that is, the Battle of Ard Lemnacht in Uí Cennselaig. Each of them whom they wounded used to lie in the milk. The venom did not have any power against anyone after that. The Tuath Fidga were slain afterwards. Then four Cruithni died: that is, Drostan, Solen, Nechtan, Ulfa. Gub with his son Cathluan gained great power in Ireland, so that they banished Éremón (*sic*) and he gave to them the wives of the men who had been drowned together with Donn: that is, the wife of Bres and the wife of Basse, etc. Six of them stayed on(?) Bregmach, and it is from them every taboo and every omen and every prophetic sneeze and songs of birds, and every portent, besides. It is Cathluan who was king over all of them and he is the first king of them who ruled in Alba. Seventy kings of them over Alba from Cathluan to Constantine(?). He is the last Cruithnian who ruled. Two sons of Cathluan took [over] the Cruithni(?): that is, Cadnolodor and Catainlacach. Two heroes then: Im son of Pern/Pert and Cing father of Cruithne. Crus son of Cirig, their soldier. Uaisnem, their seer; Cruithne, their artisan. Domnall mac Alpín is first who ruled, till Britus wife of Isacon killed him. Descendants of Nemed took it after Britus: that is, Erglan. Cruithni took it after their coming from Ireland. Gaels then took it after that: that is, the sons of Erc son of Eochaid/Eochu.

VARIATION P#G(Bal.)

De Cruithneac'aib incípít

A t'ír Traicia tra tancadar Cruít'nigh .i. clanda Gleoín meic Ercoil iad.
Aganthirsi a nanmanda Seisiur brat'ar tangadar toiseac' .i. Solen. Ulfa.
Nechtan. Drostan. Aengus. Letend. Fat'a a tiac'tana .i. Policornus rí Traigía do
rad grad' da siair. co ro triall a bret' gan toc'ra. lodar iarsin tar Romanchu co
Frangcu ET cumtaig'it sit cat'air ann .i· Pictauís a pictís .i· o narmtaib'. Ocus do
rat rí Frangc grad' dia s'iair. lodar for muír iar neg in ts'eisead' brat'ar .i·
Leitcínd I Cínd da laa iar ndul for muír atbath a siur gabsat Cruit'nig' ínber
Slaine i nUíb' Ceindselaigh Atbert ríu Cremht'and Sciat'b'el rí Laigen doberad'
failtí doib' ar dic'ur Tuait'e Fid'b'a atbert Drostan drui Cruit'neac' .i· bleagon
uíí.xx bo find d'o d'ortug' maille is fearfaid'i in cath Do ronnad' indí sin, 7 do
ronnad' in cat' doib' .i· cath Arda Leamnac'ta i nUib' Ceindselaig' gac' aen no
g'ontís no laig'ed is in leamnac't ni cum'gad[h] a neím' ní do neoc' dibh Ro
marb't'a dna iartain Tuat'a Fid'b'ha Marb' ceatrar do Cruit'neac'aib' iar sin ·i.
Drostan Solen Neac'tain. Ulfa. Gabais Gub 7 a mac ·i· Cathluan neart mór a
nErinn goríndarbadar Erímhoin 7 go tarda mna na fear ro baitea immaille fri
Dond doib' ·i· mna Bresse 7 Buanaisse et reliqua. Anaís s'eiser dib' os
Breag'maíg'· IS uaidib' gach geiss 7 gach sen 7 gach sreod', got'a en 7 gac'
mana Cat'luan ba haird ri orro uilí 7 is e ·c· rí ro gab' dib' a nAlbain .lxx. rig'
dib' for Albain o C'at'luan gu Constantin 7 is e Cruít'neac' deid'enac'. ros cab'
Da mac Cathluain .i· Catínolod'or 7 Catínolac'an in da c'uraid' Im mac Pírn 7
Cínd athaír Cuithne Crus mac Cirig' a milid' Uisnemh a filid' Cruít'ne a ceard
Domnall mac Ailpín is e toísec' go ro marb Britus im ní mac Isícon Clanna
Neimíd' ro gabsat iar m-Britus ·i· Iarglun. Cruíthnigh ro gabsat iar sin iar iar
tec't doib' a hErinn. Gaedil im- ro gabsat iar sin ·i. meic Eirc meic Eac'd'ach
(P#E(Bal.))...

Of the Cruithni commencing. Out of the land of Thrace, then, came the Cruithni; that is, the children of Gelon son of Ercal [were] they. Agathyrsi their name. Six brothers came first: that is, Solen, Ulfa/Ulpa, Nechtan, Drostan, Óengus, Letenn. The cause of their coming: Policornius, King of Thrace, had given love to their sister so that he attempted her carrying away without a bride-price. Then they went past the Romans to the Franks. And they constructed a city there: that is, Pictabis from "pictis"; that is, from their battle-equipment. And the king of the Franks fell in love with their sister. They went across the sea after the death of the sixth brother: that is, Letenn. At the end of two days after going across the sea, their sister perished. The Cruithni settled Inber Slaine in Uí Cennselaig. Crimthann Shield-mouth, king of Laigin, told them(?) that he would give welcome to them in return for the extirpation of the Tuath Figda. Drostan, druid of the Cruithni, said: that is, the milking of seven score of white cows should be poured in the place in which the battle would be fought. That was done and the battle was given to them: that is, the Battle of Ard Lemnacht in Ui Cennselaig. Each of them whom they wounded used to lie in the milk. The venom did not have any power against anyone after that. The Tuath Fidga were slain afterwards. Then four Cruithni died: that is, Drostan, Solen, Nechtan, Ulfa/Ulpa. Gub with his son Cathluan gained great power in Ireland, till Éremón banished them, and he gave to them the wives of the men who had been drowned together with Donn: that is, the wife of Bres and the wife of Basse, "and the rest." Six of them stayed on(?) Bregmach, and it is from them every taboo and every omen and every prophetic sneeze and songs of birds, and every portent. Cathluan who was high-king over all of them and he is the first king of them who ruled in Alba. Seventy kings of them over Alba from Cathluan to Constantine(?). He is the last Cruithni who ruled. Two sons of Cathluan: that is, Cadnolodor and Catainlacach. The two heroes then: Im son of Pern/Pert and Cing father of Cruithne. Crus son of Cirig, their soldier. Uaisnem, their seer; Cruithne, their artisan. Domnall mac Alpín is the first who ruled, until Britus son of Isacon killed him. The children of Nemed took it after Britus: that is, Erglan (after Glun?). Cruithni took it after their coming from Ireland. Gaels then took it after that: that is, the sons of Erc son of Eochaid/Eochu.

VARIATION P#G(B 512)

De Cruithnechaib annso beus A tir Tracia tancatar Cruithnig ·i· clanda Geloin meic Ercoil iadside Agathirsi a nanmand   Seisir toisech ·ui· braithir sin ón Solen· Ulfa· Nechtan· Drostan Oengus· Letennd· Fath a tichtana ·i· Poilicornus rig Tracia dorat grad dia siair· co ro triallsat ar a brith cen tinscra no tochra· Lotar iarsin dar Romanchu co Francu ⁊ cumdaigsed cathir and .i. Pictauis a pictis o na rindtaib· Dorat do nrig Franc grad dia siair Lotar for muir iar nec a seisead brathair ·i· Letind· I Ciund da la iar ndul for muir atbath a siur Gabsat Cruithnich Inber Slaine ⁊ ferais Crimthan failte friu ar dichar Tuathe Fidga ⁊ Ro chuirsit an cath Arda Lemnacht ⁊ cech fer no gonta no luiged isin lemnacht ⁊ ni chumgad an neim ni doib iarn Ro marbtha Tuatha Figba ann ⁊ romarbad cethror do Chruithnechaib ann dano ·i· Drostan ⁊ Solen· Nechtan ⁊ Ulfa Gabsat nert et reliqua inarbais Erimon et reliqua Lotar do cuinngid ban co hErind iartain ·i· mna Breise ⁊ Buaise Anais seiser dib os Bregmaig· ⁊ is uaidib cech ngeis ⁊ cech sén ⁊ cech sreod ⁊ gotha en ⁊ cech mana Cat[']luan ba hairdri forru uile ⁊ is e ·c· rig rogab i nAlbain dib ·lxx· rig dib for sin Albain o Cathluan co Cusantin IS e Cusantin Cruithnech deigenach rotasgab Da mac Cathluain Catanilodor ⁊ Catanilachtan na da cauraid ·Im· mac Firn ⁊ Cinn athair Cruithne· Crus mac Cirig a milig. Uasnem a file· Cruithne a cerd· Domnall mac Alpin is e toisech rogab Albain· Co ro marb Britus mac Isicon Clanna Nemid rogabsat iar mBritus ·i· Erglan et reliqua Cruithnig rogabsat iarsin iar tuidecht doib a hErind Goidil rogabsat iarsin ·i· meic Eirc meic Echach

(P#E(B 512))...

Of the Cruithni here, then. Out of the land of Thrace, then, came the Cruithni; that is, the children of Gelon son of Ercal [were] they. Agathyrsi their name. Six leaders. Six brothers then: that is, Solen, Ulfa/Ulpa, Nechtan, Drostan, Óengus, Letenn. The cause of their coming: Policornus, king of Thrace, had given love to their sister so that he attempted her carrying away without a bride-price or payment. Then they went past the Romans to the Franks. And they constructed a city there: that is, Pictabis from "pictis"; that is, from their battle-equipment. And the king of the Franks fell in love with their sister. They went across the sea after the death of the sixth brother: that is, Letenn. At the end of two days after going across the sea, their sister perished. The Cruithni settled Inber Slaine. Crimthann, king of Laigin, told them(?) that he would give welcome to them in return for the extirpation of the Tuath Figda. Drostan, druid of the Cruithni, said that the milking of seven score of white cows should be poured in the place in which the battle would be fought. That was done and the battle was given to them: that is, the Battle of Ard Lemnacht in Uí Cennselaig. Each of them whom they wounded used to lie in the milk. The venom did not have any power against anyone after that. The Tuath Fidga were slain afterwards. Then four Cruithni died: that is, Drostan, Solen, Nechtan, Ulfa. They took power "and the rest." They were banished by Éremón "and the rest." They went seeking wives as far Ireland then(?): that is, the wife of Bres and the wife of Basse, etc. Six of them stayed over Bregmach, and it is from them every taboo and every omen and every prophetic sneeze and songs of birds, and every portent. It is Cathluan who was high-king over all of them and he is the first king of them who ruled in Alba. Seventy kings of them over Alba from Cathluan to Constantine(?). Constantine(?) is the last Cruithni who ruled. Two sons of Cathluan: that is, Cadnolodor and Catainlacach. The two heroes then: Im son of Pern/Pert and Cing father of Cruithne. Crus son of Cirig, their soldier. Uaisnem, their seer; Cruithne, their artisan. Domnall mac Alpín is the first who ruled, until Britus son of Isacon killed him. The children of Nemed took it after Britus: that is, Erglan "and the rest." The Cruithni took it after their coming from Ireland. Gaels then took it after that: that is, the sons of Erc son of Eochu.

VARIATION P#G(1295)

　　　　　De Cruit'neac'aib' ínc'ipít

A TÍR TRAÍCÍA tra thangadair Cruít'nig' ·i· clanda Gleoín meic Ercoil.iád.
Agat'irsi a nanmanda; Seisiur brat'air t'angadair toiseac' ·i· Solen. Ulfa.
Nechtan. Drostan, Aengus. Let'e[a]nd. fat'a a t'iac'tana ·i· Polícornus rig' Tragia
do rad grad' da siair co ró t'riall a bret' gan toc'ra. lodair iar sin tar Rom'anchu
có Frangcu ·7 cum'taig'it sit cat'air ann .i· Pictauís a pictís ·i· o nármtaib'. Ocus
do rat rí Frangc grad' dia s'iair. lodar fon muir íar neg ín tseisead' brat'air ·i·
Leit'c'ind I Cind da laa iar ndul for M'uir atbat' a síur· g'ab'sat Cruit'nig' Inb'ir
Slaine í nUib' C'ennselaig'· Atbert ríu Cream't'an'd Sciat'b'el rí Laig'en doberad'
failtí d'oib' ar díc'ur Tuait'e Fit'b'a adbert Drostan drúi Cruit'neac' ·i· bleag'on.
uíí.xx· bo find do d'ortug maille is fearfaid' in cat' do ronnad' índí sin ·7 do
ronnad' ín cat' doib' .i· cat' Arda Leam'nac'ta í nUib' C'eindselaig' gac' aen nó
g'ontís nó laig'ed' is in Leam'nac't ní cumgad' a neim' ní do neoc' dib'· Ro
mairb't'a iartáin Tuat'a Fid'ba· Marb' ceat'rar do Cruit'neac'aib' iar sin ·i·
Drostan Solén Neac'táin. Ulfa. gab'ais Gub ·7 a mac ·i· Cat'luán neart mór a
nErinn goríndarbadar Erim'óin ·7 go tarda mna na fear ró bait'ea ímmaille [?]
fri Dond doib' ·i· mna Bresse ·7 Buanaisse et reliqua. Anais seisir dib' os
Breag'maig'· IS uaid'ib' gac' geiss ·7 gac' sen ·7 gach sreod' ·7 got'a én et gac'
Mamana. Catluan ba haird rí orra uilí ·7 is é ced ró g'ab' dib' a nAlbáin lxx· ríg'
dib' for Albáin ba ·{haird}· ó C'at'luán gú Constantín 7 is e Cruit'neac'
deid'enac' ros cab' da mac Cat'luáin ·i· Catínolod'or ·7 Catínolac'a in da curaid'
Im mac Pírn ·7 Cind athair C'r[a]uithne Crus mac Círig' a, a milid'· Uaisneim'
a f'ilid' Cruit'ne a c'eard Dom'naill Mac Ailpín is é toiseac' go ró m'airb' Britus
ím ní mac Isicon, Clanda Neim'idh ró g'ab'sat iarsin iar mBrítus ·i· Iárg'lun
Cruit'[nig'?]· ro g'ab'sat iar sin iar teac't doib' a hEirin. Gaed'il im⁻ ro g'ab'sat
iar sin ·i· meic Eirc Meic Eac'dach

　　　　　(P#E(1295))...

Of the Cruithni commencing. Out of the land of Thrace, then, came the Cruithni; that is, the children of Gelon son of Ercal [were] they. Agathyrsi their name. Six brothers came first: that is, Solen, Ulfa/Ulpa, Nechtan, Drostan, Óengus, Letenn. The cause of their coming: Policornus, king of Thrace, had given love to their sister so that he attempted her carrying away without a bride-price. Then they went past the Romans to the Franks. And they constructed a city there: that is, Pictabis from "pictis"; that is, from their battle-equipment. And the king of the Franks fell in love with their sister. They went across the sea after the death of the sixth brother: that is, Letenn. At the end of two days after going upon the sea, their sister perished. The Cruithni settled Inber Slaine in Uí Cennselaig. Crimthann Shield-mouth, king of Laigin, told them(?) that he would give welcome to them in return for the extirpation of the Tuath Figda. Drostan, druid of the Cruithni, said: that is, the milking of seven score of white cows should be poured in the place in which the battle would be fought. That was done and the battle was given to them: that is, the Battle of Ard Lemnacht in Uí Cennselaig. Each of them whom they wounded used to lie in the milk. The venom did not have any power against anyone after that. The Tuath Fidga were slain afterwards. Then four Cruithni died: that is, Drostan, Solen, Nechtan, Ulfa/Ulpa. Gub with his son Cathluan gained great power in Ireland, till Éremón banished them and he gave to them the wives of the men who had been drowned together with Donn: that is, the wife of Bres and the wife of Basse "and the rest." Six of them stayed on(?) Bregmach, and it is from them every taboo and every omen and every prophetic sneeze and songs of birds, and every portent. Cathluan who was high-king over all of them, and he is the first king of them who ruled in Alba. Seventy kings of them over Alba from Cathluan to Constantine(?). He is the last Cruithni who ruled. Two sons of Cathluan: that is, Cadnolodor and Catainlacach. The two heroes then: Im son of Pern/Pert and Cing father of Cruithne. Crus son of Cirig, their soldier. Uaisnem, their seer; Cruithne, their artisan. Domnall mac Alpín is the first who ruled, until Britus son of Isacon killed him. The children of Nemed took it after Britus: that is, Erglan (after Glun?). The Cruithni took it after their coming from Ireland. Gaels then took it after that: that is, the sons of Erc son of Eochaid/Eochu.

VARIATION P#H(Lein.)

Hisind amsirsin tancatar Cruthnig co ngabsat Inber Sláne i nhUib·
Cendselaig. Ros léic Crimthan chuce. arin leges fuair druí Cruithnech dó do
chath fri Tuaith Fidga i Fothartaib .i. tuath de Bretnaib. cach oen fori ndergtaís
ba marb. ⁊ nis gaibtís acht iarna nemide. Conid é in leges blegon sé fichet bó
mael find do dórtud isna hettrigib bale i ferfaithe in cath. Unde cath Ardda
Lemnacht. Et dorochratar uile Tuath Fidba triasin ceilgsin. Cora gaib Catluan
mac Cing do Chruthentuaid. nert mór for hErind. Coros innarb hErimon. *IS
and sin tanic Cruithnechan mac Cinge do chungid ban for hErimon.* Co tarat
hErimon dó mnaa na fer robatte ocna Dumachaib .i. Bres ⁊ Broes ⁊ Buagne. Et
ráth grene ⁊ ésca forra connabad lugu ro gabtha ferand ó feraib i Cruithentuaith
indás ó mnáib co bráth

⁻ This is Mac Eoin's 3(a).

VARIATION P#H(D.iii.1)

ISin naimsir sin tangatar Cruithnig con'gabhsat in Indber S'lane i
nhUib Ceindselaig ros leíc Crimthand cuici ar[in] leíges fuair drai Cruithnech
do cath fri Tuaith Fid'ba ·i· tuath do Bretnaib robui i Fothartaib· Marb cach aen
forí nddergtais i nis geibthis· acht· íarna neimmidhe Conad he in leges blegon·
uí· xx. bo mael finn do dhortadh isna [he]gib baile i fifithe in cath· am⁻ cath
Arda Lemnachta ⁊ do rocratar uile Tuata Fidbha triasin ceilgsin· co rogab
Cathluan mac Gud do Cruithentuaith nert mor for Erind· coro índarbad a
hErimon IS andsin taínic Cruithhni mac Cinge do chuingidh mna no ban fer
nErind cotard Eremon do mhnaí na fer robaitea maraen re Dond ·i· da
mnhaidg no tri .c. ban occna Dumadhaib .i. Bres ⁊ Braes ⁊ Buas ⁊ Buaighne ⁊
rath greíne ⁊ esca connabad' lughu do gebt'a do rige ⁊ domon o mhnaib inás o
feraib ic Cruithentuathaib co brath.

VARIATION P#H(D.i.3)

ISin aimsir sin tancatar Cruithnigh congabsat in nInbir Slane i nhUib
Cendsilaig Ros leic Crimthand chuicce arin leighis fuair Drostan drai
Cruithnech do chathugud fri Tuaith Fidga ·i· tuath do Bretnaib robae hi
Fothartaib· marb gach aen no gondaís conid hé leiges tuc Drostan· doib blegon·
uíí· ficit bo find do dortad for eitrighib airm i ferfaig'e in cath· unde cath Arda
Lemnachta ⁊ torcratar Tuatha ·Fidga· uile desin· Co rogab Gid ⁊ a mac
Catluan· do Cruithentuaith nert mor for ·hErind· coros innarb Erimon isi a rom
tanic do chuinngidh ban· co hErimon ·i· mna na fer ro baiti maille la Dond et
reliqua·

<In that time the Cruithni came until they seized Inber Slaine in Uí Cennselaig. Crimthann allowed them [to settle] there because of the cure that the Cruithni's druid found for him for battle against the Tuath Fidga in Fotharta: that is, a people of the Britons. Every one whom they would manage to hit was dead. And they would only take poisoned blades. So that this is the cure: milking of six score hornless, white cows to be poured out in the furrows where the battle would be fought. Whence, the Battle of Ard Lemnacht. And all the Tuath Fidga fell on account of that stratagem. Until Cathluan son of Cing from Pictland took great power over Ireland. Till Éremón expelled them. It is then Cruithnechan son of Cing came to Éremón requesting wives. So that Éremón gave to him the wives of the men who were drowned close to the Sand-banks: that is, Bres and Basse(?) and Buaigne. And the guarantee of the sun and moon [placed] upon them so that it would not be less that landed property would be taken (inherited?) from men in Pictland than from women forever.>

<In that time the Cruithni came until they seized Inber Slaine in Uí Cennselaig. Crimthann allowed them [to settle] there because of the cure that the Cruithni's druid found for him for battle against the Tuath Fidga: that is, a people of the Britons who lived in Fotharta. Every one whom they would manage to hit was dead. And they would only take poisoned blades. So that this is the cure: milking of six score hornless, white cows to be poured out in the furrows(?) where the battle would be fought(?). Whence, the Battle of Ard Lemnacht. And all the Tuath Fidga fell on account of that stratagem. Until Cathluan son of Gub from Pictland took great power over Ireland. Till Éremón expelled them. It is then Cruithne son of Cing came to Éremón requesting wives or women of the men of Ireland. So that Éremón gave to him wives of the men who were drowned with Donn: that is, from women or three hundred wives close to the Sand-banks: that is, Bres and Basse(?), and Buaigne. And the guarantee of the sun and moon so that women should ot partake of rule and sovereignty any less than men in Pictland forever.>

<In that time the Cruithni came until they seized Inber Slaine in Uí Cennselaig. Crimthann allowed them [to settle] there because of the cure that Drostan, the Cruithni's druid, found for him for battle against the Tuath Fidga: that is, a people of the Britons who were in Fotharta. Every one whom they would wound was dead of weapon(?). And they would only take poisoned blades. So that this is the cure: milking of six score hornless, white cows to be poured out in furrows where the battle would be fought. Whence, the Battle of Ard Lemnacht. And all the Tuath Fidga fell on account of that stratagem. Until Gub and his son Cathluan from Pictland took great power over Ireland. Till Éremón expelled them. It is then they came to Éremón requesting wives: that is, wives of men who were drowned together with Donn "and the rest.">

VARIATION P#H(Lec.)

ISin aimsir sin tancatar Cruithnig congabsat in Inber Slane i nhuib
Cennsilaig Ros leic Crimthann chuicce arin leigis fuair Drostan drui
Cruithnech do chathugud fri Tuaith Fid'ga ·i· tuath do Bretnaib roboi hi
Fothartaib· marb gach aen no gondais conad he legess tuc Drostan doib· blegon·
uii· xx.^it bo find do dortad' for etrig'ib airm hi ferfaig'i in cath· im⁻ cath Arda
Lemnachta 7 do roc[rai]tar Tuatha Fidga uile desin Co rogab Cid' 7 a mac
Catluan do Cruithentuaid nert mor for Erind· coros inarb hErimon· isi a rom
tanic do chuindig ban· co hErimon ·i· mna na fer ro bata maille la Donn et
reliqua·

VARIATION P#H(B 512)

ISin aimsir sin tancatar Cruithnig congabsat a nInber Slane a nUib
Ceindselaig Dos leic Crimthan cuice arin legis fuair Drostan drui Cruithnech
do cathugud fri Tuaith Fidga ·i· Tuath do Bretnaib bói i Fothartaib cach oen no
gontais marb iarna conid e leges tug Drostan doib· Blegon· uii· xx. mbo mael
bfind do dortad airm i ferfaide in cath isna heitrigib fotha· unde cath Arda·
Lemnachta· 7 torchoir Tuath ·Fidga· desin uili Co rogaib Giid 7 a mac Catluan
do Cruithnechaib en nert mor for· hErind· coros innarb hErimon· isi a rum
tancatar do chuinngid ban co hErimon ·i· mna na fer ro baite maille la Dond et
reliqua·

          (P#G(B 512))...

<In that time the Cruithni came until they seized Inber Slaine in Uí Cennselaig. Crimthann allowed them [to settle] there because of the cure that Drostan, the Cruithni's druid, found for him for battle against the Tuath Fidga: that is, a people of the Britons who were in Fotharta. Every one whom they would wound was dead of weapon(?). And they would only take poisoned blades. So that this is the cure: milking of six score hornless, white cows to be poured out in the furrows where the battle would be fought. Whence, the Battle of Ard Lemnacht. And all the Tuath Fidga fell on account of that stratagem. Until Gub and his son Cathluan from Pictland took great power over Ireland. Till Éremón expelled them. It is then they came to Éremón requesting wives: that is, the wives of the men who were drowned together with Donn "and the rest.">

<In that time the Cruithni came until they seized Inber Slaine in Uí Cennselaig. Crimthann allowed them [to settle] there because of the cure that Drostan, the Cruithni's druid, found for him for battle against the Tuath Fidga: that is, a people of the Britons who were in Fotharta. Every one whom they would wound was dead of weapon(?). And they would only take poisoned blades. So that this is the cure: milking of six score hornless, white cows to be poured out in the furrows where the battle would be fought. Whence, the Battle of Ard Lemnacht. And all the Tuath Fidga fell on account of that stratagem. Until Gub and his son Cathluan from the Cruithni people took great power over Ireland. Till Éremón expelled them. It is then they came to Éremón requesting wives: that is, the wives of the men who were drowned together with Donn "and the rest.">

VARIATION P#I(Lein.)

Senchass Ardda Lemnacht lain. fail lim fri ferdacht findcháid.
adbar dia fríth tuachle tra do marbad Tuathi Fidga.

Crimthand Sciathbel, ro scaíl scíam. ba rí ós gasraid Galian.
is dó ropdar birda baill. Tuatha Fidga 7 Fochmaind.

Nis laimed turbaid ar bith. nis gaibed aurgail armgrith.'
cach a n'gontais cian ind ail. ni blaissed biad no bethaid.

Comlund cét cech oenfer díb. forlund a mmét ria mórrím.
gabsat na fichaib tall tair coros dithaig cland Chruthnig.

Solen. Ulfa. Nechtain. nar. Óengus Lethend is Drostán
sé meic Gleoin cen gním n'gand fríth a ndegfóir do Crimthand.

IArum asbert Drostan drui. fri muntir Crimthaind clethnui.
mad ail a mmarbad co mer. is é a ndamnad a ndíchned.

A na n'gonfat Fidgai fir. mescthar i llind lemnacht gil.
dáig na narm n'dremun n'drechtach atré slemun slánchrechtach.

Tuctha coíca ar chét bó m'boc. co hoenmagin co hoenphort.'
ro tomlacht cen luag a llacht. i cnucc úar Ardda Lemnacht.

Fríth in cach dagammum don draimm. ferand Fidga 7 Fochmaind.'
ar chlód na fer mairda mass. dianid sód saerda senchas. S.

The tradition of famous Ard Lemnacht, which is with me in respect of(?) fine,
    noble (pure?) heroism,
[is the] reason where by a cunning discovery indeed for the killing of the Tuath
    Fidga;

Crimthann Shield-mouth whose beauty spread about, he was king over the
    warriors of the Gaileoin;
it is to him they were sharp-pointed tackle the Tuath Fidga and Fochmaind;

No disaster whatever was affecting them, clangor of battle was not prevailing
    over them;
each whom they would wound, long-standing is the misfortune, he would not
    taste food or life;

A match for a hundred every single man of them; superior was their size to be
    proudly calculated;
they settled in their lands yonder, easterly until the offspring of Cruithne
    destroyed them;

Solen, Ulfa/Ulpa, honorable Nechtan, Óengus, Letenn, and Drostan;
the six sons of Gelon, without a meager deed; there was found their noble help
    to Crimthann;

Then said Drostan the druid to the community of bright-speared(?) Crimthann:
"If you desire their swift killing this is their subduing, their beheading;

"Whomever the men of the Fidga shall wound, let him be plunged in a pool of
    pure milk;
from the slaughter of furious, numerous arms he will arise smooth, healthy in
    body;"

One hundred and fifty gentle cows were brought to a single place, to a single
    stead;
their milk was yielded without compensation/payment on the cold hill of Ard
    Lemnacht;

There has been found in every noble division/name of the people, territory of
    the Fidga and Fochmaind;
because of the vanquishing of the noble, fine men whence the tale is a lofty
    delight.

Pictish Sourcebook

<u>VARIATION P#I(Uí Ma.)</u>

(P#J(Uí Ma.))...

Sencas <u>Ar</u>da Lea<u>mn</u>ac<u>h</u>ta loir fil lim <u>fri</u> feirrda<u>cht</u> fi<u>nn</u> coir
a{n}dbar dia <u>frith</u> [t]uaithli <u>tra</u> da <u>mar</u>bad Tuati Fi[d']ga

Crim<u>th</u>a<u>nn</u> Sciat<u>h</u>bel ro scail sciam os gasraig <u>garda</u> Gailia<u>n</u>
is dob<u>at</u>ar birrda boill Tuatha Fidga ₇ Fochmain

Comland ·c· ca<u>ch</u> ae<u>n</u>fir dib <u>for</u>lund a met re morri<u>m</u>
gabsad na fiacaib tall <u>t</u>air coras ditaig cl<u>and</u> Cri<u>mth</u>ai<u>n</u>

Solen Ulf<u>ha</u> Nectan na Ae<u>ngus</u> Leith[f]i<u>nn</u> is D<u>ros</u>dan
·ui· m<u>ai</u>c Gaileoi<u>n</u> gan gni<u>m</u> gni<u>m</u> ngan<u>d</u> frit a ndegoir do Cri<u>m</u>tann

Iarsi<u>n</u> adb<u>ert</u> D<u>ros</u>[d]an drui <u>fri</u> mui<u>ntir</u> Crimthai<u>nn</u> clet<u>h</u>nai
mad ail a <u>mar</u>bad co me<u>ar</u> is e a ndamnad' a nditned

A na ngon[s/f]ad Fidga fir mesct<u>air</u> a li<u>nn</u> lemn<u>acht</u> gil
o ag na n<u>ar</u>m ndre<u>m</u>un ndrectach adre sleaman slan slancrectach

Tucat<u>ar</u> ·l· <u>ar</u> ·c· bo [·n]boc co hae<u>n</u>maigi<u>n</u> cu henport·
ro ta<u>m</u>la<u>cht</u> can luag a la<u>cht</u> a cnuc uag <u>Ar</u>da Leamn<u>acht</u>

Frith in ca<u>ch</u> [degam<u>m</u>?/degain<u>m</u>?] don drei<u>m</u> f<u>ear</u>a<u>nn</u> Figda ₇ Foc[<u>h</u>]main<u>n</u>
<u>ar</u> clod na fe<u>ar</u> maerda mas dianad sod saerda an sen<u>ch</u>as· Se⁻

The tradition of famous(?) Ard Lemnacht: which is with me in respect of(?)
       fine, proper heroism,
[is the] reason where by a cunning discovery indeed for the killing of the Tuath
       Fidga;

Crimthann Shield-mouth whose beauty spread about, over the warriors, the
       court of the Gaileoin;
it is to him they were sharp-pointed tackle, the Tuath Fidga and Fochmaind

A match for a hundred every single man of them; superior was their size to be
       proudly calculated;
they settled in their lands yonder, easterly until the offspring of Crimthann
       destroyed them;

Solen, Ulfa/Ulpa, honorable Nechtan, Óengus, Letenn, and Drostan;
the six sons of Gelon, without a deed, a meager deed; there was found their
       noble help to Crimthann;

Then said Drostan the druid to the community of bright-speared(?) Crimthann:
"If you desire their swift killing this is their subduing, their beheading;

"Whomever the men of the Fidga shall wound, let him be plunged in a pool of
       pure milk;
from the battle of furious, numerous arms he will arise smooth, whole, healthy
       in body;"

One hundred and fifty gentle cows were brought to a single place, to a single
       stead;
their milk was yielded without compensation/payment on the cold hill of Ard
       Lemnacht

There has been found in every noble division/name of the people, territory of
       the Fidga and Fochmaind;
because of the vanquishing of the noble, fine men whence the tale is a lofty
       delight.

VARIATION P#I(Lec.)

(P#J(Lec.))...

Seanchus Aird Leamnachta loir fil leam fri fearrdacht fir choir·
adbar dia frith tuaichli tra da marbad Tuatha Fidga

Crimthand sciathbel rosclai sciam os gasraid garda Gailian·
is dobadar birrda boill Tuatha Fidga ⁊ Fochaind

Nis lamaid tarbaid ar bith nis cailit urgail armgrith·
cach a ngondais cian an oil ni blaisead biad na beathaid

Comlond cet cach enfear dib forlund a med re morrim·
gabsad na fidgaid tall tair co rusdithaid cland Crimthain

Soilen Ulpha Nechtain nar Aengus Leitend is Drostan·
se maic Gaileoin can gnim ngand frith a ndegfoir do Crimthand

Arsin adbeart Drostan drai fri muintir Crimthaind cleathnai·
mad ail a marbad co mer as e anamnad a ndithcnead

A na nconsad Fidga fir mescthar a lind leamnacht gil·
oca arm ndreaman ndrechtach a drai sleamain slainchrechtach

Tucthar caeca ar cead mbo mbog co haenmaigin co henport·
ro thomlacht can luad a lacht a cnoc uar Arda Leamnacht·

Frith in cach deagainm don drem fearann Figa ⁊ Fochaind·
ar clod na fer maerda mas dianad sod saerda in senchus S·

The tradition of famous(?) Ard Lemnacht: which is with me in respect of(?)
	true, proper heroism,
[is the] reason where by a cunning discovery indeed for the killing of the Tuath
	Fidga;

Crimthann Shield-mouth whose beauty spread about, over the warriors, court of
	the Gaileoin;
it is to him they were sharp-pointed tackle, the Tuath Fidga and Fochmaind;

No disaster whatever was affecting them, clamour of battle was not
	prevailing(?) over them;
each whom they would wound, long-standing is the misfortune, he would not
	taste food or life;

A match for a hundred every single man of them; superior was their size to be
	proudly calculated;
they settled in their lands yonder, easterly until the offspring of Cruithne
	destroyed them;

Solen, Ulfa/Ulpa, honorable Nechtan, Óengus, Letenn, and Drostan;
the six sons of Gelon, without a meager deed; there was found their noble help
	to Crimthann;

Then said Drostan the druid to the community of bright-speared(?) Crimthann:
"If you desire their swift killing this is their subduing, their beheading;

"Whomever the men of the Fidga shall wound, let him be plunged in a pool of
	pure milk;
from the slaughter of furious, numerous arms he will arise smooth, healthy in
	body;"

One hundred and fifty gentle cows were brought to a single place, to a single
	stead;
their milk was yielded without compensation/payment on the cold hill of Ard
	Lemnacht

There has been found in every noble name of the people, territory of the Fidga
	and Fochmaind;
because of the vanquishing of the noble, fine men whence the tale is a lofty
	delight.

VARIATION P#I(Bal.)

(P#J(Bal.))...

Senc'as Arda Lemnacht loir. fil lim fri feardacht fir coir.
adbar dia frith túaicli tra do marbad Tuait'í Fid'g'a.

Crímthand Sciat'bel ro scail sciam os gasraid gasta Gailian.
is dó robdar bird'a baill Túat['] Fidg'a ⁊ Foc'maínd.

Nis laimed turbaid ar bit' nis gaibed urgail armgrith
gach a ngondais cian índ ail ní blaissed bíad ná beathaid.

Comlund ·c· gac' enfear dib forlund a meid ria morrím'
gabsat nar fiacaib tall tair coros díthaig cland Cruithnig.

Soilen Ulpa Nechtan nár Aengus Leitfind' is Trosdan
si maic Geloin con gnim ngann. frít' a ndegfoir do Crímthand.

IArum asbert Dro[ac]an druí fri muintir Crimthaind clet'nuí
mad ail a marbad go mer a ndamnad a ndic'nead'

A na ngonfat Fidgai fir mescdar i linn lemnacht gil
o ag arm ndremun ndrec'tac atre slemun slanc'rechtac.

Tugad ·l. ar ·c. mbo mbog. co henmaigin co hencnoc.
ro tomlacht cen luag a lacht i cnuc uag Arda Lemnacht.

Frit' in gach degainm don dreim. ferund Fidga Focmaínd.
ar clod' na fer maerda mas. dianad sod saerda ín seanc'as.
                    Seanc'as·

The tradition of famous(?) Ard Lemnacht, which is with me in respect of(?)
    fine, noble (pure?) heroism,
[is the] reason where by a cunning discovery indeed for the killing of the Tuath
    Fidga;

Crimthann Shield-mouth whose beauty spread about, over the alert warriors of
    the Gaileoin;
it is to him they were sharp-pointed tackle the Tuath Fidga and Fochmaind;

No disaster whatever was affecting them, clangor of battle was not prevailing
    over them;
each whom they would wound, long-standing is the misfortune, he would not
    taste food or life;

A match for a hundred every single man of them; superior was their size to be
    proudly calculated;
they settled in their lands yonder, easterly until the offspring of Cruithne
    destroyed them;

Solen, Ulfa/Ulpa, honorable Nechtan, Óengus, Letenn, and Drostan;
the six sons of Gelon, without a meager deed; there was found their noble help
    to Crimthann;

Then said Drostan the druid to the community of bright-speared(?) Crimthann:
"If you desire their swift killing their subduing, their beheading;

"Whomever the men of the Figda shall wound, let him be plunged in a pool of
    pure milk;
from the battle of furious, numerous arms he will arise smooth, healthy in
    body;"

One hundred and fifty gentle cows were brought to a single place, to a single
    hill;
their milk was yielded without compensation/payment on the grave(?) hill of
    Ard Lemnacht;

There has been found in every noble name of the people, territory of the Figda
    [and] Fochmaind;
because of the vanquishing of the noble, fine men whence the tale is a lofty
    delight.

VARIATION P#I(D.ii.2)

(P#J(D.ii.2))...

Seanchas Arda Lemnachta loír fuil sund' fri ferrdacht fir c'oir
ad'bur día frith tuaic'le tra do marbad Thuaithe Fid'g'a

Crímthann Sciathbel ros cail sciám ós gasraigh gasta Galian
as do robdar birrdha a mbaill Tuáta Fidhg'a 7 Fochmaind

Ni lamadh turbaigh ar bith nis gabadh urgail armgrith
gach a ngondais cian i ndail ní blaisdís biadh na beathaigh

Comlonn .c. cach ainf'ir dib' forlonn a méd re m'ór rim
gabsat na fíc'aib' tall tair corus dit'aig' cland Crimthain

Solen Ulpa Nechtan nár. Aengus Leit'end is Drostán.
uíí. maic Gealóin ní gnim gand frith a ndeghf'ór do Crimt'and

IArsin asbert Drostan draí fría muintir Chrimthainn clethnaí
mad' áil a marbad co mer asse ndamnadh a ndítean

A na ngonsat Fidhgai fir mescthar i línd lemnacht ghil.
o ag' arm ndremha[in] ndréchtach. a draid' slemain slán c'rechtach

Tucadh .l. ar .c. mbo mboc co haen maighin co haenphort
ro tomloc'ht gan luagh a lacht a cnoc uár Arda Lemnac't.

Frith in gach deghainm don drem. ferand Fidgha 7 Fochmaind
ar clod' na fear maerdha mais. dianadh saadh saerda seanchass.
		Sencas . Arda. L.

The tradition of famous(?) Ard Lemnacht, which is here in respect of(?) true,
        proper heroism,
[is the] reason where by a cunning discovery indeed for the killing of the Tuath
        Fidga;

Crimthann Shield-mouth whose beauty spread about, over the alert warriors of
        the Gaileoin;
it is to him they were sharp-pointed tackle the Tuath Fidga and Fochmaind;

No disaster whatever was affecting [them], clangor of battle was not prevailing
        over them;
each whom they would wound, long-standing is the misfortune, they would not
        taste food or life;

A match for a hundred every single man of them; superior was their size to be
        proudly calculated;
they settled in their lands yonder, easterly until the offspring of Crimthann
        destroyed them;

Solen, Ulfa/Ulpa, honorable Nechtan, Óengus, Letenn, and Drostan;
the six sons of Gelon, without a meager deed; ther was found their noble help
        to Crimthann;

Then said Drostan the druid to the community of bright-speared(?) Crimthann:
"If you desire their swift killing this is their subduing, their beheading;

"Whomever the men of the Figda shall wound, let him be plunged in a pool of
        pure milk;
from the battle of furious, numerous arms he will arise smooth, healthy in
        body;"

One hundred and fifty gentle cows were brought to a single place, to a single
        stead;
their milk was yielded without compensation/payment on the cold hill of Ard
        Lemnacht;

There has been found in every noble name of the people, territory of the Figda
        and Fochmaind;
because of the vanquishing of the noble, fine men whence the tale is a lofty
        delight.

VARIATION P#I(1322)

(P#J(1322))...

Seanchus Ardau Lemnacht loir. fuil liom fri ferrdacht finncoir
adber dia frith toaithli tra. do marbad Tuaithi Fidga

Criomhthann Sciathbel roscail sciam. for gassruid gasta Gailian
is do robt[ar] birrdá boill. Toatha Fidgá, agus Fochmoinn

NIS laimeth turbuid' ár bith. nis gáibadh urgail airmgrith
cech a ngondaois Scien an ail. ní blaised bied no bethaid

Comlond cet gach aoinfer dib. forlunn a met re á morrim.
gabsát nau fichaib tall tair. corus dithaig clann Cruitnig

Solen Ulpu Nectuin nar. Oengus Lethfinn IS Trosdan
secht maic Gaileoin gon gnim ngand. frith a ndegfoir. la Crimtann

IARsin isbert Drosdan drai. fri muintir Crimtainn clethnui
mad ail a marbad go mer. IS e a ndamnad á ndicnedh.

I Na ngon[sad] Fidga fir. mescur a llind lemnacht gil.
dag arm ndremuin ndrechtuch. adroei slemoin slain crechtuch

Tugath .l. ar cet mbo mbog. co haenmaigin go haencnoc
rotomlucht can luad a llacht. a cnoc uar Ardu Lemnacht

Frith in gach degam don drem. ferund Fidga. ⁊ Fochmuinn
ar clod na fer maorda masS. dianut sod saord'a in sencas.

The tradition of famous(?) Ard Lemnacht, which is with me in respect of(?)
     fine, proper heroism,
[is the] reason where by a cunning discovery indeed for the killing of the Tuath
     Fidga;

Crimthann Shield-mouth whose beauty spread about, over the alert warriors of
     the Gaileoin;
it is to him they were sharp-pointed tackle the Tuath Fidga and Fochmaind;

No disaster whatever was affecting them, clangor of battle was not prevailing
     over them;
each whom they would wound, long-standing is the misfortune, he would not
     taste food or life;

A match for a hundred every single man of them; superior was their size to be
     proudly calculated;
they settled in their lands yonder, easterly until the offspring of Cruithne
     destroyed them;

Solen, Ulfa/Ulpa, honorable Nechtan, Óengus, Letenn, and Drostan;
the six sons of Gelon(?), without a meager deed; there was found their noble
     help to Crimthann;

Then said Drostan the druid to the community of bright-speared(?) Crimthann:
"If you desire their swift killing this is their subduing, their beheading;

"Whomever the men of the Figda shall wound, let him be plunged in a pool of
     pure milk;
from the slaughter of furious, numerous arms he will arise smooth, healthy in
     body;"

One hundred and fifty gentle cows were brought to a single place, to a single
     stead;
their milk was yielded without compensation/payment on the cold hill of Ard
     Lemnacht;

There has been found in every noble division/name of the people, territory of
     the Figda and Fochmaind;
because of the vanquishing of the noble, fine men whence the tale is a lofty
     delight.

VARIATION P#I(B.iii.1)

(P#J(B.iii.1))...

Senchas Arda Lemnacht lóir, fail liom fri ferrd'acht fionnchóir
adhbar dia u frith túaichli tra, do marb'ad Tuaithe Fiodhghá

Criomhtann Sciathbel rosgaoil sgíam, os gasraid' gasda Gailián
as do robert biorrda boill, Tuatha Fiodhgha, et Fochmuinn

Nís laimhadh turbaid' ar biot', nis gab'adh urg'oil airmgrioth
gach a ngondais cían an oil, ni blaised' bíadh no bethoidh

Comlann ced gac' aoinfear diobh, forlonn a méd re móirríomh
gab'sat nar bfichaib' tall toir, gorros dithaig clann Cruithnigh

Soilen, Elpa, Neachtan, nár· Aongus, Leit'find is Drosdan
.uii. maic Gaileoin con gniom ngann, frit' a ndagfoir la Criomt'ann

Iársin atbert Drosdan draoi, fri muintir Criomt'ainn clethnaoí
mad ail a marbad' go mer as é a ndamnad a ndíchnedh

I na ngonfad Fiodhga fir, mescctar i linn leamnacht ghil
dág a narm ndreamuin ndrechtac' atráe slemhun slain crechtac'

Tugad' caoga ar ched mbo mbog, co haonmaig'in go haenport
rotomlacht gan luag' a lacht, i ccnoc uar Arda Lem'nacht

Frit' in gach degham don draingm, ferann Fiodhg'a, $_7$ Fochmuinn
ar clod' na bfer maordha mass, dianadh sodh saord'a an sencas.
     SENCAS.

The tradition of famous(?) Ard Lemnacht, which is with me in respect of(?)
       fine, proper heroism,
[is the] reason where by a cunning discovery indeed for the killing of the Tuath
       Fidga;

Crimthann Shield-mouth whose beauty spread about, over the alert warriors of
       the Gaileoin;
it is to him they were sharp-pointed tackle the Tuath Fidga and Fochmaind;

No disaster whatever was affecting them, clangor of battle was not prevailing
       over them;
each whom they would wound, long-standing is the misfortune, he would not
       taste food or life;

A match for a hundred every single man of them; superior was their size to be
       proudly calculated;
they settled in their lands yonder, easterly until the offspring of Cruithne
       destroyed them;

Solen, Ulfa/Ulpa, honorable Nechtan, Óengus, Letenn, and Drostan;
the six sons of Gelon(?), without a meager deed; there was found their noble
       help to Crimthann;

Then said Drostan the druid to the community of bright-speared(?) Crimthann:
"If you desire their swift killing this is their subduing, their beheading;

"Whomever the men of the Figda shall wound, let him be plunged in a pool of
       pure milk;
from the slaughter of furious, numerous arms he will arise smooth, healthy in
       body;"

One hundred and fifty gentle cows were brought to a single place, to a single
       stead;
their milk was yielded without compensation/payment on the cold hill of Ard
       Lemnacht;

There has been found in every noble division/name of the people, territory of
       the Figda and Fochmaind;
because of the vanquishing of the noble, fine men whence the tale is a lofty
       delight.

VARIATION P#J(Uí Ma.)

Ard Leamnachta canus roainmniged ·ni¯· Cath tuc Crimtand Sciatbel ·r· Laigin do Tua[th]aib Fidba 7 Focomaind nert ·c· [cach] fir dib adbailed fora nderggais 7 ni [g]abdais [re]anna no faebair friu· Tuc dano Cri[mthan]d [cland] Cruithnig do cobraid cuca 7 [do ruaichill] f[ai]rb fear Fidga doib dia [mbidis?/mdar?] coscraid is and asp[er]t Drostan drai Cruithnech tomlachtaiter ·lll· laulgach naendata a naen clasaig[h] 7 no ngonfad Fidhgaid fotruictear sin leamhnacht sin 7 atre slan o neimhib a narm ana laigfiter dibsin ·im¯· dichnedar uili fogni samlaig 7 ba cosrach Crimtand 7 torc[ra]da Tuatha Fidba im¯ Ard Leamnachta dicitur

(P#I(Uí Ma.))...

VARIATION P#J(Lec.)

Ard Leamnachta canus ro hainm· ni¯· Cath thuc Crimthand Sciathbel rig Laigen do Thuathaib Fidba 7 Fochuind co neart cet cach fir dib adbailed fora ndeargdais 7 ni gabdais reanna na faebair friu Tuc do no Crimthand cland Chruithnig do chobra chucu 7 do ruaichill forb fear Fidba doib dia in mdar coscraid Is and asbert Drostan drai Crimthaind Tomlaithther tri caeca lulgach naendatha a noen clasaich 7 na n'gonfad fir daidi[sic] fothruichthear sin leamnachta sin 7 adrai slan o neimib a narm ana slaidfaidear dibseom ·im¯ dichnetar uile fogni samla 7 ba coscrach Crimthand 7 tochradar Tuatha Fidga ·im¯ Ard Leamnachta dicitur· dia buaid thear annso beos

(P#I(Lec.))...

VARIATION P#J(Bal.)

Ard Leamnachta canair¯. ni¯ cath t'ug Crim't'ann Sciat'be rí Laigen do T'uat'aib' Fid'g'a 7 Focmaínd' nert ·c· gac' fir dib' atbailed fora nderdais 7 ni g'abdais renna no faebra friu Tug don Crimthann clann Cruit'nig' doc'obraid' c'ucu 7 do ruaicill foír f'ear doib' dia mbidis coscraig' is ann asbert trosdan drai Cruithnech tomlactaiter. lll. lulgach. ndaend'at' i naen claisaig 7 nangonfat Fid'g'ai[?] d'i fot'uicter sin lemnacht sin 7 atre slan o nem'ib' a narm ana slaidfid'er dib'seom' im¯ dic'netar uili fognid sam'laid 7 ba coscrach Crímthann. 7 torc'radar Tuat'a Fid'g'a. unde Ard Leamnac'ta de quibus dicitúr hoc carmen

(P#I(Bal.))...

<Ard Lemnacht, whence was it named? Not difficult. Crimthann Shield-mouth, king of the Laigin (people of Leinster), gave battle to the peoples of Fidga and Fochmaind. The strength of one hundred in each man of them, anyone whom they wounded would die, and [neither] points nor blades would have effect against them. Thereafter, Crimthann brought the offspring of the Cruithni to help against them and promised the landed property of the men of Fidga to them when they were triumphant(?). Then Drostan, druid of the Cruithni said: "Let one hundred and fifty milch-cows of one color be milked into one pit, and let anyone whom the Fidga shall wound be immersed in that milk and he shall arise, sound from the poisons of their weapons. But anyone of them that shall be slain, let them all lose their heads." He performed thus, and Crimthann was triumphant, and the Tuath Fidga were killed moreover. It is called Ard Lemnacht.>

<Ard Lemnacht, whence was it named? Not difficult. Crimthann Shield-mouth, king of the Laigin (people of Leinster), gave battle to the peoples of Fidga and Fochmaind. With the strength of one hundred in each man of them, anyone whom they wounded would die, and [neither] points nor blades would have effect against them. Thereafter, Crimthann brought the offspring of the Cruithni to help against them and promised the landed property of the men of Fidga to them when they were triumphant(?). Then Drostan, druid of Crimthann, said: "Let one hundred and fifty milch-cows of one color be milked into one pit, and let anyone whom the men of Fidga(?) shall wound be immersed in that milk and he shall arise, sound from the poisons of their weapons. But anyone of them that shall be slain, let them all lose their heads." He performed thus, and Crimthann was triumphant, and the Tuath Fidga were killed moreover. It is still called Ard Lemnacht from their victory in the east(??) here.>

<Ard Lemnacht, whence was it named?(?) Not difficult. Crimthann Shield-mouth, king of the Laigin (people of Leinster), gave battle to the peoples of Fidga and Fochmaind. The strength of one hundred in each man of them, anyone whom they wounded would die, and [neither] points nor blades would have effect against them. Thereafter, Crimthann brought the offspring of the Cruithni to help against them and promised the landed property of the men to them when they were triumphant(?). Then Drostan, druid of Crimthann, said: "Let one hundred and fifty milch-cows of one color be milked into one pit, and let anyone whom the Fidga shall wound be immersed(?) in that milk and he shall arise, sound from the poisons of their weapons. But anyone of them that shall be slain, let them all lose their heads." He performed thus, and Crimthann was triumphant, and the Tuath Fidga were killed moreover. Whence Ard Lemnacht from which it is called. This poem: (or, Whence Ard Lemnacht. From which this poem is said: (?))>

VARIATION P#J(Ren.)(TR.WS)

Ard Lemnacht, canas roainmniged?

Ni ansa. Cath tuc Crimthann Sciathbel ri Laigen do Tuathaib Fidhgha ⁊ Fochmaind. Nert cét cach fir dib. Atbailedh [intí] fora ndergdáis, ⁊ ni gabdais renda no faebra friu.

Tuc dano Crimthann clainn Cruithnig do cobraidh cucu, ⁊ doruaichill foirb Fer Fidh[gh]a doib dia mbidis coscraigh. As ann isbert Trostan drai Cruithnech: << Tomlactaiter .lll. Iulgach n-aenndatha i n-aen clasaig, ⁊ nan-gonfat Fidhghaide fothraicther sin lemnacht sin, ⁊ atré slan o neimib a n-arm. Ana slaidfider dibseom immorro dichnetar uile. >>

Fognid samlaid ⁊ ba coscrach Crimthann ⁊ torcradar Tuatha Fidhga, Unde Ard Lemnacht.

VARIATION P#J(D.ii.2)

Ard Leamnachta canus rohainmniged'. ni⁻. Cath tuc Crimthand Scíathbel rí Laig'en do Thuathaib' Fidhgha ⁊ Fochmuind nert ·c· cachfir dibh adbailedh forandergáis ⁊ ní gabdais renda ná faebair íat. Tangadar seiser toiseach Cruithnech a tír Tracia .i. Solén. Ulfa. Nechtan. Drostán. Aengus. Leitend a nanmanna. A nInber S'láine a nUib Cennsilaig rog'absat. [Con]ebairt friu Crímthann rí Laigen. na tibredh failti na ferand doib' co tucdáis cath leis do Tuathaibh Fidhgha batar in a ferand a nUib Cennsilaig ⁊ rogellsat athabeart. Adubert fríu Drostan drai Cruithnech bleghon .l. bó fínn naendath do d'ortadh baile a fearfaidhe an cath. Dorighnead' sin ⁊ do feradh an cath ar faiche Arda Leamnac'ta. Cach aen nogontá o na harmaib nemid'aibh na naithech thuat' no loig'ed' isin lemhnacht ⁊ ní c'umcedh an neim. ní do ⁊ ticedh slánc'réchtach as unde. Ard Leam'nachta. bá coscrach Crímt'and de sin ⁊ torcradar Tuat'a Fid'ga. ut dicitur

(P#I(D.ii.2))...

VARIATION P#J(1322)

Ard Lemnuchta canus. ro ainmniged. ni⁻. cath tuc Crimhtann Sciátbel ri Laigen do Tuathaib Fidga et Focmuinn nert .c. cac a fir di[b?/d?] adbailed anti fora ndergduis. ⁊ ni gabhdaeis reanna inaoit faou[er?] friu. co tucc don Crimtan[n] cloinn Cruithnigh do cobruidcucu Et duruaicill foirb u fer u Fidga doib die mdaeis cosccruigh is ann ismbert Trostan drai Cruithniuch. Tomluchtaid tri ocha tri [caoga?] Iultach nendatha a n[áe?/áo?]n clasáig Et na ngonfuiti la Fidgaid mescar isin lemnacht sin. ⁊ adroifed slan o nemib a narm. Ana slaidfither ['Aná slaidfither' repeated] dipsium uo dicendtur uile. Fognid samloidh agus ba cosgruch Crimthann et torcrutor Fidgaidh ⁊ unde Ard Lemnachta dicitur

(P#I(1322))...

<Ard Lemnacht, whence was it named? Not difficult.   Crimthann Shield-mouth, king of Laigin, gave battle to the peoples of Fidga and Fochmaind. The strength of one hundred in each man of them, anyone whom they wounded would die, and [neither] points nor blades would have effect against them. Thereafter, Crimthann brought the offspring of the Cruithni to help against them and promised the landed property of the men of Fidba to them when they were triumphant(?). Then Drostan, druid of the Cruithni, said: "Let one hundred and fifty milch-cows of one color be milked into one pit, and let anyone whom the men of Fidga shall wound be immersed in that milk and he shall arise, sound from the poisons of their weapons. But anyone of them that shall be slain, let them all lose their heads." He performed thus, and Crimthann was triumphant, and the Tuath Fidga were killed moreover. Whence Ard Lemnacht.>

<Ard Lemnacht, whence was it named? Not difficult.   Crimthann Shield-mouth, king of Laigin, gave battle to the peoples of Fidga and Fochmaind. Strength of one hundred in each man of them. Anyone whom they wounded would die, and [neither] points nor blades would have effect against them. Six leaders of the Cruithni came from the land of Thrace: that is, Solen, Ulfa/Ulpa, Nechtan, Óengus, Letenn their names. They took Inber Slaine in Uí Cennselaig. Till Crimthann, king of Laigin, said to them that he would give the welcome of his land to them in return battling the Tuath Fidga, who were in the land in Uí Cennselaig. And they pledged an additional deed(?). Drostan, Cruithni druid, told them: the milking of fifty, fine cows of one color to be poured in the place in which the battle would be fought. They did(?) that, and the battle was fought before the green meadow of Ard Lemnacht. Any one who was wounded from poisoned weapons of the giant people would lie in the milk, and the poison would do no harm; and he was healed, healthy in body. It is whence Ard Lemnacht. Crimthann was triumphant, and the Tuath Fidga were killed. That is said.>

<Ard Lemnacht, whence was it named? Not difficult.   Crimthann Shield-mouth, king of Laigin, gave battle to the peoples of Fidga and Fochmaind. Strength of one hundred was in each man of them. Anyone whom they wounded would die, [and] [neither] points nor blades would have effect against them. Till the Cruithni were deposited by Crimthann thereafter to help, and he promised the landed property of the men of Fidga with respect to them when they were triumphant(?). Then Drostan, druid of the Cruithni, said: "Let one hundred and fifty milch-cows of one color be milked into one pit, and let anyone whom the people of Fidga shall wound be plunged in that milk and he shall arise, sound from the poisons of their weapons. But anyone of them that shall be slain, let them all lose their heads." He performed thus, and Crimthann was triumphant, and the Tuath Fidga were killed. Whence Ard Lemnacht. It is said...>

VARIATION P#J(B.iii.1)

ARD Lem'nachta canas ro hainmniged. Ni⁻. cath tug Criomhthann Sgiait'bel Rí Laigen do Thuathaib Fiodhga et Fochmainn go ro neinntighset e co mor arbai nert .c. gac' fir diobh. atbailed' anti fora ndergdáis, ni gabdais reanna inaid faob'ra friu, co rostochuir dano Criomt'ann Cruithnig' do chobraid' arga, et doruaichill foirb fer bFiodga fríu dia mdais cosccraig'. As ann asmbert Drostan draoi Cruithneuch, Tomlachtaidh tri .l. lulg'ach naondat'a i naen clasaig', ₇ i na ngonfait[?] dia b'ar [muintir] La Tuathaib Fiod'ga, mescthar isin leamnacht sin, ₇ atraeset slan ó neimib' a narm. Ana slaid'fit'er diob'som uo. dicheanntar uile. Foghinad samhlaid', ₇ torcratar Fiodhgaidh, ₇ ba cosgrac' CRiomthann ₇ [Conid'] desin ata ARd Leamhnachta; in aimser Erimhóin inn sin.

(P#I(B.iii.1))...

<Ard Lemnacht, whence was it named? Not difficult. Crimthann Shield-mouth, king of the Laigin (people of Leinster), gave battle to the peoples of Fidga and Fochmaind. So that they honored him greatly(?). The strength of one hundred was in each man of them. Anyone whom they wounded would die, [and] [neither] points nor blades would have effect against them. Till the Cruithni were deposited by Crimthann thereafter to help arga(?), and he promised the landed property of the men of Fidga with respect to them when they were triumphant(?). Then Drostan, druid of the Cruithni, said: "Let one hundred and fifty milch-cows of one color be milked into one pit, and let anyone whom the people of Fidga shall wound be plunged in that milk and he shall arise, sound from the poisons of their weapons. But anyone of them that shall be slain, let them all lose their heads." He performed thus, and the Tuath Fidga were killed, and Crimthann was triumphant. So that it is hence Ard Lemnacht in that time of Éremón.>

VARIATION P#K(D.iv.1)

No comad isin ·bliadain· sin do dechaidh Cruithnechan mac Cinge meic Lochit la Bretno Fortrend do cath fri Saxancho ⁊ ro selaig t'ir doib ·i· Cruithentuath ⁊ tarastair tir acco acht ni latar mna leo ar beabais bandtracht Alban ⁊ doluidh· im⁻· Cruithnechan for culo co macaib Miled ⁊ rogabadh neam ⁊ talom ⁊ grian ⁊ esca muir ⁊ tir druc't ⁊ daithe comadh o mnaib· flaithus forro co brath ⁊ atbert di mnai déc for craid batar ic macaib Miled robatea a fir issin fairrgi thiar araen re Donn conid' ó feraib Ereand flaithus for Cruithentuaith o saín do gres·

VARIATION P#K(Lec.1)

No comad isin bliadain sin do d[e]chaid Cruithnechan mac Cinge meic Lochit la Bretno Fortrend do cath fri Saxancho ⁊ ro selaig tir doib ·i· Cruithentuath ⁊ tarastiair tir acco acht ni batar mna [leo] ar beabais banntracht Alban Doluid im- Cruithnechan for culo co macaib Miled ⁊ rogabad neam ⁊ talum ⁊ grian ⁊ esca muir ⁊ tir drucht ⁊ daithe comad o mnaib flacht forro co brath di mnai dec for c[ra]idbatar ic macaib miled ro baitea a fir issin fairrgi thiar ar aen re Donn conid do feraib Ereand flacht for Cruithentuath o sin do gres

VARIATION P#K(Lec.2)

(P#G(Lec.))...

Dochuaid o macaib Miled Cruithnechan mac Lochit meic In'gi la Breatnu Foirtre[n]n do chathugud fri Saxanu ⁊ ro chosain tir doib [·i·] Cruithentuaith ⁊ anais fen aco Acht ni badar mna leo ar bebas bandtrocht Alban Doluid iarum· Cruithnechan for culo docum mac Miled ⁊ rogab nem ⁊ talam ⁊ grian ⁊ esca drucht ⁊ daithi muir ⁊ tir ba do maith riu flaith forro co brath ⁊ dobert da mnai dec for craidi badar oc macaib Miled a robatea a fir isin fairrge tiar araen re Donn conad do feraib hErind flaith for Cruithnib o sin dogres

(P#E(Lec.))...

VARIATION P#K(Bal.)

No gomad' isín blian sin do dheachaid' Cruithneachan mac Lochit meic Cínge la Breatnu Forrenn do chat' for Saxanachu ⁊ ro sealaig' tir doib' ·i· Cruithíntuath ⁊ taraístir accaib' acht ni badar mna leo ar beab' ais bandtrocht Alban ⁊ doluid im⁻. Cruithneachan for culu go macaib' Miled ⁊ rogabhad neamh ⁊ talum' grian ⁊ esga. muir ⁊ tír druc't ⁊ dait'i gomad o mnaib' flaic'us forro co ⁊ atbert di mnai deg for craidi badar ag macaib' Miled robaitea a fir isin fhairgi tiar araen rédond gonad o fhearaib Erinn flaithus for Cruithentuaith o sin do gres.

<Till it should be in that year that Cruithne(chan), son of Cing, son of Loichet, went with the Britons of Fortriu for battle against the Saxons, and he cleared land for them: that is, Pictland. And he settled land among them. But women did not go with them because Alba's womenfolk had died. And Cruithne(chan), moreover, then came back to the Sons of Míl, and he took the sky and earth and sun and moon, sea and land, dew and light so that sovereignty should be from women over them forever. And he brought twelve women who were in excess among the sons of Míl, whose husbands had been drowned in the ocean in the west at the same time with Donn. So that the sovereignty over the Cruithni is from the men of Ireland from then on.>

<Till it should be in that year that Cruithne(chan), son of Cing, son of Loichet, went with the Britons of Fortriu for battle against the Saxons, and he cleared land for them: that is, Pictland. And he settled land among them. But they had no wives [with them] because Alba's womenfolk had died. Cruithne(chan) then came back to the sons of Míl, and he took sky and earth, sun and moon, sea and land, dew and light so that sovereignty should be from women over them forever. Twelve women who were in excess among the sons of Míl, whose husbands had been drowned in the ocean in the west at the same time with Donn. So that the sovereignty over the Cruithni is from the men of Ireland from then on.>

<Cruithne(chan), son of Loichet, son of Cing, went with the Britons of Fortriu to give battle against the Saxons, and he won land for them: [that is,] Pictland. And he himself remained among them. But they had no wives with them because Alba's womenfolk had died. Cruithne(chan) then came back towards the sons of Mil, and he took sky and earth and sun and moon, dew and light, sea and land that it would be to their advantage [to have] a lord [ruling] over them forever. And he brought twelve women who were in excess among the sons of Mil, whose husbands had been drowned in the ocean in the west at the same time with Donn. So that the sovereignty over the Cruithni is from the men of Ireland from then on.>

<Till it should be in that year that Cruithne(chan), son of Loichet, son of Cing, went with the Britons of Fortriu for battle against the Saxons, and he cleared land for them: that is, Pictland. And he settled among them. But they had no wives with them because the womenfolk of Alba had died. And Cruithne(chan), moreover, then came back to the sons of Míl, and he took the sky and earth, sun and moon, sea and land, dew and light so that sovereignty should be from women over them forever. And he brought twelve women who were in excess among the sons of Míl, whose husbands had been drowned in the ocean in the west at the same time with Donn. So that the sovereignty over the Cruithni is from the men of Ireland from then on.>

VARIATION P#K(24.P.13)

No gumad' isin bliadain sin do dechaid' Cruithneachan mac Lochit meic Cinge meic Breathnu Fortrenn do chath for Saxanachu .7 ru seallaig' tir doib' ·i· Cruithenthúath .7 tarrasdair ogaib' acht ni ru b'adar mna léo ar beab'ais banntrachta Alban .7 doluidh Cruithnechan for gcúlu co macaib' Miled' .7 dogab' nemh .7 talomh grián .7 ésccu. muir .7 tír tracht .7 daithe comadh o macaib' Miled' .7 ó mnaib' flaithesa forra co brath .7 do bert di mnaoi dheg for cruidh badar occ macaib' Miled' dobaite a fir isin fairrge ' thiar aráon ré Donn gumad o feraib' Erinn flaithes for Cruithnec'an o sin do grés.

VARIATION P#K(1295)

No gomad' isin b'liad'aín sin do deac'aid' Cruit'neac'an mac Loc'hit meic Cínge la Breat'nu Fortrenn do c'at' for Saxanac'u ·7 ró sealaig' tír doib' ·i· Cruit'íntuath ·7 taraistir accaib' acht mbadair *im⁻. Cr{u}i{t}'neac'an for c'{u}lá {g}{o} ma{c}:* mna leo ar beab'as bandtrocht Alban ·7 doluid im⁻. Cruithneac'an for c'ula go macaib' Miled' ·7 rog'ab'ad nem' ·7 talam' grian ·7 esga. muír ·7 tír druc't agus dait'í gomad' o m'naib' flait'iús forro co brat ·7 atbert dí m'nai deg for craid'i b'adair ag macaib' Miled' robait'ea a fir isin fairgí t'iar araen re Donn gonad' ó fearaib' Erinn flait'us for Cruit'entuait' o sin do g'reas.

*⁻*It seems that this phrase is intended to be deleted.

VARIATION P#K(1289)

no gomad' isin blia'duin do deac'aid' Cruit'nec'an m'ac Loc'it m'ic Cinge la Bret'nu Fortrén do c'at' for Sacsanam., 7 ro sealaid' tír díob' .i. Cruit'enntúait'· 7 tairaistir, acht ni b'ádar mnaib leo ar bfheab'as bantracht Albonn. 7 doluid Cruinnec'an for chulad' go macaib' Miliod', 7 rog'ab' nemh, 7 talam', grian, 7 Easga, muir, 7 tír, druchт, 7 daithe gomadh o mhnaib' flaithris forra go brat', 7 adbert di mnaib' dég for chraid'e b'adar ag macu Miliod' robait'e[d'] a b'fir isin fhairge t'iar araon re Donn gonad' o fhearaib' Éirenn flait'es for C'ruitnec'aib' ós sin do ghres

VARIATION P#K(D.iii.2)

no gomad' isin bliad'uin sin do deac'aid' Cruit'nec'an m'ac Loc'it m'ic Cínge la Bret'nu Fortren do c'at' for Sacsanam., 7 ro sealaid' tír díobh ·i· Cruit'enntúait'· 7 tairaístír, acht ni badar mnaibh léo ar bfeab'as banntracht Albonn, 7 doluidh Cruinnec'an for c'ulad' go macaib' Milead', 7 rog'ab' nem' Et talam', grian, 7 easga, muir, 7 tir, drucht Et dait'e gomadh o m'naib' flait'ris forra go brat', 7 adbert di mnaibh deg for craid'e badair ag macu Miliod' robait'ed' a bfir ionnsa isin fairge t'iar airáen re Donn gonad' ó fearaib' Eirenn flaithes for C'ruit'nec'aibh o sin do g'reis

<Till it should be in that year that Cruithne(chan), son of Loichet, son of Cing, went with Britons of Fortriu for battle against Saxons, and he cleared land for them: that is, Pictland. And he settled among them. But they had no wives with them because the womenfolk of Alba had died. And Cruithne(chan) then came back to the sons of Míl, and he took the sky and earth, sun and moon, sea and land, dew and light so that sovereignty should be from women over them forever. And he brought twelve women who were in excess among the sons of Míl, whose husbands had been drowned in the ocean in the west at the same time with Donn. So that sovereignty over the Cruithni should be from the men of Ireland from then on.>

<Till it should be in that year that Cruithne(chan), son of Loichet, son of Cing, went with Britons of Fortriu for battle against Saxons, and he cleared land for them: that is, Pictland. And he settled among them. But they had no wives with them because the womenfolk of Alba had died. And Cruithne(chan), moreover, then came back to the sons of Míl, and he took the sky and earth, sun and moon, sea and land, dew and light so that sovereignty should be from women over them forever. And he brought twelve women who were in excess among the sons of Míl, whose husbands had been drowned in the ocean in the west at the same time with Donn. So that sovereignty over the Cruithni is from the men of Ireland from then on.>

<Till it should be in that year that Cruithne(chan), son of Loichet, son of Cing, went with Britons of Fortriu for battle against Saxons, and he cleared land for them: that is, Pictland. And he settled among them. But they had no wives with them because Alba's womenfolk had died. And Cruithne(chan) then came back to the sons of Míl, and he took sky and earth, sun and moon, sea and land, dew and light so that sovereignty should be from women over them forever. And he brought twelve women who were in excess among the sons of Míl, whose husbands had been drowned in the ocean in the west at the same time with Donn. So that sovereignty over the Cruithni is from men of Ireland from then on.>

<Till it should be in that year that Cruithne(chan), son of Loichet, son of Cing, went with Britons of Fortriu for battle against Saxons, and he cleared land for them: that is, Pictland. And he settled among them. But they had no wives with them because Alba's womenfolk had died. And Cruithne(chan) then came back to the sons of Míl, and he took sky and earth, sun and moon, sea and land, dew and light so that sovereignty should be from women over them forever. And he brought twelve women who were in excess among the sons of Míl, whose husbands had been drowned in the ocean in the west at the same time with Donn. So that sovereignty over the Cruithni is from men of Ireland from then on.>

VARIATION P#L(Uí Ma.)

Tainic iartain dam ochtair cona loingis coroaitreabsead a nErind ⁊
corghabh rand mor Fir Bolg ·uo· a Manaind ⁊ araili insi archeana .i. Ara ⁊ Ila
Raca. Clanda Gailioin meic Earcoil rogabhsad indsi hOrc .i. Istoreth mac
Istorine mac Againi meic Agaitheris Roscailsead aris a nindsib Orc Dachuaidh
·uo· Cruithni mac Ingi meic Lugnn meic Pairti meic Istoirith meic Agnomain
meic Buain meic Mhair meic Faitheach meic Iuaith meic Iathbeth conroghabhi
tuaisceart insi Breatan ⁊ cororoindsid a seacht maic a a fearanda a ·uii· randaib,
⁊ as e ainm gach fhir dhib ata fora ferand S'eacht meic Cruithni .i. Pib
Fidhach Fodhlaigh Fortreand Cat· Ce· Cirig Dagabh Aenbeagan mac Cait meic
Cruithni airdrigi na ·uii· rand· Finachta ba flaith Erenn in tan sin re sin
rog'abs'ad geill Cruithneach Dacuadar ·u· ear da Cruithneachaib an indsib Orc
.i. ·u· brathair athar Cruithni co Francu corcumdaigsid cathair and i Picctatus
no Inpictus .i. ona rinntaib an ainm ⁊ cotancadair aris dochum na hindsi ·i·
docum Erenn corabadair fria re cian corasdichuirsead Gaighil tar muir docum a
mbraithar Clanda Liathain meic Earcail rogabsad fearand Dimetorum ⁊ Guer
⁊ Guiteilli corosindarb Cohenda cona macaib a Breatnaib.

<Afterwards there came a retinue of eight with their fleet so that they settled in Ireland and occupied a large portion of it. The Fir Bolg, however, seized the Isle of Man and certain islands besides: that is, Ara and Ile [and] Rachra. The offspring of Gaileoin (Gelon?), the son of Ercal, took the Orc Islands: that is, Istoreth, son of Istorine, son of Aigine, son of Agathyrsus. They moved on again from the islands of Orc. There went Cruithne, moreover, son of Cing, son of Loichet, son of Pairte (Partholon?), son of Istoreth, son of Agnaman, son of Buan, son of Mar, son of Fathecht, son of Javad, son of Japheth; until he took it, the far-north of the island of Britain, and until his seven sons divided his territory into seven parts, and it is the name of each man of them that is on his domain. Seven sons of Cruithne: that is, Fib, Fidach, Fotla, Fortrenn, Cat, Ce, Cirig. Aenbegan, son of Cat, took the high-kingship of the seven regions. Finachta was prince of Ireland at that time. They took the hostages of the Cruithni. However, there went five from the tribes of the Cruithni from the Islands of Orc (that is, the five brothers of the father of Cruithne) to the Franks so that they founded a city there: that is, Pictatus or Inpictus (that is, from their tattoos the name); and until they came back towards the island: that is, towards Ireland. So that they were for a long time there until the Gaels put them over the seas towards their brothers. The descendants of Liathan, son of Ercal, took the territory of the Dimeti and Guer and Guigell, until Cunedda with his sons expelled them from the Britons.>

VARIATION P#L(Lec.)

Tanic iartain dam eachtair con loingeas coroaitrebsadar i nErind ꝛ
corogabsadar rind moir inti Fir· im⁻· rogabsad Manaind ꝛ rogabsad araile
olchena ·i· Ara ꝛ Ile ꝛ Racca Clanna Geloim meic Ercoil rogobsad i nindsib
Orcc ·i· in Istoireand(?) meic hIstoirim meic Agnumna meic Agathairsi ro
scailsead arisidi o indsib Orcc ·i· dochuaid Cruithne mac In'ge meic Luchta
meic Parthalon meic Agnon meic Buain meic Mais meic F'athecht meic Iauad
meic Iathfeth meic Nae IS he athair Cruithnech ꝛ cet bliadain do i rrige Seacht
meic Cruithne indso ·i· Fid ꝛ Fidach ꝛ Fotla ꝛ Fortrenn· Cait ꝛ Ce ꝛ Ciric ut·
dixit· Colamcilli

        Moirfeisear do Chruithne claind
        roindsed Albain a seacht raind
        Cait Ce Cireach cetach cland
        Fib Fidach Fotla Foirtreand

Cororoindsead i secht rannaib in fearann ꝛ ise ainm cach fir dib fil fora
fearand ut est Fib Ce Cait et reliqua xiii· ri congabsad dib forro ꝛ gabais
Onbecan mac Cait meic Cruithne airdrigi na secht renn sin Findachta fa flaith
nErenn isin re sin ꝛ rogob giallu Cruithnech Dochuaidar ·im⁻· coicfear do
Chruithentuaith a hindsib Orc ·i· u· er brathar athar do Chruithne co Frangcaib
corocumdaiged cathraid ann ·i· Pictabis a hainm cotancadar doridise dochum
na hindse sea ·i· co hErind co robadár re ciana and corusdichuirsead Gaedil tar
muir docum a mbrathar Clanda Liathain· im⁻· rogabsadar fearand Diemtoram ꝛ
Cuher ꝛ Cugeilli corusinnarbsadar Cuanna cona macaib a Bretain

<Afterwards there came a retinue of eight with their fleet so that they settled in Ireland and occupied a large portion of it. The Fir [Bolg?], moreover, seized the Isle of Man, and they took certain islands besides: that is, Ara and Ile and Rachra. The offspring of Gelon, moreover, the son of Ercal, took the Orc Islands: that is, that Istoreth(?), son of Istorine, son of Aigine, son of Agathyrsus. They moved on again from the islands of Orc: that is, there went Cruithne, son of Cing, son of Loichet, son of Pairte (Partholon?), son of Istoreth, son of Agnaman, son of Buan, son of Mar, son of Fathecht, son of Javad, son of Japheth, son of Noah. He is the father of the Cruithni, and [he was] a hundred years in the sovereignty. Seven sons of Cruithne here(?): that is, Fib and Fidach and Fotla and Fortrenn, Cat and Ce and Cirig.
As Columba said:

> Seven sons of Cruithne of the clan
> divided Alba into seven parts
> Cat, Ce, Cirig, a warlike clan,
> Fib, Fidach, Fotla, Fortrenn.

So that they divided the land into seven parts, and this is the name of each man of them which is upon his domain. As it is Fib, Ce, Cat, "and the rest." So that thirteen kings of them took control over them. And Aenbegan, son of Cat, took the high-kingship of the seven regions then. Finachta was prince of Ireland at that time. They took the hostages of the Cruithni. However, there went five from the tribes of the Cruithni from the Islands of Orc (that is, the five brothers of the father of Cruithne) to the Franks so that they founded a city there: that is, Pictatus the name. Till they came back towards this island: that is, to Ireland for a long time there until the Gaels put them over the seas towards their brothers. The descendants of Liathan, moreover, took the territory of the Dimeti and Guer and Guigell, until Cunedda with his sons expelled them from the Britons.>

VARIATION P#L(Bal.)

Tangadar iarsin dam' ac'tor gona loingis goroaitreib' i nErinn ₇ gorogaib raind mora idte Fir Bolg uo rogobsat Manaind ₇ frogab'sat alaile indsi orcheana .i. Ara ₇ Ila ₇ Recca. Clanda Gleoin im⁻ hErcoil rogabsat indsi Orcc. .i· hIstoirend meic hIstorím meic Agom meic Agait'irsi roscailsead dorid'ísi a hindsib Orc ·i· docoid Cruit'ne mac Cínge meic Luc'taí meic Partaí meic Istoirech meic corogaib tuaiscert indsi Bretan ₇ gororoindsed a sec't meic ín fearand i secht randaib' ₇ coraigaib Onbécan mac Cait meic Cruitne airdrige na secht rand   Finach ba flaíth Erenn isín re sin rogab' gialla Cruit'neach. Doc'odar coiccar uo coigear do Cruit'neac'aib' a hindsib' Orcc .i. cuíg brat'ar at'ar Cruit'ne co Frangco gurocumdaigsead cat'raig' and .i. Pictauís a hainm gotangadar dorid'isi doc'um na hindsi .i· go hErenn corabadar re ciana ann corosdícoirsead Gaed'il dar muir docum a mbrat'ar Clanda Liat'ain uo rogabsas ferand Díamtorad' ₇ Guer ₇ Gugellí corasindarbastar Cuanda gona macaib' a Breatnaib'

<Afterwards there came a retinue of eight with their fleet so that they settled in Ireland and occupied a large portion of it. The Fir Bolg, however, seized the Isle of Man and certain islands besides: that is, Ara and Ile and Rachra. The offspring of Gelon, moreover, [the son] of Ercal, took the Orc Islands: that is, Istoreth, son of Istorine, son of Aigine, son of Agathyrsus. They moved on again from the islands of Orc. There went Cruithne, son of Cing, son of Loichet, son of Pairte (Partholon?), son of Istoreth, son of. Until he took it, the far-north of the island of Britain, and until his seven sons divided his territory into seven parts.   And Aenbegan, son of Cat, took the high-kingship of the seven regions. Finachta was prince of Ireland at that time. They took the hostages of the Cruithni. However, there went five from the tribes of the Cruithni from the Islands of Orc (that is, the five brothers of the father of Cruithne) to the Franks so that they founded a city there, that is, Pictabis the name. Until they came back towards the island: that is to Ireland. So that they were for a long time there until the Gaels put them over the seas towards their brothers. The descendants of Liathan took the territory of the Dimeti and Guer and Guigell, until Cunedda with his sons expelled them from the Britons.>

VARIATION P#L(1336)

Tainig iardain dam ochtair cona [{oc}h] l[ong]is coroaitreabsead a nErinn ⁊ corogab rand mor de Fir bolg im⁻ rogabsat a Manaind ⁊ araile innisi ar[ce]ana Ara ⁊ Ili ⁊ Raca. Clanda Ga[il]eoin im⁻ meic Earcail rogabsat indsi Orc ·i· Istoreth mac Istorine meic Aigíne meic Agathirir rosgailseat aris A nindsib Orc docuaid Cruithne mac Ingu meic Luithe meic Pairti [meic] .Istoreth meic Agnamain meic Buain meic Mair meic Faith[ea]cht meic Iauad meic Iafeth conadrogab tuasceart innsi Breatan ⁊ cororoindseat a ·uii· meic ua ferann a ·uii· rannaib ⁊ as e ainm cach fir dib [ata] fora ferann Se[act] meic Cruithnig ·i· Fib· Fidach· Fotdlaid· Fortrean· Cat· Ce· Cirig ⁊ coragab Aenbegan [mac] Caitt meic Cruithní ardrig na ·uii· rand· Finachta ba flaith· nEirenn· isin re sin rogabsat giall Crithneach Docuadar coiccar do Cruthantuathaib a hindsib Orcc .i. cuic brathri athar Cruithne co Francaib gorocumdaigsead cathraigh [ann] ·i· [P]icctatus no Inpictus ona rinntaib ainm ⁊ codancadar doris docum na hinnsi ·i· docum na hErenn corabadar re cian ann gorasdichuirseat Gaedil tar muir docum a mbrathar Clanna Liathain meic Earcail rogabsad fearann Dienntorum ⁊ Guer ⁊ Gaigelle gorosinnarb Cohen[da cona] macaib a Breatnaib.

<Afterwards there came a retinue of eight with their fleet so that they settled in Ireland and occupied a large portion of it. The Fir Bolg, however, seized the Isle of Man and certain islands besides: Ara and Ile and Rachra. The offspring of Gaileoin (Gelon?), moreover, the son of Ercal, took the Orc Islands: that is, Istoreth, son of Istorine, son of Aigine, son of Agathyrsus. They moved on again from the islands of Orc. There went Cruithne, son of Cing, son of Loichet, son of Pairte (Partholon?), son of Istoreth, son of Agnaman, son of Buan, son of Mar, son of Fathecht, son of Javad, son of Japheth; until he took it, the far-north of the island of Britain, and until his seven sons divided his territory into seven parts, and it is the name of each man of them that is on his domain. Seven sons of Cruithne: that is, Fib, Fidach, Fotla, Fortrenn, Cat, Ce, Cirig. And Aenbegan, son of Cat, took the high-kingship of the seven regions. Finachta was prince of Ireland at that time. They took hostages of the Cruithni. However, there went five from the tribes of the Cruithni from the Islands of Orc (that is, five brothers of the father of Cruithne) to the Franks so that they founded a city there: that is, Pictatus or Inpictus (that is, from their tattoos the name); and until they came back towards the island: that is towards Ireland. So that they were for a long time there until the Gaels put them over the seas towards their brothers. The descendants of Liathan, son of Ercal, took the territory of the Dimeti and Guer and Guigell, until Cunedda with his sons expelled them from the Britons.>

VARIATION P#L(1295)

Tangadair iarsin dam' ac'dór gona loingis goróaitreib' i nEirinn ·7
goroghaib' raind mora índte; Fir Bolg ·uo· g'ab'sat Manaind ·7 rog'ab'sad alaile
indsi {orcc ·i· hIstoiren'd·} orcheana ·i· Ara ·7 Ila ·7 Recca· Clanda Gleoín· im⁻
hErcoil rog'ab'sat indsi Orcc ·i· hIstoirend meic hIstorim meic Agom Meic
Agat'irsi roscailseád doríd'sí a hindsib' Orc ·i· docoid' C'ruit'ne Mac Cinge meic
Luc'tai Meic Part'aí meic Istoirec' meic coragaib' tuaiscert indsi Breatán ·7
cororoindsed a seac't íi fearond a secht randaib' 7 coraigaib no innti Onbecan
mac Cait Meic Cruit'ne airdrige na secht rand Fínach ba flait' Eirenn isin re sin
rógab' gialla Cruit'neac'· doc'odar coiccar uo coiger do C'ruit'neac'aib' a
hindsib' Orcc ·i· cuig brat'air at'air co Frangca gurocuim'daig'seád cat'raig' and
·i· Pictauís a hainm go tangadair dorid'isi doc'um na hindsí ·i· co hEarinn
gorabadair re cián ann corosdic'oirseád Gaed'il tar múir doc'um a mbrat'air
Clanda Liat'áin ·uo· rogabsad ferand Diamtorad' ·7 Guear ·7 Gugellí
corósindarbastair Cuanda gona macaib' a Breatnaib';

<Afterwards there came a retinue of eight with their fleet so that they settled in Ireland and occupied a large portion of it. The Fir Bolg, however, seized the Isle of Man and certain islands besides: that is, Ara and Ile and Rachra. The offspring of Gelon, moreover, [the son] of Ercal, took the Orc Islands: that is, Istoreth, son of Istorine, son of Aigine, son of Agathyrsus. They moved on again from the islands of Orc. There went Cruithne, son of Cing, son of Loichet, son of Pairte (Partholon?), son of Istoreth, son of [.?.]. Until he took it, the far-north of the island of Britain, and until his seven sons divided his territory into seven parts. And Aenbegan, son of Cat, took the high-kingship of the seven regions. Finachta was prince of Ireland at that time. They took hostages of the Cruithni. However, there went five from the tribes of the Cruithni from the Islands of Orc (that is, five brothers of the father of Cruithne) to the Franks so that they founded a city there: that is, Pictabis the name. Until they came back towards the island: that is, to Ireland. So that they were for a long time there until the Gaels put them over the seas towards their brothers. The descendants of Liathan took the territory of the Dimeti and Guer and Guigell, until Cunedda with his sons expelled them from the Britons.>

VARIATION P#L(G47)

Tanic iartain dam eac'tair cona loingeas coroaitrebsadar i nErind ⁊ corogabsadar rind moir inti Fir· im⁻· rogabsad Manaind   ⁊ rogabsad araile olceana ·i· Ara ⁊ Ile ⁊ Racca Clanna Geloim meic Ercoil rogobsad i nindsib Orcc ·i· in Isdoireand(?) meic hIstoirim meic Agnumna meic Agat'airsi ro scailsead arisidi o indsib Orcc ·i· doc'uaid Cruit'ne mac Inge meic Luc'ta meic Part'alon meic Agnon meic Buain meic Mais meic Fatec't meic Iaud meic Iat'feat' meic Nae is he atair Cruit'nec' ⁊ ceat bliadain do i rrige Seac't m Cruit'ne indso ·i. Fid ⁊ Fidac' ⁊ Fotla ⁊ Fortreann Cait ⁊ Ce ⁊ Ciric ut· dixit· Colamcilli

> Moirfeisear do Chruit'ne claind
> roindsed Albain a seac't raind
> Cait Ce Cireach ceata cland
> Fib Fidac' Fotla Foirtreand

Cororoindsead i secht ranaib in fearand ⁊ ise {resin} anim cac fir dib fil fora fearand ut est Fib Ce Cait et reliqua xiii· ri congobsad dib forro ⁊ gabais Onbecan mac Cait meic Cruit'ne airdrigi na sec't renn sin Findachta fa flaith nEreann isin re sin ⁊ rogob giallu Cruit'nec' Doc'uadar im⁻. coic-fear do Cruit'eantuait a hindsib Orc ·i· u· Er brathar atar do C'ruit'ne co Frangcaib corocumdaigead cat'raid ann .i. Pictabis a hainm cotancadar doridise dochim na hindse sea ·i· co hEarind co ro badar re ciana and corusdich'irsead Gaeidil tar muir docum a mbratar Clanda Liat'ain· im⁻· rogabsadar fearand Dieamtoram ⁊ Cuher ⁊ Cugeilli corusinnarbsadar Cuanna cona macaib a Bretain

<Afterwards there came a retinue of eight with their fleet so that they settled in Ireland and occupied a large portion of it. The Fir [Bolg?], moreover, seized the Isle of Man, and they took certain islands besides: that is, Ara and Ile and Rachra. The offspring of Gelon, moreover, the son of Ercal, took the Orc Islands: that is, that Istoreth(?), son of Istorine, son of Aigine, son of Agathyrsus. They moved on again from the islands of Orc: that is, there went Cruithne, son of Cing, son of Loichet, son of Pairte (Partholon?), son of Istoreth, son of Agnaman, son of Buan, son of Mar, son of Fathecht, son of Javad, son of Japheth, son of Noah. He is the father of the Cruithni, and [he was] a hundred years in the sovereignty. Seven sons of Cruithne here(?): that is, Fib and Fidach and Fotla and Fortrenn, Cat and Ce and Cirig.
As Columba said:

> Seven sons of Cruithne of the clan
> divided Alba into seven parts
> Cat, Ce, Cirig, a warlike clan,
> Fib, Fidach, Fotla, Fortrenn.

So that they divided the land into seven parts, and this is the name of each man of them which is upon his domain. As it is Fib, Ce, Cat, "and the rest." So that thirteen kings of them took control over them. And Aenbegan, son of Cat, took the high-kingship of the seven regions then. Finachta was prince of Ireland at that time. They took the hostages of the Cruithni. However, there went five from the tribes of the Cruithni from the Islands of Orc (that is, the five brothers of the father of Cruithne) to the Franks so that they founded a city there: that is, Pictatus the name. Till they came back towards this island: that is, to Ireland for a long time there until the Gaels put them over the seas towards their brothers. The descendants of Liathan, moreover, took the territory of the Dimeti and Guer and Guigell, until Cunedda with his sons expelled them from the Britons.>

PICTISH REGNAL SUCCESSION AND THE ORIGIN LEGENDS

It now seems pertinent to briefly remark on subjects that have long incited much discussion and speculation: the acquisition of wives, sovereignty, and matrilineal succession in relation to the Picts and the Origin Legends. P#A(B 506), P#A(Uí Ma.), P#A(Lec.), and P#A(C.vi.2) record that soldiers from Thrace (apparently, Cruithni (Picts?)) were given wives from the Sons of Míl because they had brought no women with them from Thrace. In return for this, the sovereignty was held by the "mothers." This could mean that the Picts practiced matrilineal succession; however, it could also indicate that the Irish line, which derives from the "mothers," should take precedence in sovereignty. Therefore, the control of the Picts by the Scots could be justified by this account. It is interesting to note that there were nine forms of marriage or sexual union in Medieval Irish law.[83] One of these, "lánamnas mná for ferthinchur," refers to a situation in which the wife is given to the husband without a dowry. This seems to correspond to the account in this legend, where wives are given to the Picts in return for "sovereignty." T.M. Charles-Edwards indicates that this concept is also present in the Welsh law "agweddi." It seems to correspond to the Hindu law "prājāpatya" in which a wife is given as a gift. However, the "ārsha union" in which a wife is given in return for cattle may be more appropriate if "sovereignty" can be considered equivalent to material goods.[84] P#C(Lein.), P#C(Uí Ma.), P#C(Lec.), and P#C(G131) only indicate that Cruithne stole wives from the Sons of Míl. Another Irish law, "lánamnas foxail," refers to abduction without the consent of the woman's kin.[85] T.M. Charles-Edwards indicates that "lánamnas foxail" corresponds to the Welsh law of "llathlud twyll" and the Hindu concept of "rākshasa."[86] P#E(Bal.) and P#E(1295) state that "it is the nobility of mothers that has been customary in the kingship." P#F(D.iv.1), P#F(Lec.1), P#F(Bal.), P#F(24.P.13), P#F(1295), and P#F(1289), P#F(D.iii.2) record that Éremón gave the Picts the widows of the men who drowned with Donn. They mention that "sovereignty" would be equally divided between men and women. P#F(Lec.2) mentions this event but possibly states that sovereignty came "from the mothers." However, this could simply mean that the Irish line would have precedence and not an indication of matrilineal succession. It does indicate that the "sovereignty" over Pictland would be from the "men of Ireland." P#G(Lec.), P#G(Bal.), P#G(B 512), and P#G(1295) also state that Éremón gave the widows to the Picts ("Cruithni") but make no mention of "sovereignty." P#H(Lein.) and P#H(D.iii.1) make the same comments as P#F(D.iv.1), P#F(Lec.1), P#F(Bal.), and P#F(24.P.13) regarding widows and equal sovereignty. P#H(B 512), P#H(D.i.3), and P#H(Lec.) merely mention that Éremón gave wives to Cathluan without mentioning sovereignty. P#K(D.iv.1), P#K(Lec.1), P#K(Bal.), P#K(24.P.13), P#K(1295), P#K(1289), and P#K(D.iii.2) make similar comments as in P#F(Lec.2). They record that the Sons of Míl gave the Picts ("Cruithni") the widows of the drowning victims. They also mention that the sovereignty would be from women; however, the texts state that the "sovereignty" would be with the "men ofIreland from then   on." P#K(24.P.13) also mentions that the sovereignty would be from the Sons of Míl as in P#F(Lec.2). This could be a justification for the rule of the Scots over the Picts as in P#A(B 506), P#A(Uí Ma.), and P#A(Lec.). P#K(Lec.2) repeats the same information without mentioning that the sovereignty would be from women. Bede records that the Irish gave wives to the Picts and that the female line was used when there was doubt about the succession.[87] This seems to indicate that Pictish sovereignty was not primarily through matrilineal succession but through some other system. M.O. Anderson indicates that the Regnal Lists show no patrilineal succession before Bede's time. She suggests that Bede was used to succession by brothers and meant that the female line was used if the ruler had no brother. However, Nora Chadwick asserts that Bede meant that the female line is used to settle regnal succession "whenever the throne becomes vacant." That is, "doubt" simply refers to any question of sovereignty.[88] Geoffrey of Monmouth states that the Picts received wives from the Irish after the Britons had refused.[89] Most of these texts do not explicitly mention matrilineal succession although some may allude to it; however, they do all reflect marriage practices that must have been common in Irish, Welsh, and even Hindu society. D.A. Binchy states that in early Irish society a ruler's successor was appointed during the ruler's lifetime and was called "tánaise ríg," a term which may be equivalent to the Welsh "gwrthrych" and "qwrthrychiat." This practice meant that a son would rarely succeed his father.[90] As a Celtic people, it seems probable that the Picts had similar succession customs as the Irish and Welsh.

In conclusion, it seems that the Origin Legends served two main functions. The first was to establish or explain the connection, albeit non-historical, between the Cruithni of Ireland and the Cruithni (Picts) of Scotland. This was probably due to an understanding that the Cruithni in Ireland had originally come from Britain. Also, it may have derived from an analogy with the historical movement of the Scots. Just as the Scots of Irish Dál Riata had established Scottish Dál Riata, the Cruithni of Dál n-Araide had founded Pictland. The second was to justify the historical dominance of the Scots over the Picts through the tale of the Picts receiving wives from the Gaels (or Irish), which appears to have been adapted from Bede's account. Because the Origin Legends written in Irish were all composed during or after the time in which the Scots gained dominance over the Picts, it is not unreasonable to consider that they were a form of Irish-centered political propaganda which combined legendary, mythological, and historical elements in order to convey their message.

3

PICTISH AND SCOTTISH REGNAL LISTS

In her article, "Matriliny by Treaty: The Pictish Foundation Legend," Molly Miller re-categorized and catalogued one group of the Pictish and Scottish Regnal Lists which she entitled the "Series Longior."[1] This group consists of the lists which M.O. Anderson had referred to as "Pictish List P" as well as several shorter texts which Anderson had not discussed. Although Anderson has published two of these lists, SL1 and SL2 O (which she called A and B, respectively), most of these texts have not been recently or at all published separately.[2] In an effort to begin to remedy this situation, I have undertaken to present here diplomatic transcriptions of some of these lists: SL2 M and SL2 H (Anderson's C2 and C1, respectively) and several of the SL3 lists.

REGNAL LIST SL2 M (*Book of Uí Maine*)[3]

This list occurs in the 14th-15th century *Book of Uí Maine* (37[93]va40-vb38), where it is appended to its version of the *Lebor Bretnach*, although it did not originally belong to it.[4] Van Hamel used it in his edition of the *Lebor Bretnach* (his text H), where he printed a composite text of the list with SL1 (his text P) and SL2 H (his text D). As Van Hamel used SL2 H as his main text, the readings from SL2 M are difficult to decipher.[5]

Cruithni mac Cingi pater Pictor[im] habidand in aca insola ·c· aninis regnaibid Seacht maccu rotheact at e andseo a namanna ·i· Fib· Fidach· Foltlaig· Fortreann· Cat· Ce· Circind Circind· lx· anínís reignnn Fidhach· xl· anínís ·regnauit· Fortrend· xl· annis a regnauit Fodlid· xxx· annis· regnauit· Got ·xii· annis regnauit· Ce· xu annis regnauit· Fidbhaidh ·xxx·íííí· annis regnauit Geid[h]e ollghothach ·lxxx· annis regnauit· Ollfindachta ·lx· annis regnauit· Enbecan· anno regnauit· Guidedh gaeth bre[it]nach ·l· annis· regnauit· Geas cuirdi ·lx· annis regnauit· Uirges ·lxx· annis regnauit· Bruig bont ·xxx· and uagh 7 Bruíndi ba hainm da ga[ch] aen fer dibh 7 regnauerunt Hiberniam 7 Alboniam ·per ·c·l· and ut inuenitur a leabraid na Cruithneach \\\ Bruidi painti

[·anno·regnauit]· int Bruidhi gnuth Bruidhi urpant· Bruídhi leo· Bruidhi gant Bruidhi gnuth Bruidhi uirgint· Bruidi· feth· Bruidhi urfexir Bruidhi fechir Bruidi· cal· Bruidhi urcal Bruidi cínd Bruidi arcind Bruidhi feth Bruidhi urfeth Bruidhi ru Bruigh i{d}h eru Bruidhi gart Bruighi cinidh Bruidi incind Bruidhi uip Bruídi tiruip Bruidhi gruith Bruidi urgruith Bruidhi munigh Bruidhi ur Bruidhi gidighe Bruídhi crín Bruidhi urmuin regnauerunnt ·c·l· and unt diximus

ET robi Alba gan rig fria aire uili co haimsir gut ced righ rogab Albáin uili tri comairli no areigin Adbearaid araili comadh he Cathluan mac Cathmidh nogabad rig[h]i ar eigín a Cruithintuaith 7 a nErind ·i· lx· bliadna 7 iarsin rogabh Gud ·i· l· Tarín ·c· and regnaid Morleo a ·xu· annis· rem Deocillmon ·xl· ante regnauit Cinicioid mac Artcois ·uíí· annis· regnauit· Deort ·l· annis· regnauit Blieberlit ·[ii?/u?]· annis· regnauit· Deotatreig frater Tui ·xl· annis· regnauit· Usconbust ·xx· annis· regnauit· Crutreig ·xl· annis regnauit Deorommois ·xx· annis· regnauit· Uis[t] ·l· annis reignim Ru ·c· and· ·regnauit· Gairtnid bolc ·iiii· annis regnauit Gartnid ·iiíí·ix· a[r]d· ·regnauit· Bret mac Butud ·uii· annis· regnauit· Uipoig nauait ·xxx· ·annis· regnauit· Cantulacma ·iíí· annis· regnauit· r· Uiridach uetla ·ii· annis· regnauit· Gartnaid dupeir ·lx· annis· regnauit· Tolorc mac Aciur ·lxx· [b·u·] Drosd mac Erp ·c· annis· regnauit· 7 ·c· cath rogín Nono decimo annis regni [con] Patricius sanctus sanctus episcopus· ad [berniam] peruenit Tolorc mac Amel ·iííí· annis regnauit· Neachta[n] morbreac mac Eirip ·xx·iiii· annis· regnauit· Tertio anno reigni [eius] D[ar]lugdach abbati[s]ta C[h]illidara de Ibierniam exulat p[ro] Xristo ad B[ri?/u?]taniam secundo ·autem· anndo adue[ni]ti tui immolauit Nectonius anno uno Apuirnighi deo 7 sanctae Brigitae presente Darlugdach air cántáuit alleluia super istam

Deirt· guitimoth ·xxx· annis· reignauit Galánarbith ·xu· annis· reig da Dreist ·i· Dreist filius· Giron 7 Drest fin Budrost ·xu· annis regnauerunt Deirts fi[n?/u?] Girum ·uíí· annis· regnauit Casolus ·u· annis· regnauit· Gartaid fi[u?/n?] Girom ·uíí· annis· regnauit· Cailtairni fiu Girom anno anno· regnauit· Talorc· fin Urtoloic xi ánnis· regnauit· Drest fin Monaid uno· anno· regnauit· Galum cenna ap ·iííí· annis· regnauit· Cum Ruidhino ·i· annis· regnauit· Bruidhi mac Maelcon ·xxx· annis· regnauit· Moctano anno reigni eius babtisconatus est Escon Columba Gartnaith ·filius· Domech ·xi· annis· regnauit· Neáchtán nepos Uer· annis· regnauit· Cínirot ·filius· Luitriu ·xix· annis· regnauit· Gartnait mac Muit ·u· ·annis· reganuit· Tolorc frater eorom ducdecim· annis· regnauit· Tolorcan ·filius· Enfreit ·iííí· annis· regnauit· Gartnáid ·filius· Donuel ·uí· annis· regnauit· 7 deimidhium ai Druisc [frater] eius ·uí· annis· regnauit· Bruidi· filius· Fili ·xx· ánnis· regnauit· Tárun· filius· Enfidáigh ·iííí· annis· regnauit· Brei· filius· Deirilei ·xi annis regnauit Neactan ·filius· Deirilei ·x· ánnis· regnauit· Dreeist 7 Elpín connegána[uin]t ·u· ánnis· regnauit· Onuis ·filius· Urgust ·xxx· ánnis· Breit fín Nurgut ·x·u· ánnis· regnauit· Ciníod Iuireidig ·xíí· ánnis· regnauit· Alpín· filius· Uroid ·ííí· annis· regnauit· Talorcein· filius· Dru ·no· u deg Tolorgein fi[lius] [Um]ust ·xíí· 7 dimídío ·annis·regnauit·Can'ul·filius·Tan[n]g·u·annis·regnauit ·Cusántin·filius· Uurguist

·xxx·u· annis· regnauit·Uidhmuisc· filius· Nugust ·xíí· annis·regnauit· Dreist·
filius· Constántin 7 Tolorc· filius· Nutmol ·ííí· ánnis· regnauit· conregnauerunt
Unen· filius· Unes ·ííí· annis· regnauit· Uread Bargoid ·ííí· ·annis· regnauit· 7
Bred ·uno· anno· regnauit·

    Cináed· filius· Alpín ·x·ui· annis· regnauit· Domnall· filius· Ailpin ·ííí·
annis· regnauit· 7 Cusántín· filius· Cinaed ·xx· ánnis ·regnauit· Aed· filius·
Cínaed ·uno· annis· regnauit· Garig mac Dungaili ·xi· no ·ííí· ·annis· regnauit·
Domnall· filius· Consántín ·xi· annis· reganuit· Consantin· filius· Aedha ·xl·u·
annis· regnauit· Maelcoloím· filius· Domnaill ·ix· annis· regnauit· Cuilen· filius·
Illdoib ·ííí· annis· regnauit· Cinaeth· filius· Máelcoloim ·xx·iiii· annis· regnauit·
Consantin· filius· Cuilen ·i· dimidio· ánnis· regnauit· Cínaeth· filius· Duib[h]
octor Maelcoloim· filius· Cínaetha ·xxx· annis· regnauit· Donchad· hua·
Mailcoloim ·ui· annis· regnauit· Macbeatadh mac Fin meic laidh ·x·iii· annis·
regnauit· Liáuach ·u· inís Maelcoloim mac Dondchaid iarsin \\

REGNAL LIST SL2 H (T.C.D. *MS. #1336*)[6]

This list occurs in the Trinity College Dublin *MS. #1336* (c.1500?) (col. 823 l.27-col. 825 l.24), where it is appended to its version of the *Lebor Bretnach*, although it did not originally belong to it.[7] Skene had previously printed a separate edition of this list, but his readings were not always accurate.[8] Van Hamel also used the list (his text D) in a composite text with SL1 (his text P) and SL2 M (his text H). Although he used SL2 H as his main text, his notes sometimes make it difficult to interprete its content.[9]

Cruithne mac Cingi pater Pictorum habidann in aca insola ·c· annis renabait ·uii· mac rotheact at e annso a nanmand ·i· Fib· Fidach· Foltlaig· Fortrend Cait· Ce· Circing Circin· lx annais regnan Fidach· xl annis regnauit Fortrend ·xl· annis ara regnauit· Foltlaid xxx· annis regnauit· Gatt xii· annis regnauit· Ce xu· annis regnauit· Fidbaid ·xxxiiii· annis regnauit· Geide ollgothach ·lxxx· annis regnauit[·] Oenbegan b⁻ Ollfinachta ·lx· annis regnauit· Guided gaeth breatnach ·l· annis regnauit· Ges cuirti Bont ·xxx· and uad 7 Bruige ba hainm do gach aen fer 7 renauerunt Hiberniam 7 Alboniam ·per ·c·l· annos uit ineenitur i leabraib na Cruithneach Bruide painte [arm] in ·c· Bruide Bruide unpann Bruige leo Bruigi gant Bruide gund Bruige urgann Bruide un[g]aint Bruigi fet Bruige urfexir Bruigi fecir Bruigi cal Brigi uncal· B· cint· B· arcint B· fet B· urfet· B· ru· B· eru B· gart B· cinit B· cind· B· uip· B· uiruip· B· gruith B· ungrith B· munaig B· ur B· gidgie B· crin B· urcrin Bruige urmain reg·nauerunnt ·cl· annos ut dixiumus

7 ro·bai Alba cen rig fria re uile co haimsir Gud cet rig rogab Albain uile tri comarli la reigin adberait araili comad he Catluan mac Catming nogabad rige a regin i Cruithentuaith a nEirind ·i· lx· bliadna 7 iar sin rogabh Gud ·i· l· Tarain ·c· ann regnauit Morleo· a xu· annis· regnauit· Deocillimon ·xl· annis regnauit Cinioiod mac Airtcois ·uii· annis· regnauit· Deort ·l· annis regnauit Blieberlith ·u· annis regnauit· e Deototreic frater Tui ·xl· annis regnauit· Usconbest ·xx· annis regnauit· Crutbolc ·uii· annis regnauit· Deordiuois ·xx· annis regnauit· Uist ·l· an[ini]s regnauit· Ru ·c· annis· regnauit· Gartnait ·iiii·ix· annis· regnauit· Breth mac Buithed ·uii· annis· regnauit· Uipoig nauit ·xxx· Canatulacma ·iii· annis· annis· regnauit· Uradach uetla ·ii· annis· regnauit· Gartnait diupeir ·lx· annis· regnauit Tolorc mac Aithiuir ·lxxu· Drust mac Erp ·c[:] regnauit· 7 ·c· catri ro reigin Nono decimo annis reigni eius Patricius [c sanctus] episcopus ad Hiberniam peruenit Tolorc mac Aniel ·iiii· annis· regnauit· Nectan morbreac mac Eirip ·xxxiiii· annis· regnauit· Tertio anno regni [eius] Darlugdach abbatista Cilledara de Aberniam axulat p[ro] Xristo ad Britiniam secundo R anno aduenitus tui immolaueit Nectonnius anno uno Apuirnige deo 7 sancteae Brigitea presente Darlugdach quae cantauit alleluia super istam

Dairt guitimoth ·xxx· annis regnauit Galanarbith ·xu· annis· regnauit Da Drerst ·i· Drest filius Budros ·xu· annis regnauertunt· Derst filius Girum solus ·u· annis· regnauit· Galum cenamlapeh ·iiii· annis· regnauit Gartnait filius

Girom ·uii· annis· regnauit· Cailtaine filius Girom anno regnauit· Talorg· filius [M?/Ui?]urtoloic ·xi· annis· regnauit· Drest filius Manaith ·uno· anno· regnauit· Cum Brideno ·uno· Bruide mac Maelcon ·xxx· annis· regnauit· Mochta anno anuo regni eit baibtisconatus est Escon Columba Gartnait ·filius· Domnach ·xi· annis· regnauit· Nechtan nepos Uerp ·xx· annis· regnauit· Cinhoint ·filius· Luitriu ·xix· annis· regnauit· Gartnait mac Uiud ·u· ·annis· reganuit· Tolorc frater eorum duc deicim· annis· regnauit· Tolorcan ·filius· Enfret ·iiii· Gartnairt ·filius· Donuel ·ui· annis· regnauit· 7 deimidium anni Druisc frater eius ·uii· annis· regnauit· Bride filius· File xx· annis· regnauit· Taran· filius· En·fidaid ·iiii· Brei· filius· Deirilei ·xi· annis regnauit Nechtan ·filius· Deirile ·x· annis· regnauit· Drest 7 Elpen con·neganaueint ·u· annis· regnauit· Onbes ·filius· Urgurt ·xxx· annis· regnauit· Breite filius Uugut ·xu· annis· regnauit· Ciniod filius Iuuredeg ·xii· annis· regnauit· Alpin· filius· Uuoid ·iii· [annis· regnauit·] 7 dimidon regni Drest ·filius· Talorcan ·uno· anno· regnauit Talorcan· filius· Drostan no· u· deg Tolorcen filius Omust ·xii· 7 dimidoin ·annis· regnauit· Canul· filius· Tanng ·u· annis· regnauit· Cuastantin ·filius· Uurguist ·xxxu· Uidn[u]st· filius· Uurgust ·xii· ann· annis· regnauit· Dr[ost] ·filius· Constantin 7 Tolorc· filius· Uuthoil ·iii· annis regnauit· conregnauerunt Unen· filius· Unest ·iii· Urad· filius Bargoit ·iii· annis· regnauit· 7 Brot ·uno· anno· regnauit·

Cinaed· filius· Alpin ·xui· annis· regnauit· Domnall· filius· Alpin ·iiii· annis regnauit· 7 Custan[ti]n· filius· Cinaeda ·xx· annis ·regnauit· Aed ·filius· Cinaed ·uno· annis· regnauit· Girig mac Dungaile ·xi· no· iii· ·annis· regnauit· Domnall· filius· Consanttin ·xi· annis· [reganuit·] Constanntin· filius· Aed ·xlu· annis· regnauit· Maelcol[aim] ·filius· Domnaill ·ix· annis· regnauit· Cuilein· filius· Ildoib ·filii· Constandtin ·iiii· annis· regnauit· Cinaed no Dub ·filius· Maelcolaim ·uii· annis· regnauit Cuilein ·i· dimidoin [regnauit·] Cinaed· filius· Duib· ocht annis· regnauit Maelcolaim mac Cinaeda ·xxx· annis· regnauit· Donchad ua· Mailcolaim ·uii· annis· regnauit· Macbethad mac Fin meic laig ·xiii· annis· regnauit· Lulach ·u· inis Maelcolaim mac Colaim Donncaid iarsin

SL3 REGNAL LISTS

This list is expanded and revised to include SL3 Regnal Lists which were not part of Molly Miller's bibliography. Lists from *Book of Lecan* are printed in my Ph.D. thesis.[10]

SL3(Lec.1) (Miller's SL3 L): *Book of Lecan*, 4vb26-50. (1418, scribe: Adam Ó Cuirin). Recension b of *Lebor Gabála*.

SL3(Lec.2) (Miller's SL3 La): *Book of Lecan*, 139ra8-24. (1416-1417, scribe: Gilla Isu Mac Fir Bhisigh). Interpolation in *Lebor Bretnach*.

SL3(Lec.3) (Miller's SL3 Lb): *Book of Lecan*, 143rb35-143va9. (1416-1417, scribe: Gilla Isu Mac Fir Bhisigh). Interpolation in *Lebor Bretnach*.

SL3(Lec.4) (Miller's SL3 M): *Book of Lecan*, 287ra10-30. 1417-1418, scribe: Gilla Isu Mac Fir Bhisigh). Part of Recension c of *Lebor Gabála*.

SL3(Bal.1) (Miller's SL3 Bii): *Book of Ballymote*, 43all-33. (1384-1406, scribe: Magnus Ó Duibgennáin). Part of Recension c of *Lebor Gabála*.

SL3(Bal.2) (Miller's SL3 Bi): *Book of Ballymote*, 203a12-a^{2}37. (1384-1406, scribe: Magnus Ó Duibgennáin). Interpolation in *Lebor Bretnach*.

SL3(D.iv.1) (Miller's SL3 V): Royal Irish Academy, *MS. Stowe D.iv.1*, 3ra51-b22. (1391-1399, possibly part of original Yellow Book of Lecan). Recension b of *Lebor Gabála*.

SL3(24.P.13): R.I.A., *MS. 24.P.13*, 26 ll.6-21. (1621, scribe: Luán (mhac) Taidg). Part of Recension c of *Lebor Gabála*.

SL3(23.G.4): R.I.A., *MS. 23.G.4.*, 366 l.27-367 l.2. (18th cent.). Interpolation in *Lebor Bretnach*.

SL3(1295.1): Trinity College Dublin, *MS #1295*, 83 ll.25-41. (1728, scribe: Richard Tipper. Copy of *Book of Ballymote*). Recension c of *Lebor Gabála*.

SL3(1295.2): T.C.D., *MS #1295*, 378a7-a^{2}27. (1728, scribe: Richard Tipper. Copy of *Book of Ballymote*). Interpolation in *Lebor Bretnach*.

SL3(1289): T.C.D., *MS. #1289*, 93 ll.3-22. (c.1745: scribe: Tadhg Ó Neachtain. Copy of *Book of Ballymote*). Part of Recension c of *Lebor Gabála*.

SL3(D.iii.2): R.I.A., *MS. Stowe D.iii.2*, 95 l.33-96 l.21. (1746: scribe: Aodh Ó Dálaigh. Copy of *Book of Ballymote*). Part of Recension c of *Lebor Gabála*.

SL3(G47): National Library of Ireland, *Gaelic MS. 47*, 1 ll.5-15 (1807). Interpolation in *Lebor Bretnach*.

Other lists may exist in R.I.A. *MS. 23.G.5.* and British Library *MS. Egerton 134*. These contain the same *Lebor Bretnach* material as in *MS. 23.G.4.*[11] I have not examined these texts.

REGNAL LIST SL3(Lec.1)

ISin bliadain· Cetna sin tancatar Cruithnig a tir Tracia ·i· clanna Geloin mac Ercail iat ·i· Cruithne mac Cinge meic Luchtai meic Parrtolain meicc Agnoin meic Buain meic Mais meic Fathecht meic Iafedh meic Noe ISe athair Cruithnech ⁊ ·c· bliadain do irrighi· Secht meic Cruithne annso ·i· Fib· Fidach· Fotla Fortrenn· Cait· Cee· Cirig ⁊ a uii· randaib ro ranndsat a forba

> Morseieser meic Cruithne ia[r]sin
> a uíj· ro rannsat Albain·
> Ca[it]· Cee Ciri Cetach clann·
> Fib Fidach Fotla Fortrend

ET ise ainm cach a fir dib fuil for a fearunn Fibh xxiiij· bliadain irrigi nAlban· Fidach xl· b· Fortrend· lxx· urpont· Cait· xxii· b· ur⁻leo Ce xíj· b· uileo Ciricc· lxxx· b· grant·Aenbecan ·u· b· urgant Cait xxx· b· gnith Finnecta .lx· b· b uirgnith· b· feth ·i· ges· uirfechtair Gest .xl· b· cal Urgeist. xxx. Brude urcal Bruide pont· xxx· b· i rrighi nUlad· is de asbertha Bruighe fer a gach fer dib edrenda na fer Bruighi cinnt .b· fet ·b· uirfet· b· ruaile Rogabastair ·i· ar da ·c· b· ut est a lebraib na Cruithnech Brude ero. Brude· gart· b· argart ·b· cind· Brude· urchind. b. uip ·b. uruip· b. grith· b. urgrith .b. muin· b· urmuin. b· Do rigaib Cruith[neach] andsin

REGNAL LIST SL3(Lec·2)

do bunad Cruithnech so
Cruithne mac Cin'ge meic Luchta meic Parthalon meic Agnon meic Buain meic Mais meic Fathecht meic Iauad meic Iathfed meic Nae meic Laimiach IS he athair Cruithnech ⁊ Ced bliadain do i rrigi amail a dear ar reamaind seacht meic Cruithnech inso ·i· Fid ⁊ Fidach· Foltla· Fortrend· Cait Ce Cirig ⁊ i seacht reandaib randsad a ferand amail adbert int eolach

> Moir feiser do Chruithne claind
> rainn Albain i sseacht raind·
> Cait Ce Cirig cetach clainn
> Fib Fidach Foltla Foirtreand

ET is e ainm cach fir dib fil fora fearand ut Fib ⁊ Ce ⁊ Cait et reliqua ·xiii· rig dec do gobsad dib Bruda Pont ·xxx· a rig uad ⁊ Bruide atberte fri cach fear dib ⁊ ranna na fear aili rogabsad ar tre ·l· ar ·c· ut est i llebraib na Cruithnech

REGNAL LIST SL3(Lec.3)

Do bunadaib na Cruithnech andso bo deas da
Cruithne mac In'ge meic Luchta meic Parrthalon meic Buain meic Mais meic
Fathecht meic Iathfeth meic Naei IS he athair Cruithnech ⁊ Ced bliadain do
irige Seacht meic Cruithne andso ·i· Fib ⁊ Ce ⁊ Cirich· et reliqua ⁊ i seacht
randaib ro rannsad a ferand ⁊ ise ainm cach fir dib fil for a fearann aniug Fib
·im⁻· Ceathra bliadain fichit do irigi Fidach ·xl· bliadain Bruid puint Foirtrenn
·lxxx· b· Urponn Cait ·xx.ii· Urleo Ce ·xi· Urleo Cirich· ·lxx· b· Gant
Aenbeccan· mac· b· Urgant Cait ·xxx· b· Gnith Findachta· lx· Bru gnith Guidid
gadbre ·b· feth ·i· ges ·i· b· b· Urfechtair Gest guirid ·i· xl· b· Cla Urgast tricha·
b· b· Urscal Bruidi pont tricha b· rig Ulad de adberther fria cach fer dib ⁊ randa
na fer· b· cint ·b· Urchindt· b· fet· b· urfed ·b· Ruale robabsad ar· b· Ar bliadain·
ut· dicitur· a lebraib na Cruithneach Bruid bliadain ero· b· Gart· b· Argart ·b·
Cinn· b· Urchind· b· Uip· b· Uruip· b· Groth· Urgroth ·b· Muin· b· Urumam· b·
IS amlaid sin fo frith

REGNAL LIST SL3(Lec.4)

ISin bliadain chetna sin tancadar Cruithnich a tir Thraigia ·i· clanda
Golain mac Ercail iat Icathirsi ananmanda Cruithnig meic In'ge meic Luchta
meic Parrthaloin meic Agnoin meic Buain meic Mais meic Faithfeacht meic
Iathfed meic Naei IS he athair Cruithneach ⁊ Cet bliadain do irigi seacht meic
Cruithnich and ·i· Fib ra· Fidach· Fotla· Foirtrenn· Cait Che· Arig Cetach ⁊ a
seacht randaib do randsad a fearanna amail adfed in file

> Moirfeser meic Cruithnech ann
> randsad ar seacht a fearand·
> Cait Che Airig Cetach cland
> Fib Fidach Fotla Foirtrend

ET ise ainm cach fir dib fuil for a fearand Fib· im⁻· bliadain a fichit do a rigi
Fidach ·xl· bliadain Foirtrend ·lxx· b· urpann Cait da bliadain ar fichit urloi Ci
da ·x· b· uileo Ciric ·lxxx· bliadain Gant Aenbecan ·im⁻· bliadain urgant Cait
tricha ·b· gnith Findechta ·lx· b· b urgnith Guidit gadbre ·b· feth ges ·b·
uirfechtair Gest· guirid· xl· b· cal Uirgset tricha ·b· urchal Bruidi pont tricha ·b·
rig Ulad de adbartha Bruidi fria cach fear dib ⁊ ranna na fear Bruidi cind
uirchind ·b· fet ·b· uirseat ·b· ruaile ro gabsad caeca ar da cheo bliadain ut est i
llebraib na Cruithnech · Bruide · ero· Bruind· gart· Bruind· argart· Bruind·
cind· urcind· Bruind· uip· bruidi uirip· Bruind· grith· Bruind· urgrith· Bruind·
muin· Bruind· urmuin· do rigaib Cruithneach annsin

REGNAL LIST SL3(Bal.1)

ISin bliadain .c.na sin tangadar Cruithnig a tir Traigia tra tangadar ·i· a clanda Gloin mac hErcoil Acathirsi a namnanda Cruithne mac Inge meic Luchtai meic Parrtholon meic Aghnoin meic Buain meic Maís meic F'at'eacht meic Iafeth meic Nae· IS e at'air Cruithneach ꝛ c· bliadain do i righe ·uií meic Cruithne andso Fid'b' Fidhach· Fodla· Fortrenn· Caít
Che Ciríg ꝛ a uíí· randaibh ro roindsead a fherand
      Morseiser fear meic Cruithne andsin
      roindsead Albu ·i· uíí randaibh·
      Cait Che Círíg cedach cland
      Fibh Fíd'ach Fodla Fortrenn
ꝛ is e ainm gach a fir dibh fuil for a fearand Fibh. íííí. bliadain .xx· í rrígí nAlban· Fidhach ·xl· bliadain Forthrenn· lxx· bliadain Urpond· Caít· xxíí· bliadain· Urleo Ce· xíí· Uileo Ciríc· lxxx· bliadain· gant Aenbeca. im-· bliadain· Urgant Caít. xxx· bliadain· gnith Finechta .lx. bliadain· B uirgníth Guidíd gatbre feth ·i· ges b· Uirfechtair Gest guiríd .xl b· Cal Urgest. xxx. bliadain urchal Bruide pont xxx· b· rig' Ulad de adberthea Bruide fria gach fear dib' ꝛ randa na fear. Bruídi cínt. b· urcínt· b· fed. b· [n]írfed· b· ruaile Rogab'sadar ·l· ar da ·c· b· ut est i llebhraib' na Cruithneach Bruide ero. Bruide gart. Bruide argart· Bruide cínd Bruide· uircínd. Bruide uip. Bruide uruíp· Bruide grith· b. urgrith Bruide muin· Bruide urmuin. Do rigaib Cruithneach índsin·

REGNAL LIST SL3(Bal.2)

de bunad' Cruithneac' andseo
Crúithne Mac Cínge Meic Luc'taí Meic Parrt'alan Meic Agnoin Meic Buain Meic Mais Meic Fathec't Meic Iafeth Meic Noe IS e athair Crúithneach ꝛ cet bl[iadain] do í rrig'i Sec't meic Cruithneac' annso·i· Fib ꝛ Fidach Fodla Fortrend cathach Cait Ce Ciríg et sec't randaib' ro roindset í nferand ut dixit Colum Cíllí
      Moirseiser do Cruithne clainn·
      rainset Albain i sec't raind·
      Caít. Ce. Cirig cethac'. clann.
      Fib Fídac' Fotla Fortrenn.
Ocus is e ainm gach fir dib fil fora fearand ut est. Fib ꝛ Ce ꝛ Cait et reliqua. Fib xxiiii. bli[adain] i rrige Fidac' .xl- bl[iadain] Bruide pont Fort[']rend lxx. Fortrenn lxx. b. urpont Cait da bliadain ar xx. uleo Cirig .lxxx. b. b. gant Ce xíi. b. b. uleo Aenbeccan .im⁻. b. urgant Cait .xxx. ar b. b. gníth Finecta .lx. b. b urgnith Guidid' gadbre. b. fet i. geís .i. b. b. urfeic'ir Gest gurid .xl- xl- b. cab. Urges .xxx. ar b. b. urcal Bruide pont .xxx. b. cínt rí Ulad' li. urcínt de adbertea fri .b. fet' gac' fir dib' ꝛ .b. urfet' randa na fear. b. ruaile rogabsadar .l. ut est i llebraib' na Cruit'neac' Bruide ero. b. gart. b. argart b. cind. b. urcínd. b. uip .b. uruíp. b. grith. urgrith. b. muin. b. urmuin.

REGNAL LIST SL3(D.iv.1)

ISin ·bliadain .cetna sin tancatar Cruithnig' a tir· Tracia ·i· clanda
Gelóin mac Ercail íat ·i· Cruithne mac Cinge meic Luchta meic Parrtholain
meic Agnoin meic Buain meic MaiS meic Fathecht meic Iafedh meic Noe IS e
athair Cruithnech ₇ ·c· bliadain· do i rrigi· Secht meic Cruith andso ·i· Fib·
Fidach· Fot'la· Fortren[d']· Cait· Cee· Cirig ₇ a sec't ran[d']aib
ro randSat a forba.
    MorSeiSer meic Cruit'ne iairsin
    a secht ro rannsat Albaín·
    Cait· Cé Ciric cetach clann·
    Fíb'· Fidhach· Fotla· Fortrend·
ET is é ainm cach a fir dib fuil for a ferand· Fibh· xxíííí· bliadain· i rrigi
nAlban Fidach ·xl· b· Fortrend· lxx· urpont Cait· xxii· b· ur¯leo· Ce· xíí· b· uiléo
Ciric· lxxx· b· grant Aenbecan ·u· b· urgant Cait· xxx· b· gnith Fínnectha· lx· b·
b uirgnith· b· feth ·i· ges· b· uirfec'tair Gest· xl· b· cal Urgest· xxx· b· urcal
Bruite pont· xxx· b· i rrighi nUladh is de atberth Bruighe fer a gach fer dib·
edrenda na fer· Bruighi cinnt· b· uircinnt· b· fet· b· uirfet· b· ruáile Rogabsatar
·i· ar da ·c· b· ut est a lebraib na Cruithnech Brude ero· Brude gart· b· argart· b·
cind· b· urchind. b. uip· b. uruip· b· grith· b· urgrith· b· m'uin· b· urmuin· b· Do
rigaib Cruithnec' andsin

REGNAL LIST SL3(24·P·13)

ISin bliadhoin ced[h]na sin tancadar Cruithnich a tír Traicchia ·i· a
clanda Gelóin mac Ercail iet· Cruithne mac Cinge meic Luchta meic Partolóin
meic Agnoin meic Buain meic MaiS meic Aithechta meic Maghócc meic Iafeth
meic Noe· IS e athair Cruitnech ·i· ceud bliadhain do a ricche uii· meic
Cruithne annso ·i· Fibra Fidhach Fod'la Fortren Cait Chi Arig cedach ·₇ a secht
randaibh ab ferand amail atfed an filidh
    Morseiser meic Crúithne andsin·
    ranndsat Alba a secht rannaibh
    Cait Che Ricch cedach clann·
    Fip Fidhach Fodla Fortrenn
·₇ is e ainm gach fir dibh fuil for a ferann· Fib. uo. bliadain ar .xx. a ricche·
Fid[i]ch ·xl· bliadain· Fortren lxx· bliadain urpond Caid da bliadain ar fichit·
Urlai Ce da bliadain dh¯· Uilio Ciricc· lxxx· bliadain gant Aenbeccan. uo.
bliadain· Urgant Cait. xxx· bliadain gni Findechto lx. b uirgnit Guidhicc
gadbre bliadain· fed ges bliadain· Uirfechtair Gest guirrid ·xl· b· Cal Uirccsed·
xxx· bliadain rig' Ulad'· De dbeite Bruidi re gach fear dib' ·₇ ranna na fear.
Bruide a cinn bliadain· Uircind ·b· fed. ·b· uired bliadain· ruaile Rogab'sadar ·l·
ar da ceud ·b· ut est a leab'raib' na Cruithneach· Bruide br[eo] Bruinde gart
Bruinde Do ricchaib' Cruithneach annsin

REGNAL LIST SL3(23.G.4)

do b'únúg'ad' Cruitnec' inso·
Cruitne, mac Cinge, meic Luc'ta, meic Part'oláin, meic Agnoman, meic
Buaed'aín, meic Máis, meic Fat'ec't, meic Iauad, meic Iafet, meic Nóe, meic
Lamiec IS é at'ir Cruit'neach ·₇ cét bliadain do i ríge am'ail a der ar rom'ainn·
Secht meic Cruithnech anso ·i· Fid ·₇ Fid'ag, Foltla Fortrenn, Cait, Ce C'irig, ·₇
a secht rannaib' raindsad a f'erann am'ail adb'ert an teolac'
        Mors'eiser do C'ruit'ne clainn:
        roinn Albain a seac't rainn:
        Cait, Ce, Cirig, cet'ach clainn,
        Fid', Fidac, Foltla, Fo[r]treand
·₇ is e ainm gac' fir d'íob' fil foral ferann ug'ad Fib', ·₇ Ce, ·₇ Caít et reliqua· trí
rí deúcc rogab'sad díob'· Bruda Pont ·xxx· úad' ·₇ Brúide abert' áoi fria gac' fer
d'íob', ·₇ ranna nalfer oile, rog'ab'sadur tre ·l· ar ·c· ut est a leab'raib' nag
Cruithnech·

REGNAL LIST SL3(1295.1)

ISín bliad'ain c·na t'angadair Cruit'nig' a tír Tragía tra tangadair
Cruit'nig' ·i· clanna Gloin mac hEircoil Acat'írsi ananmanda· Cruit'ne mac Inge
meic Luc'ta meic Parrt'oloin meic Ag'noin meic Buain meic Mais meic Fat'eac't
meic Iafet' meic [ix]·I·S e at'air Cruit'nec' ·₇· c· bliad'aín do a rig'e .uíí· meic
Cruithne andso; Fid'b'· Fid'ac'· Fod'la: Fort'renn· Cait C'e Cirig ·₇ a uíí·
randaib' ro roinnséd a f'erand·
        Morseisf'ear meic Cruit'ne andsin·
        roinnsed Albú ·i· uíí randaib'·
        Cait C'e Cirig' cedac' cland
        Fid'b' Fídac' Fodla Fortrén
·₇ is e ainm gac' a fír dib' fuil for a ferand· Fidb. íííí· bliad'na ·xx· i rig'í· Fid'ac'
·xl· bliadain· Fortren ·lxx· bliadain·urpond Caít· xxíí· urleo Ce· xíí· uileo Ciric·
lxxx· bliadain· gant Aenbeca· im⁻· bliadain· urgant Cait' xxx· bliadain· gnit'
Finec'ta lx. bliadain· cal Urgest xxx· bliadain. urcal pont xxx. b urgnít Guidid'·
gatbre fet' ·i· ges b· uirfec'tair Gest guirid ·xl· bliadain· rig' Ulad de adbert'ea
Bruide fria gac' fer dib' ·₇ randa na feair {dib} Bruid'e cínt. b· urc'ínt· bliadain·
fed· bliadain· nírféd· bliadain· ruaile· rog'ab'sadair ·l· ar da ·c· bliadain· ut est i
lleb'raib' na Cruit'neac'· b. ero. Bruide[?] gairt. b. argart. Bruide cind. b.
uircínd. Bruide uip. b· uruíp [b]· grith· b. urgrith Bruid'e· Bruide gnit'· b· urgrit·
b· muín· Bruide urmuin. Do rig'[i]aib' Cruit'neac' índsi:

REGNAL LIST SL3(1295.2)

de bunad' Cruit'neac' andséo;
Crúit'ne Mac Cínge Meic Luc'taí Meic Parrt'alan Meic Agnoín Meic Buaín
Meic Maís Meic Fat'ec't Meic Iafeth Meic Noe; IS é at'air Cruithneac' ·₇ ced
bliadaín do i rrig'i Seac't Meic Cruithneac' annso ·i· Fib· Fid'ac'· Fodla·
Fortrend· cat'ac' Cait C'e Cirig ·₇ secht randaib' ro roindset í nferand ut dixit;
Colum Cille

 Móirseisir do Cruit'ne clainn
 raindset Albaín í secht rainn
 Caít C'e Cirig cet'ac' clann
 Fib Fid'ac' Fodla Fortren·

agus is e ainm gac' fir dib' fil fora fearand. ut est· Fib ·₇ Ce ₇ Cait et relíqua
Fib· xxíííí bliad'na i rrig'e Fid'ac' xl- bliadaín Bruite pont Fortrend ·lxx: Fortren
·lxx· b. urpont Cait da bliadain ar xx· uleo Cirig ·lxxx· .b[ruide]· bliadain gant.
Ce xíí· b. b. uleo· Aenbeccan ·im⁻. b. urgant Cait ·xxx [ur]· b· b· gnith Fínec'ta
.lx· b. b urgnit' Guidíd' gadbre· b· feth ·i· geis .i. b. b. urfeic'ir Gest gurid ·xl-·
b· cab. Urges .xxx [ur]. b. b. urcal Bruide pont ·xxx· ·b· cínt rí Ulad' b. urcint
de adbertea fri· b. fet' gac' fir dib' ·₇ ·b. urfet' randa na· fear· b· ruaile
róg'absadar ·l· ut est i lleb'raib' na Cruit'neac'. Bruide ero· b· gart. b· argart· b.
cinnd· b· urc'ind· b. uip· b· uruip· b. grit'· urgrith· b· Muín ·b· urmuín· b·

REGNAL LIST SL3(1289)

ISin b'liad'uin c'edna t'angadar Cruithnigh a [t]tír Tracia go hEirinn ·i·
clann G'loin mhac hEarcuil, Arsí a na[nm]onna ó Chruit'ne mhac Uige mh[i]c
Luchtad' mhic Parrthaloin mhic Agnoin mhic Buain, mhic Mais, mhic Fat'acht
mhic Iafet mhic Naoi. ced bliad'uin do i rigi secht macu Cruithne .i. Fid'b',
Fiodhac', Fodhla, Foirtren, Cait, Che, Ciríg cedach. ₇ is é ainim gac' fir díb' for
a b'ferann, b'á rointed' etiorrad' .i. Albuin roinedar na secht rannaib'. Fid'b'
ceit're bliadna fit'c'et a righe. Fiodhach cetrac'ad bliad'uin Foirtren sechtmhod'
blíadna· Urpannt Cait da b'liaduin is fithc'e. uirleoi Ce da bliadhuin dég, Uileo
Ciric ochtmhad' bliadhuin gant Aonbega im⁻. bliadhuin. Urgant Cait. triothchat
blíadhuin, gníth Finechtad' seigad blíadhuin· Cal Urges't treadhchad blíaduin·
Urcal pont triot'c'at, b uirgnit, Guidíd. gabre fet .i. ges b. Uirfechtar. Geit,
guirid cethrathc'ad bliadui[n] a righe uile de adberted' Bruide fria gac' fer díob',
₇ rantad' na fer. Bruidhe cínt ·b· urcint· bliaduin nir fed. bliaduin ruaile,
rogabsat caogad ar dha céd bliad'uin mar ata a leab'raib' na Cruit'neac'·
bliadhuin Ero, bliadhuin Gairt bliadhuin Argart, Bride cinn bliadhuin uircínn
Brid'e uip bliadhuin uiruip bliadhuin, grit· bliadhuin, Uirgrit Bruide Bride grith
bliadhuin, Uirgrit bliaduin muin Bruid'e urmuin, do rioghaib' Cruithneac'
insin·

REGNAL LIST SL3(D.iii.2)

ISin b'liad'uin· ced'na t'angadair Cruit'nig' a tír Tracía go hEirinn ·i· clann G'loin m'ic hEarcuil, Arsi a [nan]onna· O C'ruit'ne mhac Uige m'ic Luchtad' m'ic Pairtaloin m'ic Agnoin m'ic Buaín m'ic Mais, m'ic Fat'acht mic Iafet mic Naoi· ced bliad'an do rig' secht maca Ced b'liad'uin do rig'e secht macu Cruithne .i. Fid'b', Fiodhac', Fod'la, Foirtren Cai't, C'e, Cirig cedac' ⁊ is é ainim gac' fir d'ib' foir a b'ferann, b'á roinnted' ettorrad' .i· Albuin roinedair na secht rannaib' Fid'b' ceit're bliad'uin fit'c'et a rig'e· Fiod'ac' cetrac'ad bliaduin· Foirtren sechtm'od' bliad'na. Urpannt Cait da b'liad'uin, is fit'c'e uirleoi Ce da bliad'uin deg, Uileo Ciric ochtm'ad' bliad'uin gant Aonbega bliad'ain· Urgant Cait= trioc'at bliad'uin, gnit' Finnechtad' seigad bliad'uin Cal Uirgest tread'cad bliad'uin· UrCal Pont triot'c'ad, b uirgnit, Guidid, gabre, fet ·i· ges ·b· Uiricef[echarair?]. Geit, guirid cet'rat'cad bliaduin a rig'e uile de adberted' Bruide fria gac' fer díobh ET rantad' na fer Bruid'e cinnt[?] ·b· Urcint bliad'uin fed' bliaduin nir fed bliaduin· ruaile, rogabsat caogad air= d'á c'éd bliad'uin mair ata a leab'raib' Cruit'nec'. bliad'uin Eirc,bliad'uin· Gairrt bliad'uin Argart, Bride cinn bliad'uin uircinn, Brid'e, Uip bliad'uin, uiruip bliad'uin, grit' bliad'uin· Uirgrit Bruide Bride grit' bliad'uin Uirgrit bliad'uin, muin Brid'e urmuin, do riog'aibh Cruit'n['[]ec' insin

REGNAL LIST SL3(G47)

do bunad Cruithnech so
Cruitne mac Cínge meic Luchta meic Part'alon meic Agnon meic Buain m[{i}]eic Mais meic Fat'ec't meic Iauad meic Iat'fead meic Nae meic Laimiac' IS e atair Cruit'nec' ⁊ cead bliadain do i rrigi amail a dear ar reamaind Seac't meic Cruit'nec' inso .i. Fid ⁊ Fidac' Foltla· Ftreand· Cait Cé Cirig ⁊ i seac't reandaib randsad a ferand amail adbert int eolac'

Moirfeisear do C'ruit'ne claind
rainn Albain i sseacht raind.
Cait C[e] Cirig ceatac' clainn
Fib' Fidac' Foltla Foirtreand
ET is e ainm cac' fir dib fil fora fearand ut Fib ⁊ Ce ⁊ Cait et reliqua ·xiii· rig dec do gobsad dib Bruda Pont ·xxx· a rig uad ⁊ Bruide atberde fri cach fear dib ⁊ ranna na fear aili rogabsad ar tre ·l· ar ·c· ut est i llebraib na Cruit'nec'

4

APPENDICES TO THE EDITED TEXTS

APPENDIX I

Pictish Kings with Approximate Dates
(Time periods are adapted from M. Miller and M.O. Anderson)[1]

(Mythological Period)
Kings prior to Brude (30)

(Pseudo-historical Period)
Kings from Brude (30) to Talorc f. Achivir (Talorg I/Talorc I)

(Legendary Period)
Drust f. Erp (Drest I/Drust I))	(414-456)
Talorc f. Aniel (Talorg II/Talorc II)	(456-460)
Necton f. Erip (Nechton I/Nechtan I)	(460-484)
Drest Gurthinmoch (Drest II/Drust II))	(484-514)
Galanan (Galam I)	(514-526)

(Early Historical Period)
Drest f. Uudrost (Drest III/Drust III)
and Drest f. Gyrom (Drest IV/Drust IV)	(526-531)
Drest f. Gyrom (Drest IV/Drust IV) alone	(531-536)
Garthnach f. Girom (Gartnait III)	(536-543)
Cailtram f. Girom	(543-544)
Talorg f. Muircholaich (Talorg III/Talorc III)	(544-555)
Drest f. Munait (Drest V/Drust V)	(555-556)

(Historical Period)
0. Galam (Galam II)   (556-557)
   (and one year with Bridei f. Mailcon)
1. Bridei f. Mailcon (Bridei I/Bruide I)   (555/56/57-584/86/87)
2. Gartnart f. Domelch (Gartnait IV)   (586/87-597/98/601)
3. Nectu n. Uerb (Nechton II/Nechtan II)   (598/602-618/21)
4. Cinioch f. Lutrin (Ciniod I/Cináed I)   (618/21-631/33/37)
5. Garnard f. Uuid (Gartnait V)   (631/33/37-635/37/41)
6. Breidei f. Uuid (Bridei II/Bruide II)   (635/37/41-641/42/46)
7. Talorc f. Uuid (Talorg IV/Talorc IV)   (641/42/46-653/58)
8. Talorcen f. Enfret (Talorgen I/Talorcan I)   (653/58-657/62)

(Archival Period)
9. Gartnait f. Donuel (Gartnait VI)   (657/62-663/68)
10. Drest f. Donuel (Drest VI/Drust VI)   (663/68-671/72/75)
11. Bredei f. Bili (Bridei III/Bruide III)   (671/72/75-692/93/96)
12. Taran f. Entifidich   (692/93/96-696/97/700)
13. Bredei f. Derelei (Bridei IV/Bruide IV))   (696/97/700-706/11)
14. Necthon f. Derelei (Nechton III/Nechtan III)   (706/11-724/26)
15. Drest (c.728) (Drest VII/Drust VII)   (724/26-726/31)
16. Elpín (c.728) (Alpin I/Elpin I)   (726-728/31)
Necthon f. Derelei (second reign)   (728-729)
17. Onuist f. Urguist (Onuist I/Óengus I)   (729/31-761)
18. Bredei f. Uuirguist (Bridei V/Bruide V)   (761-763)
19. Ciniod f. Uuredech (Ciniod II/Cináed II)   (763-775)
20. Elpin f. Uuroid (Alpin II/Elpin II)   (775-780)
21. Drest f. Talorgen (Drest VIII/Drust VIII)   (780-781)
22. Talorgen f. Druisten (Talorgen II/Talorcan II)   (780/81-782/85)
23. Talorgen f. Onuist (Talorgen III/Talorcan III)   (782/85-784/87)
24. Canaul f. Tarl'a (Conall)   (784/85-789)
25. Castantin f. Uurguist (Causantín)   (789-820)
26. Unuist f. Uurguist (Onuist II/Óengus II)   (820-834)
27. Drest f. Constantini (Drest IX/Drust IX)   (834-836/37)
28. Talorgen f. Uuthoil (Talorgen IV/Talorcan IV)   (834-836/37)
29. Uuen f. Unuist (Eoganan)   (836/37-839)
30. Uurad f. Bargoit (Ferad)   (839-842?)
31. Bred (Bridei VI/Bruide VI)   (842)
32. Kineth f. Ferat (Ciniod III/Cináed III)   (842-843)
33. Brude f. Fochel (Bridei VII/ Bruide VII)   (843-845)
34. Drust f. Ferat (Drest X/Drust X)   (845-848)
(End of independent kingdom of Picts)
Cináed mac Alpín (Kenneth mac Alpín)   (843/48?-58)
Domnall mac Alpín   (858-862)
Causantín mac Cináeda   (862-877)
Áed mac Cináeda   (877-878)

APPENDIX II

Comparison of Annals: Pictish Events

	ACam	AI	AT	AC	AU	AFM	CS
Birth?(wrongly "death") of Bridei f. Mailcon			506.1	509	505		
Flight before Bridei f. Mailcon			560.3	563?	558.2 560.2		560
Death of Galam (Cennalath)			580.2		580.3		580
Death of Bridei f. Mailcon		584	584.1	584	584.3		
Death of Gartnart f. Domelch			599.2	590			
Martyrdom of Donnán of Eigg and 150 others		619	617.1		617.1		
Death of Nechtan mac Canand (Nectu n. Uerb?)			621.3		621.3		621
Death of Uineus of Nér (?)					623.2		
Death of Cinioch f. Lutrin		633	631.2	632	631		631
Death of Garnard f. Uuid					635.6		
Death of Garnard f. Uuid(?)					635.8		
Death of Breidei f. Uuid			641.0		641.2		639
Burning of Iarnnbodb f. Gartnat (?)			643.3		643.4		
War of families of Áedan mac Gabrain and Gartnait f. Accidan(?)					649.4		
Death of Talorc f. Uuid			653.2	649	653.1		
Battle of Sráith Ethairt			654.4		654.5		651
Death of Talorcen f. Enfret			657.4		657.3		
Death of Gartnait f. Donuel			663.3	659	663.3		659
Battle of Luith Feirn in Fortriu					664.3		
Family(?) of Gartnait to Ireland(?)			668.1	666	668.3		664
Death of Itarnan and Corindu among Picts			669.2		669.2		
Family of Gartnait from Ireland (?)			670.4		670.4		
Expulsion of Drest f. Donuel			672.5		672.6		
Capture of Conamail f. Cano					673.3		
Founding of Apor Crosan			673.4		673.5	671.2	669
Drowning of Picts at Lann Abae					676.3		
Death of Drest f. Donuel			678.6	674	678.6		674
Death of Nechtan of Nér			679.4		679.4	677.3	675
Siege of Dún Foithir					681.5		
Orc (Orkney) destroyed by Bredei f. Bili			682.5		682.4		
Siege of Dún Duirn					683.3		
Battle of Dún Nechtain		685	686.1		686.1		
Cano f. Gartnait enters into religion (?)				683			
Death of Cano f. Gartnait			688.2		688.2		684
Death of Coblaith daughter of Cano			690.3		690.3		
Death of Bredei f. Bili		691	693.2		693.1		
Siege of Dún Foithir (?)					694.4		
Expulsion of Taran f. Entifidich			697.1		697.1		
Battle between Picts and Saxons			698.2	693	698.2		
Taran f. Entifidich to Ireland					699.3		
Killing of Conamail f. Cano					705.4		
Death of Bredei f. Derelei			706.2		706.2		
Battle of Mag Manand			711.3		711.3		
Death of Ciniod f. Derelei			713.5		713.4		
Capture of Tolargg f. Drostan			713.8	710	713.7		
Expulsion of Iona community by Necthon			717.3		717.4		713

Pictish Sourcebook

Comparison of Annals: Pictish Events

	ACam	AI	AT	AC	AU	AFM	CS
Death of Drostán of Derthach in Ard Breccáin			719.2		719.2	713.3	
Imprisonment of Simul f. Drest			725.3		725.3		
Death of Brecc of Fortriu					725.7		
Imprisonment of Necthon f. Derelei			726.1		726.1		
Battle of Monad Croibh			728.4		728.4		
Battle of Caislen Credi			728.5	725	728.4		
Pictish ships wreck at Ros Cuissine			729.2				
Battle of Monad Carno					729.2		
Battle of Druim Dergblathuig			729.4		729.3		
Battle: Bruide f. Onuist v. Talorg mac Congusa			731.4	728	731.6		
Death of Kentigerna					734.4		
Drowning of Talorg mac Congusa			734.4		734.5		
Capture of Talorgan f. Drostan					734.6		
Dúngal mac Selbaich flees Onuist f. Urguist					734.7		
Onuist f. Urguist attacks Dál Riata Capture of Dúngal f. Selbaich and Feradach f. Selbaich			736.1	733	736.1		
Battle of Cnoc Coirpri					736.2		
Death of "Ougen," king of Picts (?)	736						
Death of Bruide f. Onuist	736?		736.1	733	736.1		
Drowning of Failbe of Apor Crosan and sailors			737.2		737.2	732.5	
Sinking of "work done" in Apor Crosan (?)				734			
Drowning of Talorgan f. Drostan			739.6		739.7		
Onuist f. Urguist attacks Scots Dal Riata					741.10		
Death of Tuathalán, abbot of Cenn Righmona			747.11	746	747.11		
Battle of Catoic	750		750.4	746	750.4		
Reign ends for Onuist f. Urguist					750.11		
Death of Bridei f. Mailcon at Asreth (?)			752.4				
Death of Elpin of Glass Noíde (Glasnevin)			758.1		758.1	753.3	
Death of Onuist f. Urguist	736?		761.3	755	761.4		
Death of Bredei f. Uuirguist			763.8		763.10		
Battle in Fortriu			N/A		768.7		
Death of Ciniod f. Uuredech	776		N/A		775.1		
Death of Eithne, daughter of Ciniod f. Uuredech			N/A		778.11	773.7	
Death of Elpin f. Uuroid			N/A	773	780.5		
Death of Dub Tholarg, king of Picts (?)			N/A		782.1		
Battle: Canaul f. Tarl'a					789.11		
v. Castantin f. Uurguist			N/A		790.7		
Death of Mac Oige of Apor Crosan			N/A		802.5	797.6	
Death of Canaul f. Tarl'a		807	N/A		807.3		
Death of Castantin f. Uurguist		820	N/A		820.3		
Death of Unuist f. Uurguist			N/A		834.1		
Death of Uuen f. Unuist			N/A		839.9		
Death of Cináed mac Alpín	856	858	N/A		858.2		
Death of Domnall mac Alpín		861	N/A		862.1		862
Death of Cellach mac Ailella			N/A	863	865.2	863.4	
Óláfr and Ívarr take captives of Picts			N/A		871.2		871
Picts slaughtered by Vikings			N/A		875.3		
Death of Causantin mac Cináeda			N/A		876.1		876
Death of Áed mac Cináeda			N/A		878.2		904?
Death of "Ead, king of Pictland" (?)			N/A				904
Death of Cináed mac Alpín's daughter			N/A		905.0		

APPENDIX III

Comparison of Pictish Regnal Lists (5th-9th centuries)

List SL1	List SL2 M	List SL2 O	List SL2 H
Drust f. Erp (100)	Drosd mac Erp (100)	Drust mac Erp (100)	Drust mac Erp (100)
Talore f. Aniel (4)	Tolorc mac Amel (4)	Talorc mac Amel (4)	Tolorc mac Aniel (4)
Necton morbet f. Erip (24)	Neachtan morbreac mac Eirip (24)	Nectan mor brec mac Erip (24)	Nectan mor breac mac Eirip (34)
Drest Gurthinmoch (30)	Deirt Guitimoth (30)	Drest gurthimoth (30)	Dartguitimoth (30)
Galanan erilich (12)	Galanarbith (15)	Galanarilith (15)	Galanarbith (15)
Drest f. Gyrom et Drest f. Wdrost(5)	Dreist f. Giron and Drest fin Budrost (15)	Drest f. Giron et Drest fin Budros (12)	Drest f. Budros (15)
Drest f. Girom (5)	Deirts fi[u] Girum (7)	Drest fin Girom (5)	Derst f. Girum (5)
Garthnach f. Girom (7)	Gartaid fi[u] Girom (7)	Gartnait fin Girom (7)	Galum Cenamlapeh (4)
Cailtram f. Girom (1)	Cailtairni fiu Girom(1?)	Cailtarni fin Girom (1)	Gartnait f. Girom (7)
Talorg f. Muircholaich (11)	Talorc fin Urtoloic (11)	Talorg f. Murtholoic(11)	Cailtaine f. Girom (1)
	Drest fin Monaid (1)	Drest f. Munaith (1)	Talorg f. [M/Ui]rtolic(11)
Drest f. Munait (1)	Galum cenna ap (4)	Galam cennaleph (4)	Drest f. Manaith (1)
Galam cennaleph (1) cum Briduo (1)	cum Ruidhino (1)	cum Bridiuo (1)	cum Brideno (1)
Bridei f. Mailcon (30)	Bruidhi mac Maelcon (30)	Bruide mac Melcon (30)	Bruide mac Maelcon(30)
Gartnart f. Domelch(11)	Garnaith f. Domech (11)	Gartnait f. Domech(11)	Gartnait f.Domnach(11)
Nectu n. Uerd (20)	Neachtan n. Uer	Nectan n. Uerb (20)	Nechtan n. Uerp (20)
Cinioch f. Lutrin (19)	Cinirot f. Luitru (19)	Ciniath f. Lutrin (19)	Cinhoint f.Luitriu(19)
Garnard f. Wid (4)	Gartnait mac muit (5)	Gartnait mac Uuid (5)	Gartnairt mac Uiud (5)
Breidei f. Wid (5)	Tolorc fr. eorom (12)	Talorc fr. eorum (12)	Tolorc fr. Eorum (12)
Talore fr. eorum (12)	Tolorcan f. Enfreit (4)	Talorcan f. Enfret (4)	Tolorcan f. Enfret (4)
Talorcen f. Enfret (4)	Gartnaid f. Donuel (6.5)	Gartnait f. Donuel (6.5)	Gartnait f.Donuel(6.5)
Gartnait f. Donuel (6)	Druisc [fr-] eius (6)	Drust fr. eius (7)	Drusc fr. eius (7)
	Tarun f. Enfidaigh (4)	Bruide f. File (21)	Bride f. File (20)
	Bruidi f. Fili (20)		Taran f. Enfidaid (4)
Drest fr. ejus (7)	Brei f. Deirilei (11)	Taran f. Enfidaig (4)	Brei f. Deirilei (11)
Bredei f. Bili (21)	Neactan f. Deirilei (10)	Brei f. Derelei (11)	Nechtan f.Deirile(10)
Taran f. Entifidich(4)	Dreeist and Elpin (5)	Nechtan f. Derilei (10)	Drest and Elpen (5)
Bredei f. Derelei (11)	Onuis f. Urgust (30)	Drest et Elpin (5)	Onbes f. Urgurt (30)
Necthon f. Derelei (15)	Breit fin Nurgut (15)	Onuis f. Urguist (30)	Breite f. Uugut (15)
Drest et Elpin (5)	Ciniod Iuireidig (12)	Brete Uugut (15)	Ciniod f.Iuuredeg(15?)
Onuist(?) f.Vrguist(30)	Alpin f. Uroid (3)	Ciniod f. Uuredeg (12)	Alpin f. Uuoid (3.5)
Bredei f. Wirguist (2)	Tolorcein f. Dru (5?)	Elpin f. Uuroid (3.5)	Drest f. Tolorcan (1)
Ciniod f. Wredech (12)	Tolorgein f. Umust(12.5)	Drest f. Talorcen (1)	Talorcan f.Drostan(5?)
Elpin f. Wroid (3)	Canul f. Tanng (5)	Talorgen f.Druisten(4/5)	Talorcen f.Omust(12.5)
Drest f. Talorgen (4)	Cusantin f. Uurguist(35)	Talorcen f.Oinuist(12.5)	Canul f. Tan[n]g (5)
Talorgen f. Onuist (2)	Uidhmuisc f. Nugust (12)	Canaul f. Tang (5)	Cuastantin f.Uurguist(35)
Canaul f. Tarl'a (5)	Dreist f. Constantin and Tolorc f. Nutmol (3)	Caustantin f.Uurguist(35)	Uidnust f. Uurgust(11)
Castantin f.Wrguist(35)	Unen f. Unes (3)	Uidnuist f.Uurguist (12)	Drost f. Consatin and Tolorc f. Uuthoil(3)
Vnuist f. Wrguist (12)	Uread Bargoid (3)	Drest f. Constantin et Talorc f. Uuthoil (3)	Unen f. Unest (3)
Drest f. Constantini et Talorgen f. Wthoil(3)	Bred (1)	Unen f. Unuist (3)	Urad f. Bargoit (3)
Vuen f. Vnuist (3)	Cinaedh f. Alpin (16)	Uurad f. Bargoit (3)	Brot (1)
Wrad f. Bargoit (3)	Domnall f. Ailpin (3)	Bred (1)	Cinaed f. Ailpin (16)
Bred (1)	Cusantin f. Cinaed (20)	Cinaed f. Alpin (4)	Domnall f. Alpin (4)
[SL1 ends]	Aed f. Cinaedh (1)	Domnall f. Alpin (4)	Custan[ti]n f. Cinaeda(20)
		Custantin f. Cinaed (20)	Aed f. Cinaed (1)
		Aed f. Cinaeda (1)	

List D	List F1	List F2	List I
Drust f. Ws (100)	Drust f. Urb (100)	Drust f. Irb (100)	Drust f. Yrb (100)
Tolarag f. Anuf (2)	Talarg f. Amil (2)	Tholarg f. Amile (2)	Tolarg f. Anul (2)
Rechan chelemot (10)	Nethan Thelcamot (10)	Netthan thelcamoth (10)	Nectan celchamoch(10)
Drust f. Gurum (5)	Drust Gormot (30)	Durst gernot (30)	Drest gocineht (30)
Drust f. Hudrossig (8)	Galam (15)	Gulam (25)	Galany (15)
iterum primus Drust (4)	Drust f. Gigurum (5)	Drust f. Gigurum (5)	Drust f. Gygurn (6)
Ganach f. Gigurum (6)	Drust f. Hydrossig (8)	Drust f. Hudresseg (8)	Frust f. Hudrosig (8)
Kelturam fr. eius (6)	Ganut f. Gigurum (6)	Ganat f. Gigurum (6)	Gauach f. Gygurn (6)
Tolorg f. Mordeleg (11)	Kelturan fr. ejus (6)	Kelturan fr. ejus (6)	Kelturan fr. eius (6)
Durst f. Moneth (1)	Golorg f. Mordeleg (12)	Golorg f. Madoleg (11)	Tolorg f.Murdeleg(11)
Talalad (4)	Drust f. Moneth (1)	Drust f. Moneth (1)	Drust f. Monehet (1)
Brud f. Methon (30)	Tagalad (4)	Tagaled (4)	Tagalad (4)
Carnac f. Dornach' (20)	Brude f. Melchon (30)	Brude f. Melchon (30)	Brude f. Melcon (30)
Kynel f. Luchren (24)	Garnat f. Domnach (20)	Gernerd f. Dompneth(20)	Sauiach f. Donath(20)
Nechan f. Fide (8)	Nethan f. Ub (21)	Necthad f. Irb (21)	Nact'an f. Yrb (21)
Brude f. Fruch (5)	Kinel f. Luthren (14)	Kinet f. Luthren (14)	Kynel f. Kuchrem (14)
Tollarg f. Fechar (11)	Nectan f. Fottle (5)	Nectan f. Fotle (5)	Nact'am f. Fochle (8)
Talargan f. Amfrud (4)	Brude f. Fathe (5)	Brude f. Fathe (5)	Brude f. Fochle (5)
Cornach f. Dunal (5)	Telarg f. Fetobar (11)	Tolerg f. Fetebar (11)	Tolarg f.Fecharus(11)
Durst fr. Eius (6)	Talargan f. Amfrude (5)	Thalargan f. Confrud(4)	Talargan f. Aufrud(4)
Brud f. Bile (20)	Garnat f. Domnal (5)	Garnard f. Donnall (5)	Garcuad f. Domnal (6)
Taran f. Amfredech (14)	Drust fr. ejus (6)	Drust fr. ejus (6)	Drust fr. eius (6)
Nectan fr. Eius (18)	Brude f. Bile (21)	Brude f. Bile (21)	Brude f. Bile (21)
Brud f. Dergard (31)	Taram f. Amfredech (14)	Turan f. Amsedeth (14)	Taran f. Anfudeg (14)
Carnach f. Ferach' (24)	Brude f. Derili (31)	Brude f. Decili (31)	Brude f. Detili (31)
Onegussa f. Frud (6)	Nectan fr. ejus (18)	Ferthen fr. ejus (18)	Nett'an fr. eius (18)
Alpin f. Feret	Garnath f. Ferath (24)	Garnath f. Ferath (24)	Garnach f. Ferach(24)
Brud f. Denegus (8)	Oengusa f. Fergusa (16)	Oengusu f. Ferguse (16)	Oengusa f. Fergus(16)
Durst f. Talargagani (1)	Nethan f. Derili (9m.)	Netthan f. Decili (9m.)	Nectan f. Derili(9m.)
Thalargane f. Drustan (4)	Alpin f. Feret (6m.)	Alpin f. Feret (6m.)	Oengus f. Brude (6m.)
Falagan f. Denegus (5)	Oengus f. Brude (6m.)	Oengussa f. Brude (6m.)	Alpinus f. Engus (8)
Constantinus	idem iterum (36)	idem iterum (36)	Drust f. Tarlagan (5)
f. Fergusari (45)	Brude f. Tenegus (8)	Brude f. Tonegus (8)	Himgus f. Fergus (10)
Hungus f. Fergusane (9)	Drust f. Talargan (1)	Durst f. Talergan (1)	Engus f. Brude
			iterum(36)
Dostolorg (4)	Talargan f. Drustan (4)	Talargan f. Drustan (4)	Brude f. Engus (2)
Cogana f. Hungus (3)	Talargan f. Tenegus (5)	Talargan f. Tenegus (5)	Alpin f. Engus (8)
Fergus f. Barot (3)	Constantin f. Fergusa(42)	Constantinus	Drust f. Talargan (1)
Brude f. Ferant (1m.)	Hungus f. Fergusa (10)	f. Fergusa (42)	Talargan f.Drustan(4)
Kynat f. Ferant (1)	Dustalorg (4)	Hungus f. Fergusa (20)	Talargan f. Engus (5)
Brud f. Fodel (2)	Eoganan f. Hungus (3)	Drustilorg (4)	Constantinus
			f.Fergus(42)
Durst f. Ferant (3)	Ferat f. Batot (3)	Coganan f. Hungus (3)	Himgus f. Fergus (10)
Kynat mac Alpin (16)	Brude f. Ferat (1m.)	Ferat f. Batot (3)	Dustalorg (4)
Douenald macAlpin (4)	Kinat f. Ferat (1m.)	Brunde f. Ferat (1m.)	Doganan f. Himge (3)
Constantinus macKynat(15)	Brude f. Fotel (2)	Kinat f. Ferat (1)	Ferach f. Bacoc (3)
Edh macKynnath (1)	Drust f. Ferat (3)	Brude f. Fetal (2)	Brude f. Ferech (1)
	Kinath Mac-Alpin (16)	Drust f. Ferat (3)	Kineth f. Ferech (1)
	Dovenald Mac-Alpin (4)	Kinart mac Alpin (4)	Brude f. Fokel (2)
	Constantin Mac-Kinath(16)	Douenall macalpin (4)	Drust f. Ferech (3)
	Ed Mac-Kinet (1)	Constantinus	[Picts End.
		mackinet (16)	Scots follow]
		Edh Mackinet (1)	Kineth f. Alpin (16)
			Douenald f. Alpin (4)
			Constantinus
			f.Kineth (16)
			Edh f. Kineth (1)

List K	Fordun's List
Drust fitz Irb (100)	Durst f. Irbii (45)
Talarg fitz Amil (2)	Thalarg f. Anile (2)
Nectane Celtanieth (10)	Nectane chalcamoch (10)
Drust Gortinoch (30)	Durst gornoth (30)
Galan (15)	Galaam (15)
Drust fitz Gigurnus (50)	Durst f. Gigurum (5)
Drust fitz Hirofigus (8)	Durst f. Othred (8)
Autrefoitz le primer Drust(4)	Durst f. Gigurum (4)
Garnard' fitz Gigurnus (6)	Garnard f. Gigurum (6)
Kyburcan soun freir (6)	frater eius Kelturan (6)
Talarg fitz Mendelegh' (11)	Tholorg f. Mordeleth (11)
Drust fitz Menech (1)	Durst f. Moneth (1)
Tagalach (4)	Thalagath (4)
Drust fitz Methor (30)	Brud f. Merlochon (19)
Garnald fitz Dompnach (30)	Garnard f. Dampnach (20)
Kenech fitz Sugthen (24)	Nectane f. Irb (11)
Nectan fitz Fode (8)	Kenel f. Luchtren (14)
Bride fitz Fathe (5)	Nectane f. Fode (8)
Drust soun Freir (6)	Brude f. Fachna (5)
Drust fitz Hole (20)	Thalarg' f. Farchar (11)
Tharan fitz Amfodech (4)	Talargan f. Amfrud (4)
Brude fitz Degert (31)	Garnard f. Dompnal (5)
Jactan frer Brude (18)	frater eius Durst (6)
Garnard' fitz Feradhegh (24)	Brud f. Bile (11)
Denegul fitz Fergusagin (16)	Gharan f. Amfedeth (4)
Nectan Fitz Fergaleg (9)	Brud f. Decili (21)
Fergus fitz Frude (1m.)	frater eius Nactane (18)
Alpin fitz Eferadhech' (6m.)	Garnard f. Feredach (14)
Brude fitz Tenegus (2)	Oengussa f. Fergusa (16)
Alpin fitz Tenagus (2)	Nectane f. Dereli (9m.)
Drust fitz Talargbin (1)	Oengussa f. Brude (6m.)
Talargan fitz Drustane (4)	Alpyn f. Feredeth (6m.)
Talargan fitz Tenagus (5)	Alpinus iterum (26)
Costantin fitz Fersusa (40)	Brude f. Tenegus (2)
Hungus fitz Fergusa (10)	Alpini f. Tenegus (2)
Duf Tolorg (4)	Thalarg' f. Drusken (4)
Egganus fitz Hungus (3)	Thalarg' f. Tenegus (5)
Feradagus fitz Badogh' (3)	Constantinus f. Fergusa(40)
Brud fitz Feradhach (1m.)	Hungus f. Fergus' (10)
Kenech fitz Feradhach (1)	Durstolorg' (4)
Brude fitz Fochel (2)	Eoghane f. Hungus (3)
Drust fitz Feradhach (3)	Feredeth f. Badoc (3)
Kynet fitz Alpin (16)	Brude f. Feredeth (1m.)
Donald fitz Alpin (4)	Keneth f. Feredeth (1)
Costantin fitz Kynath' (16)	Brude f. Fothel (2)
Ath' mak Kinath (1)	Drusken f. Feredeth (3)

APPENDIX IV

Pictish Names and Their Possible Equivalents[2]

(This chart is a reference guide and not intended to be exhaustive.)

Pictish	Brittonic	Gaulish	Gaelic	Gaelicized	Derived From
Alpin, Elpin	Elffin,				
Ailpin?	Elpin				Albinus?
Artcois, Arcois					*Artocoxos?
Bridei, Bre(i)dei			Bruide,		
Bred			Brude		*Brodios
					*Wroican?
					*Uroican?,
Broichan			Froichan?	*Uroichan?	Vroichan?
Ciniod, Cinaed?			Cinaed		
Custantin					
Constantin	Custennhin		Causantín		Constantinus
Drest			Drust	Druist	
	*Drosten,				
	*Dristen,				
	Drystan,				
Drosten, Drostan	Trystan			Druistan	Drustagnos
Emchath, *Amcat	Ammecatus	Ambicatus	Imchath	Emchatus	
Gartnait,					
Gartnart, Gartnat					
Lutrin	*Loutrin				*Lugutrinos
Mailcon, Maelcon,					
Meilochon	Maelgwn		Malchon (gen.)		Maglocunos
Nechton, Nehhton,					
Nehton, *Neiton,					
Naiton	Neithon		Nechtan		
Onuist, Unuist			óengus, Aengus	óengus?	*Oinogustos
Simul	Hywel?				
Talorg, Talorc,					
Talorgg	Tallwch?				
Talorgen, Talorgan,					
Talorcan, Talorcen					
Talorggan	*Talorgan				*Talorgagnos
Tarain, Tarachin					Taranis
Uipoig namet					Uepogenus?
Ulfa, Ulpha					Ulpius?
			Eoganan,		
Uuen			Iogenan		
Uuid, Wid	Gwid, Ueda			Foith	
Uurad, Wrad	Uoret?			Ferad	*Vo-retos?
Urgest	*Gworwrst,				
Uurguist	Gorwst,		Forggus		
Wirguist, Wurgest	Gwrst		Forcus		*Ver-gustos
Uuredeg, Uuradech			Feradach	Uuradech?	*Uuradec

APPENDIX V

Picts and the *Anglo-Saxon Chronicle*

The *Anglo-Saxon Chronicle* is a West Saxon chronological history which dates from the ninth century but may have originated in the eighth. It is similar to the Irish Annals, which are the source for some of its early events.[3] It exists in eight main manuscripts known as A, A[2] (also, G or W), B, C, D, E, F, and H. These range from the ninth through twelfth centuries.[4] It contains some references to the Picts; however, as it is not a Celtic text and does not mention any Picts by name, it was not included in the main body of this work. Nevertheless, its historical importance dictates that the relevant entries be cited here.

Preface or **Introduction** (D, E) states that Pictish was one of the five languages of Britain. It also states that the Picts came from Scythia and received wives from the Scots in return for the sovereignty of the female line.[5] This passage is adapted from Bede.[6]

47[43] (D, E) records that Emperor Claudius (41-54)[7] came to Britain and subjugated the Picts and Welsh.[8]

443 (A, E) mentions that the Britons asked the Romans for help against the Picts. However, the Romans were occupied fighting the Huns, and the Britons then requested aid of the Angles.[9]

449 (A, C, E) records that Vortigern invited the Angles to Britain to help fight the Picts. They arrived in three ships and were led by Hengest and Horsa.[10]

565 (A, E, F) states that Columba converted the Picts, whose king gave him Iona. The abbot of Iona was to have control of the bishops of the Scots. It also records that Ninian had previously converted the southern Picts.[11]

597 (A, B, C, E) mentions that Ceolwulf, king of Wessex (597-611),[12] fought against the Picts, Angles, Welsh, and Scots.[13]

681 (E, F) records that Trumwine became bishop of the Picts (apparently "Wihtum" (Isle of Wight) in E).[14]

685 (A, B, C, E) records that Ecgfrith was killed "north of the sea" (Firth of Forth) but does not mention the Picts or Dún Nechtain.[15]

699 (D, E) states that Bertred was killed by the Picts.[16]

709 (C) and **710** (A, D, E) mention that Bertfrid fought the Picts.[17]

875[874] (A, B, D, E) and **876** (C) record that Halfdan, brother of Ivarr,[18] attacked the Picts and Strathclyde Britons.[19]

5

PERSONAL NAMES ASSOCIATED WITH THE PICTS

Biographical and Textual Notes

Note: The use of letters **a**, **ae**, **ai**, **ao**, **e**, **o**, and **oe**; **e**, **i**, **o**, **u**, and **ui**; **c**, **d**, **g**, **k**, and **t**; and **f**, **u**, **uu**, **v**, and **w** varies in texts according to time period and provenance. **Cruithni**, **Picts**, and **Scots** are not cross-referenced. See Chapter 6 for Population and Place Names.

        Adomnán (c.624/28-704). Ninth Abbot of Iona and author of *Vita Columbae* ("Life of Columba") (see **Columba**).[1]
        Book of Leinster includes the poem "Scrín Adomnáin" ("Shrine of Adomnán") ascribed to Adomnán. Adomnán is included in "Mothers of Irish Saints," where the genealogy of his mother Ronnat is listed and he is the son of Rónán.[2]
        AI 625 record Adomnán's birth. AT 624 mistakes his birth for his death. AU 624 and CS 624 record his birth. AT 687, AC 682 mentions that he took sixty captives to Ireland (**q.v.**). AFM 684 records that he brought captives from the northern Saxons (**q.v.**). CS 684 mentions his taking of the captives to Ireland. AT 692 and CS 688 say that Adomnán went to Ireland. AI 696, AT 697, AU 697, and CS 693 record the institution of his *Cáin Adamnáin* (or "Law of the Innocents"). ACam. 704, AI 704, AT 704, AC 700, AU 704, AFM 703, and CS 700 record Adomnán's death.
        Lists D, F1, F2, and K seem to state that Adomnán lived during the reign of Bredei f. Bili (**q.v.**). Lists which refer to Adomnán belong to the group of lists which Marjorie Anderson calls Pictish List Q and not to Pictish List P.[3]
        In *Life of Servanus*, Servanus visits Adomnán in Scotland and encounters Picts. *Félire Óengusso* lists him under 23 September and states that he freed the women of the Gaels, an allusion to his *Cáin Adomnáin*. *Martyrology of Tallaght* (Lein.) lists him under ".IX. KL- OCTIMBIR." (23 September).[4]
        Bede discusses how Adomnán convinced Irish churches to use the

the Roman Easter. He also describes Adomnán's book *On the Holy Places.*
Regarding Adomnán's relation to the Picts, Bede only gives a tenuous link
through the letter which Ceolfrith (**q.v.**) sent to Necthon f. Derelei (**q.v.**).
Ceolfrith states that Adomnán was instrumental in introducing the Roman
Easter and tonsure when he returned to Scotland.[5]

   Áed Dub (d.588). King of the Irish Cruithni dynasty of Dál n-Araide
(**q.v.**). Son of Suibne Araide.[6]
   AI 564, AU 565, and AFM 558 record that Áed Dub killed Diarmait
mac Cerbaill at Ráith Bec. AU 588 says that Áed Dub was killed in a ship.
AFM 592 states that Áed Dub was killed without naming the place.
   Adomnán states that Áed Dub was of the race of the Cruithni and was
brought to Britain (**q.v.**) by Findchán (**q.v.**) as a pilgrim after having murdered
Diarmait mac Cerbaill and others. Columba (**q.v.**) foretold at Áed's ordination
that Áed Dub would return to his violent ways and be slain by a spear aboard a
ship.[7]

   Áed Find mac Domongairt m. Domnaill. King of Scots Dál Riata
(**q.v.**) (c.748-78).[8]
   Rawl. B. 502 and *Book of Leinster* list Áed Find in a genealogy of the
kings of Alba (**q.v.**), where he is an ancestor of Cináed mac Alpín (**q.v.**) and a
descendant of Áedán mac Gabráin (**q.v.**) and Fergus Mór (**q.v.**).[9]
   AU 768 records a battle in Fortriu (**q.v.**) between Áed and Ciniod f.
Uuredech (**q.v.**). AI 778 records the death of "Áed m. m. Fergaile." This
seems to correspond to the date of the death of Áed Find. However, Seán Mac
Airt indicates that this entry is an error for "Niall (Frosach), son of Fergal" as is
recorded in AU 778. Interestingly, the death of Áed Find is also recorded in
this same entry. This could indicate that the AI entry was contracted from a
longer original. However, this is speculative. AFM 771 mentions his death.
   Áed Find is given a thirty year reign between Eogan/Ewen mac
Muiredaich and Fergus mac Echdach (called "Fergus son of Áed Find") in Lists
D, F1, F2, and I. List N repeats this and adds that he was killed.[10]
   Duan Albanach seems to give Áed a thirty year reign between
Muiredach mac Ainbcellaich (see **Ainbcellach (& son)**) and Domnall mac
Causantín.[11] However, this disagrees with the Regnal Lists.

   Áed mac Cináeda m. Alpín (Áed son of Kenneth). King of Scots
(877-8).[12]
   Áed is son of Cináed mac Alpín (**q.v.**) in *Book of Leinster.*[13]
AU 878 calls Áed "rex Pictorum" ("king of Picts") and states that he was
murdered by his comrades. CS 904 records the killing of an "Ead, king of
Pictland" (see **Pictland**) by the grandsons of Ívarr (**q.v.**) and by Caitil. W.M.
Hennessy thinks that this could be the same Áed and that the entry could

simply be misplaced. However, A.O. Anderson thinks that this "Ead" may have ruled part of Pictland either before Causantín mac Áeda (900-43) or as his appointee. He also remarks that "Ead" is similar to the Irish form of Æthelweald of Northumbria which Anderson translates as "Eadulf."[14] In AU 913 this king's name is given as "Etulbb."

Áed is mentioned in Regnal Lists SL2 M, SL2 O, and SL2 H as having reigned for one year between Causantín mac Cináeda (**q.v.**) and Giric (**q.v.**). Lists D, F1, F2, and I repeat this and say that Giric killed Áed in a battle at Strathallan and that Áed was buried on Iona. List K repeats this but only mentions that Giric killed him without mentioning the battle or Áed's burial place.[15] The evidence of the Regnal Lists seems to indicate that the "Ead" of CS is not the same as Áed mac Cináeda.

Áedán mac Gabráin m. Domongairt. King of Scots Dál Riata (574-608) who may have had a Pictish wife.[16]

Rawl. B. 502 mentions Áedán in a poem and lists him in a genealogy of kings of Alba (**q.v.**) as an ancestor of Eochaid Buide (**q.v.**). *Book of Leinster* mentions Áedán in a genealogy of Laigin (**q.v.**) as son of Eochaid mac Muiredaig and his wife Feidelm and brother of Brandub. This is an alternative Irish genealogy for Áedán, who may have had a British mother and a grandfather who was king of Strathclyde. It also mentions that Áedán became a hostage of Báetán mac Cairill of Dál Fiataich after Báetán had conquered Manu (**q.v.**). However, the Dál Fiataich left Manu after Báetán's death. This may refer to Isle of Man (**q.v.**), which Áedán may have retaken from the Dál Fiataich. Áedán is also mentioned in a genealogy of kings of Alba between Gabrán mac Domongairt and Eochaid Buide. *Jes. 20* mentions that Luan daughter of Brachan was Áedan's mother. *Book of Lecan* mentions Áedán in a similar poem as in *Rawl. B. 502*. *Laud 610* mentions Áedán's conquest of Manu. *Bonhed Gwyr y Gogled yv Hyn* ("Descent of the Men of the North") calls him "Gauran m. Aedan Uradavc" and a descendant of Maximus (**q.v.**).[17]

In AU 580 and AU 581 Orc (**q.v.**) is recorded as having been invaded. The 580 entry mentions Áedán as the invader; however, the 581 entry does not mention Áedán. AI 583, AT 582, AT 583(?), AC 504, AU 504, and AU 583 record that Áedán won the Battle of Manu. This is most likely the battle mentioned in the genealogies. AC 587 records that Áedán met Áed mac Ainmerech and Columba (**q.v.**) at Druim Cett. Áedán is mentioned as the victor at Leithri in AT 590, AC 590, and AU 590. AT also says that Áedán won the battles of Circhend (**q.v.**) and Corann in 596. AT 600 states that Áedán was defeated in a battle against Saxons (**q.v.**) in which Eanfrith, brother of Æthelfrith (**q.v.**) was killed. In AC 603 Áedán's battle against Saxons is recorded; however, Áedán is called the victor. In AU 600 Áedán's defeat by Saxons is recorded without naming specific foes. ACam 607, AI 609, AT 606, AC 604, AU 606, and CS 606 record Áedán's death.

In Regnal Lists D, F1, and F2, Áedán is given a reign-length of thirty-four years after Conall mac Comgaill and before Eochaid Buide. List I mentions that Áedán fought the battle of Degsastan in 513. Degsastan was probably in 603 and is recorded in AT 600, AC 603, AU 600 (see **Æthelfrith** and **Cadfred**). The list places Áedán between Gabrán mac Domongairt and Eochaid Buide with a thirty-four year reign. List K records that Áedán reigned for thirty-four years between "Constan fiz Doengard" (Gabrán mac Domongairt?) and Conall mac Comgaill. List N places him between Conall and Eochaid Buide and is given a reign of thirty-three years.[18]

In *Vita Columbae*, the monks of Iona (**q.v.**) pray for Áedán's victory over the Miathi (**q.v.**). This may have been Manu of the Genealogies and Annals or Circhend. Columba instituted Áedán as king and predicted that his sons Artuir (Artúr), Eochaid Find, and Domingart (Domongart) would die in battle and that Eochaid Buide would succeed Áedán. *Martyrology of Tallaght* (Lein.) lists Áedán under ".XU. KL- MAII." (17 April).[19]

Y Gododdin mentions an "Aedan" as part of Mynyddawg's retinue. This may be Áedán mac Gabráin, but this is uncertain. *Senchus Fer nAlban* calls Áedán one of five sons of Gabrán and father of seven sons. In *Duan Albanach* Áedán is given a twenty-four year reign between Conall son of Comgall and Eochaid Buide. Áedán features in *Scéla Cano* as a contender for the kingship of Alba (**q.v.**) against Gartnán mac Áeda maic Gabráin (see **Gartnait f. Accidan** and **Gartnart f. Domelch**). *Welsh Triads* call Áedán "Gauran mab Aedan" and is among "Tri Diweir Deulu Enys Prydein." Rachel Bromwich says that it was common for early Welsh records to confuse Áedán with his father.[20]

Ælfflæd (7th-8th cent.). Abbess of Whitby and sister of Ecgfrith (**q.v.**) and daughter of Oswiu (**q.v.**).[21]

AU 713 record's Ælfflæd's death but simply calls her "Filia Ossu" ("daughter of Oswiu").

Anonymous Cuthbert remarks that Ælfflæd was visited by Cuthbert, who predicted that her brother Ecgfrith would be succeeded as king by Aldfrith (**q.v.**) who was then on Iona (**q.v.**). In this same work Cuthbert predicts the death of a member of Ælfflæd's household. In *Bede's Cuthbert*, Cuthbert's girdle heals Ælfflæd. Bede also relates the same prediction regarding Ecgfrith. To this version Bede adds that Ecgfrith was killed by the Picts in battle (see **Dún Nechtain**). Bede also recounts the story of the death of the member of Ælfflæd's household. *Life of Wilfrid* states that Theodore, archbishop of Canterbury, wrote to Ælfflæd requesting that she obey Wilfrid (**q.v.**). Ælfflæd gave an account of Aldfrith's death. She was also present at the Synod of Nidd (706), which determined that Wilfrid be restored to his former powers after they had been previously taken from him.[22]

Bede mentions that Trumwine (**q.v.**) visited Ælfflæd and her mother at their monastery.[23]

Ælfwine (d.679). Son of Oswiu (**q.v.**).[24]

AT 680, AU 680, and CS 676 state that Ælfwine was killed in the "Battle of the Saxons."

Life of Wilfrid records that Ælfwine had died a year after Wilfrid had been removed from office at the instigation of Ecgfrith (**q.v.**) and his wife Iuminburgh.[25]

Bede records that Ælfwine was killed in a battle between his brother Ecgfrith (**q.v.**) and Æthelred of Mercia near the river Trent. *Historia Brittonum* says that Ælfwine was son of Oswiu and brother of Ecgfrith, who was killed by Picts.[26]

Aenbegan (Oenbecan). Mythological king of the Picts.

In Legends P#L(Uí Ma.), P#L(Lec.), P#L(Bal.), P#L(1336), P#L(1295), and P#L(G47), Aenbegan is called son of Cat (**q.v.**) and is given control of the seven regions of Alba (**q.v.**) or the far-north of Britain (**q.v.**).

Regnal List SL1 records that Aenbegan had a reign of one hundred years between Géde Ollgothach (**q.v.**) and Olfinecta (**q.v.**). Lists SL2 M and SL2 H give him a reign of one year between Olfinecta and Guided gaed brechach (**q.v.**). In List SL3(Lec.3), Aenbegan is listed after "b. Gant" and before "b. Urgant" (see **Brude (30)**). List SL3(Lec.1) records for Aenbegan a reign of five years in the same position. List SL3(Lec.4) seems to give Aenbegan a one year reign between the same two kings. SL3(Bal.2) lists Aenbegan between "B. Uleo" and "B. Urgant," and SL3(Bal.1) places him between "Gant" and "Urgant." These last five lists intersperse the thirty "Brudes" amongst the other kings, thereby creating a confused chronology.[27]

M.O. Anderson believes the "Oenbecan" form of Aenbegan's name to be Irish rather than Pictish, which would have "On-" or "Un-." This idea came from Kenneth Jackson who cites the difference between the Gaelic "Óengus" and Pictish "Onuist."[28]

Æthelfrith. King of Northumbria and Bernicia (592/93-616/617).[29]

In AT 600 the death of Æthelfrith's brother, Eanfrith (see **Cadfred**), is recorded as having occurred in battle against Áedán mac Gabráin (**q.v.**). Stokes sees this name as a mistake for Theobald. Eanfrith (**q.v.**) was the name of Æthelfrith's son. This was probably Degsastan in 603. Æthelfrith is named as the victor at Caerleon against the Britons (**q.v.**). It also says that he died shortly afterwards. This battle was most likely Chester fought c.613.[30] In AC 603 the battle against Áedán is again recorded including the death of Æthelfrith's brother. AC 613 mentions the battle against the Britons. Æthelfrith killed the British king and then died immediately. In AU 600 the battle against Áedán is recorded, but neither Æthelfrith nor his brother is named. Again Æthelfrith is absent from the account of Caerleon in AU 613. He is called the father of Oswiu (**q.v.**) in AU 671 and CS 667.

Bede mentions the military exploits of Æthelfrith and his cruelty

towards the Britons.   He discusses Degsastan and records the death of
Theobald, Æthelfrith's brother.   Caerleon/Chester is extensively recalled.   In a
vision given to Edwin (d.633) (**q.v**), Æthelfrith persuades Rædwald, king of the
Angles (see **Angles/English**), to kill Edwin.   While Edwin was king, the sons
of Æthelfrith were exiled among Scots and Picts.   In *Historia Brittonum*,
Æthelfrith is father of seven sons and is given a reign of twelve years in
Bernicia and twelve years in Deira.   Geoffrey of Monmouth names Æthelfrith
as king of Northumbria and recalls his attacks upon the Britons.[31]

  Æthelwulf. King of Wessex (c.839-58).[32]
  AU 858 records the death of Æthelwulf.
  Fordun's List calls Æthelwulf's son Athelstan (**q.v.**) the contemporary
of Unuist f. Urguist (**q.v.**).[33]

  Agathyrsus (Agatheris). Mythological Pictish ancestor.
  In   Legends   P#L(Uí   Ma.),   P#L(Lec.),   P#L(Bal.),   P#L(1336),
P#L(1295), and P#L(G47), Agathyrsus is amongst the ancestors of the family
of Gelon (**q.v.**). Agathyrsus seems to be the ancestor of the Agathyrsi (**q.v.**), a
population name in some of the Origin Legends.

  Agnaman. Irish mythological figure. He is father of Nemed (**q.v.**).[34]
  In   Legends   P#L(Uí   Ma.),   P#L(Lec.),   P#L(G47),   P#L(Bal.),
P#L(1336), and P#L(1295), Agnaman is mentioned as an ancestor of Cruithne
(**q.v.**) and son of Buan (**q.v.**).
  In *Rawl. B. 502* Agnaman is included in a section relating to the
Laigin (**q.v.**).   Here he is called son of Tóe and grandson of Buan ("Banb").
Mac Firbis's Genealogies call Agnaman father of Nemed.[35]
  AC calls Agnaman (Agamemnon) the father of Nemed.[36]
  Agnaman is ancestor of Cruithne, son of Buan, and father of Pairte
(Partholon?) (**q.v.**) in SL3(Lec.1), SL3(Lec.3), SL3(Lec.4), SL3(Bal.1), and
SL3(Bal.2).[37]
  Historia Brittonum records that Nemed, son of Agnaman, came to
Ireland after Pairte (Partholon?).[38]

  Aigine. Pictish ancestor.
  In Legends P#L(Uí ma.), P#L(Lec.), P#L(G47), P#L(1336), and
P#L(1295), Aigine is son of Agathyrsus (**q.v.**) and father of Istorine (**q.v.**).

  Ainbcellach (& son) (Ainfcellach).   King of Scots Dál Riata (**q.v.**)
(c.697-698).[39]
  AU 698 mentions that Ainbcellach was expelled from his kingship and
taken to Ireland (**q.v.**). AT 719 and AU 719 record that Ainbcellach was killed
at Findglenn. In AU 736 Ainbcellach's son is pursued by Talorgan (d. 750)
(**q.v.**) after Cnoc Cairpri (**q.v.**) fought between Dál Riata and Fortriu (**q.v.**).

Aldfrith (Flann Fína mac Ossu/Gossa). Son of Oswiu (**q.v.**) and king of Northumbria (685-705).[40]

Rawl. B 502 calls Aldfrith ("Flann") son of Oswiu and Fína, daughter of Colmán Rímid, who is one of five sons of Báetán mac Muirchertaich. *Book of Lecan* and *Laud 610* give Aldfrith the same pedigree without mentioning Oswiu.[41]

ACam. 704 seems to record the death of Aldfrith, "king of the Saxons" (see **Saxons**). AI 705 mentions the death of Aldfrith ("Flann"). AT 704 records Aldfrith's death and calls him "Altfrith" and "Fland Fína" and calls him wise. AC 700 and AU 704 also mention his death.

Vita Columbae relates that Adomnán (**q.v**) visited Aldfrith during terrible plague. In *Anonymous Cuthbert*, Cuthbert (**q.v.**) predicts that Aldfrith, who is living on Iona (**q.v.**), will succeed his brother Ecgfrith (**q.v.**). Also Cuthbert heals the wife of one of Aldfrith's companions. *Bede's Cuthbert* also relates Cuthbert's prediction about Aldfrith's succession. and remarks that the prediction came true when Ecgfrith was killed by Picts. *Life of Wilfrid* mentions that Aldfrith became king after Ecgfrith's killing by Picts (see **Dún Nechtain**). Aldfrith was asked by Theodore, archbishop of Canterbury, to reinstate Wilfrid. However, Aldfrith banished Wilfrid from Northumbria. Eventually, Pope John VI wrote to Aldfrith and Æthelred of Mercia requesting that a synod be held to settle Wilfrid's situation. Wilfrid sent representatives to Aldfrith, who would not be reconciled with Wilfrid. Aldfrith died before the commencement of the Synod of Nidd, which finally restored Wilfrid.[42]

Bede makes several references to Aldfrith. He describes the events leading to Aldfrith's succession and says that he reigned for nineteen years. Bede also relates how Aldfrith requested that a resurrected man be admitted to a monastery. Adomnán visited Aldfrith in order to observe the religious practices and return to Iona and change any uncanonical observances. Adomnán gave Aldfrith a copy of his book *On the Holy Places*. Bede records that Aldfrith died in 705 and was succeeded by his eight year old son Osred. Pope John VI wrote to Aldfrith requesting that the bishop Wilfrid, who had been wrongly expelled by Aldfrith, be returned to his diocese. Bede relates that Aldfrith would not do this during the remainder of his reign. *Historia Brittonum* does not list Aldfrith among the kings of Northumbria and the Angles but mentions three other sons of Oswiu.[43]

Alpia (7th cent.). Mother of Servanus (Serf) (**q.v.**).[44]

In *Life of Servanus* Alpia is called daughter of the king of Arabia and wife of Obeth.[45]

In *Book of Uí Maine, Book of Lecan,* and *Book of Ballymote*, the mother (Alma) of Servanus is daughter of the king of the Cruithni (Picts?).[46]

Alpín f. Eochaid (Alpín mac Echdach).   King of Scots Dál Riata **(q.v.)** (c.839).   Father of Cináed mac Alpín **(q.v.)**.   He was sometimes confused with Elpín (c.728) **(q.v.)**.[47]

Alpín f. Eochaid appears in neither the Genealogies nor the Annals. This omission is unusual considering that other Dál Riatan kings are mentioned in them.

Regnal List D gives Alpín f. Eochaid a three year reign between Dúngal mac Selbaich **(q.v.)** and the kingship of the Picts. This could be Elpín (c.728) because Dúngal ruled 723-6. The chronology of the list is confused because it places the Picts after the Scots and has contemporary kings live at different times. The appearance of Dúngal's contemporary Necthon f. Derelei **(q.v.)** as "Nectan frater eius" in the second half of the Pictish kings clearly shows this. List F1 gives the same account of this king. The same is true of List F2 except for a five year reign. This is probably Elpín (c.728). Yet, only one king resembling "Alpin f. Eochaid" is mentioned in these lists. This could indicate that both "Alpíns" were assumed to be the same regardless of the chronology. M.O. Anderson believes that Alpín f. Eochaid was "telescoped" with Elpín (c.728). List I gives Alpín f. Eochaid a three year reign between Dúngal mac Selbaich and Cináed mac Alpín **(q.v)**. This "Alpín" may be a conflation of Elpín (c.728) and Alpín f. Eochaid. List K places Alpín after Dúngal mac Selbaich with a three year reign. This is likely to be Elpín (c.728); yet, the order of the list is confused as in Lists D, F1, and F2. List N follows the same account as in List K, making the identity of this "Alpín" uncertain.[48]

Alpín f. Óengus. Pictish king, who appears in several of the Regnal Lists but could actually be Elpín (c.728) **(q.v.)** or Elpin f. Uuroid **(q.v.)**.[49]

Regnal List I gives Alpín f. Óengus an eight year reign between Óengus f. Bruide **(q.v.)** and Drest (c.728) **(q.v.)**. It also includes another Alpín f. Óengus with an eight year reign between Bredei f. Uuirguist **(q.v.)** and Drest f. Talorgen (q.v.). According to M.O. Anderson the first of these kings could be Elpín (c.728) and the second could be Elpin f. Uuroid. However, the eight year reign recorded for the second of these could be simply copied from the first. This seems likely because Elpin f. Uuroid had a reign of four or five years. List K gives Alpín f. Óengus a reign of two years between Bredei f. Uuirguist **(q.v.)** and Drest f. Talorgen. This king appears to be Elpin f. Uuroid considering his position in the list. Fordun's List gives the same information. M.O. Anderson suggests that originally the name of this king's father was not given but was added later.[50]   Since Alpín f. Óengus appears in neither the Annals nor the Genealogies, his independent existence is dubious.

Ambrosius (Ambrosius Aurelianus?). British leader (c.460-c.475), who may have been confused with another figure of the same name (?c.412/25) and with Merlin.[51]

Jes. 20 lists Ambrosius among kings of the Britons (**q.v.**) after Gwertheuyr (Vortimer) and before Utherpendragon (**q.v.**).[52]

Gildas seems to ascribe a victory over the Saxons (**q.v.** and see also **Angles/English**) at Mount Badon to Ambrosius. According to Bede, Ambrosius was of Roman lineage and led the Britons against the Angles at Badon Hill in c.493. *Historia Brittonum* lists Ambrosius amongst the problems of Vortigern (**q.v.**) along with the Picts, Irish (**q.v.**), and Romans (**q.v.**). He is given the position of an over-king above the other kings of the Britons (**q.v.**). Geoffrey of Monmouth mentions Ambrosius frequently. He records that Gildas wrote of Ambrosius's victory. Ambrosius is called the second son of Constantine III (**q.v.**) and brother of Constans (**q.v.**) and Utherpendragon (**q.v.**). After the murder of Constantine III by a Pict, Ambrosius and Utherpendragon were both supported for the kingship but were too young and Constans, a monk, was made king by Vortigern. Ambrosius and Utherpendragon were exiles at the court of Budicius (**q.v.**) in Brittany after Vortigern had prompted the Picts to kill Constans. Upon his return from Brittany, Ambrosius set about killing Vortigern, gaining the kingship, and defeating Hengest (**q.v.**) and the rest of the Saxons. Ambrosius defeated Vortigern's son Paschent in battle and was later poisoned by a follower of Paschent.[53]

Artbranan (c.6th cent.). Pict converted by Columba (**q.v.**).[54]

Adomnán (**q.v.**) tells how Columba predicts that Artbranan will be baptized. Artbranan was an old military leader of the cohort of Geona (Geon?).[55]

A.O. and M.O. Anderson state that "Artbrananus" is a Latin version of an Irish or North-British name possibly meaning "small raven-bear" or "small bear-raven." William Reeves thinks that "Geona" was a Pictish military unit named after its district, which is uncertain but may have been an island. Richard Sharpe believes that Artbranan's identity as a Pict is indicated by Artbranan's use of an interpreter when listening to Columba. Sharpe also seems to agree with David Dumville that "Geonus" is an adjectival form of "Cé," (see **Ce**) a place-name of a Pictish province in Banffshire and Aberdeenshire according to W.J. Watson.[56]

Arthur. British leader. At least four figures of the sixth and seventh centuries bore the name "Arthur." It is, therefore, often difficult to identify which of these figures is the Arthur of legend.[57]

Jes. 20 lists Arthur among kings of the Britons (**q.v.**) between Utherpendragon (**q.v.**) and "Constantinus."[58]

AU 467 records the death of Utherpendragon (**q.v.**) and Arthur's succession as "king," who created the Round Table. ACam. 516 records the Battle of Badon in which Arthur was victorious. In ACam. 537 Arthur and Mordred (**q.v.**) were killed in the Battle of Camlann (**q.v.**).

In *Vita Cadoci*, Arthur fought against the enemies of Gundleius (Gwynllyw) after the latter had taken away Guladus (Gwladus), daughter of Brachanus (Brychan), to be his wife. Ligessauc killed three of Arthur's knights. This caused him to hunt Ligessauc until Cadoc (**q.v.**) became involved in the deliberations about the reparations that Ligessauc would pay Arthur. Arthur gave refuge to Cadoc against Maelgwn of Gwynedd (**q.v.**). This was later agreed upon by Rein (Rhain), son of Brachanus.[59]

Y Gododdin discusses the battle prowess of Gwardur but states that "he was no Arthur." It is interesting to note that *Vita Columbae* mentions that Áedán mac Gabráin (**q.v.**), who may appear in *Y Gododdin* in conjuction with Gwardur, had a son named "Artuir" who was killed in battle with the Miathi (**q.v.**). In addition, *Senchus Fer nAlban* states that Áedán had a grandson named "Artúr." Given the possible mention of Áedán in *Y Gododdin* and the link with Gwardur, Artuir/Artúr may be the "Arthur" in question, but this is uncertain. *Historia Brittonum* records that Arthur engaged in twelve battles against the Saxons (**q.v.**) under Octha (**q.v.**), the son of Hengest (**q.v.**). It also mentions a magical stone with the pawprint of Arthur's dog and the magical tomb of Arthur's son "Amr." Among its numerous references to Arthur, *Culhwch and Olwen* mentions that there was hatred between Arthur and Hueil son of Caw (**q.v.**) because Hueil had wounded his own nephew Gwydre, who was one of Arthur's warriors. It also refers to some of the events surrounding the Battle of Camlann (**q.v.**). Caw is mentioned as part of Arthur's retinue. Geoffrey of Monmouth says much about Arthur; however, the most significant citations are those in which the Picts feature. Arthur's first victory after gaining power was against an army of Saxons, Scots, and Picts under the leadership of Colgrin (**q.v.**) of the Saxons near Eboracum (York). Later, Arthur broke up the siege of Badon by the Saxons, Scots, and Picts. Picts and Scots attacked the city of Alclud (Dumbarton), where Hoel (**q.v.**) was residing. Arthur proceeded to defeat the siege and attack Scots and Picts elsewhere, an action which led to their near annihilation. Picts along with the Saxons, Scots, and Irish allied with Mordred against Arthur and were defeated at Camlann (**q.v.**). In Triad 1 of the *Welsh Triads*, Arthur is mentioned as "Pen Teyrned" ("Chief Prince") of three areas in Triad 1. His generosity is highly praised in Triad 2. Triad 12 calls an "Arthur" a "frivolous" or "scurrilous" "bard." Triad 20 includes Arthur amongst the "Ruduavc" ("Red Ravagers") of Britain. Arthur removed the head of Bendigeidvran (Brân the Blessed) from the "White Hill" in Triad 37R. Triad 51 tells the story of how Mordred allied with the Picts, Saxons, and Scots against Arthur after Arthur had entrusted Mordred with the control of Britain. Arthur and Mordred killed one another at Camlann. This is similar to Geoffrey's account.[60]

Arvirargus (Arviragus) (c.first century A.D.?). Legendary king of Britain and younger son of Cymbeline.[61]

According to Geoffrey of Monmouth, Arvirargus was the second son of Cymbeline, who governed Britain. When his brother Guiderius was killed while fighting Claudius and the Romans (**q.v.**), Arvirargus took control of the Britons (**q.v.**) and made peace with the Romans, which he broke after the departure of Claudius. Vespasian (**q.v.**) brought troops to Britain to subjugate Arvirargus, which caused a stalemate. Vespasian then returned to Rome. The Picts came to Britain during the reign of his son, Marius (**q.v.**).[62]

Athelstan (d.c.851). Saxon king (see **Saxons**) and son of Æthelwulf (**q.v.**). "Legend of St. Andrew" (*Harl. MS. 4628*) states that he was killed by Unuist f. Uurguist (**q.v.**).[63]

Fordun's List calls Athelstan the son of Æthelwulf and the contemporary of Unuist f. Uurguist.[64]

Audgisl (Auisle) (9th cent.). Brother of Óláfr (**q.v.**) of Dublin.[65]

AU 863 states that Audgisl, Óláfr, Ivarr (**q.v.**), and Lorcan mac Cathail attacked the lands of Flann mac Conaing. AU 866 says that Óláfr and Audgisl harried Fortriu (**q.v.**) and the rest of Pictland (**q.v.**). AC 864 states that Audgisl and Óláfr ravaged Pictland and took hostages in 871. In AC 865 and AU 867, Audgisl's kinsmen killed him.

Bagag ollfiacha (Fíac?). Mythological king of Alba (**q.v.**) and Ireland (**q.v.**) from the Cruithni (Picts?).[66]

P#A(B 506), P#A(Uí Ma.), P#A(Lec.), and P#A(C.vi.2) mention Bagag as one of seven Cruithni from Alba (**q.v.**) who were kings of Ireland. He reigned for thirty years in Temair (**q.v.**) between Slanoll and Berngal (**q.q.v.**). Wars first started in Ireland during his rule. In P#L(Uí Ma.), P#L(Lec.), P#L(G47), P#L(Bal.), P#L(1336), and P#L(1295), Finachta (**q.v.**) is ruler of Ireland when the Cruithni divided northern Britain into seven parts. Finachta could be Bagag, Finachta, or Eilim ollfhinachta (**q.v.**).

Book of Leinster, *Book of Lecan*, and *Laud 610* list a "Fíac" among kings of Dál n-Araide (**q.v.**) of Ulaid (Ulster) from the family of Ollam Fótla (**q.v.**). This could be Bagag.[67]

In AC Bagag seems to be "Fiagha 4th son of king Ollow" and is given an eight year reign between Géde Ollgothach (**q.v.**) and Berngal. He is called "a good king" with nothing important occurring during his reign. Later, AC includes this "Fiagha" among the ancestors of one Arthur Magennis, who was outlawed in 1642.[68] However, he could be confused with Eilim ollfhinachta. AFM 3971 mentions a "Fiacha mac Fionnachta," whose identity is uncertain.

Regnal Lists SL1, SL2 M, and SL2 H give Olfinecta (**q.v.**) a sixty year reign between Aenbegan (**q.v.**) and Guidid gaed brechach (**q.v.**). This could either be Bagag or Eilim ollfhinachta. It is also possible that the reigns of these two kings were combined into one reign because each is given a thirty year reign in P#A(B 506), P#A(Uí Ma.), P#A(Lec.2), and P#A(C.vi.2). List SL3(Lec.3) gives a sixty year reign to "Findachta." This is probably "Olfinecta" of the previous lists; therefore, he could be Bagag, Eilim ollfhinachta, or both monarchs combined into one. Lists SL3(Lec.1), SL3(Lec.4), SL3(Bal.1), and SL3(Bal.2) record the same information, thus causing the same problems of identity.[69]

Banba. Personification of Ireland who encountered the Sons of Míl (**q.v.**) in the *Lebor Gabála* ("Book of Invasions").[70]

In Legends P#C(Lein.), P#C(Uí Ma.), P#C(Lec.), and P#C(G131), it is uncertain whether the sons of Míl or the Cruithni (Picts?) encountered Banba at Sliab Mis (**q.v.**). Banba features in P#D(D.iv.1), P#D(Lec.1), P#D(Lec.2), P#D(Bal.), and P#D(24.P.13), and P#D(1295) as an enemy of the Cruithni. This seems to indicate that P#C(Lein.), P#C(Uí Ma.), and P#C(Lec.) have the Cruithni encounter Banba, but this is not certain.

AFM 3500 records that Banba, Eire (**q.v.**), and Fotla (**q.v.**) were killed by the Sons of Míl.

Basse (Buas (Boas) mac Anbuais (Anfóis) m. Ébir). One of the chiefs of the sons of Míl (**q.v.**) in the *Lebor Gabála* ("Book of Invasions"). He was drowned with Donn (**q.v.**).[71]

In Legends P#C(Lein.), P#C(Uí Ma.), P#C(Lec.), the wife of Basse travelled with either the Cruithni or with the sons of Míl. In P#F(Div.1), P#F(Lec.1), P#F(Lec.2), P#F(Bal.), and P#F(24.P.13), the wife of Basse was given to the Cruithni by Éremón (**q.v.**) after Basse had drowned. This is also true of P#G(Lec.), P#G(Bal.), P#G(B 512), and P#G(1295). P#H(Lein.) and P#H(D.iii.1) tell the same story, but P#H(Lein.) seems to call Basse "Bróes."

Rawl. B. 502 includes Basse in "Ciarraige" as a descendant of Míl (**q.v.**) between Célebair mac Anbuais and Anbuas mac Ébir. In "Genelach Ciarraige" in *Book of Leinster*, he is an ancestor of Mathgamain mac Meic-beithad and descendant of Míl. Basse is positioned between Ilebuir (Célebair?) and Anbuas. In "Genelach Ciarraige Luachra," Basse is an ancestor of Mathgamain, a descendant of Míl, and placed between Célebair and Anbuas. *Book of Lecan* and *Laud 610* give him a similar pedigree.[72]

Bassianus (Caracalla). Roman Emperor (211-217). King of Britain (**q.v.**) and son of Severus (**q.v.**).[73]

Bede says that Bassianus was son of Severus and became emperor after the execution of his brother Geta. Geoffrey of Monmouth states that Bassianus, who had a British mother, was one of Severus's two sons and was made king by the Britons (**q.v.**), who had rejected his half-brother Geta who had a Roman mother. Picts gave Bassianus to Carausius (**q.v.**), who then killed him.[74]

Beli map Neithon (7th cent.). King of Strathclyde Britons (**q.v.**). Son of Neithon map Gwyddno (**q.v.**), who has been equated with Nectu n. Uerb (**q.v.**). Possibly father of Bredei f. Bili (**q.v.**).[75]

Harl. 3859 lists Beli in a genealogy of Strathclyde as son of Neithon map Gwyddno and descendant of Coroticus (**q.v.**).[76]

ACam 627 records the death of "Belin," who could be Beli. Beli could also be the "Beli," who is mentioned in *Y Gododdin*, and/or the "Belen o Leyn," who is mentioned in Triad 62 of *Welsh Triads*.[77]

Berngal mac Géide Ollgothaig (Bearngal). Mythological king of Ireland and Alba (**q.q.v.**) from the Cruithni (Picts?).

In Origin Legends P#A (B 506), P#A(Uí Ma.), P#A(Lec.), and P#A(C.vi.2), Berngal reigned for thirty years after Bagag (see **Bagag ollfiacha**). His reign was marked by wars which ruined the crops.

Rawl B. 502 mentions Berngal as king of Ulaid from the family of Ollam Fótla (**q.v.**). He is listed between Géde Ollgothach (**q.v.**) and Eilim ollfhinachta (**q.v.**). *Book of Leinster*, *Book of Lecan*, and *Laud 610* seem to place Berngal between Bagag ollfiacha and Eilim in similar passages.[78]

AC calls Berngal was the son of Géde Ollgothach and grandson of Ollam Fótla. He reigned for twelve years in which wars caused famine. He was killed by his cousin "Olleal." However, AC does not call Berngal a Pict.[79] AFM 3991 mentions that Berngal was the son of Géde and victor at "Breagh." AFM 3992 records his succession. AFM 4003 mentions his death.

Bertfrid. Northumbrian ealdorman.
Bede says that Bertfrid fought the Picts in 711 (see **Mag Manand**).[80]

Bertred (d.698). Northumbrian commander.[81]
AT 698, AC 693, and AU 698 record that Bertred, son of Berníth, was killed in battle against the Picts.
Bede records that Picts killed Bertred in 698.[82]

Blarehassereth. Pseudo-historical Pictish king.
Only Fordun's List includes this king. He is given a seventeen year reign between Uipoig namet (**q.v.**) and Fiacua albus (**q.v.**). Molly Miller suggests that Blarehassereth could occur in other Lists abbreviated as "Breth" (see **Breth f. Buthut**).[83]

Blieiblituth. Pseudo-historical Pictish king.
Lists SL1 and SL2 O give him a five year reign between Deoord (**q.v.**) and Dectotr'ic fr. Diu (**q.v.**). Skene interprets the name as "Bliesblituth." SL2 M gives Blieiblituth a two year reign between the same kings. SL2 H places Blieiblituth between Dectotr'íc and Deoord. He only appears in those Lists which M.O. Anderson calls "Pictish List P."[84]

Boisil (d.c.664). Priest and prior of Melrose in Scotland.[85]

In *Bede's Cuthbert*, Cuthbert (**q.v.**) goes to Melrose to study under Boisil and enter monastic life. Boisil healed Cuthbert of an ailment before dying himself. Boisil foresaw Cuthbert as bishop.[86]

Bede records how a vision of Boisil told Ecgberht (saint) (**q.v.**) to visit Columba (**q.v.**).[87]

Brecc of Fortriu (d.725). Unidentified figure who may have been a Pict. He is apparently mentioned in only one source. "Brecc" seems to be the Irish for "speckled" or "speckled one." Interestingly, it occurs in Domnall Brecc, seventh century king of Scots Dál Ríata (**q.v.**) and grandson of Áedán mac Gabráin (**q.v.**).[88]

AU 725 records the death of Brecc of Fortriu (**q.v.**).

Bred (Bridei VI, Brude son of Ferat/Wrad). Pictish king (?842).[89]

Regnal List SL1 records a one year reign for Bred after Uurad f. Bargoit (**q.v.**). This is also true of List SL2 M, where Cináed mac Alpín (**q.v.**) follows Bred. This is repeated in Lists SL2 O and SL2 H. Lists D, F1, and F2 give Bred a one month reign between Uurad f. Bargoit and Kineth f. Ferat (**q.v.**). List I gives a one year between Uurad f. Bargoit and Kineth f. Ferat. List K and Fordun's List place him between the same kings with a one month reign.[90]

M.O. Anderson thinks that "Bred" could be the same as "Bridei," "Bre(i)dei," "Breth," and "Bru(i)de" and could derive from Celtic "*brodios."[91]

Bredei f. Bili (Bridei III, Brude son of Bile). King of Picts (671-692). Possibly son of Beli map Neithon (**q.v.**).[92]

AT 682 and AU 682 record that Bredei destroyed Orc (**q.v.**). AI 691, AT 693, and AU 693 mention Bredei's death.

List SL1 gives Bredei a twenty-one year reign between Drest f. Donuel (**q.v.**) and Taran f. Entifidich (**q.v.**). SL2 M gives Bredei a twenty year reign between the same two monarchs. SL2 O places him between the same kings with a twenty-one year reign. SL2 H and D give him a twenty year reign in the same position. Lists F1, F2, and I record a twenty-one year reign between Drest and Taran. List K gives him a twenty year reign in the same position. Fordun's List gives him an eleven year reign between Drest and Taran.[93]

A poem ascribed to Adomnán (**q.v.**) in the tenth century *Betha Adomnáin* (*Life of Adomnán*) appears to be the only text which identifies Bredei as the son of Beli map Neithon.[94]

Historia Brittonum call Bredei king of Picts and "fratuelem" of Ecgfrith (**q.v.**), whom he defeated in battle (see **Dún Nechtain**). "Fratuelem" has been translated as "cousin." It appears to be the accusative form of "fratuelus" which can also mean "nephew" and which derives from "frater" ("brother").[95] Regarding the name, see **Bred**.

Bredei f. Derelei (Bridei IV, Brude son of Derile). Pictish king (696-?706).[96]

AT 706 and AU 706 record the death of Bredei.

Regnal Lists SL1, SL2 M, SL2 O, and SL2 H record an eleven year reign for Bredei between Taran f. Entifidich (**q.v.**) and Necthon f. Derelei (**q.v.**). M.O. Anderson suggests that "Derile" is an Irish woman's name. List D gives him a thirty-one year reign between Necthon and Ciniod f. Uuredech (**q.v.**). Bredei has a thirty-one year reign between Taran and Necthon in Lists F1, F2, I, and K. Fordun's List places him between Taran and Necthon with a twenty-one year reign. This could be a mistake for Bredei f. Bili (**q.v.**), who has an eleven year reign in Fordun's List.[97]

In *Life of Servanus*, Bredei tries to murder Servanus (**q.v.**) and his followers. However, Servanus cures Bredei of an illness, and he gives Servanus land for a monastery.[98] Regarding the name, see **Bred**.

Bredei f. Uuirguist (Bridei V, Brude son of Forgus/Brude son of Óengus?). Pictish king (761-3).[99]

AT 763 and AU 763 record his death and call him king of Fortriu (**q.v.**).

Regnal List SL1 gives Bredei a two year reign after Onuist f. Urguist (**q.v.**) and before Ciniod f. Uuredech (**q.v.**). In Lists SL2 M, SL2 O, SL2 H and Bredei is placed between the same two kings with a fifteen year reign.[100]

M.O. Anderson thinks that Bredei is the "Brude son of Óengus" who is mentioned in the other lists. List D, F1 and F2 give this king an eight year reign between Elpin f. Uuroid (**q.v.**) and Drest f. Talorgen (**q.v.**). List I records a two year reign for "Brude son of Óengus," which agrees with List SL2. However, this list places him between Óengus f. Bruide (**q.v.**) and Alpín f. Óengus (**q.v.**). List K and Fordun's List give him a two year reign between Elpin f. Uuroid and Alpín f. Óengus.[101] Regarding the name, see **Bred**.

Breidei f. Uuid (Bridei II, Brude/Breidei son of Uuid). Pictish king (635-641).[102]

AT 641, AU 641, and CS 639 record the death of Breidei.

List SL1 records a five year reign between Garnard f. Uuid (**q.v.**) and Talorc f. Uuid (**q.v.**). Lists D F1, F2, and I give Breidei a five year reign between Garnard f. Uuid and Talorc f. Uuid. List K gives him a five year reign between Garnard f. Uuid and Drest f. Donuel (**q.v.**), leaving out several intervening kings. Fordun's List gives him a five year reign between Garnard f. Uuid and Talorc f. Uuid.[103] Regarding the name, see **Bred**.

Bres (Bress Rí mac Airt Inflig). A chief of the Sons of Míl (**q.v.**) in *Lebor Gabála* ("Book of Invasions").[104]

In P#C(Lein.), P#C(Uí Ma.), P#C(Lec.), and P#C(G131), Cruithne (**q.v.**) seems to have carried off Bres's wife although the poem is ambiguous.

In P#F(D.iv.1), P#F(Lec.1), P#F(Lec.2), P#F(Bal.), and P#F(24.P.13), and P#F(1295), Bres had drowned with Donn (**q.v.**) and his wife was given to the Cruithni (**q.v.**) by Éremón (**q.v.**) along with two other widows (see **Basse** and **Buaigne**). This event is recalled in P#G(B 512), P#G(Lec.), P#G(Bal.), P#G(1295), P#H(Lein.), and P#H(D.iii.1).

In *Rawl. B. 502*, Bres is included amongst kings of Ireland (**q.v.**) with a nine year reign and victory in many battles against the Fomuire. Bres is in a list of kings from the family of Éber mac Míled with a nine year reign. Bres is listed between Sétnae Innarraid and Artt Imblech, and he is said to have fought twenty battles against the Fomuire. Bres is also placed in a list between Findsruth (Findroth) and Imblech (Imbrech). *Book of Leinster* places Bres in a list between Artt Imblech and Sétnae Innarraid. "Genelach Eoganachta Casil" lists Bres between Findsruth and Imblech with thirty battles to his credit. *Book of Lecan* gives Bres a nine year reign between Artt and Sétnae and mentions similar facts as in *Rawl B. 502*.[105]

CS A.M. 2390 mentions a "Bress" amongst the Tuatha Dé Danann (**q.v.**) who defeated the Fir Bolg (**q.v.**). This could be the same person as Bres.

Bretach (son of) (Macbeth/Mac Bethad). King of Scotland (1040-1057).[106]

Legends P#E(Bal.) and P#E(1295) claim that there were fifty kings of Alba (**q.v.**) from Fergus (see **Fergus Mór**) to "mac mbrigach mBretach" ("the son of mighty Bretach"). Skene equates the latter monarch with Macbeth. Gearóid Mac Eoin also makes this equation. There were thirty-two kings of Dál Riata (**q.v.**) from the Cenél nGabráin Dynasty starting with Fergus and ending with Cináed mac Alpín (**q.v.**). If one adds these thirty-two kings to the eighteen kings of the Scots from Domnall mac Alpín (**q.v.**) to Macbeth, one does indeed have fifty kings.[107]

Rawl. B. 502 includes the genealogy of Macbeth in "Item Ríg Alban." *Book of Leinster* mentions Macbeth's pedigree in a genealogy of the family of Lulach.[108]

AT 1058 and CS 1056 record the killing of Macbeth by Malcolm, son of Duncan.

List SL2 M gives Macbeth a thirteen year reign between Duncan I son of Crínan and Lulach. Lists SL2 O and SL2 H place him between the same kings with a sixteen year reign. Lists D, F1, F, and I give him a seventeen year reign between Duncan and Lulach and mention that Macbeth killed Duncan and that Malcolm killed Macbeth, who was buried on Iona (**q.v.**). List K gives Macbeth a reign of sixteen years between Duncan and Lulach. List N records a seventeen year reign between the same kings and mentions Macbeth's slaying.[109]

Duan Albanach gives Macbeth a reign of seventeen years between Duncan and Lulach.[110]

Breth f. Buthut. Pseudo-historical Pictish king.

Regnal List SL1 records a seven year reign for Breth between "Gartnait .iiii" (see **Gartnart (4)**) and Uipoig namet (**q.v.**). List SL2 M repeats this. This is also true of SL2 O; however, Breth follows "Gartnait ini," which M.O. Anderson says should be read as "Garnait iiii." SL2 H records a seven year reign between "Garnart .iiii." and Uipoig namet.[111]

Molly Miller states that "Blarehassereth" (**q.v.**) of Fordun's List could be Breth in an abbreviated form. M.O. Anderson asserts that the name "Breth" could be the same as "Bridei," "Bre(i)dei," "Bred," and "Bru(i)de" and could derive from the Celtic "*brodios."[112]

Bridei f. Mailcon (Bridei I, Brude son of Maelchon). Pictish king (c.556-86).[113]

AT 506, AC 509 (with the note "hiec erratum est"), and AU 505 mistakenly record his death. AT 560 mentions that the "men of Alba" (see **Alba**) fled before Bridei. In AC 563 Bridei defeated the Scots. AU 558 remarks on "fuga ante filium Maelchon" ("flight before the son of Mailcon"), which could be the event of AC 563. CS 560 records Bridei's defeat of the Scots, here called "Teithedh Dalbancoibh" ("retreat of the inhabitants of Alba"). AI 584, AT 584, AT 752 (mistakenly), AC 584, and AU 584 record Bridei's death.

Lists SL1, SL2 M, SL2 O, and SL2 H record that Bridei reigned for one year with Galam (**q.v.**) after the latter's solitary reign and for thirty years alone before Gartnart f. Domelch (**q.v.**). Columba (**q.v.**) baptized him during the eighth year of Bridei's reign. Lists D, F1, and F2 record a thirty year reign between Galam and Gartnart f. Domelch. They also record that "Saint Columba converted him to the faith." List I records the same information and adds that Columba came to the Picts in 565 and lived among them for thirty-two years. It mentions that Columba died in 592 at the time of Bridei. List K gives Bridei a thirty year reign between Galam and Gartnart f. Domelch. It also records that both Columba and Palladius (**q.v.**) (possibly, Torannán (**q.v.**)) converted Bridei. Fordun's List gives Bridei a nineteen year reign between Galam and Gartnart f. Domelch.[114]

Vita Columbae mentions that in front of Bridei, Columba endowed a stone with the ability to heal and float in water. Columba scared Bridei with his thunderous singing voice. In Bridei's presence, Columba threatened the magician Broichan (**q.v.**) to gain the release of an Irish slave held by him. When Columba first visited Bridei, the king would not let him enter. Therefore, Columba caused the gates to open. This disturbed Bridei, who then greeted Columba. Columba asked Bridei to have the king of Orc (**q.v.**) protect Columba's followers who might land there.[115]

Bede says that Bridei was in the ninth year of his reign when Columba arrived. Columba then converted the Picts, who gave him Iona (**q.v.**).[116] Regarding the name, see **Bred**. Regarding Bridei's father, see **Mailcon.**

Brigid (Brigit) (455-524). Saint of Kildare.[117]

In *Rawl. B. 502*, Brigid is called part of the family of Artt Cerp (Cert) mac Cairpri Niad, daughter of Dubthach mac Deimre, and part of the "Húi Bresail." Brigid is also mentioned in a section on the Laigis (**q.v.**), where her birth is predicted by a druid. Brigid is also descended from Eochaid (Eocho) Find Fuath nAirt. *Book of Leinster* gives the same genealogy in "Genealogies of Irish Saints." Brigid's poems are counted among the three great accomplishments of Ireland, and "Irish Saints and Places" claims that "the subjects of Saint Brigid, these were all holy virgins of whom connected places and names were reckoned." *Book of Lecan* mentions that Brigid was of the family of Artt Cerp and daughter of Dubthach. *Laud 610* records Brigid's descent from Eochaid (Eocho). Brigid is given a separate genealogy, where she is called Dubthach's daughter. *MacFirbis Genealogies* apparently includes Brigid in "Naomhsheanchus" ("History of Saints").[118]

AI 455, AC 425, AU 452, AU 456, and CS 439 record the birth of Brigid. Brigid's death is mentioned in AI 524. AT 524 records Brigid's death. AC 522 records Brigid's death at the age of either twenty-seven or seventy years of age and that she was of noble lineage. AU 524, AU 526, AU 528, and AFM 524 mention the death of Brigid. CS 523 mentions her death at the age of either eighty-seven or seventy-seven.

List SL1 records that Necton f. Erip (**q.v.**) dedicated Aburnethige (**q.v.**) to Brigid and that Necton saw Brigid in Ireland after being expelled by his brother Drust f. Erp (**q.v.**). She told him that he "would possess the kingdom of the Picts in peace." SL2 M, SL2 O, and SL2 H also mention the dedication of Aburnethige to Brigid. M.O. Anderson postulates that the foundation date of the church at Aburnethige is uncertain and that "Brigid" to whom it is dedicated may have been another saint with a similar name.[119]

Betha Coluim Cille says that Brigid predicted that Columba (**q.v.**) would be successful and without blemish. While in his church, Columba became aware of Brigid walking on a plain and wishing to dedicate it to God. *Félire Óengusso* lists Brigid under 1 February and calls her "chaste head of Erin's nuns."[120]

Britus (Brutus).   Legendary first king of the Britons, who was of Trojan ancestry.[121]

P#G(B 512), P#G(Lec.), P#G(Bal.), and P#G(1295) record that Britus killed Domnall and implies that he ruled Alba (**q.v.**) before the offspring of Nemed (**q.v.**). P#G(Lec.) mistakenly calls Britus the "wife" of Isicon (**q.v.**).

Jes. 20 lists Britus in a genealogy of kings of Britons (**q.v.**) as grandson of "Ascanius," son of the Trojan hero Aeneas, and an ancestor of Arthur (**q.v.**).[122]

Vita Niniani says that Britus gave his name to Britain (**q.v.**).[123] *Historia Brittonum* calls Britus a Roman consul and mentions that Britain was named after him. It also recounts that Britus was the son of "Silvius" and the grandson of "Ascanius," the son of the Trojan refugee Aeneas. Britus is said to have ruled in Britain at the time that "Heli" ruled in Israel. While Britus reigned, the Scots went to Dál Riata (**q.v.**) in Ireland one thousand and two years after the Egyptians were drowned in the Red Sea. A different origin says that Britus was descended from Japheth (**q.v.**), son of Noah (**q.v.**). *Duan Albanach* says that Britus took control of Alba from his brother Albanus and reigned before the offspring of Nemed. Geoffrey of Monmouth calls Britus the first king of the Britons (**q.v.**) and gives him a Trojan ancestry. However, he relates an elaborate tale about his exploits which ends with Britus's death in the twenty-fourth year after he had come to Britain. Among his feats, Britus defeats "Goffarius Pictus," who reigns in Aquitaine. It is possible that this individual is meant to be a Pict. However, it seems likely that "Pictus" is meant to be Poitiers, which has been associated with the Picts (see **Pictabis**). Geoffrey says that Britus had twenty sons, twenty wives, and thirty daughters. Britus's descent from the Trojans is repeated when the Roman invasion of Britain is discussed.[124]

Broichan (sixth century). Wizard and foster-father of the Bridei f. Mailcon (**q.v.**). Broichan is sometimes associated with Irish druid Fráechán mentioned in some of the Annals.[125]

AT 561, AU 561, AFM 555, CS 561 record that Fráechán mac Temnáin aided Diarmait mac Cerbaill when Diarmait was defeated at Cúl Dremne (**q.v.**) through the intercession of Columba (**q.v.**).

Vita Columbae calls Broichan a magician and Bridei's foster-father. Adomnán relates how Columba predicted that Broichan would die if he refused to free an Irish woman slave. Broichan became ill because he did not do as Columba said; however, Columba later cured Broichan with water into which a magic stone had been dipped after he promised to free the slave. Broichan used magic to bring forth a tempest in order to prevent Columba from sailing; however, Columba was able to counteract the storm.[126]

T.F. O'Rahilly claims that "Broichanus" used by Adomnán is a Latinized Irish name. It would have been "*Vroichán" in the sixth century and "Froíchan/Fróechan" in Old Irish, deriving from "froích/froéch" ("heather"). Kenneth Jackson thinks that it is not a Latinization but a Gaelicized P-Celtic cognate of "*Uroican." A.O. and M.O. Anderson believe that Broichan may be Fráechán of the Annals. They state that because Adomnán does not say that Columba needed an interpreter to speak with Broichan, Broichan must have known Irish. They also cite the intercession of Columba against Diarmait as further proof that Fráechán is Broichan. Richard Sharpe disagrees with the speculation that Fráechán is the same person as Broichan, and declares that the accounts in the Annals are traditions about the battle that developed independently of *Vita Columbae*.[127] Although there is a linguistic basis for the equation of Broichan with Fráechán, the historical evidence is inconclusive.

Brude f. Fochel (Bridei VII, Brude son of Fothel) Pictish king (?843-?845).[128]

Regnal Lists D, F1, F2, I, K, and Fordun's List record a two year reign for Brude between Kineth f. Ferat (**q.v.**) and Drust f. Ferat (**q.v.**).[129] Regarding the name, see **Bred**.

Brude (30). Thirty pseudo-historical Pictish kings mentioned in some of the Regnal Lists although there are not always thirty named.

Regnal List SL1 says that these kings reigned for 150 years in Ireland and Scotland between Wurgest (**q.v.**) and "Gilgidi" (see **Gub/Gib**). The first of these, "Brude Bont," is given a forty-eight year reign. The others are not given reign lengths. The "Brudes" seem to be arranged in pairs with the second of the pair given a prefix (usually "Ur-") to his epithet (i.e.: "Brude Pant" and "Brude Urpant"). List SL2 M gives the same information; however, no individual reign lengths are given. Also, there is a note which states that this is recorded in the books of the Cruithni. List SL2 O only records the reign of "Bruide urmum," who starts the list and is given a reign of 150 years over all of Alba (**q.v.**) before Gub/Gib (**q.v.**). List SL2 H repeats the information in SL2 M. List SL3(Lec.2) states that there were thirty kings named "Bruide" who reigned for one hundred and fifty years but only names "Bruda Pont." Lists SL3(Lec.1), SL3(Lec.3), SL3(Lec.4), and SL3(Bal.2) intersperse the "Brudes" amongst the other kings in the lists.[130]

M.O. Anderson says that "Brude" could be a title and that some have apparently Pictish names, while the rest have apparently Irish names. The account of "Brudes" in SL1 influenced Regnal Lists contained in *Lebor Bretnach* and *Lebor Gabála*. W.A. Cummins believes that the "thirty Brudes" were neither actual kings nor names created to add to the lists. He suggests that "Brude" is related to Old Welsh "brud" or "brut" meaning "prophecy" or "chronicle." Cummins postulates that Regnal Lists were recited during festivals, where "chronicles" would be called out. He cites the example of "*Brude Pant*' (valley chronicle)" and "'*Brude Urpant*' (great valley chronicle)."[131] See also **Bred**.

Bruide f. Onuist (Brude son of Óengus I) (eighth century). Son of Onuist f. Urguist (**q.v.**).[132]

AT 731, AC 728, AU 731 state that Bruide defeated Talorg mac Congusa (**q.v.**). AT 736 says that he died after Onuist had ravaged Dál Riata (**q.v.**). AC 733 and AU 736 mention his death. Regarding the name, see **Bred**.

Bruning. Saxon leader killed at Camlann (**q.v.**).[133]

Geoffrey of Monmouth calls Bruning a Saxon (see **Saxons**) who was allied with Picts and Irish (**q.v.**) on the side of Mordred (**q.v.**) against Arthur (**q.v.**).[134]

Buaigne. A chief of the Sons of Míl (**q.v.**) in the *Lebor Gabála* ("Book of Invasions").[135]

P#C(Lein.), P#C(Uí Ma.), and P#C(G131) mention the wife of Buaigne after saying that Cruithne (**q.v.**) had stolen wives and state "great difficulty they all suffer ... with the wives of Bres (**q.v.**), Basse (**q.v.**), and Buaigne." The identity of "they" is uncertain. It could mean the Picts or the Sons of Míl. P#C(Lec.) may mention the wife of Buaigne in the phrase "la mna Buaise." However, this may refer to another person. P#F(D.iv.1), P#F(Lec.1), P#F(Lec.2), P#F(Bal.), P#F(24.P.13), and P#F(1295) say that the wife of Buaigne was given to the Cruithni (Picts) by Éremón (**q.v.**) after Buaigne had been drowned. P#H(Lein.) and P#H(D.iii.1) record that the wife of Buaigne was given to the Picts by Éremón.

Buan (Banb mac Séim m. Máir). Pictish ancestor.[136]

Legends P#L(Uí Ma.), P#L(Lec.), P#L(G47), and P#L(1336) state that Buan was the father of Agnaman (**q.v.**) and the son of Mar (**q.v.**). Buan was also the ancestor of Cruithne (**q.v.**), the eponymous progenitor of the Picts. This would make the Picts relatives of the Sons of Míl (**q.v.**).

Rawl. B. 502 three times calls him Tóe's father, Agnaman's grandfather, Sém's father, and Mar's grandson.[137]

SL3(Lec.1) and SL3(Lec.4) repeat the information in P#L(Uí Ma.), P#L(Lec.), P#L(G47). SL3(Lec.2), SL3(Bal.1), and SL3(Bal.2) call Buan Mar's son and Agnaman's father. SL3(Lec.3) calls Buan Mar's son and father of Pairte (Partholon?) (**q.v.**).[138]

Bubon (c.600). Possibly a Pict or a Briton from north of Manaw (see **Mag Manand**).[139]

Y Gododdin mentions Bubon's fierceness in battle.[140]

The name may be related to "Buan," "Biguan," "Biuguan (Biwan)," "Biuan," "Biuon," and "Biuonui." Buan (**q.v.**) is the name of a Pictish ancestor. It could be read as "Eubon."[141]

Budicius. King of Brittany and foster-father of Ambrosius (**q.v.**) and Utherpendragon (**q.v.**). Welsh tradition identified him as "Emyr Llydaw."[142] Geoffrey of Monmouth says that Budicius cared for Ambrosius and Utherpendragon after Picts had murdered Constans (**q.v.**).[143]

Buite mac Brónaig (Boecius of Monasterboice, Boethius) (d.521). Irish or Italian saint who preached among the Picts. *Book of Leinster, Book of Lecan,* and *Book of Ballymote* call him son of Brónach. The 13th century *Vita Sancti Boecii* states that he raised Necton f. Erip (**q.v.**) from the dead.[144]

AI 521, AT 520, AC 521, AU 519, AU 523, and CS 518 record the death of Buite and the birth of Columba (**q.v.**)

Félire Óengusso lists him under 7 December.[145]

Cadfred (?).

List I mistakenly records the battle of Degsastan between Áedán mac Gabráin (**q.v.**) and Cadfred in 513. Degsastan was actually fought in 603 between Áedán and Æthelfrith (**q.v.**). AC 603 records this battle and states that "Canfrith" (Eanfrith), brother of Æthelfrith was killed. Cadfred may actually be Eanfrith or Æthelfrith. AT 600 also records this battle and the death of Eanfrith, but Whitley Stokes sees "Eanfrith" as a mistake for Theobald.[146] Æthelfrith had a son named Eanfrith (**q.v.**).

Cadnolodor. Pseudo-historical Pict.

P#E(Lec.), P#E(Bal.), and P#E(1295) call Cadnolodor son of Cathluan (**q.v.**) and leader of the Cruithni (Picts?) when they left Ireland. P#F(D.iv.i), P#F(Lec.1), P#F(Lec.2), P#F(Bal.), P#F(24.P.13), P#F(1295), P#F(1289), P#F(D.iii.2) state that Cadnolodor was one of two heroes of the Cruithni and son of Cathluan. P#G(B 512), P#G(Lec.), P#G(Bal.), and P#G(1295) say that Cadnolodor and Catainlacach (**q.v.**) ruled the Cruithni in Alba (**q.v.**).

"Cadnolodor" could be an Irish version of Welsh "Cadwaladr." Cadwaladr (**q.v.**) was a seventh century king of Gwynedd, whose father was Cadwallon. O'Rahilly suggests that "Catluan" (Cathluan) is an Irish version of Welsh "Cadwallon."[147] Although Cadnolodor and Cadwaladr are unlikely to be the same, it is possible that Cadwaladr was used as a model for Cadnolodor.

Cadoc (saint) (Cadog) (c.580).   British saint associated with Llancarfan (Nantcarvan). An abbot who was said to have been a king. *Jes. 20* records his pedigree, where he is descended from Maximus (**q.v.**). 12th century *Bonedd Y Saint* ("Descent of the Saints") calls Cadoc son of Gwynllyw.[148]

Vita Cadoci says that he went to Scotland and encountered the dead giant Caw (**q.v.**), who may be a Pict. Cadoc resurrected Caw and was given property by Scottish kings.[149]

Cador. Legendary duke of Cornwall.

Geoffrey of Monmouth relates that Arthur (**q.v.**) gave Cador the task of fighting Saxons (**q.v.**). He defeated them and their leader Baldulfus near York (Eboracum). Cador pursued the Saxons while Arthur's nephew Hoel (**q.v**) was being attacked by Scots and Picts. In a list of visitors to the "City of Legions" (Caerleon or Chester), Cador is called king of Cornwall.[150]

Cadwaladr (7th cent.). King of Gwynedd and son of Cadwallon, who was an enemy of Edwin (d.633) (**q.v.**).[151]

Harl. 3859 and *Bonedd Y Saint* record his genealogy as son of Cadwallon and descendant of Maelgwn of Gwynedd and Cunedda (**q.q.v.**).[152]

ACam 682 records his death.

Geoffrey of Monmouth states that when Cadwaladr left Britain (**q.v.**), Cadwaladr declared that it would be open to Picts, Scots, Saxons, Romans, and

Ambrones (**q.q.v.**).   Rachel Bromwich indicates that Geoffrey confused Cadwaladr with Cædwalla, king of Wessex, who had died as a pilgrim in Rome in 689. Triads 17 and 53 both call him "blessed." Triad 53 also states that he was struck by the poet Golydan.[153] Regarding the name, see **Cadnolodor**.

Cailtram f. Girom. Pictish king (453-544(?)).[154]

Lists SL1, SL2 M, SL2 O, and SL2 H give Cailtram a reign of one year between Garthnach f. Girom (**q.v.**) and Talorg f. Muírcholaich (**q.v.**). D, F1, and F2, I, K, and Fordun's List record a six year reign between Garthnach and Talorg.[155]

Cainnech Mocu Dalon of Achadh Bó (Aghaboe, County Leix in Ireland) (d.599/600). Friend of Columba active in Pictland (**q.v.**). He visited Bridei f. Mailcon (**q.v.**). *Book of Leinster*, *Book of Lecan*, and *Book of Ballymote* call him the son of Luigthech.[156]

AT 518, AC 519, AU 521, AU 527, and CS 516 record Cainnech's birth. AI 603, AT 600, AC 599, AU 599, AU 600, AFM 598, and CS 600 mention his death.

Vita Columbae states that Columba had predicted the circumstances of Cainnech's arrival at Iona (**q.v.**). Cainnech miraculously aided Columba, who was in a storm at sea. Later, Columba, who was at Iona, miraculously returned a staff to Cainnech, who had left it on his return to Ireland. Cainnech visited Columba on Hinba. *Félire Óengusso* and *Martyrology of Tallaght* (Lein.) list him under 11 October.[157]

Cairpre Cruithnechan (Cairpre Cruithnechan (or Luachra) mac Cuircc m. Luigdech). Son of Conall Corc and Mongfind (**q.q.v.**). Grandson of Feradach Find Fechtnach (**q.v.**).[158]

Rawl. B. 502 and *Book of Lecan* call Cairpre one of the seven sons of Conall Corc and son of Mongfind, daughter of Feradach. He is named as an ancestor of "Óengus king of Alba," who may be Onuist f. Urguist (**q.v.**). *Book of Leinster* also calls Cairpre one of the seven sons of Conall Corc and mentions Mongfind as his mother. *Book of Lecan* gives similar information about Cairpre as in *Rawl B. 502*. *Laud 610* calls Cairpre one of seven sons of Conall Corc without naming his mother. *Laud 610* includes "Conall Corc and the Corco Luigde" (c.700), which calls Cairpre one of two sons of the unnamed daughter of Feradach. After arriving in Ireland, Cairpre incurred his father's wrath and was exiled.   It also discusses the Uí Carpri population in Pictland (**q.v.**), a tribe descended from Cairpre and related to the Eóganacht of Munster. His conception and birth seem to be discussed in *Longes Chonaill* although he is not named.   W.J. Watson states that "Cruithnechan" means "little Pict" or "Pict-sprung."[159] Some of the Origin Legends refer to Cruithne (**q.v.**) as "Cruithnechan."

Caitnind. Pseudo-historical Pict.

Legends P#E(Lec.), P#E(Bal.), and P#E(1295) state that Caitnind was the father of Cathluan (**q.v.**) who led the Cruithni (Picts?) out of Ireland. Interestingly, other Legends say that Cathluan's father was Gub/Gib (**q.v.**).

Regnal Lists SL2 M, SL2 O, and SL2 H call Caitnind the father of Cathluan.[160]

Canaul f. Tarl'a (Conall son of Tadg). King of Picts (?784-89) and Scots Dál Riata (**q.v.**) (?805-807).[161]

AU 789 and AU 790 mention a battle between Canaul and Castantin f. Uurguist (**q.v.**) in which Canaul was forced to flee. AI 807 records that Canaul was killed in Alba (**q.v.**). AU 807 states that Conall mac Áedáin (**q.v.**) slew Canaul in Kintyre.

Regnal Lists SL1, Lists SL2 M, SL2 O, and SL2 H record a five year reign for Canaul between Talorgen f. Onuist and Castantin f. Uurguist (**q.q.v.**).[162]

Cano f. Gartnait. Possibly two individuals who were the sons of two Pictish rulers (c.6th-7th cent.) who have been confused with one another.[163]

Cano 1 (c.621). Possibly Son of Gartnart f. Domelch (**q.v.**) and grandson of Áedán mac Gabráin (**q.v.**). A note in the *Book of Deer* mentions a "Clann Chanann" ("clan of Cano") in Buchan, which may have descended from this Cano.[164] AT 621 and AU 621 record the death of Cano's son, "Nechtan" (see **Nectu n. Uerb**).

Cano 2 (c. 688). Son of Pictish ruler named Gartnait (see **Gartnait f. Accidan, Gartnait f. Donuel**). AU 668 and CS 664 state that Gartnait's sons went from Skye to Ireland. This may include Cano. AT 688, AU 688, and CS 684 record Cano's murder. AC 683 states that he "entered into religion." This is probably a mistake.[165]

Cano is the hero of *Scéla Cano*, where he is the son of Gartnán mac Áeda maic Gabráin (see **Garnait f. Accidan, Gartnait f. Donuel, Gartnart f. Domelch**). M.O. Anderson states that the tale relates events that occurred later than the time of Áedán mac Gabráin (**q.v.**), who appears in the story. John Bannerman says that it combines each Cano into one character.[166]

Canutulachama. Pseudo-historical Pictish king.

List SL1 gives Canutulachama a reign of four years between Uipoig namet (**q.v.**) and Uuradech (**q.v.**). Canutulachama has a three year reign between these same kings in SL2 M, SL2 O, and SL2 H. List D records a six year reign for him between Fiacua albus (**q.v.**) and Donornauch (**q.v.**). This is also true of Lists F1, F2, I, and K. Fordun's List gives him a reign of six years between Chalag amfrud (**q.v.**) and Donornauch (**q.v.**).[167]

According to Kenneth Jackson, "Canutulachama" is not Celtic. H.M. Chadwick asserts that Canutulachama is the same as Catainlacach (**q.v.**).[168]

Carausius (c.286). British Ruler.[169]

According to Bede, Carausius was a soldier during the joint reign of Diocletian and Maximian and took control of Britain (**q.v.**). After ruling for seven years, he was killed by Allectus. *Historia Brittonum* calls Carausius a tyrant, who became fourth Emperor after murdering Severus (**q.v.**). He rebuilt a wall which separated the Picts and Scots from the Britons (**q.v.**). Geoffrey of Monmouth gives an extended record of Bede's account of Carausius' life. He states that Carausius killed Severus's son Bassianus (**q.v.**) in order to gain control of Britain (**q.v.**). The Picts had betrayed Bassianus to Carausius and were given land in Albania (Scotland) (see **Alba**) in return.[170]

Carausius looks similar to Caruorst (**q.v.**), who appears in Regnal List SL1. However, this is merely an observation.

Caruorst (Carvorst). Pseudo-historical Pictish King.

Regnal Lists SL1, SL2 M, and SL2 O give Caruorst a forty year reign between Usconbuts (**q.v.**) and Deo Artíuois (**q.v.**). In List SL2 H, Caruorst is given a reign of seven years between the same two kings. Starting with List D, the form of Caruorst's name changes drastically. In this list he is called "Fevanacherche" and is given a forty year reign between Usconbuts and Gartnaith loc (**q.v.**). Lists F1, F2, and I give Caruorst the same reign length between the same kings. Fordun's List records a forty year reign for Caruorst after Deoord (**q.v.**) and before Gartnaith loc.[171]

Caruorst looks similar to Carausius (**q.v.**). However, they are unlikely to be the same person.

Castantin f. Uurguist (Causantín mac Fergusa, Constantine son of Fergus). King of Picts and Scots Dál Riata (**q.v.**) (789-820).[172]

Legends P#F(D.iv.i), P#F(Lec.1), P#F(Lec.2), P#F(Bal.), and P#F(24.P.13) state that there were seventy Cruithnian kings of Alba (**q.v.**) from Cathluan (**q.v.**) to "Constantine." It is uncertain which "Constantine" is meant. P#F(1295), P#F(1289), and P#F(D.iii.2) repeat this without mentioning Cathluan as the starting point. H.M. Chadwick thinks that it could be Castantin or Causantín mac Cináeda (**q.v.**).[173] P#G(B 512), P#G(Lec.), P#G(Bal.), and P#G(1295) make the same remarks about "Constantine."

AU 789 and AU 790 recount a Pictish battle between Castantin and Canaul f. Tarl'a (**q.v.**) with Castantin victorious. AI 820 records the death of Castantin and calls him "king of Alba." AU 820 records the death of Castantin and calls him "king of Fortriu" (**q.v.**).

Regnal Lists SL1, SL2 M, SL2 O, and SL2 H give Castantin a reign of thirty-five years between Canaul f. Tarl'a and Unuist f. Uurguist (**q.q.v.**). List D records a forty-five year reign for Castantin between Talorgen f. Onuist (**q.v.**) and Unuist f. Uurguist. It also states that he founded Dunkeld (**q.v.**). This refers to the building of a church to replace Iona (**q.v.**), which had been deserted because of Viking raids. Lists F1 and F2 give him a forty-two year reign between the same kings and record his founding of Dunkeld. List I records the same reign between Talorgen and Unuist and states that Castantin founded Cenn Righmona (**q.v.**). M.O. Anderson indicates that this may be a mistake for Unuist f. Uurguist. List K and Fordun's List give him a forty year reign between Talorgen and Unuist and state that he founded Dunkeld.[174]

Duan Albanach mentions that Cathluan was the first of the Cruithni kings and "Cusaintín" was the last. This "Cusaintín" could be Castantin or Causantín mac Cináeda. It also states that Castantin reigned for nine years between Canaul f. Tarl'a and Unuist f. Uurguist.[175]

Cat. Mythological Pictish king and eponym for Caithness (see **Cat (Caithness)**).[176]

Legends P#L(Uí Ma.), P#L(Lec.), P#L(G47), P#L(Bal.), and P#L(1336) state that Cat was one of the seven sons of Cruithne (**q.v.**) and that he was given one-seventh of the far-north of Britain (**q.v.**). Cat is also said to be the father of Aenbegan (**q.v.**). P#L(1295) states that Cat was son of Cruithne and father of Aenbegan.

Lists SL1, SL2 M, and SL2 H call Cat one of the seven sons of Cruithne and give him a reign of twelve years between Fotla (**q.v.**) and Ce (**q.v.**). Lists SL3(Lec.1), SL3(Bal.1), and SL3(Bal.2) call Cat one of the seven sons of Cruithne and ruler of one seventh of Alba. He is apparently given a reign of twenty-two years between Fortrenn and Ce. A second reign of thirty years is seemingly recorded for Cat after Aenbegan and before Olfinecta (**q.v.**). Brude (30) (**q.v.**) are interspersed within the list. This is also true of List SL3(Lec.4), which gives Cat a second reign of twenty-two years. List SL3(Lec.2) also calls Cat one of the sons of Cruithne and one of thirteen Cruithni kings. List SL3(Lec.3) gives Cat a reign of twenty-two years seemingly between Fortrenn (**q.v.**) and Ce. However, this list has a confused chronology because it intersperses Brude (30) amongst the other kings. He is also called son of Cruithne and possibly father of Aenbegan. He is apparently given a reign of twenty-two years between Fortrenn and Cirig (**q.v.**). A second reign of thirty years is seemingly recorded for Cat after Aenbegan and before Olfinecta (**q.v.**). Again, Brude (30) are interspersed within the list.[177]

F.T. Wainwright equates the story of the seven sons of Cruithne with the text De Situ Albanie, which describes the provinces of Scotland. He says that "Cait" (Cat) is the same as the "Cathanesia" mentioned in the text.[178]

Catainlacach. Pseudo-historical Pict.

P#E(Lec.), P#E(Bal.), P#E(1295), P#F(D.iv.1), P#F(Lec.1), P#F(Lec.2), P#F(Bal.), P#F(24.P.13), P#F(1295), P#F(1289), P#F(D.iii.2), P#G(B 512), P#G(Lec.), and P#G(Bal.) state that Catainlacach is son of Cathluan (**q.v.**), brother of Cadnolodor (**q.v.**), and one of the Cruithni heroes.

H.M. Chadwick asserts that "Cathanalachan" (Catainlacach) is the same as Canutulachama (**q.v.**), who appears in some of the Regnal Lists.[179]

Cathluan. Pseudo-historical Pictish King.

Origin Legend P#E(Lec.) says that Cathluan was killed among the Cruithni or Picts. This is probably a mistake because he is mentioned later in the poem. Also, Cathluan is the son of Caitnind (**q.v.**), who leads the Cruithni out of Ireland. He is called the father of Cadnolodor (**q.v.**) and Catainlacach (**q.v.**). P#E(Bal.) and P#E(1295) says that "Cathluan was glorified by them" rather than being killed. This is more likely the correct intent of the passage. The rest of the poem repeats the same information. In P#F(D.iv.1), P#F(Lec.1), P#F(Lec.2), P#F(Bal.), P#F(24.P.13), P#F(1295), P#F(1289), P#G(B 512), P#G(Lec.), P#G(Bal.), and P#G(1295), Cathluan is called the son of Gub/Gib (**q.v.**). Éremón (**q.v.**) banished Cathluan and Gub from Ireland. They also say that Cathluan was the first king of Alba (**q.v.**) from the Cruithni and father of Cadnolodor and Catainlacach. P#F(D.iii.) repeats this but omits Gub/Gib. P#H(Lein.), P#H(D.iii.1), P#H(B 512), P#H(D.i.3), and P#H(Lec.) call Cathluan son of Cing (**q.v.**) and say that Cathluan and the Cruithni were expelled from Ireland by Éremón. P#H(B 512), P#H(D.i.3), and P#H(Lec.) state that Cathluan (**q.v.**) received wives of men who drowned with Donn (**q.v.**) from Éremón.

MacFirbis Genealogies mention the "Teallach Cathluain" ("Family(?) of Cathluan"). Whether or not this is the same Cathluan is uncertain without further examination of the text. This could be Cadwallon (d.634).[180]

Lists SL2 M, SL2 O, and SL2 H record that Cathluan may have been first king of Alba and Ireland for sixty years.[181]

Duan Albanach states that Cathluan was the first Cruithnian king of Alba.[182] T.F. O"Rahilly suggests that "Catluan" (Cathluan) is an Irish version of Welsh "Cadwallon," the name of the father of Cadwaladr (**q.v.**).[183]

Causantín mac Cináeda (Constantine son of Kenneth). King of Scots (862-77). Son of Cináed mac Alpín (**q.v.**).[184]

P#F(D.iv.1), P#F(Lec.1), P#F(Lec.2), P#F(Bal.), F#F(24.P.13), P#F(1295), P#F(1289), P#F(D.iii.2), P#G(Lec.), P#G(Bal.), P#G(B 512), and P#G(1295) state that there were seventy Cruithni kings of Alba (**q.v.**) to "Constantine." This could be Causantín or Castantin f. Uurguist (**q.v.**).

Rawl B. 502 and *Book of Leinster* list him in genealogies of kings of Alba as Domnall mac Causantín's father and son of Cináed mac Alpín .[185]

AU 872 and CS 872 state that Causantín had Artgal of the Strathclyde Britons (**q.v.**) killed. AU 876 records Causantín's death and calls him "rex Pictorum" ("king of Picts). CS 876 also mentions his death.

Lists SL2 M, SL2 O, and SL2 H give him a twenty year reign between Domnall mac Alpín (**q.v.**) and Áed mac Cináeda (**q.v.**). Lists D, F1, F2, I, and K give him a fifteen year reign between Domnall and Áed. He was killed in battle by Norwegians (**q.v.**) and buried on Iona (**q.v.**). List N gives him a twenty year reign between Domnall and Áed and states that he was killed by Norwegians.[186]

Duan Albanach gives Causantín a thirty year reign between Domnall and Áed and mentions the seventy kings from Cathluan to an uncertain "Cusaintín."[187]

Caw (Cau Pritdin, Cauus of Arecluta (Alclud (Dumbarton)), Caw O Brydein) (5th-6th cent.). Father of Gildas. Possibly king of northern Picts.[188]

Bonedd Y Saint calls Caw father of Gildas and Gurhei.[189]

Vita Cadoci recounts how Cadoc (saint) (**q.v.**) went to Albania (Scotland) (see **Alba**) and encountered the already deceased Caw (also "Cawr"), who had ruled beyond Bannog (**q.v.**). Cadoc resurrected him in return for service and reform. *Vita Sancti Dauid* mentions Caw as father of Gildas.[190]

Culhwch and Olwen records that Caw was part of the retinue of Arthur (**q.v.**) and that he had nineteen sons (including Gildas) and one daughter. He killed Ysgithrwn Chief-boar while riding Arthur's mare. He also collected the blood from a witch whom Arthur had killed. Triad 21 of *Welsh Triads* calls Caw father of Hueil. Triads 81.C18 and 96 state Caw was the ancestor of a family of saints with Welsh mothers.[191]

John Morris states that legend made Caw a giant because "Cawr" is Welsh for "giant." H.M. Chadwick states that Caw is also in *Life of Gildas* and *Dream of Rhonabwy*. K.H. Jackson indicates that "Cauuus" would have been the original form.[192]

Ce. Mythological Pictish king of Marr (Mar) and Buchan.[193]

Legends P#L(Uí Ma.), P#L(Lec.), P#L(G47), and P#L(1336) record that Ce was one of seven sons of Cruithne who divided Alba (**q.v.**) or the far-north of Britain (**q.v.**).

Lists SL1, SL2 M, and SL2 H call Ce one of Cruithne's seven sons and give him a fifteen year reign between Cat (**q.v.**) and Fib (**q.v.**). Skene's SL2 H has twelve years. List SL3(Lec.1) gives him a twelve twelve reign year. SL3(Lec.2) calls Ce one of Cruithne's seven sons and one of thirteen Cruithni kings. SL3(Lec.3) calls Ce one of Cruithne's seven sons and seems to give him an eleven year reign between Cat and Cirig (**q.v.**). However the interspersing of Brude (30) (**q.v.**) confuses the list. SL3(Lec.4) gives a twenty year reign. SL3(Bal.1) and SL3(Bal.2) seem to give him a twelve year reign between Cirig and Aenbegan (**q.v.**), but the lists are again confused.[194]

F.T. Wainwright equates Ce's territory with "Marr cum Buchen" described in *De Situ Albanie*. H.M. Chadwick is uncertain about its location but states that it included areas of "Marr with Buchan" and "Moray with Ross" in *De Situ Albanie*. M.O. Anderson asserts that his territory must have been north of the Dee.[195]

Celestine (pope) (Celestinus). Pope (422-432).[196]

AI § 389, AC (p.65), AU 431, and AFM 430 record that Celestine sent Palladius (**q.v.**) to Ireland (**q.v.**) to convert the Scots (see also **Irish**). This was during the eighth year of the reign of Theodosius. AC records both of these events and states that Palladius died in Pictland (**q.v.**). Celestine's death is mentioned in AI § 389 and AC 425 (p.65). AC 658 mentions the third General Council held at Ephesus by Celestine and Theodosius. AFM 431 records that Celestine sent Patricius (Patrick) (**q.v.**) to Ireland.

Cellach mac Ailella (d.865). Abbot of Iona (**q.v.**) and Kildare.[197]

AC 863, AU 865, AFM 863 state that Cellach died in Pictish territory. CS 865 mentions Cellach's death but does not give a location.

Ceolfrith (d.716). Saint. Abbot of Jarrow (682-716). Abbot of Monkwearmouth (c.689-716).[198]

Bede states that Ceolfrith went to Rome in 680 with Abbot Benedict, whom Ceolfrith would succeed. Necthon f. Derelei (**q.v.**) sent messengers to Ceolfrith to help establish the Roman Easter, and Ceolfrith sent a response to Necthon in 710. Ceolfrith and Benedict were Bede's teachers.[199]

Chalag amfrud. Pseudo-historical Pictish king.

Fordun's List gives Chalag amfrud a seventeen year reign between Fiacua albus and Canutulachama (**q.q.v.**). Molly Miller points out that Chalag amfrud seems like Talorcen f. Enfret (**q.v.**), who appears in Fordun's List as well as others but that he may be another individual.[200]

Chelric. Legendary Saxon leader (see **Saxons**).

Geoffrey of Monmouth records that Chelric supported Mordred (**q.v.**) against Arthur (**q.v**) in return for land. He was killed at Camlann (**q.v.**).[201]

Cináed mac Alpin (Kenneth mac Alpín, Kenneth son of Alpín). King of Scots Dál Riata (?841-858) and Picts (c.843/48?-858), although he was not the first to rule over both peoples.[202]

Origin Legend P#E(Lec.) states that the Cruithni controlled Alba (**q.v.**) until Cináed. P#E(Bal.) and P#E(1295) record that Cináed ruled Alba.

Rawl. B. 502 records that he was son of Alpín (see **Alpín f. Eochaid**) and father of Causantín mac Cináeda (**q.v.**). *Book of Leinster* repeats this and calls him father of Áed mac Cínáeda (**q.v.**).[203]

ACam. 856, AI 858, and AU 858 record Cináed's death. AC 905 records the death of Cináed's daughter.

Regnal Lists SL2 M, SL2 O, and SL2 H give Cináed a sixteen year reign between Bred and Domnall mac Alpín (**q.q.v.**). Lists D, F1, F2,and I give a sixteen year reign between Drust f. Ferat (**q.v.**) and Domnall. Cináed destroyed the Picts, was killed at Forteviot (**q.v.**), and was buried on Iona (**q.v.**).

This is also true of List K which wrongly calls him first king of the Picts and Scots. List N gives Cináed a sixteen year reign between Alpín f. Eochaid and Domnall and states that he destroyed the Picts and was buried on Iona. Fordun's List states that Cináed reigned after Drust f. Ferat.[204]

Duan Albanach records a thirty year reign between Uuen f. Unuist (**q.v.**) and Domnall mac Alpín.[205]

Cing (Inge in some of the Origin Legends). Pictish ancestor and father of Cruithne (**q.v.**).[206]

Origin Legends P#E(Lec.), P#E(Bal.), and P#E(1295) call Cing a victorious warrior and father of Cruithne. P#F(D.iv.1), P#F(Lec.1), P#F(Lec.2), P#F(Bal.), P#F(1295), P#F(1289), P#F(24.P.13), and P#F(D.iii.2) state that Cing and possibly Im (**q.v.**) were Cruithni elders and call Cing Cruithne's father (P#F(1289) and P#F(D.iii.2) omit Cruithne's name). They also call Cing father of Loichet (**q.v.**) and Cruithne's grandfather. P#G(B 512), P#G(Lec.), P#G(Bal.), and P#G(1295) call Cing one of two heroes of the Cruithni. P#K(D.iv.1) and P#K(Lec.1) record that Cing was Cruithne's father and Loichet's son. P#K(Lec.2), P#K(Bal.), P#K(24.P.13), P#K(1295), P#K(1289), and P#K(D.iii.2) state that Cing was father of Loichet and grandfather of Cruithne. In P#L(Uí Ma.), P#L(Lec.), P#L(G47), P#L(Bal.), and P#L(1295), Cing is Cruithne's father and Loichet's son.

Rawl B. 502 records an Ingai (Cingai, Ginga) m. Rudraige m. Sittride from the prehistory of Dál n-Araide (**q.v.**). This could be Cing and is worth examining. Ingai is father of Cappa mac Ingai (Cingai, Ginga) and son of Rudraige mac Sittride. This genealogy goes back to Ollam Fótla (**q.v.**) and Ír son of Míl (**q.v.**). Irél Glúnmár (**q.v.**), who appears in Origin Legends, is among descendants of Ingai. This would make the Cruithni related to the Sons of Míl, who appear in some of the Legends as contemporaries of the Cruithni. Ollam was a Cruithni king of Alba and Ireland (**q.q.v.**). *Book of Lecan* gives the same genealogy for "Ginga." *Laud 610* has a similar genealogy for Ingai ("Cingai") excluding Ollam. *Book of Lecan* also seems to state that Nadbroicc, mother of Niall mac Trichim of Ulaid (Ulster), was from the "genus nInge de Pictis" ("family of Inge of the Picts"). H.M. Chadwick indicates that early Irish scholars saw Ír's offspring as Scottish Cruithni. Cing, Ingai, and Inge could be the same person in an attempt to combine different traditions.[207]

Regnal Lists SL1, SL2 M, and SL2 H call Cing father of Cruithne. SL3(Lec.1), SL3(Lec.2), SL3(Lec.3), SL3(Lec.4), SL3(Bal.1), SL3(Bal.2), and List D call Cing Cruithne's father and Loichet's son. In Lists F1, F2, and I, Cing is father of Cruithne. List K has "Cruthene Kenek" as first king of Picts. "Kenek" is no doubt Cing. Cing is father of Cruithne in Fordun's List.[208]

H.M. Chadwick states that "Cing" is Gaelic for "champion." R.I.A. *Dictionary* corroborates this.[209]

Cinioch f. Lutrin (Ciniod I, Cinioch/Kenneth son of Luchtren). Pictish king (621-631).[210]

AI 633 records Cinioch's death and calls him king of Alba (**q.v.**). Cinioch's death is mentioned in AT 631, AC 632, AU 631, and CS 631, where he is king of Picts.

Regnal Lists SL1, SL2 M, SL2 O, and SL2 H give Cinioch a reign of nineteen years between Nectu n. Uerb (**q.v.**) and Garnard f. Uuid (**q.v.**). M.O. Anderson suggests that "Cinioch" could be "Cinioth" or "Ciniod," which appears to be Pictish. List D records a reign of twenty-four years for Cinioch between Gartnart f. Domelch (**q.v.**) and Garnard f. Uuid. Lists F1, F2, and I give Cinioch a fourteen year reign between Nectu n. Uerb and Garnard f. Uuid. List K gives Cinioch a twenty-four year reign between Gartnart f. Domelch and Garnard f. Uuid. Fordun's List records a fourteen year reign between Nectu n. Uerb and Garnard f. Uuid.[211]

Ciniod f. Derelei (d.713). Brother of Bredei f. Derelei and Necthon f. Derelei (**q.q.v.**).[212]

AT 713 and AU 713 record that Ciniod was murdered.

Alfred Smyth refers to Ciniod as a Pict with a Gaelic name. A.O. Anderson states that Ciniod was the brother of Necthon f. Derelei.[213]

Ciniod f. Uuredech (Ciniod II, Cinaed/Ciniod son of Uuredech/?Feradach of Lorn). Pictish king (763-75).[214]

AU 768 records a battle between Ciniod and Áed Find (**q.v.**) in Fortriu (**q.v.**). ACam. 776 and AU 775 record Ciniod's death.

Lists SL1, SL2 M, SL2 O, and Van Hamel's SL2 H record a twelve year reign between Bredei f. Uuirguist (**q.v.**) and Elpin f. Uuroid (**q.v.**). Skene's SL2 H gives a fifteen year reign.[215]

M.O. Anderson postulates that "Garnard son of Ferath/Feradach" (Carnach f. Ferach) mentioned in the later Lists is Ciniod f. Uuredech. List D records a twenty-four year reign for Garnard between Bredei f. Derelei (**q.v.**) and Óengus f. Bruide (**q.v.**). Lists F1, F2, I, and K give Garnard a twenty-four year reign between Necthon f. Derelei (**q.v.**) and Onuist f. Urguist (**q.v.**). Fordun's List records a fourteen year reign between the same kings.[216]

Cinioiod f. Arcois (Cimoiod, Ciniod). Pseudo-historical Pictish king.

Lists SL1, SL2 M, SL2 O, and SL2 H give Cinioiod a seven year reign between Deocilinion (**q.v.**) and Deoord (**q.v.**). SL1(Sk.) has "Cimoiod."[217]

M.O. Anderson states that Cinioiod could be "Ciniod," a Pictish name. H.M. Chadwick sees "Cinioiod" as an earlier form of "Ciniod." Kenneth Jackson asserts that "Artcois" (Arcois) means "Bear's Leg" or "Bear's Paw" and is more related to Gaulish than British.[218]

Cirig (Circinn). Mythological Pictish king.

P#E(Lec.), P#E(Bal.), and P#E(1295) call Cirig father of the warrior Crus (**q.v.**). P#F(D.iv.1), P#F(Lec.1), P#F(Lec.2), P#F(Bal.), P#F(24.P.13), P#F(1295), P#F(1289), and P#F(D.iii.2) call Cirig and Crus two soldiers of the Cruithni. P#G(B 512), P#G(Lec.), P#G(Bal.), and P#G(1295) state that Cirig is father of Crus. P#L(Uí Ma.), P#L(Lec.), P#L(G47), and P#L(1336) count Cirig as one of seven sons of Cruithne (**q.v.**).

Regnal Lists SL1, SL2 M, and SL2 H call him (apparently as "Circinn") a son of Cruithne and the first to rule with a sixty year reign before Fidach (**q.v.**). SL3(Lec.2) calls Cirig one of seven sons of Cruithne. SL3(Lec.1) and SL3(Lec.4) call him Cruithne's son but seem to record an eighty year reign between Ce (**q.v.**) and Aenbegan (**q.v.**). The lists are confused because they intersperse the "thirty Brudes" (see **Brude (30)**) among the other kings. This is true of SL3(Lec.3), which gives a seventy year reign. SL3(Bal.1) gives Cirig an eighty year reign between Ce and Aenbegan. SL3(Bal.2) calls him Cruithne's son with an eighty year reign between Cat (**q.v.**) and Ce. The lists also intersperse the "thirty Brudes."[219]

F.T. Wainwright postulates that Cirig's territory corresponds to "Enegus cum Moerne" described in *De Situ Albanie*, which was printed by Skene and M.O. Anderson. H.M. Chadwick equates "Angus with the Mearns" ("Enegus cum Moerne") with "Circinn," "Magh Circinn", and "Magh Gergend" (see **Circhend**). M.O. Anderson says that "Cirig" is a different name from "Circinn."[220] However, they seem to fill the same function in the texts. This would indicate that they are meant to be the same person.

Coblaith daughter of Cano. Her father could be either of the individuals named Cano f. Gartnait (**q.v.**).

AT 690 and AU 690 record her death.

Colcu mac Mongáin (Colcu mac Mongáin m. Fiachnai of Ulaid (?)).[221]

Origin Legends P#A(B 506), P#A(Uí Ma.), P#A(Lec.), and P#A(C.vi.2) quote a poem attributed to Colcu about the fifty battles of Irél Glúnmár (**q.v.**).

Book of Leinster and *Laud 610* mention Colcu mac Mongáin, son of Cumne Dub ben Mongáin, and brother of Conall mac Mongáin. *Book of Lecan* gives the same pedigree but seems to call him "Colmán."[222]

Colgrin. Legendary leader of the Saxons (**q.v.**).[223]

Geoffrey of Monmouth recounts that Colgrin gathered an army of Saxons (**q.v.**), Scots, and Picts in order to fight Arthur (**q.v.**). Arthur defeated him near "flumen Duglas" ("River Douglas") and Colgrin escaped to York (Eboracum) where Arthur attacked him. Colgrin was killed in battle against Arthur.[224]

Columba (Colum Cille, Columb Cille mac Feidelmtheo m. Fergusa) (521-597). Founder and first abbot of Iona (**q.v.**). He was from the Cenél Chonaill Uí Neill dynasty of north-western Ireland (**q.v.**).[225]

Legend P#L(Lec.), P#L(G47) records a poem that Columba recited about Cruithne (**q.v.**) and his seven sons. This poem is also contained in some of the Regnal Lists.

Rawl. B. 502 names Ethne ingen Óengusa nó Dímmae as Columba's mother and calls him one of the two sons of Fedelmid mac Fergusa Cennfota. *Book of Leinster* lists the pedigree of Columba in the "Genealogies of Irish Saints," where he is called the son of Fedelmid. It also states that "Crimthann" is another name of Columba. It is interesting to note that Crimthann (**q.v.**) is also the king of Laigin (**q.v.**) in some of the Origin Legends. Columba is included in a list of priests. A list of Irish saints also mentions Columba. "Comananmand Naebúag Herenn" mentions Columba's mother Ethne. *Laud 610* states that Fóelchú received a blessing from Columba. Columba is also called one of two sons of Fedelmid. *MacFirbis Genealogies* include Columba in a section about Irish saints.[226]

ACam. 521, AI 521, AT 520, AC 521, AU 519, AU 523, and CS 518 record the birth of Columba. The birth of Baithine, ward of Columba, is recorded in AT 536 and AC 536. An enigmatic entry in AI 537 records the "ruin of the bread of Columba." Seán Mac Airt suggests that this is an abridged entry. AU 553 relates that an angel gave Columba one of relics of Patricius (Patrick) (**q.v.**): the "Soiscela in Aingil" ("Gospel of the Angel"). AU 561, AFM 554, AFM 555, CS 560, and CS 561 record that Columba caused the defeat of Diarmait mac Cerbaill at Cúl Dremne (**q.v.**). Columba travelled to Britain in ACam. 562 and AI 563. AT 563 also records that Columba travelled to Iona (**q.v.**). AC 547 records that after he went to Scotland, Columba helped to heal Diarmait mac Cerbaill. Columba went to Scotland in AC 563. Columba's journey to Iona is mentioned in AU 563. AFM 557 records Columba's journey to Alba (**q.v.**). CS 563 records Columba's journey to Iona. AC 569 states that Conall mac Comgaill, king of Scots Dál Riata (**q.v**) (558-74) gave Iona to Columba. AU 574 implies the donation of Iona to Columba by Conall. Columba was in Druim Cett with Áedán mac Gabráin (**q.v.**) in AC 587. The Convention of Druim Cett in Derry is recorded in AU 575. AT 589, AU 589, and AFM 585 mention that Durrow was given to Columba. ACam. 595, AT 595, AC 590, AU 595, AU 601, AFM 592, and CS 595 record his death.

Regnal Lists SL1, SL2 M, SL2 O, SL2 H record that Columba baptized Bridei f. Mailcon (**q.v.**) during the eighth year of his reign. List SL3(Bal.2) attributes a poem about the sons of Cruithne (**q.v.**) to Columba. Lists D, F1, and F2 record that Columba converted Bridei. This is also true of List I, which states that Columba died during Bridei's reign. List K states that both Columba and Palladius (**q.v.**) (perhaps, Torannán (**q.v.**)) converted Bridei. Columba converted Bridei in Fordun's List.[227]

Vita Niniani refers to Bede's account of Columba's journey to the northern Picts. *Amra Choluimb Chille* (c.600) alludes to Columba as having preached to Pictish tribes around the Tay. *Vita Columbae* frequently mentions the Picts in connection with Columba. He defeated the efforts of magicians to prevent him from sailing back from Pictish territory. At the court of Bridei, Columba endowed a stone with healing powers. In Pictish territory, Columba blessed a magic well so that it cured illness rather than causing it. On the banks of the river Ness, Columba repelled a river monster that had attacked Luigne moccu Min (**q.v.**) while he was swimming. Adomnán also mentions that the presence of Columba and his monasteries twice protected the Picts and the Scots from plague. Columba had a foster-father named Cruithnechan. Interestingly, this is also a name applied to Pictish ancestor Cruithne (**q.v.**) and to Cairpe Cruithnechan (**q.v.**), son of Conall Corc (**q.v.**). *Betha Coluim Cille* records that Columba was in Alba for thirty-four years. After establishing Iona, Columba travelled as a missionary around Britain. *Félire Óengusso* lists him under 9 June.[228]

Bede twice records that Columba converted the northern Picts in the ninth year of Bridei's reign. He was also given Iona and became its first abbot. *Historia Brittonum* records that there were four years between the birth of Columba and the death of Brigid (**q.v.**).[229]

Comgan (Congan) (c.8th cent.). Saint of Turriff in Aberdeenshire. Supposedly the brother of Kentigerna (**q.v.**).[229a]

Félire Óengusso lists him under 13 October, and *Martyrology of Tallaght* (Lein.) lists him under ".III. IDUS OCTIMBIR" (13 October).[229b]

Conall Cernach mac Amargin m. Caiss. Red Branch hero and ancestor of the Cruithni. Father of Irél Glúnmár (**q.v.**).[230]

P#A(B 506), P#A(Uí Ma.), P#A(Lec.), and P#A(C.vi.2) state that Conall was father of Irél Glúnmár and ancestor of the "Clan of Conall Cernach" (see **Cenél Conaill**).

Rawl. B. 502 says that Conall is from the Ulaid, son of Amargein, and father of Lugaid Loígsech (Loíchse) Cennmár. Also, the seven "Loíchsi Lagen" (see **Laigis** and **Laigin**) are descended from Conall. Conall is also the ancestor of the Dál n-Araide (**q.v.**), "Húi Echdach," the seven Sodain (**q.v.**), and the "Conailli Murthemni." Conall's mother Findchóem is given a genealogy in "Senchas Síl Ir." Conall is mentioned in a prophetic poem, and "Conmaicne" also gives Conall ancestor status. *Book of Leinster* lists the clans descended from Conall and calls him father of Irél Glúnmár and Loígsech and son of Amargein and Findchóem. "Genelach hEli Descirt" includes further clans descended from Conall. *Book of Lecan* calls Conall son of Amargein and ancestor of the Loichsi. *Laud 610* says that Findchóem is the mother of Conall and lists the clans descended from Conall in the section "Clanna Conchobuir maic Nessa." Conall was son of Amargein and father of Irél. *MacFirbis Genealogies* and *MacFirbis Abstract* have sections on his descendants.[231]

TBF records that Fróech (**q.v.**) visited Conall in search of his cattle. Later, the two went to Pictland (**q.v.**) to retrieve three of Fróech's cattle.[232]

Conall Corc (Corcc mac Luigdech, Corc mac Luigthig) (c.400). King of Munster from the Eóganacht.[233]

Rawl. B. 502, *Book of Leinster*, and *Book of Lecan* call him father of Cairpre Cruithnechan (**q.v.**), whose mother was Mongfind (**q.v.**) daughter of Feradach Find Fechtnach (**q.v.**). Conall Corc is son of Lugaid mac Dáiri Cherrba and father of Nad-fraích mac Cuircc, Cass mac Cuircc, Mac-Iair, and Daig mac Cuircc. *Laud 610* states that Conall Corc had seven sons including Cairpre Cruithnechan. "Conall Corc and the Corco Luigde" states that he was exiled to Alba (**q.v.**), where he was to be killed by Feradach. However, Gruibne (**q.v.**), whom he had saved from captivity, saved him. In Alba, he has two sons by Feradach's anonymous daughter: Cairpre and Lughid.[234]

Conall Corc is the hero of *Longes Chonaill* in which he sails to Alba and is nearly killed by a snowstorm. He is rescued by Gruibne, poet of Feradach, who discovers an ogham death sentence on Conall's shield. However, Gruibne tells Feradach that Conall is to be given the king's daughter. The king refuses but is deceived so that it occurs surreptitiously. A son is born of this union; however, the mother is to be burned because they are unmarried. Conall manages to save her and his son from punishment. Finally, Feradach sanctions the marriage, and Conall Corc takes his new family back to Ireland. Vernam Hull states that "Feradach" is Feradach Find Fechtnach.[235] Therefore, the daughter would be Mongfind and the son would be Cairpre Cruithnechan.

Conall mac Áedáin (c.807). Possible pretender to the kingship of Scottish Dál Riata (**q.v.**).[236]

AU 807 states that Conall slew Canaul f. Tarl'a (**q.v.**) in Kintyre.

Duan Albanach gives him a four year reign between Canaul f. Tarl'a (**q.v.**) and Castantin f. Uurguist (**q.v.**).[237]

Conamail f. Cano. His father could be either of the individuals named Cano f. Gartnait (**q.v.**). However, the *Genelaig Albanensium* mentions that Cano grandson of Áedán mac Gabráin (**q.v.**) had a son named Conamail.[237a]

AU 673 records the capture of Conamail and Elén. AU 705 mentions the killing of Conamail.

Congal mac Rónáin (d.c.654).[238]

AT 654 and CS 651 state that he died at Sráith Ethairt (**q.v.**). AU 654 records the battle without naming Congal.

Constans f. Constantine III (c.409).   Monk and   British emperor. Son of Constantine III (**q.v.**).[239]

Bede records that after his father's murder, Constans became emperor and was killed by Gerontius. Geoffrey of Monmouth calls Constans, Ambrosius, and Utherpendragon (**q.q.v.**) three sons of Constantine III. Constans became a monk at his father's request. After Constantine had been murdered by a Pict, Vortigern (**q.v.**) elevated Constans to the kingship. Vortigern later incited Picts to assassinate him and took the throne himself.[240] In the *Welsh Triads*, Triad 51 says that Vortigern betrayed Constans and brought about his death.[241]

Rachel Bromwich says that Geoffrey's story of Constans derives from that related by Orosius. He may have been confused with Constans, son of Constantine the Great.[242]

Constantin (Constantinus rex Cornubiensis) (d.c.596/600). King of Cornwall who became a monk and may have travelled among Picts and Scots. He may have given his name to Scottish locations. He was confused with others of the same name.[242a]

ACam 589, AT 588, AC 587, and AU 588 record his conversion.

Constantine III.   Western Roman emperor (406-411). Also called Constantine II, king of Britain.[243]

Bede says that he became emperor after the death of Gratian (**q.v.**) but was later murdered and succeeded by his son Constans. *Historia Brittonum* records that he was emperor for sixteen years and died in Britain. Geoffrey of Monmouth states that he was made king of Britain after his brother refused it. He was murdered by a Pict and had three sons: Constans (his successsor), Ambrosius, and Utherpendragon (**q.q.v.**).

Rachel Bromwich indicates that Geoffrey possibly conflated Constantine of the Dumnonian royal dynasty with Constantine III and/or Constantine the Great to create his "Constantinus." In the *Welsh Triads*, Triad 51 states that Constantine was father of Constans.[244]

Corindu (?) (d.c.669). AT 669, AU 669, and CS 665 record that Corindu and Itarnan (**q.v.**) died among the Picts.[245]

Cormac Ua Liathain (late 6th cent.) Irish explorer and monk of the Uí Liathain (see **Liathan**).[246]

Book of Leinster calls Cormac son of Dímma mac Commáin and includes him in a list of priests.[247] *Vita Columbae* records that Columba (**q.v.**) predicted that Cormac would have an unsuccessful quest in the ocean. Columba later asks Bridei f. Mailcon (**q.v.**) to ensure that the king of Orc (**q.v.**) would guarantee the safety of Cormac. Also, Cormac is helped out of danger on the sea through the prayers of Columba. Cormac and three other founders of monasteries travelled to Hinba to see Columba. *Betha Coluim Cille* says that Columba left Cormac in Durrow. *Félire Óengusso* list him under 21 June.[248]

Coroticus (Ceretic) (5th cent.).   Probably king of Strathclyde Britons (**q.v.**); however, this identification is uncertain.[249]

   Harl. 3859 includes Coroticus in a genealogy of Strathclyde, where he is an ancestor of Neithon map Gwyddno (**q.v.**) and Beli map Neithon (**q.v.**).[250]

   In his *Epistola*, Patricius (Patrick) (**q.v.**) reprimands Coroticus for selling Christians into slavery to Scots and Picts.[251]

Crimthann (Crimthann Sciathbel ("Shield-mouth")).
Legendary king of Laigin (**q.v.**).[252]

   P#D(D.iv.1), P#D(Lec.1), P#D(Lec.2), P#D(Bal.), P#D(24.P.13), P#D(1295), P#D(1289), and P#D(D.iii.2) recount the Battle of Ard Lemnacht (**q.v.**) in which the Cruithni aided Crimthann.   P#E(Lec.), P#E(Bal.), and P#E(1295) mention that Crimthann brought cattle to be milked as a magic cure against the poisoned weapons of Fea (**q.v.**).   Crimthann survived Ard Lemnacht.   P#F(D.iv.1), P#F(Lec.1), P#F(Lec.2), P#F(Bal.), P#F(24.P.13), P#F(1295), P#F(1289), P#F(D.iii.2), P#G(B 512), P#G(Lec.), P#G(Bal.), P#G(1295), P#H(Lein.), P#H(D.iii.1), P#H(B 512), P#H(D.i.3), P#H(Lec.), P#I(Lein.), P#I(Bal.), and P#I(B.iii.1) state that Crimthann would befriend the Cruithni if they expelled the Tuath Fidga (**q.v.**).   Ard Lemnacht is also described.   P#I(Uí Ma.), P#I(Lec.), P#I(D.ii.2) mention that Crimthann's offspring destroyed the Tuath Fidga.   P#J(Uí Ma.), P#J(Lec.), P#J(Bal.), P#J(Ren.)(TR.WS), P#J(D.ii.2), and P#J(B.iii.1) record that Crimthann engaged the Cruithni to defeat the Tuath Fidga at Ard Lemnacht.

   "Crimthann" occurs frequently in Geneaologies, but none seem to be this Crimthann. However, there is Crimthann mac Énnai Chennselaig, who is associated with Uí Cennselaig (**q.v.**). Given that some of the Legends have the Cruithni (Picts?) land at Uí Cennselaig, this Crimthann seems a possible candidate although he is not called "Sciathbel." *Rawl.B. 502* and *Book of Lecan* list him in "Genelach Síl Chormaicc." He is a contemporary of Patricius (Patrick) (**q.v.**) in *Book of Leinster* and *Book of Lecan*.[253]

   AC records that Éremón (**q.v.**) made Crimthann "King of Dowrancha." AFM 3502 and the *Lebor Gabála* in the *Book of Leinster* make similar comments concerning Crimthann.[254]

   Denis Murphy says that Crimthann aided the sons of Míl (**q.v.**) against the Britons (**q.v.**). T.F. O'Rahilly states that Crimthann was descended from the "Dumnonii" of Devon and Cornwall.[255]

Crodai. Another name for Irél Glúnmár (**q.v.**).
   Legends P#A(B 506), P#A(Uí Ma.), and P#A(Lec.), and P#A(C.vi.2) state that Crodai was used for Irél Glúnmár. "Crodai" seems to derive from the Irish adjective "cródae" meaning "cruel," "bloody," or "fierce."[256]

Cruithne. Mythological and eponymous ancestor of the Cruithni (Picts?) and Picts.[257]

Legends P#A(B 506), P#A(Uí Ma.), P#A(Lec.), and P#A(C.vi.2) seem to state that Irél Glúnmár (**q.v.**) was descended from Cruithne's sister.[258] P#C(Lein.), P#C(Uí Ma.), P#C(Lec.), and P#C(G131) call Cruithne son of Cing (**q.v.**) and say that he stole the wives of the Gaels (**q.v.**) except for Tea (**q.v.**). P#E(Lec.), P#E(Bal.), and P#E(1295) say that Cruithne brought women for the Cruithni.   P#F(D.iv.1), P#F(Lec.1),   P#F(Bal.), P#F(24.P.13), and P#F(1295) record that Cruithne received wives of those drowned with Donn (**q.v.**) from Éremón. He was the artisan of the Cruithni. He is called both the son of Inge (Cing) and Loichet (**q.v.**). P#F(Lec.2) repeats this and mentions that Cruithne (called "Cruithnechan") with the Britons (**q.v.**) of Fortriu (**q.v.**) battled against the Saxons (**q.v.**). P#F(1289) and P#F(D.iii.) call Cruithne the artisan of the Cruithni and the son of both Loichet and Cing. P#G(B 512), P#G(Lec.), P#G(Bal.), and P#G(1295) record that Cruithne was son of Cing and the artisan of the Cruithni. P#H(Lein.) and P#H(D.iii.1) state that Éremón gave the widows of those who drowned with Donn to Cruithne. P#I(Lein.), P#I(Bal.), and P#I(B.iii.1) mention that the offspring of Cruithne destroyed the Tuath Fidga (**q.v.**). P#K(D.iv.1) and P#K(Lec.1) call Cruithne the son of Cing and the grandson of Loichet.   P#K(Lec.2), P#K(Bal.), P#K(24.P.13), P#K(1295), P#K(1289), and P#K(D.iii.2) call Cruithne the son of Loichet and the grandson of Cing. All these texts state that after leaving the Sons of Míl (**q.v.**) with the Britons (**q.v.**) of Fortriu (**q.v.**), he battled against the Saxons. He returned to the Sons of Míl and received the widows. P#L(Lec.), P#L(G47) and P#L(1336) state that Cruithne took the Cruithni to Orc (**q.v.**). They also give extended genealogies of Cruithne and record that he took control of Alba (**q.v.**).and had seven sons who divided it amongst themselves P#L(Uí Ma.), P#L(Bal.), and P#L(1295) state that Cruithne took the Cruithni to Orkney (**q.v.**) and record that he took control of the far-north of the island of Britain.

Regnal Lists SL1, SL2 M, and SL2 H call Cruithne the son of Cing. Cruithne is named "pater Pictorum" ("father of the Picts") and is given a hundred year reign before his seven sons.   Lists SL3(Lec.1), SL3(Lec.2), SL3(Lec.3), SL3(Lec.4), SL3(Bal.1), and SL3(Bal.2) give Cruithne's genealogy back to Noah (**q.v.**) and give him a hundred year reign. List D calls Cruithne "clemens judex" ("merciful judge") and says that he reigned for fifty years before Gub/Gib (**q.v.**). Lists F1, F2, I, and K repeat this. Molly Miller suggests that "deboner" used in this text is the eqivalent of "judex" and indicates that Cruithne might not have been a king. However, it could simply be an epithet. Fordun's List says that Cruithne reigned for one year. M.O Anderson asserts that this should be fifty.[259]

"Cruithne" is an eponym derived from "Cruithni." Kenneth Jackson relates it to "*Priteni," "*Pritani," "Britanni," "Prydain," "*Quriteni," and "*Quritenii." These terms refer to Britain and its inhabitants. M.O. Anderson compares the idea of Cruithne as a judge with judges in ancient Israel.[260]

Crus. Mythological Pict.

Origin Legends P#E(Lec.), P#E(Bal.), P#E(1295), P#F(D.iv.1), P#F(Lec.1), P#F(Lec.2), P#F(Bal.), P#F(24.P.13), P#F(1295), P#F(1289), P#F(D.iii.2), P#G(B 512), P#G(Lec.), P#G(Bal.), and P#G(1295) call Crus one of the soldiers of the Cruithni (Picts?) and son of Cirig (**q.v.**).

Cú Chulainn (Cú-Chulaind (-Chaulaind) mac Soaltaich (Sualtaim) m. Becalta). Legendary champion of Ulster and hero of *Táin Bó Cuailgne*.[261]

Origin Legends P#A(B 506), P#A(Uí Ma.), P#A(Lec.), and P#A(C.vi.2) say that Cú Chulainn and Cú Roi mac Daire (**q.v.**) went from Alba (**q.v.**) to Ireland (**q.v.**) because of Echde eachbheoil (**q.v.**). H.M. Chadwick states that this refers to a tale in which Cú Chulainn and Cú Roi stole cattle from Echde.[262]

Rawl. B. 502 mentions a poem which Cú Chulainn recited in "Ríg Érenn." "Senchas Síl Ir" mentions him in a poem. Cú Chulainn's genealogy is listed in "Item Genelach Con-Caulaind," where he is "Sétanta id est Cú-Chaulaind. m. Soaltaich." *Book of Leinster* records that Cú Chulainn had two sons with Lebarcham: Caulnia and Condluan. It repeats the genealogy of Cú Chulainn back to Míl (**q.v.**). *Laud 610* mistakenly calls Cú Chulainn the father of Findscóp (Findscuap). Conchobor was actually her father.[263]

AI § 206 records the death of Cú Chulainn.

Cunedda (c.4th-5th cent.). Founder of the First Dynasty of Gwynedd in Wales. He may have been from Pictland (**q.v.**).[264]

After discussing the Cruithni (Pict?), Origin Legends P#L(Uí Ma.), P#L(Lec.), P#L(G47), P#L(Bal.), P#L(1336), and P#L(1295) state that Cunedda expelled the sons of Liathan (**q.v.**) from the Britons (**q.v.**) (possibly, land of the Britons).

Harl. 3859 includes Cunneda in a genealogy of Gwynedd, where he is the son of Etern and an ancestor of Maelgwn of Gwynedd (**q.v.**) and Cadwaladr (**q.v.**). He was also ancestor of many others including the "Manaú Guodotin," who were associated with Mag Manand (**q.v.**). *Jes. 20* mentions Cunedda in several genealogies. *Bonedd Y Saint* mentions Cunedda as an ancestor of several individuals.[265]

Vita Cadoci states that Cunedda was son of Etern and father of Ceretic.[266]

Historia Brittonum mentions that Cunedda drove the sons of Liathan out of Britain without discussing the Picts or Cruithni. Cunedda is an ancestor of Maelgwn of Gwynedd (**q.v.**). In *Welsh Triads*, Triad 43 calls him father of Brwyn m. Kynadaf. Triad 81 states that Cunedda was the ancestor of one of three groups of Welsh saints.[267]

Cú Roí mac Dáire (Cú-ruí mac Dáiri). Legendary Irish hero.

Legends P#A(B 506), P#A(Uí Ma.), P#A(Lec.), and P#A(C.vi.2) say that Cú Roí and Cú Chulainn (**q.v.**) went from Alba (**q.v.**) to Ireland (**q.v.**) because of Echde eachbheoil (**q.v.**). H.M. Chadwick states that this refers to a tale in which Cú Chulainn and Cú Roí stole cattle from Echde.[268]

In *Rawl. B. 502*, Cú Roí is listed in "Genelach Cimbáeda" as one of the five provincial kings. "Airgialla" records Cú Roí as the ancestor of the "Dál Fiatach" of Munster. Cú Roí was son of Daire and was apparently killed. This is also true of *Book of Leinster*.[269]

Cuthbert (saint) (634-687). Bishop of Lindisfarne (685-687).[270]

AFM 686 records Cuthbert's death.

Anonymous Cuthbert records that Cuthbert and his followers were miraculously fed with dolphin meat on their return from Pictland (**q.v.**). Cuthbert also predicted that Ecgfrith (**q.v.**) would be killed in battle against the Picts. *Bede's Cuthbert* again records both of these events. *Martyrology of Tallaght* (Lein.) lists him under ".XIII. KL- APRILIS." (20 March).[271]

Bede records that Cuthbert warned Ecgfrith against battling the Picts. However, he ignored Cuthbert and was killed during a Pictish victory. This was Dún Nechtain (**q.v.**). Bede gives an extensive account of Cuthbert's life. *Historia Brittonum* wrongly records that Cuthbert died during Ecgfrith's reign.[272]

Darlugdach (d.525). Saint of Kildare. Successor of Brigid (**q.v.**).[273]

Book of Leinster places Darlugdach in Lemdruimm in "[Irish saints and places associated with them]."[274]

Lists SL1, SL2 M, SL2 O, and SL2 H state that Darlugdach visited Necton f. Erip (**q.v.**) in the third year of his reign and sang when he dedicated Aburnethige (**q.v.**) to Brigid.[275]

Dectotr'ic fr. Diu. Pseudo-historical Pictish king.

Regnal Lists SL1, SL2 M, SL2 O, and SL2 H give him a forty year reign between Blieibliuth (**q.v.**) and Usconbuts (**q.v.**). List D gives him reign of forty years between "Derordegeli" (see **Deoord**) and Usconbuts. Lists F1, F2, and I record a sixty year reign between the same kings.[276]

M.O. Anderson mentions that "Dectotr'ic" is similar to "Decdric (for Theodoric son of Ida)" mentioned in *Historia Brittonum*.[277] There is also a slight similarity between Dectotr'ic and Sodric (**q.v.**).

Deo Artíuois (Deo ardivois). Pseudo-historical Pictish king.

Regnal Lists SL1, SL2 M, SL2 O, and SL2 H give him twenty year reign between Caruorst (**q.v.**) and Uist (**q.v.**).[278]

Deocilinion (Deocilunon). Pseudo-historical Pictish king.

Regnal Lists SL1, SL2 M, SL2 O, and SL2 H give Deocilinion a forty year reign between Morleo (**q.v.**) and Cinioiod f. Arcois (**q.v.**). List D records a forty year reign between Tharain (**q.v.**) and Deoord (**q.v.**). Lists F1 and F2 repeat this. This is also true of List I. List K records a forty year reign between Dínortechest (**q.v.**) and Gartnaith loc (**q.v.**). Fordun's List records a forty year reign between Dínortechest and Deoord.[279]

Deoord. Pseudo-historical Pictish king.

Regnal Lists SL1, SL2 M, SL2 O, and SL2 H give Deoord a fifty year reign between Cinioiod f. Arcois (**q.v.**) and Blieiblituth (**q.v.**). Lists D, F1, F2, and I give a twenty year reign between Deocilinion (**q.v.**) and Dectotr'ic fr. Diu (**q.v.**). Fordun's List gives a twenty year reign between Deocilinion and Caruorst (**q.v.**).[280]

Dínortechest. Pseudo-historical Pictish king.

Regnal List K gives Dínortechest a twenty year reign between Tharain (**q.v.**) and Deocilinion (**q.v.**). This is also true of Fordun's List.[281]

H.M. Chadwick equates Dínortechest with "Duordeghall" (see **Deoord**), whom he sees as different from Deoord. Molly Miller states that Dínortechest only occurs in List K and Fordun's List. Contrary to Chadwick's assertion, both "Duordeghall" and Dínortechest occur in Fordun's List.[282]

Domnall mac Alpín (Donald I). King of Scots (858-862).[283]

Legends P#F(D.iv.1), P#F(Lec.1), P#F(Lec.2), P#F(Bal.), P#F(1295), P#F(1289), P#F(24.P.13), and P#F(D.iii.2) state that Domnall was leader of the Cruithni. This seems anachronistically to make Domnall a contemporary of the legendary Pictish ancestors. P#G(B 512), P#G(Lec.), and P#G(1295) record that Domnall was their first leader until Britus (**q.v.**) killed him.

AI 861 records the death of Domnall, who is called "ri Alba" ("king of Alba") (see **Alba**). AU 862 and CS 862 also record this and call him "rex Pictorum" ("king of Picts").

List SL2 M gives Domnall a three year reign between Cináed mac Alpín and Causantín mac Cináed (**q.q.v.**). In Lists SL2 O and SL2 H, and K, Domnall is given a four year reign between these same two kings. Lists D, F1, F2, I, and N record that he reigned for four years between Cináed and Causantín, died at the Rath of Inveralmond (see **Inveralmond**), and was buried on Iona (**q.v.**).[284]

Duan Albanach gives Domnall a four year reign between Cináed mac Alpín and Causantín mac Cináeda.[285]

Donn. A chief of the Sons of Míl (**q.v.**) in the *Lebor Gabála* ("Book of Invasions").[286]

Origin Legends P#C(Lein.), P#C(Uí Ma.), P#C(Lec.), and P#C(G131) record that Donn died at Tech Duinn (**q.v.**). P#F(D.iv.1), P#F(Lec.1), P#F(Lec.2), P#F(Bal.), P#F(24.P.13), P#F(1295), P#F(1289), P#F(D.iii.2), P#G(B 512), P#G(Lec.), P#G(Bal.), and P#G(1295) state that the wives of men who drowned with Donn were given to the Cruithni by Éremón (**q.v.**).

Rawl. B. 502 and *Book of Lecan* describe the drowning of Donn.[287]

AI § 35 calls Donn one of the four sons of Míl and records his drowning. AC states that Donn died at Tech Duinn and that the wives of the men who drowned with Donn were given to the Picts. CS also records the drowning of Donn, son of Míl.[288]

Donnán of Eigg (d.617). Martyr killed on the island of Eigg, which probably had a monastery and was in Pictland (**q.v.**).[288a]

Book of Leinster relates a legend about Donnán.[288b]

AI 619, AT 617, and AU 617 record the martyrdom of Donnán and 150 others on the fifteenth of the kalends of May (17 April).

Félire Óengusso lists him under 17 April, and *Martyrology of Tallaght* (Lein.) lists him under ".XU. KL- MAII." (17 April).[288c]

Donornauch (Donornauch necales). Pseudo-historical Pictish king.

Lists D, F1, F2, I, K, and Fordun's List give Donornauch a reign of one year between Canutulachama (**q.v.**) and Uuradech (**q.v.**).[289]

Drest (c.728) (Drest VII, Drust). Pictish king (?724-26).[290]

AT 725 mentions that Drest's son was imprisoned. AU 725 records the imprisonment of Drest's son Simul (see **Simul f. Drest**). AT 726 and AU 726 record that Drest imprisoned Necthon f. Derelei (**q.v.**). Drest and Elpín (c.728) (**q.v.**) had joint rule of the Picts in AT 726. AC 722 records that Drest succeeded Necthon. AT 729 and AU 729 record that Drest was killed at Druim Dergblaithug (**q.v.**) fighting Onuist f. Urguist (**q.v.**). Drest's death is also mentioned in AC 726.

Lists SL1, SL2 M, SL2 O, and SL2 H give Drest and Elpín (c.728) a five year reign between Necthon and Onuist.[291]

Drest f. Constantini (Drest IX, Drust/Drest son of Constantine). Pictish king (?834-837). Son of Castantin f. Uurguist (**q.v.**).[292]

Regnal Lists SL1, SL2 M, SL2 O, and SL2 H record a three year joint reign for Drest and Talorgen f. Uuthoil (q.v.) between Unuist f. Uurguist (**q.v.**) and Uuen f. Unuist (**q.v.**). The remaining lists, which M.O. Anderson classifies as "Q," combine Drest and Talorgen into one person. Lists D, F1, F2, I, K, and Fordun's List give this contracted "Dostolorg" a four year reign between Unuist f. Uurguist (**q.v.**) and Uuen f. Unuist (**q.v.**).[293]

Drest f. Donuel (Drest VI) (Drust son of Donuel (?Domnall)). Pictish king (?663-71).[294]

AT 672 and AU 672 record that Drest was deposed. AT 678, AC 674, AU 678, and CS 674 mention Drest's death.

List SL1 gives Drest a seven year reign between Gartnait f. Donuel (**q.v.**) and Bredei f. Bili (**q.v.**). List SL2 M gives Drest a six year reign between these same kings. List SL2 O and SL2 H give him a seven year reign between Gartnait and Bredei. Lists D, F1, F2, I, K, and Fordun's List record a six year reign for Drest between Gartnait and Bredei.[295]

Drest f. Gyrom (Drest IV). Pictish king (526-531 with Drest f. Uudrost (**q.v.**), 531-536 alone(?)).[296]

Regnal List SL1 gives Drest a five year reign with Drest f. Uudrost between Galanan (**q.v.**) and Drest f. Gyrom's solo reign. Drest was followed by Garthnach f. Girom (**q.v.**). List SL2 M give the two Drests a fifteen year reign after Galanan. It gives Drest f. Gyrom a seven year solo reign before Garthnach. List SL2 O gives the two Drests a twelve year reign with the same details. List SL2 H only records a five year solo reign for Drest f. Gyrom between Drest f. Uudrost and Galanan. List D records a five year reign for Drest f. Gyrom after Necton f. Erip (**q.v.**) and before Drest f. Uudrost. Lists F2 and F2 record the same reign for Drest between Galanan and Drest f. Uudrost. List I gives Drest a six year reign between these same kings. List K records a fifty year reign for Drest between Galanan and Drest f. Uudrost. He is given a second reign of four years between Drest f. Uudrost and Garthnach f. Girom. Fordun's List gives a five year between Galanan and Drest f. Uudrost and four year reign between Drest f. Uudrost and Garthnach.[297]

Drest f. Munait (Drest V). Pictish king (555-556(?)).[298]

Regnal Lists SL1, SL2 M, SL2 O, D, F1, F2, I, K, and Fordun's List give Drest a one year reign between Talorg f. Muircholaich (**q.v.**) and Galam (**q.v.**). List SL2 H gives Drest a one year reign Talorg and a one year joint reign with Bridei f. Mailcon before Bridei f. Mailcon (**q.v.**) before Bridei's solo reign.[299]

Drest f. Talorgen (Drest VIII, Drest/Drest son of Talorcen). Pictish king (?780-781).[300]

List D records a four year reign between Elpin f. Uuroid (**q.v.**) and Talorgen f. Onuist (**q.v.**). SL2 O and SL2 H give him a one year reign between Elpin and Talorgen f. Druisten (**q.v.**). Lists D, F1, and F2 seem to record a four year reign between Bredei f. Uuirguist (**q.v.**) and Talorgen f. Druisten. Lists I, K, and Fordun's List give a one year reign between Alpín f. Óengus (**q.v.**) and Talorgen f. Druisten.[301]

Drest f. Uudrost (Drest III).   Pictish king   (526-531 with Drest f. Gyrom (**q.v.**)(?)).[302]

Regnal List SL1 records a joint reign for Drest f. Uudrost and Drest f. Gyrom of five years between Galanan (**q.v.**) and the solo reign of Drest f. Gyrom. List SL2 M gives Drest and Drest f. Gyrom a reign of fifteen years between Galanan and Drest f. Gyrom's reign. List SL2 O records a twelve year reign for the two Drests between Galanan and Drest f. Gyrom. List SL2 H only records a fifteen year solo reign for Drest f. Uudrost between Galanan and Drest f. Gyrom. Lists D, F1, F2, I, K, and Fordun's List give Drest an eight year reign between Drest f. Gyrom and another reign by Drest f. Gyrom.[303]

Drest Gurthinmoch (Drest II). Pictish king (484-514(?)).

Lists SL1, SL2 M, SL2 O, SL2 H, F1, F2, I, K, and Fordun's List give him a thirty year reign for between Necton f. Erip and Galanan (**q.q.v.**).[304]

Drostan. Legendary Pict.

Legends   P#D(D.iv.1),   P#D(Lec.1),   P#D(Lec.2),   P#D(Bal.), P#D(24.P.13), P#D(1295), P#F(1289), and P#D(D.iii.2) record that Drostan was one of six Cruithni brothers who fought the Battle of Ard Lemnacht (**q.v.**). P#E(Lec.), P#E(Bal.), and P#E(1295) state that Drostan was one of six brothers and mentions that he died after the battle. P#F(D.iv.1), P#F(Lec.1), P#F(Lec.2), P#F(Bal.), P#F(24.P.13), P#F(1295), P#F(1289), and P#F(D.iii.2) repeat this and also say that Drostan was the druid of the Cruithni and found a cure for the poisoned weapons of the Tuath Fidga (**q.v.**). This is also true of P#G(B 512), P#G(Lec.), P#G(Bal.), P#G(1295), P#I(Lein.), P#I(Uí Ma.), P#I(Lec.), P#I(Bal.), P#I(D.ii.2), P#I(B.iii.1), and P#J(D.ii.2). P#H(B 512), P#H(D.i.3), P#H(Lec.), P#J(Uí Ma.), P#J(Lec.), P#J(Bal.), P#J(Ren.)(TR.WS), and P#J(B.iii.1) credit Drostan with the cure but do not mention his brothers.

K. H. Jackson states that "Drosten" (Drostan) is related to Welsh "Trystan"/"Drystan," is probably not Gaelic, and "Drostan" derives from Celtic "Drustagnos." He asserts that the Pictish language is related to Brittonic.[305]

Drostán of Aberdour (c.6th-7th cent.). Possible Pictish saint in Buchan and student of Columba (**q.v.**). He has been called son of Cosgrach (*Book of Deer*), nephew of Columba (*Aberdeen Breviary*), and great-grandson of Áedán mac Gabráin (**q.v.**) (Fordun). He may have been patron saint of Deer (see **Nér**) in Buchan. Although there seems to be no early historical record of him, he may be commemorated on the St Vigeans stone in Forfarshire, which may date to the 8th century.[305a]

A twelfth century note in the *Book of Deer* records that Drostán and Columba travelled from Iona (**q.v.**) to Aberdour, and Bede the Pict, mormaer (approximately, "earl") of Buchan, granted them the monastery there. Later, they were given land after healing one of Bede's sons. Columba then gave Drostán the monastery of Deer.[305b]

Drostán of Derthach. Possible Pict who died in Ard Breccáin monastery.[306]

AT 719, AU 719, and AFM 713 record Drostán's death.

Drust f. Erp (Drest I) Pictish king (414-456(?)).[307]

AC 449 records the death of Drust. CS 457 apparently had a note recording the death of Drust.

Regnal List SL1 gives Drust a hundred year reign and one hundred victories in battle between Talorc f. Achivir (**q.v.**) and Talorc f. Aniel (**q.v.**). It also records that Patricius (Patrick) (**q.v.**) went to Ireland (**q.v.**) during the nineteenth year of Drust's reign. In addition, the list mentions that Drust expelled his brother Necton f. Erip (**q.v.**). Lists SL2 M, SL2 O, and SL2 H record the same information except for the expulsion of Necton. Lists D, F1, and F2 record a hundred year reign and a hundred battle victories for Drust between Talorc f. Achivir and Talorc f. Aniel. List I gives Drust a hundred year reign after Talorc f. Achivir and before Talorc f. Aniel. List K and Fordun's List record the same reign and gives Drust the hundred battle victories. Fordun's List also says that Drust was also called "Nectane."[308] This could be a confusion of Drust with his brother Necton.

The tale *Tochmarc Emere* ("Wooing of Emer") mentions the similarly named Drust mac Serb, who journeys with Cú Chulainn (**q.v.**) to rescue Dervorgil from robbers. Drust f. Erp may have been the model for Drust mac Serb and for the hero Drystan (Tristan) m. Tallwch of Medieval legend, who appears in Triads 19, 21, 26, 41 (Pen. 47), 71, 72, 73 of *Welsh Triads*.[309]

Drust f. Ferat (Drest X, Drust son of Ferat/Wrad). Pictish king (?845-?848).[310]

Regnal Lists D, F1, and F2 give Drust a three year reign between Brude f. Fochel (**q.v.**) and Cináed mac Alpín (**q.v.**). The lists also state that Drust was killed at (or near) Forteviot (**q.v.**) or Scone (**q.v.**). List I gives a three year reign to Drust after Brude f. Fochel and wrongly before the reign of the Scots starting with Fergus f. Erc (**q.v.**). List K records that Drust reigned for three years between Brude and Cináed mac Alpín. It also says that he was treasonously killed at Scone (**q.v.**). Fordun's List gives Drust a three year reign between Brude and Cináed. It also seems to indicate that Drust was overthrown in a revolt which resulted in the succession of Cináed.[311]

Drusticc (6th cent.). Possible Pictish princess, who may have been the daughter of Drest f. Gyrom, Drest f. Munait, or Drest f. Uudrost (**q.q.v.**).[312]

Book of Leinster includes Drusticc in "[Mothers of Irish Saints]" as daughter of "Trust, king of the northern Britons" (see **Britons**) and mother of Lonan of Treóit, son of Talmach. *Book of Uí Maine* has a similar passage without her father's name. *Liber Hymnorum* recounts a tale in which Drusticc, daughter of "Drust rex Bretan" ("Drust, king of Britain"), travels to Whithorn (see **Ninian**) to study with Mugint. There, she has an affair with Talmach (who is disguised as Rioc) and has a son named Lonan, who would later become a monk and saint.[313]

Dúnchad mac Conaing (Duncan son of Duban?). King of Scots Dál Riata (**q.v.**) (?c.651-654). Grandson of Áedán mac Gabráin (**q.v.**).[314]

AT 654, AU 654, and CS 651 record that Dúnchad was killed at Sráith Ethairt (**q.v.**).

Dúngal mac Selbaich. King of Scots Dál Riata (**q.v.**)(733-736).[315]

AU 734 records that Dúngal fled from Onuist f. Urguist (**q.v.**). AT 736, AC 733, and AU 736 record that Onuist captured Dúngal and his brother Feradach mac Selbaich (**q.v.**).

Lists D, F1, F2, I, K, and N record a seven year reign for Dúngal after Fergus mac Echdach and before Alpin f. Eochaid(?) (see **Alpín f. Eochaid, Elpín (c.728)**).[316]

Eanfrith (Enfret). King of Bernicia (633-634). Son of Æthelfrith (**q.v.**). Father of Talorcen f. Enfret (**q.v.**).[317]

AT 632 records a battle involving Eanfrith and Cadwallon, king of the Britons (**q.v.**), father of Cadwaladr (**q.v.**). AC 634 also mentions this event and says that Eanfrith was decapitated. AU 632 also records the battle.

Regnal Lists SL1, SL2 M, SL2 O, SL2 H, D, F1, F2, I, and Fordun's List call Eanfrith the father of Talorcen.[318]

Ebissa.

Historia Brittonum states that Ebissa and Octha (**q.v.**) were invited to Britain by Hengest (**q.v.**) and Vortigern (**q.v.**) to fight against the Picts.[319]

Ecgberht (saint) (Egbert) (c.640-729). English bishop who died on Iona (**q.v.**).[320]

AT 729, AC 726, and AU 729 record Ecgberht's death.

Bede records that in 716 Ecgberht, an English noble, caused Iona to accept the Roman Easter. He went to Ireland (**q.v.**) and miraculously recovered from a disease. He was also an exile amongst the Picts and Scots and warned Ecgfrith (**q.v.**) against attacking Ireland. Also, Ecgberht wished to preach amongst the Germans but was unable to do so because of supernatural interference. Bede records that he died in 729.[321]

Ecgfrith. King of Northumbria (670/71-685). Son of Oswiu (**q.v.**).[322]

AT 686 and AU 686 record that Ecgfrith was killed by Bredei f. Bili (**q.v.**) at Dún Nechtain (**q.v.**).

Vita Columbae recounts that Adomnán (**q.v.**) visited England after Dún Nechtain (called "Bellum Ecfridi"). *Anonymous Cuthbert* records that Cuthbert (**q.v.**) predicted to Ælfflæd (**q.v.**) that Ecgfrith, her brother, would die in battle and be succeeded by his brother Aldfrith (**q.v.**). Ecgfrith and the Saxon (see **Saxons**) bishops elected Cuthbert bishop of Lindisfarne. Ecgfrith died in battle against the Picts. *Bede's Cuthbert* repeats Cuthbert's prediction concerning Dún Nechtain. Cuthbert also had a vision of Ecgfrith ravaging the lands of the Picts and being killed at a fountain. *Life of Wilfrid* records that Ecgfrith was at the dedication of Ripon. Ecgfrith ruled over the Picts, who revolted early in his reign. He vanquished them in many battles and enslaved them. Ecgfrith and his wife Iurminburgh caused Wilfrid (**q.v.**) to be deposed and later refused the order of the pope to reinstate him. Evenually, Ecgfrith was killed in battle against the Picts.[323]

Bede says that Ecgfrith was a hostage at the court of Queen Cynwise while his father Oswiu (**q.v.**) fought against Mercia. Ecgfrith succeeded his father as king in 670. In the eighth year of Ecgfrith's reign, a comet appeared and Ecgfrith had a dispute with deposed bishop Wilfrid. In 680 Ecgfrith gave Ceolfrith (**q.v.**) approval to build Monkwearmouth monastery. Bede also records that Ecgfrith's wife Æthelreda had an incorrupt corpse. Archbishop Theodore arranged a truce between Ecgfrith and Æthelred of Mercia after Ecgberht's brother Ælfwine (**q.v.**) had been killed by Mercians. Bede mentions Dún Nechtain and its aftermath. Ecgfrith appointed Cuthbert bishop of Lindisfarne. Bede mentions that Ecgfrith was at the Synod at Twyford. *Historia Brittonum* records that Ecgfrith was Oswiu's son and Ælfwine's brother. Ecgfrith reigned for nine years and died fighting Picts.[324]

Echdhe eachbheoil. Legendary ruler in Mull of Kintyre.[325]
Origin Legends P#A(B 506), P#A(Uí Ma.), P#A(Lec.), and P#A(C.vi.2) say that Echdhe was father of Lonceta (**q.v.**) and grandfather of Irél Glúnmár (**q.v.**).
H.M. Chadwick says that in a saga Cú Chulainn (**q.v.**) and Cú Roí mac Dáire (**q.v.**) stole cattle from Echdhe. He discusses the similarity of Echdhe eachbheoil ("Horse-lip") with "Errge Echbel," who appears in the tale *Mesca Ulad*.[326]

Edwin (d.633). King of Northumbria (617-33).[327]
ACam. 617 records the beginning of Edwin's reign. In ACam. 626 Edwin is baptized by Paulinus ("Run filius Urbgen"). AT 625 records the baptism of Edwin. The death of Edwin at Meicen (Haethfelth) is recorded in ACam. 630. His death in battle is also mentioned in AT 631. Penda (**q.v.**) is recorded as the victor. AC 630 also mentions the battle but not the death of Edwin. AU 631 records the "Bellum filii Ailli" ("Battle of the son of Ælle") but neither mentions Edwin by name nor his death.
Bede devotes chapters 9-17 of Book II to Edwin's reign. He records his

baptism by Paulinus and death at Haethfelth (Meicen) against Cadwallon and Penda in 633. *Historia Brittonum* calls Edwin father of Eanflæd (wife of Oswiu (**q.v.**)), son of Ælle, father of Osfrid and Eadfrid and states that Edwin was killed at Meicen (Haethfelth). Edwin is given a seventeen year reign. Geoffrey of Monmouth recounts a long feud between Edwin and Cadwallon, father of Cadwaladr (**q.v.**), which ended with Cadwallon killing him. In *Welsh Triads*, Triad 26 W calls Edwin "vrenhin Lloegr" ("king of England") and one of three "invasions" of Anglesey. Triad 62 records a battle between Edwin and Belen o Leyn (see **Beli map Neithon**) at Bryn Edwin. Triad 69 records a battle between Edwin and Cadwallon.[328]

Eilim ollfhinachta (Fínnacta mac Ollaman Fótla). Mythological king of Alba (**q.v.**) and Ireland (**q.v.**) from the Cruithni (Picts?).
Legends P#A(B506), P#A(Uí Ma.), P#A(Lec.), and P#A(C.vi.2) record a thirty year reign for Eilim after Ollam Fótla (**q.v.**) and before Findoll cisirne (**q.v.**). During his reign, the "wine snow" fell in the winter. In P#L(Uí Ma.), P#L(Lec.), P#L(G47), P#L(Bal.), P#L(1336), and P#L(1295), a "Finachta" ruled in Ireland (**q.v.**) at the same time that Aenbegan (**q.v.**) ruled in Alba. This could be Eilim or Bagag ollfiacha (**q.v.**). This may refer to a different person (see **Finachta** and **Olfinecta**).
Rawl. B. 502, Book of Leinster, Book of Lecan, and *Laud 610* apparently call him "Fínnachta" and list him as one of four sons of Ollam Fótla. *Book of Leinster* and *Laud 610* also list him amongst the kings of Ulaid (Ulster) from the Dál n-Araide (**q.v.**).[329]
AFM 3923 and AFM 3942 seem to record Eilim's reign and mention the abundance of snow.[330]
SL1, SL2 M, and SL2 H state that Olfinecta (**q.v.**) reigned for sixty years between Aenbegan (**q.v.**) and Guidid gaed brechach (**q.v.**).[331]
H.M. Chadwick asserts that Olfinecta of the Regnal Lists is the same as Eilim ollfhinachta. T.F. O'Rahilly seems to agree with this assessment. This is also true of M.O. Anderson.[332]

Eire (Eriu). Eponymous figure representing Ireland.[333]
Legends P#C(Lein.), P#C(Uí Ma.), P#C(Lec.), and P#C(G131) state that a group including the wives of Bres, Basse, and Buaigne (**q.q.v.**) met Eire. It is unclear whether they were the followers of Cruithne (**q.v.**) or the Gaels (**q.v.**).
AC calls Eire the sister of Banba and Fotla (**q.q.v.**) and daughter of "Fiagha m^cDealvoye." AC also records that Eire with her husband and her sisters with their husbands were killed by the Sons of Míl (**q.v.**).[334] AFM 3500 mentions that Eire and her sisters were killed by the Sons of Míl.

Eithne (Eithni) (d.778). Daughter of Ciniod f. Uuradech (**q.v.**).[335]
AU 778 and AFM 773 record her death.

Elaf. Saxon leader killed at Camlann (**q.v.**).[336]

Geoffrey of Monmouth states that Elaf was allied with Mordred (**q.v.**) against Arthur (**q.v.**) at Camlann.[337]

Elair (Hilary) (c.320-68). Saint and bishop of Poitiers (353-68).[338]

Legends P#E(Lec.), P#E(Bal.), and P#E(1295) state that the Cruithni were famous at the home of Elair. This refers to the founding of Pictabis (**q.v.**) in France.

Félire Óengusso and *Martyrology of Tallaght* (Lein.) list him under 13 January.[338a]

Elpín (c.728) (Alpin I, ?Alpin son of Eochaid son of (?)Domangart). King of Picts (726-28) and possibly of Scots Dál Riata (**q.v.**) (733-36?). There is some confusion between him and Alpín f. Eochaid (**q.v.**), the father of Cináed mac Alpín (**q.v.**).[339]

AT 728, AC 725, and AU 728 record Mónad Croibh (**q.v.**) in which Onuist f. Urguist (**q.v.**) defeated Elpín and Elpín's son was killed. AT 728, AC 725, and AU 728 mention Caislén Credi (**q.v.**) where Elpín was defeated.

SL1, SL2 M, SL2 O, and SL2 H give Elpín a five year joint reign with Drest (c.728) (**q.v.**) between Necthon f. Derelei (**q.v.**) and Onuist f. Urguist (**q.v.**). List D mentions that Alpín f. Eochaid ruled the Scots (**q.v.**) for three years after Dúngal mac Selbaich (**q.v.**). In this case it seems that this Alpín could be Elpín (c.728). After this king's reign the list indicates that Picts began to rule. Lists F1 and F2 mention the same circumstances of Elpín's reign; however, List F2 gives him a five year reign over the Scots. List I mentions several "Alpíns." The Pictish section includes Alpín f. Óengus (**q.v.**) with an eight year reign between Óengus f. Bruide (**q.v.**) and Drest (c.728) (**q.v.**). Another Alpín f. Óengus has an eight year reign between Bredei f. Uuirguist (**q.v.**) and Drest f. Talorgen (**q.v.**). These kings are not mentioned in the earlier lists; however, M.O. Anderson seems to suggest that they could be Elpín (c.728) from the earlier lists or Elpin f. Uuroid (**q.v.**). It appears likely that the first Alpín f. Óengus is Elpín (c.728) and the second is Elpin f. Uuroid although his predecessor Ciniod f. Uuredech (**q.v.**) is omitted. The Scottish section gives Alpín f. Eochaid a three year reign between Dúngal mac Selbaich and Cináed mac Alpín (**q.v.**). This could be the result of confusion between Elpín (c.728) and Alpín f. Eochaid given that Cináed reigned over a hundred years later than Dúngal. List K records that "Alpyn fitz Beghach" reigned over the Scots (**q.v.**) for three years after Dúngal mac Selbaich and before the Picts began to rule. This is could be Elpín (c.728). List N also places an "Alpín" in this position with Cináed succeeding him.[340]

H.M. Chadwick claims that Elpín's father was Eochu (Eochaid), king of Dál Riata in 697. This could account for the confusion about Elpín (c.728) and Alpín f. Eochaid. M.O. Anderson suggests that Elpín was brother of Drest (c.728) and son of a sister of Necthon f. Derelei (**q.v.**).[341]

Elpin f. Uuroid (Alpin II, Alpin son of Feret/Wroid). Pictish king (775-?780).[342]

AC 773 records Elpin's death. AU 780 repeats this but calls him "king of the Saxons" (q.v.). A.O. Anderson suggests that his name is Anglo-Saxon (Ælfwine) and he may have had an English mother.[343]

SL1, SL2 M, SL2 O, and SL2 H give Elpin a three-and-a-half year reign between Ciniod f. Uuredech and Drest f. Talorgen (q.q.v.). List D gives him an unspecified reign between Óengus f. Bruide and Bredei f. Uuirguist (q.q.v.). Lists F1 and F2 give him a six month reign between Necthon f. Derelei (q.v.) and Óengus f. Bruide. List I may call him Alpín f. Óengus (q.v.) with an eight year reign (which could be a repeat of the reign for Alpín f. Óengus) between Bredei f. Uuirguist and Drest f. Talorgen. List K appears to give a six month reign (with a later thirty year reign) between Óengus f. Bruide and Bredei f. Uuirguist. Fordun's List repeats this but gives his second reign as twenty six years. M.O. Anderson points out that his second reign is sometimes given to Óengus f. Bruide. She suggests that Elpin f. Uuroid is "Elpin" of AC and AU and "Alpin son of Feret/Feredeth" of the Regnal Lists.[344]

Elpin of Glass Noíde (Glasnevin). Possible Pict.[345]
AT 758, AU 758, and AFM 753 record Elpin's death.

Emchath. A Pict converted by Columba (q.v.).
Vita Columbae records that Columba's preaching converted Emchath (an old man near Loch Ness) and his family.[346]

A.O. and M.O. Anderson suggest that "Emchatus" is a "partly-Irish" version of the British "Ambicatus." Kenneth Jackson remarks that "Emcat or Emchat" has been associated with the Gaelic "Imchath" and used to show the Goedelic nature of the Picts but points out that it is related to Gaulish "Ambicatus" and British "Ammecatus" which would have become "*Amcat" in Columba's time and Gaelicized in *Vita Columbae*.[347]

Eochaid Buide (Eochu Buide).   King of Scots Dál Riata (q.v.) (608?-29). Son of Áedán mac Gabráin.[348]

Rawl. B. 502 and *Book of Leinster* call Eochaid father of Domnall Brecc and son of Áedán mac Gabráin (q.v.).[349]

AC 590 calls Eochaid one of four kings who reigned in Scotland during a forty-three year period. AI 631 and AT 629 record Eochaid's death. Eochaid's death is recorded in AU 629, where he is "king of the Picts." CS 629 states that Eochaid died during the twentieth year of his reign. List D records a fifteen year reign between Áedán mac Gabráin (q.v.) and Connad Cerr. Lists F1, F2, and I give Eochaid a sixteen year reign. List K gives a sixteen year reign between Conall mac Comgaill and Connad Cerr. List N gives a six year reign between Áedán and Connad Cerr and says that Eochaid was killed.[350]

Vita Columbae states that he became king after his father Áedán.[351]

Senchus Fer nAlban calls Eochaid one of seven sons of Áedán mac Gabráin and father of eight sons. *Duan Albanach* appears to give Eochaid a seventy year reign between Áedán mac Gabráin and Connad Cerr.[352]

A.O. and M.O. Anderson suggest Eochaid may have claimed Fortriu (**q.v.**) through his mother, explaining why AU calls him "king of Picts."[353]

Eochaid/Eochu (Eochaid Munremor, Eochaid Muinremur mac Óengusa m. Fergusa (Feidelmid)). Ancestor of "Scots in Britain" from Irish Dál Riata (**q.v.**). Father of Erc (**q.v.**) and grandfather of Fergus Mór (**q.v.**).[354]

P#E(Bal.) and P#E(1295) state that fifty kings of Alba (**q.v.**) were descended from Eochaid. P#G(B 512), P#G(Lec.), P#G(Bal.), and P#G(1295) say that his descendants, the Gaels (**q.v.**), controlled Alba after the Cruithni.

Rawl. B. 502 and *Book of Leinster* call Eochaid son of Óengus mac Fergusa, or Óengus mac Feidelmid, and father of Muirecht ingen Echach Muinremair and Erc. *Book of Lecan* seems to include him in a genealogy of the family of Lóegaire mac Néill Noígiallaig.[355]

According to *Senchus Fer nAlban*, Eochaid was the father of Erc and Olchu. *Duan Albanach* states that the descendants of Eochaid controlled Alba after the Cruithni (Picts?).[356]

Eolchu. Mythological Pictish ancestor.
Origin Legend P#E(Lec.) states that the Picts were descended from Eolchu, son of Ercal (**q.v.**).

Erc (Erc mac Echdach Muinremuir). Legendary ancestor of the "Scots in Britain" from Irish Dál Riata (**q.v.**). Father of Fergus Mór (**q.v.**) and son of Eochaid/Eochu (**q.v.**).[357]

Rawl. B. 502 calls Erc father of Fergus and Loarn Mór (**q.v.**) and son of Eochaid/Eochu. *Book of Leinster* mentions Erc as father of Loarn and son of Eochaid/Eochu.[358] AC 454 records that Erc's sons went to Scotland in 498.

Lists D, F1, F2, I, K, and N call Erc father of Fergus. List K also says that he was from Ireland.[359]

Senchus Fer nAlban calls Erc one of two sons of Eochaid/Eochu. *Duan Albanach* says that he had three sons.[360]

Ercal (Hercules). Mythological ancestor of the Picts. Father of Gelon (**q.v.**) and Agathyrsus (**q.v**), an idea taken from Virgil.[361]

P#E(Lec.) states that the Picts lived in the region of Ercal and were Ercal's descendants through Eolchu (**q.v.**). P#E(Bal.) and P#E(1295) repeat this but say that the Picts were descended from Ercal's son Gelon. P#G(B 512), P#G(Lec.), P#G(Bal.), P#G(1295), P#L(Uí Ma.), P#L(Lec.), P#L(G47), P#L(Bal.), P#L(1336), and P#L(1295) call Ercal Gelon's father.

Regnal Lists SL3(Lec.1), SL3(Lec.4), and SL3(Bal.1) call Ercal the father of Gelon.[362]

Éremón mac Míled (Érimón). A chief of the Sons of Míl (**q.v.**) in *Lebor Gabála* ("Book of Invasions").[363]

Legends P#C(Lein.), P#C(Uí Ma.), P#C(Lec.), and P#C(G131) record that Cruithne (**q.v.**) stole wives from the Sons of Míl (**q.v.**) except for Tea (**q.v.**), the wife of Éremón. P#F(D.iv.1), P#F(Lec.1), P#F(Lec.2), P#F(Bal.), P#F(24.P.13), P#F(1295), P#F(1289), P#F(D.iii.2), P#G(B 512), P#G(Bal.), P#G(1295), P#H(Lein.), P#H(D.iii.1), P#H(B 512), P#H(D.i.3), and P#H(Lec.) state that the Cruithni (Picts?) were powerful during the time of Éremón. Éremón expelled them and gave them the widows of the men drowned with Donn (**q.v.**). P#G(Lec.) seems to state that the Cruithni expelled Éremón.

Rawl. B. 502 includes Éremón in two genealogies going back to Adam and calls him an ancestor of Laigin (**q.v.**). Éremón is father of Irél (Irial, Ireor) Fáith and son of Míl. "Ríg Érenn" ("Kings of Ireland") calls Éremón one of two sons of Míl who divided Ireland (**q.v.**) into two parts. It also states that Éremón reigned for sixteen years and had five sons. Éremón is the first name included in "Hec Sunt Nomina Incredentium." *Rawl. B. 502* also names four of Éremón's sons. Éremón is included as an ancestor of the Scots. *Book of Leinster* mentions that Éremón may have defined or controlled the area of Connacht. Éremón is mentioned in the "Genelach Muscraige Mittine." *Book of Lecan* describes the descendants of Éremón and includes him as an ancestor of the Scots. *Laud 610* calls Éremón one of two sons of Míl and father of six sons. He is listed as an ancestor of kings. *MacFirbis Genealogies* appear to have a section about the descendants of Éremón.[364]

AI §35 states that Éremón was one of four sons of Míl and was born in Spain (**q.v.**). AI §41 records Éremón's death. AC states that Éremón was born in Spain and ruled Ireland with his brother.   AC discusses Éremón's involvement in the conquests of the Sons of Míl. AFM 3501, AFM 3502, AFM 3503, AFM 3510, and AFM 3516 mention similar information. CS states that Éremón was the son of Míl and was born in Spain.[365]

Erglan. Mythological ruler of Alba (**q.v.**). He was one of three sons of Beóán from the race of Nemed (**q.v.**) in *Lebor Gabála* ("Book of Invasions").[366]

Legends P#G(B 512), P#G(Lec.), P#G(Bal.), and P#G(1295) state that Erglan was a descendant of Nemed, who took control of Alba before the Cruithni.

Duan Albanach states that Erglan took control of Alba after Britus (**q.v.**). T.F. O'Rahilly states that this idea was borrowed from *Lebor Gabála*.[367]

Failbe mac Guaire (d.737). Cleric in Apor Crosan (**q.v.**) in Pictland (**q.v.**). Successor of Maelrubai (**q.v.**).[368]

AT 737, AU 737, and AFM 732 record that Failbe drowned along with 22 sailors.

Fathecht (Ethecht mac Aurthecht). Mythological Pictish ancestor.

Origin Legends P#L(Uí Ma.), P#L(Lec.), P#L(G47), and P#L(1336) state that Fathecht was son of Javad (**q.v.**), father of Mar (**q.v.**), and ancestor of Cruithne (**q.v.**). *Rawl. B. 502* three times calls Fathecht "Ethecht" and the father of Mar and son of Aurtecht (Aurtacht, Aurthecht) mac Aboth. He seems to be a descendant of Japheth (**q.v.**). *Book of Lecan* also seems to call him Japheth's descendant. SL3(Lec.2) calls Fathecht Cruithne's ancestor, son of Javad (**q.v.**), and father of Mar (**q.v.**). SL3(Lec.1), SL3(Lec.3), SL3(Lec.4), SL3(Bal.1), and SL3(Bal.2) call him Cruithne's ancestor, Mar's father, and Japheth's son.[369]

Fea. Mythological enemy of the Picts. Possible leader of the Tuath Fidga (**q.v.**). P#E(Lec.), P#E(Bal.), and P#E(1295) state that Fea used magic against the Cruithni in the Battle of Ard Lemnacht (**q.v.**) and was defeated by them. The role of Fea is given to the Tuath Fidga in other Origin Legends. "Fea" appears to be the personification of Mag Fea in Uí Cennselaig (**q.v.**).[370]

Feradach Find Fechtnach rí Cruthentuaithe. Legendary Pictish king of Alba (**q.v.**). *Rawl. B. 502*, *Book of Leinster,* and *Book of Lecan* call Feradach king of Pictland (**q.v.**), father of Mongfind (**q.v.**), and grandfather of Cairpre Cruithnechan (**q.v.**). "Conall Corc and the Corco Luigde" in *Laud 610* states that he is king of the Picts of Alba who gives Conall Corc (**q.v.**) his anonymous daughter with whom Conall has two sons: Cairpre and Lughid.[371]

Longes Chonaill calls Feradach king of Alba and relates how Feradach intended to execute his daughter when she bore a child by Conall Corc but later spared her.[372] Regarding the name of this monarch, see **Uuradech**.

Another Feradach Find Fechtnach appears in the Genealogies and *Audacht Morainn*. He is king of Laigin (**q.v.**) and has a Pictish mother. The two figures may derive from the same tradition.[373]

Feradach mac Selbaich (d. 736). Brother of Dúngal mac Selbaich (**q.v.**).[374] AT 736, AC 733, and AU 736 record that Feradach was killed in battle against Onuist f. Uurguist (**q.v.**). Regarding the name, see **Uuradech**.

Feradach of Ile. Rich man on Ile (**q.v.**). *Vita Columbae* records that Feradach hosted an exiled Pict (see **Tarain (exile)**), whom he betrayed and killed. After this act, Feradach died suddenly as predicted by Columba (**q.v.**).[375] Regarding the name of this person, see **Uuradech**.

Fergus Mór (Fergus Mór mac Eirc) (c.500). King of Scots Dál Riata (**q.v.**), who moved the dynasty from Ireland (**q.v.**).[376]

P#E(Bal.) and P#E(1295) call Fergus first of fifty kings of Alba (**q.v.**) descended from Eochaid/Eochu (**q.v.**). AC states that Fergus was the son of the king of Ireland and that he went to Scotland and became king.[377]

Regnal Lists D, F1, F2, I, and K state that Fergus reigned for three years before Domongart mac Fergusa.[378]

Senchus Fer nAlban calls Fergus one of the sons of Erc (**q.v.**). Fergus is one of three sons of Erc in *Duan Albanach*.[379]

Fergus of Strageath (c.6th-7th cent.). Irish bishop based in Strageath (Strogeth) near Crieff in Perthshire who preached among the Picts in Caithness and Buchan. He may have been a companion of Fóelán of St Fillans (**q.v.**). The St Vigeans stone in Forfarshire may commemorate him.[380]

Fergus the Pict (Fergus Cruithnech) (8th cent.). Pictish bishop present at council in Rome in 721. He may have been an Iona (**q.v.**) monk, who was a bishop in Scots or Irish Dál Riata (**q.v.**). *Martyrology of Tallaght* (Lein.) lists him under "Nonas [*recte* .UI. IDUS]. SEPTIMBIR." (8 September).[381]

Fiachna mac Báetáin (Fiachna Lurcan (Luscan, Find) mac Báetáin)) (d.626). King of Dál n-Araide (**q.v.**) and Ulaid (Ulster) from the Irish Cruithni. He is referred to as king of Alba (**q.v.**) and Ireland (**q.v.**) from the Cruithni (Picts?) in some of the Origin Legends.[382]

Legends P#A(B 506), P#A(Uí Ma.), P#A(Lec.), and P#A(C.vi.2) state that Fiachna was the last of thirty Cruithni kings of Alba and Ireland beginning with Ollam Fótla (**q.v.**).

Rawl. B. 502, *Book of Lecan*, and *Laud 610* associate him with Dál n-Araide (**q.v.**) and call him son of Báetán mac Echdach m. Condlae and father of Eochaid Iarlaithe.[383]

AT 594 and AU 594 record that Fiachna was victorious at Éudann Mór. AT 597, AC 590, AU 597, and CS 597 mention Fiachna's victory at Sliab Cua. Fiachna was victorious at Cúil Caíl in AT 602, AU 602, and CS 602. AI 624, AT 623, AU 623, and CS 623 record that Fiachna besieged Ráith Guali. AT 625, AC 627, AU 625 mention the killing of Fiachna's son. AT 626, AC 627, AU 626, and CS 626 record Fiachna's death at Lethet Midind.

Fiachra of Aberdeen and Perthshire (c.6th-7th cent.?). Probably an Irish cleric active among Picts. He is apparently known only from location names.[384]

Fiachu nAraide (Fiachu (Fiachra) Araide Óengusa Goibnenn). Mythological and eponymous ancestor of Dál n-Araide (**q.v.**).[385]

Legends P#A(B 506) and P#A(Lec.) associate Fiachu with Dál n-Araide. *Rawl. B. 502* gives Fiachu a twenty year reign between Lugaid Menn mac Óengusa Find and Fedelmid mac Fiachach. He is the last name in "Genelach Dál Araide." He is father of Cass mac Fiachach Araidi and son of Óengus Goibnenn mac Fergusa Gallíni. *Book of Leinster* includes him in "Genelach Laigsi Cúle" between Cathaír Már mac Fedelmid Fir Aurglais and

Ailill Aulomm mac Mogoa-Nuadat. Fiachu is given a twenty year reign between Lugaid and Fedelmid. Fiachu is listed in two genealogies of Dál n-Araide as father of Cass and son of Óengus. *Book of Lecan* gives similar information as in *Rawl. B. 502*. *Laud 610* gives Fiachu a twenty year reign between Lugaid and Fedelmid. "Itim Síl Fergusa" places Fiachu in a list between Cass and Óengus.[386]

AI §281 records that Fiachu nAraide and the Irish Cruithni were defeated by Fiachu Mullaillethan and Cormac at Fochart Muirthemne.

Fiacua albus. Pseudo-historical Pictish king.

Lists D, F1, F2, I, and K record a thirty year reign for Fiacua between Uipoig namet and Canutulachama (**q.q.v.**). Fordun's List gives Fiacua a thirty year reign after Blarehassereth (**q.v.**) and before Chalag amfrud (**q.v.**).[387]

Fial. Daughter of Míl (**q.v.**) and wife of Lugaid (**q.v.**) in the *Lebor Gabála* ("Book of Invasions").[388]

Legends P#C(Lein.), P#C(Uí Ma.), P#C(Lec.), and P#C(G131) indicate that either the Gaels (**q.v.**) or the Cruithni (Picts?) landed in Ireland (**q.v.**) at Inber Scene (**q.v.**), where Fial bathed. The text is somewhat confused.

Fib. Mythological Pictish king and son of Cruithne (**q.v.**). His name appears to be an eponym for Fife.[389]

Legends P#L(Uí Ma.), P#L(Lec.), P#L(G47), P#L(1336) call Fib one of seven sons of Cruithne who divided the north of Britain (**q.v.**).

Lists SL1, SL2 M, and SL2 H call Fib one of seven sons of Cruithne and gives him a reign of twenty-four years between Ce (**q.v.**) and Géde Ollgothach (**q.v.**). SL3(Lec.1), SL3(Lec.3), and SL3(Bal.1) and SL3(Bal.2) call Fib son of Cruithne and give him a twenty-four year reign before Fidach (**q.v.**). List SL3(Lec.2) calls Fib son of Cruithne and one of thirteen Cruithni kings. Fib reigned for twenty-one years before Fidach in List SL3(Lec.4). F.T. Wainwright equates Fib with Fife by using the divisions of Alba (**q.v.**) occurring in *De Situ Albanie*, which calls one area "Fif cum Fothreue."[390]

Fidach. Mythological Pictish king. Son of Cruithne (**q.v.**).[391]

P#L(Uí Ma.), P#L(Lec.), P#L(G47), and P#L(1336) call Fidach one of Cruithne's seven sons who divided northern Britain (**q.v.**).

SL1, SL2 M, and SL2 H call Fidach one of Cruithne's seven sons and give him a forty year reign between Cirig (**q.v.**) and Fortrenn (**q.v.**). SL3(Lec.1) and SL3(Lec.4) record a forty year reign between Fib and Fortrenn. SL3(Lec.2) calls Fidach one of Cruithne's son. SL3(Lec.3), SL3(Bal.1), and SL3(Bal.2) repeat this; however, they give a forty year reign at the start of the list. F.T. Wainwright suggests that Fidach controlled "Muref et Ross" as described in *De Situ Albanie*. This had been asserted by H.M. Chadwick, who equated it with "Moray and Ross."[392]

Finachta. Mythological king of Ireland (**q.v**).

P#A(B 506), P#A(Uí Ma.), P#A(Lec.), and P#A(C.vi.2) mention kings with similar names (see **Bagag ollfiacha, Eilim ollfhinachta, Olfinecta**). Whether or not one of these is Finachta is uncertain. Finachta is mentioned in P#L(Uí Ma.), P#L(Lec.), P#L(G47), P#L(Bal.), P#L(1336), and P#L(1295) as ruler of Ireland when the Cruithni took control of northern Britain. This could be one of those mentioned in P#A(B 506), P#A(Uí Ma.), P#A(Lec.), and P#A(C.vi.2) or another person.

Rawl. B. 502, Book of Leinster, Book of Lecan, and *Laud 610* mention a "Fínnachta" (probably, Eilim ollfhinachta) as one of four sons of Ollam Fótla (**q.v.**). If any one of these is Finachta, this one seems the most likely.[393]

AC (p.35) records that "Fineaghty," son of Ollam reigned for twenty years in which there was much snow. This is no doubt the same person as the "Finnachta" from the Genealogies. It could also be Finachta. AFM 3923 also mentions this person.

Fínán of Aberdeenshire (6th-7th cent.). Irish saint active among Picts of Aberdeenshire and Perthshire, where there are many dedications to him. His feast is 18 March, which is close to that of Fínán of Swords, listed in *Félire Óengusso* under 16 March and in *Martyrology of Tallaght* (Lein.) under ".XUII. KL- APRILIS." (16 March). Fínán of Aberdeenshire and Fínán of Swords may be the same individual.[394]

Findbar (Fimbarrus, Barr, Finbar) (6th cent.?). Irish cleric who may have been active among Picts. He may be identical with Bairre (Findbarr, Barre, Barra) of Cork, who is son of Amargein in *Book of Leinster* and *Book of Lecan.* Bairre is listed in *Félire Óengusso* under 25 September and in *Martyrology of Tallaght* (Lein.) under ".UII. KL- OCTIMBIR." (25 September) and ".UI. KL- OCTIMBIR" (26 September). [395]

Findchán. Unidentified priest. Possibly patron of Kilfinichen on Mull. *Vita Columbae* states that Findchán founded a monastery named Artchain. Findchán wrongly ordained Áed Dub (**q.v.**) and was punished with a decaying hand as predicted by Columba (**q.v.**).[396]

Findoll cisirne. Mythological king of Alba (**q.v.**) and Ireland (**q.v.**) from the Cruithni (Picts?).[397]

P#A(B 506), P#A(Uí Ma.), P#A(Lec.), and P#A(C.vi.2)state that he was one of the Cruithni and give him a thirty year reign between Eilim ollfhinachta (**q.v.**) and Géde Ollgothach (**q.v.**). During his reign, every cow had a white head.

Finnguine f. Deileroith (d.711). AT 711 and AU 711 states that Finnguine was killed at Mag Manand (**q.v.**) in a battle between the Picts and the Saxons (**q.v.**). This was during the reign of Necthon f. Derelei (**q.v.**).[398]

Flannán (c.6th/7th cent.?). Irish saint of the Flannan Isles (Lewis) active among the Picts. He may have been Flannán of Cell da Lua (Killaloe, Clare), listed in *Book of Leinster* as one of two sons of Tairdelbach and in *Martyrology of Tallaght* (Lein.) under ".XU. KL- IANUARII." (18 December).[399]

Fóelán of St Fillans (Fáelán, Faolán) (6th-7th cent.?). Irish saint active among Picts with his main center at St Fillans on Loch Earn. The exact details of his life are uncertain because there are about 20 saints with the same name and the hagiographical material varies greatly. He has been called son of Kentigerna (**q.v.**) and nephew of Comgan (**q.v.**). He has been equated with Fóelán of Fosses (Belgium) (d.c.655) and Fóelán of Fertullagh in West Meath (Fáelán of Cluain Moescna) with whom he apparently shares a feast day (9 January). Fóelán of Fertullagh is listed in *Félire Óengusso* under 9 January and in *Martyrology of Tallaght* (Lein.) under ".U. IDUS. IANUARII." (9 January).[400]

Fortrenn (Fortrean). Mythological Pictish king and eponym of Fortriu (**q.v.**).[401] P#L(Uí Ma.), P#L(Lec.), P#L(1336), and P#L(G47) call him one of seven sons of Cruithni who divided Alba (**q.v.**) or northern Britain (**q.v.**).

SL1 calls Fortrenn one of seven sons of Cruithne and gives him a seventy year reign between Fidach (**q.v.**) and Fotla (**q.v.**). SL2 M and SL2 H record a forty year reign between these same two monarchs. SL3(Lec.1), SL3(Lec.3), and SL3(Lec.4) seem to give him a seventy year reign between Fidach and Cat (**q.v.**). SL3(Lec.2) calls Fortrenn one of Cruithne's sons. SL3(Bal.1) gives him a seventy year reign between Fidach and Cat, and SL3(Bal.2) seems to give two seventy year reigns between Fidach and Cat.[402]

F.T. Wainwright uses the description in *De Situ Albanie* to equate Fortrenn's territory with "Sradeern cum Meneted." H.M. Chadwick had previously equated the territory of Fortrenn with "Strathearn with Menteith."[403]

Fotla. Personification of Ireland (**q.v.**).[404]

P#C(Lein.), P#C(Uí Ma.), P#C(Lec.), and P#C(G131) states that Fotla fought the Cruithni or Gaels (**q.v.**).

AC calls Fotla the sister of Banba (**q.v.**) and Eire (**q.v.**) and the daughter of "Fiagha mᶜDealvoye." AC records the killing of Fotla, her sisters, and their husbands by the Sons of Míl (**q.v.**).[405] AFM 3500 mentions that Fotla and her sisters were killed by the Sons of Míl.

Fotla (Fotlaid). Mythological Pictish king. Son of Cruithne (**q.v.**).[406]

Origin Legends P#L(Uí Ma.), P#L(Lec.), P#L(G47), and P#L(1336) state that Fotla was one of the seven sons of Cruithne who divided Alba (**q.v.**) or northern Britain (**q.v.**).

Lists SL1, SL2 M, and SL2 H call Fotla son of Cruithne and record a thirty year reign for him between Fortrenn (**q.v.**) and Cat (**q.v.**). SL3(Lec.1), SL3(Lec.2), SL3(Lec.4), SL3(Bal.1), and SL3(Bal.2) call Fotla one of Cruithne's sons.[407]

H.M. Chadwick and F.T. Wainwright equate Fotla's territory with "Adtheodle et Gouerin" ("Atholl and Gowrie") described in *De Situ Albanie*. "Atholl" derives from Irish "Athfotla" ("new Ireland") (see previous **Fotla**).[408]

Fróech (Fráech/Fróech mac Idaith). Connacht hero.

TBF records that three of Fróech's cattle were taken by the Cruithni (Picts) of Alba (**q.v.**). Fróech and Conall Cernach (**q.v.**) went to Pictland (**q.v.**) to retrieve these cattle.[409]

Galam (Galam II, Galam Cennaleph, Cennalath) (d.c.580). Pictish king (556-557(?)(solo)).[410]

AT 580 records his death and calls him "Cindaeladh rex Pictorum." AC 580 and AU 580 mention Galam's death.

SL1 gives Galam a one year solo reign and a one year joint reign with Bridei f. Mailcon (**q.v.**) between Drest f. Munait (**q.v.**) and Bridei's solo reign. SL2 M records a four year solo reign for him and a one year joint reign with Bridei. SL2 O lists a four year solo reign and a one year reign with Bridei between Drest f. Munait and Bridei's solo reign. SL2 H gives a four year reign between Drest f. Gyrom and Garthnach f. Girom (**q.q.v.**). Lists D, F1, F, I, K, and Fordun's List give a four year reign between Drest f. Munait and Bridei.[411]

H.M. Chadwick speculates that Galam may have been overthrown by Bridei but retained an under-kingship over the southern Picts.   F.T. Wainwright also suggests that he was under Bridei's rule.   M.O. Anderson states that "Cennaleph" or "Cennalath" may be an Irish phrase meaning "with particoloured head."[412]

Galan f. Barrfhind. In *Senchus Fer nAlban*, Galan is great-grandson of Erc (**q.v.**) by a mother who may have been of the Cruithni (Picts?).[413]

Galanan (Galam I). Pictish king (514-526(?)).[414]

List SL1 gives Galanan a twelve year reign between Drest Gurthinmoch (**q.v.**) and the joint reign of Drest f. Gyrom and Drest f. Uudrost (**q.q.v.**). Lists SL2 M and SL2 O give him fifteen years. Lists SL2 H and F1 give him a fifteen year reign between Drest f. Gurthinmoch and Drest f. Uudrost. He has a twenty-five year reign between the same kings in Lists F2, I, K, and Fordun's List. H.M. Chadwick states that "Galanan" may be Pictish.[415]

Garnard f. Uuid (Gartnait V, Gartnait son of Foth). Pictish king (631-635).[416]

AU 635 records the death of Garnard at Segais (**q.v.**). AT 643 and AU 643 record the killing of Iarnnbodb f. Gartnat (**q.v.**). He could have been the son of Garnard or Gartnait f. Accidan (**q.v.**).

List SL1 gives Garnard a four year reign between Cinioch f. Lutrin (**q.v.**) and Breidei f. Uuid (**q.v.**). SL2 M, SL2 O, and SL2 H give Garnard a five year reign between Cinioch and Talorc f. Uuid (**q.v.**). M.O. Anderson indicates that the remaining Regnal Lists call Garnard "*Nectan* son of Fode." List D gives him an eight year reign between Cinioch and Breidei. Lists F1 and F2 give him a five year reign between these same kings. List I, List K, and Fordun's List give him an eight year reign between Cinioch and Breidei.[417]

Garthnach f. Girom (Gartnait III). King of Picts (536-543(?)).[418]

Regnal Lists SL1, SL2 M, and SL2 O records for Garthnach a seven year reign between Drest f. Gyrom (**q.v.**) and Cailtram f. Girom (**q.v.**). List SL2 H gives him a seven year reign between Galam (**q.v.**) and Cailtram. List D gives Garthnach a six year reign between. Drest f. Gyrom and Cailtram. Lists F1, F2, I, K, and Fordun's List record a six year reign for Garthnach between Drest f. Uudrost (**q.v.**) and Cailtram.[419]

Gartnaich diuberr (Gartnait II). Pseudo-historical Pictish king.

SL1, SL2 M, SL2 O, SL2 H, D, F1, F2,I, and K give Gartnaich a sixty year reign between Uuardech (**q.v.**) and Talorc f. Achivir (**q.v.**). Fordun's List gives a sixty year reign between Uuaradech and Hurgust f. Forgso (**q.v.**).[420]

Gartnaich f. Accidan (?) (7th cent.) Possibly father of Cano (see **Cano f. Gartnait**: Cano 2).[421]

AU 649 records a war between the family of Áedán mac Gabráin (**q.v.**) and Garnait. AT 668, AC 666, AU 668, and CS 664 state that the family of "Gartnait" went to Ireland (**q.v.**). This could be Gartnait. AT 670 and AU 670 mention that the family of Gartnait left Ireland.

Scéla Cano may call him "Gartnán mac Áeda maic Gabráin" and rival of Áedán mac Gabráin. This could also be Gartnart f. Domelch or Gartnait f. Donuel (**q.q.v.**).[422]

There is confusion concerning the identity of Gartnait f. Accidan and his relationship to Cano f. Gartnait and the "family of Gartnait" who went to Ireland. T.F. O'Rahhilly asserts that Gartnait f. Accidan is not the "Gartnait" whose family went to Ireland. M.O. Anderson suggests this and that this "Gartnait" was son of Áedán mac Gabráin. John Bannerman thinks that the Gartnán of *Scéla Cano* is Áedán's son who appears in *Senchus Fer nAlban* (see **Gartnart f. Domelch**) and that the father of Cano 2 might be Gartnait f. Donuel. The tale may combine Gartnart f. Domelch and Gartnait f. Donuel (**q.v.**) into one character.[423]

Gartnait f. Donuel (Gartnait VI). Pictish king (657-?663). Possibly father of Cano (see **Cano f. Gartnait**: <u>Cano 2</u>) and son of Domnall Brecc, grandson of Áedán mac Gabráin (**q.v.**).[424]

AT 663, AC 659, AU 663, and CS 659 record the death of Gartnait. AT 668, AC 666, AU 668, and CS 664 record that the family of "Gartnait" went to Ireland (**q.v.**). This could be Gartnait f. Donuel.

Lists SL1, SL2 M, SL2 O, and SL2 H give Gartnait a six and a half year reign between Talorcen f. Enfret (**q.v.**) and Drest f. Donuel (**q.v.**). Lists D, F1, and F2 record a five year reign for him between Talorcen and Drest. List I gives a six year reign between Talorcen and Drest. Fordun's List gives him a five year reign between Talorcen and Drest.[425]

A.O. Anderson asserts that Gartnait f. Donuel is not <u>Cano 2</u>'s father but could be Domnall Brecc's son. John Bannerman suggests that he is <u>Cano 2</u>'s father and "Gartnait" whose sons went to Ireland rather than Gartnait f. Accidan (**q.v.**). M.O. Anderson suggests that Domnall Brecc could be his father or that "Donuel" may have been from Strathclyde or "lord of Dunnichen," (see **Dún Nechtain**) who married the sister of Talorcen f. Enfret (**q.v.**).[426]

Gartnaith loc (Gartnait I). Pseudo-historical Pictish king.

Regnal List SL1 records that Gartnaith loc reigned between Ru (**q.v.**) and Gartnart (4) (**q.v.**). List SL2 M gives Gartnaith loc a four year reign between the same monarchs. List SL2 O repeats this. Lists D, F1, F2, and I give a nine year reign between Caruorst (**q.v.**) and Uipog namet (**q.v.**). The nine year reign could be a confusion with Gartnart (4), who do not appear in this list. List K gives Gartnaith loc a nine year reign between Deocilinion (**q.v.**) and Uipoig namet. Fordun's List records a nine year reign between Caruorst and Uipoig namet.[427]

Gartnart (4) (Garnart, Gartnait). Four pseudo-historical Pictish kings.

Regnal List SL1 seems to record that four kings with this name reigned for nine years between Gartnaith loc (**q.v.**) and Breth f. Buthut (**q.v.**). List SL2 M gives the same information. List SL2 O gives "Gartnait ini" a nine year reign between the same kings. M.O. Anderson suggests that "ini" be read "iiii," as in the other lists. List SL2 H gives them a nine year reign between Ru (**q.v.**) and Breth.[428]

T.F. O'Rahilly suggests that the form "Gartnait" is related to the Old Irish "gart" ("head").[429]

Gartnart f. Domelch (Gartnait, Gartnait/Garnard son of Dome(l)ch/Dompnach). King of Picts (c.586-597/601/602).[430]

AT 599 and AC 590 record his death.

Lists SL1, SL2 M, SL2 O, and SL2 H give Gartnart an eleven year reign between Bridei f. Mailcon (**q.v.**) and Nectu n. Uerb (**q.v.**). List D gives him a twenty year reign between Bridei and Cinioch f. Lutrin (**q.v.**) and states that he established Aburnethige (**q.v.**). Lists F1, F2, and I give a twenty year reign between Bridei and Nectu. List K records a thirty year reign between Bridei and Cinioch and the foundation of Aburnethige. Fordun's List gives him twenty years between Bridei and Nectu and mentions his founding of Aburnethige.[431]

Senchus Fer nAlban may call Gartnart the son of Áedán mac Gabráin (**q.v.**). John Bannerman suggests that "Domelch" may have been Gartnart's Pictish mother and that Áedán was his father. *Scéla Cano* mentions Gartnán mac Áeda maic Gabráin, nephew of Áedán. The tale may confuse Gartnart f. Domelch with another Pictish ruler (see **Gartnait f. Accidan, Gartnait f. Donuel**) who was father of the Cano who went from Skye to Ireland (see **Cano f. Garnait**). Bannerman states that *Scéla Cano* has merged Gartnait f. Donuel and Gartnart f. Domelch into one character, thus causing "chronological difficulties."[432]

Géde Ollgothach (Ollgóethach) mac Ollaman Fótla (Gede olgudach). Mythological king of Alba and Ireland (**q.q.v.**) from the Cruithni (Picts?).[433]

Legends P#A(B 506), P#A(Uí Ma.), P#A(Lec.), and P#A(C.vi.2) call Géde one of seven Cruithni kings of Alba (**q.v.**) who ruled Ireland for thirty years between Findoll cisirne (**q.v.**) and Slanoll (**q.v.**).

Rawl. B. 502 states that Géde was one of four sons of Ollam Fótla (**q.v.**). Géde is included in a list of kings from Dal n-Araide (**q.v.**) between Slanoll (**q.v.**) and Bearngal (**q.v.**). *Book of Leinster* and *Book of Lecan* call Géde one of four sons of Ollam Fótla. Géde is listed among kings of Dal n-Araide between Slanoll and Fiac (see **Bagag ollfiacha**). *Laud 610* includes Géde among four sons of Ollam Fótla between Slanoll and Fiac.[434]

AC calls Géde third son of Ollam Fótla with a peaceful, eighteen year reign between Slanoll and Bagag ollfiacha.[435] AFM 3969 records his reign, and AFM 3971 mentions his death.

Regnal List SL1 gives Géde an eighty year reign between Fib (**q.v.**) and Aenbegan (**q.v.**). Lists SL2 M and SL2 H give an eighty year reign between Fib and Olfinecta (**q.v.**).[436]

M.O. Anderson suggests that Géde's inclusion as one of the Cruithni king of Ireland may have been influenced by the Regnal Lists. She points out the similarities among Géde Ollgothach, "Gede" (see **Gub/Gib**) who succeeded Cruithne (**q.v.**), and "Gilgidi/Gidige" (see **Gub/Gib**) with a hundred and fifty year reign.[437]

Gelon. Mythological Pictish ancestor.

Origin Legends P#E(Bal.), P#E(1295), P#G(B 512), P#G(Lec.), P#G(Bal.), and P#G(1295) state that the Cruithni, or Picts, were descended from Gelon son of Ercal (**q.v.**) who came from Thrace (**q.v.**). P#I(Lein.), P#I(Uí Ma.), P#I(Lec.), P#I(Bal.), P#I(D.ii.2), and P#I(B.iii.1) state that Gelon had six sons (see **Drostan, Letenn, Nechtan, Óengus, Solen, Ulfa/Ulpa**).

P#L(Uí Ma.), P#L(Lec.), P#L(G47),   P#L(Bal.), P#L(1336), and P#L(1295) state that offspring of Gelon conquered Orc (**q.v.**).

Regnal Lists SL3(Lec.1), SL3(Lec.4), and SL3(Bal.1)   call Gelon Ercal's son and a Cruithnian ancestor.[438]

The use of Gelon as an ancestor of the Picts seems to derive from the reference to "pictosque Gelonos" in Virgil's *Georgics*. W.J. Watson states this idea and mentions that the descent of Gelon and Agathyrsus (**q.v.**) from Hercules (Ercal) comes from Herodotus.[439] This may have caused confusion of Gelon with the tribe of Gaileoin (**q.v.**).

Gest gurcich. Mythological Pictish king.

Regnal List SL1 records a forty year reign for Gest between Guidid gaed brechach (**q.v.**) and Wurgest (**q.v.**). List SL2 M gives Gest a sixty year reign between these same monarchs. List SL2 H lists Gest between Guidid and the thirty Brudes (see **Brude (30)**) without a reign length. List SL3(Lec.1) records a forty year reign for Gest seemingly between Olfinecta (**q.v.**) and Wurgest. List SL3(Lec.3) gives Gest a forty year reign apparently between Guidid and Wurgest. This list intersperses the "thirty Brudes" among the other kings. SL3(Lec.4) and SL3(Bal.1) appear to give him a forty year reign between Guidid and Wurgest. SL3(Bal.2) seems to repeat this but records "xl. xl." as his reign.[440]

W.F. Skene suggests that Gest might be one of the thirty Brudes which would bring their total to thirty. H.M. Chadwick indicates that Gest gurcich and Wurgest follow a pattern similar to that of Brude (30).[441]

Gillabor(?). Irish leader killed at Camlann (**q.v.**)

Geoffrey of Monmouth states that Gillabor was allied with Mordred (**q.v.**) at Camlann.[442] "Gilla" is Irish for "a youth of an age to bear arms" or "servant." It is commonly used as a prefix in names.[443]

Gillafer (?). Irish leader killed at Camlann.
Geoffrey of Monmouth recounts that Gillafer was allied with Mordred (**q.v.**) at Camlann (**q.v.**).[444] The name "Gillafer" appears to derive from the Irish "gilla" (see **Gillabor**) and "fer" ("man").[445]

Gillapatric (?). Irish leader killed at Camlann.

The Genealogies mention many "Gillapatrics" although none of these is likely to be this person.[446]

Geoffrey of Monmouth recounts that Gillapatric was allied with Mordred at Camlann (**q.v.**).[447] Regarding the prefix "Gilla," see **Gillabor**.

Gillarum (?). Irish leader killed at Camlann.

Geoffrey of Monmouth recounts that Gillarum was allied with Mordred at Camlann (**q.v.**).[448] Regarding the prefix "Gilla," see **Gillabor**.

Giric (Giric/Girg/Grig son of Dúngal). King of Scots (?878-889) possibly with Eochaid ap Rhun.[449]

Regnal Lists SL2 M, SL2 O, and SL2 H give Giric an eleven or three year reign between Áed mac Cináeda (**q.v.**) and Domnall mac Causantín. Lists D, F1, F2, and I record that Giric killed Áed mac Cináeda and gives him a twelve year reign between Áed and Domnall. He defeated Ireland and the Angles (**q.v.**), freed the Scottish church from Pictish influence, and was buried on Iona (**q.v.**). List K gives the same account without mentioning his burial.[450]

Gratian. Roman emperor (375-383).[451]

Vita Cadoci states that Maximus (**q.v.**) killed Gratian.[452] Bede also mentions that Maximus killed Gratian. *Historia Brittonum* states that Gratian ruled with his brother Valentinianus (**q.v.**) and was killed by Maximus.

Geoffrey of Monmouth repeats this in an extended account. Gratian and Valentinianus were supported by Melga (**q.v.**) and Wanius (**q.v.**).[453]

Gruibne. Legendary poet.

Longes Chonaill calls Gruibne poet of Feradach Find Fechtnach (**q.v.**). He saves Conall Corc (**q.v.**) from freezing in snow and from an ogam death sentence on Conall's shield.[454]

In "Conall Corc and the Corco Luigde," Gruibne had been a captive freed by Conall.[455]

Gub/Gib (Gud). Pseudo-historical Pictish king.

Legends P#F(D.iv.1), P#F(Lec.1), P#F(Lec.2), P#F(Bal.), P#F(24.P.13), P#F(1295), P#F(1289), and P#F(D.iii.) call Gub the father of Cathluan (**q.v.**). They became powerful in Ireland (**q.v.**) and were expelled by Éremón (**q.v.**). P#G(B 512), P#G(Lec.), P#G(Bal.), and P#G(1295) seem to state that Gub expelled Éremón.

List SL1 appears to call Gub "Gilgidi" and gives him a hundred and fifty year reign between thirty Brudes (see **Brude (30)**) and Tharain (**q.v.**). Lists SL2 M, SL2 O, and SL2 H state that Gub either reigned between Brude (30) and Tharain or reigned for fifty years between Cathluan and Tharain. List D seems to call Gub/Gib "Cede" and gives him a hundred year reign between Cruithne (**q.v.**) and Tharain. Lists F1 and F2 give "Gede" a hundred and one year reign between the same two kings. List I gives "Gede" a hundred and fifty year reign between Cruithne and Tharain. List K records the same information. Fordun's List gives this same king a reign between Cruithne and Tharain.[456]

M. Miller states that "Gud" (Gub) replaced "Gilgidi" from List SL1. M.O Anderson points out the similarities among Géde Ollgothach (**q.v.**), "Gede" (Gub/Gib) who succeeded Cruithne (**q.v.**), and "Gilgidi/Gidige" who reigned for one hundred and fifty years.[457]

Guidid gaed brechach. Mythological Pictish king.

SL1 gives him a forty year reign between Olfinecta and Gest gurcich (**q.q.v.**). SL2 M and SL2 H record a fifty year reign between Aenbegan (**q.v.**) and Gest gurcich. SL3(Lec.3) gives a one year reign between Olfinecta and Gest. SL3(Lec.4), SL3(Bal.1), and SL3(Bal.2) give an unspecified reign between the same kings.[458] W.J. Watson suggests that "Guidid" is British for "woodsman" and it may be the equivalent of Fidach (**q.v.**).[459]

Gwid f. Peithan (c.600). Northern British chief or southern Pict. "Gwid" seems to be present in the form "Uuid" or "Wid" in names of seventh century Pictish kings Bredei f. Uuid, Garnard f. Uuid, and Talorc f. Uuid (**q.q.v.**). This may indicate that Gwid f. Peithan is their father. "Peithan" may actually be "Neithon," and he may have been Nectu f. Uerb or Neithon map Gwyddno (**q.q.v.**).[460]

Y Gododdin calls Gwid f. Peithan a steadfast warrior.[461]

Hengest (c.428/40/50). Legendary Germanic invader (see **Angles/English** and **Saxons**) and ruler of Kent.[462]

Bede states that Hengest and Horsa (**q.v.**) were the first rulers of the invaders from Germany (**q.v.**). Hengest was ancestor of the kings of Kent. In *Historia Brittonum*, Hengest and Horsa came to Britain (**q.v.**) with three ships during the reign of Vortigern (**q.v.**). Vortigern gave Kent to Hengest in return for Hengest's daughter as a bride. After gaining Vortigern's favor, he invited Octha (**q.v.**) and Ebissa (**q.v.**) to fight the Picts. Vortigern's son Vortimer repelled Hengest and Horsa. Hengest captured Vortigern after slaughtering his followers during a contrived "peace conference." Hengest was succeeded by Octha. Geoffrey of Monmouth states that Hengest and Horsa came to Kent with three ships during Vortigern's reign. Hengest received land after defeating the Picts. He repeats the tale of Vortigern's marriage and Hengest's rise to power. The Britons (**q.v.**), not trusting Hengest, gave the kingship to Vortigern's son Vortimer, who defeated Hengest four times. When Vortimer had died and Vortigern had regained the kingship, Hengest instigated the "peace conference" slaughter. Hengest was concerned by Vortigern's death because he feared Ambrosius (**q.v.**). Hengest was defeated by Ambrosius and executed. Triad 59 of the *Welsh Triads* laments the advice which brought Hengest, Horsa, and Hengest's daughter to Britain.[463]

Hoel (Howel m. Emyr Llydaw). Legendary king of Brittany. Nephew or cousin of Arthur (**q.v.**). Son of Budicius (**q.v.**).[464]

Geoffrey of Monmouth states that Hoel came to Britain to aid Arthur against Colgrin (**q.v.**), Picts, Saxons (**q.v.**), and Scots. Arthur left Hoel in Alclud (Dumbarton), besieged by Scots and Picts but returned to defeat them. Hoel commanded half of Arthur's army in France and defeated Guitard. Hoel stayed in France and was probably there at the time of Camlann (**q.v.**).[465]

Horsa (c.428/40/50). Brother of Hengest (**q.v.**).[466]

Bede states that Horsa and Hengest came from Germany (**q.v.**) and Horsa was killed in battle. *Historia Brittonum* says that Horsa and Hengest arrived during the time of Vortigern (**q.v.**). Horsa was killed during the second of four battles which Vortigern's son Vortimer fought against Hengest. Geoffrey of Monmouth states that Horsa and Hengest came with three ships during Vortigern's reign. Horsa agreed that Hengest should receive Kent in exchange for Vortigern's marriage to Hengest's daughter. Horsa was killed in battle by Vortigern's second son. Triad 59 of *Welsh Triads* laments the advice which brought Hengest, Horsa, and Hengest's daughter to Britain.[467]

Hurgust f. Forgso. Pseudo-historical Pictish king.

Fordun's List gives Hurgust a twenty-seven year reign between Gartnaich diuberr (**q.v.**) and Talorc f. Achivir (**q.v.**). It says that Regulus (**q.v.**) brought St. Andrew's relics to Scotland during Hurgust's reign (see **Cenn Righmona**).[468]

Hurgust only appears in this list, and Molly Miller states that Onuist f. Urguist (**q.v.**) is the king usually associated with the St. Andrew legend. She also notes the similarity of Hurgust f. Forgso with Onuist f. Urguist and Unuist f. Uurguist (**q.v.**).[469]

Iarnnbodb f. Gartnat (d.c.644). Possibly son of Garnard f. Uuid (**q.v.**) or Gartnait f. Accidan (**q.v.**).[470]

AT 643 and AU 643 record that Iarnnbodb was burned.

Im. Mythological Pictish leader.

Origin Legend P#E(Lec.) seems to indicate that Im was son of Pern/Pert (**q.v.**) and a warrior of the Cruithni. The text may say "uii" instead of "Im." P#E(Bal.) and P#E(1295) give the same information. P#F(D.iv.1), P#F(Lec.1), P#F(Lec.2), P#F(Bal.), P#F(24.P.13), P#F(1295), P#F(1289), and P#F(D.iii.2) may mention Im, but they are unclear. P#G(B 512), P#G(Lec.), P#G(Bal.), and P#G(1295) state that Im was a Cruithni elder.

Iogenan. Possible Pictish priest in Ireland (**q.v.**).[471]

Vita Columbae states that Iogenan had a book written by Columba (**q.v.**).[472] William Reeves equates the "Pictum" of the text with the idea of "Irish Picts" and claims that Iogenan was from Ireland. T.F. O'Rahilly indicates that the Latin "Picti" was never used for the Irish "Cruithin" (see **Cruithni (Picts?)**). Richard Sharpe agrees with this and says that "Éoganán" (Iogenan) is an Irish name unknown in Pictland (**q.v.**) until the ninth century. He indicates that Iogenan may have altered his original name. Kenneth Jackson states that "Iogenan" is Gaelic but used for the Pictish "Uuen" (which probably came from British), the name of a Pictish king (see **Uuen f. Unuist**).[473]

Irél Glúnmár mac Conaill Chernaich (Irial Glunmar). Nephew of Cruithne (**q.v.**) and ancestor of Dál n-Araide (**q.v.**).[474]

P#A(B 506), P#A(Uí Ma.), and P#A(Lec.), P#A(C.vi.2) state that Irél was called Crodai (**q.v.**) from which derived "Nat Crodu," a term used for the Cruithni. They also state that Irél was son of Conall Cernach (**q.v.**), nephew of Cruithne, and Lonceta (**q.v.**), daughter of Echdhe Eachbeoil (**q.v.**). M.O. Anderson suggests that "nia Cruithni" ("nephew of Cruithne") may have been "nia Cruithne" ("champion of the Cruithni").[475]

In *Rawl. B. 502* and *Book of Lecan*, Irél is called the ancestor of Dál n-Araide. He is son of Conall Cernach and father of Rochaid mac Iréil Glúnmáir, Dáire mac Iréil Glúnmáir, and Fiachu Findamnas. Irél was the grandfather of Rechtaid Rigderg, king of Ireland and Alba (**q.q.v.**). Irél is included in a list beginning with "Maicnia pater na Fothud." He is given a forty year reign. *Book of Leinster* calls Irél son of Conall Cernach and father of Rochaid and Fiachu Findamnas and gives him a forty year reign. *Laud 610* gives him a forty year reign and calls him Conall Cernach's son and father of Fiachu Findamnas.[476]

Isicon. Mythological father or grandfather of Britus (**q.v.**).

P#G(B 512), P#G(Bal.), and P#G(1295) call Isicon father of Britus. P#G(Lec.) wrongly calls Britus wife of Isicon.

Historia Brittonum seems to call Isicon "Ascanius" and makes him Britus's grandfather and son of the Trojan hero Aeneas. "Ascanius" may not be Isicon. His son killed him as predicted by fortune-tellers. He is given a 37 year reign in Italy. It seems to say that Britus was great-great grandson of Ascanius. *Duan Albanach* calls Britus Isicon's son. Geoffrey of Monmouth calls Ascanius son of Aeneas and says that he went to Italy with his father after the Trojan War. In Italy he established a city called Alba, which is also a Gaelic name for Scotland. Geoffrey repeats the tale of how Ascanius was killed by his son him, a story taken from *Historia Brittonum*. Ascanius is called grandfather of Britus.[477]

Istoreth. Mythological Pictish ancestor.

P#L(Uí Ma.) calls Istoreth both son of Istorine (**q.v.**) and son of Agnaman (**q.v.**). He is father of Pairte (see **Pairte (Partholon?)**) and ancestor of Gelon (**q.v.**). This difference probably results from new material added to the account in *Historia Brittonum*. P#L(Lec.), P#L(G47) may refer to Istoreth in the phrase "in Istoireand" and call him son of Istorine. P#L(Bal.), P#L(1336), and P#L(1295) call Istoreth son of Istorine and father of Pairte. *Historia Brittonum* says that Istoreth controlled Dál Riata (**q.v.**).[478]

Istorine. Mythological Pictish ancestor.

P#L(Uí Ma.) calls both Istorine and Agnaman (**q.v.**) the father of Istoreth (**q.v.**). This difference probably results from the addition of new material to the *Historia Brittonum*. P#L(Lec.), P#L(G47) seems to call Istorine the son of Aigine. P#L(Bal.), P#L(1336), and P#L(1295) call Istorine father of Istoreth. *Historia Brittonum* calls Istorine father of Istoreth.[479]

Itarnan (Etharnanus) (d.669). Possibly founder and first bishop of Rathin in Buchan.[480]

In AT 669 and AU 669, Itarnan and Corindu (**q.v.**) died amongst Picts. Kenneth Jackson states that "Itarnan" is apparently not Celtic and is similar to "Edarnon" and "Idarnoin," names that appear in inscriptions. He suggests that Itarnan may be "Ethernan or Ithernan," bishop of Rathin.[481]

Ívarr (the Boneless?) (9th cent.). King of Dublin.[482]

AC 830 includes Ívarr amongst the Danes (**q.v.**) who intended to invade Ireland (**q.v.**). AU 857 and CS 857 state that Ívarr and Óláfr (**q.v.**) defeated Caitil the Fair (Ketil Find). CS 858 records that Ívarr and Cerball defeated the "[Cinel] Fiachach." AU 859 mentions that Ívarr and Óláfr led an army in Meath. Ívarr, Óláfr, and Audgisl (**q.v.**) devastated the land of Flann mac Conaing in AU 863. AU 870 states that Ívarr and Óláfr besieged Dublin. Ívarr and Óláfr brought back Angles (**q.v.**), Britons (**q.v.**), and Picts as captives to Ireland. In CS 871, Ívarr brought back hostages from Alba (**q.v.**) but Picts are not mentioned. AU 873 and CS 873 record Ívarr's death.

Japheth (Iaféth).[483] Pictish ancestor.

P#L(Uí Ma.) and P#L(1336) call Japheth father of Javad (**q.v.**) and an ancestor of Cruithne (**q.v.**). P#L(Lec.), P#L(G47) call him son of Noah (**q.v.**) and Javad's father.

Rawl. B. 502 includes Japheth in two genealogies of the Laigin (**q.v.**). He is also called Noah's son and seems to be ancestor of Fathecht (**q.v.**). *Book of Lecan* also seems to call him an ancestor of Fathecht. *MacFirbis Genealogies* call him son of Noah and ancestor of the Gaels (**q.v.**).[484]

AC says that Japheth was the ancestor of Míl (**q.v.**). AC calls Japheth Noah's son and father of Magog.[485]

Lists SL3(Lec.1), SL3(Lec.3), SL3(Lec.4), SL3(Bal.1), and SL3(Bal.2) state that he was Cruithne's ancestor, Noah's son, and father of Fathecht. List SL3(Lec.2) calls him Cruithne's ancestor, Noah's son, and Javad's father.[486]

Historia Brittonum states that Japheth was son of Noah, ancestor of Europeans, and had seven sons.[487]

Javad. Pictish ancestor. P#L(Uí Ma.), P#L(Lec.), P#L(G47), and P#L(1336) state that Javad was an ancestor of Cruithne (**q.v.**), son of Japheth (**q.v.**), and father of Fathecht (**q.v.**).

Regnal List SL3(Lec.2) gives the same information.[488]

Historia Brittonum seems to call Javad the fourth son of Japheth and the father of "Iobobaath."[489]

Justin the Younger (Justin II). Roman emperor (565-578).[490]
AU 566 records the beginning of Justin's eleven year reign.
Vita Niniani states that Justin succeeded Justinian and that Columba
(**q.v.**) preached to the Picts during his reign.[491]

Kentigerna (Cáintighearnd) (d.734). Daughter of Cellach Cualan,
king of Laigin (**q.v.**) (d.AU 715). Irish saint active in Pictland (**q.v.**), who may
have died on Inch Cailleach ("nuns' isle") in Loch Lomond. She was reputed to
be the mother of Fóelán of St Fillans (**q.v.**), but the chronology makes this
uncertain. Her name is of British origin.[491a] AU 734 records her death.

Kineth f. Ferat (Ciniod III, Kinat, Cinaed son of Ferat/Wrad). King
of Picts (842-843). Son of Uurad f. Bargoit (**q.v.**).[492]
List D gives him a one year reign between Bred and Drust f. Ferat
(**q.q.v.**). List F1 gives him a one month reign between Bred and Brude f. Fochel
(**q.v.**). F2, I, K, and Fordun's List give him one year in the same position.[493]

Letenn. Mythological Pict.
P#D(D.iv.1), P#D(Lec.1), P#D(Lec.2), P#D(Bal.), P#D(24.P.13),
P#D(1295), P#D(1289), P#D(D.iii.2), P#E(Lec.), P#E(Bal.), and P#E(1295)
state that Letenn was one of six Cruithni who came from Thrace (**q.v.**).
P#F(D.iv.1), P#F(Lec.1), P#F(Lec.2), P#F(Bal.), P#F(24.P.13), P#F(1295),
P#F(1289), P#F(D.iii.2), P#G(B 512), P#G(Lec.), P#G(Bal.), and P#G(1295)
call Letenn one of six Cruithni from Thrace and mention that he died before
the others left the Franks (**q.v.**). P#I(Lein.), P#I(Uí Ma.), P#I(Lec.), P#I(Bal.),
P#I(D.ii.2), and P#I(B.iii.1) say that Letenn was one of six sons of Gelon (**q.v.**).
It is possible that "Letenn" is related to "Letavia" the Latinized form of
the Welsh "Llydaw," meaning "Brittany, Armorica." The Irish form of this
place was "Letha." The name may also occur in the Scottish place Dún
Leithfinn, which is mentioned in AU 734.[494]

Liathan. Mythological ancestor.
Legends P#L(Uí Ma.), P#L(Lec.), P#L(G47), P#L(Bal.), P#L(1336),
and P#L(1295) call Liathan son of Ercal (**q.v.**) and state that his descendants
controlled the area of the Dimeti (**q.v.**), Guer (**q.v.**), and Guigell (**q.v.**).
Historia Brittonum gives similar information.[495]
The accounts seem to be related to a settlement of the Uí Liatháin from
east Cork into Cornwall and Dyfed in Wales, a migration which may have
occurred by the third century.[496]

Llif f. Cian (Llifiau) (c.600). Possible Pictish warrior from Maen
Gwyngwn (**q.v.**) beyond Bannog (**q.v.**).[497] *Y Gododdin* recounts the exploits
of Llif, who is called a "foreign horseman" from Maen Gwyngwn and from
beyond Bannog.[498]

Loarn Mór (Loarn Mór mac Eirc). Legendary Scot.

Rawl. B. 502 and *Book of Leinster* include Loarn in genealogies of kings of Alba (**q.v.**) as father of Muiredach mac Loairn and the son of Erc (**q.v.**). *MacFirbis Genealogies* have a section about descendants of Loarn.[499]

Lists D, F1, F, I, and K state that Loarn was buried on Iona (**q.v.**).[500]

Vita Columbae says that Adomnán was forced to remain with descendants of Loarn while returning to Iona from a synod.[501]

Senchus Fer nAlban calls Loarn one of the sons of Erc and progenitor of the Cenél Loairn. *Duan Albanach* calls Loarn one of Erc's three sons with a ten year reign in Alba (**q.v.**) before Fergus Mór (**q.v.**).[502]

Loichet (Luchta). Mythological Pictish ancestor.

P#F(D.iv.1), P#F(Lec.1), P#F(Lec.2), P#F(Bal.), P#F(24.P.13), P#F(1295), P#F(1289), P#F(D.iii.2), P#K(Lec.2), P#K(Bal.), P#K(24.P.13), P#K(1295), P#K(1289), and P#K(D.iii.2) call Loichet the father of Cruithne (**q.v.**) and son of Cing (**q.v.**). P#K(D.iv.1) and P#K(Lec.1) call him Cing's father and Cruithne's grandfather. P#L(Uí Ma.), P#L(Lec.), P#L(G47), P#L(Bal.), and P#L(1295) call Loichet Cing's father and son of Pairte (Partholon?) (**q.v.**).

Lists SL3(Lec.1), SL3(Lec.2), SL3(Lec.3), SL3(Lec.4), SL3(Bal.1), and SL3(Bal.2) call Loichet father of Cing and the son of Pairte (Partholon?). The form "Luchta," which occurs in the Regnal Lists and some of the Origin Legends is the name of a Tuatha Dé Danann (**q.v.**) woodwright god.[503]

Lonceta. Mythological ancestor of Dál n-Araide (**q.v.**) and the Cruithni (Picts?).

Legends P#A(B 506), P#A(Uí Ma.), P#A(Lec.), and P#A(C.vi.2) call Lonceta daughter of Echde eachbeoil (**q.v.**) and mother of Irél Glúnmár (**q.v.**).

Lugaid. Chief of the Sons of Míl (**q.v.**) in the *Lebor Gabála* ("Book of Invasions").[504]

Origin Legends P#C(Lein.), P#C(Uí Ma.), P#C(Lec.), and P#C(G131) call Lugaid the husband of Fial (**q.v.**).

Rawl. B. 502 calls Lugaid son of Ith mac Míled Espáin and grandson of Míl. *Book of Leinster* calls Lugaid son of Ith and the progenitor of various families.[505]

Luigne moccu Min. Associate of Columba (**q.v.**).

Vita Columbae records that Columba permanently cured Luigne of a nosebleed. Adomnán mentions that Luigne encountered a monster in the river Ness in the territory of the Picts. Columba prevented the monster from attacking Luigne. Richard Sharpe calls this the oldest account of the "Loch Ness Monster."[506]

Mac Oige (d.c.802).

AU 802 and AFM 797 record the death of Mac Oige of Apor Crosan (**q.v.**), abbot of Bangor.

Machar (Macarius, Machorius, Mo-Chonna, Tochannu) (6th-7th cent.). Irish saint active among the Picts. He was one of the twelve followers of Columba (**q.v.**) who travelled with him from Ireland (**q.v.**) to Iona (**q.v.**).[506a]

Vitae Columbae includes Machar ("Tochannu") in a list of Columba's followers appended to the main text.[506b]

Maelgwn of Gwynedd (d.547/49 or 597/99). King of Gwynedd in Wales. Great-grandson of Cunedda (**q.v.**). He has been equated with Mailcon (**q.v.**), father of Bridei f. Mailcon (**q.v.**).[507]

Harl. 3859 includes him in a Gwynedd genealogy as a descendant of Cunedda and an ancestor of Cadwaladr (**q.v.**). *Jes. 20* mentions his wife, traces his descent from Cunedda, and includes him in a list of kings of Britons (**q.v.**) along with Vortigern, Ambrosius, Utherpendragon, Arthur, and Cadwaladr (**q.q.v.**). *Bonedd y Saint* mentions his son Run and daughter Eurgein.[508]

ACam. 547 records the death of Maelgwn, king of Gwynedd.

Vita Cadoci records that Maelgwn ruled all of Britain and was a contemporary of Arthur. He gave protection to Cadoc (**q.v.**) as had Arthur.[509]

Gildas mentions a "Maglocune" as a tyrant. A.O. and M.O. Anderson state that this individual is the same as the "Mailcun" in ACam. 547. *Historia Brittonum* mentions that Maelgwn ruled the Britons in Gwynedd. Geoffrey of Monmouth calls Maelgwn a British leader who was brave but full of vice and records that he had two sons: Ennianus and Run. Maelgwn is Arthur's chief elder in Triad 1 of *Welsh Triads*.[510]

Maelrubai (Maelrubha) (642-722). Irish cleric from Bangor. He founded the monastery of Apor Crosan (**q.v.**) in Pictland (**q.v.**).[511]

AT 671, AU 671, and CS 667 record that Maelrubai travelled to Britain (**q.v.**). AT 673, AU 673, AFM 671, and CS 669 record that Maelrubai founded Apor Crosan. AT 722, AU 722, and AFM 721 mention his death.

Félire Óengusso lists him under 21 April and states that he died with his mother. *Martyrology of Tallaght* (Lein.) lists him under ".XI. KL- MAII." (21 April).[511a]

Mailcon (Maelcon). Father of Pictish king Bridei f. Mailcon (**q.v.**). M.O. Anderson states that he could be Maelgwn of Gwynedd (**q.v.**).[512]

AI 584 and AT 584 record the death of Bridei f. Mailcon. AC 509, 563, and 584 all call Mailcon the father of Bridei. AU 505, 558, 560, and 584 all discuss the son of Mailcon. CS 560 also calls Mailcon the father of Bridei.

Regnal Lists SL1, SL2 M, SL2 O, SL2 H, D, F1, F2, I, K, and Fordun's List mention Mailcon as Bridei's father.[513]

Bede mentions Mailcon as the father of Bridei. H.M. Chadwick indicates that "Mailcon" is a "Welsh-Pictish" form and the equivalent of "Maelgwn;" therefore, Maelgwn of Gwynedd could be the father of Bridei f. Mailcon. Kenneth Jackson states that the name of Bridei's father is not clearly Goidelic as the genitive would be "Málchon" rather than "Mailcon" or "Maelchon." Jackson also indicates that "Maelcon" derived from "Maglocunos."[514]

Mar (Már mac Ethecht m. Aurtecht). Pictish ancestor.

Legends P#L(Uí Ma.), P#L(Lec.), P#L(G47), and P#L(1336) record Mar as an ancestor of Cruithne (**q.v.**) and the son of Fathecht (**q.v.**) and father of Buan (**q.v.**).

Rawl. B. 502 twice mentions Mar as the son of Fathecht and the father of Sém mac Máir.[515]

Regnal Lists SL3(Lec.1), SL3(Lec.2), SL3(Lec.3), SL3(Lec.4), SL3(Bal.1), and SL3(Bal.2) call Mar an ancestor of Cruithne, son of Fathecht, and father of Buan.[516]

Marius. Son of Arvirargus (**q.v.**) and legendary king of Britain (**q.v.**).[517]

Geoffrey of Monmouth records that Marius defeated the Picts and killed their leader Sodric (**q.v.**). Marius gave the Picts land in Caithness (see **Cat (Caithness)**).[518]

Maximus (Magnus Maximus, Maxen Wledic). Western Roman emperor (383-388).[519]

Harl. 3859 mentions Maximus in two genealogies and states that he killed Gratian (**q.v.**). *Jes. 20* lists him as an ancestor of Cadoc (saint) (**q.v.**) and several royal dynasties. *Bonedd Y Saint* calls Maximus emperor and father of Peblic.[520]

Vita Cadoci states that Maximus killed Gratian and controlled all Europe (**q.v.**). It also says that Maximus was an ancestor of Cadoc (saint) (**q.v.**).[521]

Gildas records that Maximus was a tyrant who had become emperor through military strength and not legal claim. Bede states that Maximus was made emperor by his soldiers and that he betrayed and killed Gratian in Gaul. Later Maximus was defeated by Gratian's brother Valentinianus (**q.v.**) and killed. *Historia Brittonum* calls Maximus the seventh emperor who reigned in Britain and records that he killed Gratian. It mentions that Maximus was executed after his defeat by Valentinianus. Geoffrey of Monmouth mentions that Melga (**q.v.**) and Wanius (**q.v.**) fought against Maximus because they were allied with Gratian and Valentinianus. Gratian's friends killed Maximus. Triad 35R of the *Welsh Trads* states that Maximus and Elen went with an army to Llychlyn and never returned.[522]

Melga. Legendary king of Picts.[523]

Rawl. B. 502 refers to a prehistoric "Meilge" and two others of the same name. *Book of Leinster* mentions "Milige" in "Genelach Laigsi." *Book of Lecan* repeats this and includes Conall Cernach (**q.v.**) in the genealogy. *Laud 610* lists the previously mentioned "Meilge" as "Melge Mol-."[524] Although none of these is probably Melga, the similarity is interesting to note.

Geoffrey of Monmouth records that Melga was allied with Wanius (**q.v.**) of the Huns (**q.v.**) against Maximus (**q.v.**). Melga and Wanius invaded Britain in support of Gratian (**q.v.**) and Valentinianus (**q.v.**). The text uses both "Melge" and "Melga."[525]

Míl Espáine mac Bili. Ancestor of the Sons of Míl (**q.v.**) in *Lebor Gabála* ("Book of Invasions").[526]

P#A(B 506), P#A(Uí Ma.), P#A(Lec.), and P#A(C.vi.2) state that descendants of Míl gave wives to the Cruithni (Picts?). P#B(Lec.), P#B(Bal.), P#B(1295), P#B(1289), and P#B(D.iii.2) seem to state that the Sons of Míl gave land to the Cruithni. P#C(Lein.), P#C(Uí Ma.), P#C(Lec.), and P#C(G131) say that Cruithne (**q.v.**) stole wives from the Sons of Míl. P#K(D.iv.1), P#K(Lec.1), P#K(Lec.2), P#K(24.P.13), P#K(1295), P#K(1289). and P#K(D.iii.2) state that the Sons of Míl gave widows of the men who had drowned with Donn (**q.v.**) to the Cruithni because the women of Alba (**q.v.**) had died. AC (pp.25-26) records a similar tale.

Rawl. B. 502 calls Míl father of Éremón (**q.v.**) and Éber and son of Bile mac Nemáin, or Nem. *Book of Leinster* calls Míl father of Éremón and Éber. It also states that Míl is father of Ír, an ancestor of Ollam Fótla (**q.v.**). *Book of Lecan* seems to give a similar pedigree as in *Rawl. B. 502. Laud 610* records that two of Míl's sons, Éremón and Éber, divided Ireland (**q.v.**) into two parts. *MacFirbis Genealogies* seem to have a section about the Sons of Míl. *MacFirbis Abstract* also includes a section about the Sons of Míl.[527]

AI §35 records that Míl died in Spain (**q.v.**). AC mentions that Míl was of the "Race of Japhett" (see **Japheth**). AC records that Míl had eight sons. There are numerous other references to Míl in AC. AFM 3500 recounts Míl's career. CS calls Míl the son of Bile, states that he travelled from Spain to Scythia (**q.v.**), from Scythia to Egypt, and records that he died in Spain.[528]

Modan (Modanus, M'Áedán, M'Aodhán) (6th-7th cent.?). Irish missionary among Picts and Scots. Active in Dumbarton and Stirling and was saint of Rosneath (Neveth). He may be identical with Modan who gives his name to Cill Mhaodháin (Kilmodan, Kilmadan) in Glendaruel, Cowal.[528a]

Modwenna (Monenna). (7th cent.). Presumably English saint. Abbess of Faughart, Louth in Ireland. She founded churches in northern England, Pictland (**q.v.**) and other parts of Scotland. She was a friend of Aldfrith (**q.v.**) and was confused with Darerca of Killevy, whose *Life* contains her story.[528b]

Mongfind ingen Feradach Find Fechtnaig ríg Cruthentuathi. Daughter of Feradach Find Fechtnach (**q.v.**).[529]

Rawl. B. 502, *Book of Leinster*, and *Book of Lecan* record that Mongfind was Feradach's daughter and the mother of Cairpre Cruithnechan (**q.v.**). *Rawl. B. 502*, *Book of Lecan*, and *Laud 610* mention another Mongfind who is daughter of Fidach and sister of Crimthann mac Fidaig, who appears in "Conall Corc and the Corco Luigde." It is possible that the two are actually the same individual. She is alluded to in the tale but not named.[530]

Longes Chonaill mentions that Feradach had a daughter who had a son with Conall Corc (**q.v.**). However, neither the daughter nor the son are given a name.[531] Presumably, they are Mongfind and Cairpre Cruithnechan.

Mordred (Medraut). Legendary nephew of Arthur (**q.v.**).[532]

ACam. 537 records that Mordred and Arthur killed each other at Camlann (**q.v.**).

Geoffrey of Monmouth mentions Mordred often. Mordred is called the son of the sister of Ambrosius (**q.v.**) and Loth. Lewis Thorpe states that this is a mistake for Arthur's sister. Geoffrey records that Mordred was allied with Picts, Scots, and Irish (**q.v.**) against Arthur. Mordred was killed at Camlann (**q.v.**). Triad 51 of *Welsh Triads* also discusses Camlann. Triad 54 states that Mordred ate and drank everything at Arthur's court and attacked Guinevere.[533]

Morleo. Pseudo-historical Pictish king.

Regnal Lists SL1, SL2 M, and SL2 O record a fifteen year reign for Morleo between Tharain (**q.v.**) and Deocilinion (**q.v.**). SL2 H records a twelve year reign for Morleo between Tharain and Deocilinion.[534]

Nechtan. Mythological Pict.

Legends P#D(D.vi.1), P#D(Lec.1), P#D(Lec.2), P#D(Bal.), P#D(24.P.13), P#D(1295), P#D(1289), and P#D(D.iii.2) call Nechtan one of six Cruithni who came from Thrace (**q.v.**). This is also true of P#E(Lec.), P#E(Bal.), and P#E(1295). P#E(Bal.), P#E(1295), P#F(D.vi.1), P#F(Lec.1), P#F(Lec.2), P#F(Bal.), P#F(24.P.13), P#F(1295), P#F(1289), P#F(D.iii.2) P#G(B 512), P#G(Lec.), P#G(Bal.), and P#G(1295) record that Nechtan died with three of his brothers after Ard Lemnacht (**q.v.**).. P#I(Lein.), P#I(Uí Ma.), P#I(Lec.), P#I(Bal.), P#I(D.ii.2), and P#I(B.iii.1) call Nechtan one of six sons of Gelon (**q.v.**).

Kenneth Jackson states that "Nechtan" is equivalent to "Nechton," "Nehhton," "Nehton," and "Naiton" and that "Nechtan" is Gaelic. He indicates that "Nechton" or "Nehhton" is Celtic but not Gaelic and that "Nechton" would have been the early Pictish form. F.J. Byrne points out that "Nechtan" is used for the god Nuada Necht, who is the source of the Boyne (**q.v.**) and husband of its goddess. This god is the counterpart of the Roman god Neptunus. Interestingly, Nechtan is called "Nechtan nár" ("noble Nechtan") in all the versions of P#D and P#I. This is also how Nechtan of Nér (**q.v.**) is described in *Félire Óengusso*.[535]

Nechtan of Nér (Nathalan) (d.c.679). Possibly British cleric in Pictland (**q.v.**). Nér (**q.v.**) has been identified with Deer in Buchan.[536]
AT 679, AU 679, AFM 677, and CS 675 record Nechtan's death.
Félire Óengusso lists him under 8 January.[536a] Regarding the name, see **Nechtan**.

Necthon f. Derelei (Nechtan III/Nechton III, Nechtan son of Derile). Pictish King (?706-?724, 729).[537]
AT 713 and AU 713 record that Necthon captured his brother Tolargg f. Drostan (**q.v.**). Necthon also drove out the "familia" of Iona (**q.v.**) in AT 717, AU 717, and CS 713. This refers to a community on the Tay, which had been set up from Iona.[538] AT 724 mentions that Necthon entered the religious life, and AT 726 records that Drest (c.728) (**q.v.**) held Necthon captive. AT 728 records the Battle of Caislén Credi (**q.v.**) in which Necthon defeated Elpín (c.728) (**q.v.**). AC 725 records Caislén Credi. AU 726 mentions that Necthon was the prisoner of Drest (c.728). AU 729 records that Onuist f. Urguist (**q.v.**) defeated Necthon at Monad Carno (**q.v.**). AT 732 mentions Necthon's death.
List SL1 records a fifteen year reign for Necthon between Bredei f. Derelei (**q.v.**) and the joint reign of "Drest et Elpín" (see **Drest (c.728)** and **Elpín (c.728)**). Lists SL2 M, SL2 O, and SL2 H give him a ten year reign between the same monarchs. List D gives him an eighteen year reign between Taran f. Entifidich (**q.v.**) and Bredei f. Derelei. Lists F1 and F2 give an eighteen year reign between Bredei and Ciniod f. Uuredech (**q.v.**) and a second nine month reign between Onuist f. Urguist and Elpín (c.728). Lists I, K, and Fordun's List give the same information and place the second reign between Onuist and Óengus f. Bruide (**q.v.**).[539]
Bede mentions a letter to Necthon from Ceolfrith (**q.v.**) concerning the proper observance of Easter.[540] Regarding the name, see **Nechtan**.

Necton f. Erip (Nechtan I/Nechton I). Pictish king (460-484(?)).[541]
Lists SL1, SL2 M, and SL2 O record a twenty-four year reign for Necton between Talorc f. Aniel (**q.v.**) and Drest Gurthinmoch (**q.v.**). SL2 H gives a thirty-four year reign. Necton was visited by Darlugdach (**q.v.**) during the third year of his reign and he founded Aburnethige (**q.v.**). Necton visited Brigid (**q.v.**) when he was driven out by his brother Drust f. Erp (**q.v.**). Lists D, F1, F2, I, K, and Fordun's List give Necton a ten year reign between Talorc f. Aniel and Drest Gurthinmoch.[542] Regarding the name of this monarch, see **Nechtan**.

Nectu n. Uerb (Nechtan II/Nechton II, Nectu n. Uerd, Nechtan grandson of Verb, Nechtan *nepos* of Uerb, or son of Irb). Pictish king (c.601/02-621). Possibly son of Cano f. Gartnait (see **Cano f. Gartnait:** Cano 1). He has been equated with Neithon map Gwyddno (**q.v.**) of Strathclyde.[543]

AT 621, AU 621, and CS 621 record the death of "Nechtan mac Canand." This seems to be Nectu.

Regnal List SL1 gives Nectu a reign of twenty years after Gartnart f. Domelch (**q.v.**) and before Cinioch f. Lutrin (**q.v.**). Lists SL2 M, SL2 O, and SL2 H record the same information without a reign length. Lists F1 and F2 record a twenty-one year reign between Gartnart f. Domelch and Cinioch f. Lutrin and that he founded Aburnethige (**q.v.**). This is also said of Necton f. Erip (**q.v.**). List I gives him a twenty-one year reign between Gartnart and Cinioch, and Fordun's List gives Nectu a nine year reign between the same two monarchs.[544] Regarding the name of this monarch, see **Nechtan**.

Neithon map Gwyddno (Neithon map Guipno, Neithon son of Gwyddno). King of Strathclyde (7th cent.). He has been equated with Nectu n. Uerb (**q.v.**).[545]

Harl. 3859 includes him in a genealogy of Strathclyde, where he is father of Beli map Neithon (**q.v.**) and descendant of Coroticus (**q.v.**).[546]

Nemed. Legendary son of Agnaman (**q.v.**) in *Lebor Gabála* ("Book of Invasions").[547]

Legends P#C(Lein.), P#C(Uí Ma.), P#C(Lec.), and P#C(G131) seem to record that the children of Nemed allied themselves with the Gaels (**q.v.**). The text is confused and may indicate the Cruithni (Picts?) instead of the Gaels.

MacFirbis Genealogies appear to associate him with Partholon (see **Pairte (Partholon?)**).[548]

AC (p.14) calls Nemed the son of Agnaman. AFM 2820, AFM 2850, AFM 2859, and AFM 3066 recount the career of Nemed and his descendants.

Historia Brittonum records that Nemed went to Ireland (**q.v.**) from Spain (**q.v.**) in a journey that took a year and a half. *Duan Albanach* mentions that the clan of Nemed ruled Alba (**q.v.**) after Britus (**q.v.**).[549]

Ninian (Nynia) (5th or 6th cent.). Bishop of Whithorn in Galloway. The exact extent of his contact with the Picts has been subject to much debate due to the idea that there were Picts in Galloway during Ninian's career. It is now clear that his subjects were Britons (**q.v.**) of Strathclyde.[550]

Miracula Ninie describes how Ninian converted a Pictish tribe, the Niduari (**q.v.**). *Vita Niniani* twice records Bede's account of Ninian.[551]

Bede says that Ninian preached to the southern Picts. *Culhwch* and *Olwen* calls Ninian one of "two oxen of Bannog." This may allude to Ninian having been a chief of the Picts north of Bannog (**q.v.**) before becoming a cleric.[552]

Noah (Nóe mac Laméch).[553] Pictish ancestor and Biblical shipwright.
P#L(Lec.), P#L(G47) call Noah father of Japheth (**q.v.**) and ancestor
of Cruithne (**q.v.**).

Rawl. B. 502 calls Noah son of Laméch and father of Japheth (**q.v.**)
and Cam (Ham). *Book of Lecan* repeats this. *MacFirbis Genealogies* seem to
call Noah father of Japheth.[554]

AC states that Noah was Laméch's son and Japheth's father. It records
how Noah built his ark.[555]

Regnal List SL3(Lec.2) calls Noah Lamech's son and Japheth's father.
He is also the ancestor of Cruithne (**q.v.**). Lists SL3(Lec.1), SL3(Lec.3), and
SL3(Lec.4) again makes Noah the father of Japheth and ancestor of Cruithne.
This is also true of SL3(Bal.1) and SL3(Bal.2).[556]

Historia Brittonum records that the second age of the world began
with Noah, father of Cam (Ham) (who laughed at Noah) and two other sons.[557]

Octha. Legendary son or grandson of Hengest (**q.v.**).[558]

Historia Brittonum records that Octha and Ebissa (**q.v.**) came to
Britain at Hengest's urging and fought against Picts. After Hengest's death,
Octha took control of Kent. Octha is Ossa's father and ancestor of Kentish
kings. Geoffrey of Monmouth mentions Octha frequently. Octha arrived in
Britain with Ebissa and three hundred ships. After Hengest had been defeated
by Ambrosius (**q.v.**), Octha fled to York. Octha was eventually killed in battle
against the Britons (**q.v.**) under the leadership of Utherpendragon (**q.v.**).[559]

Óengus. Mythological Pict.

Origin Legends P#D(D.iv.1), P#D(Lec.1), P#D(Lec.2), P#D(Bal.),
P#D(24.P.13), P#D(1295), P#D(1289), and P#D(D.iii.2) record that Óengus
was one of six Cruithni from Thrace (**q.v.**). P#E(Lec.), P#E(Bal.), and
P#3(1295) repeat this and state that Óengus died after Ard Lemnacht (**q.v.**).
P#F(D.iv.1), P#F(Lec.1), P#F(Lec.2), P#F(Bal.), P#F(24.P.13), P#F(1295),
P#F(1289), P#F(D.iii.2), P#G(B 512), P#G(Lec.), P#G(Bal.), and P#G(1295)
also call Óengus one of the six Cruithni from Thrace. P#I(Lein.), P#I(Uí Ma.),
P#I(Lec.), P#I(Bal.), P#I(D.ii.2), and P#I(B.iii.1) call Óengus one of the six
sons of Gelon (**q.v.**).

Kenneth Jackson states that "Óengus" is Gaelic and derives from
Celtic "*Oinogustus" and that the Pictish forms are "Onuist" and "Unuist."[560]

Óengus f. Bruide. Pictish king (?). M.O. Anderson suggests that he
is a repetition of Onuist f. Urguist (**q.v.**) as he only occurs in some of the
Regnal Lists.[561]

Regnal List D seems to give a Óengus a six month reign between
Ciniod f. Uuredech (**q.v.**) and Elpin f. Uuroid (**q.v.**). Lists F1 and F2 repeats
this and records a second reign for him of thirty-six years immediately
following his first reign. List I gives a thirty-six year reign between Onuist f.

Urguist and Bredei f. Uuirguist (**q.v.**). List K seems to give him a one month reign between Necthon f. Derelei (**q.v.**) and Elpin f. Uuroid. Fordun's List records a sixth month reign for Óengus between the same two kings.[562] Regarding the name, see **Óengus**.

Óengus Mór mac Eirc. Third son of Erc (**q.v.**) with descendants on Ile (**q.v.**).[563]

MacFirbis Genealogies appear to discuss descendants of Óengus. *MacFirbis Abstract* mentions "Mac Aongusa." It is uncertain if this refers to Óengus.[564]

Regnal Lists D, F1, F2, and I state that Óengus was one of three sons of Erc who were buried on Iona (**q.v.**).[565]

Senchus Fer nAlban frequently mentions Óengus. He is one of twelve (or thirteen) sons of Erc and has descendants in Scotland. He had two sons, whose descendants settled on Ile (Islay). *Duan Albanach* calls Óengus one of the three sons of Erc. *Longes Chonaill* mentions that Conall Corc (**q.v.**) will be famous amongst the "tuathe Óengusa" ("people of Óengus"). This could refer to Óengus Mór or Onuist f. Urguist (**q.v.**). T.F. O'Rahilly indicates that Conall Corc had a grandson named Óengus mac nad Froích (d.490). It is possible that this Óengus is meant.[566] Regarding the name, see **Óengus**.

Óláfr (Olaf, Amlaib) (fl. 9th cent.). Scandinavian prince and king of Dublin based in Ireland (**q.v.**).[567]

CS 853 states that Óláfr came to Ireland and gained the service of Scandinavians there and received payment from the Gaels (**q.v.**). AI 867 states that he conspired against Les Mór (Lismore) and lost Mártan. AC 864 records that Óláfr and Audgisl (**q.v.**), who were Danish princes (see **Danes**), took troops to Pictland (**q.v.**) and returned with hostages. AU 857 and CS 857 mention that Óláfr and Ívarr (**q.v.**) defeated Caitil the Fair (Ketil Find) in Munster. Óláfr, Ívarr, and Cerball took a large army into Meath in AU 859. AU 863 records that Óláfr, Ívarr, and Audgisl raided the territory of Flann mac Conaing. In AU 864 and CS 864, Óláfr drowned Conchobor mac Donnchada, king of Meath. AU 866 mentions that Óláfr and Audgisl pillaged Pictland and captured hostages. In CS 869 Óláfr burned Ard Macha (Armagh) and took one thousand captives. Óláfr and Ívarr attacked the fortress of Ail Cluaithe (Dumbarton) for four months and then destroyed it in AU 870. AU 871 states that Óláfr and Ívarr returned to Dublin with hostages consisting of Angles (**q.v.**), Britons (**q.v.**), and Picts. Óláfr and Ívarr arrived in Dublin from Alba (**q.v.**) with Saxons (**q.v.**), Britons, and two hundred ships in CS 871.

Olfinecta. Mythological Pictish king.

P#A(B 506), P#A(Uí Ma.), P#A(Lec.), and P#A(C.vi.2) record the reigns of Eilim ollfhinachta (**q.v.**) and Bagag ollfiacha (**q.v.**). It is uncertain if either one is Olfinecta.

Rawl B. 502, *Book of Leinster*, *Book of Lecan*, and *Laud 610* mention a "Fínnachta" (probably, Eilim ollfhinachta), one of four sons of Ollam Fótla (**q.v.**). It is unclear if this is Olfinecta.[568]

AC discusses the reign of "Fiagha," son of Ollam Fótla. It is uncertain if this is Olfinecta. AFM 3923 and AFM 3942 mention a "Fionachta" son of Ollam.[569] These could be Olfinecta, Eilim ollfhinachta, Bagag ollfiacha, or Finachta (**q.v.**).

Lists SL1 and SL2 H record a sixty year reign for Olfinecta between Aenbegan (**q.v.**) and Guidid gaed brechach (**q.v.**). List SL2 M gives Olfinecta the same reign between Aenbegan and Géde Ollgothach (**q.v.**). List SL3(Lec.1) appears to give Olfinecta a sixty year reign after Cat (**q.v.**) and before Gest gurcich (**q.v.**). However, the list is somewhat confused because it intersperses the "thirty Brudes" (see **Brude (30)**) throughout the list. List SL3(Lec.3) seems to give Olfinecta a sixty year reign between Aenbegan and Guidid gaed brechach. Again, this list intersperses the "thirty Brudes." The similarly confused SL3(Lec.4) seems to record a sixty year reign for Olfinecta between Cat and Guidid gaed brechach. This is also true of SL3(Bal.1) and SL3(Bal.2).[570] H.M. Chadwick equates Olfinecta with Eilim ollfhinachta.[571]

Ollam Fótla mac Fiachach Finscothaig. Mythological king of Ireland (**q.v.**) and Alba (**q.v.**) from the Cruithni (Picts?).

Legends P#A(B 506), P#A(Uí Ma.), P#A(Lec.), and P#A(C.vi.2) record that Ollam Fótla was one of seven Cruithnian kings of Alba who ruled Ireland and mention that he instituted the "Feast of Temair" (see **Temair**).

Rawl. B. 502 mentions Ollam Fótla frequently. Ollam Fótla is included in a list of kings of Ireland as the father of Cairpre mac Ollaman Fótla. Ollam Fótla reigned for forty years and that he had four sons. *Book of Leinster* also records that Ollam Fótla reigned for forty years and had four sons. It also mentions that he is of the Ulaid from Dál n-Araide (**q.v.**). *Book of Lecan* and *Laud 610* record the same information.[572]

AFM 3883 and AFM 3922 dicuss the reign of Ollam Fótla.

Onuist f. Urguist (Onuist I, Onnist, Óengus I son of Forgus/Fergus). Pictish king (729-61) and king of Scots Dál Riata (**q.v.**) (736-750). He may have been viewed as a descendant of Cairpre Cruithnechan (**q.v.**).[573]

AT 728 and AU 728 record that Onuist defeated Elpín (c.728) (**q.v.**) at the Battle of Mónad Croibh (**q.v.**). AT 729 and AU 729 record that Onuist defeated Drest (c. 728) (**q.v.**) at the Battle of Druim Dergblathuig (**q.v.**). AU 729 states that Onuist defeated Necthon f. Derelei (**q.v.**) at Monad Carno (**q.v.**). AU 734 records that Dúngal mac Selbaich (**q.v.**) escaped from Onuist.

AC 733 and AU 736 record that Onuist attacked Dál Riata. ACam. 736 records the death of "Ougen rex Pictorum." This could be misplaced or a mistake for Bruide f. Onuist (**q.v**) or another person.[574] AT 739 and AU 739 record that Onuist drowned Talorgan f. Drostan (c.734) (**q.v.**). AU 741 mentions that Onuist again attacked Dál Riata. AU 750 records the end of Onuist's reign. The death of Onuist is recorded in AT 759, AT 761, AC 755, and AU 761.

Regnal Lists SL1, SL2 M, SL2 O, and SL2 H record a thirty year reign for Onuist after "Drest et Elpín" (see **Drest (c.728)** and **Elpín (c.728)**) and before Bredei f. Uuirguist (**q.v.**). Lists F1 and F2 gives Onuist a sixteen year reign between Ciniod f. Uuredech (**q.v.**) and Necthon f. Derelei. Lists I, K, and Fordun's List repeat this.[575]

Regarding the name of this monarch, see **Óengus**.

Osric f. Ælfric. King of Deira (633-634).[576]

AT 629, AC 627, and CS 629 record that Osric was killed in the Battle of Fid Eoin.

Bede states that Osric was baptized by Paulinus but later renounced Christianity. Osric was killed in battle against Cadwallon, father of Cadwaladr (**q.v.**).[577]

The accounts of Osric in the Annals may be misplaced because they record that Osric died before his predecessor Edwin (d.633) (**q.v.**). Because Osric was killed in 634, the Annals may have had Osric instead of one of the sons of Æthelfrith (**q.v.**).[578]

Oswiu (Oswy). King of Northumbria (642-70/71). Son of Æthelfrith (**q.v.**).[579]

AT 642 and AU 642 mention that Oswiu fought against the Britons (**q.v.**). AC 642 mentions a battle fought between Oswiu and Penda (**q.v.**). AT 650, AT 656, and AC 652 record a battle between Oswiu and Penda in which Penda and thirty kings were killed. Battles between Oswiu and Penda are mentioned in AU 650 and AU 656. CS 647 records that Oswiu defeated Penda in battle. ACam. 658 records that Oswiu plundered. ACam. 669, AI 670, AT 671, AC 667, AU 671 and CS 667 mention Oswiu's death.

Bede's Cuthbert states that Cuthbert (**q.v.**) visited the nun Æbbe who was Oswiu's sister.[580]

Bede records that Oswiu conquered many of the Picts and Scots in Britain (**q.v.**). According to Bede, Oswiu killed Oswin son of Osric f. Ælfric (**q.v.**). Oswiu's battles against Penda are also recorded by Bede. Bede states that Oswiu died in 670. *Historia Brittonum* records that Oswiu had three sons and was one of Æthelfrith's seven sons. It also records that he reigned for twenty-eight and a half years. Geoffrey of Monmouth records that Oswiu killed Penda in battle after Penda aided a revolt led by Oswiu's son Aldfrith (**q.v.**).[581]

Pairte (Partholon?). Mythological Pictish ancestor who seems to be the same as Partholon from the *Lebor Gabála* ("Book of Invasions").[582]

Legends P#L(Uí Ma.), P#L(Bal.), P#L(1336), and P#L(1295) call Pairte (Partholon?) the ancestor of Cruithne, father of Loichet and son of Istoreth (**q.v.**). P#L(Lec.), P#L(G47) calls Pairte (Partholon?) the ancestor of Cruithne (**q.v.**), the father of Loichet (**q.v.**) and the son of Agnaman (**q.v.**).

MacFirbis Genealogies seem to include a section on descendants of Partholon.[583]

AFM 2520, AFM 2546, and AFM 2550 discuss Partholon's career. CS A.M. 1859 records that Partholon went Ireland (**q.v.**) and cleared four plains, and his people occupied the country. Eventually, they all died.

SL3(Lec.1), SL3(Lec.2), SL3(Lec.3), SL3(Lec.4), SL3(Bal.1), and SL3(Bal.2) call him ancestor of Cruithne, father of Loichet, and son of Agnaman.[584]

Historia Brittonum records that Partholon came to Ireland (**q.v.**) from Spain (**q.v.**) with a thousand people who subsequently died from disease. Geoffrey of Monmouth records that Partholon came from Spain and was given land by Gurguint Barbtruc.[585]

Palladius. Bishop (early fifth cent.), probably of Italian origin and died in southern Britain. He was apparently later identified with Torannán (**q.v.**), who preached and died among the Picts.[586]

AI §389, AU 431, and AFM 430 record that Celestine (**q.v.**) sent Palladius to Ireland (**q.v.**) to preach. AI § 390 mentions that he died in Britain. AC states that Palladius was sent to Ireland before Patricius (Patrick) (**q.v.**) and that he died in Pictland (**q.v.**).[587]

List K states that Palladius (Torannán?) and Columba (**q.v.**) converted Bridei f. Mailcon (**q.v.**). Fordun's List says Celestine sent Palladius during the reign of Drust f. Erp (**q.v.**). Molly Miller thinks that this is meant to be Patricius.[588]

Bede records that Celestine sent Palladius to preach to the Scots (**q.v.** and see **Irish**). *Historia Brittonum* records that Palladius went to convert the Scots and that he died amongst the Picts.[589]

Patricius (Patrick) (Padraig) (d.c.461/493). British saint and bishop (see **Britons**), who founded Ard Macha (Armagh) in Ireland.[590]

Rawl. B. 502 records that Patricius converted the Irish (**q.v.**). It also quotes a blessing concerning Patricius. *Book of Leinster* records that Crimthann believed in Patricius in "Genelach .h. Cendselaig" and mentions that Patricius blessed Muiredach Muinderg in "Senchas Dáil Fiatach." *Book of Lecan* quotes Patricius and mentions his benediction of Muiredach. *Laud 610* records Patricius's conversion of the Irish and his benediction of Muiredach Muinderg. *MacFirbis Genealogies* include Patricius in a section about Irish saints.[591]

AI §313 and AT record his birth.[592]   CS 353 mentions Patricius's birth.   AI §315 mentions his baptism.   AI §320 and CS 369 record that Patricius was released from captivity. His captivity is recorded in AT. AC states that Patricius was brought to Ireland as a captive and remained so for seven years. AC records how Patricius converted Ireland.[593] AI §390, AI §391, AU 432, and CS 489 mention that het went to Ireland (**q.v.**).   AI 441, AU 441 state that he was approved. AFM 431, AFM 432, AFM 447, AFM 448, AFM 457, and AFM 493 discuss his life and achievements. ACam. 457, AI 496, AT 492, AC 487, AU 492, and CS 489 record his death. It is possible that the earlier and later dates refer to different individuals, but this is uncertain.

Regnal Lists SL1, SL2 M, SL2 O, and SL2 H state that Patricius went to Ireland during the nineteenth year of the reign of Drust f. Erp (**q.v.**).[594]

Vita Columbae records that a follower of Patricius predicted the emergence and career of Columba (**q.v.**).   *Betha Coluim Cille* states that Patricius himself predicted the career of Columba. *Félire Óengusso* lists him under 17 March and calls him "apostle of virginal Erin." *Martyrology of Tallaght* (Lein.) lists him under .XUI. KL- APRILIS." (17 March).[595]

In his *Epistola* ("Letter") discussing the Strathclyde king Coroticus (**q.v.**), Patricius reprimands the ruler for selling Christians into slavery to Picts and Scots. He describes the Picts as apostate (or "unrighteous"/"immoral").[596] *Historia Brittonum* seems to indicate that Patricius went to Ireland around 405 and that he died sixty years before Brigid (**q.v.**). It also gives an account of his career, describes his miracles, and compares him to Moses. *Duan Albanach* states that the three sons of Erc (**q.v.**) received a benediction from Patricius.[597]

Penda. King of Mercia (626-655).[598]

AC 638 mentions that Penda defeated Oswald in battle. ACam. 657 records the death of Penda. AT 650 and 656 mention that Penda and thirty kings fought against Oswiu (**q.v.**) and were killed. AC 642 and AC 652 both state that Penda was killed in battle against Oswiu. AU 650 records a battle between Penda and Oswiu. AU 656 mentions that Penda was defeated in battle against Oswiu.

Bede records that Penda killed Edwin (d.633) (**q.v.**) in battle. Penda later burned Bamburgh. Around 635 Penda attacked the East Angles (see **Angles/English**). According to Bede, Penda was killed in battle against Oswiu. *Historia Brittonum* records that Penda was one of twelve sons of Pybba ("Pubba") and states that Penda was killed in battle. Penda reigned for ten years. Geoffrey of Monmouth states that Penda was defeated and captured by Cadwallon and later killed Oswald in battle. Oswiu killed Penda in battle.[599]

Pern/Pert. Mythological Pict.

Origin Legend P#E(Lec.) calls Pern/Pert the father of the Pictish warrior Im (**q.v.**). However, the text could also state that he had seven sons. P#E(Bal.) and P#E(1295) again call Pern/Pert the father of Im. P#F(D.iv.1), P#F(Lec.1),

P#F(Lec.2), P#F(Bal.), P#F(24.P.13), P#F(1295), P#F(1289), P#F(D.iii.2),
P#G(B 512), P#G(Lec.), P#G(Bal.), and P#G(1295) call him a hero of the
Cruithni. They may also call him father of Im.

Kenneth Jackson points out that "pert" is an apparently P-Celtic form
used in northern Scottish place-names.[600]

Policornus. Mythological king of Thrace (**q.v.**).

Origin Legends P#F(D.iv.1), P#F(Lec.1), P#F(Lec.2), P#F(Bal.),
P#F(24.P.13), P#F(1295), P#F(1289), P#F(D.iii.2), P#G(B 512), P#G(Lec.),
P#G(Bal.), and P#G(1295) record that Policornus fell in love with the sister of
the six Cruithni brothers (see **Drostan**, **Letenn**, **Nechtan**, **Óengus**, **Solen**, and
Ulfa/Ulpa).

Interestingly, there was a bishop of Babylon with the similar name
Policronius (Polycronius) who was martyred during the reign of the emperor
Decius (249-251). He is listed in *Félire Óengussuo* under 20 March and in
Martyrology of Tallaght (Lein.) under ".XIII. KL- APRILIS." (20 March).
Apparently, other martyrologies have him listed under 17 February.[600a]

Regulus (4th, 8th, or 9th cent.). Saint reputed to have brought relics of
St. Andrew to Cenn Righmona (**q.v.**), a tale which is related in at least five
texts. He was said to be a Greek from Patras or Constantinople and was
confused with Regulus of Senlis and Riaguil of Mucc-Inis.[601]

List K records that Regulus went to Cenn Righmona during the time
of Unuist f. Uurguist (**q.v.**). Fordun's List mentions that Regulus brought the
relics of St. Andrew during the reign of Hurgust f. Forgso (**q.v.**).[602]

Ru. Mythological Pictish king.

Lists SL1, SL2 M, and SL2 O record a hundred year reign between
Uist (**q.v.**) and Gartnaith loc (**q.v.**). SL2 H gives a hundred year reign between
Uist and Gartnart (4) (**q.v.**).[603]

Servanus (Serf) (between 450 and 700). Saint of Culross in Fife.
There may have been two saints with the name who were confused with one
another. List K places him in Fife during the reign of Bredei f. Derelei
(**q.v.**).[604]

Life of Servanus states that he was son of Alpia (**q.v.**) and Obeth.
Bredei f. Derelei attempted to kill Servanus and his followers but was healed by
Servanus.   Bredei granted land in Culross for an ecclesiastical community.
Vita Kentigerni Imperfecta (12th cent.) states that Servanus was a student of
Palladius (**q.v.**) (perhaps, a mistake for Torannán (**q.v.**)) and teacher of
Kentigern (d.c.612). *Vita Kentigerni* (c.1185) also says that Servanus taught
Kentigern.[605]

Book of Uí Maine, Book of Lecan, and *Book of Ballymote* call
Servanus's mother Alma, daughter of the king of the Cruithni (Picts?).[606]

Severus (Septimus Severus). Roman emperor (193-211).[607]

Vita Cadoci calls Severus the ancestor of Cadoc (saint) (**q.v.**) and the father of Meobus and the son of Antonius.[608]

Bede records that Severus became Emperor in 189, ruled for seventeen years, and built an earthwork boundary for Roman Britain. *Historia Brittonum* states that he was the third emperor to come to Britain and he built a wall to separate Britons (**q.v.**) from Picts and Scots. Severus was killed by Carausius (**q.v.**). Geoffrey of Monmouth says that Severus built a wall in Britain. Sulgenius (**q.v.**) besieged Severus at York and Severus was killed, leaving two sons: Bassianus (**q.v.**) and Geta.[609]

Simul f. Drest (c.725). Son of Drest (c.728) (**q.v.**).

AT 725 and AU 725 record that Simul was imprisoned.

Slanoll mac Ollaman Fótla. Mythological king of Ireland (**q.v.**) and Alba (**q.v.**) from the Cruithni (Picts?).

P#A(B 506), P#A(Uí Ma.), P#A(Lec.), and P#A(C.vi.2) record that Slanoll reigned between Géde Ollgothach and Bagag ollfiacha (**q.q.v.**) for thirty years in which no one was ill.

Rawl. B. 502, *Book of Leinster*, *Book of Lecan*, and *Laud 610* call Slanoll one of four sons of Ollam Fótla (**q.v.**). He reigned between "Fínnachta" (see **Eilim ollfhinachta, Finachta, Olfinecta**) and Géde Ollgothach.[610]

AC records that Slanoll reigned for twenty-six years between Finachta and Géde Ollgothach, that there was no disease during his reign, and that his body remained incorrupt.[611] AFM 3943 record's Slanoll's reign, and AFM 3959 mentions his death and incorrupt body.

Sodric. Legendary Pictish king.

Geoffrey of Monmouth records that Sodric was the king of the Picts and that he came to Alba (**q.v.**) from Scythia (**q.v.**). He was defeated and killed in battle against Marius (**q.v.**).[612]

Solen. Mythological Cruithni and Pict.

Legends P#D(D.iv.1), P#D(Lec.1), P#D(Lec.2), P#D(Bal.), P#D(24.P.13), P#D(1295), P#D(1289), and P#D(D.iii.2) record that Solen was one of six Cruithni who came from Thrace (**q.v.**). P#E(Lec.), P#E(Bal.), P#E(1295), P#F(D.iv.1), P#F(Lec.1), P#F(Lec.2), P#F(Bal.), P#F(24.P.13), P#F(1295), P#F(189), P#F(24.P.13), P#G(B 512), P#G(Lec.), P#G(Bal.), and P#G(1295) give the same information and state that he died after the Battle of Ard Lemnacht (**q.v.**). P#I(Lein.), P#I(Uí Ma.), P#I(Lec.), P#I(Bal.), P#I(D.ii.2), and P#I(B.iii.1) call Solen of one of the six sons of Gelon (**q.v.**).

The name "Solen" has been compared to the Old Breton "Sulan" derived from "sul" from the Latin "sōl."[613]

Sulgenius. Legendary foe of Severus (**q.v.**).

Geoffrey of Monmouth records that Sulgenius went to Scythia (**q.v.**) to enlist the aid of the Picts against Severus. He besieged and defeated Severus at York. However, Sulgenius died as a result of the siege.[614]

Talorc f. Achivir (Talorc I). Pseudo-historical Pictish king.

Lists SL1, SL2 M, SL2 O, and SL2 H record a seventy-five year reign for Talorc between Gartnaich diuberr (**q.v.**) and Drust f. Erp (**q.v.**). Lists D, F1, F2, I, and K give him a twenty-five year reign between and Gartnaich diuberr and Drust f. Erp. Fordun's List gives Talorc a twenty-five year reign after Hurgust f. Forgso (**q.v.**) and before Drust f. Erp.[615]

Kenneth Jackson states that "Talorc" is an alternative spelling of "Talorg" and is a Celtic name.[616]

Talorc f. Aniel (Talorc II, Talore filius Aniel). Pictish king (456-460(?)).[617]

Regnal Lists SL1, SL2 M, SL2 O, and SL2 H record a four year reign for Talorc between Drust f. Erp (**q.v.**) and Necton f. Erip (**q.v.**). Lists D, F1, F2, I, K, and Fordun's List give a two year reign between Drust f. Erp and Necton f. Erip.[618] Regarding the name, see **Talorc f. Achivir**.

Talorc f. Uuid (Talorc IV, Talorg son of Foth). Pictish king (641-653).[619]

AT 653, AC 649, and AU 653 record Talorc's death.

List SL1 gives Talorc a twelve year reign between Breidei f. Uuid (**q.v.**) and Talorcen f. Enfret (**q.v.**). List SL2 M gives a twelve year reign between Garnard f. Uuid (**q.v.**) and Talorcen f. Enfret. Lists SL2 O and SL2 H record a twelve year reign between Garnard and Talorcen. Lists D, F1, F2, I, and Fordun's List give an eleven year reign between Breidei and Talorcen.[620] Regarding the name, see **Talorc f. Achivir**.

Talorcen f. Enfret (Talorcan I, Talorcen son of Eanfrith (**q.v.**)). Pictish king (653-657 or 658-62).[621]

AT 654 and CS 653 record his victory at Sráith Ethairt (**q.v.**). AT 657, AC 653, and AU 657 mention his death.

Lists SL1, SL2 M, SL2 O, SL2 H, and D record a four year reign for Talorcen between Talorc f. Uuid (**q.v.**) and Gartnait f. Donuel (**q.v.**). List F1 gives him a five year reign between the same kings. List F2, I, and Fordun's List record a four year reign for Talorcen between Talorc and Gartnait.[622]

K.H. Jackson states that "Talorgen" and "Talorgan" come from Celtic "*Talorgagnos" and are related to "Talorcan" and "Talorggan." "Talorgen" is different from the Brittonic form which would be "*Talorgan" in Old Welsh.[623]

Talorg f. Muircholaich (Talorc III). Pictish king (544-555(?).[624]
Regnal Lists SL1, SL2 M, SL2 O, SL2 H, D, F2, I, K, and Fordun's List give Talorg an eleven year reign between Cailtram f. Girom (**q.v.**) and Drest f. Munait (**q.v.**). List F1 records a twelve year reign between Cailtram and Drest.[625] Regarding the name, see **Talorc f. Achivir**.

Talorg mac Congusa (Talorc son of Congus) (c.734). He seems to be a descendant of Áedán mac Gabráin (**q.v.**).[626]
AT 731 and AU 731 record that Talorg was defeated and put to flight by Bruide f. Onuist (**q.v.**). AT 734 state that Talorg gave his brother to the Picts, who drowned him. AC 731 and AU 734 mention that Talorg's brother gave him to the Picts, who drowned him. Regarding the name, see **Talorc f. Achivir**.

Talorgan (d.750) (Talorgan son of Forgus). Brother of Bredei f. Uuirguist and Onuist f. Urguist (**q.q.v.**).[627]
AU 736 mentions that Talorgan defeated Dál Riata (**q.v.**) at Cnoc Cairpri (**q.v.**). ACam. 750, AT 750, AC 746, and AU 750 record that Talorgan was killed in battle by the Britons (**q.v.** and see **Catoic**). Regarding the name, see **Talorcen f. Enfret**.

Talorgan f. Drostan (c.734) (Talorgan son of Drostan, ?Talorc son of Drostan). Pictish king of Atholl.[628]
AU 734 records that Talorgan was captured at Dún Ollaig (**q.v.**). AT 739 and AU 739 mention that Talorgan was drowned by Onuist f. Urguist (**q.v.**). Regarding the name, see **Talorcen f. Enfret**.

Talorgen f. Druisten (Talorcan II, Talorgan son of Drostan). Pictish king (?781-?785).[629]
AU 782 records the death of a "Dub Tholargg, king of Picts." M.O. Anderson remarks that this could be either Talorgen f. Druisten or Talorgen f. Onuist (**q.v.**).[630]
Regnal Lists SL2 M and SL2 H give Talorgen a five year reign between Drest f. Talorgen and Talorgen f. Onuist (**q.q.v.**). SL2 O records a four or five year reign between the same kings. Lists D, F1, F2, I, K, and Fordun's List give a four year reign in the same position.[631] Regarding the name, see **Talorcen f. Enfret**.

Talorgen f. Onuist (Talorcan III, Talorgen f. Onnist, Talorgen son of Óengus). Pictish king (?785-?787).[632]

AU 782 records the death of a "Dub Tholargg rex Pictorum," who could be Talorgen f. Onuist or Talorgen f. Druisten (**q.v.**).[633]

SL1 gives Talorgen a two-and-a-half year reign between Drest f. Talorgen and Canaul f. Tarl'a (**q.q.v.**) SL2 M, SL2 O, and SL2 H give him a twelve and a half year reign between Talorgen f. Druisten (**q.v.**) and Canaul f. Tarl'a. Lists D, F1, F2, I, K, and Fordun's List give a five year reign between Talorgen f. Druisten and Castantin f. Uurguist (**q.v.**).[634] Regarding the name, see **Talorcen f. Enfret**.

Talorgen f. Uuthoil (Talorcan IV, Talorgen/Talorc son of Uuthoil). Pictish king (834-?837).[635]

Lists SL1, SL2 M, SL2 O, and SL2 H give a joint reign of three years for Talorgen and Drest f. Constantini (**q.v.**) between Unuist f. Uurguist (**q.v.**) and Uuen f. Unuist (**q.v.**). Lists D, F1, F2, I, K, and Fordun's List seem to combine Talorgen and Drest in "Dostolorg" and record a four year reign between Unuist f. Uurguist and Uuen f. Unuist. "Uuthoil" could be the equivalent of the Irish "Fothol" or "Fethol," names which occur in prehistoric genealogies.[636] Regarding the name, see **Talorcen f. Enfret**.

Tarain (exile). Pictish noble and friend of Columba (**q.v.**). He may have been seen as an ancestor of Taran f. Entifidich (**q.v.**).[637]

Vita Columbae records that Tarain was killed by Feradach of Ile (**q.v.**), who had given him protection on Ile (**q.v.**).[638]

K.H. Jackson indicates that "Tarain" is a non-Goedelic Celtic name derived from "Taranis." A.O. and M.O. Anderson state that "Taranis" was the Gallic for "thunder-god" and that "Tarachin" is another form of "Tarain."[639]

Taran f. Entifidich. Pictish king (692-696).[640]

AT 697 and AU 697 record that Taran was deposed. AU 699 records that Taran went to Ireland (**q.v.**).

List SL1, SL2 O, SL2 H, List K and Fordun's List record a four year reign for him between Bredei f. Bili (**q.v.**) and Bredei f. Derelei (**q.v.**). List SL2 M gives Taran a four year reign between Drest f. Donuel (**q.v.**) and Bredei f. Derelei. List D records a fourteen year reign for him between Bredei f. Bili and Necthon f. Derelei (**q.v.**). Lists F1, F2, and I give Taran a fourteen year reign between Bredei f. Bili and Bredei f. Derelei.[641] Regarding the name, see **Tarain (exile)**.

Tea. Legendary wife of Éremón (**q.v.**).

P#C(Lein.), P#C(Uí Ma.), P#C(Lec.), and P#C(G131) states that Cruithne (**q.v.**) stole all the wives of the Sons of Míl (**q.v.**) except for Tea. AFM 3502 records her death and burial.

Tharain (Taran). Pseudo-historical Pictish king.

List SL1 records a hundred year reign for him between "Gilgidi" (see **Gub/Gib**) and Morleo (**q.v.**). SL2 O and SL2 H give him a hundred year reign between Gub/Gib or Cathluan (**q.v.**) and Morleo. List D gives a hundred year reign between Gub/Gib and Deocilinion (**q.v.**). Lists F1 and F2 repeat this. List I gives the same information. List K gives Tharain a hundred year reign between Gub/Gib and Dínortechest (**q.v.**). Fordun's List seems to indicate that Gub/Gib and Tharain reigned for two hundred and fifty years before Dínortechest.[642] Regarding the name, see **Tarain (exile)**.

Tolargg f. Drostan (c.712). Possibly the brother or half-brother of Necthon f. Derelei (**q.v.**). M.O. Anderson discusses the identity of Tolargg and the possibility that he is Talorgan f. Drostan (c.734) (**q.v.**).[643]

AT 713, AC 710, and AU 713 record that Tolargg was captured by Necthon. Regarding the name, see **Talorc f. Achivir**.

Torannán (Mothairén, Ternan, Torannán of Sligo) (6th cent.). Irish abbot of Banchory-Ternan on the Dee in Aberdeenshire. He apparently became identified with Palladius (**q.v.**).[644]

Book of Leinster, *Book of Lecan*, and *Book of Ballymote* calls him one of seven sons of Óengus mac Áeda and grandson of Erc (**q.v.**). *Betha Coluim Cille* records that Columba, when travelling in Ireland, visited Torannán in Drumcliff and gave Torannán a crozier which he had made. *Félire Óengusso* lists him under 12 June and notes the confusion of him with Palladius.[645]

Trumwine (Tuma). Bishop of Picts (678-685) based in Aebbercurnig (**q.v.**).[646] *Anonymous Cuthbert* and *Bede's Cuthbert* state that Trumwine reported that a child had predicted the career choice of Cuthbert (**q.v.**). Trumwine and Ecgfrith (**q.v.**) chose Cuthbert as bishop of Lindisfarne.[647]

Bede records that Trumwine was "to be bishop of those Picts subject to English rule" (see **Angles/English**). He mentions that Trumwine and his followers fled from Aebbercurnig after the death of Ecgfrith in battle against the Picts (see **Dún Nechtain**). The choice of Cuthbert as bishop of Lindisfarne is also recorded by Bede.[648]

Uaisnem. Mythological Pict.

P#E(Lec.), P#E(Bal.), P#E(1295), P#F(D.iv.1), P#F(Lec.1), P#F(Lec.2), P#F(Bal.), P#F(24.P.13), P#F(1295), P#F(1289), P#F(D.iii.2), P#G(B 512), P#G(Lec.), P#G(Bal.), and P#G(1295) call Uaisnem seer (or poet) of the Cruithni (Picts?).

Uineus of Nér (Finnia) (d.622/623). Abbot of Nér (**q.v.**) which could be Deer in Buchan in Pictland (**q.v.**). The name could be the equivalent of the Irish "Fine."[649] AU 623 records the death of Uineus.

Uipoig namet (Vipoig namet). Pseudo-historical Pictish king.

Regnal Lists SL1, SL2 M, SL2 O, and SL2 H record a thirty year reign for Uipoig between Breth f. Buthut (**q.v.**) and Canutulachama (**q.v.**). Lists D, F1, F2, I, and K give Uipoig a thirty year reign between Gartnaith loc (**q.v.**) and Fiacua albus (**q.v.**). Fordun's List gives Uipoig a thirty year reign between Gartnaith loc and Blarehassereth (**q.v.**).[650]

Kenneth Jackson indicates that "Uipoig namet" or "Uipo ignauiet" may be "Uepogenus," the name of a Caledonian in a third century inscription at Colchester. He also states that the correct form is difficult to ascertain because the manuscripts have so many different variations.[651]

Uist (Vist). Pseudo-historical Pictish king.

Lists SL1, SL2 M, SL2 O, and SL2 H record a fifty year reign for Uist between Deo Artíuois (**q.v.**) and Ru (**q.v.**).[652]

There is a similarity between "Uist" and the place-name Uist in the Hebrides. Kenneth Jackson states that the Old Norse for "food" was "uist."[653]

Ulfa/Ulpa. Mythological Pict.

Legends P#D(D.iv.1), P#D(Lec.1), P#D(Lec.2), P#D(Bal.), P#D(24.P.13), P#D(1295), P#D(1289), and P#D(D.iii.2) call Ulfa/Ulpa one of six Cruithni who came from Thrace (**q.v.**). P#E(Lec.) also call Ulfa/Ulpa one of six Cruithni from Thrace. Ulfa/Ulpa went to Rachru (**q.v.**) after four of his brothers died. P#E(Bal.), P#E(1295), P#F(D.iv.1), P#F(Lec.1), P#F(Lec.2), P#F(Bal.), P#F(24.P.13), P#F(1295), P#F(1289), P#F(D.iii.2), P#G(B 512), P#G(Lec.), P#G(Bal.), and P#G(1295) record that Ulfa/Ulpa was one of six brothers and that Ulfa/Ulpa died with three of them after Ard Lemnacht (**q.v.**). P#I(Uí Ma.), P#I(Lein.), P#I(Lec.), P#I(Bal.), P#I(D.ii.2), and P#I(B.iii.1) call Ulfa/Ulpa one of six sons of Gelon (**q.v.**).

Unuist f. Uurguist (Onuist II, Óengus II/Unuist/Hungus son of Fergus/Urguist). King of Scots Dál Riata (**q.v.**) and Picts (820-834).[654]

AU 834 records the death of Unuist ("Óengus").

Lists SL1, SL2 M, SL2 O, and SL2 H record a twelve year reign for Unuist between Castantin f. Uurguist and Drest f. Constantini and Talorgen f. Uuthoil (**q.q.v.**). List D gives him a nine year reign between Castantin f. Uurguist and "Dostolorg" (see **Drest f. Constantini, Talorgen f. Uuthoil**). It also states that he founded Cenn Righmona (**q.v.**). Lists F1 and F2 give the same information but with a ten year reign. List I gives Unuist a ten year reign between Castantin f. Uurguist and "Dustalorg." List K repeats this and states that Unuist founded Cenn Righmona. It records that Regulus (**q.v.**) came to Cenn Righmona during Unuist's reign. M. Miller states that Onuist f. Urguist (**q.v.**) is the monarch usually associated with Cenn Righmona. Fordun's List gives him a ten year reign between Castantin and "Durstolorg'." It also states that Athelstan (**q.v.**) reigned in Wessex at the same time as Unuist.[655]

Usconbuts. Pseudo-historical Pictish king.

Regnal List SL1 records a thirty year reign for Usconbuts between Dectotr'ic fr. Diu (**q.v.**) and Caruorst (**q.v.**). Lists SL2 M, SL2 O, SL2 H, D, F1, F2, and I give Usconbuts a twenty year reign between the same two monarchs.[656]

Kenneth Jackson states that "Usconbuts" is not Celtic.[657]

Utherpendragon. Legendary king of Britain and father of Arthur (**q.v.**).[658]

Jes. 20 includes Utherpendragon in a record of kings of the Britons (**q.v.**) between Ambrosius (**q.v.**) and Arthur (**q.v.**). The list also includes Britus, Vortigern, Maelgwn of Gwynedd, and Cadwaladr (**q.q.v.**).[659]

AU 467 records the death of Utherpendragon.

Geoffrey of Monmouth mentions Utherpendragon often. He is called the third son of Constantine III (**q.v.**) and the brother of Constans f. Constantine III (**q.v.**) and Ambrosius (**q.v.**). Utherpendragon and Ambrosius were raised by Budicius (**q.v.**) to protect them from Vortigern (**q.v.**), who had incited the Picts to murder Constans. Utherpendragon became ill but managed to defeat Octha (**q.v.**) and Ebissa (**q.v.**). However, Utherpendragon was fatally poisoned by the Saxons (**q.v.**). Triad 28 of the *Welsh Triads* states that the enchantment of Utherpendragon was one of the three prime enchantments of Britain. Triad 51 remarks that Utherpendragon and Ambrosius were banished by Vortigern.[660]

Uuen f. Unuist (Uven f. Vnuist, Eoganán son of Óengus II). King of Scots Dál Riata (**q.v.**) and Picts (?837-839). Son of Unuist f. Uurguist (**q.v.**).[661]

AU 839 records that Uuen was killed in battle against the "gentiles" (see **Norwegians**), resulting in the deaths of many Pictish nobles. This helped Cináed mac Alpín (**q.v.**) to become king.[662]

Regnal Lists SL1, SL2 M, SL2 O, and SL2 H record a three year reign between the joint reign of Drest f. Constantini and Talorgen f. Uuthoil (**q.v.**) and Uurad f. Bargoit (**q.v.**). Lists D, F1, F, I, K, and Fordun's List give Uuen a three year reign between "Dostolorg" (see **Drest f. Constantini** and **Talorgen f. Uuthoil**) and Uurad f. Bargoit.[663] Regarding the name of this monarch, see **Iogenan**.

Uurad f. Bargoit (Ferat/Wrad son of Bargoit). Pictish king (839-842?).[664]

Regnal Lists SL1, SL2 M, SL O, and SL2 H give Uurad a three year reign between Uuen f. Unuist (**q.v.**) and Bred (**q.v.**). Lists D, F1, F2, I, and K give a three year reign between Uuen f. Unuist and Bred. This is also true of Fordun's List.[665] Kenneth Jackson indicates that "Uurad" is the Gaelicizing "Ferad."[666]

Uuradech (Uuradechuecla). Pseudo-historical Pictish king.

Lists SL1, SL2 M, SL2 O, and SL2 H give Uuradech a two year reign between Canutulachama and Gartnaich diuberr (**q.q.v.**). Lists D, F1, F2, I, K, and Fordun's List record a two year reign between Donornauch (**q.v.**) and Gartnaich diuberr.[667]

K.H. Jackson states that "Uuradech" may be a Gaelicization of "*Uuradec" and "Uuredeg" may be a Pictish form. H.M. Chadwick and M.O. Anderson mention the similarity of "Uuradechuecla" and Feradach Find Fechtnach (**q.v.**).[668]

Valentinianus (Valentinian II).Western Roman emperor (375-93).[669]

Historia Brittonum states that Valentnianus and his brother Gratian (**q.v.**) reigned for six years and that Valentinianus reigned for a further eight years with Theodosius. Valentinianus and Theodosius defeated and executed Maximus (**q.v.**). Geoffrey of Monmouth remarks that he was Gratian's brother and that Maximus was their rival. Valentinianus fled Rome after Maximus killed Gratian. Valentinianus was backed by Melga and Wanius (**q.q.v.**).[670]

Vespasian. Roman emperor (69-79).[671]

Harl. 3859 includes Vespasian in a record of emperors as son of Claudius and father of Titus.[672]

AC remarks mentions that Vespasian was the father of Domitian.[673]

Bede records that Claudius sent Vespasian to subdue the Isle of Wight. Geoffrey of Monmouth mentions that Claudius sent Vespasian to make an agreement with Arvirargus (**q.v.**). However, Arvirargus would not let Vespasian land. At Vespasian's siege of Exeter, Arvirargus attacked Vespasian and forced a stalemate. Vespasian then went back to Rome.[674]

Volocus (Makwoloch) (5th cent.). Possibly a Gaulish or British saint active in Marr (Mar), which was in Pictland (**q.v.**). He may have been a follower of Ninian (**q.v.**). His tale is contained in the *Aberdeen Breviary*.[674a]

Vortigern (Gyrtheyrn Gvrtheneu. Guorthigirn).   British ruler (c.425-459), possibly confused with a later ruler.[675]

Harl. 3859 includes the "city of Vortigern" in a list of cities. *Jes. 20* records Vortigern as son of Gwidawl and places him among the kings of the Britons (**q.v.**) along with Britus, Ambrosius, Utherpendragon, Arthur, Maelgwn of Gwynedd, and Cadwaladr (**q.q.v.**).[676]

Gildas seems to discuss the career of Vortigern without naming him. Bede records that Vortigern invited Angles (see **Angles/English**) or Saxons (**q.v.**) and Hengest (**q.v.**) to Britain. *Historia Brittonum* mentions Vortigern frequently. During his reign, Vortigern was threatened by Picts, Scots, and Ambosius (**q.v.**). Vortigern also welcomed Hengest and Horsa (**q.v.**) in 347. Vortigern made Hengest an advisor in return for Hengest's daughter. At

Hengest's request, Vortigern had Octha (**q.v.**) and Ebissa (**q.v.**) come to Britain in order to fight the Picts. Later, Vortigern was betrayed by Hengest during a "peace conference." Vortigern was killed in a fire at his fortress. Geoffrey of Monmouth also mentions Vortigern frequently. According to Geoffrey, Vortigern had Constans crowned but later incited the Picts to murder him. The sovereignty then passed to Vortigern. During Vortigern's reign, Hengest and Horsa came to Kent with three ships full of Saxons (**q.v.**). These Saxons helped Vortigern to defeat the Picts. Later, Vortigern married Hengest's daughter in return for his giving Kent to Hengest. Geoffrey also records the slaughter of Vortigern's men by the Saxons during the "peace conference." Vortigern was burnt to death by Ambrosius. Triad 37(R) of the *Welsh Triads* mentions that Vortigern exhumed the bones of a saint which protected Britain from Saxon invasion. Triad 51 gives an account of Vortigern's treacherous acts.[677]

Wanius. Legendary king of the Huns (**q.v.**).[678]

Geoffrey of Monmouth states that Wanius was allied with Melga, Gratian, and Valentinianus (**q.q.v.**). He was driven off to Ireland (**q.v.**) by followers of Maximus (**q.v.**).[679]

Wilfrid (Wilfred) (634-709). Bishop of Northumbria and Hexham. He was trained at Lindisfarne.[680]

Life of Wilfrid recounts that he had jurisdiction over Saxons, Britons, Scots, and Picts (**q.q.v.**) until Ecgfrith (**q.v.**) and his wife Iurminburgh caused his deposition. After Ecgfrith's death, Wilfrid became enemies with Aldfrith (**q.v.**). In a synod at Rome, Wilfrid accepted Catholic doctrine for the Angles (see **Angles/English**), Britons, Picts, and Scots. He was later reinstated by the Synod of Nidd, which was instituted at the request of Pope John VI.[681]

Bede discusses Wilfrid's participation at the Synod of Whitby as a defender of Roman Easter practice against the Picts, Scots, and Britons. He records that Wilfrid was expelled during the reign of Ecgfrith and repeats the other information given in *Life of Wilfrid*.[682]

Wurgest. Mythological Pictish king.

Regnal Lists SL1 and SL2 M give Wurgest a thirty year reign between Gest gurcich (**q.v.**) and "Bruide Bont" (see **Brude (30)**). Lists SL3(Lec.1), SL3(Lec.2), SL3(Lec.4), SL3(Bal.1), and SL3(Bal.2) seem to give Wurgest a thirty year reign after Gest gurcich. However, the lists are confused by the interspersing of the "thirty Brudes."[683]

W.F. Skene believes that "Urgest" (Wurgest) is probably one of the "thirty Brudes." It is possible that "Wurgest" and its variations are related to the Pictish form "Uurguist," which K.H. Jackson says is the Gaelic "Forcus." T.F. O'Rahilly indicates that "Forcus" is the same as "Forggus," an Old Irish form that is mistakenly used for "Fergus."[684]

6

POPULATION AND PLACE NAMES ASSOCIATED WITH THE PICTS

Identifying and Textual Notes

Aburnethige (Apurnethige, Abirnithin, Abernethy). Pictish ecclesiastical center near Perth. The name means "confluence of the Nethy." "Nethy" may derive from "Neithon" (see **Nechtan**) or a river name.[1]

Regnal Lists SL1, SL2 M, SL2 O, and SL2 H record that Necton f. Erip (**q.v.**) dedicated Aburnethige to Brigid (**q.v.**). List D records that Gartnart f. Domelch (**q.v.**) founded Aburnethige. Lists F1 and F2 mention that Nectu n. Uerb (**q.v.**) founded Aburnethige. List K and Fordun's List record that Gartnart f. Domelch founded Aburnethige.[2]

M.O. Anderson states that it is likely that Aburnethige was founded during the reign of Gartnart f. Domelch or Nectu n. Uerb rather than Necton f. Erip.[3]

Aebbercurnig (Aber Curnaig, Abercorn). Pictish ecclesiastical center in Linlithgow founded in 681 under the jurisdiction of the Northumbrian church. Trumwine (**q.v.**) was its first bishop.[4]

Bede records that Trumwine and his followers fled Aebbercurnig after the defeat of Ecgfrith (**q.v.**) by the Picts (see **Dún Nechtain**).[5]

Agathyrsi (Agantirsi, Agthairius). Mythological name for the Picts, which alludes to their descent from Agathyrsus (**q.v.**) and Hercules (see **Ercal**).[6]

Legends P#E(Lec.), P#E(Bal.), P#E(1295), P#G(B 512), P#G(Lec.), P#G(Bal.), and P#G(1295) use Agathyrsi as a name for the Cruithni (Picts?).

J.H. Todd mentions that the Agathyrsi were a tribe from Scythia (**q.v.**) which derived from Agathyrsus, who was son of Hercules (Ercal). W.J. Watson states that the use of "Agathyrsi" as a name for the Picts derives from Virgil and Herodotus. In the *Aeneid*, Virgil uses the phrase "pictique Agathyrsi." M.O. Anderson states that the reference to "Picti" provided the link between the

Picts and Thrace (**q.v.**) given in the Origin Legends. Interestingly, the Irish version of the *Aeneid* from the *Book of Ballymote* does not appear to have the equivalent passage in its text.[7]

      Alba (Albania). Irish term generally used for Scotland but can be used for Great Britain as a whole.[8]
      Legends P#A(B 506), P#A(Uí Ma.), P#A(Lec.), and P#A(C.vi.2) record that thirty kings from the Cruithni ruled Alba and Ireland (**q.v.**) and seven kings of the Cruithni from Alba reigned at Temair (**q.v.**). P#E(Lec.), P#E(Bal.), and P#E(1295) state that the Cruithni settled in Alba after journeying from Thrace (**q.v.**). P#F(D.iv.1), P#F(Lec.1), P#F(Lec.2), P#F(Bal.), P#F(1295), P#F(1289), P#F(24.P.13), P#F(D.iii.2), P#G(B 512), P#G(Lec.), P#G(Bal.), and P#G(1295) record that Cathluan (**q.v.**) was the first of seventy Cruithni to rule Alba. P#K(D.iv.1), P#K(Lec.1), P#K(Lec.2), P#K(Bal.), P#K(24.P.13), P#K(1295), P#K(1289), and P#K(D.iii.2) indicate that the Cruithni had no wives because the women of Alba had died. P#L(Lec.), P#L(G47) states that the sons of Cruithne (**q.v.**) controlled and divided Alba.
      Rawl. B. 502 discusses the family of Cairpre Cruithnechan (**q.v.**) in Alba and also contains genealogies of kings of Alba. *Book of Leinster* also has a genealogy of the kings of Alba. *Book of Lecan* mentions the family of Cairpre Cruithnechan in Alba. *MacFirbis Genealogies* appear to have a genealogy of kings of Alba and seem to contain "A eolcha Alban uile," which is *Duan Albanach*.[9]
      CS 560 records the defeat of the "men of Alba" by Bridei f. Mailcon (**q.v.**). AI 563 records the arrival of Columba (**q.v.**) in Alba. AU 606 calls Áedán mac Gabráin (**q.v.**) "king of Alba" when recording his death. AT 759 and AT 761 mention the death of Onuist f. Urguist (**q.v.**) and call him "king of Alba" and "king of the Picts." AI 807 states that Canaul f. Tarl'a (**q.v.**) was killed in Alba. AI 820 records that Castantin f. Uurguist (**q.v.**), king of Alba, was killed. AU 829 records that the relics of Columba (**q.v.**) were taken to Alba. AI 858 mentions the death of Cináed mac Alpín (**q.v.**), king of Alba. The death of Domnall f. Alpín (**q.v.**), king of Alba, is recorded in AI 861. AU 866 states that Óláfr (**q.v.**) and Audgisl (**q.v.**) led the foreigners of Ireland (**q.v.**) and Alba in the devastation of Pictish lands. AU 871 records that Óláfr and Audgisl brought various hostages to Dublin from Alba.
      List SL1 states that "thirty Brudes" (see **Brude (30)**) ruled Ireland and Albania (Alba) for a hundred and fifty years. List SL2 M says that Alba was without a ruler between the "thirty Brudes" and Gub/Gib (**q.v.**), who controlled all of Alba. SL2 O gives similar information. List SL3(Lec.1) states that Fib (**q.v.**) ruled Alba for twenty-four years.[10]
      The Cruithni (Picts) of Alba stole cattle from Fróech (**q.v.**) in *TBF*, and he journeys there to retrieve them.[11] In *Longes Chonaill*, the exiled Conall Corc (**q.v.**) travels to the court of Feradach Find Fechtnach (**q.v.**) in Alba.

Scéla Cano describes the conflict over Alba between Áedán mac Gabráin (**q.v.**) and Gartnán mac Áeda maic Gabráin (see **Gartnait f. Accidan, Gartnait f. Donuel, Gartnart f. Domelch**). Geoffrey of Monmouth records that Sodric (**q.v.**) and the Picts came to Albania from Scythia (**q.v.**). Carausius (**q.v.**) gave land in Albania to the Picts. Wanius (**q.v.**), king of the Huns (**q.v.**), and Pictish king Melga (**q.v.**) landed in Albania to further the cause of Gratian (**q.v.**) and Valentinianus (**q.v.**). After the Romans (**q.v.**) left Britain, Albania was overrun by Picts, Scots, Norwegians (**q.v.**), and Daci to the wall built by Severus (**q.v.**). Lewis Thorpe identifies "Daci" as Danes (**q.v.**). Allies of the Picts who had been brought to Albania revolted against Vortigern (**q.v.**). Picts went from Albania to attack the rest of Britain during Vortigern's reign. Arthur (**q.v.**) went to Albania to aid Hoel (**q.v.**) against Picts and Scots.[12]

W.J. Watson states that "Albion," which is related to the Latin "albus" ("white"), was used for all Britain from c.500 B.C. The earliest Irish form of the name is "Alpe, Albe (nom.)," which became "Alba, Albu." Watson says that the term became limited to the Gaelic part of Scotland when Dál Riata (**q.v.**) was founded in western Scotland to distinguish it from "Cruithentuath" (see **Pictland**). "Alba" was later used for the kingdom of Scone (**q.v.**). T.F. O'Rahilly and Dauvit Broun state that "Alba" was originally used for Britain as a whole and around 900 became a term for Scotland alone, superseding "Pictland."[13]

Alt na n-ingen. Irish place in Dál n-Araide (**q.v.**). M.E. Dobbs indicates that the identity of Alt na n-ingen is uncertain but that it may be near Larne.[14]

Legends P#A(B 506), P#A(Uí Ma.), P#A(Lec.), and P#A(C.vi.2) state that Alt na n-ingen received its name ("Cliff of the Maidens") because one hundred fifty maidens from there went to Britain with the Cruithni (Picts?).

Ambrones. Name used by Geoffrey of Monmouth for Picts, Huns (**q.v.**), and Saxons (**q.v.**).[15]

Geoffrey of Monmouth states that the Ambrones (Picts and Huns) were allied with Gratian (**q.v.**) against Maximus (**q.v.**) and slew the daughters of British noblemen. Geoffrey indicates that the Ambrones had often harried Britain. It is unclear to whom he is applying the term as he uses it separately from the Picts, Scots, and Saxons.[16]

As the name does not seem to appear in other sources, its meaning is uncertain. "Ambrones" may contain the same root ("amber") as in Ambrosius (**q.v.**), which is contained in English place-names and is related to the Welsh "Emrys." The root "Amber" present in "Ambrosius" Kenneth Jackson states is of unknown origin.[17]

Angles/English. Term used for the Germanic invaders of Britain (**q.v.**) who arrived in the fifth century.[18]

AU 871 records that Óláfr (**q.v.**) and Ívarr (**q.v.**) brought captive Angles and others to Ireland (**q.v.**).

Bede states that the Angles were one of the four nations of Britain (**q.v.**) along with the British (see **Britons**), Scots (see also **Irish**), and Picts. The Angles allied themselves with the Picts after the former had arrived in Britain. The English king Oswiu (**q.v.**) conquered the Picts and Irish. Bede also states that English along with British, Pictish, and Irish was one of the four languages of Britain.[19]

"Angle" is a modern transliteration of the Latin term "Angli," the equivalent of "Engle" or "Englisc" ("English") used by the Germanic settlers for themselves. "Saxon" (see **Saxons**) was used by Celts in Irish and Welsh to describe the Angles/English but not used to describe an English person in the English language. "*Saxones*" apparently was the only term used in sources before Bede to describe the Germanic raiders in Roman Britain. "Saxon" was later used for the English in northern and midland England.[20] The presence of either "Angle" or "Saxon" in a text could give an indication as to its original source.

Apor Crosan (Applecross). Pictish ecclesiastical center in Ross opposite Skye founded in 672 or 673 by Maelrubai (**q.v.**) of Bangor in Ireland (**q.v.**). It is possible that its foundation was related to the exile and return of the family of Gartnait of Skye (see **Cano f. Gartnait**, **Gartnait f. Accidan**, **Gartnait f. Donuel**). Site of scriptorium which may have been the source for some of the Annals.[21]

AT 673, AU 673, AFM 671, and CS 669 record that Maelrubai founded Apor Crosan. AT 722, AU 722, and AFM 721 record that Maelrubai died in Apor Crosan.   AT 737, AU 737, and AFM 732 mention that Maelrubai's successor, Failbe (see **Failbe mac Guaire**), drowned along with 22 sailors. AC 734 mistakenly says that the "work done" in Apor Crosan sank. AU 802 and AFM 797 state that Mac Oige (**q.v.**) of Apor Crosan, abbot of Bangor, died.

Ara (Arran). Scottish island between Alba and Pictland (**q.q.v.**).[22]

P#L(Uí Ma.), P#L(Bal.), P#L(1336), and P#L(1295) state that the Fir Bolg (**q.v.**) took Ara, the Isle of Man (**q.v.**), Islay (**q.v.**), and Rachra (**q.v.**) when the Cruithni went to Britain (**q.v.**). P#L(Lec.), P#L(G47) gives the same account without specifically mentioning the Fir Bolg.

Ard Lemnacht (Ard Lemnachta ("New-milk-height")). Location in Uí Cennselaig (**q.v.**) where a battle was fought between Crimthann (**q.v.**) and the Tuath Figda (**q.v.**).[23]

Legends P#D(D.iv.1), P#D(Lec.1), P#D(Lec.2), P#D(Bal.), P#D(24.P.13), P#D(1295), P#D(1289), P#D(D.iii.2), P#E(Lec.), P#E(Bal.), P#E(1295), P#F(D.iv.1), P#F(Lec.1), P#F(Lec.2), P#F(Bal.), P#F(24.P.13), P#F(1295), P#F(1289), P#F(D.iii.2), P#G(B 512), P#G(Lec.), P#G(Bal.), P#G(1295), P#H(Lein.), P#H(D.iii.1), P#H(B 512), P#H(D.i.3), P#H(Lec.), P#I(Lein.), P#I(Uí Ma.), P#I(Lec.), P#I(Bal.), P#I(D.ii.2), P#I(B.iii.1) indicate that Crimthann won at Ard Lemnacht with the aid of the Cruithni, who gave him a magical means of resisting the poison weapons of the Tuath Figda with the use of a milk bath. P#J(Uí Ma.), P#J(Lec.), P#J(Bal.), P#J(Ren.)(TR.WS), P#J(D.ii.2), and P#J(B.iii.1) again discuss Ard Lemnacht and its name.

Ath. Uncertain location in Scotland.

Origin Legends P#E(Bal.) and P#E(1295) state that the Cruithni took control of Alba (**q.v.**) and dwelled from "Ath" to "Forcu" (see **Fortriu**).

Origin Legend P#E(Lec.) uses "Cat" (see **Cat (Caithness)**) instead of "Ath." It is possible that "Cat" or the Pictish kingdom of Atholl is meant. "Ath" means "ford" or "open space" in Irish.[24]

Athgort. Location in Ireland. J.H. Todd indicates that its identity is unknown.[25]

P#E(Lec.), P#E(Bal.), and P#E(1295) state that Cruithne (**q.v.**) carried women "across Athgort" for the Cruithni (Picts?).

"Ath" means "ford" or "open space." "Gort" could be the Irish for "field," "corn-crop," or "ivy."[26]

Athmagh (Athmag). Location in Ireland. J.H. Todd indicates that its identity is unknown.[27]

Origin Legend P#E(Lec.) states that Cruithne (**q.v.**) carried women "across Athmagh" for the Cruithni (Picts?).

Concerning the meaning of "ath," see **Ath**. "Mag" is the Irish term for "plain" or "field."[28]

Bannog (Banawc). Scottish mountainous area between Stirling and Dumbarton on the southern boundary of Pictland (**q.v.**). It may have possibly been the Grampians or the Mounth.[29]

In *Vita Cadoci* Caw of Pictland (**q.v.**) indicates that he ruled beyond Bannog when he was alive.[30]

Y Gododdin states that the Llif f. Cian (**q.v.**) was from Maen Gwyngwn (**q.v.**) and from beyond Bannog. *Culhwch and Olwen* may allude to Ninian (**q.v.**) as having come from north of Bannog.[31]

Boyne (Bóand). Irish river between Ulaid (Ulster) and Brega (**q.v.**).[32]
Origin Legends P#E(Lec.), P#E(Bal.), and P#E(1295) record that the Cruithni (Picts?) controlled the mouth of the Boyne.
The Boyne goddess was aunt of Fróech (**q.v.**) in *TBF*.[33]

Brega (Bregia). Irish place and population located in Meath associated with Bregmach (**q.v.**).[34]
Legends P#E(Lec.), P#E(Bal.), and P#E(1295) indicate that Ulfa/Ulpa (**q.v.**) was killed in Brega.

Bregmach (Bregmag). Place in Ireland (**q.v.**) associated with Brega (**q.v.**).[35]
P#E(Lec.), P#E(Bal.), and P#E(1295) record that those Cruithni (Picts?) who did not settle in Bregmach landed in Alba (**q.v.**). P#F(D.iv.1), P#F(Lec.1), P#F(Lec.2), P#F(Bal.), P#F(24.P.13), P#F(1295), P#F(1289), P#F(D.iii.2), P#G(B 512), P#G(Lec.), P#G(Bal.), P#G(1295) state that six Cruithni stayed in Bregmach.

Britain. Island in northern Europe (**q.v.**), the northern part of which became home to the Picts.
Legends P#L(Uí Ma.), P#L(Bal.), P#L(1336), and P#L(1295) state that Cruithne (**q.v.**) took control of the most northerly part of Britain.
Miracula Ninie records that Columba (**q.v.**) went to Britain to preach to the northern Picts.[36]
Bede records that the Picts came to Britain after leaving Ireland (**q.v.**). *Historia Brittonum* records that Scots, Picts, Saxons (**q.v.**), and Britons (**q.v.**) are the four ethnic groups that inhabit Britain. Picts held one-third of Britain in the north. During the reign of Vortigern (**q.v.**) in Britain, He was under threat from Picts, Scots and Ambrosius (**q.v.**). Palladius travelled from Ireland to Britain and died among the Picts. Geoffrey of Monmouth states that Britain was inhabited by Normans (**q.v.**), Britons, Saxons, Picts, and Scots. The Picts came to Britain from Scythia (**q.v.**) and setled in Albania (see **Alba**). Sulgenius (**q.v.**) brought Picts from Scythia to Britain to regain power. Picts and Huns (**q.v.**) under their leaders Melga (**q.v.**) and Wanius (**q.v.**) invaded Britain in support of the cause of Gratian (**q.v.**) and Valentianus (**q.v.**). Vortigern convinced the Picts that he should be ruler of Britain instead of Constans (see **Constans f. Constantine III**). Britain was vulnerable to the Picts, Romans (**q.v.**), Scots, Ambrones (**q.v.**), and Saxons when Cadwaladr (**q.v.**) left Britain.[37]

Britons (British/Welsh). Native population of Britain south of the Forth-Clyde line.[38]

P#A(B 506), P#A(Uí Ma.), P#A(Lec.), P#A(C.vi.2) record that the Cruithni (Picts?) took land among the Britons. P#E(Lec.), P#E(Bal.), P#E(1295) state that the Cruithni travelled from the Franks (**q.v.**) past the Britons to Ireland (**q.v.**). P#F(Lec.2), P#K(D.iv.1), P#K(Lec.1), P#K(Lec.2), P#K(Bal.), P#K(D.iii.2), P#K(24.P.13) mention that Cruithne (**q.v.**) was allied with Britons of Fortriu (**q.v.**) against Saxons (**q.v.**). P#H(Lein.), P#H(D.iii.1), P#H(B 512), P#H(D.i.3), P#H(Lec.) state that the Cruithni fought at Ard Lemnacht (**q.v.**) against the Tuath Fidga (**q.v.**), who were Britons. P#L(Uí Ma.), P#L(Lec.), P#L(G47), P#L(Bal.), P#L(1336), P#L(1295) state that Cunedda (**q.v.**) expelled the descendants of Liathan (**q.v.**) from the Britons.

AT 750, AC 746, and AU 750 record a battle between the Picts and Britons in which Talorgan (d. 750) (**q.v.**) was killed. AU 871 states that Óláfr (**q.v.**) and Ívarr (**q.v.**) took captives of Angles (see **Angles/English**), Picts, and Britons to Ireland. CS 871 states that Óláfr and Ívarr took captives of Saxons (**q.v.**) and Britons to Ireland with no mention of Picts.

Bede states that Britons were the original inhabitants of Britain which during his time also had English, Scots (see also **Irish**), and Picts. He also states that the languages of these groups were the four languages of Britain. Britons were enemies of the English who were allied with the Picts during Bede's time. *Historia Brittonum* states that the four inhabitants of Britain were Britons, Scots, Picts, and Saxons. Severus (**q.v.**) built a wall separating the Britons from the Picts and Scots. Britons enlisted the aid of the Romans (**q.v.**) when they were threatened by the Picts and Scots. Geoffrey of Monmouth records that the Picts asked the Britons for wives but the request was refused. Some Britons allied with Sulgenius (**q.v.**) and the Picts against Severus (**q.v.**). After Carausius had given land to the Picts, they began to mix with Britons.[39]

The native Britons called themselves "cives" in Latin and "combrogi" in their own language. These mean "fellow-countrymen" and survive in modern Welsh as "Cymry" and modern English as "Cumber." The English called them "wealas," "wealh," or "wylisc" in Old English, terms which mean "foreigners" and survive in modern English as "Welsh."[40]

Caislén Credi. Place in Scotland. Moorhill, now Boothill, near the old Abbey of Scone (**q.v.**).[41]

AT 728, AC 725, and AU 728 record the Battle of Caislén Credi in which Necthon f. Derelei (**q.v.**) defeated Elpín (c.728) (**q.v.**) and became king of Picts.

Camlann ("Crooked Glen"). Unidentified place in England. Several places in England bore the name.[42]

ACam. 537 record that Arthur (**q.v.**) and Mordred (**q.v.**) both fell in the Battle of Camlann.

Geoffrey of Monmouth states that at the Battle of Camlann, Picts, Saxons (**q.v.**), Scots, and Irish (**q.v.**) fought on Mordred's side.[43]

Lewis Thorpe indicates that in Camelford at the bank of the Camel there is an inscribed stone which could mark the location of Camlann, which local legend attaches to the area. John Morris states that a Roman fort at Hadrian's Wall and a place in Merionethshire had the name "crooked glen." He calculates the date of the battle as c.515. Leslie Alcock indicates that it could have been "Cambolanda" ("crooked enclosure") or Camboglanna" ("crooked bank") in British, which would have been "Camglann" in Early Welsh. Camboglanna was the Roman fort of Birdoswald at the western end of Hadrian's Wall. He gives 511 as a possible date for the battle.[44]

Cat (Caithness) (Cait). Place in Scotland and one of seven divisions under Cruithne (**q.v.**). Associated with the legendary Pict Cat (**q.v.**).[45]

P#E(Lec.) records that Cruithni occupied Alba (**q.v.**) from Cat to Forcu (see **Fortriu**). P#L(Uí Ma.), P#L(Lec.), P#L(G47), and P#L(1336) call Cat one of seven regions of the far-north of Britain and associates it with Cat.

SL3(Lec.1), SL3(Lec.2), SL3(Lec.4) seem to repeat this.[46]

Geoffrey of Monmouth states that Colgrin (**q.v.**) and the Saxons (**q.v.**), who were allied with Picts and Scots, controlled part of Britain from the Humber to Caithness (here called a "sea").[47]

Catoic (Catohic). Unidentified location in Scotland, perhaps in Pictland (**q.v.**).[48]

ACam. 750, AT 750, AC 746, and AU 750 record the Battle of Catoic (using various names) between the Picts and Britons (**q.v.**) in which Talorgan (d.750) (**q.v.**) was killed.

Cenannus (Cenandas, Kells). Irish place in Meath.[49] P#A(B 506), P#A(Uí Ma.), P#A(Lec.), and P#A(C.vi.2) record that Cenannus was named from the white-headed cows born during the reign of Findoll Cisirne (**q.v.**).

Cenél Conaill (Cenél Conaill Cernaig). Irish population who were the Laigis (**q.v.**) of Leinster.

Legends P#A(B 506), P#A(Uí Ma.), P#A(Lec.), and P#A(C.vi.2) state that the family of Conall Cernach (**q.v.**) was descended from Cruithni.

Cenn Righmona (Cenrigmonaid, Kilremont(h), St Andrews). Pictish ecclesiastical center in Fife. The legend of Regulus (**q.v.**) bringing relics of St. Andrew to Cenn Righmona is related in the Poppleton Manuscript, British Museum *Additional MS. 25014*, *Polychronicon* (Higden), *Brit. Eccles. Ant. XV* and *Works* (Archbishop Ussher), and *Harleian MS. 4628*.[50]

AT 747 and AU 747 record the death of Tuathalán, abbot of Cenn Righmona.

Regnal List D, F1, and F2 record that Unuist F. Uurguist (**q.v.**) founded Cenn Righmona. List I states that Castantin f. Uuirguist founded Cenn Righmona. Fordun's List mentions that Hurgust f. Forgso (**q.v.**) founded Cenn Righmona. Molly Miller states that Onuist f. Urguist (**q.v.**) is the actual king associated with the foundation of Cenn Righmona.[51]

Circhend (Circinn, Cirgen). Pictish province north of the Tay. Alternately, Kirkintulloch northeast of Glasgow.[52]

P#A(B 506), P#A(Uí Ma.), P#A(Lec.), and P#A(C.vi.2) state that the Cruithni took land in Fortriu (**q.v.**) and Circhend.

AT 596 records that Áedán mac Gabráin (**q.v.**) was victorious at Circhend. A.O. and M.O. Anderson indicate that this battle may have been fought earlier involving Bridei f. Mailcon (**q.v.**), who may have been killed there.[53]

Scela Cano mentions that there were territories of the Cruithni in "Gergin" (Circhend).[54]

Cnoc Coirpri (Cnoc Cairbre, Cnoc Cairpri). Scottish place in Calathros at Etarlindu.[55]

AU 736 records the Battle of Cnoc Coirpri in which Talorgan (d.750) (**q.v.**) of Fortriu (**q.v.**) defeated Dál Riata (**q.v.**).

W.F. Skene claims that Cnoc Coirpri is the modern place "Knock Cariber." W.J. Watson dismisses this assertion on the grounds that "Carriber is a compound term."[56] "Coirpri" appears to be present in the figure of Cairpre Cruithnechan (**q.v.**).

Crúachu (Croghan). Irish place in Roscommon in Connacht.[57]

P#A(B 506), P#A(Uí Ma.), and P#A(Lec.) record that Ollam Fótla (**q.v.**) ruled at Temair (**q.v.**) and Crúachu for thirty years.

Cruithni (Picts?) (Cruithne). Irish term for Picts. In Medieval Irish texts the form "Cruithnig" is also used for an unrelated population in Ireland as well as Scotland.[58]

Legends P#A(B 506), P#A(Uí Ma.), P#A(Lec.), and P#A(C.vi.2) state that the Cruithni were the same as the Dál n-Araide (**q.v.**). They also record that the Cruithni were the ancestors of Irél Glúnmár (**q.v.**). Thrace (**q.v.**) was the original home of the Cruithni, and there were thirty kings of the Cruithni who ruled Alba (**q.v.**) and Ireland (**q.v.**). P#B(Lec.), P#B(Bal.), P#B(1295), P#B(1289), and P#B(D.iii.2) record that the Cruithni came from Thrace and that the Sons of Míl (**q.v.**) promised them land in Pictland (**q.v.**), where they later settled. P#D(D.iv.1), P#D(Lec.1), P#D(Lec.2), P#D(Bal.), P#D(24.P.13), P#D(1295), P#D(1289), and P#D(D.iii.2) record how the Cruithni won the Battle of Ard Lemnacht (**q.v.**). P#E(Lec.), P#E(Bal.), and P#E(1295) recount the whole story of how the Cruithni (also called "Picts") went from Thrace through the lands of the Franks (**q.v.**) to Ireland and eventually settled in Alba (**q.v.**).   P#F(D.iv.1),   P#F(Lec.1),   P#F(Lec.2),   P#F(Bal.),   P#F(24.P.13), P#F(1295), P#F(1289), and P#F(D.iii.2) give similar information but do not use the term "Picts." P#F(D.iv.1), P#F(Lec.1), P#F(Bal.), P#F(24.P.13), and P#F(1295) state that sovereignty was divided equally amongst men and women because the Cruithni had received wives from the Gaels (**q.v.** and see **Donn**). P#F(Lec.2) states that sovereignty was with the "men of Ireland." P#G(B 512), P#G(Lec.), P#G(Bal.), and P#G(1295) record a truncated account of the travels of the Cruithni.   P#H(Lein.), P#H(D.iii.1), P#H(B 512), P#H(D.i.3), and P#H(Lec.) record the Battle of Ard Lemnacht. It also records that Éremón expelled them from Ireland.   P#I(Lein.), P#I(Uí Ma.), P#I(Lec.), P#I(Bal.), P#I(D.ii.2), P#I(B.iii.1), P#J(Uí Ma.), P#J(Lec.), P#J(Bal.), P#J(Ren.)(TR.WS), P#J(D.ii.2), and P#J(B.iii.1) also tell the story of Ard Lemnacht. P#K(D.iv.1), P#K(Lec.1),   P#K(Lec.2),   P#K(Bal.),   P#K(24.P.13),   P#K(1295),   P#K(1289), and P#K(D.iii.2) record that the Cruithni and the Britons (**q.v.**) of Fortriu (**q.v.**) fought against the Saxons (**q.v.**) and gained land. It states that the Cruithni had no wives and were given wives by the Sons of Míl.   P#L(Uí Ma.), P#L(Lec.), P#L(G47), P#L(Bal.), P#L(1336), and P#L(1295) record that the Cruithni were descended from Gelon (**q.v.**) and that they took Orc (**q.v.**) and then the far-north of Britain (**q.v.**), which they divided into seven parts (see **Cat**, **Ce**, **Cirig**, **Fib**, **Fidach**, **Fotla**, **Fortrenn**) under Cruithne (**q.v.**).   They went to the land of the Franks and to Ireland (**q.v.**) and were later expelled from the lands of the Britons by Cunedda (**q.v.**).   The order of events is different from the other legends concerning their travels.

AI § 257 records that there were seven kings of the Cruithni who ruled Ireland. AT 560 mentions that Bridei f. Mailcon (**q.v.**), king of the Cruithni, won a battle against the men of Alba. Talorcen f. Enfret (**q.v.**) won at Sráith Ethairt (**q.v.**) in CS 651.   CS 659 records the death of Gartnait f. Donuel (**q.v.**). AI 685 records a battle among the Cruithni (Picts). This is no doubt Dún Nechtain (**q.v.**). AI 691 records the death of Bredei f. Bili and calls him king of the Cruithni. AI uses the term "Cruithni" and its variations for groups in both Ireland and Scotland. AT also uses "Cruithni" for populations in both Ireland and Scotland but seems to use it more often of "Cruithni" in Ireland. Because AC only exists in translation, it is not possible here to assess its use of the term "Cruithni."   It uses "Picts" for populations in both Ireland and Scotland although this may not have originally been the case. However, AC does state that Pictland (**q.v.**) is called "criocha cruithneach" in Irish.[59] AU appears to only the term "Cruithni" and its variants only for populations in Ireland and not in Scotland. CS uses "Cruithni" for populations in both Ireland and Scotland.

Regnal Lists SL2 M and SL2 H state that the books of the Cruithni record that thirty kings named Brude (see **Brude (30)**) ruled Ireland and Scotland. SL3(Lec.1) and SL3(Lec.4) record that the Cruithni came from Thrace (**q.v.**) and also that Cruithne was the father of the Cruithni. The books of the Cruithni are again mentioned. List SL3(Lec.2) and SL3(Lec.3) record the reign of some of the legendary kings of the Cruithni in Scotland. It states that Cruithne (**q.v.**) was the father of the Cruithni and also mentions that the books of the Cruithni record the reign of the "thirty Brudes." This is also true of SL3(Bal.1) and SL3(Bal.2).[60]

TBF mentions that the Cruithni of Alba (**q.v.**) had stolen three cattle from Fróech (**q.v.**). *Senchus Fer nAlban* states that the mother of Galan f. Barrfhind (**q.v.**) was of the Cruithni. *Duan Albanach* records that the Cruithni took control of Alba and Pictland (**q.v.**) after leaving Ireland (**q.v.**). *Scéla Cano* mentions "red ales" in the territory of the Cruithni about Circhend (**q.v.**).[61]

The use of the term "Cruithni" in texts for both populations in Ireland and Scotland has long caused much speculation. W.F. Skene asserts that the Cruithni of Scotland and Ireland are the same group and that they settled in Meath from Ulster. W.J Watson indicates that the terms "Cruthen," "Cruithne," "Cruthnech," "Cruithnigh," and "Cruithnich" are also used in relation to the Cruithni. He also states that the Old Irish term "Cruthen" (pl. "Cruithin") is equivalent to the Welsh "Pryden" and "Prydyn." "Prydyn" refers to inhabitants of Britain (**q.v.**) and means "Picts" but originally meant the Britons (**q.v.**). It is related to the Welsh term "Prydain" ("Britain") and the Latin term "Britannia." Watson also states that "Cruthen" was at first used for any inhabitant of Britain but later was only used for those north of the Antonine Wall. Because the term "Cruthen" became interchangeable with "Pict," Watson remarks that the "Cruithnigh" of Ireland became identified as "Picts" although they are not the same group.[62] T.F. O'Rahilly indicates that the "Cruthin (Priteni)" gave the Greeks their name for Britain and Ireland ("the Pretanic Islands") and that they were non-Goidelic Celts who had been one of the groups of invaders of Ireland mentioned in tradition. O'Rahilly asserts that this means that the "Priteni" were in control of Britain and Ireland when the Greeks first became aware of them. According to O'Rahilly, Irish writers used the Latin term "Picti" and the Irish term "Cruithni" when discussing the inhabitants of northern Scotland but never used "Picti" of the "Irish Cruthin." He agrees with Watson's view on the Irish Cruithni. H.M. Chadwick discusses in depth the relationship between the Cruithni in Ireland and Scotland as evidenced in legend. He concludes that the Irish Cruithni were similar to the other peoples of Ireland and did not seem to share the culture of the Cruithni in Scotland although the two were often connected to one another. This connection may have had its basis in the remains of La Téne culture in Ulster which may have come from southwestern Scotland in the second century B.C.[63] Kenneth Jackson states that the terms "*Priteni," "*Pritani," and "Cruithni" are Celtic and mean "'the people of the designs'" (referring to tattoos). According to

Jackson, the use of "Pritanic Islands" to designate the British Isles seems to date from the late fourth century B.C.; therefore, the term "*Pritani" would have applied to Iron Age A tribes in southern England. Tribes in the north would have been "*Priteni." Jackson asserts that it is not known if the La Téne culture used "Pritani" as a name for themselves; however, the inhabitants of Roman Britain used the term "Brittones," which was related to what may have been the Latin form of "Pritani," "Britanni." He also states that the term "Priteni" was later used by the Roman Britons for the inhabitants north of the Antonine Wall, just as "Cruthen" was used by the Irish. Jackson also says that although the terms "Cruithin" and "Cruithni" were used in the Old Irish period to indicate both the historical Picts of Scotland and supposed British immigrants in Ireland, the two groups were not connected with one another in any way. The Irish Cruithni were probably immigrants from Britain who spoke Irish in historical times. M.O. Anderson has a similar view concerning the Irish and Scottish Cruithni. She also asserts that the existence of Irish "Picts" first appeared in AC, where the term "Cruithni(g)" was translated as "Picts," regardless of context.[64] It is now apparent that the Cruithni (Picts) of Scotland and the Cruithni of Ireland were neither linguistically nor ethnically connected. Hence, one can see that the term "Cruithni" and its variants should not automatically be translated "Picts" until its exact reference is determined.

Cúl Dremne (Cúil Dreimne, Cúl Drebene). Irish place in Carbury between Drumcliff and Sligo. Site of a battle in which Columba (**q.v.**) was involved. This involvement may have caused Columba's excommunication and subsequent exile to Dál Riata (**q.v.**) in Scotland.[65]

AI 561, AT 561, AU 561, and CS 561 record that Ainmere mac Sétnai, Domnall mac Muirchertaig, and Ninnid mac Duach won the Battle of Cúl Dremne against Diarmait mac Cerbaill.

Vita Columbae states that Columba left Ireland (**q.v.**) two years after Cúl Dremne.[66]

Dál n-Araide (Dál Araide). Irish place and population name in area from Newry to Sliab Mis (**q.v.**) and associated in legend with the Cruithni of both Ireland and Scotland.[67]

Legends P#A(B 506), P#A(Uí Ma.), P#A(Lec.), and P#A(C.vi.2) record that the Dál n-Araide are descended from Conall Cernach (**q.v.**) and are also called "Cruithni."

Rawl. B 502 and *Laud 610* equate Dál n-Araide with the Cruithni.[68]

Dál Riata (Dál Riada). Population and place in Ireland (**q.v.**) from Dál n-Araide (**q.v.**) to northern Antrim and in Scotland north of the Firth of Clyde and west of Pictland (**q.v.**) with Druim Alban as the boundary.[69]

AT 736, AC 733, and AU 736 record the devastation of Scottish Dál Riata by the Pictish king Onuist f. Urguist (**q.v.**). AU 736 states that Dál Riata was defeted by Talorgan (d.750) at Cnoc Cairpri (**q.v.**). AU 741 records that the Battle of Druim Cathmail (**q.v.**) was fought by Dál Riata and the Cruithni and that Onuist f. Urguist attacked Dál Riata.

Bede records that Dál Riata was named for the leader of the Scots from Ireland, "Reuda," who settled in Britain (**q.v.**). The Scots obtained Dál Riata from the Picts either by force or as a gift. *Historia Brittonum* seems to indicate that the ancestors of the Picts took control of Dál Riata under Istoreth (**q.v.**).[70]

Danes. Scandinavian population from islands between the Jutland peninsula and the Scanian peninsula.[71]

AC 864 records that the Danish princes Óláfr (**q.v.**) and Audgisl (**q.v.**) attacked Pictland (**q.v.**) and took hostages in 871.

Geoffrey of Monmouth records that the "Daci" along with the Picts, Scots and Norwegians (**q.v.**) attacked Britain (**q.v.**). "Daci" is a form of the Medieval Latin term "Dacus" ("Dane, Danish"). Geoffrey also states that the Danes, Picts, Scots, and Norwegians took control of Albania (see **Alba**) when the Romans (**q.v.**) left. Vortigern (**q.v.**) was concerned that the Picts would enlist the aid of the Danes and Norwegians to fight the Britons (**q.v.**). According to Geoffrey, Scotland was vulnerable to Danes, Picts, Scots, and Norwegians.[72]

Dimeti (Demetians). Population of Demetia (Dyfed) in southwest Wales.[73]

Legends P#L(Uí Ma.), P#L(Lec.), P#L(G47), P#L(Bal.), P#L(1336), and P#L(1295) record that the descendants of Liathan (**q.v.**), took control of the land of the Dimeti and Guer (**q.v.**) and Guigell (**q.v.**).

Historia Brittonum repeats this information.[74]

Druim Cathmail. Place in the territory of the Cruithni and Dál Riata (**q.v.**). It could be in either Antrim or Scotland. It may have some connection to the conflict between Onuist f. Urguist (**q.v.**) and Scots Dál Riata.[75]

AU 741 records the Battle of Druim Cathmail between the Cruithni and the Dál Riata.

Druim Dergblathuig (Druim Derg Blathug). Place in Pictland (**q.v.**) in Forfar.[76]

AT 729, AC 726, and AU 729 record the Battle of Druim Dergblathuig between Drest (c.728) and the Pictish king Onuist f. Urguist (**q.v.**) in which Drest was killed.

Dún Duirn (Dundurn). Pictish fortress above the east end of Loch Earn.[77] AU 683 records the siege of Dún Duirn.

Dún Foithir (Dún Fother, Dunottar). Pictish fortress near Stonehaven in Kincardine in the Mearns.[78]

AU 681 and AU 694 record the siege of Dún Foithir. The second is probably a repeat.

Dunkeld (Dunkeldin, Dún Cailden). Scottish ecclesiastical center in Perthshire. It was founded to replace Iona (**q.v.**), which had been abandoned because of Viking raids.[79]

Lists D, F1, F2, K, and Furdun's List record that Dunkeld was founded by Castantin f. Uurguist (**q.v.**).[80]

Dún Nechtain (Dunnichen, Nechtansmere). Scottish place in Forfarshire near Strathmore. Site of battle between Picts and English (see **Angles/English**) in 685.[81]

AI 685 records Dún Nechtain without naming it. AT 686 and AU 686 mention that Ecgfrith (**q.v.**) was killed by Bredei f. Bili (**q.v.**) at Dún Nechtain.

Anonymous Cuthbert, *Bede's Cuthbert*, and *Life of Wilfrid* record that Ecgfrith was killed by the Picts without naming the battle.[82]

Bede recounts that Ecgfrith ignored the advice of Cuthbert (**q.v.**) and attacked the Picts. He was killed in an unnamed battle. *Historia Brittonum* also records Dún Nechtain without naming it.[83]

Dún Ollaig. Place in Scotland. Dunolly Castle in Argyll (Argyle), near Oban.[84] AU 734 records that Talorgan f. Drostan (c.734) (**q.v.**) was captured near Dún Ollaig.

Ealga (Ealca, i.e. Éire). Irish term for Ireland (**q.v.**).[85]

Origin Legends P#E(Lec.), P#E(Bal.), and P#E(1295) record that some of the Cruithni remained in Ealga.

Eiblinn (Sliab Eiblinne). Irish place in Munster.[86]

Legends P#C(Lein.), P#C(Uí Ma.), P#C(Lec.), and P#C(G131) record that the Picts or the Gaels (**q.v.**) fought Fotla (**q.v.**) at Eiblinn. The meaning of the text is unclear.

Europe (Eoraip).

Legends P#E(Lec.), P#E(Bal.), and P#E(1295) record that the Cruithni travelled in the east of Europe from Thrace (**q.v.**) before moving westward and establishing their own country.

Fain-Laibe. Irish place in Mugdorn (**q.v.**).[87]

P#A(B 506), P#A(Uí Ma.), P#A(Lec.), and P#A(C.vi.2) record that Gede olgudach (**q.v.**) ruled over Fain-Laibe and Tara (**q.v.**) for thirty years.

Fir Bolg.   Legendary Irish population in Mag Luirg, about the Calaid.[88]

Legends P#C(Lein.), P#C(Uí Ma.), P#C(Lec.), and P#C(G131) record that either the Cruithni or the Gaels (**q.v.**) allied themselves with the Fir Bolg.   The meaning of the text is uncertain.   P#L(Uí Ma.), P#L(Bal.), P#L(1336), and P#L(1295) state that the Fir Bolg controlled the Isle of Man (**q.v.**), Ara (**q.v.**), Ile (**q.v.**), and Rachra (**q.v.**). This prevented the Cruithni from controlling them and caused them to take Orc (**q.v.**).   P#L(Lec.), P#L(G47) has the same account but does not specifically mention the Fir Bolg.

Fochmaind. Irish population or place.[89]

Origin Legends P#I(Lein.), P#I(Uí Ma.), P#I(Lec.), P#I(Bal.), P#I(D.ii.2), and P#I(B.iii.1) record that the Fochmaind allied themselves with the Tuath Fidga (**q.v.**) against Crimthann (**q.v.**) and the Cruithni in the Battle of Ard Lemnacht (**q.v.**). This is also true of P#J(Uí Ma.), P#J(Lec.), P#J(Bal.) and P#J(Ren.)(TR.WS).

Forteviot. Scottish place in Perthshire.[90]

Regnal Lists D, F1, and F2 record that Drust f. Ferat (**q.v.**) was killed at Forteviot or Scone (**q.v.**) and that Cináed mac Alpín (**q.v.**) died at Forteviot. "Scottish Chronicle" in Poppleton Manuscript, List I, and List K mention that Cináed mac Alpín died in Forteviot.[91]

Fortriu (gen. Fortrenn). Scottish place associated with Strathearn and Menteith and the mythological person Fortrenn (**q.v.**).   Edmund Hogan indicates that Fortriu could be in Pictland (**q.v.**) or another name for Pictland. M.O. Anderson states that it may have been the primary seat of Pictish power.[92]

Legends P#E(Lec.), P#E(Bal.), and P#E(1295) record that the Cruithni (Picts?) settled in Alba (**q.v.**) from either Ath (**q.v.**) or Cat (Caithness) (**q,v.**) to Forcu (Fortriu?). W.J. Watson indicates that "Forcu" could be "the Fords of Frew on Forth."[93]   P#F(Lec.2), P#K(D.iv.1), P#K(Lec.1), P#K(Lec.2), P#K(Bal.), P#K(24.P.13), P#K(1295), P#K(1289), and P#K(D.iii.2) state that the Britons (**q.v.**) of Fortriu and Cruithne (**q.v.**) fought the Saxons (**q.v.**).

AU 664 mentions the Battle of Luith Feirn (**q.v.**) in Fortriu. AT 693 and AU 693 record the death of Bredei f. Bili (**q.v.**) and calls him king of Fortriu. AU 725 records the death of Brecc (**q.v.**) of Fortriu. AT 763 and AU 763 mention the death of Bredei f. Uuirguist (**q.v.**), king of Fortriu.   AU 768 records a battle fought in Fortriu between Ciniod f. Uuredech (**q.v.**) and Áed Find (**q.v.**). Also, AU 820 calls Castantin f. Uurguist (**q.v.**) "rex Foirtrenn" ("king of Fortriu").   when recording his death. AU 834 records the death of Onuist f. Urguist (**q.v.**), "rex Fortrenn." AU 865 mentions the death of Tuathal mac Artgusso, bishop of Fortriu.

Fotharta. Irish place in barony of Forth in county Carlow.[94]
P#F(D.iv.1),   P#F(Lec.1),   P#F(Lec.2),   P#F(Bal.),   P#F(24.P.13),
P#F(1295), P#F(1289), P#F(D.iii.2), P#H(Lein.), P#H(D.iii.1), P#H(B512),
P#H(D.i.3), P#H(Lec.) state that the Cruithni fought the Battle of Ard
Lemnacht(**q.v.**) against the Tuath Fidga (**q.v.**), Britons (**q.v.**) living in Fotharta.

Franks (Frainc). Population of France.[95]
Legends P#E(Lec.), P#E(Bal.) P#F(D.iv.1), P#F(Lec.1), P#F(Lec.2),
P#F(Bal.), P#F(24.P.13), P#F(1295), P#F(1289), P#F(D.iii.2), P#G(B 512),
P#G(Lec.), P#G(Bal.), and P#G(1295) record that the Cruithni settled in the
territory of the Franks and established a city there (see **Pictabis** and **Pictatus**).

Gaels (Gaedil). Gaelic speakers (see **Irish** and **Scots**).[96]
Legends P#B(Lec.),   P#B(Bal.),   P#B(1295),   P#B(1289),   and
P#B(D.iii.2) record that the Gaels cleared the land of the Cruithni (Picts?).
This is also true of P#G(B 512), P#G(Lec.), P#G(Bal.), and P#G(1295).
P#L(Uí Ma.), P#L(Lec.), P#L(Bal.), P#L(1336), P#L(1295), and P#L(G47)
record that the Gaels drove the Cruithni out of Ireland (**q.v.**).
Duan Albanach states that Gaels controlled Alba after the Cruithni.[97]

Gaileoin. Population in Leinster (see **Laigin**).[98]
P#I(Lein.), P#I(Uí Ma.), P#I(Lec.), P#I(Bal.), P#I(D.ii.2), P#I(B.iii.1)
state that Crimthann (**q.v.**) ruled the Gaileoin.   P#L(Uí Ma.), P#L(Lec.),
P#L(Bal.), P#L(1336), P#L(1295), P#L(G47) seem to state that the Cruithni
were related to the Gaileoin through the son of Ercal (**q.v.** and see **Gelon**).

Germany. See also **Saxons**.
Legends P#A(B 506), P#A(Uí Ma.), P#A(Lec.), P#A(C.vi.2),
P#B(Lec.), P#B(Bal.), P#B(1295), P#B(1289), and P#B(D.iii.2) record that the
Cruithni travelled with the Sons of Míl (**q.v.**) from Thrace (**q.v.**) to Germany.
Geoffrey of Monmouth records that Melga (**q.v.**) and Wanius (**q.v.**)
ravaged Germany.[99]

Guer (Gower). Place in Wales.[100]
P#L(Uí Ma.), P#L(Lec.), P#L(Bal.), P#L(1336), P#L(1295), P#L(G47)
state that descendants of Liathan (**q.v.**) controlled the territories of Guer and of
Dimeti (**q.v.**) and Guigell (**q.v.**). This is also true of *Historia Brittonum*.[101]

Guigell   (Cetgueli,   Kidwelly).   Welsh   place   in   eastern
Camarthenshire.[102]
P#L(Uí Ma.), P#L(Lec.), P#L(Bal.), P#L(1336), P#L(1295), P#L(G47)
record that descendants of Liathan (**q.v.**) controlled the territory of Guigell,
the Dimeti (**q.v.**), and Guer (**q.v.**).This is also true of *Historia Brittonum*.[103]

Huns. Turkic-speaking steppe nomads from Asia.[104]

Geoffrey of Monmouth records that the Huns under Wanius (**q.v.**) and the Picts under Melga (**q.v.**) plundered Germany (**q.v.**). The Huns and Picts invaded and ravaged Albania (see **Alba**) until Maximus (**q.v.**) defeated them, and they fled to Ireland (**q.v.**).[105]

Ile (Islay). Scottish island off the Argyll coast.[106]

Origin Legends P#E(Lec.), P#E(Bal.), and P#E(1295) record that the Cruithni landed on Ile after leaving Ireland (**q.v.** and see **Ealga**) and before capturing Alba (**q.v.**). P#L(Uí Ma.), P#L(Bal.), P#L(1336), and P#L(1295) state that the Fir Bolg (**q.v.**) captured Ile, the Isle of Man (**q.v.**), Ara (**q.v.**), and Rachra (**q.v.**) before the Cruithni could control them. P#L(Lec.), P#L(G47) give the same account but do not specifically mention the Fir Bolg.

Vita Columbae recounts that Tarain (see **Tarain (exile)**) was exiled on Ile but was betrayed and killed by his host Feradach (see **Feradach of Ile**).[107]

Senchus Fer nAlban records that Galan f. Barrfhind (**q.v.**) possessed land on Ile.[108]

Inber Colpa (Inber Colptha). Irish place at Droiched Atha, near the Brug na Bóinne.[109]

P#C(Lein.), P#C(Uí Ma.), P#C(Lec.), and P#C(G131) state that Éremón (**q.v.**) took half of a host to Inber Colpa.

Inber Scéne. Irish place. Mouth of Kenmare River or River Corrane, Kerry, North. Seems connected with Loch Luigdech in West Munster.[110]

P#C(Lein.), P#C(Uí Ma.), P#C(Lec.), P#C(G131) state that Éremón (**q.v.**) landed with half a host at Inber Scéne after leaving Inber Colpa (**q.v.**).

Inber Sláine. Irish place in Uí Cennselaig (**q.v.**).[111]

Origin Legends P#E(Lec.), P#E(Bal.), and P#E(1295) record that the Cruithni captured Inber Sláine after leaving the Franks (**q.v.**). P#F(D.iv.1), P#F(Lec.1), P#F(Lec.2), P#F(Bal.), P#F(24.P.13), P#F(1295), P#F(1289), P#F(D.iii.2), P#G(B 512), P#G(Lec.), P#G(Bal.), P#G(1295), P#H(Lein.), P#H(D.iii.1), P#H(B 512), P#H(D.i.3), and P#H(Lec.) mention that the Cruithni took Inber Sláine.

Inpictus. Pictish city among the Franks (**q.v.**).

Legends P#L(Uí Ma.) and P#L(1295) record that Inpictus was a name for Pictatus (**q.v.**), founded by the Cruithni (see also **Pictabis**).

Inveralmond (Inbher Amon). Scottish place. Mouth of the River Almond in West Lothian.[112]

Regnal Lists D, F1, F2, and I state that Domnall mac Alpín (**q.v.**) died at the Rath of Inveralmond.[113]

Iona (Í, Í Choluim Chille). Scottish island off Mull. Site of monastic community established by Columba (**q.v.**). It had a scriptorium which produced a chronicle used for the Irish Annals.[114]

AT 563, AU 563, and CS 563 states that Columba travelled to Iona. AU 574 and CS 574 record the death of Conall mac Comgaill, who gave Iona to Columba. Columba's death on Iona is recorded in AT 595, AC 590, and CS 595. AT 624 mentions Adomnán's birth. AI 704, AT 704, AC 700, AU 704, and CS 700 mention the death of Adomnán (**q.v.**), abbot of Iona. Necthon f. Derelei (**q.v.**) expelled the Iona "familia" in AT 717, AU 717, and CS 713. This refers to a group of monks on the Tay, who had come from Iona.[115] AI 795 records that Iona was attacked. AC 863, CS 865 records the death of Cellach mac Ailella (**q.v.**), abbot of Iona.

Regnal Lists D, F1, F2, I, and K state that Cináed mac Alpín (**q.v.**), Erc (**q.v.**), Fergus Mór (**q.v.**), Loarn Mór (**q.v.**), Óengus Mór (**q.v.**), Domnall mac Alpín (**q.v.**), Causantín mac Cináeda (**q.v**), Áed mac Cináeda (**q.v.**), and Giric (**q.v.**) were buried on Iona. List N records that Cináed mac Alpín, Domnall mac Alpín, and Giric were buried on Iona.[116]

Betha Coluim Cille mentions that after he had founded Iona, Columba preached to the people of Alba (**q.v.**), Britons (**q.v.**), and Saxons (**q.v.**).[117]

Bede records that Bridei f. Mailcon (**q.v.**) gave Iona to Columba.[118]

Ireland (Ériu). "Hibernia" in Latin.[119]

Legends P#A(B 506), P#A(Uí Ma.), P#A(Lec.), and P#A(C.vi.2) record that the Cruithni (Picts?) were given wives from the nobility of Ireland. Thirty kings from the Cruithni ruled Ireland and Alba (**q.v.**). P#C(Lein.), P#C(Uí Ma.), P#C(Lec.), and P#C(G131) mention that Donn (**q.v.**) died while trying to capture the southern part of Ireland. P#E(Lec.), P#E(Bal.), and P#E(1295) record that the Cruithni left Ireland under Cathluan (**q.v.**). P#F(D.iv.1), P#F(Lec.1), P#F(Lec.2), P#F(Bal.), P#F(24.P.13), P#F(1295), P#F(1289), P#F(D.iii.2), P#G(B 512), P#G(Bal.), and P#G(1295) mention that six brothers came to Ireland (see **Drostan**, **Nechtan**, **Óengus**, **Solen**, **Ulfa/Ulpa**). They also record that the Cruithni gained power in Ireland but were expelled by Éremón (**q.v.**). P#G(Lec.) seems to state that the Cruithni gained power in Ireland and then expelled Éremón. The Cruithni later took control of Alba after leaving Ireland. P#H(Lein.), P#H(D.iii.1), P#H(B 512), P#H(D.i.3), and P#H(Lec.) record that the Cruithni were expelled from Ireland by Éremón after gaining power. P#L(Uí Ma.), P#L(Lec.), P#L(Bal.), P#L(1336), P#L(1295), and P#L(G47) state that a company of eight settled in Ireland. These are presumably meant to be Cruithni. It mentions that Finachta (**q.v.**) was prince of Ireland at the time.

AI § 257 records that seven kings from the Cruithni (Picts?) ruled Ireland. AT 668, AT 670, AC 666, AU 668, AU 670 mention that the sons of Gartnait (see **Gartnait f. Accidan** and **Gartnait f. Donuel**) went to Ireland. AC (pp.25-26) states that the Picts received wives from Ireland. AU 699 seems to record that Taran f. Entifidich (**q.v.**) went to Ireland.

Lists D, F1, F2, K, N record that Giric (**q.v.**) controlled Ireland.[120]

Miracula Ninie records that Bede stated that Columba (**q.v.**) went from Ireland to Britain (**q.v.**).[121]

Bede states that the Picts went to Ireland from Scythia (**q.v.**) and that Columba went from Ireland to Britain. *Duan Albanach* says that the Cruithni went to Pictland (**q.v.**) after leaving Ireland. Geoffrey of Monmouth says that the Picts went to Ireland to gain wives after the Britons (**q.v.**) had refused them. Picts and Huns (**q.v.**) fled to Ireland after Maximus (**q.v.**) had defeated them. Picts, Huns, Norwegians (**q.v.**), and Danes (**q.v.**) returned to Britain from Ireland.[122]

Irish. Gaelic-speaking inhabitants of Ireland (**q.v.**) and Scotland (see also **Alba**, **Gaels**, and **Scots**).

For Bede's comments on the Irish, see **Scots**. Geoffrey of Monmouth records that the Scots were descended from the Picts and Irish. Mordred (**q.v.**) was allied with Irish, Scots, Picts, and Saxons (**q.v.**) at Camlann (**q.v.**).[123]

Isle of Man (Mana).[124]

Legends P#L(Uí Ma.), P#L(Bal.), P#L(1336), and P#L(1295) record that the Fir Bolg (**q.v.**) captured the Isle of Man, Ile (**q.v.**), Ara (**q.v.**), and Rachra (**q.v.**) before the Cruithni could control them. P#L(Lec.) and P#L(G47) give the same account but do not specifically mention the Fir Bolg.

Historia Brittonum seems to state that the Fir Bolg controlled the Isle of Man ("Eubonia").[125]

Laigin. Population of Leinster.[126]

Origin Legends P#F(D.iv.1), P#F(Lec.1), P#F(Lec.2), P#F(Bal.), P#F(24.P.13), P#F(1295), P#F(1289), and P#F(D.iii.2) record that Crimthann (**q.v.**) was king of Laigin when the Cruithni arrived in Ireland (**q.v.**). P#J(Uí Ma.), P#J(Lec.), P#J(Bal.), P#J(Ren.)(TR.WS), P#J(D.ii.2), and P#J(B.iii.1) state that Crimthann was king of Laigin.

Laigis (pl. Laigsi). Irish population and place. Leix and the people of Leix.[127]

Legends P#A(B 506), P#A(Uí Ma.), P#A(Lec.2), P#A(C.vi.2) record that the seven Laigsi of Laigin (**q.v.**) are descended from the Cruithni (Picts?).

Lann Abae. Scottish or Irish place. Possibly Lundaff in Perthshire.[128]
AU 676 records that a multitude of Picts drowned off Lann Abae.

Luith Feirn (Lutho-feirnn). Unidentified location in Fortriu (**q.v.**) in Pictland (**q.v.**).[129]
AU 664 records the battle of Luith Feirn in Fortriu.

Maen Gwyngwn. Unidentified location in Scotland beyond Bannog (**q.v.**), which would locate it in Pictland (**q.v.**).[130]

Y Gododdin records that Llif f. Cian (**q.v.**) was from Maen Gwyngwn and beyond Bannog.[131]

Mag Manand (Mag Manonn, Manaw). Scottish place. "Manau Gododdin" in Welsh. West of Calathros, included parish of Slanannan.[132] See also **Isle of Man**, **Manu**, and **Miathi**.

AT 711 and AU 711 record a "Battle of the Picts" among the Saxons (**q.v.**) at Mag Manand, where Finguinne f. Deileroith (**q.v.**) was killed.

Bede mentions that Bertfrid (**q.v.**) fought the Picts in 711. This seems to be Mag Manand.[133]

Manu (Mana). Uncertain location of battle fought by Áedán mac Gabráin (**q.v.**). Sometimes used of Mag Manand (**q.v.**) in Scotland, the Isle of Man (**q.v.**), or a place in Ireland.[134]

AI 583, AT 582, AT 583(?), AC 580, AU 582, and AU 583 record that Áedán mac Gabráin (**q.v.**) won the Battle of Manu.

M.O. Anderson suggests that this battle may have been fought in Manau on the Forth (see **Mag Manand** and **Miathi**). John Bannerman asserts that the Isle of Man is meant. "Manu" appears to be the equivalent of the Welsh "Manaw," which refers to the territory of Scotland near Stirling and along the River Forth, which is Mag Manand. However, it is not certain if this territory is implied.[135]

Miathi (Maeatae?). A Pictish tribe, who may have dwelled near Mag Manand (**q.v.**).[136]

Vita Columbae records that Áedán mac Gabráin (**q.v.**) defeated the Miathi in a battle in which his sons Artuir (Artúr) and Eochaid Find were killed. T.F. O'Rahilly believes that this is Circhend (**q.v.**), mentioned in AT 596, and rejects the notion that this was the Battle of Manu (**q.v.**), also fought by Áedán. A.O. and M.O. Anderson disagree that it was Circhend but favor the idea that it was Manu. John Bannerman dismisses both of these suggestions and indicates that it may have been the Battle of Leithri mentioned in AT 590, AC 590, and AU 590.[137]

Monad Carno. Scottish place near Loch Loogdae. Cairn O' Mounth in the Mearns.[138]

ACam. 728 records the Battle of Monad Carno. AU 729 recounts that Monad Carno was fought between Necthon f. Derelei (**q.v.**) and Onuist f. Urguist (**q.v.**) in which Onuist was victorious and in which Biceot son of Monet and his son, Finnguine son of Drostan, and Feroth son of Finnguine were killed.

Mónad Croibh (Moncrieffe). Place in Perthshire, which would have been in Pictland (**q.v.**).[139]

AT 728, AC 725, and AU 728 record the Battle of Mónad Croibh between Alpín (c. 728) (**q.v.**) and Onuist f. Urguist (**q.v.**) in which Onuist was the victor.

Mugdorn (Mugdornai). Irish place. North of Meath, now Cremourne, Crích Mogdorne.[140]

P#A(B 506), P#A(Uí Ma.), P#A(Lec.), and P#A(C.vi.2) record that Fain-Laibe (**q.v.**), which Gede olgudach (**q.v.**) ruled, was in Mugdorn.

Nér (Neir). Possibly monastery of Deer (Der) in Buchan in Pictland (**q.v.**).[141]

AU 623 records the death of Uineus of Nér (**q.v.**). AU 679, AFM 677, and CS 675 record the death of Nechtan of Nér (**q.v.**). AT 679 mentions Nechtan's death but not Nér.

Niduari. Scottish population.

Miracula Ninie records that Ninian (**q.v.**) converted the Niduari, who were tribes of Picts. Alan Macquarrie states that "Niduari" is an unacceptable emendation by scholars from "Naturae," an unidentifiable population. *Anonymous Cuthbert* and *Bede's Cuthbert* state that Cuthbert (**q.v.**) travelled to the land of the Picts called "Niduera" (Niduari) and was miraculously fed with dolphin meat.[142]

Bertram Colgrave associates them with the River Nid. John MacQueen asserts that the Niduari were thought to have lived near the River Nith (Nid) in Dumfriesshire but were probably in eastern Scotland. This opinion is shared by F.T. Wainwright.[143]

Normans.

Geoffrey of Monmouth anachronistically states that Normans, Britons (**q.v.**), Saxons (**q.v.**), Picts, and Scots were the peoples of Britain (**q.v.**).[144]

Norwegians. Scandinavian population which settled in northern and western Scotland.[145]

Regnal Lists D, F1, F2, I, K, and N record that Causantín mac Cináeda (**q.v.**) was killed by Norwegians.[146]

Geoffrey of Monmouth records that Norwegians, Danes (**q.v.**), Picts, and Scots invaded and controlled northern Britain after the Romans (**q.v.**) had departed. Vortigern (**q.v.**) told Constans (see **Constans f. Constantine III**) that the Picts were going to lead the Norwegians and Danes in an attack against the Britons (**q.v.**). Scotland was always open to attacks by the Norwegians, Picts, Scots, and Danes.[147]

Orc (Orcades, Orkney).[148]

Legends P#L(Uí Ma.), P#L(Lec.), P#L(G47), P#L(Bal.), P#L(1336), and P#L(1295) record that the offspring of Gelon (**q.v.** and see **Cruithni (Picts?)** and **Picts**) took control of Orc.

AT 682 and AU 682 record that Bredei f. Bili (**q.v.**) attacked Orc.

In *Vita Columbae*, Columba (**q.v.**) entreated Bridei f. Mailcon (**q.v.**) to guarantee that the king of Orc would protect any monks that should land at Orc.[149]

Historia Brittonum records that Orc is one of three islands off Britain (**q.v.**) and that it lies beyond the Picts. Picts settled Orc and used it as a base to control northern Britain. Octha (**q.v.**) and Ebissa (**q.v.**) travelled around the Picts and ravaged Orc at the invitation of Vortigern (**q.v.**) and Hengest (**q.v.**).[150]

Pictabis. City in the land of the Franks (**q.v.**) founded by the Picts (see also **Cruithni (Picts?)**). See also **Pictatus**.

Origin Legends P#E(Lec.), P#E(Bal.), and P#E(1295) record that the Cruithni built a city in the land of the Franks and called it "Pictabis" from "pictis." Presumably, this means that the Picts named the city after themselves. P#F(D.iv.1), P#F(Lec.1), P#F(Lec.2), P#F(Bal.), P#F(1295), P#F(1289), and P#F(D.iii.2) give a similar account although the city was named from "points." This is true of P#G(B 512), P#G(Lec.), P#G(Bal.), and P#G(1295); however, they indicate that the name derived from their "battle-equipment." This could be the previously mentioned "points." P#L(Lec.), P#L(G47), P#L(Bal.), and P#L(1295) state that the Cruithni built a city called Pictabis.

J.H. Todd indicates that "Pictavis" (Pictabis) is "Poictiers" (Poitiers) in France, which was "Pictavia" (**q.v.**), "Pictaviae," "Pictava," and "Pictavae." He also states that the name comes from the notion that the Picts painted themselves and the possible relation of the name of the city to weapon terms "pike" in English, "pioc" in Irish, "pig" in Welsh, "picca" in Italian, and "pica" among Du Cange. He states that the people of "Poictou" (Poitou) were called "Pictones" during the time of Caesar and sees the connections of the Picts with France as somewhat fabulous due to similar sounds of words. H.M. Chadwick states that the use of "Pictavis" (Pictabis) is an equation of "Pictavi" and "Picti." This would lead to the idea that the Picts founded Poitiers. Interestingly, the terms "pictavensis," "pictavus," and other related terms were used from the eleventh century in British and Irish manuscripts to describe "Poitevin."[151]

Pictatus (Picctatus). City in the land of the Franks (**q.v.**) founded by the Picts (see also **Cruithni (Picts?)**). See also **Pictabis**.

P#L(Uí Ma.) and P#L(1336) record that the Picts built a city in the land of the Franks and called it "Picctatus" or Inpictus (**q.v.**) after their "tattoos."

Pictaue (Pictavia, Pictava). Poitiers (Poictiers) in France.[152] See also **Pictabis** and **Pictatus**.

Origin Legends P#E(Lec.), P#E(Bal.), and P#E(1295) seem to record that the Cruithni were in Pictaue from which they derived their name and where Elair (**q.v.**) was when the king of the Franks (**q.v.**) fell in love with their sister.

M.O. Anderson indicates that the Poppleton Manuscript uses the term "Pictavia" for the country of the Picts (see **Pictland**) in Scotland until the reign of Domnall mac Causantín (Donald son of Constantine) at the end of the ninth century when it uses the term "Albania" (see **Alba**).[153]

Pictland (Cruithen-tuath in Scotland).[154] See also **Alba**, **Cruithni (Picts?)**, and **Pictaue**.

Legends P#B(Lec.), P#B(Bal.), P#B(1295), P#B(1289), and P#B(D.iii.2) indicate that thirty-six soldiers came from Thrace (**q.v.**) into Pictland. These appear to be the Picts. P#H(Lein.), P#H(D.iii.1), P#H(D.i.3), and P#H(Lec.) record that Cathluan (**q.v.**) came from Pictland.

AC (p.26) states that the land of the Picts is "pictland" in English and "criocha cruithneach" in Irish. AC records that Palladius (**q.v.**) died in Pictland sometime around 432, and AC 449 mentions the death of Drust f. Erp (**q.v.**), "K. of Pictland."[155] AC 509 erroneously records the death of Bridei f. Mailcon (**q.v.**) and calls him "K. of Pictland." AC 666 records that "the race of Gartnayt of Pictland returned to Ireland" (see **Gartnait f. Accidan**, **Gartnait f. Donuel**, and **Ireland**). AC 757 mentions the death of Onuist f. Urguist (**q.v.**) and calls him "K. of Pictland." AC 864 records that Óláfr (**q.v.**) and Audgisl (**q.v.**) invaded Pictland. CS 904 records the death of "Ead Rí Cruithentuaithe" (see **Áed mac Cináeda**).

Vita Cadoci relates that Cadoc (see **Cadoc (saint)**) encountered the deceased Caw (**q.v.**), who is called "Cau Pritdin" with "Pritdin" being used for "Pictland" (see **Cruithni (Picts?)**).[156]

TBF records that Fróech (**q.v.**) and Conall Cernach (**q.v.**) travelled to Pictland to retrieve Fróech's cattle. *Duan Albanach* uses the term "Cruithenchlár" in reference to Pictland and states that the Cruithni controlled Pictland after leaving Ireland. "Chlár" seems to be the Irish term "clár," which has numerous meanings including "level expanse" or "plain." *Welsh Triads* 81. C 18 and 96 mention that one family of saints with Welsh mothers derived from Caw of Pictland (here called "Brydyn").[157]

W.J. Watson states that the term "Cruithentuath" ("Briton-land," "Pictland") was used for "the eastern side of Scotland north of Forth" to distinguish it from the Gaelic area of "Alba" (**q.v.**). Kenneth Jackson indicates that in Medieval Welsh "Prydyn" was used for "the Picts, Pictland, northern Scotland."[158]

Picts (Latin: Picti).   Population of Scotland of probable Gallo-Brittonic, Celtic origin.[159] See also **Cruithni (Picts?)**.

Legend P#E(Lec.) records that the Picts were the descendants of Eolchu (**q.v.**), son of Ercal (**q.v.**). P#E(Bal.) and P#E(1295) call the Picts the descendants of Gelon (**q.v.**), son of Ercal.

In AC (pp.25-26), the Picts receive the wives of the men who drowned with Donn (**q.v.**). It also states that they were named from the practice of painting their faces. AC 427 records that the Picts fought wars against the Britons (**q.v.**). AT 580, AC 580, records the death of Galam (**q.v.**). AU 584 records the death of Bridei f. Mailcon (**q.v.**). The death of Gartnart f. Domelch (**q.v.**), is mentioned in AC 590. AU 629 mentions the death of Eochaid Buide (**q.v.**), where he is called "king of the Picts." AC 632, AU 631, and CS 630 record the death of the Pictish king Cinioch f. Lutrin (**q.v.**). AC 649 and AU 653 record the death of Talorc f. Uuid (**q.v.**). AC 653 and AU 657 mention the death of Talorcen f. Enfret (**q.v.**). The death of Gartnait f. Donuel (**q.v.**) is recorded in AC 659. Itarnan (**q.v.**) and Corindu (**q.v.**) died amongst the Picts in AT 669 and AU 667. AU 676 records the drowning of Picts at Lann Abae (**q.v.**). Bertred (**q.v.**) was killed in a battle between the Picts and Saxons (**q.v.**) in AT 698, AC 693, an AU 698. AT 711 and AU 711 record the Battle of Mag Manand (**q.v.**) fought by the Picts amongst the Saxons. Necthon f. Derelei (**q.v.**) entered religious life in AT 724 and AC 724 and was succeeded by Drest (c. 728) (**q.v.**). Drest was expelled from the kingship by Elpín (c.728) (**q.v.**) in AT 726. AT 728, AU 728, and AC 725 mentions the battles of Mónad Croibh (**q.v.**) and Caislén Credi amongst the Picts. At Ros Cuissine (**q.v.**) one hundred and fifty Pictish ships crashed ("Picardach" is used) in AT 729. AT 729 and AU 729 mention the Battle of Druim Dergblathuig (**q.v.**) fought between the Onuist f. Urguist (**q.v.**) and Drest (c. 728) (**q.v.**). AC 731 and AU 734 record that Talorg mac Congusa (**q.v.**) was drowned by the Picts after his brother had given him to them. Onuist f. Urguist ravaged Scots Dál Riata (**q.v.**) in AT 736, AC 733, and AU 736. ACam. 736 seems to mistakenly record the death of the Onuist f. Urguist (**q.v.**). ACam. 750, AT 750, AC 746, and AU 750 record a battle fought by the Picts against the Britons (**q.v.**) in which Talorgan (d. 750) (**q.v.**) was killed and the Picts were defeated. The death of Onuist f. Urguist is mentioned in AT 761 and AU 761. AC 773 recounts the death of Elpin f. Uuroid (**q.v.**), which is probably a mistake. ACam. 776 and AU 775 mention the death of Ciniod f. Uuredech (**q.v.**). AU 782 recounts the death of "Dub Tholargg." This could be either Talorgen f. Druisten (**q.v.**) or Talorgen f. Onuist (**q.v.**). AU 789 records a battle involving the Picts in which Castantin f. Uurguist (**q.v.**) defeated Canaul f. Tarl'a (**q.v.**). ACam. 856 and AU 858 record the death of Cináed mac Alpín (**q.v.**). AU 862 and CS 862 record that Domnall mac Alpín (**q.v.**), "king of Picts," died. Óláfr (**q.v.**) and Ívarr (**q.v.**) brought Picts, Angles (**q.v.**), and Britons as captives to Ireland (**q.v.**) in AU

871. AU 875 records that the Picts were defeated in battle against the "Black Foreigners." According to Barbara Crawford, the term "Dubh-Gall" (Black Foreigners) was used of Danes and Northmen (see **Danes** and **Norwegians**) as a means of identifying a specific group of "Vikings."[160] The killing of Áed mac Cináeda (**q.v.**) is mentioned in AU 878. CS 876 records the death of Causantín mac Cináeda (**q.v.**), "king of Picts." As it is a translation, AC uses the term "Picts" for populations in Scotland and Ireland (**q.v.** and see also **Cruithni (Picts?)**).

List SL1 calls Cruithne (**q.v.**) "father of the Picts." The list states that Necton f. Erip (**q.v.**) was "King of all the provinces of the Picts." Brigid (**q.v.**) declared that Necton "would possess the kingdom of Picts in peace." Lists SL2 M and SL2 H state that Cruithne was "father of the Picts." List D records that the Picts ruled Scotland for 1061 years after the Scots under Alpín f. Eochaid and before more Scots. It also mentions that Cruithne ruled the Picts for fifty years. Cináed mac Alpín is recorded as destroying the Picts. Giric freed the Scottish church from Pictish influence. Lists F1, F2, I, and K mention that the Kingdom of the Scots became Kingdom of the Picts after the reign of Alpín f. Eochaid. Again, Cruithne ruled the Picts for fifty years. Cináed mac Alpín is recorded as destroying the Picts. Giric freed the Scottish church from Pictish influence. List N mentions that Cináed mac Alpín destroyed the Picts. Fordun's List states that the Kingdom of Picts became Kingdom of Scots after Drust f. Ferat (**q.v.**).[161]

Miracula Ninie states that Ninian (**q.v.**) converted the group of Picts called Niduari (**q.v.**). *Vita Niniani* recounts Bede's description of Columba's journey to the northern Picts. It also mentions that Ninian converted the southern Picts. *Vita Columbae* records that Columba defeated the efforts of magicians to prevent him from sailing back from Pictish territory. In Pictish territory, Columba blessed a magic well so that it cured illness rather than causing it. On the banks of the river Ness, Columba repelled a river monster that had attacked Luigne moccu Min (**q.v.**) while he was swimming. Adomnán also mentions that Columba and his monasteries twice protected the Picts and Scots from plague. *Anonymous Cuthbert* states that Cuthbert travelled to the land of the Picts called Niduari and was miraculously fed on dolphin meat when he and his followers were starving on their return. It also records that the Picts were attacked by Ecgfrith (**q.v.**), who was eventually killed by them. *Bede's Cuthbert* recounts the same events. *Life of Servanus* records that the Pictish king Bredei f. Derelei (**q.v.**) attempted to kill Servanus (**q.v.**) but was cured by Servanus, to whom Bredei granted land. *Life of Wilfrid* records that the Picts revolted against Ecgfrith (**q.v.**) and were defeated. Wilfrid (**q.v.**) had jurisdiction over them, and at a synod in Rome, Wilfrid accepted Catholic doctrine on behalf of the Picts. Ecgfrith was killed by Picts in battle (see **Dún Nechtain**).[162]

Gildas records that Britain (**q.v.**) was attacked from the north by the Picts and from the northwest by the Scots. He later states that the Picts and Scots attacked from across the sea in boats but that later they were relatively peaceful. This seems to describe events which took place between the late 4th and late 5th centuries.[163]

Bede remarks that the Picts, English (see **Angles/English** and **Saxons**), British (see **Britons**), and Scots (see also **Irish**) are the four groups that inhabit Britain (**q.v.**). He records that the Picts came from Scythia (**q.v.**) to Ireland (**q.v.**). Then, the Picts settled in Britain and received wives from the Scots (Irish) because they had none of their own. This established the custom of using the female line if the royal succession were in doubt. The Britons were constantly under attack from the Picts and Scots. The Picts and Scots controlled northern Britain when the Romans (**q.v.**) left in the fifth century. The Picts allied themselves with the Angles soon after the Angles had arrived in Britain. The Picts and Scots in northern Britain were controlled by Oswiu (**q.v.**) in the seventh century. Bede recounts that the Picts and Scots were the hosts of the exiled sons of Æthelfrith (**q.v.**) while Edwin (d.633) (**q.v.**) ruled Deira. Bede also states that the Picts had given Iona (**q.v.**) to Columba (**q.v.**) and monks from Ireland. According to Bede, the northern Picts were converted to Christianity by Columba and the southern Picts were converted by Ninian. At the Synod of Whitby, the Picts, Scots, and Britons contended against the Roman practice of Easter. Bede states that Ecgberht (saint) (**q.v.**) was exiled among the Picts and Scots. Bede also records that Trumwine (**q.v.**) became the bishop of the Picts ruled by the English in 678. The Picts defeated and killed Ecgfrith in battle and regained their lands as a result. This was Dún Nechtain (**q.v.**). Bede states that the northern Picts were first taught about Christianity by Columba, who founded Iona. At a Synod in Rome at the behest of the peoples of northern Britain (including the Picts), Wilfrid "affirmed the true and Catholic Faith." Bede records that a letter written by Ceolfrith (**q.v.**) to the Necthon f. Derelei (**q.v.**) caused Necthon to institute the correct Easter cycles amongst the Picts. Bede remarks that at the time of his writing the Picts and English were at peace.[164]

Historia Brittonum records that Picts, Scots, Saxons, and Britons were the four inhabitants of Britain. The island of Orc (**q.v.**) is beyond the Picts, who settled it and used it as a base to control northern Britain. It also states that Picts and Scots constantly attacked the Britons. Severus (**q.v.**) built a wall to stop the Picts and Scots. When the Picts and Scots attacked the Britons, the Britons asked the Romans for help. During his reign, Vortigern (**q.v.**) feared attack from the Picts and Scots. Vortigern invited Octha (**q.v.**) and Ebissa (**q.v.**) to fight the Scots. They sailed past the Picts and ravaged Orc. Palladius (**q.v.**) died in Pictish territory. Picts under Bredei f. Bili (**q.v.**) defeated and killed Ecgfrith at "Gueith Lin Garan" (Dún Nechtain).[165]

Geoffrey of Monmouth states that the Picts, Normans (**q.v.**), Britons, Saxons (**q.v.**), and Scots were the five groups that inhabited Britain. According to Geoffrey, the Picts came from Scythia (**q.v.**) under Sodric (**q.v.**) during the time of Marius (**q.v.**). After Marius had killed Sodric, he gave the Picts land in Albania (see **Alba**). However, the Picts had no wives and requested them from the Britons, who refused. Therefore, they acquired wives in Ireland (**q.v.**). In order to reinforce his rebellion against Severus (**q.v.**), Sulgenius (**q.v.**) went to Scythia to enlist the aid of the Picts. Bassianus (**q.v.**), son of Severus, was betrayed by the Picts in their support of Carausius (**q.v.**). As a result the Picts were given land in Albania (Alba). In support of Gratian (**q.v.**) and Valentinianus (**q.v.**), the Picts under Melga (**q.v.**) and the Huns (**q.v.**) under Wanius (**q.v.**) attacked the supporters of Maximus (**q.v.**) in Germany (**q.v.**) and invaded Britain. Later, Picts, Scots, Norwegians (**q.v.**), and Danes (**q.v.**) came from Ireland and captured Albania (Alba). Constantine III (**q.v.**) was killed by a Pict. Vortigern warned Constans (see **Constans f. Constantine III**) that the Picts and Danes planned to invade and that Constans should use Picts in his court as spies; however, Vortigern (**q.v.**) secretly convinced the Picts to kill Constans and make him ruler. As a result, these Picts were betrayed by Vortigern and executed. Their kinsmen sought vengeance on Vortigern and attacked Vortigern but were defeated with the help of the Saxons, who had recently come from Germany. Geoffrey remarks that Scotland was always vulnerable to the Picts, Scots, Danes, and Norwegians. The Picts, Saxons, and Scots under Colgrin (**q.v.**) were defeated by Arthur (**q.v.**). Arthur postponed his war against the Picts and Scots to break the Saxon siege of Bath. Arthur came to the aid of Hoel (**q.v.**), who was under attack from Picts and Scots. Mordred (**q.v.**) enlisted the aid of the Picts, Scots, Irish (**q.v.**), and Saxons to fight against Arthur at Camlann (**q.v.**). When Cadwaladr (**q.v.**) left Britain, he declared that Britain was open to Picts, Scots, Saxons, Romans (**q.v.**), and Ambrones (**q.v.**).[166]

Triad 36 of the *Welsh Triads* calls the Picts (here "Gwydyl Fychti") one of the "Three Oppressions" of Britain. Rachel Bromwich indicates that the term "Gwydyl Fychti" occurs in the "*Bruts*" and in poetry.[167]

W.J. Watson states that the "Picti" (Picts) were first described by Eumenius in A.D. 297 as enemies of the Britons. He indicates that the term "Picti" is "Pettr" in Old Norse, "Peohta" in Old English, "Pecht" in Old Scots, and occurs in the Welsh "Peithwyr" ("Pict-men"). Because of this, Watson thinks that these forms come from "Pecht-," which is similar to "Pecti" used once by Ammanius in 360. Watson suggests that the Latin "Picti" comes from a Pictish term which can be seen in the Welsh "Peithnant." T.F. O'Rahilly indicates that when writing in Latin, Irish writers used the terms "Picti," "Pictones," or "Pictores" to describe the people of northern Scotland. When writing in Irish, they used "Cruithni" or "Cruithnig"; however, "Picti" was never used for the Cruithni in Ireland. F.T. Wainwright remarks that "Picti" originated from the notion that the Picts painted or tattooed themselves and that it is similar to the Latin "pictus." He states that Julius Caesar observed the practice amongst the "Britanni" (Britons). Wainwright is uncertain about the notion that "Picti" derived from a native term.[168] Kenneth Jackson states that Romans used the term "Picti" for the inhabitants of Britain north of the Antonine Wall and that they used the term to mean "the Painted People," regardless of whether or not it derived from a Pictish term. He asserts that "Picti" was used as a translation of "Priteni" (see **Cruithni (Picts?)**) and that the "proto-Picts" had a Gallo-Brittonic "Priteni" character. However, the native name for the proto-Picts and Picts is unknown. Nora Chadwick analyzes the use of the term "Picti" and its relation to painting or tattooing extensively and indicates that "Picti" was not used by carefully observant authors writing about the inhabitants of northern Britain. She repeats that the first use of "Picti" was in 297 but states that the panegyric was not written by Eumenius. In conclusion, Chadwick suggests that dyeing of the skin or clothes may lie behind the accounts of the "Picti" but this needs further study. Isabel Henderson agrees with Kenneth Jackson and asserts that "Pictish" should only be used to describe periods after A.D. 300. She indicates that the earlier "Priteni" ("people of the designs") was used of the people of northern Britain before "Picti." It is possible that the Picts were tattooed in the fourth century if "Picti" were not merely a Latinized form of a native term.[169] M.O. Anderson also states that the Picts" name for themselves is unknown, if they indeed had one. She indicates that the first use of the term "Picti" in 297 was actually anachronistic as it referred to the wars of Julius Caesar. "Picti" was a general term for the people of northern Britain. Anna Ritchie indicates that only four classical authors refer to the Picts by name. She mentions the first in the panegyric of 297 and agrees with its ascription to Eumenius. The last of these, fifth century poet Claudius Claudianus, is the only one who directly associates the Picts with tattooing. Katherine Forsyth asserts that Pictish derived from "Pritenic" (see **Cruithni (Picts?)**), a Brittonic language and the only one used in Roman times in the north of Britain.[170]

      Rachra (Rathlin). Irish island in the north.[171]
      Legends P#L(Uí Ma.), P#L(Bal.), P#L(1336), and P#L(1295) record that the Fir Bolg (**q.v.**) captured Rachra, Isle of Man (**q.v.**), and Ile (**q.v.**) before the Cruithni (Picts?) were able to control them. P#L(Lec.) and P#L(G47) give the same account without specifically mentioning the Fir Bolg.

      Rachru (Rachrann). Irish Place in Brega (**q.v.**).[172]
      Legend P#E(Lec.) seems to record that Ulfa/Ulpa (**q.v.**) was killed in Rachru.

Romans. Legends P#F(D.iv.1), P#F(Lec.1), P#F(Lec.2), P#F(Bal.), P#F(1295), P#F(1289), P#F(24.P.13), P#F(D.iii.2), P#G(B512), P#G(Lec.), P#G(Bal.), P#G(1295) say that the Cruithni travelled past the Romans after leaving Thrace (**q.v.**).

Gildas records that after the Romans left, the Picts and Scots invaded Britain (**q.v.**). Bede states that the Romans defeated the Picts for the Britons (**q.v.**) in return for allegiance. *Historia Brittonum* records that Britons requested Roman aid against the Picts and Scots even after the Britons had killed Roman generals. Vortigern (**q.v.**) feared Romans, Picts, Scots, and Ambrosius (**q.v.**). Geoffrey of Monmouth states that Sulgenius (**q.v.**) enlisted Pictish aid in his rebellion against Severus (**q.v.**). After the Romans left Britain, Picts, Scots, Norwegians (**q.v.**), and Danes (**q.v.**) invaded. When Cadwaladr (**q.v.**) left Britain, he declared that Britain was open to Picts, Scots, Saxons, Romans, and Ambrones (**q.v.**).[173]

Ros Cuissine. Place on the coast of Scotland. Possibly, Troup Head in Banffshire.[174]

In AT 729, 150 Pictish ships sank off Ros Cuissine.

Saxons (Saxain). Population of England (see also **Angles/English**).[175]

P#F(Lec.2), P#K(D.iv.1), P#K(Lec.1), P#K(Lec.2), P#K(Bal.), P#K(24.P.13), P#K(1295), P#K(1289), and P#K(D.iii.2) state that Cruithne (**q.v.**) and the Britons (**q.v.**) of Fortriu (**q.v.**) fought against the Saxons.

AT 698, AC 693, and AU 698 record a battle between Saxons and Picts in which Bertred (**q.v.**) was killed. AT 711 and AU 711 record the Battle of Mag Manand (**q.v.**) involving Picts and Saxons.

Historia Brittonum states that Saxons, Picts, Scots, and Britons (**q.v.**) were the four groups that inhabited Britain (**q.v.**). *Scéla Cano* remarks that Saxons had "bitter ales" in contrast to the "red ales" of the Cruithni (Picts?). Geoffrey of Monmouth records that Saxons, Normans (**q.v.**), Britons, Picts, and Scots were the five populations of Britain. After they had arrived in Britain, the Saxons defeated the Picts on behalf of Vortigern (**q.v.**) and the Britons, who rewarded them. Saxons under Colgrin (**q.v.**) along with the Picts and Scots were defeat by Arthur (**q.v.**) at "flumen Duglas" ("River Douglas"). At Camlann (**q.v.**), Saxons, Picts, Scots, and Irish (**q.v.**) fought on the side of Mordred (**q.v.**). When Cadwaladr (**q.v.**) left Britain, he declared that Britain was open to the Saxons, Scots, Picts, Romans (**q.v.**), and Ambrones (**q.v.**). Triad 36 calls the Saxons with Hengest (**q.v.**) and Horsa (**q.v.**) and the Picts two of the "Three Oppressions" of Britain.[176]

"Saxon" and "Saxones" ("Saxons") were used by outsiders to describe settlers from Germany (**q.v.**). It survives in Welsh as "Saesnaeg" and Irish as "Sasanach," terms which mean "English." These settlers called themselves "Engle" or "Englisc" (see **Angles/English**) or "Angli" in Latin.[177]

Scone (Scona, Scoan). Scottish place in Perthshire. Possibly the place of inauguration of Pictish kings.[178]

Lists D, F1, and F2 record that Drust f. Ferat (**q.v.**) was either killed at Forteviot (**q.v.**) or at Scone by the Scots. List I records that Drust was killed at Scone.[179]

Scots (Scot, Scoti, Scotti). Population of Ireland (**q.v.** and see **Irish**)) and Scotland (see **Alba**).[180]

Regnal List D records that the Scots ruled Scotland for two hundred sixty years and three months before the Picts and for three hundred thirty-eight years and five months after the Picts. In addition it indicates that after the reign of Alpín f. Eochaid (**q.v.**) the kingdom of the Scots became the kingdom of the Picts. It also states that the Scots killed the Pictish King Drust f. Ferat (**q.v.**) and then controlled Pictish territory. Lists F1 and F2 mention that the Scots reigned before and after the Picts.   It also states that after the reign of Alpín f. Eochaid (**q.v.**) the kingdom of the Scots became the kingdom of the Picts. List I states that the Scots reigned after the Picts and that after the reign of Alpín f. Eochaid (**q.v.**) the kingdom of the Scots became the kingdom of the Picts. List K indicates that the Picts reigned after the Scots and that Cináed mac Alpín (**q.v.**) was the first Scots king to rule the Picts. List N states that Cináed mac Alpín destroyed the Picts. Fordun's List records that after the reign of Drust f. Ferat the kingdom of the Picts became the kingdom of the Scots.[181]

Gildas records that Scots and Picts frequently attacked Britain (**q.v.**). After the Romans (**q.v.**) left Britain, Scots and Picts captured the north of Britain. Bede, who uses "Scots" for Gaels in both Ireland and Scotland, records that Scots along with the English (see **Angles/English**), Britons (**q.v.**), and Picts were one of the four nations of Britain (**q.v.**). The Picts received wives from the Scots (Irish) because they had taken no women of their own kind. The Scots and Picts attacked the Britons. Oswiu (**q.v.**) gained control over the Picts and Scots in Britain.   The Scots, Picts, and Britons held unorthodox Easter observances at the Synod of Whitby (A.D. 664). *Historia Brittonum* also mentions that Scots and Picts frequently attacked Britons (**q.v.**). Geoffrey of Monmouth records that Scots, Normans (**q.v.**), Picts, Saxons (**q.v.**), and Britons were the five inhabitants of Britain. Scots were descended from Picts and Irish (**q.v.**).   After Romans (**q.v.**) left Britain, Scots, Picts, Norwegians (**q.v.**), Danes (**q.v.**) took control of northern Britain. Scotland was always vulnerable to these groups. Under Colgrin (**q.v.**) Scots, Picts, and Saxons (**q.v.**) were defeated by Arthur (**q.v.**) at "River Douglas."   Arthur postponed attacking Scots and Picts in order to fight the Saxons besieging Bath. Scots and Picts later attacked Arthur's nephew Hoel (**q.v.**) at Alclud (Dumbarton), but Arthur defeated them there and elsewhere.   Scots, Picts, Irish, and Saxons fought with Mordred (**q.v.**) at Camlann (**q.v.**).   When Cadwaladr (**q.v.**) left Britain, he declared that Britain was open to Saxons, Scots, Picts, Romans, and Ambrones (**q.v.**).[182]

Scythia. Legendary place of origin for the Picts. The historical Scythians spoke an Iranian language and originated north of the Black Sea.[183]

Bede records that Scythia was the home of the Picts. Leo Sherley-Price suggests that Bede meant "Scandinavia." Geoffrey of Monmouth also states that the Picts came from Scythia. When rebelling against the emperor Severus (**q.v.**), Sulgenius (**q.v.**) travelled to Scythia to enlist the aid of the Picts.[184]

Thrace (**q.v.**) is used as home of the Picts in other texts. "Scythia" is also used for the home of the Scots in many texts.[185]

Segais. One of three Irish places: Curlieu Hills, River Boyle, or River Boyne in the Síd.[186]

AU 635 mistakenly seems to record that Garnard f. Uuid (**q.v.**) was killed in a battle at Segais.

Sliab Mis. One of three Irish places: Slieve Mish in Kerry, Slemish in center of Racavan in Antrim, or near Cenntsaile.[187]

Legends P#C(Lein.), P#C(Uí Ma.), P#C(Lec.), and P#C(G131) state that either the Cruithni or Sons of Míl (**q.v.**) encountered Banba (**q.v.**) at Sliab Mis. The text is somewhat confused.

Sodain (Soghains). Irish place and population. Sodain Midi and South Aichti in Fernmag. The descendants of Conall Cernach (**q.v.** and see **Dál n-Araide**).[188]

Legends P#A(B 506), P#A(Uí Ma.), P#A(Lec.), and P#A(C.vi.2) record that the seven Soghains (Sodain) of Ireland (**q.v.**) were from the Cruithni of Ireland.

Spain (Espáin).[189]

Legends P#A(B 506), P#A(Uí Ma.), P#A(Lec.), and P#A(C.vi.2) record that the Sons of Míl (**q.v.**) of Spain travelled to Germany (**q.v.**) with the Cruithni, who came from Thrace (**q.v.**).

Bede states that Picts went to Ireland (**q.v.**) and wrongly indicates that Ireland extends further south than Britain (**q.v.**) to the coast of Spain.[190]

Sráith Ethairt. Scottish place possibly in Pictland (**q.v.**) in Perthshire. Location of battle fought in 654 between Picts and Scots Dál Riata (**q.v.**).[191]

AT 654, AU 654, and CS 651 record that the Pictish king Talorcen f. Enfret (**q.v.**) won the Battle of Sráith Ethairt in which Dúnchad mac Conaing (**q.v.**) and Congal mac Rónáin (**q.v.**) were killed.

Tech Duinn. Irish place in Corca Duibne in Kerry. Island off Dursey Island, south of Kenmare Bay.[192]

Legends P#C(Lein.), P#C(Uí Ma.), P#C(Lec.), and P#C(G131) record that Tech Duinn was a cairn honoring Donn (**q.v.**) who drowned there.

AC (pp.25-26) mentions that Donn drowned at Tech Duinn.

Temair (Temair Breg, Tara). Irish place in County Meath.[193]

Legends P#A(B 506), P#A(Uí Ma.), P#A(Lec.), and P#A(C.vi.2) record that there were seven kings (see **Bagag ollfiacha**, **Berngal**, **Eilim ollfhinachta**, **Findoll cisirne**, **Géde Ollgothach**, **Ollam Fótla**, **Slanoll**) from the Cruithni of Alba (**q.v.**) who ruled Ireland (**q.v.**) at Temair. P#E(Lec.), P#E(Bal.), and P#E(1295) record that the Cruithni were told by Cathluan (**q.v.**) to leave Ireland in order to avoid a conflict over Temair.

Thrace (Tracia). Place used as the home of the Cruithni (Picts?) in some of the Origin Legends. The historical Thracians lived in the eastern half of the Balkans and spoke an Indo-European language.[194]

Legends P#A(B 506), P#A(Uí Ma.), P#A(Lec.), and P#A(C.vi.2) record that thirty-six soldiers (probably, Cruithni) travelled from Thrace to Germany (**q.v.**) with the Sons of Míl (**q.v.**). This is also true of P#B(Lec.), P#B(Bal.), P#B(1295), P#B(1289), and P#B(D.iii.2). P#D(D.iv.1), P#D(Lec.1), P#D(Lec.2), P#D(Bal.), P#D(24.P.13), P#D(1295), P#D(1289), P#E(Lec.), P#E(Bal.), and P#E(1295) state that the Cruithni came from Thrace. P#F(D.iv.1), P#F(Lec.1), P#F(Lec.2), P#F(Bal.), P#F(1295), P#F(1289), P#F(24.P.13), P#F(D.iii.2), P#G(B 512), P#G(Lec.), P#G(Bal.), and P#G(1295) repeat this.

M.O. Anderson indicates that the association of the Picts with Thrace derives from Virgil (see **Agathyrsus**, **Gelon**, **Istoreth**, and **Agathyrsi**). Scythia (**q.v.**) is also used as the home of the Picts in other sources.[195]

Tuatha Dé Danann (Tuath Dé Danann). Irish population related to the Fir Bolg (**q.v.**). In the *Lebor Gabála* ("Book of Invasions"), the Tuatha Dé Danann defeated the Fir Bolg and took control of Ireland.[196]

Origin Legends P#C(Lein.), P#C(Uí Ma.), P#C(Lec.), and P#C(G131) state that the Tuatha Dé Danann sent the Cruithni (Picts?) or Sons of Míl (**q.v.**) out on the sea. It seems to state that the Tuatha Dé Danann made a marriage alliance with the Sons of Míl. The text is ambiguous.

Tuath Fidga. British tribe living in Fotharta (**q.v.**) of Laigin (**q.v.**) and Uí Cennselaig (**q.v.**).[197]

Legends P#F(D.iv.1), P#F(Lec.1), P#F(Lec.2), P#F(Bal.), P#F(24.P.13), P#F(1295), P#F(1295), and P#F(D.iii.2) record that the Cruithni (Picts?) helped Crimthann (**q.v.**) defeat the Tuath Fidga and their poisoned weapons at Ard Lemnacht (**q.v.**). P#G(B 512), P#G(Lec.), P#G(Bal.), and P#G(1295) repeat this. This is also true of P#H(Lein.), P#H(D.iii.1), P#H(B 512), P#D(D.i.3), P#H(Lec.), P#I(Lein.), P#I(Uí Ma.), P#I(Lec.), P#I(Bal.), P#I(D.ii.2), P#I(B.iii.1), P#J(Uí Ma.), P#J(Lec.), P#J(Bal.), P#J(Ren.)(TR.WS), P#J(D.ii.2), and P#J(B.iii.1).

The role of the Tuath Fidga is given to Fea (**q.v.**) in P#E(Lec.), P#E(Bal.), and P#E(1295).

Uí Cennselaig (Uí Chennselaig). Irish place comprising all of County Wexford, part of County Wicklow, and part of County Carlow.[198]
Origin Legends P#F(D.iv.1), P#F(Lec.1), P#F(Lec.2), P#F(Bal.), P#F(24.P.13), P#F(1295), P#F(1289), and P#F(D.iii.2) record that the Cruithni landed at Inber Sláine (**q.v.**) in Uí Cennselaig and fought at Ard Lemnacht (**q.v.**) in Uí Cennselaig. P#G(Lec.), P#G(Bal.), and P#G(1295) repeat this. P#H(Lein.), P#H(D.iii.1), P#H(B 512), P#H(D.i.3), and P#H(Lec.) also mention that the Cruithni took control of Inber Sláine in Uí Cennselaig.

Uisnech. Irish place in the Connacht part of Meath.[199]
Legends P#C(Lein.), P#C(Uí Ma.), P#C(Lec.), and P#C(G131) state that the Cruithni or Sons of Míl (**q.v.**) met Eire (**q.v.**) at Uisnech. The text is ambiguous.

ENDNOTES

INTRODUCTION

[1] George Gordon, Lord Byron, *The Poetical Works of Lord Byron* (London: Oxford University Press, 1960), 196.

[2] Wainwright, F.T., *The Problem of the Picts* (Edinburgh: Nelson, 1956), 100.

[3] Hughes, Kathleen, *Early Christian Ireland*, in G.R. Elton, gen. ed., *The Sources of History* (London: The sources of History Limited in Association with Hodder and Stoughton Limited, 1972), 99.

[4] Wainwright, *Problem*, vi.

[5] Gearóid S. Mac Eoin, "On the Irish Legend of the Origin of the Picts," in *Studia Hibernica*, No. 4 (1964), 138-154.

[6] Mac Eoin, "Irish Legend," 140-144. Molly Miller, "Matriliny by Treaty: The Pictish Foundation-Legend," in Dorothy Whitelock, Rosamond McKitterick, and David Dumville, eds., *Ireland in Early Mediaeval Europe* (Cambridge: Cambridge University Press, 1982), 161.

[7] R. Mark Scowcroft, "*Leabhar Gabhála*, Part I: The Growth of the Text," in *Ériu*, Vol. XXXVIII (1987), 79-140.

[8] A.G. Van Hamel, *Lebor Bretnach* (Dublin: The Stationery Office, 1932). David Dumville, "The Textual History of 'Lebor Bretnach': A Preliminary Study," *Éigse*, Vol. XVI (1975-6), 255-264.

[9] Kathleen Hughes, David Dumville, ed., *Celtic Britain in the Early Middle Ages* (Woodbridge, Suffolk: The Boydell Press, 1980), 67. M.A. O'Brien, ed., *Corpus Genealogiarum Hiberniae* (Dublin: Dublin Institute for Advanced Studies, 1976), ix, 1-333.

[10] R.I. Best and M.A. O'Brien, eds. *The Book of Leinster*, Vol. I (Dublin: Dublin Institute for Advanced Studies, 1954), xviii. and Anne O'Sullivan, ed., *Book of Leinster*, Vol. VI (Dublin: Dublin Institute for Advanced Studies, 1983).

[11] O'Brien, *CGH*, ix. John Morris, ed., *Genealogies and Texts*, Vol. 5 of *Arthurian Period Sources*, in John Morris, gen. ed. History from the Sources (Chichester: Phillimore, 1995), 3.

[12] Elizabeth FitzPatrick, "Fasciculus XV," in Royal Irish Academy, *Catalogue of Irish Manuscripts in the Royal Irish Academy* (Dublin: Royal Irish Academy), pp. 1811-1862.

[13] Nollaig Ó Muraíle, *The Celebrated Antiquary*, Maynooth Monographs 6 (Maynooth: An Sagart, 1996), xv-xvi.

[14] Beryl Smalley, *Historians in the Middle Ages* (New York: Charles Scribner's Sons, 1974), 15.

[15] John Morris, *Annals and Charters*, Vol. 2 in *Arthurian Period Sources*, John Morris, gen. ed., History from the Sources (Chichester: Phillimore & Co. LTD., 1995), 33.

[16] Hughes, *Celtic Britain*, 86-100, 87.

[17] Morris, *Annals*, 11.

[18] Hughes, *Early Christian*, 99-159.

[19] M.O. Anderson, *Kings and Kingship in Early Scotland* (Edinburgh & London: Scottish Academic Press, 1980), 77-78, 85-86, 88.

[20] Miller, "Matriliny," 159-161.

[21] M.O. Anderson, *KKES*, 77.

[22] Ibid., 290-291.

[23] Hughes, *Early Christian*, 219.

[24] John and Winifred MacQueen, *St Nynia* (Edinburgh: Polygon Books, 1990), 86. Alan Macquarrie, *The Saints of Scotland* (Edinburgh: John Donald Publishers Ltd., 1997), 50-2.

[25] John MacQueen, "Myth and the Legends of Lowland Scottish Saints," *Scottish Studies*, Vol.24 (1980), 2.

[26] Ibid.

[27] John Morris, *Persons: Ecclesiastics and Laypeople*, Vol. 3 of *Arthurian Period Sources*, gen. ed., John Morris, History from the Sources (London and Chichester: Phillimore & Co. LTD., 1995), 24.

[28] Hughes, *Celtic Britain*, 53.

[29] Morris, *Persons*, 34.

[30] MacQueen, "Myth and Legends," 4-5.

[31] Máire Herbert, *Iona, Kells, and Derry* (Blackrock, Co. Dublin: Four Courts Press, 1996), 180-181.

[32] Morris, *Persons*, 43. Bertram Colgrave, *Two Lives of Cuthbert* (Cambridge: The University Press, 1940), 13, 16. J.F. Webb, and D.H. Farmer, *The Age of Bede*, 4th ed. (London: Penguin Books, 1998), 9-10.

[33] Morris, *Persons*, 147. Webb and Farmer, *Age of Bede*, 10. J.F. Webb and D.H. Farmer, "Eddius Stephanus: Life of Wilfrid," in J.F. Webb, trans. and D.H. Farmer, ed. and trans., *The Age of Bede*, 4th ed. (London: Penguin Books, 1998), 105-184.

[34] MacQueen, "Myth and Legends," 3, 4, 9. Morris, *Persons*, 131-132.

[35] Smalley, *Historians*, 15.

[36] Michael Winterbottom, ed., trans., *Gildas*, Vol. 7, *Arthurian Period Sources*, gen. ed. John Morris, History from the Sources (London, Chichester: Phillimore & Co., 1978), 1.

[37] A.O.H. Jarman, *Aneirin: Y Gododdin, Britain's Oldest Heroic Poem* (Llandysul, Dyfed: Gomer Press, 1990), xiii.

[38] Bede, *Ecclesiastical History of the English People*, Leo Sherley-Price, trans., rev. R.E. Latham and D.H. Farmer (London: Penguin Books, 1990), 19.

[39] Wolfgang Meid, *Táin Bó Fraích* (Dublin: Dublin Institute for Advanced Studies, 1974), xvii-xviii, xxv.

[40] John Morris, *Nennius: British History and the Welsh Annals*, Vol. 8 of *Arthurian Period Sources*, gen. ed., John Morris, History from the Sources (London and Chichester: Phillimore and Co. LTD., 1980), 1-2.

[41] John Bannerman, *Studies in the History of Dalriada* (Edinburgh: Scottish Academic Press, 1974), 28-39.

[42] Kenneth Jackson, "*Duan Albanach*" in *Scottish Historical Review*. Vol. XXXVI (1957), 125-127.

[43] Vernam Hull, "Exile of Conall Corc," *Publications of the Modern Language Association of America*, Vol. 56.2 (1941), 937-939. Dr. T.O. Clancy brought this text to my attention.

[44] D.A. Binchy, *Scéla Cano Meic Gartnáin* (Dublin: The Dublin Istitute for Advanced Studies, 1975), ix, xiv.

[45] Geoffrey of Monmouth, *The History of the Kings of Britain*, trans. Lewis Thorpe (Harmondsworth, Middlesex: Penguin Books, 1987), 9. Brynley Roberts, *Brut y Brenhinedd: Llanstephan MS. 1 Version* (Dublin: Dublin Institute for Advanced Studies, 1971), xxiv states that there are about sixty manuscripts which contain Welsh versions of the Latin *Historia Regum*. Their analysis and examination would require a separate study from this current work.

[46] Neil Wright, ed., *The Historia Regum Britannie of Geoffrey of Monmouth*, I (Cambridge: D.S. Brewer, 1984), xx.

[47] Rachel Bromwich, ed. and trans, *Trioedd Ynys Prydein*, 2nd ed. (Cardiff: University of Wales Press, 1978), xi-lxiv, lxxviii-lxxix.

[48] O'Brien, *CGH*.

[49] Morris, *Persons*, 1-7.

[50] Edmund Hogan, *Onomasticon Goedelicum* (Dublin: Four Courts Press, 1994).

[51] M.O. Anderson, *KKES*, 231-233.

[52] Kenneth Jackson, "Pictish Language" in F.T. Wainwright, *The Problem of the Picts* (Edinburgh: Thomas Nelson and Sons LTD., 1955), 129-66.

[53] Egerton Phillimore, "The *Annales Cambriae* and Old-Welsh Genealogies From Harleian Ms. 3859," in John Morris, ed., *Genealogies and Texts*, Vol. 5 of *Arthurian Period Sources*, gen. ed., John Morris, History from the Sources (London and Chichester: Phillimore & Co. LTD., 1995), 41-55.

[54] O'Brien, *CGH*, 1-333.

[55] Anne O'Sullivan, ed., *Book of Leinster*, Vol. VI (Dublin: Dublin Institute for Advanced Studies, 1983).

[56] O'Brien, *CGH*, 334-440.

[57] Egerton Phillimore, "Pedigrees from Jesus Collge MS. 20," in John Morris, ed., *Genealogies and Texts*, Vol. 5 of *Arthurian Period Sources*, gen. ed., John Morris, History from the Sources (London and Chichester: Phillimore & Co. LTD., 1995), 56-65.

[58] Mulchrone, *Lecan*, 53c-228d.

[59] Kuno Meyer, "The Laud Genealogies and Tribal Histories," in *Zeitschrift für Celtische Philologie*, Vol. VIII (1912), 291-339.

[60] FitzPatrick, "Fasciculus XV," 1811-1850.

[61] Ibid., 1850-1862.

[62] Phillimore, "*Annales Cambriae*," 13-41.

[63] Morris, *Nennius*, 85-91, 45-49.

[64] Seán Mac Airt, ed. and trans., *The Annals of Inisfallen* (Dublin: Dublin Institute for Advanced Studies, 1977).

[65] Whitley Stokes, "The Annals of Tigernach: Second Fragment. A.D. 143-361," "The Annals of Tigernach: Third Fragment. A.D. 489-766," and "The Annals of Tigernach: Fourth Fragment. A.D. 973-1088" in *Revue Celtique*, Vol. XVII (1896), 6-33, 119-263, 337-420.

[66] Donnchadh Ó Corráin and Tiarnáin Ó Corráin, eds., *Annals of Tigernach: Corpus of Electronic Texts Edition*, Cork: Corpus of Electronic Texts (CELT), University College Cork, 1996. <http//www.ucc.ie/celt/online/G10002.html>.

[67] Kathryn Grabowski and David Dumville, *Chronicles and Annals of Mediaeval Ireland and Wales* (Woodbridge, Suffolk: The Boydell Press, 1984), 128-152, 190-205.

[68] Denis Murphy, ed., *The Annals of Clonmacnoise* (Dublin: University Press, 1896).

[69] Seán Mac Airt and Gearóid Mac Niocaill, eds., *The Annals of Ulster (To A.D. 1131): Part I, Text and Translation* (Dublin: Dublin Institute for Advanced Studies, 1983).

[70] Donnchadh Ó Corráin and Mavis Cournane, eds., *Annals of the Four Masters: Corpus of Electronic Texts Edition*, Vol. I. Cork: Corpus of Electronic Texts, University College Cork, 1997.
<http://www.ucc.ie/celt/online/G100005A.html>.
Donnchadh Ó Corráin and Mavis Cournane, eds., *Annals of the Four Master: Corpus of Electronic Texts Edition*, Vol. II. Cork: Corpus of Electronic Texts (CELT), University College Cork, 1997.
<http://www.ucc.ie/celt/online/G100005B.html>.

[71] William M. Hennessy, ed., *Chronicum Scotorum* (London: Longmans, Green, Reader, and Dyer, 1866).

[72] M. Miller, "Matriliny by Treaty: The Pictish Foundation-Legend," in Dorothy Whitelock, Rosamond McKitterick, and David Dumville, eds., *Ireland in Early Mediaeval Europe* (Cambridge: Cambridge University Press,1982), 159-61.

[73] William F. Skene, *Chronicles of the Picts, Chronicles of the Scots* (Edinburgh: H.M. General Register House,1867), 1ra-1va, 4-8.

[74] M.O. Anderson, *KKES*, 245-49.

[75] R.A.S. MacAlister, *The Book of Uí Maine* (Dublin: The Irish Manuscripts Commisssion, 1942), 37[93]va40-vb38. Van Hamel, *Bretnach*, 82-87 and notes.

[76] M.O. Anderson, *KKES*, 261-3.

[77] T.C.D., *MS. #1336*, microfilm printout, col. 823 1.27- col. 825 1.24 Skene, *CPS*, 396-400.

[78] Van Hamel, *Bretnach*, 82-7 and notes.

[79] Mulchrone, *Lecan*, 4vb26-50. Miller, "Matriliny," 161.

[80] Mulchrone, *Lecan*, 139ra8-24. Miller, "Matriliny," 161.

[81] Mulchrone, *Lecan*, 143rb35-143va9. Miller, "Matriliny," 161.

[82] Mulchrone, *Lecan*, 287ra10-30. Miller, "Matriliny," 161.

[83] Atkinson, *Ballymote*, 43a11-13. Miller,"Matriliny," 161.

[84] Atkinson, *Ballymote*, 203a12-a237. Miller,"Matriliny," 161

[85] Royal Irish Academy, *MS. Stowe D.iv.1*, microfilm printout, 3ra51-b22. Miller, "Matriliny," 161.

[86] R.I.A., *MS. 24.P.13*, microfilm printout, 26 ll.6-21.

[89] Ibid., 378a7-a227.

[87] R.I.A., *MS. 23.G.4*, microfilm printout, 366 1.27-367 1.2.

[88] T.C.D., *MS. #1295*, microfilm printout, 83 ll.25-41.

[90] T.C.D., *MS. #1289*, microfilm printout, 93 ll.3-22.

[91] R.I.A., *MS. Stowe D.iii.2*, microfilm printout, 95 1.33-96 1.21.

[92] N.L.I.,*Gaelic MS. 47*,1 ll.5-15.

[93] M.O. Anderson, *KKES*, 264-8.

[94] Ibid., 269-278.

[95] Ibid.

[96] Ibid., 279-285.

[97] Ibid., 286-289.

[98]Ibid., 290-291.

[99]Molly Miller, "The Disputed Historical Horizon of the Pictish King-Lists" in *Scottish Historical Review*, Vol. 58 (1979), 1-34. M.O. Anderson, *KKES*, 292.

[100]John and Winifred MacQueen, *St. Nynia*, 88-101.

[101]Alexander Penrose Forbes, *Lives of S. Ninian and S. Kentigern*, Historians of Scotland, Vol. V (Edinburgh: Edmonston and Douglas, 1874), 137-57. John and Winifred MacQueen, *St. Nynia*, 102-124.

[102]A.W. Wade-Evans, *Vitae Sanctorum Britanniae et Genealogiae* in Board of Celtic Studies, *History and Law Series*, Vol. 9 (Cardiff: University of Wales Press Board, 1944), 24-141.

[103]William Reeves, ed. and trans., *Life of Saint Columba, Founder of HY*, Vol. VI in Historians of Scotland (Edinburgh: Edmonston and Douglas, 1874).

[104]A.O. and M.O. Anderson, *Adomnán's Life of Columba* (London: Thomas Nelson & Sons, 1961). A.O. and M.O. Anderson, *Adomnán's Life of Columba*, 2nd. ed. (Oxford: Clarendon Press, 1991).

[105]Adomnán, *Life of St Columba*, trans. Richard Sharpe (London: Penguin Books, 1991).

[106]Herbert, *Iona, Kells*, 211-265.

[107]Colgrave, *Lives of Cuthbert*, 60-139.

[108]Ibid., 142-307.

[109]Webb and Farmer, "Life of Wilfrid," 105-184.

[110]Skene,*CPS*, 412-420.

[111]Whitley Stokes, *Félire Óengusso Céli Dé: The Martyrology of Oengus the Culdee*, 2nd ed. (Dublin: Dublin Institute for Advanced Studies, 1984).

[112]O'Sullivan, *Leinster*, Vol. VI, 1596-1648.

[113]A.B.E. Hood, "*Epistola*" and "Letter," in A.B.E. Hood, *Sources*, in John Morris, gen. ed., History from the Sources (London and Chichester: Phillimore, 1978), 35-38, 55-59.

[114]Winterbottom, *Gildas*.

[115]Ifor Williams, *Canu Aneirin* (Caerdydd, 1978). Jarman, *Y Gododdin*.

[116]Bede, *Historia Ecclesiastica Gentis Anglorum*, in Bede, *Historical Works*, 2 Vols., 5th ed., ed. and trans. J.E. King, in G.P. Goold, ed. Loeb Classical Library (Cambridge, Massachusetts and London: Harvard University Press, 1994). Bede, *EHEP*.

[117]Wolfgang Meid, *Táin Bó Fraích*, 2nd. ed. (Dublin: Dublin Institute for Advanced Studies, 1974). R.I. Best and M.A. O'Brien, *Book of Leinster*, Vol. V (Dublin: Dublin Institute for Advanced Studies, 1967), 1127-1135.

[118]Morris, *Nennius*, 59-83, 9-43.

[119]Bannerman, *SIHD*, 27-156.

[120]Jackson, "*Albanach*." Kenneth Jackson, "The Poem *A Eolcha Alban Uile*" in *Celtica*, Vol. III (1956), 149-167.

[121]Hull, "Exile of Conall." Best and O'Brien, *Leinster*, Vol. V, 1249-51.

[122]Binchy, *Scéla Cano*.

[123]Rachel Bromwich and D. Simon Evans, eds., *Culhwch and Olwen: An Edition and Study of the Oldest Arthurian Tale* (Cardiff: University of Wales

Press, 1992). Patrick K. Ford, "Culhwch and Olwen," in Patrick K. Ford, ed. and trans., *The Mabinogi and Other Medieval Welsh Tales* (Berkeley, Los Angeles, London: University of California Press, 1977), 119-157.

[124]Wright, *Regum*. Geoffrey of Monmouth, *History*.

[125]Bromwich, *Trioedd*.

PICTISH ORIGIN LEGENDS

[1]Mac Eoin, "Irish Legend," 141, 153. Bodleian Library, *Rawlinson B 506*, microfilm printout, 3vbb31-4rb9. Also the digital images of *Rawlinson B 506* at Bodleian Library website, <http://image.ox.ac.uk/list?collection=bodleian>. Ó Muraíle, *Antiquary*, 163.

[2]Mac Eoin, "Irish Legend," 141, 153. MacAlister, *Uí Maine*, 15[67]ra8. Dumville, "Textual" 260-62.

[3]Mac Eoin, "Irish Legend," 141, 153. Mulchrone, *Lecan*, xiii, 131vb250-132ra49. Dumville, "Textual" 258-59.

[4]Mac Eoin, "Irish Legend," 141, 153. R.I.A., *MS. C.vi.2*, microfilm printout, 298b16-299b4. FitzPatrick, "Fasiculus XII," 1181.

[5]Mac Eoin, "Irish Legend," 141, 153. Mulchrone, *Lecan*, xiii, 270b2-12. Scowcroft, "*Leabhar Gabhála*, Part I," 87.

[6]Mac Eoin, "Irish Legend," 141, 153. Atkinson, *Ballymote*, Intro.1, 19a39-47. Scowcroft, *Leabhar Gabhála*, Part I," 87.

[7]Mac Eoin, "Irish Legend," 141, 153. Trinity College Dublin, *MS. #1295*, microfilm printout, 40 ll.19-23. Scowcroft, "*Leabhar Gabhála*, Part I," 87.

[8]Mac Eoin, "Irish Legend," 141, 153. Trinity College Dublin, *MS. 1289*, microfilm printout, 41 ll.19-24. Scowcroft, "*Leabhar Gabhála*, Part I," 87.

[9]Mac Eoin, "Irish Legend," 141, 153. R.I.A., *Stowe MS. D.iii.2*, microfilm printout, 20 ll.20-27. Scowcroft, "*Leabhar Gabhála*, Part I," 87.

[10]Mac Eoin, "Irish Legend," 140, 153. Atkinson, *Leinster*, 134a48-b21. Scowcroft, "*Leabhar Gabhála*, Part I," 85.

[11]Mac Eoin, "Irish Legend," 144, 153. MacAlister, *Uí Maine*, 150[208]ra20. Dumville, "Textual" 260-262.

[12]Mac Eoin, "Irish Legend," 144, 153. Mulchrone, *Lecan*, xiii, 144vb46-145a20. Dumville, "Textual" 258-59.

[13]Mac Eoin, "Irish Legend," 144, 153. National Library of Ireland, *Gaelic Manuscript G 131*, microfilm, 28v[52] l.6-29r[53] l.4. Date and scribal information provided by Elizabeth Kirwan of N.L.I. via e-mail.

[14]Mac Eoin, "Irish Legend," 144, 153. R.I.A., *Stowe MS. D.iv.1*, microfilm printout, 3rb46-3va6. Scowcroft, "*Leabhar Gabhála*, Part I," 86.

[15]Mac Eoin, "Irish Legend," 144, 153. Mulchrone, *Lecan*, xiii, 5a17-28. Scowcroft, "*Leabhar Gabhála*, Part I," 86.

[16]Mac Eoin, "Irish Legend," 144, 153. Mulchrone, *Lecan*, xiii, 287b11-23. Scowcroft, "*Leabhar Gabhála*, Part I," 87.

[17]Mac Eoin, "Irish Legend," 144, 153. Atkinson, *Ballymote*, 43a56-43b12. Scowcroft, "*Leabhar Gabhála*, Part I," 87.

[18]Mac Eoin, "Irish Legend," 144, 153. R.I.A., *24.P.13*, microfilm printout, 27 ll.8-19. Scowcroft, "*Leabhar Gabhála*, Part I," 86, 87.

[19]Mac Eoin, "Irish Legend," 144, 153. T.C.D., *1295*, microfilm printout, 84 ll.15-24. Scowcroft, "*Leabhar Gabhála*, Part I," 87.

[20]Mac Eoin, "Irish Legend," 144, 153. T.C.D., *1289*, microfilm printout, 93 l.38-94 l.8. Scowcroft, "*Leabhar Gabhála*, Part I," 87.

[21]Mac Eoin, "Irish Legend," 144, 153. Scowcroft, "*Leabhar Gabhála*, Part I," 87. R.I.A., *D.iii.2*, 97 ll.12-21.

[22]Mac Eoin, "Irish Legend," 144, 153. Mulchrone, *Lecan*, xiii, 144a14-144va6. Dumville, "Textual" 258-259.

[23]Mac Eoin, "Irish Legend," 144, 153. Atkinson, *Ballymote*, Intro.1, 204a34-205a24. Dumville, "Textual" 257.

[24]Mac Eoin, "Irish Legend," 144, 153. Bodleian Library, *Rawl. B 512*, microfilm printout, 95rb29-32. Also the digital images of *Rawlinson B 512* at Bodleian Library website,
<http://image.ox.ac.uk/pages/bodleian/celtcanon.htm>
<http://image.ox.ac.uk/list?collection=bodleian>.
Scowcroft, "*Leabhar Gabhála*, Part I," 87.

[25]Mac Eoin, "Irish Legend," 144, 153. T.C.D, *1295*, 380 l.1-381 l.9. Dumville, "Textual" 257. Scowcroft, "*Leabhar Gabhála*, Part I," 87.

[26]Mac Eoin, "Irish Legend," 142, 153. R.I.A., *D.iv.1*, 3rb22-45, 3va7-28. Scowcroft, "*Leabhar Gabhála*, Part I," 86. Dumville, "Textual" 258.

[27]Mac Eoin, "Irish Legend," 142, 153. Mulchrone, *Lecan*, xiii, 4vb50-5a16, 5a29-49. Scowcroft, "*Leabhar Gabhála*, Part I," 86.

[28]Mac Eoin, "Irish Legend," 142, 153. Mulchrone, *Lecan*, xiii, 287ra33-b10, 287rb24-287va4. Scowcroft, "*Leabhar Gabhála*, Part I," 87.

[29]Mac Eoin, "Irish Legend," 142, 153. Atkinson, *Ballymote*, Intro.1., 43a33-55, 43b13-32. Scowcroft, "*Leabhar Gabhála*, Part I," 87.

[30]Mac Eoin, "Irish Legend," 142, 153. R.I.A., *24.P.13*, 26 l.21-27 l.8, 27 l.20-28 l.4. Scowcroft, "*Leabhar Gabhála*, Part I," 86, 87.

[31]Mac Eoin, "Irish Legend," 143, 153. T.C.D., *1295*, 83 l.41-84 l.14, 84 ll.25-39. Scowcroft, "*Leabhar Gabhála*, Part I," 87.

[32]Mac Eoin, "Irish Legend," 142, 153. T.C.D., *1289*, 93 ll.22-37, 94 ll.9-20. Scowcroft, "*Leabhar Gabhála*, Part I," 87.

[33]Mac Eoin, "Irish Legend," 142, 153. T.C.D., *D.iii.2*, 96 l.21-97 l.11, 97 ll.22-37. Scowcroft, "*Leabhar Gabhála*, Part I," 87.

[34]Mac Eoin, "Irish Legend," 143, 153. Mulchrone, *Lecan*, xiii, 143vb11-144ra3. Dumville, "Textual" 258-9.

[35]Mac Eoin, "Irish Legend," 143, 153. Atkinson, *Ballymote*, Intro.1, 203c37-204a33. Dumville, "Textual" 257.

[36]Mac Eoin, "Irish Legend," 143, 153. Bodleian, *Rawl. B 512*, 95ra18-529.
I have also consulted the digital images of *Rawl B 512* at Bodleian Library Oxford website, <http://image.ox.ac.uk/pages/bodleian/celtcanon.htm>
<http://image.ox.ac.uk/ist/collection=bodleian>.
Scowcroft, "*Leabhar Gabhála*, Part I," 87.

[37]Mac Eoin, "Irish Legend," 143, 153. T.C.D., *1295*, 379 ll.13-40.

Scowcroft, "*Leabhar Gabhála*, Part I," 87. Dumville, "Textual," 257.

[38]Mac Eoin, "Irish Legend," 143-144. Atkinson, *Leinster*, 15a22-37. Scowcroft, "*Leabhar Gabhála*, Part I," 85.

[39]Mac Eoin, "Irish Legend," 144, 153. R.I.A., *Stowe D.iii.1*, microfilm printout, 1vb38-2ra18. Scowcroft, "*Leabhar Gabhála*, Part I," 85.

[40]Mac Eoin, "Irish Legend," 144, 153. R.I.A., *Stowe D.i.3*, microfilm printout, 3rb13-23. Scowcroft, "*Leabhar Gabhála*, Part I," 87. Dumville, "Textual," 258.

[41]Mac Eoin, "Irish Legend," 144, 153. Mulchrone, *Lecan*, xiii, 20v6-16. Scowcroft, "*Leabhar Gabhála*, Part I," 87.

[42]Mac Eoin, "Irish Legend," 144, 153. Bodleian, *Rawl. B 512*, 95ra1-18. Digital images at Bodleian Library website, <http://image/ox.ac.uk/pages/bodleian/celtcanon.htm>. <http://image.ox.ac.uk/list?collection=bodleian>. Scowcroft, "*Leabhar Gabhála*, Part I," 87.

[43]Mac Eoin, "Irish Legend," 144, 153. Atkinson, *Leinster*, 196a11-31. Scowcroft, "*Leabhar Gabhála*, Part I," 85.

[44]Mac Eoin, "Irish Legend," 144, 153. MacAlister, *Uí Maine*, 93[152]vb6-21. Dumville, "Textual," 260-262.

[45]Mac Eoin, "Irish Legend," 144, 153. Mulchrone, *Lecan*, xiii, 234va12-35.

[46]Mac Eoin, "Irish Legend," 144, 153. Atkinson, *Ballymote*, Intro.1, 370b1-25.

[47]Mac Eoin, "Irish Legend," 144, 153. Whitley Stokes, "The Prose Tales in the Rennes Dinds'enchas" in *Revue Celtique*, Vol. XV, 272, 427-28. Gwynn, *Metrical Dindshenchas, Part III*, 164-167.

[48]Mac Eoin, "Irish Legend," 144, 153. R.I.A., *MS. Stowe D.ii.2*, microfilm printout, 26vb23-27ra22. R.I.A., *Catalogue of Manuscripts in the Royal Irish Academy*, 1221.

[49]Mac Eoin, "Irish Legend," 144, 153. T.C.D., *MS. #1322*, microfilm, 24b3-20. Gwynn, *Metrical Dindshenchas, Part III*, 164-167. Date information provided by Felicity O'Mahony of T.C.D. Library via e-mail.

[50]Mac Eoin, "Irish Legend," 144, 153. R.I.A., *MS. Stowe B.iii.1*, microfilm printout, 30v l.26-31r l.14. R.I.A., *Catalogue*, 741-742.

[51]Mac Eoin, "Irish Legend," 144, 153. MacAlister, *Uí Maine*, 93[152]va51-vb5. Dumville, "Textual," 260-62.

[52]Mac Eoin, "Irish Legend," 144, 153. Mulchrone, *Lecan*, xiii, 234b43-234va11.

[53]Mac Eoin, "Irish Legend," 144, 153. Atkinson, *Ballymote*, Intro.1, 370a38-51.

[54]Mac Eoin, "Irish Legend," 144, 153. Whitley Stokes, "The Prose Tales in the Rennes Dinds'enchas" in *Revue Celtique*, Vol. XV, 272, 427-28.

[55]Mac Eoin, "Irish Legend," 144, 153. R.I.A., *MS. Stowe D.ii.2*, microfilm printout, 26va26-26vb22. R.I.A., *Catalogue*, 1221.

[56]Mac Eoin, "Irish Legend," 144, 153. T.C.D., *MS. #1322*, microfilm, 24a36-24b2. Date information provided by Felicity O'Mahony of T.C.D. Library

via e-mail.

[56a]Mac Eoin, "Irish Legend," 144, 153. R.I.A., *MS. Stowe B.iii.1*, microfilm printout, 30v ll. 17-25. R.I.A., *Catalogue*, 741-742.

[57]Mac Eoin, "Irish Legend, 141-2, 153. R.I.A., *D.iv.1*, 3va35-46. Scowcroft, "*Leabhar Gabhála*, Part I," 86.

[58]Mac Eoin, "Irish Legend," 141-2, 153. Mulchrone, *Lecan*, xiii, 5rb2-12. Scowcroft, "*Leabhar Gabhála*, Part I," 86.

[59]Mac Eoin, "Irish Legend," 141-2, 153. Mulchrone, *Lecan*, xiii, 144ra4-14. Dumville, "Textual," 258-59.

[60]Mac Eoin, "Irish Legend," 141-2, 153. Atkinson, *Ballymote*, Intro.1, 43b49-44a3. Scowcroft, "*Leabhar Gabhála*, Part I," 87.

[61]Mac Eoin, "Irish Legend," 141-2, 153. R.I.A., *24.P.13*, 28 ll.17-25. Scowcroft, "*Leabhar Gabhála*, Part I," 87.

[62]Mac Eoin, "Irish Legend," 141-2, 153. T.C.D., *1295*, 85 ll.10-17. Scowcroft, "*Leabhar Gabhála*, Part I," 87.

[63]Mac Eoin, "Irish Legend," 141-2, 153. T.C.D., *1289*, 94 1.34-95 1.2. Scowcroft, "*Leabhar Gabhála*, Part I," 87.

[64]Mac Eoin, "Irish Legend," 141-2, 153. R.I.A., *D.iii.2*, 98 ll.20-31. Scowcroft, "*Leabhar Gabhála*, Part I," 87.

[65]Mac Eoin, "Irish Legend," 145-6, 152-3. MacAlister, *Uí Maine*, 36[92]ra44-65. Dumville, "Textual," 260-2.

[66]Mac Eoin, "Irish Legend," 145-6, 152-3. Mulchrone, *Lecan*, xiii, 141ra. Dumville, "Textual," 258-9.

[67]Mac Eoin, "Irish Legend," 145-6, 152-3. Atkinson, *Ballymote*, Intro.1, 206a24-48. Dumville, "Textual," 257.

[68]Mac Eoin, "Irish Legend," 14-6, 152-3. T.C.D., *MS. #1336*, microfilm printout, cols. 809 1.36-810 1.21. Dumville, "Textual," 263.

[69]Mac Eoin, "Irish Legend," 145-6, 152-3, T.C.D., *1295*, 382 ll.7-40. Scowcroft, "*Leabhar Gabhála*, Part I," 87. Dumville, "Textual," 257.

[70]Mac Eoin, "Irish Legend," 145-6, 152-3, N.L.I., *Gaelic MS. G 47*, 1 1.13-11 1.6. Dumville, "Textual," 260.

[71]Skene, *CPS*, 318-21. M.E. Dobbs, "The History of the Descendants of Ir," *Zeitschrift für Celtische Philologie*, Vol. XIII, 308 and Vol. XIV, 62-68.

[72]Skene, *CPS*, 322, Todd, *Irish Nennius*, 246-51.

[73]MacAlister, *Lebor Gabála, Part II*, 70. Skene, *CPS*, 45, 47-8. Best, *Leinster*, Vol. III, 19-20.

[74]Todd,*Irish Nennius*, 244. Skene, *CPS*, 326-8. MacAlister, *Lebor Gabála, Part I*, vi-vii and *Lebor Gabála, Part V*, 424-5.

[75]Todd, *Irish Nennius*, 126-53. Skene, *CPS*, 30, 32-44. Van Hamel, *Bretnach*, 10-14.

[76]Todd, *Irish Nennius*, 120-7. Skene, *CPS*, 323, 325-6, 328-9. MacAlister, *Lebor Gabála, Part I*, vi-vii and *Lebor Gabála, Part V*, 174-80.

[77]Todd, *Irish Nennius*, 120-6. Skene, *CPS*, 30-2. Van Hamel, *Bretnach*, 8.

[78]Skene, *CPS*, 125-6. MacAlister, *Lebor Gabála, Part I*, vi-vii and *Lebor Gabála, Prt V*, 174-80. Scowcroft, "*Leabhar Gabhála*, Part I," 85-7. Best, *Leinster*, Vol. I, 7.

[79]Gwynn, *Dindshechas*, 164-7. Best, *Leinster*, IV, 906-7.

[80]Stokes, *Prose Dindshenchas*," 427-8.

[81]Todd, *Irish Nennius*,126-7. Skene, *CPS*, 323. MacAlister, *Lebor Gabála, Part II*, 70. Mac Eoin, "Legend," 141.

[82]Skene, *CPS*, 3-4. Van Hamel, *Bretnach*, vi-viii, 23-4.

[83]Fergus Kelly, *A Guide to Early Irish Law* in Fergus Kelly, gen. ed., *Early Irish Law Series* (Dublin: Dublin Institute for Advanced Studies, 1988), 70.

[84]T.M. Charles-Edwards, "Nau Kynywedi Teithiauc" in Dafydd Jenkins and Morfydd E. Owen, eds., *The Welsh Law of Women* (Cardiff: University of Wales Press, 1980), 37.

[85]Kelly, *Irish Law*, 70-71.

[86]Charles-Edwards, "Nau Kynywedi," 38-39.

[87]Bede, *HEGA*, Vol. I, 18-9. Bede, *EHEP*, 46.

[88]M.O. Anderson, *KKES* 165 n.180. Nora K. Chadwick, "Pictish and Celtic Marriage," in *Scottish Gaelic Studies*, Vol. VIII (1955-58), 68.

[89]Wright, *Regum*, 45.

[90]D.A. Binchy, *Celtic and Anglo-Saxon Kingship* (Oxford: Clarendon Press. 1970), 26-28.

PICTISH AND SCOTTISH REGNAL LISTS

[1]Molly Miller, "Matriliny by Treaty," 159-161.

[2]Anderson, *KKES*, 77, 237, 245-249, 261-263. Miller, "Matriliny," 159, 160, 161.

[3]MacAlister, *Uí Maine*, 37[93]va40-vb38.

[4]Dumville, "Textual," 260-262, 266.

[5]Van Hamel, *Bretnach*, 82-87. Miller, "Matriliny," 160.

[6]T.C.D., *MS. #1336*, col. 823, l.27 - col. 825, l.24.

[7]Dumville, "Textual," 263, 266.

[8]Skene, *CPS*, 396-400. Miller, "Matriliny," 160.

[9]Van Hamel, *Bretnach*, 82-87. Miller, "Matriliny, 160.

[10]J.M.P. Calise, "Medieval Celtic Texts Relating to the Picts and Scots," Ph.D. thesis (Edinburgh University, 1999), 70-72. Dumville, "Textual," 257-60, 265. Miller, "Matriliny," 160, 161. Scowcroft, "*Leabhar Gabhála* Part I," 86, 87. Mulchrone, *Lecan*, xii-xiii, 4vb26-50, 139ra8-24, 143rb35-143va9, 287ra10-30. Atkinson, *Ballymote*, Intro.1, 43a11-33, 203a12-a237. R.I.A., *Stowe D.iv.1*, 3ra51-b22. R.I.A., *24.P.13*, 26 ll.6-21. R.I.A., *23.G.4*, 366 l.27-367 l.2. T.C.D., *#1295*, 83 ll.25-41, 378a7-a227. T.C.D., *#1289*, 93 ll.3-22. R.I.A., *Stowe D.iii.2*, 95 l33-96 l.21. N.L.I., *Gaelic MS. 47*, 1 ll.5-15.

[11]Dumville,"Textual," 259-60.

APPENDICES

[1]A.O. Anderson, *ESSH*, Vol. I, cxiii; M.O. Anderson, *KKES*, 169; M. Miller, "Disputed," 4, 10-12, 24. M. Miller, "Last Century of Pictish Succession," *Scottish Studies*, Vol. 23 (1979), 47.

[2]M.O. Anderson, *KKES*, 97 n.82, 246 n.77, 248 nn.104, 105; Bromwich, *Trioedd*, 512. Jackson, "Pictish Language," 129-166; T.F. O'Rahilly, *Irish History*, 353-384.

[3]Morris, *Annals and Charters*, 7.

[4]Michael Swanton, *Anglo-Saxon Chronicle* (New York: Routledge, 1998), xxi-xxviii.

[5]Swanton, *Anglo-Saxon Chronicle*, 3. T. Jebson, *MS. D*, 1. <http://lonestar.texas.net/~ jebbo/asc/d.html>. T. Jebson, *MS. E*, 1. <http://lonestar.texas.net/~ jebbo/asc/d.html>.

[6]Swanton, *Anglo-Saxon Chronicle*, 3 n.6.

[7]Morby, *Kings & Queens*, 43.

[8]Jebson, *MS. D*, 2. Jebson, *MS. E*, 2. Swanton, *Anglo-Saxon Chronicle*, 6, 7.

[9]Tony Jebson, *MS. A: Parker MS; CCCC 173 ff.1-32*, <http://lonestar.texas.net/~jebbo/asc/a.html>, 1995, p.3. Jebson, *MS. E*, 3-4. Swanton, *Anglo-Saxon Chronicle*,12-13

[10]Swanton, *Anglo-Saxon Chronicle*, 12-13. Jebson, *MS. A*, 4. Jebson, *MS. C: Cotton Tiberius B.*, 1996, p.2. <http://lonestar.texas.net/~ jebbo/asc/c.html> Jebson, *MS. E*, 4.

[11]Jebson, *MS. A*, 5. Jebson, *MS. E*, 5. Swanton, *Anglo-Saxon Chronicle*, 18-19. A.O. Anderson, *Scottish Annals*, 6-7 n.5.

[12]Morby, *Kings & Queens*, 66.

[13]Jebson, *MS. A*, 6. Jebson, *MS. C*, 4. Jebson, *MS. E*, 6. Swanton, *Anglo-Saxon Chronicle*, 20-21. A.O. Anderson, *Scottish Annals*, 10-11.

[14]Jebson, *MS. E*, 13. Swanton, *Anglo-Saxon Chronicle*, 38n.10, 39. A.O. Anderson, *Scottish Annals*, 38n.1.

[15]Jebson, *MS. A*, 9. Jebson, *MS. C*, 7. Jebson, *MS. E*, 13. Swanton, *Anglo-Saxon Chronicle*, 38-39. A.O. Anderson, *Scottish Annals*, 42 n.4.

[16]Jebson, *MS. D*, 7. Jebson, *MS. E*, 14. Swanton, *Anglo-Saxon Chronicle*, 41. A.O. Anderson, *Scottish Annals*, 47 n.2.

[17]Jebson, *MS. A*, 10. Jebson, *MS. C*, 8. Jebson, *MS. D*, 3. Jebson, *MS. E*, 14. Swanton, *Anglo-Saxon Chronicle*, 42-3. A.O. Anderson, *Scottish Annals*, 49, nn.1, 2.

[18]Crawford, *Scandinavian*, 131, 197, 267. Hudson, *Kings of Celtic*, 53.

[19]Jebson, *MS. A*, 10. Jebson, *MS. C*, 876. Jebson, *MS. D*, 12. Jebson, *MS. E*, 24. Swanton, *Anglo-Saxon Chronicle*, 72-5. A.O. Anderson, *Scottish Annals*, 62.

PERSONAL NAMES ASSOCIATED WITH THE PICTS

[1]Adomnán and Sharpe, *Life of Columba*, 3. Morris, *Persons*,11.

[2]O'Sullivan, *Leinster*, 1684-1686, 1692.

[3]M.O. Anderson, *KKES*, 77, 266, 272, 287.

[4]Skene, *CPS*, 416-417. O'Sullivan, *Leinster*, Vol. VI, 1634. Stokes, *Félire Óengusso*, 196, 211.

[5]Bede, *HEGA*, Vol. II, 280-83, 356-57. Bede, *EHEP*, 293-294, 319.

[6]Francis John Byrne, *Irish Kings and High-Kings* (New York: St. Martin's Press, 1973), 287. Adomnán and Sharpe, *Life of Columba*, 297.

[7]Reeves, *Saint Columba*, 135, 136, 138, 139.

[8]A.O. Anderson, *Early Sources of Scottish History*, Vol.I (Stamford: Paul Watkins, 1990), cxii.

[9]O'Brien, *CGH*, 328. O'Sullivan, *Leinster*, 1471.

[10]M.O. Anderson, *KKES*, 265, 271, 282, 290, 301. Hudson, *Kings of Celtic*, 191.

[11]Jackson, "*Albanach*," 4. M.O. Anderson, *KKES*, 191-193, 228, 229, 298, 306. O'Brien, *CGH*, 591.

[12]A.O. Anderson, *ESSH*, Vol. I, cxiii.

[13]O'Brien, *CGH*, 426.

[14]Hennessy, *Chronicum*, 180, n. A.O. Anderson, *ESSH*, Vol. I, cxiii, 398n.8, 403, 403 n.3. O'Brien, *CGH*, 538. Hudson, *Kings of Celtic*, 193.

[15]MacAlister, *Uí Maine*, 37[93]vb. M.O. Anderson, *KKES*, 263, 267, 274, 283, 288. Skene, *CPS*, 204, 400.

[16]A.O. Anderson, *ESSH*, Vol. I, cxii. Bannerman, *SIHD*, 93-94.

[17]O'Brien, *CGH*, 275, 329. O'Sullivan, *Leinster*, 1366, 1441, 1471. Bannerman, *SIHD*, 83-4, 88-9. Royal Irish Academy, *Dictionary of the Irish Language* (Dublin: Royal Irish Academy, 1983), 361. Mulchrone, *Lecan*, 115rc. Meyer, "Laud," 327. Phillimore, "Pedigrees," 56. Bromwich, *Trioedd*, 238-39.

[18]M.O. Anderson, *KKES*, 228, 264, 270, 281, 286, 290, 297, 300, 302.

[19]A.O. and M.O. Anderson, *ALOC*(1991), xix-xxi, 30-33. Reeves, *Columba*, 120, 196-197. T.F. O'Rahilly, *EIHM*, 504-5. O'Sullivan, *Leinster*, Vol. VI, 1615.

[20]Bannerman, *SIHD*, 41. Jackson, *Albanach*, 130-131. Binchy, *Scela Cano*, 1, 57. Bromwich, *Trioedd*, 57, 264-6. Williams, *Canu Aneirin*, 14. Jarman, *Y Gododdin*, 24-5.

[21]Bede, *EHEP*, 387. Clare Stancliffe, "Cuthbert and the Polarity between Pastor and Solitary" and Alan Thacker, "Lindisfarne and the Origins of the Cult of St Cuthbert" in Gerald Bonner, David Rollason, Clare Stancliffe, eds., *St Cuthbert*, 3rd ed. (Woodbridge, Suffolk: Boydell Press, 1998), 34-5, 117. Webb and Farmer, *Age of Bede*, 153, 277.

[22]Colgrave, *Lives of Cuthbert*, 102-105, 126-127, 230-233, 234-239, 260-265.

[23]Bede, *HEGA*, Vol. II, 162-65. Bede, *EHEP*, 255.

[24]A.O. Anderson, *ESSH*, Vol. I, 190, 190 n.2.

[25]Webb and Farmer, "Life of Wilfrid," 132-33.

[26]Bede, *HEGA*, Vol. II, 118-19. Bede, *EHEP*, 240 Morris, *Nennius*, 77.

[27]Skene, *CPS*, 1ra, 5, 396. T.C.D., *1336*, col. 823. M.O. Anderson, *KKES*, 245. MacAlister, *Uí Maine*, 37[93]va. Mulchrone, *Lecan*, 4vb, 143rb, 287ra. Atkinson, *Ballymote*, 43a, 203a.

[28]M.O. Anderson, *KKES*, 81. Jackson, "Pictish Language," 162.

[29]A.O. Anderson, *ESSH*, Vol. I, cxi. Molly Miller, "Eanfrith's Pictish Son," *Northern History*, Vol. XIV (1978), 53.

[30]A.O. Anderson, *ESSH*, Vol.I, 123, 123 nn.2,4,5, 140, 140n.2.

[31]Bede, *HEGA*, Vol. I, 178-81, 210-13, 270-3, 324-5. Bede, *EHEP*, 97, 106-107, 126, 143. Morris, *Nennius*, 77, 79. Wright, *HEGA Regum*, 135-136.

[32]A.O. Anderson, *ESSH*, Vol.I, 266n.2, 287 n.4.

[33]M.O. Anderson, *KKES*, 292.

[34]Tom Peete Cross and Clark Harris Slover, *Ancient Irish Tales* (Totowa, New Jersey: Barnes & Noble Books, 1988), 3.

[35]O'Brien, *CGH*, 4, 6. FitzPatrick, "Fasciculus XV," 1841.

[36]Murphy, *Clonmacnoise*, 14.

[37]Mulchrone, *Lecan*, 4vb, 139ra, 287ra. Atkinson, *Ballymote*, 43a, 203a.

[38]Morris, *Nennius*, 61.

[39]A.O. Anderson, *ESSH*, Vol. I, cxii.

[40]A.O. Anderson, *ESSH*, Vol. I, cxi, 210n.1. Mac Airt, *Inisfallen*, 446. O'Brien, *CGH*, 649.

[41]O'Brien, *CGH*, 135. Mulchrone, *Lecan*, 54a. Meyer, "Laud," 294.

[42]Reeves, *Columba*, 191. Colgrave, *Lives of Cuthbert*, 104, 114, 236, 238. Webb and Farmer, "Life of Wilfrid," 153-5, 167, 172-76. A.O. and M.O. Anderson, *ALOC* (1991), 178-81.

[43]Bede, *HEGA*, Vol. II, 162-165, 202-203, 266-67, 280-81, 284-85, 292-95, 310-311, 316-17. Bede, *EHEP*, 255, 267, 289, 293, 295, 298, 304, 306. Morris, *Nennius*, 77. Alex Woolf and Séamus Mac Mathúna pointed out that "Alcfrid" is not the same individual as "Aldfrith" and that Morris, *Nennius*, 36 misidentifies "Alcfrid" as "Aldfrith."

[44]Morris, *Persons*, 132.

[45]Skene, *CPS*, 412.

[46]Pádraig Ó Riain, *Corpus Genealogiarum Sanctorum Hiberniae* (Dublin: Dublin Institute for Advanced Studies, 1985), 181. MacAlister, *Uí Maine*, 55[111]vb. Mulchrone, *Lecan*, 34vb-35ra. Atkinson, *Ballymote*, 214a.

[47]M.O. Anderson, *KKES*, 195-197.

[48]A.O. Anderson, *ESSH*, Vol. I, cxii. M.O. Anderson, *KKES*, 195, 265, 266, 271, 286, 290.

[49]M.O. Anderson, *KKES*, 87

[50]Ibid., 87, 169, 181, 292.

[51]Leslie Alcock, *Arthur's Britain*, 4th ed. (London: Penguin Books, 1990), 34. John Morris, *Age of Arthur* (London: Weidenfield, 1993), 512-13. Morris, *Persons*, 154-155. Bromwich, *Trioedd*, 345.

[52]Phillimore, "Pedigrees," 63. Bromwich, *Trioedd*, 286-8.

[53]Winterbottom, *Gildas*, 98. Bede, *EHEP*, 64. Morris, *Nennius*, 67, 74.

Wright, *Regum*, 47, 62-4, 84-89, 92-43.

[54]Adomnán and Sharpe, *Life of Columba*, 294.

[55]A.O. and M.O. Anderson, *ALOC* (1961), 274; *ALOC* (1991), 62-63.

[56]A.O. and M.O. Anderson, *ALOC* (1961), 158. Reeves, *Columba*, 258. Sharpe, *Life of Columba*, 294. William J. Watson, *History of the Celtic Place-Names of Scotland*, 2nd.ed. (Edinburgh: Birlinn Limited, 1993), 108-109.

[57]Alcock, *Arthur's Britain*, 55. Morris, *Arthur*, 513. Morris, *Persons*, 156.

[58]Phillimore, "Pedigrees," 63.

[59]Wade-Evans, *VSBG*, 26-9, 68-75, 78-81.

[60]Williams, *Canu Aneirin*, 49. Jarman, *Y Gododdin*, 65. Morris, *Nennius*, 76, 83. Wright, *Regum*, 101-3, 104-5, 130-2. Alcock, *Arthur's Britain*, 73. Geoffrey of Monmouth, *History*, 213. A.O. and M.O. Anderson, *ALOC* (1991), xx, 30-2. Bromwich, *Trioedd*, 1, 5, 21, 35, 89, 131-3, 274, 264. Bromwich and Evans, *Culhwch and Olwen*, 1-4, 8-9, 14-15, 27-8, 31, 33-5, 37-42, 215. Ford, "Culhwch and Olwen," 119-21, 123-33, 143, 144, 146-57. Bannerman, *SIHD*, 41, 90-91.

[61]Geoffrey of Monmouth, *History*, 119.

[62]Wright, *Regum*, 42, 43-44, 44-45, 45.

[63]M.O. Anderson, *KKES*, 99 n.87. Skene, *CPS*, 184.

[64]Ibid., 292.

[65]A.O. Anderson, *ESSH*, Vol. I, 296 n.3. Crawford, *Scandinavian*, 50.

[66]Skene, *CPS*, 320-321.

[67]O'Sullivan, *Leinster*, 1439. Mulchrone, *Lecan*, 114vb. Meyer, "Laud," 326.

[68]Murphy, *Clonmacnoise*, 35, 212-213.

[69]Skene, *CPS*, 1ra, 5, 396. T.C.D., *1336*, col.823. M.O. Anderson, *KKES*, 245. MacAlister, *Uí Maine*, 37[93]va. Mulchrone, *Lecan*, 4vb, 143rb, 287ra. Atkinson, *Ballymote*, 43a, 203a.

[70]Cross, *Ancient Irish*, 17, n.1.

[71]Cross, *Ancient Irish*, 16, 20. O'Brien, *CGH*, 528.

[72]O'Brien, *CGH*, 287, 698. O'Sullivan, *Leinster*, 1424, 1474-1475. Mulchrone, *Lecan*, 117rd. Meyer, "Laud," 333-334.

[73]John E. Morby, *The Wordsworth Handbook of Kings and Queens* (Ware, Hertfordshire: Wordsworth Reference, 1994), 43. Geoffrey of Monmouth, *History*, 127. Alex Woolf of Edinburgh University pointed out that Bassianus=Caracalla.

[74]Bede, *HEGA*, Vol. I, 32-3. Bede, *EHEP*, 50. Wright, *Regum*, 48.

[75]A.O. Anderson, *ESSH*, Vol.I, 193n.1. Miller, "Eanfrith's,"53-4. A.P. Smyth, *Warlords*, 62-4. Thomas Owen Clancy and Gilbert Márkus, *Iona* (Edinburgh: Edinburgh University Press, 1995), 166-7.

[76]Phillimore, "*Annales Cambriae*," 44.

[77]Hughes, *Celtic Britain*, 92, 92 n.42. Bromwich, *Trioedd*, 167, 280-281. Williams, *Canu Aneirin*, 18, 181 n.449. Jarman, *Y Gododdin*, 30-31, 105 n.427.

[78]O'Brien, *CGH*, 275. O'Sullivan, *Leinster*, 1439. Mulchrone, *Lecan*, 114vb. Meyer, "Laud," 326.

[79]Murphy, *Clonmacnoise*, 35. Mac Airt, *Ulster*, 124.

[80]Bede, *HEGA*, Vol.II, 382-3. Bede, *EHEP*, 328.

[81]Ibid.

[82]Bede, *HEGA*, Vol.II, 380-1. Bede, *EHEP*, 328.

[83]Miller, "Disputed," 19.

[84]Skene, *CPS*, 1ra, 6, 398. M.O. Anderson, *KKES*, 77, 245-246, 261. MacAlister, *Uí Maine*, 37[93]v. Miller, "Disputed," 12.

[85]Morris, *Persons*, 21.

[86]Colgrave, *Lives of Cuthbert*, 172-175, 180-185.

[87]Bede, *HEGA*, Vol.II, 236-9. Bede, *EHEP*, 278-9.

[88]Bannerman, *SIHD*, 99. R.I.A., *Dictionary*, 82. Isabel Henderson, "*North Pictland*," 46.

[89]M.O. Anderson, *KKES*, 169, 295.

[90]Skene, *CPS*, 1va, 8, 400. T.C.D., *1336*, col. 825. M.O. Anderson, *KKES*, 249, 263. MacAlister, *Uí Maine*, 37[93]v. M.O. Anderson, *KKES*, 266, 273, 281, 287, 292.

[91]M.O. Anderson, *KKES*, 246 n.77.

[92]Ibid., 169. Miller, "Eanfrith's," 53-4. Clancy and Márkus, *Iona*, 166-7.

[93]Skene, *CPS*, 1va, 7, 399. T.C.D., *1336*, col. 824. M.O. Anderson, *KKES*, 266, 272, 280, 287, 248, 262-263, 292. MacAlister, *Uí Maine*, 37[93]v.

[94]Clancy and Márkus, *Iona*,166-7. Skene, *CPS*,408-9.

[95]Morris, *Nennius*, 36, 77. R.E. Latham, *Revised Medieval Latin Word-List from British and Irish Sources* (London: Oxford University Press for the British Academy, 1989), 201. D.A. Simpson, *Cassell's New Latin Dictionary* (New York: Funk & Wagnalls Company, 1959), 255. M.O. Anderson, *KKES*, 171.

[96]M.O. Anderson, *KKES*, 169, 295.

[97]Skene, *CPS*, 1va, 7, 399. T.C.D., *1336*, col. 824. M.O. Anderson, *KKES*, 175, 248, 263, 266, 272-273, 280, 287, 291. MacAlister, *Uí Maine*, 37[93]v.

[98]Skene, *CPS*, 417.

[99]M.O. Anderson, *KKES*, 169, 295-296.

[100]Skene, *CPS*, 1va, 7, 400. M.O. Anderson, *KKES*, 249, 263. MacAlister, *Uí Maine*, 37[93]v.

[101]M.O. Anderson, *KKES*, 87, 266, 273, 281, 287, 291.

[102]M.O. Anderson, *KKES*, 169, 296.

[103]Skene, *CPS*, 1va, 7. M.O. Anderson, *KKES*, 248, 266, 273, 280, 287, 292.

[104]Cross, *Ancient Irish*, 16.

[105]O'Brien, *CGH*, 117, 187, 198, 250, 512, 605, 645, 734. O'Sullivan, *Leinster*, 1373, 1378. Mulchrone, *Lecan*, 213rb, 214rc, 225rc.

[106]Mac Eoin, "Irish Legend," 139.

[107]Skene, *CPS*, 473. Mac Eoin, "Legend," 139. M.O. Anderson, *KKES*, 230. Hudson, *Kings of Celtic*, 167.

[108]O'Brien, *CGH*, 330. O'Sullivan, *Leinster*, 1472.

[109]Skene, *CPS*, 400. T.C.D., *1336*, col. 825. MacAlister, *Uí Maine*, 37[93]vb. M.O. Anderson, *KKES*, 263, 268, 276, 284, 288, 291, 299, 304.

[110]Jackson, "*Albanach*," 132.

[111]Skene, *CPS*, 1ra, 6, 398. T.C.D., 1336, col. 824. M.O. Anderson, *KKES*,

246, 262. MacAlister, *Uí Maine*, 37[93]v.

[112]Miller, "Disputed," 12, 19. M. Anderson, *KKES*, 246n.77.

[113]M.O. Anderson, *KKES*, 169, 295.

[114]Skene, *CPS*, 1rb-1va, 7, 399. M.O. Anderson, *KKES*, 201, 248, 262, 266, 272, 280, 292. MacAlister, *Uí Maine*, 37[93]v. Miller, "Disputed," 20.

[115]A.O. and M.O. Anderson, *ALOC* (1961), 196. 288, 398-400, 408, 440; *ALOC* (1991), 12-13, 70-1, 124-45, 167-7.

[116]Bede, *HEGA*, Vol.I, 340-1. Bede, *EHEP*, 148.

[117]Morris, *Persons*, 22.

[118]O'Brien, *CGH*, 82, 84, 94, 130, 133, 613. O'Sullivan, *Leinster*, 1527, 1537, 1580. Mulchrone, *Lecan*, 96va, 96vd. Meyer, "Laud," 292, 301-2. FitzPatrick, "Fasciculus XV," 1832.

[119]Skene, *CPS*, 1rb, 6, 399. T.C.D., *1336*, col. 824. M.O. Anderson, *KKES*, 92-95, 247, 262. MacAlister, *Uí Maine*, 37[93]v.

[120]Herbert, *Iona, Kells*, 224, 235. Stokes, *Félire*, 58.

[121]Geoffrey of Monmouth, *History*, 54-7.

[122]Phillimore, "Pedigrees," 63.

[123]Forbes, "Vita Niniani," 140. J. and W. MacQueen, *St. Nynia*, 105.

[124]Morris, *Nennius*, 59-63. Jackson, "*Albanach*," 128. Wright, *Regum*, 1-15, 17, 35.

[125]Adomnán and Sharpe, *Life of Columba*, 334. A.O. and M.O. Anderson, *ALOC* (1961), 84-85; *ALOC* (1991), 140-5.

[126]Anderson, *ALOC* (1961), 398-402, 404-406.

[127]T.F. O'Rahilly, *EIHM*, 533-4. Jackson, "Pictish Language," 143. A.O. and M.O. Anderson, *ALOC* (1961), 84-5, 344 and (1991), xxxiii-xxxiv.

[128]M.O. Anderson, *KKES*, 169, 295.

[129]Ibid., 266, 273, 281, 287, 292.

[130]Skene, *CPS*, 1ra, 5, 397-398. T.C.D., *1336*, cols. 823-24. M.O. Anderson, *KKES*, 245, 261. MacAlister, *Uí Maine*, 37[93]va. Mulchrone, *Lecan*, 4vb, 139ra, 143rb-143va, 287ra. Atkinson, *Ballymote*, 43a.

[131]M.O. Anderson, *KKES*, 81-84. W.A. Cummins, *The Age of the Picts* (Phoenix Mills: Alan Sutton Publishing Ltd., 1995), 150-152. M. Miller, "Disputed," 12.

[132]M.O. Anderson, *KKES*, 183, 295.

[133]Geoffrey of Monmouth, *History*, 307.

[134]Wright, *Regum*, 130-132.

[135]Cross, *Ancient Irish*, 16.

[136]O'Brien, *CGH*, 516.

[137]O'Brien, *CGH*, 4, 6, 17.

[138]Mulchrone, *Lecan*, 4vb, 139ra, 143rb, 287ra. Atkinson, *Ballymote*, 43a, 203a.

[139]Jarman, *Y Gododdin*, 147 n.946.

[140]Williams, *Canu Aneirin*, 48. Jarman, *Y Gododdin*, 62-3.

[141]Williams, *Canu Aneirin*, 339 n.1211.

[142]Geoffrey of Monmouth, *History*, 309. Bromwich, *Trioedd*, 346-7.

[143]Wright, *Regum*, 62-63.

[144]Morris, *Persons*, 20. Watson, *HCPNS*, 279, 313, 336. Ó Riain, *Corpus Sanctorum*, 230. O'Sullivan, *Leinster*, VI, 1562. Mulchrone, *Lecan*, 39vb, 43vd. Atkinson, *Ballymote*, 221d. Charles Plummer, *Vitae Sanctorum Hiberniae*, 2nd. ed., Vol. I, (Dublin: Four Courts Press, 1997), 88-9. Richard Sharpe, *Medieval Irish Saints' Lives* (Oxford: Clarendon Press, 1991), 266, 370-1, 391

[145]Stokes, *Félire Óengusso*, 250.

[146]M.O. Anderson, *KKES*, 280. Bannerman, *SIHD*, 86. A.O. Anderson, *ESSH*, I, 123 n.2. Stokes, "Tigernach," 163.

[147]Suggested by Prof. W. Gillies of Edinburgh University. Bromwich, *Trioedd*, 292. O'Rahilly, *EIHM*, 354.

[148]Bromwich, *Trioedd*, 290. Morris, *Persons*, 24. Morris, *Arthur*, 174. Wade-Evans, *VSBG*, xvii, 321, 331. Phillimore, "Pedigrees," 56, 57.

[149]Wade-Evans, *VSBG*, 84.

[150]Geoffrey of Monmouth, *History*, 309. Alcock, *Arthur's, Britain*, 63. Wright, Regum, 101, 104, 109-10. Morris, *Arthur*, 111, 125, 663.

[151]Bromwich, *Trioedd*, 292-4

[152]Phillimore, "*Annales Cambriae*," 42. Wade-Evans, *VSBG*, 320.

[153]Wright, *Regum*, 145. Bromwich, *Trioedd*, 29, 144, 293.

[154]Miller, "Disputed," 10.

[155]Skene, *CPS*, 1rb, 7, 399. T.C.D., *1336*, col. 824. M.O. Anderson, *KKES*, 247, 262, 265-6, 272, 280, 287, MacAlister, *Uí Maine*, 37[93]v. Miller, "Disputed," 20.

[156]Morris, *Persons*, 25-6. Ó Riain, *Corpus Sanctorum*, 230. Watson, *Place Names*, 276. O'Sullivan, *Leinster*, VI, 1545, Mulchrone, *Lecan*, 36vc. Atkinson, *Ballymote*, 218e.

[157]A.O. and M.O. Anderson, *ALOC* (1991), 26-9, 110-15, 206-7. O'Sullivan, *Leinster*, VI, 1638. Stokes, *Félire Óengusso*, 215.

[158]Watson, *HCPNS*, 219.

[159]Hudson, *Kings of Celtic*, 4. Vernam Hull, "Conall Corc and the Corco Luigde," *Publications of the Modern Language Association of America*, Vol. 62.2 (1947), 889, 892, 894-7. Kuno Meyer, "Conall Corc and the Corco Luigde," *Anecdota from Irish Manuscripts* (1910), Vol. iii, 58-59. O'Brien, *CGH*, 195, 196, 208. O'Sullivan, *Leinster*, VI, 1375. Mulchrone, *Lecan*, 213vb-215va. Meyer, "Laud," 304, 315 n.1. T.F. O'Rahilly, *EIHM*, 370-1. Watson, *HCPNS*, 219.

[160]MacAlister, *Uí Maine*, 37[93]v. M.O. Anderson, *KKES*, 261. T.C.D., *1336*, col. 824. Skene, *CPS*, 399

[161]A.O. Anderson, *ESSH*, Vol. I, cxii-cxiii. M.O. Anderson, *KKES*, 191-2, 296.

[162]Skene, *CPS*, 1va, 7, 400. T.C.D., *1336*, col. 825. M.O. Anderson, *KKES*, 249, 263. MacAlister, *Uí Maine*, 37[93]v.

[163]Bannerman, *SIHD*, 93.

[164]Bannerman, *SIHD*, 93. Jackson, *Gaelic Notes*, 32, 35,111.

[165]Bannerman, *SIHD*, 93. Murphy, *Clonmacnoise*, 110. Stokes "Tigernach," 210 has the entry "Occis[I]ó Canonn maic Gartnain" ("killing of Cano mac Gartnáin") followed by the entry "Finnachta clericatum susceptit"

("Finnachta received into religion"). It is probable that the two entries were conflated at some point before the original of AC was translated.

[166]Binchy, *Scéla Cano*, xi, 1. M.O. Anderson, *KKES*, 154-5. Bannerman, *SIHD*, 93.

[167]Skene, *CPS*, 1ra, 6. 398. T.C.D., *1336*, col. 824. M.O. Anderson, *KKES*, 246, 262, 265, 272, 279, 287. MacAlister, *Uí Maine*, 37[93]v. Miller, "Disputed," 12, 19.

[168]Jackson, "Pictish Language," 145. H.M. Chadwick, *Early Scotland* (Cambridge: Cambridge University Press, 1949), 7-8.

[169]Bede, *HEGA*, Vol. I 32-5. Bede, *EHEP*, 50-1.

[170]Bede, *HEGA*, Vol. I 32-5. Bede, *EHEP*, 50-1. Morris, *Nennius*, 64-65. Wright, *Regum*, 48-49.

[171]Skene, *CPS*, 1ra, 6, 398. T.C.D., *1336*, col. 824. M.O. Anderson, *KKES*, 246, 261-262, 265, 271, 279. MacAlister, *Uí Maine*, 37[93]v. Miller, "Disputed," 12, 19.

[172]M.O. Anderson, *KKES*, 169, 297.

[173]Chadwick, *Scotland*, 85, 85 n.3.

[174]Skene, *CPS*, 1va, 7-8, 400. T.C.D., *1336*, col. 825. M.O. Anderson, *KKES*, 249, 263, 266. MacAlister, *Uí Maine*, 37[93]v. Smyth, *Warlords*, 186. M.O. Anderson, *KKES*, 194, 273, 281, 287, 292.

[175]Jackson, "*Albanach*," 128, 132.

[176]Chadwick, *Scotland*, 2, 2 n.3.

[177]Skene, *CPS*, 1ra, 4, 396. T.C.D., *1336*, col. 823. M.O. Anderson, *KKES*, 245. MacAlister, *Uí Maine*, 37[93]v. Mulchrone, *Lecan*, 4vb, 139ra, 143rb, 287ra. Atkinson, *Ballymote*, 43a, 203a.

[178]F.T. Wainwright, *Problem*, 46-47. Skene, *CPS*, 135-137. M.O. Anderson, *KKES*, 240-3.

[179]Chadwick, *Scotland*, 7-8.

[180]FitzPatrick, "Fasciculus XV," 1816. Bromwich, *Trioedd*, 293-294.

[181]MacAlister, *Uí Maine*, 37[93]va. M.O. Anderson, *KKES*, 261. Skene, *CPS*, 398.

[182]Jackson, "*Albanach*," 128. Miller, "Disputed," 12.

[183]O'Rahilly, *EIHM*, 354. Bromwich, *Trioedd*, 292-294. Alex Woolf and Séamus Mac Mathúna pointed out that AU 632 (Mac Airt, *Ulster*, 116) uses "Bellum Cathloen" for "Battle of Cadwallon." This verifies O'Rahilly's suggestion.

[184]A.O. Anderson, *ESSH*, Vol. I, cxiii.

[185]O'Brien, *CGH*, 328, 591. O'Sullivan, *Leinster* VI,1471.

[186]MacAlister, *Uí Maine*, 37[93]v. M. Anderson, *KKES*, 263, 267, 274, 283, 289. Skene, *CPS*, 400. T.C.D., *1336*, col. 825.

[187]Jackson, "*Albanach*," 128, 132.

[188]Morris, *Persons*, 163. MacQueen, *St. Nynia*.

[189]Wade-Evans, *VSBG*, xvii, 323,

[190]Ibid., 82-4, 152.

[191]Bromwich and Evans, *Culhwch*, 1-8, 24, 38, 42, 215. Ford, "Culhwch," 152, 156-7. Bromwich, *Trioedd*, 159-60, 201, 227.

[192]Morris, *Persons*, 164. Bromwich, *Trioedd*, 159-60. Kenneth Jackson, *Language and History in Early Britain* (Dublin: Four Courts Press, 1994), 306.

[193]Watson, *HCPNS*, 108.

[194]M.O. Anderson, *KKES*, 245. MacAlister, *Uí Maine*, 37[93]v. Skene, *CPS*, 396. Van Hamel, *Bretnach*, 82. Mulchrone, *Lecan*, 4vb, 139ra, 143rb, 287ra. Atkinson, *Ballymote*, 43a, 203a.

[195]Wainwright, *Problem*, 46-7. Skene, *CPS*, 136-7. Chadwick, *Scotland*, 2, 38-9. M.O. Anderson, *KKES*, 143, 240-3.

[196]Morris, *Persons*, 29.

[197]Herbert, *Iona, Kells*, 73. Mac Airt, *Ulster*, 320.

[198]Webb and Farmer, *Age of Bede*, 31, 34.

[199]Bede, *HEGA*, Vol. II, 96-9, 324-61, 382-3, 388-9. Bede, *EHEP*, 234, 308-20, 329-30.

[200]Miller, "Disputed," 19, 21.

[201]Geoffrey of Monmouth, *History*, 312. Wright, *Regum*, 130-2.

[202]A.O. Anderson, *ESSH*, Vol. I, cxii-cxiii. M.O. Anderson, *KKES*, 169, 304.

[203]O'Brien, *CGH*, 328. O'Sullivan, *Leinster*, 1471.

[204]MacAlister, *Uí Maine*, 37[93]v. M.O. Anderson, *KKES*, 263, 266-7, 273-4, 282-3, 287-8, 290, 292. T.C.D., *1336*, col. 825. Skene, *CPS*, 400.

[205]Jackson, "*Albanach*," 132.

[206]Chadwick, *Scotland*, 1.

[207]O'Brien, *CGH*, 667, 325. Chadwick, *Scotland*, 105-6, 118. Mulchrone, *Lecan*, 126rb, 130vb. Meyer, "Laud,"335.

[208]Skene, *CPS*, 1ra, 4, 396. T.C.D., *1336*, col.823. M.O. Anderson, *KKES*, 245, 265, 271, 279, 286. MacAlister, *Uí Maine*, 37[93]v. Mulchrone, *Lecan*, 4vb, 139ra, 143rb, 287ra. Atkinson, *Ballymote*, 43a, 203a. Miller, "Disputed," 19.

[209]Chadwick, *Scotland*, 2. R.I.A., *Dictionary*,116.

[210]A.O. Anderson, *ESSH*, Vol. I, cxii. M.O. Anderson, *KKES*, 296.

[211]Skene, *CPS*, 1va, 7 has "Nectu nepos uerd." M.O. Anderson, *KKES*, 248 reads this as "Nectu nepos Uerb." MacAlister, *Uí Maine*, 37[93]v. M.O. Anderson, *KKES*, 248 n.104, 262, 266, 272, 280, 287, 292. T.C.D., *1336*, col. 824. Skene, *CPS*, 399.

[212]M.O. Anderson, *KKES*, 175.

[213]Smyth, *Warlords*, 177. A.O. Anderson, *ESSH*, 214 n.3.

[214]M.O. Anderson, *KKES*, 169, 296.

[215]Skene, *CPS*, 1va, 7, 400. T.C.D., *1336*, col.825. M.O. Anderson, *KKES*, 249, 263. MacAlister, *Uí Maine*, 37[93]v. Van Hamel, *Bretnach*, 86.

[216]M.O. Anderson, *KKES*, 87, 87 n.44, 266, 273, 280-281, 287, 292.

[217]Skene, *CPS*, 1ra, 6, 398. T.C.D., *1336*, col.824. MacAlister, *Uí Maine*, 37[93]v. M.O. Anderson, *KKES*, 245,261.

[218]M. Miller, "Disputed," 12. M.O. Anderson, *KKES*, 245 n.70. Chadwick, *Scotland*, 7 n.5. Jackson, "Pictish Language," 137.

[219]Skene, *CPS*, 1ra, 4, 396. T.C.D., *1336*, col.823. M.O. Anderson, *KKES*,

245. MacAlister, *Uí Maine*, 37[93]v. Mulchrone, *Lecan*, 4vb, 139ra, 143rb, 287ra. Atkinson, *Ballymote*, 43a, 203a.

[220]Wainwright, *Problem*, 46, 46 n.5. Skene, *CPS*, 135-137. Chadwick, *Scotland*, 38-39. M.O. Anderson, *KKES*, 82, 240-3.

[221]O'Brien, *CGH*, 551.

[222]O'Sullivan, *Leinster*, 1442. Mulchrone, *Lecan*, 127vb. Meyer, "Laud," 329. O'Brien, *CGH*, 551, 557, 579.

[223]Geoffrey of Monmouth, *History*, 314.

[224]Wright, *Regum*, 101, 104.

[225]Morris, *Persons*, 34. Hogan, *Onomasticon*, 217-218. Adomnán and Sharpe, *Life of Columba*, 247. Watson, *HCPNS*, 279-80.

[226]O'Brien, *CGH*, 99, 163. O'Sullivan, *Leinster*, 1528, 1595, 1653, 1660, 1674. Meyer, "Laud," 298, 301. FitzPatrick, "Fasciculus XV," 1832.

[227]Atkinson, *Ballymote*, 203a. Skene, *CPS*, 1rb-1va, 7, 399. M.O. Anderson, *KKES*, 248, 263. MacAlister, *Uí Maine*, 37[93]v. M.O. Anderson, *KKES*, 266, 272, 280, 287. Miller, "Disputed," 20.

[228]Forbes, "Vita Niniani," 139-40. J. and W. MacQueen, *St. Nynia*, 104. Clancy and Markús, *Iona*, 96, 104-105, 112-113, 117, 118. A.O. and M.O. Anderson, *ALOC* (1961), 194-196, 348-352, 386-388, 455-460, 466; *ALOC* (1991), 12-13, 108-9, 132-3, 138-48, 178-81. Herbert, *Iona, Kells*, 236, 237. Stokes, *Félire Óengusso*, 139.

[229]Bede, *HEGA*, Vol. I, 338-43 and Vol. II, 236-7. Bede, *EHEP*, 148-9, 279. Morris, *Nennius*, 62.

[229a]Watson, *HCPNS*, 281. A.O. Anderson, *ESSH*, Vol. I, 31 Stokes, *Félire Óengusso*, 216.

[229b]O'Sullivan, *Leinster*, VI, 1639.

[230]Chadwick, *Scotland*, xx, 101.

[231]O'Brien, *CGH*, 87, 137, 154-155, 280, 283, 321, 324-25, 509, 644, 677. O'Sullivan, *Leinster*, 1371, 1409, 1445, 1449, 1483. Mulchrone, *Lecan*, 114rb, 126va. Meyer, "Laud," 332, 335. FitzPatrick, "Fasciculus XV," 1828, 1855.

[232]Meid, *TBF*, 13, 15.

[233]Hull, "Corco Luigde," 887. Byrne, *Irish Kings*, 291. O'Brien, *CGH*, 565. For a detailed analysis of the tales concerning Conall Corc, see David Sproule, "Politics and Pure Narrative in the Stories about Corc of Cashel," *Ériu*, Vol. xxxvi (1985), 11-28.

[234]Hull, "Corco Luigde," 889, 894-7, 897 n.100. Meyer, "Conall Corc," 57-9. O'Brien, *CGH*, 195, 198, 208, 210-11, 215, 219, 534, 680, 682, 678, 710. O'Sullivan, *Leinster*, 1375, 1378, 1415, 1417, 1382. Mulchrone, *Lecan*, 213vb-217r. Meyer., "Laud," 304, 315n.1

[235]Hull, "Exile of Conall," 940-2. Hull, "Corco Luigde," 895.

[236]A.O. Anderson, *ESSH*, Vol. I, 255 n.1.

[237]Jackson, "*Albanach*," 132. M.O. Anderson, *KKES*, 191-3, 229, 296.

[237a]M.O. Anderson, *KKES*, 154. Bannerman, *SIHD*, 66

[238]Mac Airt, *Ulster*, 128.

[239]Morris, *Persons*, 39.

[240]Bede, *HEGA*, Vol.I, 52-3. Bede, *EHEP*, 57. Wright, *Regum*, 62, 64.

[241]Bromwich, *Trioedd*, 131.

[242]Ibid., 316.

[242a]Morris, *Persons*, 39-40. Watson, *HCPNS*, 189-9, 303.

[243]Morris, *Persons*, 39. Geoffrey of Monmouth, *History*, 315.

[244]Bede, *HEGA*, Vol.I, 52-3. Bede, *EHEP*, 57. Morris, *Nennius*, 65. Wright, *Regum*, 61-62. Bromwich, *Trioedd*, 131.

[245]A.O. Anderson, *ESSH*, Vol. I., 180.

[246]Morris, *Persons*, 41-42. Adomnán and Sharpe, *Life of Columba*, 266 n.74. Watson, *HCPNS*, 282.

[247]O'Sullivan, *Leinster*, 1562, 1654.

[248]A.O. and M.O. Anderson, *ALOC* (1961), 222-4, 440-6, 500; *ALOC* (1991), 28-31, 164-71, 206-7. Herbert, *Iona, Kells*, 232. Stokes, *Félire Óengusso*, 141.

[249]Alcock, *Arthur's Britain*, 129. Morris, *Arthur*, 18, 416. Hughes, *Celtic Britain*, 50, 117. Smyth, *Warlords*, 16-18. David Dumville, "Coroticus," 107-15.

[250]Phillimore, "*Annales Cambriae*," 44.

[251]A.B.E. Hood, *St. Patrick* in *Arthurian Period Sources*, Vol. 9, in John Morris, gen. ed., History from the Sources (Chichester: Phillimore, 1978),35,37.

[252]Chadwick, *Scotland*, 85.

[253]O'Brien, *CGH*, 14-15, 569. O'Sullivan, *Leinster*, VI, 138-60. Mulchrone, *Lecan*, 92r, 93r.

[254]Murphy, *Clonmacnoise*, 28. Ó Corráin and Cournane, *CELT Four Masters*, Vol. I, 20. Best and O'Brien, *Leinster*, Vol. I, 57.

[255]Murphy, *Clonmacnoise*, 28 n.7. O'Rahilly, *EIHM*, 92-94.

[256]R.I.A., *Dictionary*, 159.

[257]Chadwick, *Scotland*, 2.

[258]M.O. Anderson, "The List of Kings: II. Kings of the Picts," in *Scottish Historical Review*, Vol. 29 (1949), 14 n.6 suggests that "nia Cruithni" ("nephew of Cruithne") may have been "nia Cruithne" ("champion of the Cruithni").

[259]Skene, *CPS*, 1ra, 4, 396. T.C.D., *1336*, col.823. M.O. Anderson, *KKES*, 84, 245, 265, 271, 279, 286, 292. MacAlister, *Uí Maine*, 37[93]v. Mulchrone, *Lecan*, 4vb, 139ra, 143rb, 287ra. Atkinson, *Ballymote*, 43a, 203a. Miller, "Disputed," 19.

[260]Jackson, "Pictish Language," 158-159. M.O. Anderson, *KKES*, 84.

[261]Cross, *Ancient Irish*, 281.

[262]Chadwick, *Scotland*, 101-102.

[263]O'Brien, *CGH*, 121, 284, 285, 645. O'Sullivan, *Leinster*, 1371, 1450. Meyer, "Laud," 333.

[264]Alcock, *Arthur's*, 125-9. Chadwick, *Scotland*, 4, 73.

[265]Phillimore, "*Annales Cambriae*," 42, 44, 49-50, 52-54. Phillimore, "Pedigrees," 58, 60, 62-63. Wade-Evans, *VSBG*, 320, 323.

[266]Wade-Evans, *VSBG*, 118-119, Morris, *Arthur*, 204.

[267]Morris, *Nennius*,65, 79. Bromwich, *Trioedd*, 107, 201, 288.

[268]Chadwick, *Scotland*, 101-102.

[269]O'Brien, *CGH*, 120. R.I.A., *Dictionary*, 128. O'Brien, *CGH*, 154, 182,

190. O'Sullivan, *Leinster*,1373-4.

[270]Morris, *Persons*,43. Webb and Farmer, *Age of Bede*, 9-10.

[271]Colgrave, *Lives of Cuthbert*, 82-5, 122-3, 192-5, 238-9. O'Sullivan, *Leinster*, 1607.

[272]Bede, *HEGA*, Vol. II, 160-1. Bede, *EHEP*, 254, 255-66. M.O. Anderson, *KKES*, 16. Morris, *Nennius*, 80.

[273]Morris, *Persons*, 46. Watson, *HCPNS*, 275.

[274]O'Sullivan, *Leinster*, 1579.

[275]Skene, *CPS*, 1rb, 6, 399. T.C.D., *1336*, col. 824. Anderson, *KKES*, 247, 262. Watson, *HCPNS*, 275.

[276]Skene, *CPS*, 1ra, 6, 398. T.C.D., *1336*, col.824. M.O. Anderson, *KKES*, 245-246, 261. MacAlister, *Uí Maine*, 37[93]v. M.O. Anderson, *KKES*, 265, 271, 279.

[277]M.O. Anderson, *KKES*, 246 n.72. Miller, "Diputed," 12.

[278]The name is unclear in facsimile in Skene, *CPS*, 1ra. Skene, *CPS*, 6 has "Deo ardivois." M.O. Anderson, *KKES*, 246 has "Deo Artíuois." MacAlister, *Uí Maine*, 37[93]v. M.O. Anderson, *KKES*, 246, 261. Skene, *CPS*, 398. Miller, "Disputed," 12.

[279]Skene, *CPS*, 1ra, 6, 398. T.C.D., *1336*, col.824. M.O. Anderson, *KKES*, 245, 261, 265, 271, 279, 287. MacAlister, *Uí Maine*, 37[93]v. Miller, "Disputed," 12,19.

[280]Skene, *CPS*, 1ra, 6, 398. T.C.D., *1336*, col.824. M.O. Anderson, *KKES*, 245, 261, 265, 271, 279. MacAlister, *Uí Maine*, 37[93]v. Miller, "Disputed," 12, 19.

[281]M.O. Anderson, *KKES*, 286-287.

[282]Miller, "Disputed," 19. Chadwick, *Scotland*, 7.

[283]A.O. Anderson, *ESSH*, Vol. I, cxiii.

[284]MacAlister, *Uí Maine*, 37[93]v. M.O. Anderson, *KKES*, 263, 267, 274, 283, 288, 290. T.C.D., *1336*, col. 825. Skene, *CPS*, 400.

[285]Jackson, "*Albanach*," 132.

[286]Cross and Slover, *Ancient Irish*, 16.

[287]O'Brien, *CGH*, 186. Mulchrone, *Lecan*, 213ra.

[288]Murphy, *Clonmacnoise*, 25-6. Hennessy, *Chronicum*, 12-13

[288a]Bannerman, *SIHD*, 114. Watson, *HCPNS*, 283, 338.

[288b]O'Sullivan, *Leinster* VI, 1688.

[288c]O'Sullivan, *Leinster* VI, 1615. Stokes, *Félire Óengusso*, 107.

[289]M.O. Anderson, *KKES*, 265, 272, 279, 287. Miller, "Disputed," 19.

[290]M.O. Anderson, *KKES*, 169, 299.

[291]Skene, *CPS*, 1va, 7, 399-400. T.C.D., *1336*, cols. 824-5.M.O. Anderson, *KKES*, 249, 263. MacAlister, *Uí Maine*, 37[93]v.

[292]M.O. Anderson, *KKES*, 193, 169, 299.

[293]Skene, *CPS*, 1va, 8, 400. T.C.D., *1336*, col. 825. M.O. Anderson, *KKES*, 193, 249, 263, 266, 273, 281, 287, 292. MacAlister, *Uí Maine*, 37[93]v

[294]M.O. Anderson, *KKES*, 169.

[295]Skene, *CPS*, 1va, 7, 399., T.C.D., *1336*, col. 824. M.O. Anderson,

KKES, 248, 262, 266, 272,280, 287, 292. MacAlister, *Uí Maine*, 37[93]v.

[296]Miller, "Disputed," 10.

[297]Skene, *CPS*, 1rb, 399. T.C.D., *1336*, col. 824. M.O. Anderson, *KKES*, 247, 262, 266, 272, 280, 287, 292. MacAlister, *Uí Maine*, 37[93]v.

[298]Miller, "Disputed," 20.

[299]Skene, *CPS*, 1rb, 7, 399. T.C.D., *1336*, col. 824. M.O. Anderson, *KKES*, 247-248, 262, 266, 272, 280, 287. MacAlister, *Uí Maine*, 37[93]v. Miller, *Disputed*, 20.

[300]M.O. Anderson, *KKES*, 169, 299.

[301]Skene, *CPS*, 1va, 7, 400. T.C.D., *1336*, col. 825. M.O. Anderson, *KKES*, 249, 263, 266, 237, 281, 287, 292.

[302]Miller, "Disputed," 10.

[303]Skene, *CPS*, 1rb, 7, 399. T.C.D., *1336*, col.824. M.O. Anderson, *KKES*, 247, 262, 265, 272, 280, 287. MacAlister, *Uí Maine*, 37[93]v. Miller, "Disputed," 20.

[304]Miller, "Disputed," 10. Skene, *CPS*, 1rb, 7, 399. T.C.D., *1336*, col. 824. M.O. Anderson, *KKES*, 247, 262, 272, 280, 287. MacAlister, *Uí Maine*, 37[93]v. Miller, *Disputed*, 20.

[305]Jackson, "Pictish Language," 140, 163-165.

[305a]Morris, *Persons*, 51. Watson, *HCPNS*, 316-18. A.O. Anderson, *ESSH*, Vol. II, 174n.5. Jackson, *Gaelic Notes*, 4-7.

[305b]Jackson, *Gaelic Notes*, 19, 30, 33, 96-97.

[306]T.F. O'Rahilly, *EIHM*, 364 n.1.

[307]Miller, "Disputed," 10.

[308]Skene, *CPS*, 1ra-1rb, 6-7, 398. T.C.D., *1336*, col.824. M.O. Anderson, *KKES*, 247, 262, 265, 272, 280, 287. MacAlister, *Uí Maine*, 37[93]v. Miller, "Disputed," 20.

[309]Alcock, *Arthur's Britain*, 161. R.I. Best and Osborn Bergin, eds., *Lebor na hUidre*, 3rd ed. (Dublin: Dublin Institute for Advanced Studies, 1970), 315-16. Bromwich, *Trioedd*, 33, 37, 45, 103-4, 189, 192, 193, 329-333, 330n.2. Cross and Slover, *Ancient Irish*, 153, 168-19.

[310]M.O. Anderson, *KKES*, 169.

[311]Ibid., 266, 273, 281, 287, 292.

[312]J. and W. MacQueen, *St. Nynia*, 43.

[313]J. and W. MacQueen, *St. Nynia*, 42-44. Morris, *Persons*, 105. A.O. Anderson, *ESSH*, Vol. I, 7-8, 7 n.3. O'Sullivan, *Leinster*, 1665, 1697. Hogan, *Onomasticon*, 645. MacAlister, *Uí Maine*, 55[113]vb40-44.

[314]A.O. Anderson, *ESSH*, Vol. I, cxii, 177 n.7. Bannerman, *SIHD*, 94, 103.

[315]A.O. Anderson, *ESSH*, Vol. I, cxii.

[316]M.O. Anderson, *KKES*, 229, 265, 271, 282, 286, 290, 300.

[317]A.O. Anderson, *ESSH*, Vol.I, cxi. M.O. Anderson, *KKES*, 172, 300. Miller, "Eanfrith's," 53.

[318]Skene, *CPS*, 1va, 7, 399. T.C.D., *1336*, col.824. M.O. Anderson, *KKES*, 248, 262, 266, 272, 280, 292. MacAlister, *Uí Maine*, 37[93]v. Van Hamel, *Bretnach*,85.

[319]Morris, *Nennius*, 69.

[320]Morris, *Persons*, 53. Dáibhí Ó Cróinin, "Is the Augsburg Gospel Codex a Northumbrian Manuscript," in Gerald Bonner, *St Cuthbert*, 194.

[321]Bede, *HEGA*, Vol. I, 342-45, 486-89. Bede, *HEGA*, Vol. II, 160-61, 234-41, 360-65, 368-69, 382-83. Bede, *EHEP*, 149, 195-6, 254, 278-80, 321-22, 323, 328.

[322]A.O.Anderson, *ESSH*, Vol.I, cxi. Miller, "Eanfrith's,"53.

[323]A.O. and M.O. Anderson, *ALOC* (1961), 460; *ALOC* (1991), 178-9. Colgrave, *Lives of Cuthbert*, 102-105, 110-111, 122-23, 234-29, 242-3, 248-9. Webb and Farmer, "Life of Wilfrid,"125, 127-9, 132, 142-4, 149, 154.

[324]Bede, *HEGA*, Vol. I, 450-51. Bede, *HEGA*, Vol. II, 32-35, 68-71, 96-99, 102-13, 118-119, 160-167, 176-77. Bede, *EHEP*, 183, 212, 224-225, 234, 236, 240, 254-256, 259. Morris, *Nennius*, 77, 78, 80.

[325]Chadwick, *Scotland*, 109.

[326]Chadwick, *Scotland*, 101-102, 101 n.2.

[327]A.O. Anderson, *ESSH*, Vol. I, cxi.

[328]Bede, *HEGA*, Vol. I, 244-303, 314-15. Bede, *EHEP*, 117-136, 140. Morris, *Nennius*, 77, 78, 79. Bromwich, *Trioedd*, 47, 167, 182. Wright, *Regum*, 136-8, 140-2.

[329]O'Brien, *CGH*, 270. O'Sullivan, *Leinster*, 1438, 1439. Mulchrone, *Lecan*, 114r. Meyer, "Laud," 325, 326.

[330]Ó Corráin and Cournane, *CELT Four Masters*, 34.

[331]Skene, *CPS*, 1ra, 396. T.C.D., *1336*, col. 823. M.O. Anderson, *Kingship*, 245. MacAlister, *Uí Maine*, 37[93]v.

[332]Chadwick, *Scotland*, 2-3. O'Rahilly, *EIHM*, 345. M. O. Anderson, *KKES*, 81.

[333]Cross and Slover, *Ancient Irish*, 17 n.1.

[334]Murphy, *Clonmacnoise*, 18, 26.

[335]A.O. Anderson, *ESSH*, Vol. I, 249, 249 n.3.

[336]Geoffrey of Monmouth, *History*, 321.

[337]Wright, *Regum*, 131-2.

[338]Todd, *Irish Nennius*, 134 n.t. Morris, *Persons*, 78.

[338a]O'Sullivan, *Leinster* VI, 1601. Stokes, *Félire Óengusso*, 35.

[339]M.O. Anderson, *KKES*, 169, 194-5, 294.

[340]Skene, *CPS*, 1va, 7, 399-400. T.C.D., *1336*, col. 824-5. M.O. Anderson, *KKES*, 87, 232, 249, 263, 265, 271, 282, 286, 289, MacAlister, *Uí Maine*, 37[93]v. A.O. Anderson, *ESSH*, Vol. I, cxxii.

[341]H.M. Chadwick, *Scotland*, 127. A.O. Anderson, *ESSH*, Vol. I, cxii. M.O. Anderson, *KKES*, 83.

[342]M.O. Anderson, *KKES*, 169, 294.

[343]A.O. Anderson, *ESSH*, Vol. I, 249 n.4.

[344]Skene, *CPS*, 1va, 7, 400. T.C.D., *1336*, col. 825. M.O. Anderson, *KKES*, 63, 86-7, 249, 263, 266, 273, 281, 287, 292. MacAlister, *Uí Maine*, 37[93]v.

[345]T.F. O'Rahilly, *EIHM*, 364 n.1.

[346]A.O. and M.O. Anderson, *ALOC* (1961), 492; (1991), 200-3.

[347]A.O. and M.O. Anderson, *ALOC* (1961), 145, 160. Jackson, "Pictish

Language," 142-3.

[348]A.O. Anderson,*ESSH*, Vol.I, cxii, M.O. Anderson, *KKES*, 149.

[349]O'Brien, *CGH*, 328. O'Sullivan, *Leinster* VI, 1471.

[350]M.O. Anderson, *KKES*, 264, 270, 281, 286, 290.

[351]A.O. and M.O. Anderson, *ALOC* (1961), 228; (1991), 32-3.

[352]Bannerman, *SIHD*, 41, Jackson, "*Albanach*," 130.

[353]A.O. and M.O. Anderson, *ALOC* (19610, 46.

[354]M.O. Anderson, *KKES*, 9.

[355]O'Brien, *CGH*, 165, 328-9, 615, 705, 718. Mulchrone, *Lecan*, 61vb. O'Sullivan, *Leinster*, 1471.

[356]Bannerman, *SIHD*, 41. Jackson, "*Albanach*," 128.

[357]M.O. Anderson, *KKES*, 9.

[358]O'Brien, *CGH*, 328, 329. O'Sullivan, *Leinster*, 1471.

[359]M.O. Anderson, *KKES*, 264, 270, 281, 286, 290.

[360]Bannerman, *SIHD*, 41. Jackson, "*Albanach*," 130.

[361]Todd, *Irish Nennius*, 120 n.a and n.e.

[362]Mulchrone, *Lecan*, 4vb, 287ra. Atkinson, *Ballymote*, 43a.

[363]Cross, *Ancient Irish*, 16.

[364]O'Brien, *CGH*, 4, 6, 10, 17, 123, 129, 192, 668. O'Sullivan, *Leinster*, 1370, 1401. Mulchrone, *Lecan*, 53rc, 213v. Meyer, "Laud," 291, 337. FitzPatrick, "Fasciculus XV," 1815.

[365]Murphy, *Clonmacnoise*, 21, 23, 27-30. Hennessy, *Chronicum*, 12.

[366]T.F. O'Rahilly, *EIHM*, 487.

[367]Jackson, "*Albanach*," 128. T.F. O'Rahilly, *EIHM*, 537.

[368]M.O. Anderson, *KKES*, 8-9, Smyth, *Warlords*, 110.

[369]O'Brien, *CGH*, 4, 6-7, 17, 514. Mulchrone, *Lecan*, 214vb.

[370]Mulchrone, *Lecan*, 4vb, 139ra, 143rb, 287ra. Atkinson, *Ballymote*, 43a, 203a.

[371]Hogan, *Onamasticon*, 407.

[372]Hull "Corco Luigde," 894-5. Meyer, "Conall Corc," 58. O'Brien, *CGH*, 195, 629. O'Sullivan, *Leinster*, 1375. Mulchrone, *Lecan*, 213v.

[373]Hull, "Exile of Conall," 940, 941.

[374]M.O. Anderson, *KKES*, 185, 189.

[375]Adomnán and Sharpe, *Life of Columba*, 22. A.O. and M.O. Anderson, *ALOC* (1961), 376-378; *ALOC* (1991), 126-9.

[376]Bannerman, *SIHD*, 73-75.

[377]Murphy, *Clonmacnoise*, 25-26.

[378]M.O. Anderson, *KKES*, 228, 264, 270, 281, 286, 290, 298.

[379]Bannerman, *SIHD*, 41. Jackson, "*Albanach*," 130.

[380]Morris, *Persons*, 57. Watson, *HCPNS*, 317, 322-23.

[381]Morris, *Persons*, 57. Watson, *HCPNS*, 322-323. O'Sullivan, *Leinster*, Vol. VI, 1631.

[382]O'Rahilly, *EIHM*, 345. M.O. Anderson, *KKES*, 149. Byrne, *Irish Kings*, 287.

[383]O'Brien, *CGH*, 155, 323, 515, 636. O'Sullivan, *Leinster*, 1449, 1468. Mulchrone, *Lecan*, 126ra. Meyer, "Laud," 335.

[384]Morris, *Persons*, 57.

[385]O'Rahilly, *EIHM*, 95 n.2.

[386]O'Brien, *CGH*, 277, 323, 324, 501, 534, 535, 628, 679, 716. O'Sullivan, *Leinster*, 1369, 1440, 1449, 1469. Mulchrone, *Lecan*, 115ra, 126ra. Meyer, "Laud," 327, 335.

[387]M.O. Anderson, *KKES*, 265, 272, 279, 287. Miller, "Disputed," 19.

[388]Cross and Slover, *Ancient Irish*, 20.

[389]Chadwick, *Scotland*, 2.

[390]Skene, *CPS*, 1ra, 4, 396. T.C.D., *1336*, col. 823. M.O. Anderson, *KKES*, 240-3, 245. MacAlister, *Uí Maine*, 37[93]v. Atkinson, *Ballymote*, 43a, 203a. Wainwright, *Problem*, 46-7. Skene, *CPS*, 135-7. Mulchrone, *Lecan*, 4vb, 139ra, 143rb, 278ra.

[391]Chadwick, *Scotland*, 2.

[392]Skene, *CPS*, 1ra, 4, 396. T.C.D., *1336*, col. 823. M.O. Anderson, *KKES*, 240-3, 245. MacAlister, *Uí Maine*, 37[93]v. Mulchrone, *Lecan*, 4vb, 139ra, 143rb, 287ra. Atkinson, *Ballymote*, 43a, 203a. Wainwright, *Problem*, 46-47. Skene, *CPS*, 135-137. Chadwick, *Scotland*, 38-39.

[393]O'Brien, *CGH*, 270, 275, 645-646. O'Sullivan, *Leinster*, 1438-39. Mulchrone, *Lecan*, 114ra. Meyer, "Laud," 325-326.

[394]Morris, *Persons*, 58-59. Watson, *HCPNS*, 285-287. O'Sullivan, *Leinster*, Vol. VI, 1606. Stokes, *Félire Óengusso*, 82. Plummer, *V. Sanctorum Hiberniae*, Vol.I, xxxi-xxxii.

[395]Morris, *Persons*, 58-59. O'Sullivan, *Leinster*, VI, 1575, 1635. Mulchrone, *Lecan*, 39vb. Watson, *HCPNS*, 272-273. Ó Riain, *Corpus Sanctorum*, 227. Stokes, *Félire Óengusso*, 196.

[396]Adomnán and Sharpe, *Life of Columba*, 296. A.O. and M.O. Anderson, *ALOC* (1961), 278-282; *ALOC* (1991), 64-7.

[397]H.M. Chadwick, *Scotland*, 99-100.

[398]Mac Airt, *Ulster*, 167. M.O. Anderson, *KKES*, 169.

[399]Morris, *Persons*, 65. Watson, *HCPNS*, 304. O'Sullivan, *Leinster* VI, 1562, 1646.

[400]Morris, *Persons*, 65-6. Watson, *HCPNS*, 284-5. O'Sullivan, *Leinster* VI, 1599. Stokes, *Félire Óengusso*, 34.

[401]Watson, *HCPNS*, 107-8.

[402]Skene, *CPS*, 1ra, 4, 396. T.C.D., *1336*, col. 823. M.O. Anderson, *KKES*, 245. MacAlister, *Uí Maine*, 37[93]v. Mulchrone, *Lecan*, 4vb, 139ra, 143rb, 287ra. Atkinson, *Ballymote*, 43a, 203a.

[403]Wainwright, *Problem*, 46. Skene, *CPS*, 135-7. H.M. Chadwick, *Scotland*, 38-9. M.O. Anderson, *KKES*, 240-3.

[404]Cross and Slover, *Ancient Irish*, 17 n.1.

[405]Murphy, *Clonmacnoise*, 18, 26.

[406]Chadwick, *Scotland*, 2.

[407]Skene, *CPS*, 1ra, 4, 396. T.C.D., *1336*, col. 823. M.O. Anderson, *KKES*, 245. MacAlister, *Uí Maine*, 37[93]v. Mulchrone, *Lecan*, 4vb, 139ra, 287ra. Atkinson, *Ballymote*, 43a, 203a.

[408]Wainwright, *Problem*, 46-7. Skene, *CPS*, 135-7. H.M. Chadwick,

Scotland, 38-9. M.O. Anderson, *KKES*, 240-3.

[409]Meid, *TBF*, 13, 15, 73.

[410]A.O. Anderson, *ESSH*, Vol.I, 86. Miller, "Disputed,"10.

[411]Skene, *CPS*, 1rb,7, 399, T.C.D., *1336*, col. 824. M.O. Anderson, *KKES*, 248, 262, 266,272, 280, 287. MacAlister, *Uí Maine*, 37[93]v. Miller, "Disputed," 20.

[412]Chadwick, *Scotland*, 14. Wainwright, *Problem*, 21. M.O. Anderson, *KKES*, 91 n.55.

[413]Bannerman, *SIHD*, 42.

[414]Miller,"Disputed," 10.

[415]Skene, *CPS*, 1rb, 7, 399. T.C.D., *1336*,col. 824. M.O. Anderson, *KKES*, 247, 262, 272, 280, 287. MacAlister, *Uí Maine*, 37[93]v. Miller, "Disputed," 20. Chadwick, *Scotland*, 11.

[416]M.O. Anderson, *KKES*, 169.

[417]Skene, *CPS*, 1va, 7, 399. M. Anderson, *KKES*, 87n.44,248, 262, 266, 272, 280, 287, 292. MacAlister, *Uí Maine*, 37[93]v.

[418]Miller, "Disputed," 10.

[419]Skene, *CPS*, 1rb, 7, 399. T.C.D., *1336*, col.824. M.O. Anderson, *KKES*, 247, 262, 265-6, 272, 280,287. MacAlister, *Uí Maine*, 37[93]v. Miller, "Disputed,"20.

[420]Skene, *CPS*, 1ra, 6, 398. T.C.D., *1336*, col.824. M.O. Anderson, *KKES*, 246, 262, 265, 272, 279-280, 287. MacAlister, *Uí Maine*, 37[93]v. Miller, "Disputed," 12,19.

[421]A.O. Anderson, *ESSH*, Vol. I, 179 n.5.

[422]Binchy, *Scéla Cano*, 1. M.O. Anderson, *KKES*, 154. Bannerman, *SIHD*, 93.

[423]T.F. O'Rahilly, *EIHM*, 395 n.4, 361 n.1. M.O. Anderson, *KKES*, 154. Bannerman, *SIHD*, 92-93.

[424]M.O. Anderson, *KKES*, 154, 169, 172. Bannerman, *SIHD*, 92-93.

[425]Skene, *CPS*, 1va, 7, 399. T.C.D., *1336*, col. 824. M.O. Anderson, *KKES*, 248, 262, 266, 272, 280, 280. MacAlister, *Uí Maine*, 37[93]v.

[426]A.O. Anderson, *ESSH*, Vol. I, 178 n.4. Bannerman, *SIHD*, 92-93. M.O. Anderson, *KKES*, 154, 172.

[427]Skene, *CPS*, 1ra, 6. M.O. Anderson, *KKES*, 247, 262, 265, 270, 279, 287. MacAlister, *Uí Maine*, 37[93]v. Miller, "Disputed," 12, 19.

[428]"Gartnart," Skene, *CPS*, 1ra. "Garnart," Skene, *CPS*, 6. "Gartnait," M.O. Anderson, *KKES*, 246. MacAlister, *Uí Maine*, 37[93]v. M.O. Anderson, *KKES*, 262, 262 n.5. T.C.D., *1336*, col. 824. Skene, *CPS*, 398.

[429]O'Rahilly, *EIHM*, 365-366.

[430]M.O. Anderson, *KKES*, 169, 302. Bannerman, *SIHD*, 93. Skene, *CPS*, 1va appears to have "Gartnart." M.O. Anderson, *KKES*, 248 has "Gartnait."

[431]Facsimile in Skene, *CPS*, 1va has "Nectu nepos uerd." M.O. Anderson, *KKES*, 248 has "Nectu nepos Uerb." MacAlister, *Uí Maine*, 37[93]v. M.O. Anderson, *KKES*, 262, 266, 272, 280, 287, 292. T.C.D., *1336*, col. 824. Skene, *CPS*, 399.

[432]Bannerman, *SIHD*, 41, 93-4. Binchy, *Scéla Cano*, 1. M.O. Anderson, *KKES*, 154-5. Bannerman, *SIHD*,93.

[433]O'Brien, *CGH*, 659.

[434]O'Brien, *CGH*, 270, 275. O'Sullivan, *Leinster*, 1438-9. Mulchrone, *Lecan*, 114ra, 114vb. Meyer, "Laud," 325, 326.

[435]Murphy, *Clonmacnoise*, 35.

[436]Skene, *CPS*, 1ra, 4-5, 396. T.C.D., *1336*, col. 823. M.O. Anderson, *KKES*, 245. MacAlister, *Uí Maine*, 37[93]v.

[437]M.O. Anderson, *KKES*, 81, 84.

[438]Mulchrone, *Lecan*, 4vb, 287ra. Atkinson, *Ballymote*, 43a, 203a.

[439]Virgil, *The Eclogues and Georgics*, ed. R.D. Williams (New York: St. Martin'S Press, 1979), 46. Watson, *HCPNS*, 60-61.

[440]Skene, *CPS*, 1ra, 5, 396-97. T.C.D., *1336*, col. 823. M.O. Anderson, *KKES*, 245. MacAlister, *Uí Maine*, 37[93]v. Mulchrone, *Lecan*, 4vb, 143rb, 287ra. Atkinson, *Ballymote*, 203a.

[441]Skene, *CPS*, cv. Chadwick, *Scotland*, 3.

[442]Wright, *Regum*, 131-132.

[443]R.I.A., *Dictionary*, 361. O'Brien, *CGH*, 660-661.

[444]Wright, *Regum*, 131-132.

[445]R.I.A., *Dictionary*, 361, 249.

[446]O'Brien, *CGH*, 661.

[447]Wright, *Regum*, 131-132.

[448]Ibid.

[449]A.O. Anderson, *ESSH*, Vol.I, 363, 397, 397n.2. M.O. Anderson, *KKES*, 198, 303. Hudson, *Kings of Celtic*, 55.

[450]MacAlister, *Uí Maine*, 37[93]v. M.O. Anderson, *KKES*, 263, 267, 274, 283, 288, 299. T.C.D., *1336*, col. 825. Skene, *CPS*, 400.

[451]Morby, *Kings & Queens*, 45. Morris, *Arthur*, 512.

[452]Wade-Evans, *Sanctorum*, 116.

[453]Bede, *HEGA*, Vol.I, 48-9. Bede, *EHEP*,55. Morris, *Nennius*, 65-66. Wright, *Regum*, 51-54, 57.

[454]Best and O'Brien, "Longes Chonaill," 1249-50. Hull, "Exile of Conall," 940-941.

[455]Hull, "Corco Luigde," 894. Hull, "Exile of Conall," 937-8. Meyer, "Conall Corc," 57-8.

[456]Skene, *CPS*, 1ra, 5-6, 398. T.C.D., *1336*, col. 824. M.O. Anderson, *KKES*, 245, 261, 265, 271, 279, 286. MacAlister, *Uí Maine*, 37[93]v. Miller, "Disputed," 12, 19.

[457]M.O. Anderson, *KKES*, 84. Miller, "Disputed," 9.

[458]MacAlister, *Uí Maine*, 37[93]v. T.C.D., *1336*, col. 823. Skene, *CPS*, 396. Mulchrone, *Lecan*, 143rb, 287ra. Atkinson, *Ballymote*, 43a, 203a.

[459]Watson, *HCPNS*, 115.

[460]M.O. Anderson, *KKES*, 248 n.105. Jackson, "Pictish Language," 162. Jarman, *Y Gododdin*, 102 n.371. Smyth, *Warlords*, 64-66.

[461]Williams, *Canu Aneirin*, 15. Jarman, *Y Gododdin*, 26-27.

[462]Alcock, *Arthur's Britain*, 90, 108-113. Morris, *Arthur*, 38, 74-75, 512.

[463]Bede, *EHEP*, 63, 112. Bede, *HEGA*, Vol.I, 68-71, 226-7. Morris, *Nennius*, 67, 68, 72-3, 76. Wright, *Regum*, 65-71, 86-9. Bromwich, *Trioedd*, 159.

[464]Geoffrey of Monmouth, *History*, 333. Bromwich, *Trioedd*, 407-408.

[465]Wright, *Regum*, 101-105, 109, 130-132.

[466]Alcock, *Arthur's Britain*, 108-113. Morris, *Arthur*, 38, 74-75, 512.

[467]Bede, *HEGA*, Vol.I, 68-71. Bede, *EHEP*,63. Morris, *Nennius*, 67, 72. Wright, *Regum*, 65, 67, 68. Bromwich, *Trioedd*, 159.

[468]Miller, "Disputed," 19-20.

[469]Ibid., 20-21.

[470]A.O. Anderson, *ESSH*, Vol. 1, 169 n.2.

[471]A.O. and M.O. Anderson, *ALOC* (1961), 344 n.6; *ALOC* (1991), 107.

[472]A.O. and M.O. Anderson, *ALOC* (1961), 344; *ALOC* (1991), 106-7.

[473]Reeves, *Life of Columba*, 269. O'Rahilly, *EIHM*, 342. Adomnán and Sharpe, *Life of Columba*, 322 n.232. Jackson, "Pictish Language," 143, 143 n.4.

[474]O'Brien, *CGH*, 668.

[475]M.O. Anderson, "II. Kings of Picts, " 14 n.6.

[476]O'Brien, *CGH*, 154-5, 264, 265, 277, 324, 581, 638, 723, 724. O'Sullivan, *Leinster*, 1371, 1440, 1469. Mulchrone, *Lecan*, 113va, 114vd, 125va, 126rb. Meyer, "Laud," 327, 335.

[477]Morris, *Nennius*, 60-1, 63. Jackson, "*Albanach*," 128. Wright, *Regum*, 2-3, 35. Geoffrey of Monmouth, *History*, 55n.1.

[478]Morris, *Nennius*, 62.

[479]Morris, *Nennius*, 62.

[480]Jackson, "Pictish Language," 139-40. Morris, *Persons*, 55. Watson, *HCPNS*, 321.

[481]Jackson, "Pictish Language," 139-140.

[482]Barbara E. Crawford, *Scandinavian Scotland* (Leicester: Leicester University Press, 1987), 51. Hudson, *Kings of Celtic*, 49-50, 64.

[483]O'Brien, *CGH*, 664.

[484]O'Brien, *CGH*, 2, 7, 17, 201. Mulchrone, *Lecan*, 214vb. FitzPatrick, "Fasciculus XV," 1815.

[485]Murphy, *Clonmacnoise*, 12, 20.

[486]Mulchrone, *Lecan*, 4vb, 139ra, 143rb, 287ra. Atkinson, *Ballymote*, 43a, 203a.

[487]Morris, *Nennius*, 63.

[488]Mulchrone, *Lecan*, 139ra.

[489]Morris, *Nennius*, 63.

[490]Morby, *Kings & Queens*, 51. Morris, *Arthur*, 513.

[491]Forbes, "Vita Niniani," 139. J. and W. MacQueen, *St. Nynia*, 104.

[491a]Morris, *Persons*, 85. Watson, *HCPNS*, 284-85, 301-302. A.O. Anderson, *ESSH*, Vol. I, 230, 231 n.3

[492]M.O. Anderson, *KKES*, 169, 296, 301, 304.

[493]Ibid., 266, 273, 281, 287, 292.

[494]Bromwich, *Trioedd*, 82-3. Morris, *Arthur*, 565 n.159.2. John Morris, *Places & Peoples, & Saxon Archaeology*, Vol. 4 of *Arthurian Period Sources* in

John Morris, gen. ed., History from the Sources (Chichester: Phillimore & Co. LTD., 1995), 36. Suggested by Alex Woolf and Séamus Mac Mathúna. T.F. O'Rahilly, *EIHM*, 363-64 n.5.

[495]Morris, *Nennius*, 62.

[496]Dáibhi Ó Cróinín, *Early Medieval Ireland, 400-1200*, 4th ed. (London and New York: Longman, 1997).

[497]Williams, *Canu Aneirin*, 141 n.257. Jarman, *Y Gododdin*, 84 n.93, 94 nn.260 and 262. Hughes, *Celtic Britain*, 49.

[498]Williams, *Canu Aneirin*, 4, 10. Jarman, *Y Gododdin*, 8-9, 18-19.

[499]O'Brien, *CGH*, 329, 706. O'Sullivan, *Leinster*, VI, 1471. FitzPatrick, "Fasciculus XV," 1823.

[500]M.O. Anderson, *KKES*, 266-7, 273-4, 282-3, 288.

[501]A.O. and M.O. Anderson, *ALOC* (1961), 456; (1991), 176-7.

[502]Bannerman, *SIHD*, 41-3. Jackson, "*Albanach*," 130.

[503]Mulchrone, *Lecan*, 4vb, 139ra, 143rb. Atkinson, *Ballymote*, 43a, 203a. M.O. Anderson, *KKES*, 82, T.F. O'Rahilly, *EIHM*, 314.

[504]Cross and Slover, *Ancient Irish*, 16.

[505]O'Brien, *CGH*, 155, 668. O'Sullivan, *Leinster*, VI, 1371.

[506]Adomnán, Sharpe, *Life of Columba*, 288 n.22, 325 n.249.

[506a]Morris, *Persons*, 90-1. Watson, *HCPNS*, 325-6.

[506b]A.O. and M.O. Anderson, *ALOC* (1961), 364, 386-8; (1991), 238-9. Adomnán and Sharpe, *Life of Columba*, 330 n.272.

[507]M.O. Anderson, *KKES*, 167. Bromwich, *Trioedd*, 437.

[508]Phillimore, "*Annales Cambriae*," 42. Phillimore, "Pedigrees," 56, 60, 63. Wade-Evans, *VSBG*, 320, 323.

[509]Wade-Evans, *VSBG*, 72-80.

[510]Winterbottom, *Gildas*, 102. A.O. and M.O. Anderson, *ALOC* (1961), 84. Morris, *Nennius*, 79. Wright, *Regum*, 133, 140. Bromwich, *Trioedd*, 1.

[511]M.O. Anderson, *KKES*, 167-8. Morris, *Persons*, 95. Watson, *HCPNS*, 287-9.

[511a]O'Sullivan, *Leinster* VI, 1616. Stokes, *Félire*, 107.

[512]M.O. Anderson, *KKES*, 167. Bromwich, *Trioedd*, 437.

[513]Skene, *CPS*, 1rb, 7, 399. T.C.D., *1336*, col. 824. M.O. Anderson, *KKES*, 248, 262, 266, 272, 280, 287. MacAlister, *Uí Maine*, 37[93]v. Miller, "Disputed," 20.

[514]Bede, *HEGA*, Vol. I, 340-1. Bede, *EHEP*, 148. H.M. Chadwick, *Scotland*, 15. K. Jackson in Cyril Fox and B. Dickins, eds., *Early Cultures of North-West Europe* (Cambridge, 1950), 208n.2. Jackson, "Pictish Language," 163-4.

[515]O'Brien, *CGH*, 4, 17, 732.

[516]Mulchrone, *Lecan*, 4vb, 139ra, 143rb, 287ra. Atkinson, *Ballymote*, 43a, 203a.

[517]Geoffrey of Monmouth, *History*, 346.

[518]Wright, *Regum*, 45.

[519]Morris, *Arthur*, 512. Bromwich, *Trioedd*, 451-2.

[520]Phillimore, "*Annales Cambriae*," 43, 44. Phillimore, "Pedigrees," 57,

59, 60. Wade-Evans, *VSBG*, 232.

[521]Wade-Evans, *VSBG*, 116-17.

[522]Winterbottom, *Gildas*, 93. Bede, *HEGA*, Vol. I, 48-9. Bede, *EHEP*, 55-6. Morris, *Nennius*, 65, 66.Wright, *Regum*, 57, 58, 159. Bromwich, *Trioedd*, 77.

[523]Geoffrey of Monmouth, *History*, 347.

[524]O'Brien, *CGH*, 699. O'Sullivan, *Leinster* VI, 1367. Mulchrone, *Lecan*, 97rd. Meyer, "Laud," 337.

[525]Wright, *Regum*, 57-8.

[526]Cross and Slover, *Ancient Irish*, 14.

[527]O'Brien, *CGH*, 4, 6, 199, 201, 519. O'Sullivan, *Leinster*, 1328, 1379, 1438. Mulchrone, *Lecan*, 214r-214v. Meyer, "Laud," 291. FitzPatrick, "Fasciculus XV," 1815, 1852.

[528]Murphy, *Clonmacnoise*, 12, 18. Hennessy, *Chronicum*,10-12.

[528a]Morris, *Persons*, 103. Watson, *HCPNS*, 289.

[528b]Morris, *Persons*, 45-6, 103. Watson, *HCPNS*, 190, 342, 344, 366.

[529]O'Brien, *CGH*, 702.

[530]Meyer, "Conall Corc," 57-8. O'Brien, *CGH*, 122, 132, 195. O'Sullivan, *Leinster* VI, 1357. Mulchrone, *Lecan*, 213vb-214ra. Hull, "Corco Luigde," 893-4. Sproule, "Politics," 15-17. Meyer, "Laud," 303.

[531]Best and O'Brien, "Longes Chonaill," 1250. Hull, "Exile of Conall," 941.

[532]Geoffrey of Monmouth, *History*, 349.

[533]Wright, *Regum*, 106, 130-32. Geoffrey of Monmouth, *History*, 349. Bromwich, *Trioedd*, 131-132, 147.

[534]Skene, *CPS*, 1rb, 6, 398. T.C.D., *1336*, col. 824. M.O. Anderson, *KKES*, 245, 261. MacAlister, *Uí Maine*, 37[93]v. Miller, "Disputed," 12.

[535]Jackson, "Pictish Language," 140, 145, 164-165. Byrne, *Irish Kings*, 55. Watson, *HCPNS*, 308, 329-331. Stokes, *Félire Óengusso*, 34.

[536]A.O. Anderson, *ESSH*, Vol. I, 185-6 n.9. M.O. Anderson, *KKES*, 8 n.34. T.F. O'Rahilly, *EIHM*, 373-4 n.1. Watson, *HCPNS*, 308, 329-31.

[536a]Stokes, *Félire Óengusso*, 34.

[537]M.O. Anderson, *KKES*, 169.

[538]Clancy and Márkus, *Iona*, 24.

[539]Skene, *CPS*, 1va, 7, 399. T.C.D., *1336*, col. 824. M.O. Anderson, *KKES*, 248-9, 263, 266, 272-3, 280, 287, 292. MacAlister, *Uí Maine*, 37[93]v.

[540]Bede, *HEGA*, Vol. II, 324-61. Bede, *EHEP*, 308-21.

[541]Miller, "Disputed," 10.

[542]Skene, *CPS*, 1ra-1rb, 6-7, 398-9. T.C.D., *1336*, col. 824. M.O. Anderson, *KKES*, 247, 262, 265, 272, 280, 287. MacAlister, *Uí Maine*, 37[93]v. Miller, "Disputed," 20.

[543]A.O. Anderson, *ESSH*, Vol. I, cxiii. M.O. Anderson, *KKES*, 169, 306. Bannerman, *SIHD*, 92-4. Miller, "Eanfrith's," 53-5. Smyth, Warlords, 62-6.

[544]Skene, *CPS*, 1va, 7 has "Nectu nepos uerd." M.O. Anderson, *KKES*, 248 has "Nectu nepos Uerb." MacAlister, *Uí Maine*, 37[93]v. M.O. Anderson, *KKES*, 262, 272, 280, 292. T.C.D., *1336*, col. 824. Skene, *CPS*, 399.

[545]Miller, "Eanfrith's," 53-4. Smyth, *Warlords*, 62-6.

[546]Phillimore, "*Annales Cambriae*," 44-5.

[547]Cross and Slover, *Ancient Irish*, 3.

[548]FitzPatrick, "Fasciculus XV," 1815.

[549]Morris, *Nennius*, 61. Jackson, "*Albanach*," 128.

[550]J. and W. MacQueen, *St. Nynia*, 1-87, 39-53, 86. Watson, *HCPNS*, 293-7. Morris, *Persons*, 109-10. MacQuarrie, *Saints of Scotland*, 50-73.

[551]Forbes, "Vita Niniani," 139-40. 147-8. J. and W. Macqueen, *St. Nynia*, 89-90, 104, 112-13.

[552]Bede, *HEGA*, Vol. I, 340-1. Bede, *EHEP*, 148. Bromwich and Evans, *Culhwch and Olwen*, 22. Ford, "Culhwch and Olwen," 138. J. and W. MacQueen, *St. Nynia*, 75-6.

[553]O'Brien, *CGH*, 714.

[554]O'Brien, *CGH*, 4, 7, 17, 330. Mulchrone, *Lecan*, 183va. FitzPatrick. "Fasciculus XV," 1815.

[555]Murphy, *Clonmacnoise*, 11-12.

[556]Mulchrone, *Lecan*, 4vb, 139ra, 143rb, 287ra. Atkinson, *Ballymote*, 43a, 203a.

[557]Morris, *Nennius*, 59, 60, 63.

[558]Geoffrey of Monmouth, *History*, 351. Bede, *HEGA*, Vol.I, 226-7.

[559]Morris, *Nennius*, 69, 76-7. Wright, *Regum*, 68, 88, 99-100

[560]Jackson, "Pictish Language," 162.

[561]M.O. Anderson, *KKES*, 87.

[562]Ibid., 266, 272, 281, 287, 292.

[563]Ibid., 136. Bannerman, *SIHD*, 70-71.

[564]FitzPatrick, "Fasciculus XV," 1823, 1855.

[565]M.O. Anderson, *KKES*, 267, 273-4, 282-3.

[566]Bannerman, *SIHD*, 41, 42. Jackson, "*Albanach*," 130. Hull, "Exile of Conall Corc," 940, 945 n.55. Best and O'Brien, "Longes Chonaill," 1249.

[567]Crawford, *Scandinavian*, 49. Hudson, *Kings of Celtic*, 46, 49.

[568]O'Brien, *Corpus*, 270. O'Sullivan, *Leinster* VI, 1438. Mulchrone, *Lecan*, 114ra. Meyer, "Laud," 325.

[569]Murphy, *Clonmacnoise*, 32. Ó Corráin and Cournane, *CELT Four Masters*, Vol. I, 34.

[570]Skene, *CPS*, 1ra, 5, 396. T.C.D., *1336*, col. 823. M.O. Anderson, *KKES*, 245. MacAlister, *Uí Maine*, 37[93]v. Mulchrone, *Lecan*, 4vb, 143rb, 287ra. Atkinson, *Ballymote*, 43a, 203a.

[571]H.M. Chadwick, *Scotland*, 2-3.

[572]O'Brien, *Corpus*, 117, 270, 532. O'Sullivan, *Leinster*, 1439. Mulchrone, *Lecan*, 114ra. Meyer, "Laud," 325.

[573]M.O. Anderson, *KKES*, 169, 229, 307. Hudson, *Kings of Celtic*, 4

[574]Morris, *Nennius*, 88. A.O. Anderson, *ESSH*, Vol. I, 235 n.3 speculates that this refers to "Ewen" of Dál Riata.

[575]Skene, *CPS*, 1va could have "Onuist." *CPS*, 7 has "Onnist." M.O. Anderson, *KKES*, 249 has "Oniust." MacAlister, *Uí Maine*, 37[93]v. M.O. Anderson, *KKES*, 262, 273, 280-1, 287, 292. T.C.D., *1336*, col. 825. Skene, *CPS*, 399-400.

[576]A.O. Anderson, *ESSH*, Vol. I, 153 n.1.

[577]Bede, *EHEP*, 143.

[578]A.O. Anderson, *ESSH*, Vol. I, 153 n.1. Bannerman, *SIHD*, 98-9.

[579]A.O. Anderson, *ESSH*, Vol. I, cxi. Miller, "Eanfrith's," 53.

[580]Colgrave, *Lives of Cuthbert*, 188-90.

[581]Bede, *HEGA*, Vol. I, 226-7; Vol.II, 32-3. Bede, *EHEP*, 111, 164-5, 183-4, 212. Morris, *Nennius*, 77, 79. Wright, *Regum*, 142-3.

[582]Cross and Slover, *Ancient Irish*, 3.

[583]FitzPatrick, "Fasciculus XV," 1815.

[584]Mulchrone,*Lecan*, 4vb, 139ra, 143rb, 287ra. Atkinson, *Ballymote*, 43a, 203a.

[585]Morris, *Nennius*, 60. Wright, *Regum*, 31.

[586]Morris, *Persons*, 111-12, 138-9.

[587]Murphy, *Clonmacnoise*, 65.

[588]M.O. Anderson, *KKES*, 287. Miller, "Disputed," 20.

[589]Bede, *HEGA*, Vol. I, 62-3. Bede, *EHEP*, 60. Morris, *Nennius*, 74.

[590]D.N. Dumville, "The Death Date of Saint Patrick," 29-34. Morris, *Persons*, 113. Morrris, *Arthur*, 347-9. Smyth, *Warlords*, 18.

[591]O'Brien, *CGH*, 123, 317-8. O'Sullivan, *Leinster* VI 1359, 1442. O'Brien, *CGH*, 707. Mulchrone, *Lecan*, 122vb, 127va, Meyer, "Laud," 291, 328. FitzPatrick, "Fasciculus XV," 1832.

[592]Stokes, "Tigernach," 30, 32.

[593]Murphy, *Clonmacnoise*, 63, 65-9.

[594]Skene, *CPS*, 1ra, 6, 398. T.C.D., *1336*, col. 824. M.O. Anderson, *KKES*, 247, 262. MacAlister, *Uí Maine*, 37[93]v.

[595]A.O. and M.O. Anderson, *ALOC* (1961), 182; *ALOC* (1991), 4-5. Herbert, *Iona, Kells*, 224. O'Sullivan, *Leinster* VI, 1607. Stokes, *Félire Óengusso*, 82.

[596]Hood, *St. Patrick*, 35, 37. Hughes, *Celtic Britain*,50.

[597]Morris, *Nennius*, 62, 74-6. Jackson, "*Albanach*," 130.

[598]Morby, *Kings & Queens*, 43. Morris, *Arthur*, 184, 515.

[599]Bede, *HEGA*, Vol. I, 314-15, 402-3, 412-15, 448-51. Bede, *EHEP*, 140, 168, 171, 183. Morris, *Nennius*, 78-80. Wright, *Regum*, 141-144.

[600]Jackson, "Pictish Language," 148.

[600a]O'Sullivan, *Leinster*, VI, 1607. Stokes, *Félire Óengusso*, 83, 100, 441.

[601]A.O. Anderson, *ESSH*, Vol. I, 266-267 n.2. M.O. Anderson, *KKES*, 240, 258-60. M.O. Anderson, "St Andrews before Alexander I, 7-8. J. MacQueen, "Myth and Legends," 8. Watson, *HCPNS*, 190, 396-7, 516. Skene, *CPS*, 138-40, 183-93.

[602]M.O. Anderson, *KKES*, 287. Miller, "Disputed," 19.

[603]Skene, *CPS*, 1ra, 6, 398. T.C.D., *1336*, col. 824. M.O. Anderson, *KKES*, 246, 262. MacAlister, *Uí Maine*, 37[93]v. Miller, "Disputed," 12.

[604]Morris, *Persons*, 131-2. Watson, *HCPNS*, 332-3. A.O. Anderson, *ESSH*, Vol. I, 127-30. MacQueen, "Myth and Legends," 3, 4, 9. M.O. Anderson, *KKES*,287.

[605]Skene, *CPS*, 412, 417. Forbes, *Ninian and Kentigern*, 168, 170, 246.

MacQueen, "Myth and Legends," 2-3.

[606]MacAlister, *Uí Maine*, 55[111]vb. Mulchrone, *Lecan*, 34vb-35ra. Atkinson, *Ballymote*, 214a.

[607]Morby, *Kings & Queens*, 43. Morris, *Arthur*,155.

[608]Wade-Evans, *VSBG*, 72.

[609]Bede, *HEGA*, Vol.I, 30-3. Bede, *EHEP*, 50. Morris, *Nennius*, 64-65. Wright, *Regum*, 47-48.

[610]O'Brien, *CGH*, 270, 275. O'Sullivan, *Leinster*, 1438-9. Mulchrone, *Lecan*, 114ra, 114vb. Meyer, "Laud," 325-6.

[611]Murphy, *Clonmacnoise*, 35.

[612]Wright, *Regum*, 45.

[613]T.F. O'Rahilly, *EIHM*, 363-64 n.5.

[614]Geoffrey of Monmouth, *History*, 364. Wright, *Regum*, 47-8.

[615]Skene, *CPS*, 1ra, 6, 398. T.C.D., *1336*, col.824. M.O. Anderson, *KKES*, 246-247, 262, 265, 272, 280, 287. MacAlister, *Uí Maine*, 37[93]v. Miller, "Disputed," 12, 19-20.

[616]Jackson, "Pictish Language," 145, 164.

[617]Miller, "Disputed," 10.

[618]Skene, *CPS*, 1ra-1rb, 6, 398-9. T.C.D., *1336*, col.824. M.O. Anderson, *KKES*, 247, 262, 265, 272, 280, 287. MacAlister, *Uí Maine*, 37[93]v. Miller, "Disputed," 20.

[619]M.O. Anderson, *KKES*, 169.

[620]Skene. *CPS*, 1va, 7, 399. T.C.D., *1336*, col.824. M.O. Anderson, *KKES*, 248, 266, 266, 272, 280, 292. MacAlister, *Uí Maine*, 37[93]v.

[621]M. O. Anderson, *KKES*, 169, 309. Miller, "Eanfrith's," 53.

[622]Skene, *CPS*, 1va, 7, 399. T.C.D., *1336*, col.824. M.O. Anderson, *KKES*, 248, 262, 266, 272, 280, 292. MacAlister, *Uí Maine*, 37[93]v.

[623]Jackson, "Pictish Language," 164.

[624]Miller, "Disputed," 10.

[625]Skene, *CPS*, 1rb, 7, 399. T.C.D., *1336*, col.824. M.O. Anderson, *KKES*, 248, 262, 266, 272, 280, 287. MacAlister, *Uí Maine*, 37[93]v. Miller, "Disputed," 20.

[626]A.O. Anderson, *ESSH*, Vol. I, clvi, 228 n.1.

[627]M.O. Anderson, *KKES*, 186-87, 309.

[628]M.O. Anderson, *KKES*, 175-76.

[629]M.O. Anderson, *KKES*, 169, 309.

[630]M.O. Anderson, *KKES*, 191.

[631]MacAlister, *Uí Maine*, 37[93]v. T.C.D., *1336*, col.825. M.Anderson, *KKES*, 263, 266, 273, 281, 287, 292. Skene,*CPS*,400.

[632]M.O. Anderson, *KKES*, 169, 309.

[633]M.O. Anderson, *KKES*, 191.

[634]Skene, *ÇPS*, 1va, 7, 400. T.C.D., *1336*, col.825. M.O. Anderson, *KKES*, 249, 263, 266, 273, 281, 287, 292. MacAlister, *Uí Maine*, 37[93]v.

[635]M.O. Anderson, *KKES*, 169, 309.

[636]Skene, *CPS*, 1va, 8, 400. T.C.D., *1336*, col.825. M.O. Anderson, *KKES*, 249, 263, 266, 272, 281, 287, 292. MacAlister, *Uí Maine*, 37[93]v. O'Brien,

CGH, 635, 656.

[637]A.O. and M.O. Anderson, *ALOC* (1961), 60.

[638]A. O. and M.O. Anderson, *ALOC* (1961), 376; *ALOC* (1991) 126-7.

[639]Jackson, "Pictish Language," 145, 165. A.O. and M.O. Anderson, *Adomnan's Columba*, 160.

[640]M.O. Anderson, *KKES*, 169.

[641]Skene, *CPS*, 1va, 7, 399. T.C.D., *1336*, col.824. M.O. Anderson, *KKES*, 248, 262-263, 266, 272, 280. 287, 292. MacAlister, *Uí Maine*, 37[93]v.

[642]Skene, *CPS*, 1ra, 5-6, 398. T.C.D., *1336*, col.824. M.O. Anderson, *KKES*, 245, 261, 265, 271, 279, 287. MacAlister, *Uí Maine*, 37[93]v. Miller, "Disputed," 12, 19.

[643]M.O. Anderson, *KKES*, 175-177.

[644]Morris, *Persons*, 111-112, 138. Ó Riain, *Corpus Sanctorum*, 261. Watson, *HCPNS*, 298-300, 337.

[645]Ó Riain, *Corpus Sanctorum*, 35, 261. Sullivan, *Leinster*, VI, 1559, Mulchrone, *Lecan*, 43va. Atkinson, *Ballymote*, 220g-221a. Herbert, *Iona, Kells*, 236, 260. Stokes, *Félire Óengusso*, 140.

[646]Morris, *Persons*, 142. Henderson, *Picts*, 81.

[647]Colgrave, *Lives of Cuthbert*, 64-66, 110, 156, 239.

[648]Bede, *HEGA*, Vol. II, 70-71, 160-63, 176-77. Bede, *EHEP*, 225, 255, 259.

[649]M.O. Anderson, *KKES*, 8 n.34. T.F. O'Rahilly, *EIHM*, 373 n.1.

[650]Skene, *CPS*, 1ra, 6, 398. T.C.D., *1336*, col.824. M.O. Anderson, *KKES*, 246, 262, 265, 271-2, 279, 287. MacAlister, *Uí Maine*, 37[93]v. Miller, "Disputed," 19.

[651]Jackson, "Pictish Language," 137-8, 145. Miller, "Disputed," 12.

[652]Skene, *CPS*, 1ra, 6, 398. T.C.D., *1336*, col.824. M.O. Anderson, *KKES*, 246, 261-262. MacAlister, *Uí Maine*, 37[93]v.

[653]Crawford, *Scandinavian Scotland*, 23. Jackson, *Early Britain*, 531. Miller, "Disputed," 12.

[654]M.O. Anderson, *KKES*,169, 229, 307.

[655]Skene, *CPS*, 1va, 7-8, 398. T.C.D. *1336*, col.825. M.O. Anderson, *KKES*, 249, 261-2, 266, 272, 281, 287, 292. MacAlister, *Uí Maine*, 37[93]v. Miller, "Disputed," 20.

[656]Skene, *CPS*, 1va, 6, 398, T.C.D., *1336*, col.824. M.O. Anderson, *KKES*, 246, 261, 265, 271, 279. MacAlister, *Uí Maine*, 37[93]v.

[657]Jackson, "Pictish Language," 145. Miller, "Disputed,"12.

[658]Geoffrey of Monmouth, *History*, 368-9.

[659]Phillimore, "Pedigrees," 63.

[660]Wright, *Regum*, 62-4, 99-100. Bromwich, *Trioedd*, 56,131.

[661]M.O. Anderson, *KKES*, 169, 229, 301.

[662]Ibid., 194-96.

[663]Skene, *CPS*, 1va, 8, 400. T.C.D., *1336*, col. 825. M.O. Anderson, *KKES*, 249, 263, 266, 273, 281, 287, 292. MacAlister, *Uí Maine*, 37[93]v.

[664]M.O. Anderson, *KKES*, 169, 301.

[665]Skene, *CPS*, 1va, 8, 400. T.C.D., *1336*, col. 825. M.O. Anderson, *KKES*, 249, 263, 266, 273, 281, 287, 292. MacAlister, *Uí Maine*, 37[93]v.

[666]Jackson, "Pictish Language," 163.

[667]Skene, *CPS*, 1ra, 6, 398. T.C.D., *1336*, col. 824. M.O. Anderson, *KKES*, 246, 262, 265, 272, 279-280, 287. Miller, "Disputed," 19. MacAlister, *Uí Maine*, 37[93]v.

[668]Jackson, "Pictish Language," 163. M.O. Anderson, *KKES*, 90. Miller, "Disputed," 12. H.M. Chadwick, *Scotland*, 8.

[669]Morby, *Kings & Queens*, 45. Morris, *Arthur*, 512.

[670]Morris, *Nennius*, 66. Wright, *Regum*, 53, 57.

[671]Suetonius, *Caesars*, 329.

[672]Phillimore, "*Annales Cambriae*," 49. Phillimore, "Pedigrees," 59, 63.

[673]Murphy, *Clonmacnoise*, 50.

[674]Bede, *HEGA*, Vol.I, 28-9; *EHEP*, 49. Wright, *Regum*,44.

[674a]Morris, 146. Watson, *HCPNS*, 335-6.

[675]Alcock, *Arthur's Britain*, 111. Morris, *Arthur*, 512. Bromwich, *Trioedd*, 392

[676]Phillimore, "*Annales Cambriae*," 55.

[677]Winterbottom, *Gildas*, 97. Bede, *HEGA*, Vol. I, 68-9, 226-7. Bede, *EHEP*, 62, 112. Morris, *Nennius*, 67, 69, 73. Wright, *Regum*, 62-7, 70-71, 86. Bromwich, *Trioedd*, 88, 131.

[678]Geoffrey of Monmouth, *History*, 371.

[679]Wright, *Regum*, 57-8.

[680]Morris, *Persons*, 147. Webb and Farmer, *Age of Bede*,10.

[681]Webb and Farmer, "Life of Wilfrid," 129-32, 151-5, 164-7, 174-6.

[682]Bede, *HEGA*, Vol. I, 456-477, Vol. II, 308-317.

[683]M.O. Anderson, *KKES*, 245. MacAlister, *Uí Maine*, 37[93]v. Mulchrone, *Lecan*, 4vb, 143va, 287ra. Atkinson, *Ballymote*, 43a, 203a.

[684]Skene, *CPS*, cv. Jackson, "Pictish Language," 142. O'Rahilly, *EIHM*, 368 n.3, 370.

POPULATION AND PLACE NAMES

[1]Hogan, *Onomasticon*, 4, 32. Watson, *HCPNS*, 211,466.

[2]Skene, *CPS*, 1rb, 6, 399. T.C.D., *1336*, col. 824.
M.O. Anderson, *KKES*, 247, 262, 266, 272, 287, 292. MacAlister, *Uí Maine*, 37[93]v.

[3]M.O. Anderson, *KKES*, 92-93.

[4]Hogan, *Onomasticon*, 4. Henderson, *Picts*, 81. Bede, *HEGA*, Vol. II, 499.

[5]Bede, *HEGA*, Vol. II, 160-163.

[6]Watson, *HCPNS*, 60-61.

[7]Todd, *Irish Nennius*, 121 n.e. Watson, *HCPNS*, 60-61. P. Vergili Maronis, *Aeneidos: Liber Quartus*, ed. R.G. Austin (Oxford: The Clarendon Press, 1955), l. 146. M.O. Anderson, *KKES*, 83. George Calder, *Imtheacht Aeniasa: The Irish Aeneid*, Vol. VI in *Irish Texts Society* (London: David Nutt for the Irish Texts Society, 1907), 46.

[8]Hogan, *Onomasticon*, 28.

[9]O'Brien, *CGH*, 196, 328. O'Sullivan, *Leinster*, 1471-1472. Mulchrone, *Lecan*, 213v. FitzPatrick, "Fasciculus XV," 1823. Jackson, *"Albanach,"* 125.

[10]Skene, *CPS*, 1ra, 5. M.O. Anderson, *KKES*, 245, 261. MacAlister, *Uí Maine*, 37[93]v. Mulchrone, *Lecan*, 4vb.

[11]Meid, *TBF*, 13.

[12]Best and O'Brien, "Longes Chonaill," 1249-50. Hull, "Exile of Conall," 940. Binchy, *Scéla Cano*, 1. Wright, *Regum*, 45, 48, 57, 59, 64, 66, 104. Geoffrey of Monmouth, *History*, 147.

[13]Watson, *HCPNS*, 6, 11. Dauvit Broun, "The Origin of Scottish Identity in Its European Context," Barbara Crawford, ed., *Scotland in Dark Age Europe*, St John's House Papers No.5 (St Andrews, 1994), 21. T.F. O'Rahilly, *EIHM*, 385-7.

[14]Hogan, *Onomasticon*, 30. Dobbs, "Descendants of Ir," Vol. XIV, 65 n.6.

[15]Geoffrey of Monmouth, *History*, 294.

[16]Wright, *Regum*, 57, 145.

[17]Morris, *Arthur*, 100. Jackson, *Language and History*, 511.

[18]Alcock, *Arthur's Britain*, 108, 278-79. Morris, *Arthur*, 41.

[19]Bede, *HEGA*, Vol. I, 16-17, 72-3, 226-7, 350-1. Bede, *EHEP*, 45, 63, 111, 152.

[20]Alcock, *Arthur's Britain*, 278. Morris, *Arthur*, 41-2.

[21]Hogan, *Onomasticon*, 32. M.O. Anderson, *KKES*, 8-9, 12, Hughes, *Celtic Britain*, 45, 51. Henderson, *Picts*, 167-8. MacQuarrie, *Saints of Scotland*, 170.

[22]Watson, *HCPNS*, 67 n.2.

[23]Hogan, *Onomasticon*, 42.

[24]H.M. Chadwick, *Scotland*, xxi. R.I.A, *Dictionary*,56.

[25]Hogan, *Onomasticon*, 62. Todd, *Irish Nennius*, 143 n.v.

[26]R.I.A, *Dictionary*, 56, 368.

[27]Hogan, *Onomasticon*, 65. Todd, *Irish Nennius*, 143 n.v.

[28]R.I.A., *Dictionary*, 450.

[29]Hughes, *Celtic Britain*, 49. Jarman, *Y Gododdin*, 84 n.93, 94 n.260. Bromwich, *Trioedd*, 278-9. J. and W. MacQueen, *St. Nynia*, 75-76.

[30]Wade-Evans, *VSBG*, 82-83.

[31]Bromwich and Evans, *Culhwch and Olwen*, 22. Ford, "Culhwch and Olwen," 138. J. and W. MacQueen, *St. Nynia*, 75-6. Williams, *Canu Aneirin*, 4, 10. Jarman, *Y Gododdin*, 8-9, 18-19.

[32]Hogan, *Onomasticon*, 117.

[33]Meid, *TBF*, 73.

[34]Hogan, *Onomasticon*, 123-124.

[35]Hogan, *Onomasticon*, 124.

[36]John and Winifred MacQueen, *St Nynia*, 104.

[37]Bede, *HEGA*, Vol. I, 18-21. Bede, *EHEP*, 46-47. Morris, *Nennius*, 59, 61, 67, 74. Wright, *Regum*, 2, 45, 47, 57, 63, 144-145.

[38]Morris, *Arthur*, 41.

[39]Bede, *HEGA*, Vol. I, 16-17, 350-51. Bede, *HEGA*, Vol. II, 372-73. Bede, *EHEP*, 45, 152, 324. Morris, *Nennius*, 59, 64-66. Wright, *Regum*, 45, 47, 48.

[40]Alcock, *Arthur's Britain*, 310. Morris, *Arthur*, 41.

[41]Hogan, *Onomasticon*, 146.

[42]Morris, *Arthur*, 140.

[43]Wright, *Regum*, 131-132.

[44]Geoffrey of Monmouth, *History*, 259-260 n.1. Morris, *Arthur*, 140. Alcock, *Arthur's Britain*, 53-5, 67.

[45]Hogan, *Onomasticon*, 150.

[46]Mulchrone, *Lecan*, 4vb, 139ra, 287ra.

[47]Wright, *Regum*, 101.

[48]A.O. Anderson, *ESSH*, Vol. I, 239 n.4.

[49]Hogan, *Onomasticon*, 218. Byrne, *Irish Kings*, 331

[50]M.O. Anderson, *KKES*, 240, 308. Hogan, *Onomasticon*, 227.

[51]M.O. Anderson, *KKES*, 266, 273, 281, 287. Miller, "Disputed," 19-20.

[52]Bannerman, *SIHD*, 85. Hogan, *Onomasticon*, 234.

[53]A.O. and M.O. Anderson, *ALOC* (1991),xx. M.O. Anderson, *KKES*, 36-37.

[54]Binchy, *Scéla Cano*, 18.

[55]Hogan, *Onomasticon*, 274.

[56]Skene, *CPS*, 442. Watson, *HCPNS*, 105.

[57]Hogan, *Onomasticon*, 293, 312. Meid, *TBF*, 74.

[58]R.I.A, *Dictionary*, 162. Hogan, *Onomasticon*, 312.

[59]Murphy, *Clonmacnoise*, 26.

[60]MacAlister, *Uí Maine*, 37[93]v. T.C.D., *1336*, col.823. Skene, *CPS*, 397. Mulchrone, *Lecan*, 4vb, 139ra, 143rb-143va, 287ra. Atkinson, *Ballymote*, 43a, 203a.

[61]Meid, *TBF*, 13. Bannerman, *SIHD*, 42. Jackson, "*Albanach*," 128. Binchy, *Scéla Cano*, 18.

[62]Skene, *CPS*, xcvii-xcviii. Watson, *HCPNS*, 13-14, 67.

[63]O'Rahilly, *EIHM*, 15-16, 15-16 n.1, 84, 342. H.M. Chadwick, *Scotland*, 99-119.

[64]Jackson, "Pictish," 158, 159. M.O. Anderson, *KKES*, 129-130.

[65]Hogan, *Onomasticon*, 319. Herbert, *Iona, Kells*, 27-29.

[66]A.O. and M.O. Anderson, *ALOC* (1961), 224-6; *ALOC* (1991), 6-7.

[67]Hogan, *Onomasticon*, 330.

[68]O'Brien, *CGH*, 153. Meyer, "Laud," 313.

[69]Hogan, *Onomasticon*, 335.

[70]Bede, *HEGA*, Vol. I, 18-19. Bede, *EHEP*, 46. Bannerman, *SIHD*, 123-4. Hudson, *Kings of Celtic*, 3. Morris, *Nennius*, 62.

[71]Crawford, *Scandinavian*, 11-12.

[72]Wright, *Regum*, 58, 59, 63, 86. Latham, *Latin Word-List*, 129.

[73]Morris, *Arthur*, 18.

[74]Morris, *Nennius*, 62.

[75]Hogan, *Onomasticon*, 359. M.O. Anderson, *KKES*, 186.

[76]Hogan, *Onomasticon*, 362.

[77]Hogan, *Onomasticon*, 382. M.O. Anderson, *KKES*, 141.

[78]Hogan, *Onomasticon*, 384. M.O. Anderson, *KKES*, 10.

[79]M.O. Anderson, *KKES*, 300. Hogan, *Onomasticon*, 379. Smyth, *Warlords*, 186.

[80]M.O. Anderson, *KKES*, 250, 266, 273, 287, 292.

[81]M.O. Anderson, *KKES*, 16, 300. Hogan, *Onomasticon*, 388.

[82]Colgrave, *Lives of Cuthbert*, 122, 239. Webb and Farmer, "Life of Wilfrid," 154.

[83]Bede, *HEGA*, Vol. II, 160-61. Bede, *EHEP*, 254. Morris, *Nennius*, 77.

[84]Hogan, *Onomasticon*, 388.

[85]Hogan, *Onomasticon*, 391-392.

[86]Hogan, *Onomasticon*, 608.

[87]Hogan, *Onomasticon*, 405.

[88]Hogan, *Onomasticon*, 423.

[89]Hogan, *Onomasticon*, 426.

[90]Watson, *HCPNS*, 510. M.O. Anderson, *KKES*, 302.

[91]M.O. Anderson, *KKES*, 266, 273, 282, 288.

[92]Watson, *HCPNS*, 68, 107-108.Hogan, *Onomasticon*, 429. M.O. Anderson, *KKES*, 139-141, 143-146.

[93]Watson, *HCPNS*, 60.

[94]Hogan, *Onomasticon*, 480.

[95]Hogan, *Onomasticon*, 431.

[96]Hogan, *Onomasticon*, 433.

[97]Jackson, "*Albanach*," 128.

[98]Hogan, *Onomasticon*, 434.

[99]Wright, *Regum*, 57.

[100]Morris, *Nennius*, 20. Morris, *Arthur*, 208.

[101]Morris, *Nennius*, 62.

[102]Morris, *Arthur*, 66.

[103]Morris, *Nennius*, 62.

[104]J.P. Mallory, *In Search of the Indo-Europeans* (London: Thames and Hudson, 1992), 61, 223.

[105]Wright, *Regum*, 57-58.

[106]Hogan, *Onomasticon*, 454. M.O. Anderson, *KKES*, 123.

[107]A.O. and M.O. Anderson, *ALOC* (1961), 376-378; *ALOC* (1991), 126-7.

[108]Bannerman, *SIHD*, 42.

[109]Hogan, *Onomasticon*, 457.

[110]Hogan, *Onomasticon*, 459.

[111]Hogan, *Onomasticon*, 459.

[112]Hogan, *Onomasticon*, 457.

[113]M.O. Anderson, *KKES*, 267, 274, 283.

[114]Hogan, *Onomasticon*, 400. Hughes, *Celtic Britain*, 40. Crawford, *Scandinavian*, 23.

[115]Clancy and Márkus, *Iona*, 24.

[116]M.O. Anderson, *KKES*, 266-7, 273-4, 282-3, 288, 290.

[117]Herbert, *Iona, Kells*, 237.

[118]Bede, *HEGA*, Vol. I, 340-41. Bede, *EHEP*. 148.

[119]Hogan, *Onomasticon*,452. Simpson, *Latin Dictionary*, 275.

[120]M.O. Anderson, *KKES*, 267, 274, 288, 290.

[121]John and Winifred MacQueen, *St Nynia*, 104.

[122]Bede, *HEGA*, Vol. I, 16-17, 340-41. Bede, *Eccesiastical*, 45-46, 148. Jackson, "*Albanach*," 128. Wright, *Regum*, 45, 58, 59.

[123]Wright, *Regum*, 45, 130-132.

[124]Hogan, *Onomasticon*, 536.

[125]Morris, *Nennius*, 62, 20.

[126]Hogan, *Onomasticon*, 473.

[127]Hogan, *Onomasticon*, 474.

[128]Hogan, *Onomasticon*, 475.

[129]A.O. Anderson, *ESSH*, 179, 179 n.2.

[130]Hughes, *Celtic Britain*, 49. Jarman, *Y Gododdin*, 84 n.93, 94 n.260.

[131]Williams, *Canu Aneirin*, 4, 10. Jarman, *Y Gododdin*, 8-9, 18-19.

[132]Hogan, *Onomasticon*, 525.

[133]Bede, *HEGA*, Vol. II, 382-83. Bede, *EHEP*, 328. A.O. Anderson, *Scottish Annals*, 49, 49 n.2, 50, 50nn.1 and 2. A.O. Anderson, *ESSH*, Vol.I, 213, 213nn. 1 and 3.

[134]Hogan, *Onomasticon*, 536.

[135]M.O. Anderson, *KKES*, 31n.128. Bannerman, *SIHD*, 83-4. Adomnán and Sharpe, *Life of Columba*, 268-271 n.81, n.84. MacQueen, "Myth and Legends," 19 n.8.

[136]A.O. and M.O. Anderson, *ALOC*(1991), xix-xxi. Alcock, *Arthur's Britain*, 73. Morris, *Places and People*, 39.

[137]A.O. and M.O. Anderson,*ALOC* (1991), xix-xxi, 30-31. T.F. O'Rahilly, *EIHM*, 504-5. Bannerman, *SIHD*, 84-85.

[138]Hogan, *Onomasticon*, 543.

[139]Hogan, *Onomasticon*, 543.

[140]Hogan, *Onomasticon*, 544.

[141]Hogan, *Onomasticon*, 554. M.O. Anderson, *KKES*, 8n.34. T.F. O'Rahilly, *EIHM*, 373-374 n.1. A.O. Anderson, *ESSH*, Vol. I, 185-186 n.9.

[142]John and Winifred MacQueen, *St. Nynia*, 89. Colgrave, *Lives of Cuthbert*, 82, 192. Macquarrie, *Saints of Scotland*,64

[143]Colgrave, *Lives of Cuthbert*, 320-321. John and Winifred MacQueen, *St. Nynia*, 41. Wainwright, *Problem*, 42-43.

[144]Wright, *Regum*, 2.

[145]Crawford, *Scandinavian*, 35.

[146]M.O. Anderson, *KKES*, 267, 274, 283, 288, 290.

[147]Wright, *Regum*, 59, 63, 86.

[148]Hogan, *Onomasticon*, 561.

[149]A.O. and M.O. Anderson, *ALOC* (1961), 440; *ALOC* (1991), 166-7.

[150]Morris, *Nennius*, 59, 61, 69.

[151]Todd, *Irish Nennius*, 122-123 n.i. H.M. Chadwick, *Scotland*, 84-85. Latham, *Latin Word-List*, 350.

[152]Todd, *Irish Nennius*, 122-123 n.i.

[153]M.O. Anderson, *KKES*, 197-198.

[154]Hogan, *Onomasticon*, 312.

[155]Murphy, *Clonmacnoise*, 65, 71.

[156]Wade-Evans, *VSBG*, 82-84.

[157]Meid, *TBF*, 15. Jackson, "*Albanach*," 128-9. R.I.A., *Dictionary*, 119. Bromwich, *Trioedd*, 201, 227.

[158]Watson, *HCPNS*, 11. Jackson, "Pictish," 159.

[159]Wainwright, *Problem*, 2. Jackson, "Pictish," 160.

[160]Crawford, *Scandinavian*, 2.

[161]Skene, *CPS*, 1ra, 4, 396. T.C.D., *1336*, col.823. M.O. Anderson, *KKES*, 87, 245, 247, 264-267, 271, 273, 274, 279, 280, 282, 283, 286, 290, 292. MacAlister, *Uí Maine*, 37[93]v.

[162]Forbes, "Vita Niniani, 139-40, 147-8. J. and W. MacQueen, *St. Nynia*, 89, 104, 112-113. A.O. and M.O. Anderson, *ALOC* (1961), 194-96, 348-352, 386-388, 485-460; *ALOC* (1991), 1-13, 108-9, 132-3, 138-48, 178-81. Colgrave, *Lives of Cuthbert*, 82, 122, 192, 239. Skene, *CPS*, 417. Webb and Farmer, "Life of Wilfrid," 127-29, 154, 166.

[163]Winterbottom, *Gildas*, 93-95. David Dumville, "The Chronology of *De Excidio Britanniae, Book I*," in Michael Lapidge and David Dumville, eds., *Gildas: New Approaches* (Woodbridge, Suffolk: The Boydell Press, 1984), 83.

[164]Bede, *HEGA*, Vol.I, 16-19, 56-7, 60-1, 72-3, 226-7, 324-5, 338-9, 340-1, 454-5, 466-7, 488-9. Bede, *HEGA*, Vol. II, 70-1, 160-3, 236-7, 310-11, 360-1, 372-3. Bede, *EHEP*, 45-6, 58, 60, 63, 111, 143, 148, 185, 188-9, 196, 225, 254-5, 299-304, 320, 324. M.O. Anderson, *KKES*,16.

[165]Morris, *Nennius*, 59, 61, 62, 64-66, 69, 74, 77, 80.

[166]Wright, *Regum*, 2, 45, 47, 48, 57, 59, 62-4, 86, 101, 103, 104, 130-2, 145. Bromwich, *Trioedd*, 292.

[167]Ibid., 84.

[168]Watson, *HCPNS*, 9, 59, 67-8. O'Rahilly, *EIHM*, 343, Wainwright, *Problem*, 1-2.

[169]Jackson, "Pictish Language," 159-60. Nora K. Chadwick, "The Name Pict," *Scottish Gaelic Studies*. Vol. VIII (1955-58), 146-8, 176. Isabel Henderson, *The Picts* (London: Thames and Hudson, 1967), 15, 33.

[170]M.O. Anderson, *KKES*, 80, 125. Anna Ritchie, *Perceptions of the Picts* (Rosemarkie: Groam House Museum Trust, 1994), 3-5. Katherine Forsyth, *Language in Pictland* (Utrecht: de Keltische Draak, 1997), 16, 26-7.

[171]Hogan, *Onomasticon*, 565.

[172]Hogan, *Onomasticon*, 565.

[173]Winterbottom, *Gildas*, 94-5. Bede, *EHEP*, 56. Morris, *Nennius*, 66. Wright, *Regum*, 47, 59, 145. Bromwich, *Trioedd*, 292.

[174]Hogan, *Onomasticon*, 585. Watson, *HCPNS*, 507.

[175]Hogan, *Onomasticon*, 591.

[176]Morris, *Nennius*, 59. Binchy, *Scéla Cano*, 18. Wright, *Regum*, 2, 66, 101, 131-2, 145. Bromwich, *Trioedd*, 292, 84.

[177]Alcock, *Arthur's Britain*, 278. Morris, *Arthur*, 41.

[178]Hogan, *Onomasticon*, 593. M.O. Anderson, *KKES*, 308.

[179]M.O. Anderson, *KKES*, 266, 273, 287.

[180]Hogan, *Onomasticon*, 593.

[181]M.O. Anderson, *KKES*, 265-7, 270, 271, 273, 281-2, 286, 288, 290, 292.

[182]Winterbottom, *Gildas*, 93-95. Bede, *HEGA*, Vol. I, 16-19, 54-5, 456-67. Bede, *EHEP*, 45, 46, 58, 60, 111, 186-9. Morris, *Nennius*, 62. Wright, *Regum*, 2, 45, 49, 86, 101, 103-5, 130-2, 145. Bromwich, *Trioedd*, 292.

[183]Mallory, *Search*, 50.

[184]Bede, *HEGA*, Vol. I, 16-17. Bede, *EHEP*, 45, 45 n.2. Wright, *Regum*, 45, 47.

[185]Chadwick, *Scotland*, 87, 89. Skene, *CPS*, 3, 145, 292, 298, 333.

[186]Hogan, *Onomasticon*, 542.

[187]Hogan, *Onomasticon*, 610.

[188]Hogan, *Onomasticon*, 615.

[189]Hogan, *Onomasticon*, 402.

[190]Bede, *HEGA*, Vol. I, 16-17. Bede, *EHEP*, 46.

[191]Hogan, *Onomasticon*, 616. Bannerman, *SIHD*, 103.

[192]Hogan, *Onomasticon*, 623.

[193]Hogan, *Onomasticon*, 629, 630.

[194]Mallory, *Search*, 72-73.

[195]M.O. Anderson, *KKES*, 82-3, 83 n.30. H.M. Chadwick, *Scotland*, 87, 89.

[196]Hogan, *Onomasticon*, 651. Cross and Slover, *Ancient Irish*, 13-14.

[197]Hogan, *Onomasticon*, 651.

[198]Hogan, *Onomasticon*, 664.

[199]Hogan, *Onomasticon*, 878.

BIBLIOGRAPHY

MANUSCRIPTS

Atkinson, Robert. *The Book of Ballymote, A Collection of Pieces (Prose and Verse) in the Irish Language Compiled about the Beginning of the Fifteenth Century: for the First Time Published from the Original Manuscript in the Library of the Royal Irish Academy, by the Royal Irish Academy with Introduction, Analysis of Contents, and Index.* Dublin: Royal Irish Academy House. 1887.

Atkinson, Robert. *The Book of Leinster, A Collection of Pieces (Prose and Verse) in the Irish Language Compiled, in Part, about the Middle of the Twelfth Century: for the First Time Published from the Original Manuscript in the Library of Trinity College, Dublin, by the Royal Irish Academy with Introduction, Analysis of Contents, and Index.* Dublin: Royal Irish Academy House. 1880.

Bodleian Library, Oxford. *MS. Rawlinson B 506.* Microfilm Printout of 3v-4r provided by the Bodleian Library.

Bodleian Library, Oxford. *MS. Rawlinson B 512.* Microfilm Printout of 75v-97v provide by the Bodleian Library.

MacAlister, R.A.S. *The Book of Uí Maine Otherwise Called the "Book of the O'Kelly's" with Description Introduction and Indexes.* Facsimiles in Collotype of Irish Manuscripts. Vol. IV. Dublin: The Stationery Office of Éire for the Irish Manuscripts Commission. 1942.

Mulchrone, Kathleen. *The Book of Lecan: Leabhar Mór Mhic Fhirbisigh Leacain.* Facsimiles in Collotype of Irish Manuscripts. Vol. II. Dublin: The Stationery Office of Saorstát Éireann for the Irish Manuscripts Commission. 1937.

National Library of Ireland. *Gaelic Manuscript G 47.* Microfilm of pp. 1-13 provided by the National Library of Ireland.

National Library of Ireland. *Gaelic Manuscript G 131.* Microfilm of folios 27r[49]-30r[55] provided by the National Library of Ireland.

Royal Irish Academy. *MS. Stowe B.iii.1.* Microfilm Printout of folios 30v-31r provided by the Royal Irish Academy.

Royal Irish Academy. *MS. Stowe C.vi.2*. Microfilm Printout of pp. 296-300 provided by the Royal Irish Academy.

Royal Irish Academy. *MS. Stowe D.i.3*. Microfilm Printout of folios 1-17r provided by the Royal Irish Academy.

Royal Irish Academy. *MS. Stowe D.ii.2*. Microfilm Printout of folios 26v-27r provided by the Royal Irish Academy.

Royal Irish Academy. *MS. Stowe D.iii.1*. Microfilm Printout of folios 1-15 provided by the Royal Irish Academy.

Royal Irish Academy. *MS. Stowe D.iii.2*. Microfilm Printout of pp. 1-135 provided by the Royal Irish Academy.

Royal Irish Academy. *MS. Stowe D.iv.1*. Microfilm Printout of folios 1r-8v provided by the Royal Irish Academy.

Royal Irish Academy. *MS. 23.G.4*. Microfilm Printout of pp. 366-373 provided by the Royal Irish Academy.

Royal Irish Academy. *MS. 24.P.13*. Microfilm Printout of pp. 12-29, 200-257 provided by the Royal Irish Academy.

Trinity College Dublin. *MS. #1289*. Microfilm Printout of pp. 29-125 provided by Trinity College Dublin.

Trinity College Dublin. *MS. #1295*. Microfilm Printout of pp. 29-104, 378-390 provided by Trinity College Dublin.

Trinity College Dublin. *MS. #1322*. Microfilm of pp.21-28 (folios 11r-14v) provided by Trinity College Dublin.

Trinity College Dublin. *MS. #1336*. Microfilm Printout of columns 809-827 provided by Trinity College Dublin.

PRINTED SOURCES

Adomnán of Iona. *Life of St Columba*. ed. and trans. Sharpe, Richard. London: Penguin Books. 1995.

Alcock, Leslie. *Arthur's Britain: History and Archaeology AD 367-634*. 4th ed. London: Penguin Books. 1989.

Anderson, Alan Orr. *Early Sources of Scottish History*. 2 Vols. Stamford: Paul Watkins. 1990.

Anderson, Alan Orr. *Scottish Annals from English Chroniclers*. Stamford: Paul Watkins. 1991.

Anderson, A.O. and Anderson, M.O. *Adomnan's Life of Columba*. London: Thomas Nelson & Sons. 1961.

Anderson, A.O. and Anderson, M.O. rev. M.O. Anderson. *Adomnan's Life of Columba*. 2nd. ed. Oxford: Clarendon Press. 1991.

Anderson, Marjorie O. *Kings and Kingship in Early Scotland*. 2nd. ed. Edinburgh & London: Scottish Academic Press. 1980.

Anderson, M.O. "St Andrews before Alexander I." in Barrow, G.W.S. ed. *The Scottish Tradition: Essays in Honour of Ronald Gordon Cant*. Edinburgh: Scottish Academic Press. 1974. 1-13.

Bannerman, John. *Studies in the History of Dalriada.* Edinburgh: Scottish Academic Press. 1974.

Bede. *Ecclesiastical History of the English People.* ed. and trans. Sherley-Price, Leo and Farmer, D.H. London: Penguin Books. 1990.

Bede. *Historia Ecclesiastica Gentis Anglorum.* in Bede. *Historical Works*, 2 Vols. 5th edition. ed. and trans. King, J.E. in Goold, G.P. ed. Loeb Classical Library. Cambridge, Massachusetts and London: Harvard University Press. 1994.

Best, R.I. and O'Brien, M.A. eds. *The Book of Leinster.* Vol. I. Dublin: Dublin Institute of Advanced Studies. 1954.

Best, R.I. and O'Brien, M.A. eds. *The Book of Leinster.* Vol. III. Dublin: Dublin Institute of Advanced Studies. 1957.

Best, R.I. and O'Brien, M.A. eds. *The Book of Leinster.* Vol. IV. Dublin: Dublin Institute of Advanced Studies. 1957.

Best, R.I. and O'Brien, M.A. eds. *The Book of Leinster.* Vol. V. Dublin: Dublin Institute of Advanced Studies. 1967.

Binchy, D.A. *Celtic and Anglo-Saxon Kingship: The O'Donnell lectures for 1967-8 Delivered in the University of Oxford on 23 and 24 May 1968.* Oxford: The Clarendon Press. 1970.

Binchy, D.A. *Scéla Cano Meic Gartnáin.* Dublin: The Dublin Institute for Advanced Studies. 1975.

Black, Ronald. "Gaelic Paelaeography: Key to Symbols." Unpublished Course Material for Gaelic Palaeography. Edinburgh University. 1994.

Bonner, Gerald; Rollason, David; Stancliffe, Clare. eds. *St Cuthbert, His Cult and Community to AD 1200.* 3rd ed. Woodbridge, Suffolk: The Boydell Press. 1998.

Bromwich, Rachel. ed. and trans. *Trioedd Ynys Prydein: The Welsh Triads.* 2nd ed. Cardiff: University of Wales Press. 1978.

Bromwich, Rachel and Evans, D. Simon. eds. *Culhwch and Olwen: An Edition and Study of the Oldest Arthurian Tale.* Cardiff: University of Wales Press. 1992.

Broun, Dauvit. "The Origin of Scottish Identity in Its European Context." in Crawford, Barbara. ed. *Scotland in Dark Age Europe.* St John's House Papers No. 5. St Andrews. 1994.

Byrne, Francis John. *Irish Kings and High-Kings.* New York: St. Martin's Press. 1973.

Byron, George Gordon. *The Poetical Works of Lord Byron.* London: Oxford University Press. 1960.

Calder, George. *Imtheacht Aeniasa: The Irish Aeneid.* in Irish Texts Society. Vol. VI. London: David Nutt for the Irish Texts Society. 1907.

Chadwick, H.M. *Early Scotland: The Picts, the Scots, and the Welsh of Southern Scotland.* Cambridge: Cambridge University Press. 1949.

Chadwick, Nora K. "The Name Pict." in *Scottish Gaelic Studies.* Vol. VIII. 1955-1958. 146-176.

Chadwick, Nora K. "Pictish and Celtic Marriage." in *Scottish Gaelic Studies.* Vol. VIII. 1955-1958. 56-115.

Charles-Edwards, T.M. *Early Christian Ireland.* Cambridge: Cambridge University Press. 2000.

Charles-Edwards, T.M. "Nau Kynywedi Teithiauc." in Jenkins, Dafydd and Owen, Morfydd E. eds. *The Welsh Law of Women.* Cardiff: The University Press. 1980.

Clancy, Thomas Owen. and Márkus, Gilbert. *Iona: The Earliest Poetry of a Celtic Monastery.* Edinburgh: Edinburgh University Press. 1995.

Colgrave, Bertram. *Two Lives of Saint Cuthbert: A Life by an Anonymous Monk of Lindisfarne and Bede's Prose Life.* Cambridge: The University Press. 1940.

Crawford, Barbara E. *Scandinavian Scotland.* Leicester: Leicester University Press. 1987.

Cross, Tom Peete and Slover, Clark Harris. *Ancient Irish Tales.* Totowa, New Jersey: Barnes & Noble Books. 1988.

Cummins, W.A. *The Age of the Picts.* Phoenix Mills: Alan Sutton Publishing LTD. 1995.

Dobbs, M.E. "The History of the Descendants of Ir." in *Zeitschrift für Celtische Philologie.* Vol. XIV. 44-144.

Dumville, David. "The Chronology of *De Excidio Britanniae, Book I.*" in Lapidge, Michael and Dumville, David. eds. *Gildas: New Approaches.* Woodbridge, Suffolk: The Boydell Press. 1984. 61-84.

Dumville, David. "Coroticus" in Dumville, David N. ed. *Saint Patrick: A.D. 493-1993.* 3rd. ed. Woodbridge, Suffolk: Boydell Press. 1999. 107-115.

Dumville, David. "The Death-date of Saint Patrick." in Dumville, David N. ed.*Saint Patrick: A.D. 493-1993.* 3rd. ed. Woodbridge, Suffolk: Boydell Press. 1999. 29-33.

Dumville, David. "The Textual History of "Lebor Bretnach": A Preliminary Study. *Éigse.* Vol. XVI. 1975-6. 255-264.

Evans, D. Simon. *A Grammar of Middle Welsh.* Dublin: The School of Celtic Studies, Dublin Institute for Advanced Studies. 1989.

Evans, H. and Thomas, W.O. *Y Geiriadur Mawr: The Complete Welsh-English, English-Welsh Dictionary.* Christopher Davies, A Gwasg Gomer . 1989.

FitzPatrick, Elizabeth. "Fasciculus XV." in Royal Irish Academy. *Catologue of Irish Manuscripts in the Royal Irish Academy.* Dublin: Royal Irish Academy. pp. 1811-1938.

Forbes, Alexander Penrose. *Lives of S. Ninian and S. Kentigern.* Historians of Scotland. Vol. V. Edinburgh: Edmonston and Douglas. 1874.

Ford, Patrick K. "Culhwch and Olwen," in Ford, Patrick K. ed. and trans. *The Mabinogi and Other Medieval Welsh Tales.* Berkeley, Los Angeles, London: University of California Press. 1977. 119-157.

Forsyth, Katherine. *Language in Pictland: The Case Against "non-Indo-European Pictish".* Utrecht: de Keltische Draak. 1997.

Geoffrey of Monmouth. *The History of the Kings of Britain.* trans. Thorpe, Lewis. Harmondsworth, Middlesex: Penguin Books. 1987.

Grabowski, Kathryn and Dumville, David. *Chronicles and Annals of Mediaeval Ireland and Wales: The Clonmacnoise-group Texts.* Woodbridge, Suffolk: The Boydell Press. 1984.

Gwynn, Edward. *The Metrical Dindshenchas, Part III.* in Royal Irish Academy Todd Lecture Series. Dublin: Hodges, Figgis, & Co., LTD. 1913.

Henderson, Isabel. *The Picts.* in Daniel, Glyn. gen. ed. *Ancient Peoples and Places.* Vol. 54. London: Thames and Hudson. 1967.

Hennessy, William. ed. *Chronicum Scotorum: A Chronicle of Irish Affairs from the Earliest Times to A.D. 1135 with a Supplement, Containing the Events from 1141 to 1150.* London: Longmans, Green, Reader, and Dyer. 1866.

Herbert, Máire. *Iona, Kells, and Derry: The History and Hagiography of the Monastic Familia of Columba.* Dublin: Four Courts Press. 1996.

Hogan, Edmund. *Onomasticon Goedelicum: Locorum et Tribuum Hiberniae et Scotiae, an Index, with Identifications, to the Gaelic Names of Places and Tribes.* Dublin: Four Courts Press. 1994.

Hood, A.B.E. *St. Patrick: His Writings and Muirchu's Life.* in *Arthurian Period Sources.* Vol. 5. in Morris, John. gen. ed. History from the Sources. London and Chichester: Phillimore & Co. LTD. 1978.

Hudson, Benjamin T. *Kings of Celtic Scotland.* Westport, Connecticut and London: Greenwood Press. 1994.

Hughes, Kathleen. *Celtic Britain in the Early Middle Ages.* ed. Dumville, David. Rowman & Littlefield. The Boydell Press. 1980.

Hughes, Kathleen. *Early Christian Ireland: Introduction to the Sources.* in Elton, G.R. gen. ed. *The Sources of History: Studies in the Uses of Historical Evidence.* London: Sources of History Limited in Association with Hodder and Stoughton Limited. 1972.

Hull, Vernam. "Conall Corc and the Corco Luigde." in *Publications of the Modern Language Association of America.* Vol. 62.2. 1947. 887-909.

Hull, Vernam. "The Exile of Conall Corc." in *Publications of the Modern Language Association of America.* Vol. 56.2. 1941. 937-940.

Jackson, Kenneth. "*Duan Albanach.*" in *Scottish Historical Review.* Vol. XXXVI. 1957. 127-137.

Jackson, Kenneth. "Notes on the Ogam Inscriptions of Southern Britain." in Fox, Cyril and Dickins, B. eds. *The Early Cultures of North-West Europe.* Cambridge. 1950. 199-213.

Jackson, Kenneth. *Language and History in Early Britain.* Dublin: Four Courts Press. 1994.

Jackson, Kenneth. "The Pictish Language." in Wainwright, F.T. ed. *The Problem of the Picts.* Edinburgh: Thomas Nelson and sons LTD. 1955. 129-66.

Jackson, Kenneth, "The Poem *A Eolcha Alban Uile.*" in *Celtica.* Vol. III 1956. 149-67.

Jarman, A.O.H. *Aneirin: Y Gododdin, Britain's Oldest Heroic Poem.* Lladysul, Dyfed: Gomer Press. 1990.

Kelly, Fergus. *A Guide to Early Irish Law,* in Kelly, Fergus. gen. ed. *Early Irish Law Series.* Dublin: Dublin Institute for Advanced studies. 1988

Kennedy, Benjamin Hall. *The Revised Latin Primer.* ed. and rev. Mountford, James. Harlow, Middlesex: Longman. 1993.

Latham. R.E. *Revised Latin Word-List from British and Irish Sources.* London: Oxford University Press. 1989.

Lindsay, W.M. *Contractions in Early Latin Miniscule Mss.* Oxford: James Parker and Co. 1908.

Lindsay, W.M. *Early Irish Miniscule Script.* Oxford: James Parker and Co. 1910.

Lindsay, W.M. *Early Welsh Miniscule Script.* Oxford: James Parker and Co. 1912.

Lowe, Elias A. *Handwriting.* Rome: Edizioni di Storia e Letteratura. 1969.

Mac Airt, Seán. ed. and trans. *The Annals of Inisfallen (MS. Rawlinson B. 503).* Dublin: Dublin Institute for Advanced Studies. 1977.

Mac Airt, Seán and Mac Niocaill, Gearóid. eds. *The Annals of Ulster (to A.D. 1131): Part I Text and Translation.* Dublin: Dublin Institute for Advanced Studies. 1983.

MacAlister, R.A.S. ed. and trans. *Lebor Gabála Érenn: The Book of the Taking of Ireland, Part II.* in Irish Texts Society. Vol. XXXV. Dublin: The Educational Company of Ireland, LTD. 1939.

MacAlister, R.A.S. ed. and trans. *Lebor Gabála Érenn: The Book of the Taking of Ireland, Part V.* in Irish Texts Society. Vol. XLIV. Dublin: TheEducational Company of Ireland, LTD. 1956.

Mac Eoin, Gearóid S. "On the Irish Legend of the Origin of the Picts." *Studia Hibernica.* No. 4. 1964. 138-154.

Macquarrie, Alan. *The Saints of Scotland: Essays in Scottish Church History A.D. 450-1093.* Edinburgh: John Donald Publishers Ltd. 1997

MacQueen, John. "Myth and the Legends of Lowland Scottish Saints." in *Scottish Studies.* Vol. 24. 1980. 1-21.

MacQueen, John and Winifred. *St. Nynia: With a Translation of the Miracula Nynie Episcopi and the Vita Niniani.* Edinburgh: Polygon Books. 1990.

Mallory, J.P. *In Search of the Indo-Europeans: Language, Archaeology and Myth.* London: Thames and Hudson. 1992.

Meid, Wolfgang. *Táin Bó Fraích.* second ed. Dublin: Dublin Institute for Advanced Studies. 1974.

Meyer, Kuno. "Conall Corc and the Corco Luigde." *Anecdota from Irish Manscripts.* Vol. iii. 1910. 57-63.

Meyer, Kuno. "The Laud Genealogies and Tribal Histories." *Zeitschrift für Celtische Phililogie.* VIII. 1912. 291-339.

Miller, Molly. "The Disputed Historical Horizon of the Pictish King-Lists." in *The Scottish Historical Review.* Vol. 58. 1979. 1-34.

Miller, Molly. "Eanfrith's Pictish Son." in *Northern History.* Vol. XIV. 1978. 47-66.

Miller, Molly. "The Last Century of Pictish Succession," in *Scottish Studies,* Vol. 23 (1979), 39-67.

Miller, Molly. "Matriliny by Treaty: The Pictish Foundation- Legend." in Whitelock, Dorothy; McKitterick, Rosamond; and Dumville, David. eds. *Ireland in Early Mediaeval Europe: Studies in Memory of Kathleen Hughes.* Cambridge: Cambridge University Press. 1982.

Morby, John E. *The Wordsworth Handbook of Kings and Queens*. Ware, Hertfordshire: Wordsworth Reference. 1994.

Morris, John. *The Age of Arthur: A History of the British Isles from 350 to 650*. London: Weidenfield. 1993.

Morris, John. *Annals and Charters*. Vol. 2 of *Arthurian Period Sources*. in Morris, John. gen. ed. History from the Sources. Chichester: Phillimore & Co LTD. 1995.

Morris, John. ed. *Genealogies and Texts*. Vol. 5 of *Arthurian Period Sources*. in Morris, John. gen. ed. History from the Sources. Chichester: Phillimore & Co. LTD. 1995.

Morris, John. ed. and trans. *Nennius: British History and the Welsh Annals*. Vol. 8 of *Arthurian Period Sources*. in Morris, John. gen. ed. History from the Sources. London and Chichester: Phillimore & Co. LTD. 1980.

Morris, John. *Persons: Ecclesiastics and Laypeople*. Vol. 3 of *Arthurian Period Sources*. in Morris, John. gen. ed. History from the Sources. Chichester: Phillimore & Co. LTD. 1995.

Morris, John. *Places & Peoples, and Saxon Archaeology*. Vol. 4 of *Arthurian Period Sources*. in Morris, John. gen. ed. History from the Sources. Chichester: Phillimore & Co. LTD. 1995.

Murphy, Denis. ed. *The Annals of Ireland from the Earliest Period to A.D. 1408: Translated into English A.D. 1627 by Conell Mageoghagan and Now for the First Time Printed*. Dublin: The University Press. 1896.

Nicolaisen, W.F.H. *Scottish Place-Names: Their Study and Significance*. London: B.T. Batsford LTD. 1986.

O'Brien, M.A. ed. *Corpus Genealogiarum Hiberniae*. Vol. 1. Dublin: Dublin Institute for Advanced Studies. 1976.

Ó Cathasaigh, Tomás. *The Heroic Biography of Cormac Mac Airt*. Dublin: Dublin Institute for Advanced Studies. 1977.

Ó Cróinín, Dáibhí. *Early Medieval Ireland: 400-1200*. 4th ed. London and New York: Longman. 1997.

Ó Cróinín, Dáibhí. "Is the Augsburg Gospel Codex a Northumbrian Manuscript?" in Bonner, Gerald; Rollason, David; Stancliffe, Clare. eds. *St Cuthbert, His Cult and Community to AD 1200*. 3rd ed. Woodbridge, Suffolk: The Boydell Press. 1998. 189-201.

Ó Muraíle, Nollaig. *Celebrated Antiquary: Dubhaltach Mac Fhirbhisigh (c. 1600-1671), His Lineage, Life and Learning*. Maynooth Monographs 6. Maynooth: An Sagart. 1996.

O'Rahilly, Cecile. *Táin Bó Cúailnge: Recension I*. Dublin: Dublin Institute for Advanced Studies. 1976.

O'Rahilly, Thomas F. *Early Irish History and Mythology*. Dublin: Dublin Institute for Advanced Studies. 1984.

O'Sullivan, Anne. ed. *The Book of Leinster: Formerly Lebar na Núachongbála*. Vol. VI. Dublin: Dublin Institute for Advanced Studies. 1983.

Phillimore, Egerton. "The *Annales Cambriae* and Old-Welsh Genealogies from *Harleian Ms. 3859.*" in Morris, John. ed. *Genealologies and Texts.* Vol. 5 of *Arthurian Period Sources.* in Morris, John. gen. ed. History from the Sources. Chichester: Phillimore & Co. LTD. 1995.

Phillimore, Egerton. "Pedigrees from Jesus College MS. 20," in Morris, John. ed. *Genealologies and Texts.* Vol.5 of *Arthurian Period Sources.* in Morris, John. gen.ed. History from the Sources. Chichester: Phillimore & Co. LTD. 1995.

Plummer, Charles. *Vitae Sanctorum Hiberniae: Partim Hactenvs Ineneditae ad Fidem Codicvm Manuscriptorvm Recognovit Prolegomenis Notis Indicibvs Instrvxit.* 2nd. ed. 2 Vols. Dublin: Four Courts Press. 1997.

Reeves, William. *Life of Saint Columba, Founder of Hy.* in *Historians of Scotland.* Vol. VI. Edinburgh: Edmonston and Douglas. 1874.

Ritchie, Anna. *Perceptions of the Picts: From Eumenius to John Buchan.* Rosemarkie: Groam House Museum Trust. 1994.

Roberts, Brynley. ed. *Brut y Brenhinedd: Llanstephan MS. 1 Version.* Dublin: Dublin Institute for Advanced Studies. 1971.

Royal Irish Academy. *Catalogue Of Irish Manuscripts in the Royal Irish Academy.* Dublin: Royal Irish Academy.

Royal Irish Academy. *Dictionary of the Irish Language Based Mainly on Old and Middle Irish Materials: Compact Edition.* Dublin: Royal Irish Academy. 1983.

Scowcroft, R. Mark. "*Leabhar Gabhála*, Part I: The Growth of the Text." in *Ériu.* Vol. XXXVIII. 1987. 79-140.

Sharpe, Richard. *Medieval Irish Saints" Lives: An Introduction to Vitae Sanctorum Hiberniae.* Oxford: Clarendon Press. 1991.

Simpson, D.P. *Cassell's New Latin Dictionary.* New York: Funk & Wagnalls Company. 1959.

Skene, W.F. *Chronicles of the Picts, Chronicles of the Scots and Other Early Memorials of Scottish History.* Edinburgh: H.M. General Register House. 1867.

Smalley, Beryl. *Historians in the Middle Ages.* New York: Charles Scribner's Son's. 1974.

Smyth, Alfred P. *Warlords and Holy Men: Scotland AD 80-1000.* Edinburgh: Edinburgh University Press. 1984.

Stancliffe, Clare. "Cuthbert and the Polarity between Pastor and Solitary." in Bonner, Gerald; Rollason, David; Stancliffe, Clare. eds. *St Cuthbert, His Cult and Community to AD 1200.* 3rd. ed. Woodbridge, Suffolk: The Boydell Press. 1998. 21-44.

Stokes, Whitley. "The Annals of Tigernach: Second Fragment A.D. 143-361." "The Annals of Tigernach: Third Fragment A.D. 489-766." "The Annals of Tigernach: Fourth Fragment A.D. 973-1088." in *Revue Celtique.* Vol. XVII. 1896. 6-33, 119-263, 337-420.

Stokes, Whitley. *Félire Óengusso Céli Dé: The Martyrology of Oengus the Culdee.* 2nd. ed. Dublin: Dublin Institute for Advanced Studies. 1984.

Stokes, Whitley. "The Prose Tales in the Rennes Dindsenchas." in *Revue Celtique*. Vol. XV. 1894. 427-428.

Strachan, John. *Old-Irish Paradigms and Selections from the Old-Irish Glosses*. 3rd. ed. rev. Bergin, Osborn. Dublin: Royal Irish Academy. 1989.

Suetonius. *The Twelve Caesars*. trans. Graves, Robert. rev. Grant, Michael. London: Penguin Books. 1989.

Swanton, Michael. *The Anglo-Saxon Chronicle*. New York: Routledge. 1998.

Thacker, Alan. "Lindisfarne and the Origins of the Cult of St Cuthbert." in Bonner, Gerald; Rollason, David; Stancliffe, Clare. eds. *St Cuthbert, His Cult and Community to AD 1200*. 3rd ed. Woodbridge, Suffolk: The Boydell Press. 1998. 103-122.

Thurneysen, Rudolf. *A Grammar of Old Irish*. trans. Binchy, D.A. and Bergin, Osborn. Dublin: The Dublin Institute for Advanced Studies. 1980.

Todd, James Henthorn. *The Irish Version of the Historia Brittonum of Nennius*. Dublin: The Irish Archaeology Society. 1848.

Turabian, Kate L. *A Manual for Writers of Term Papers, Theses, and Dissertations*. fifth edition. revised and expanded by Honigsblum, Bonnie Birtwistle. Chicago and London: The University of Chicago Press. 1987.

Van Hamel, A.G. ed. *Lebor Bretnach: The Irish Version of the Historia Britonum Ascribed to Nennius*. Dublin: The Stationery Office. 1932.

Vergili Maronis, P. *Aeneidos: Liber Quartus*. Oxford: The Clarendon Press. 1955.

Virgil. *The Eclogues & Georgics*. New York: St. Martin's Press. 1979.

Wade-Evans, A.W. *Vitae Sanctorum Britanniae et Genealogiae*. Vol. 9 in Board of Celtic Studies. *History and Law Series*. Cardiff: University of Wales Press Board. 1944.

Wainwright, F.T. *The Problem of the Picts*. Edinburgh: Nelson. 1956.

Watson, William J. *The History of the Celtic Place-Names of Scotland*. 2nd ed. Edinburgh: Birlinn Limited. 1993.

Webb, J.F. trans. and Farmer, D.H. ed. and trans. *The Age of Bede*. 4th ed. London: Penguin Books. 1998.

Webb, J.F. and Farmer, D.H. "Eddius Stephanus: Life of Wilfrid," in Webb, J.F. trans. and Farmer, D.H. ed. and trans. *The Age of Bede*, 4th ed. London: Penguin Books. 1998.

Williams, Ifor. *Canu Aneirin*. Caerdydd. 1978.

Winterbottom, Michael. ed. and trans. *Gildas: The Ruin of Britain and Other Works*. Vol. 7 of *Arthurian Period Sources*. Morris, John. gen. ed. History from the Sources. London and Chichester: Phillimore & Co. 1978.

Wright, Neil. ed. *The Historia Regum Britannie of Geoffrey of Monmouth*. I. Cambridge: D.S. Brewer. 1984.

ONLINE PUBLICATIONS

Bodleian Library, Oxford University website.
    <http://image.ox.ac.uk/list?collection=bodleian>.
Jebson, Tony. *Manuscript A: Parker MS; CCCC 1773 ff. 1-32.*
    <http://lonestar.texas.net/~ jebbo/asc/a.html>.
Jebson, Tony. *Manuscript C: Cotton Tiberius B.I.*
    <http://lonestar.texas.net/~ jebbo/asc/c.html>.
Jebson, Tony. *Manuscript D: Cotton Tiberius B IV.*
    <http://lonestar.texas.net/~ jebbo/asc/d.html>.
Jebson, Tony. *Manuscript E: Bodleian MS Laud 636.*
    <http://lonestar.texas.net/~ jebbo/asc/e.html>.
Ó Corráin, Donnchadh and Cournane, Mavis. *Annals of the Four Masters: Corpus of Electronic Texts Edition.* Vol. I. Cork: Corpus of Electronic Texts (CELT). University College Cork. 1997. <http//www.ucc.ie/celt/online/G10005A.html>
Ó Corráin, Donnchadh and Cournane, Mavis. *Annals of the Four Masters: Corpus of Electronic Texts Edition.* Vol. II. Cork: Corpus of Electronic Texts (CELT). University College Cork. 1997. <http//www.ucc.ie/celt/online/G10005B.html>
Ó Corráin, Donnchadh and Tiarnáin. eds. *Annals of Tigernach: Corpus of Electronic Texts Edition.* Cork: Corpus of Electronic Texts (CELT). University College Cork. 1996. <http//www.ucc.ie/celt/online/G10002.html>

INDEX

Index

About the Author

J.M.P. CALISE has a Ph.D. in Celtic Studies from Edinburgh University. Dr. Calise is a fellow of the Society of Antiquaries of Scotland and has an interest in all aspects of medieval cultures and history with a special emphasis on the Dark Ages and arms and armor.